Randall Wight

ANNUAL REVIEW OF PSYCHOLOGY

EDITORIAL COMMITTEE (1983)

ANNUAL REVIEW OF PSYCHOLOGY

VOLUME 34, 1983

MARK R. ROSENZWEIG, *Editor*
University of California, Berkeley

LYMAN W. PORTER, *Editor*
University of California, Irvine

ANNUAL REVIEWS INC.   4139 EL CAMINO WAY   PALO ALTO, CALIFORNIA 94306 USA

ANNUAL REVIEWS INC.
Palo Alto, California, USA

International Standard Serial Number: 0066-4308
International Standard Book Number: 0-8243-0234-6
Library of Congress Catalog Card Number: 50-13143

PRINTED AND BOUND IN THE UNITED STATES OF AMERICA

PREFACE

We invite readers to send us comments about any aspect of the *Annual Review of Psychology*. Below are some examples of topics on which we would appreciate feedback, but comments on other subjects related to our series will also be welcome:

Special topics Several recent volumes of ARP have included "special topic" chapters on subjects not regularly treated under our Master Plan. These special chapters are prepared under shorter deadlines than usual and provide greater flexibility of coverage. Recent examples are these: "Endorphins and Behavior" (Vol. 33, 1982), "Social Dilemmas" (Vol. 31, 1980), and "Facial Expression of Emotion" (Vol. 30, 1979). We welcome suggestions of such timely topics that merit consideration for special coverage.

Form of citation Beginning with Volume 31, we have cited references in the text by author(s) and year (e.g. Brown & Henry 1981), whereas in previous volumes we had cited according to a numbered list of references (e.g. 36). Many other series published by Annual Reviews, Inc. use numerical citations, and ARP has been urged to return to that practice. Among the arguments for the numerical system are that it saves some space that could be used for increased text and that it permits the economy of automated preparation of the author index. For the present, the Editorial Committee of ARP has chosen to continue citing by author(s) and year because it gives more immediate information to the reader, but do readers really prefer this? We would appreciate your comments on this matter.

Overall coverage We would like to remind readers that the basic topics regularly covered under the Master Plan can be ascertained by referring to the list on pages 620–623 that gives the chapter titles for the last five volumes. Also, the interested reader may wish to refer to the Preface of Volume 32 (1981) for information about the scope and intent of ARP and the instructions given to the authors.

The choices of whom to invite to contribute chapters to ARP are made by the Editorial Committee at its annual meeting. It is mainly upon these choices that the quality and value of the series depends. The 1982 meeting marked the end of the five-year term of Robert Zajonc, and we will miss his wide-ranging knowledge of psychology and psychologists and his incisive comments. We welcome Edward E. Jones as the incoming member of the Committee.

M.R.R.
L.W.P.

ERRATA

Volume 33 (1982)

In the chapter titled "Environmental Psychology," by James A. Russell and Lawrence M. Ward, a line on page 654 which reads:

"that the place-specificity of behavior does not necessarily imply that the"

was transposed incorrectly. This appears as line 14, but it should have been line 1 on page 654.

In the *Literature Cited* section of the same chapter, two references are listed as Tversky, A. 1981a and 1981b. Both should have been attributed to Tversky, B.

Annual Review of Psychology
Volume 34, 1983

CONTENTS

(*continued*)

SOME ARTICLES IN OTHER *ANNUAL REVIEWS* OF INTEREST TO PSYCHOLOGISTS

From the *Annual Review of Anthropology,* Volume 11 (1982)

Forensic Anthropology, Clyde Collins Snow

The Pattern of Human Evolution: Studies on Bipedalism, Mastication, and Encephalization, Henry M. McHenry

Sociobiology: Primate Field Studies, A. F. Richard and S. R. Schulman

The Anthropologies of Illness and Sickness, Allan Young

From the *Annual Review of Sociology,* Volume 8 (1982)

The Self-Concept, Viktor Gecas

Perspectives on the Concept of Social Control, Robert F. Meier

The Social Psychology of Deviance: Toward a Reconciliation with Social Structure, Anthony R. Harris and Gary D. Hill

Sex Roles: The Division of Labor at Home and in the Workplace, Joanne Miller and Howard H. Garrison

From the *Annual Review of Public Health,* Volume 4 (1983)

Appropriate Uses of Multivariate Analysis, James A. Hanley

Design and Analysis Methods for Longitudinal Research, Nancy R. Cook and James H. Ware

Critical Issues in the Conduct and Interpretation of Clinical Trials, Thomas A. Louis and Stanley H. Shapiro

Environmental Design and Health, S. Leonard Syme and Roslyn Lindheim

The Health Consequences of Deinstitutionalization, Milton Greenblatt and Margie Norman

Lessons from Health Care Regulations, Jonathan E. Fielding

From the *Annual Review of Medicine,* Volume 34 (1983)

Cannabis and Health, Reese T. Jones

Sensory Evoked Potentials: Clinical Applications in Medicine, Leslie J. Dorfman

The Diagnosis and Treatment of Major Depressive Disorder in Childhood, Joaquim Puig-Antich and Burt Weston

(*continued*)

From the *Annual Review of Neuroscience,* Volume 6 (1983)

> *The Reorganization of the Somatosensory Cortex Following Peripheral Nerve Damage in Adult and Developing Mammals,* Jon H. Kaas, M. M. Merzenich, and H. P. Killackey
>
> *Clinical Implications of Receptor Sensitivity Modification,* Arnold J. Friedhoff and Jeannette C. Miller
>
> *Molecular Approaches to the Nervous System,* Ronald D. G. McKay
>
> *Cellular Processes of Learning and Memory in the Mammalian CNS,* Richard F. Thompson, Theodore W. Berger, and John Madden IV

From the *Annual Review of Pharmacology & Toxicology,* Volume 23 (1983)

> *The Endorphins: A Growing Family of Pharmacologically Pertinent Peptides,* Floyd E. Bloom
>
> *Nonopioid Neuropeptides in Mammalian CNS,* Leslie Iversen

Special Announcement: Volume 1 of the *Annual Review of Immunology* (Editors: William E. Paul, C. Garrison Fathman, and Henry Metzger) will be published in April, 1983.

Coming for 1984 . . .

CHAPTERS PLANNED FOR THE NEXT
ANNUAL REVIEW OF PSYCHOLOGY, VOLUME 35

Due to circumstances beyond our control, some of the articles listed above may not appear.

Neal E. Miller

Ann. Rev. Psychol. 1983. 34:1–31

BEHAVIORAL MEDICINE: SYMBIOSIS BETWEEN LABORATORY AND CLINIC

Neal E. Miller

The Rockefeller University, New York, New York 10021

CONTENTS

Symbiosis between Basic and Applied Science

Psychology has benefited, more than often is recognized, by symbiotic interactions between basic and applied science. The development of behavioral medicine illustrates how the two-way interaction between basic science in the laboratory and applied science in the clinic is contributing to the healthy development of both of these aspects of psychology. To provide a

1

0066-4308/83/0201-0001$02.00

perspective, I shall review briefly some earlier interactions between basic science in the university laboratory and practical applications in nonacademic settings.

Early basic research on individual differences led to the practical development of intelligence tests whose successful use in the army during World War I and in education gave an important impetus to the support of psychologists in university classrooms and laboratories. The training of academic psychologists in rigorous scientific methods for empirically studying complex behavioral phenomena led to their being useful in many ways when large numbers of them were called out from their ivory towers to participate in a variety of practical tasks during World War II. The fact that psychologists, along with their colleagues in the biological and physical sciences, made many practical contributions to the war effort led to the inclusion of psychology in new federal programs by the National Science Foundation and the National Institutes of Health. These programs supported graduate training and basic research in psychology at a vastly increased level. Furthermore, the problems encountered in the practical environment directed psychologists' attention to phenomena, such as information overload, the role of selective attention (filtering), and strategies of information processing, that opened up new areas of basic research. Finally, the greatly accelerated use of psychologists in clinics and in industry provided new professional opportunities that increased the popularity of psychology as a major in the universities.

To cite one more example, techniques such as avoidance learning, developed in the animal laboratory, contributed, along with many other lines of basic and applied research, to the discovery of drugs that were useful in treating mental disorders. The practical utility of those drugs helped to provide funding for basic research in psychopharmacology and physiological psychology and led the National Institute of Mental Health and the drug companies to produce new drugs and radioisotope tracers which provided research workers with powerful new tools. These, along with the funding and the enthusiasm, led to a burst of research that greatly increased our basic knowledge about neurotransmitters, interactions between hormones and the central nervous system, and many other aspects of how the brain controls behavior and visceral functions. As a result, we are learning much more about the brain mechanisms available to mediate the effects of psychosocial factors on the health of the body.

Scope of Behavioral Medicine

Behavioral medicine is an interdisciplinary field that integrates behavioral and biomedical knowledge relevant to health and disease. It involves the integration of relevant parts of epidemiology, anthropology, sociology, psychology, physiology, pharmacology, nutrition, neuroanatomy, endocrinology, immunology, and the various branches of medicine and public health, as well as related professions such as dentistry, nursing, social work, and health education. It is concerned with basic research, which at present is one of its greatest needs, and also with the application of its knowledge and techniques to prevention, diagnosis, therapy, and rehabilitation (Schwartz & Weiss 1978, Miller 1982b).

This area has been developing rapidly. The second volume of *Behavioral Medicine Abstracts* (Taylor 1981) contains abstracts of over 1000 relevant articles. This essay can delineate only some of the main themes that are contributing to the development of behavioral medicine and sample a few of the challenging areas for future research.

Emotions and Health in the Early History of Medicine

The effects of emotions on the body were recognized in the epics that antedate written history and appear in early treatises on medicine. To quote A. K. Shapiro (1978), "Galen estimated that 60% of his patients had symptoms of emotional rather than physical origin. This number is close to the contemporary estimate of 60–80%." Shapiro also points out that for many centuries most of the drugs prescribed by the medical profession were either worthless or positively harmful; thus, the continued prestige of physicians rested on purely psychological factors such as the placebo effect and on the remarkable capacity of the body to heal itself.

One of the large steps toward scientific medicine occurred around the beginning of this century when physicians began to realize the natural healing ability of the body, to discard worthless or harmful remedies, and to concentrate on simple nursing care and diagnosis. During this period, the physician's bedside manner continued to be a major component of his limited armamentarium.

Biological Progress to Impersonal Technology

In the seventeenth century, van Leeuwenhoek improved his microscopes to make the remarkable discovery of a world of creatures too small to be seen by the human eye. If Golden Fleece Awards had been given then, he certainly would have received one. What possible practical use could there be in studying such extremely minute creatures? He should have been doing something more practical like searching for ways to turn base metals into gold.

Two centuries later, Pasteur was involved in an esoteric but bitter controversy. Were the bacteria and other microorganisms that van Leeuwenhook had discovered the products of spontaneous generation? Or, as Pasteur claimed and demonstrated in a series of simple but brilliant laboratory experiments, did they originate only from other similar organisms or the spores of such organisms? Out of this and other work, Pasteur and Koch fashioned the germ theory of disease. This in turn led to two practical applications. One was the development by Lister of aseptic techniques that led to revolutionary reductions in the fatalities from operations and, along with the discovery of anesthetics, opened the way to modern surgery. The other was the development of vaccines and sanitation to prevent certain diseases.

But many generations of scientists had to spend many years in essentially basic research before they learned what specific bacteria or viruses caused what specific diseases. This slowly accumulated knowledge was essential for the development of many of the modern vaccines for the prevention of diseases but was not yet of much practical use for curing any bacterial infections. After Ehrlich's toxic but effective magic bullet against spiro-chetes (which are not bacteria), there were so many disappointments that it came to be believed that any substance that was poisonous enough to kill bacteria would necessarily have an even worse effect on human tissues and hence retard rather than help healing. This belief was so strong that in 1928, in spite of some remarkable demonstrations, Fleming was unable to get adequate biochemical support to refine penicillin, which lay dormant for an entire decade until it was revived by the discovery of sulfanilamide and the work of Florey and Chain. With the dawn of the era of antibiotics, some-thing that would have been impossible without the long history of basic research, physicians had powerful weapons that at last allowed them to cure many diseases.

In passing it should be noted that the advances in bacteriology, in sur-gery, and in antibiotics and other drugs that have made such great contribu-tions to the relief of human suffering could not have been made without causing experimental animals to suffer (Paton 1983). Concern to establish ever more rigorous regulations to govern the exploitation of the many fewer animals involved in research contrasts ironically with the lack of rigorous regulations to govern the exploitation of the vastly larger numbers involved in the sports of hunting and fishing and as pets neutered and confined to city apartments (Miller 1983).

Meanwhile, advances in other areas of science and technology had con-tributed to economic advances which led to less crowding and better sanita-tion. Knowledge about diet and vitamins helped to eliminate cretinism, rickets, and pernicious anemia.

The result of this long history of research and applications was a dramatic decrease in many diseases. As the Surgeon General's Report on Health Promotion and Disease Prevention (1979) points out, "At the beginning of this century, the leading causes of death were influenza, pneumonia, diph-theria, tuberculosis, and gastrointestinal infections. Since then, the yearly death rate from these diseases per 100,000 people has been reduced from 580 to 30!"

There has also been an impressive increase in the power of physical, microbiological, and biochemical diagnostic tests—from X rays to computerized axial tomography (CAT scanner), and from simple tests for sugar and pus cells in the urine to the autoanalyzer and radioimmune assays. Finally, in addition to antibiotics, powerful new drugs have been discovered for altering physiological processes and correcting conditions such as diabetes and gout. Yet other diseases have been all but eliminated by vaccines.

One of the side effects of the foregoing admirable process has been to emphasize attention to the physical and to downgrade attention to the emotional factors in illness. Another related side effect has been to emphasize the technology and to downgrade the personal side of the practice of medicine. Some of the pressures involved are epitomized by a statement overheard at a recent conference on gastrointestinal diseases, which went approximately as follows: "If you make the mistake of asking a patient how he feels, you'll be talking with him for about half an hour, and the most his insurance will pay is $50. But if you tell him that you will give him a complete series of tests, it will only take 5 minutes of your time and there'll be no question about a bill of $250." The foregoing developments, along with the increasing specialization of medicine, mean that many of the extremely important psychosocial functions that old family physicians used to perform are being neglected today.

The Challenge of the Changing Pattern of Disease

The remarkable progress that has just been described in the conquest of infectious diseases has produced a drastic change in the types of medical problems that are confronting industrialized countries today. The burden of illness has changed to deaths and disabilities caused by chronic diseases and by conditions such as injuries from accidents, poisonings, or violence. A number of studies have shown that a major role in current causes of mortality and morbidity is played by behavioral factors, especially by long-standing habits, such as smoking, dietary preferences, and the abuse of alcohol, that are described as life-style. For example, the Center for Disease Control (1980) of the U.S. Public Service has estimated that 50% of mortality from the 10 leading causes of death in the United States can be traced to life styles. Other authors (Lalonde 1974, Knowles 1977) come to similar conclusions and believe that the major opportunity for further improvements in health is in the area of changing unhealthful behaviors.

Rice et al (1976) estimate that the indirect costs (value of lost productivity, years of life, etc) of cardiovascular disease was $35 billion in 1975, and for accidents, poisoning, and violence $29 billion. Although seldom a direct cause of death, gastrointestinal diseases, the most common of which are functional (i.e. without recognizable injury to the involved organ), came next in impact on the national health and economy (National Commission on Digestive Diseases 1979). The behavioral components in accidents, poisoning, and violence are obvious. Those in cardiovascular and gastrointestinal diseases will become evident.

In 1977, 25 million prescriptions of a hypnotic medication were written for insomnia, and it is estimated that 35 million packages of over-the-counter pills were purchased. But the evidence for the efficacy and safety of such medications is quite limited, and evidence for harmful side effects is strong (Institute of Medicine 1979).

In 1980, the direct expenses for dental care approached $20 billion (Freeland et al 1980). Since methods for preventing many dental problems are available, Bailit & Silversin (1981) conclude that the critical need is to develop, test, and disseminate strategies for changing oral health behavior in order to increase the utilization of these preventive methods.

The relevance of behavioral factors to the foregoing changed burden of illness provides a major challenge for psychologists and other behavioral scientists to contribute to the development of behavioral medicine. Matarazzo (1982) has made a persuasive plea for psychologists to respond to this challenge.

Unhealthful Behavior and Risk Factors

Some of the unhealthful behaviors that make the greatest contribution to the current burden of disease are cigarette smoking, the abuse of alcohol and drugs, the overeating and underexercise that produce obesity, and Type A behavior. Unfortunately, these behaviors are stubbornly resistant to change and discouragingly subject to relapse. Thus, for behavioral scientists to promise to achieve too much too soon is to court disastrous disillusionment. But any contributions that behavioral scientists can make to reduce any of them will have highly significant implications for health. We are faced with a great challenge.

NONCOMPLIANCE If everyone complied with their physician's recommendations, it would be easy to eliminate types of behavior known to be unhealthful. Thus, noncompliance is a general problem. It often has been investigated in the context of failing to take prescribed drugs. That this aspect of the problem is serious is indicated by studies that estimate that approximately one-third to one-half of a patient sample are noncompliers (Davis 1966, Stamler 1974). While having the reason for the prescribed procedure adequately explained does help some, a study by Sackett et al (1975) clearly shows that information alone often is not enough.

One of the psychological principles behind the problem of noncompliance is the *Gradient of Reinforcement,* namely, that immediate rewards and punishments are much more effective than delayed ones. From this principle, one would expect that if a procedure provides immediate relief or if failing to comply produces relatively immediate discomfort, there should be relatively few problems of compliance. Unfortunately, many medical procedures, such as flossing one's teeth, exercising to strengthen one's back, giving up smoking, sticking to a diet, or taking a pill, especially if they involve some unpleasant side effects, involve the opposite conditions: delayed benefits (or avoidance of harm) but immediate effort, inconvenience, or renunciation of pleasure. Thus, the Gradient of Reinforcement is a source of noncompliance. It also is a reason why the highly cost-effective strategy of preventing illness receives so much less attention from patients, physicians, and politicians than that of treating illness after it becomes an immediate problem. One of the important strategies for dealing with problems of compliance is to try to discover or to create relatively immediate reinforcements for compliant behavior.

A reduction in fear serves as a reinforcement (Miller 1948). Thus, there is a tendency to learn to escape from thoughts that induce strong fears (Dollard & Miller 1950), a tendency that is called suppression when it is mild and repression or denial when it is strong. Therefore, messages arousing strong fear are likely to be forgotten unless some relatively clear-cut, easy course of action is immediately available to reduce the danger eliciting the fear.

One of the other suggestions from a behavioral analysis is to try to associate the compliant behavior with some perspicuous cue that always will be present at an appropriate time but not otherwise. For example, a psychologist was confronted with a group of dialysis patients who were considered to be unusually noncompliant about calling the doctor whenever their weight was outside a prescribed limit. She found that they actually were suffering from minor brain damage so that it was difficult for them to follow these directions. When she painted a distinctive yellow band on their scales and told them to call the doctor whenever the needle was outside that band, the problem was solved (D. C. McKee, personal communication).

Janis (1982) presents evidence that in inducing compliance and other health-restoring effects it is important for the patients to have a relationship with the therapist that is warm and affectionate and that bolsters their self-confidence. This book summarizes a considerable number of ingenious field studies of specific types of behavior that can enhance the role and can increase the social power of the health-care professional to influence patients. Further evidence relevant to compliance is discussed by Sackett & Haynes (1976).

The problem of noncompliance is involved in dealing with the following additional unhealthful behaviors and risk factors.

SMOKING   Converging lines of evidence show that the behavior of smoking cigarettes has a causal role in cardiovascular disease, cancer of the lung, mouth, and esophagus, and respiratory diseases such as emphysema, bronchitis, and chronic obstructive lung disease. The effect depends on the dose; the risk is reduced by quitting. Multivariate factoring out of other risks reveals an independent risk for cigarette smoking. Finally, experiments prove that cigarette smoke causes cancer in the lung and other sites in several different species of animals (Wynder & Hoffman, 1979, US Department of Health, Education, and Welfare 1979). The latest Surgeon General's Report (1982) estimates that one-third of all cancers are caused by smoking.

The immediacy of reinforcement is thought to be one of the factors responsible for the strength of the habit of smoking. Within 6 to 8 seconds after inhalation, peak concentrations of substances present in tobacco smoke reach the brain. The readiness with which the use of tobacco has been taken up wherever it has been introduced, sometimes in spite of strong sanctions against its use, indicates that a strong reinforcement must be involved. Because most people gain little satisfaction from smoke that lacks nicotine, even if it contains all the other constituents of tobacco smoke, nicotine is indicated as the primary reinforcer (Kresnegor 1979). The withdrawal symptoms and the difficulty that many people experience in trying to quit smoking suggest that nicotine must be addictive.

It has been perplexingly difficult to induce animals to choose to inhale tobacco smoke or to inject themselves with nicotine. But recently, Goldberg et al (1981) found that a combination of a visual stimulus with a nicotine injection could be used to reinforce monkeys for learning and performing bar-pressing at a high rate. This model opens up opportunities for research that may help us to learn the pharmacological details of how the smoking habit is reinforced. This knowledge could enable us to find better ways to help those smokers who want to quit.

Of the 30 million people who try to stop smoking each year, only about 3 million achieve long-term abstinence (National Center of Health Statistics 1979). Over 90% of the people who try to quit smoking do so on their own. While the initial success rate of quit clinics of various types is quite high, up to 70%, long-term success does not appear to differ from that of the spontaneous quitters, but of course the two groups may be initially different in a number of respects. There does seem to be some progress in devising more effective behavioral techniques (Pomerleau 1981). But one has to be cautious because in general the newer techniques have been tried by innovative and enthusiastic investigators on smaller numbers of cases with less opportunity for long-term follow-up. Perhaps the most optimistic thing to be said is that we are faced with a highly significant challenge and that there is a great deal of room for improvement.

The Institute of Medicine (1982) points out in an excellent chapter on smoking and health that we need to learn more about those who can successfully stop smoking on their own. A detailed analysis of why and how they succeed might suggest ways of helping others to stop. We also need more information on factors that cause people to relapse. Finally, this same report points out that even relatively ineffective methods will be useful if they can be applied to large groups of individuals at relatively little cost.

The difficulty of quitting smoking suggests the desirability of concentrating on prevention. A number of programs aimed at prevention have studied the factors associated with an increased rate of cigarette smoking and devised a combination of techniques to counteract them. They involve role-playing practice in resisting pressure from peers, adults, and advertising. Follow-up studies for 2 years indicate that the adoption of smoking among adolescent students exposed to such efforts is about half of that for controls (Evans et al 1978, McAlister et al 1979, Hurd et al 1980, Telch et al 1982). Thus, this approach appears to be promising and well worthy of longer follow-ups to evaluate the results and more research to improve them.

Some studies have used biological measures to determine objectively whether and how much the subject has been smoking; further improvements of such measures will be useful.

Smoking and behavior is considered in more detail in a report by the Institute of Medicine (1980a).

ABUSE OF ALCOHOL   Alcohol is involved in deaths from traffic accidents, cirrhosis of the liver, and various forms of cancer. It also contributes to lost production, violent crimes, and fires. In 1975, the direct and indirect costs of alcohol abuse were estimated at $43 billion (Berry et al 1977).

Although we know that both genetic and environmental factors are involved in alcoholism, most of the specific details remain to be worked out. Since only a minority of alcoholics seek treatment, and of those who do the long-term cure rate is at most 30%, it is clear that we are still a long way from being able to solve this challenging problem.

The working environment has shown promise as a setting for programs of prevention and treatment of alcoholism. A promising approach has been the "Troubled Employee" one. Employees are identified as early as possible by a drop in the quality of their work performance or by an increase in absenteeism. Then they are offered programs of counseling, support, and therapy aimed at maintaining their effectiveness as employees (e.g. Schramm 1977).

More details of the current status and research needs are presented in a report on alcoholism by the Institute of Medicine (1980b). This report calls attention to the fact that there seem to be common elements to risk-taking behavior, cigarette smoking, alcoholism, and drug use by adolescents. It suggests that these problems, which usually are studied separately, might profitably be the subject of a joint investigation.

OBESITY   The behaviors of overeating and underexercising produce obesity which is a risk factor for diabetes, gall bladder diseases, cardiovascular disease, orthopedic problems, and complication in surgery. Compared with persons of average weight, men and women 20 to 30% overweight have a mortality 20–40% greater, and those 50–60% overweight have a mortality 150–200% greater (Van Itallie 1979). Because the goal, a loss of weight, is so specific and objectively measurable, obesity provides a particularly challenging opportunity to test the efficacy of various forms of intervention. Janis (1982) and others have taken advantage of this opportunity. Like smoking and the abuse of alcohol, it is a stubborn problem; temporary successes are very likely to be followed by relapses.

Behavioral and other biological scientists have made considerable progress in discovering some of the factors involved in maintaining weight. We know that these are powerful, so that when weight is maintained at too low a level it is difficult to increase it and when it is maintained at too high a level it is difficult to decrease it. But there is still no agreement on the exact mechanisms involved. Evidence for different hypotheses is summarized in Stunkard (1980). Further knowledge about the mechanisms involved in maintenance of weight might lead to improved ways of dealing with the problem of obesity.

That obesity is subject to control by some sort of influence in the social environment is demonstrated by the fact that its incidence is much lower in people born into the upper social classes than in those born into lower ones (Stunkard 1976). Furthermore, programs ranging from psychoanalysis to behavior therapy can cause some obese people to return permanently to normal weight. These facts challenge behavioral scientists to discover more effective ways of preventing or treating obesity.

While there have been some pioneers, the interest of an appreciable number of behavioral scientists in the problems of smoking, alcohol abuse, and obesity is relatively new; we should remember the long history of basic research in microbiology that was essential for the conquest of some of the most devastating infectious diseases.

TYPE A PERSONALITY   Compared with people without such traits, those with a certain type of hard-driving, competitive, impatient, hostile personality, which has been designated as Type A, have been found in a number of studies, including one on approximately 3500 people followed up for 8½ years, to be 2½ times as likely to have heart attacks. Even when the additional risk factors of smoking, obesity, and hypertension are partialed out, Type As still are twice as likely to have heart attacks as the others called type B (Rosenman et al 1976). This observation, originally made by physicians, has been the point of departure for considerable research by psychologists and other biomedical scientists (e.g. Dembrowski et al 1978, Glass 1977, 1981, Williams et al 1981, Weiss et al 1981b).

The twofold difference shows that some significant phenomenon must be involved, but the fact that many Type As do not get heart attacks and a number of Type Bs do get them indicates that other factors must be involved. The current diagnostic tests for Type A personalities may not be aimed squarely at the right target. Thus, investigators are trying to find a better classification, to discover other relevant variables such as those that may protect Type As, and to investigate the pathophysiological mechanisms involved. Another, but difficult, line of approach is to try to modify Type A traits, ideally in ways that do not interfere with a person's productivity, and then determine whether or not such changes will reduce the risk of heart attacks.

HYPERTENSION   Massive evidence shows that hypertension is a risk factor for cardiovascular disease, stroke, kidney dysfunction, and a number of other ills. It is estimated that in the United States 35 million people have definite high blood pressure, that is, above 160 mm Hg systolic or 95 mm Hg diastolic, while 25 million more have borderline hypertension, from the foregoing levels down to 130 mm Hg systolic and 90 mm Hg diastolic (Rice & Kleinman 1980).

There is evidence, however, that defining a diastolic blood pressure of 90 mm Hg as normal because it is near the statistical average for industrialized societies sets that value too high. Massive data from life insurance companies indicate that the curve relating greater life expectancy to lower blood pressure continues progressively to a diastolic pressure of at least 70 mm Hg. This lower level is the average of people in a number of stable and relatively primitive societies. It is especially interesting that in these societies blood pressure does not go up with age as it does in modern industrialized societies. That the lower blood pressure is not genetically determined is indicated by the fact that when people from such societies migrate to industrialized cities, they develop high blood pressure which does increase with age (Cassel 1973). Apparently there is something in industrialized societies that causes blood pressure to go up so that most of the people in them should be considered to be suffering from at least some hypertension.

The foregoing evidence is reinforced by a number of studies indicating that the use of drugs to reduce the blood pressure of hypertensives can have beneficial effects. One of the most recent of these, the Hypertension Detection and Follow-up Program (1979), suggests that these drugs are useful even with patients with borderline hypertension and that reductions as small as 5 or 10 mm Hg can reduce mortality. But in spite of all the careful attempts made to control for confounding factors, the fact that at these levels there were reductions in mortality not only for diseases with a clear cardiovascular component but also somewhat similar reductions in mortality from other diseases without any apparent cardiovascular component suggests treating the conclusion with some caution. Perhaps the procedures used to insure the use of the antihypertensive drugs had unexpected side effects on hygienic behavior or health care.

The evidence for the undesirable effects of even borderline hypertension and the potential effectiveness of drugs in reducing these and higher levels of blood pressure has led to an increase in the use of such drugs and to plans for additional use in large-scale programs.

High blood pressure produces no symptoms whereas many antihypertensive drugs have unpleasant side effects. As might be expected, this unfortunate combination tends to produce serious problems of compliance. In addition to the cost of maintaining many millions of patients on these drugs for many years, the possible long-term adverse consequences of their potent physiological actions are relatively unknown. For these reasons, there is increasing interest in nonpharmacological methods of controlling hypertension. All of these methods involve behavior: reducing obesity, lowering salt intake, exercise, coping with stresses, and also the specific interventions of hypnosis, meditation, learning to relax, and biofeedback-aided learning to lower pressure. To date, evidence suggests that all of the specific interventions produce modest and approximately equal reductions in blood pressure (Shapiro et al 1977). But the evidence that we have summarized suggests that even modest reductions may be significant.

To date, the most successful procedure appears to be a package devised by Patel (Patel & North 1975, Patel et al 1981) that involves the combination of a number of procedures: imagery, training in relaxation, and biofeedback to produce a reduction in sympathetic activity as indicated by an EMG measure of muscle tension and by a reduced galvanic skin response. It has also involved procedures for transferring such training to tension-producing situations in life. A number of Patel's studies have produced reductions averaging approximately 20 mm Hg systolic and 10 diastolic that would reduce most of the 25 million borderline hypertensives in the United States to what is now considered normal, and would also have a significant effect on a considerable number of those with definite high blood pressure.

But before we can recommend mass programs, two important questions must be answered: can Patel's results be repeated on a larger scale by other investigators, and do they transfer from the clinic to everyday life? This last point is especially important because there is a possibility that the patients are able to reduce their blood pressure only when they are concentrating on doing it under the relatively undistracting circumstances of having it measured at the clinic. In that case, they might fool the physician into taking them off the hypertensive medicines that they need (Miller 1974).

Fortunately, tape-recording devices for noninvasively recording blood pressure repeatedly for 24 hours are becoming available. These are increasing our knowledge of the natural history of blood pressure outside the physician's office (Pickering et al 1982); they need to be applied to the problem of generalization of training in reducing blood pressure from the clinic to life. They also should be useful in detecting situations that produce increases in blood pressure in individual patients as a first step toward helping them to learn to cope in such situations (Miller & Dworkin 1982).

Large-Scale Efforts at Reducing Cardiovascular Risk Factors

We have seen that cardiovascular diseases are the leading cause of death in the United States, and that smoking, obesity, Type A behavior, and hypertension increase the risk for these diseases. Other such factors are serum cholesterol and lack of exercise. The prevalence of most of these factors had been going up until about the mid-1960s when increasing knowledge about them and general campaigns against them started to reverse the trend, so that they have gone down. Before then, deaths from coronary heart disease had been steadily increasing, but between 1968 and 1978 there was a decrease from this disease and from stroke that is estimated to have saved more than 800,000 lives in the United States. (Stamler 1981, Institute of Medicine 1982). But, as these authors point out, this correlation, though suggestive, is far from proof.

A study by a group at Stanford has compared results in three geographically separated communities that were of similar size and socioeconomic composition. The results of this study (Maccoby et al 1977), plus those from a somewhat similar one in Finland (Puska et al 1980), strongly suggest that behaviorally sophisticated community intervention can reduce risk factors. But the results on morbidity and mortality are unclear. The question of how the design of trials of this type affect the quality of the resulting information is discussed by Hulley & Fortman (1981).

Clinical and Epidemiological Evidence for Medically Adverse Effects of "Stress"

Another of the factors contributing to the development of behavioral medicine is increasingly strong clinical and epidemiological evidence that psychosocial factors that can loosely be described as stressful can have adverse effects on the physical health of the body. Some of the stressful situations that have been studied are combat and bombing raids, immigration to a radically different physical and social environment, rapid social changes in the same environment, social disorganization, membership in groups with markedly different social status or mores, occupations such as air-traffic controllers, and drastic life changes such as losing a spouse. Typically, the results find an increased risk of a wide variety of medically adverse consequences instead of any specific psychosomatic effect to be predicted from any particular kind of stressor. Some of the increased risks are for gastrointestinal disorders, sudden cardiac death, myocardial infarction, hypertension, stroke, diabetes, cancer, multiple sclerosis, tuberculosis, influenza, pneumonia, and a host of minor afflictions such as headaches and insomnia. Evidence for the foregoing and for some of the following statements is summarized elsewhere (Levi & Andersson 1975, Levine & Ursin 1980, Miller 1980a,b, Weiss et al 1981a, Institute of Medicine 1981, 1982).

While the increase in risk often is highly significant, both statistically and practically, situations that have a disastrous effect on some individuals may have little or no effects on the health of many others. Some part of these differences probably is accounted for by innate factors, or by acquired physiological predispositions (e.g. Weiner et al 1957). Others apparently depend on psychosocial factors.

EFFECTS OF PERCEPTION, COPING, AND SOCIAL SUPPORT   When confronted with a stressor, some people may see it as a serious threat while others, through either ignorance or perspicacity, may fail to perceive any threat and thus experience any stress. For example, observations in combat and psychotherapy show that learning a discrimination between what is dangerous and what is safe can reduce chronic exposure to the stress of fear, and that one of the ways of reducing such stress is to learn to perform a coping response that reduces the danger (Dollard & Miller 1950). Another response is the repression or denial that has been described earlier. Healthcare facilities, such as those for severely burned patients, have been used to study how people cope with stressors (e.g. Hamburg 1974, Janis & Mann 1977). In helping victims of severe stressors, it should be helpful to learn more about coping, and especially about which strategies are effective in which types of situation for which types of people.

Clinical and epidemiological evidence indicates the value of social support. In fact, severing such support may account for much of the negative effects on health in situations such as immigration, social disorganization, and the loss of a spouse. In a 9-year follow-up study of approximately 7000 adults, Berkman & Syme (1979) found that those who lacked social and community ties were more likely to die prematurely from various diseases than those with more extensive social contacts. Stout et al (1964) found an unusually low incidence of death from myocardial infarction in a closely knit Italian-American community in Pennsylvania characterized by warm social support. The incidents that did occur were in people who were marginal to or had left this socially protective environment. It is believed that social support plays a healing role in tender loving nursing care. Unfortunately, the positive effects of unusually good social support have been studied in much less detail than the negative effects of conditions that remove such support.

Experimental Proof of Effects of "Stress"

While ingenious controls have been used in some of these clinical and epidemiological studies on the effects of psychosocial factors, they have not been able to rule out completely the possible effects of confounding factors. For example, a good case has been made for the involvement of stress in the increased blood pressure of people who move from stable, primitive societies into modern cities, but one cannot rule out possible effects of increased consumption of salt and fat or exposure to pollutants. Many of the results of the clinical and epidemiological studies, however, have been confirmed by rigorously controlled experiments, most of which necessarily had to be performed on animals. Taken together, the clinical-epidemiological and the experimental evidence are convincing. Three areas in which considerable work has been done will be sampled.

CARDIOVASCULAR SYSTEM   A series of experiments summarized by Henry & Stephens (1979) placed mice reared in isolation in a colony with spaces for living and for food and water connected by narrow tubes that elicited many confrontations and prevented the formation of a stable social organization. Mice living in such a conflict-inducing colony developed progressively higher blood pressure through a series of stages analogous to those involved in human malignant hypertension and died prematurely from a variety of cardiovascular pathologies including stroke. That learning was a significant variable in these experiments is shown by the fact that if, instead of using mice reared originally in isolation they used mice that had acquired the habits of group living, the mice established more stable social organization and did not develop hypertension.

Other experiments have shown that psychological stresses interact with physiological ones and with genetic susceptibility; dogs subjected to daily sessions of avoidance learning plus salt loads develop hypertension when either of these alone is ineffective (Anderson 1982). A strain of mice bred to be susceptible to the effects of salt-loading will become hypertensive when exposed to chronic conflict while one bred to be resistant to salt-loading also is resistant to the effects of chronic conflict (Friedman & Dahl 1975). Other work shows that after an experimental infarct, stress increases susceptibility to fatal cardiac arrhythmias (Lown et al 1973, Skinner et al 1975). Eliot & Buell (1981) summarize additional evidence on psychosocial effects on the cardiovascular system.

IMMUNE SYSTEM   That stress can affect the immune system, a fact that has wide-ranging medical significance, has been shown by many experiments that have been summarized elsewhere (Stein et al 1976, Ader 1981, Riley 1981, Levy 1982). Most of the experiments have shown that stressors increase the susceptibility to experimental infections or to implants of tumors; relatively few experiments have used direct measures of some aspect of the immune system. Most of these experiments have shown that stress decreases the effectiveness of the immune system. But a significant minority of experiments that apparently are equally as good have produced the opposite results: reduced susceptibility to experimental infections and implanted tumors, or increases in a direct measure of some aspect of the immune system. Most studies have compared only two groups: a presumably nonstressed one and one exposed to a stressor. But if the dose-response curve should be a nonmonotonic one, for example with an inverted J-shape, then, depending on where on that curve the two measured points were, one could find an effect in one direction, in the opposite one, or no effect. Since this could account for some of the contradictions, there is a clear need for more detailed dose-response and time-response studies of effects of stress on direct measures of various components of the immune system and of indirect effects, such as those on susceptibility to experimental infections and implanted tumors (Miller 1980a, 1982b). Steps in this direction have been made by a number of investigators (Keller et al 1981, Riley 1981).

GASTROINTESTINAL SYSTEM   Almy (1951) has used proctoscopic examination to study the effects of emotions on the sigmoid colon, using volunteer human subjects, some of whom were normal and others suffering from irritable colon. Emotional responses were elicited by interviews that at times were bland and at other times probed topics that were emotional for the subject. He also used pain elicited by a tight headband or the cold pressor test. He found that overt moods of hostility and aggression were correlated with increased colonic tone and motility which, however, was not propulsive and thus was conducive to constipation. Helplessness and defeat correlated with reduced tone and motility and induced diarrhea. A previous study of a man with an accident-induced fistula into the stomach had shown that thoughts of food or aggressive attitudes increased stomach secretions and motor activities while disgust, repression, or fear reduced them (Wolf & Wolf 1947). While acute fear interferes with the secretion of stomach acid

(Cannon 1953), a series of experiments by Mahl on dogs and monkeys and observations on people showed that chronic fear increased acid secretion (Mahl 1949, 1950, 1952; Mahl & Karpe 1953).

ANALYSIS OF EFFECTS OF VARIABLES   In addition to rigorous controls, experiments allow an analysis of the effects of various variables. Good illustrations are experiments in which Weiss and his associates in my laboratory rigorously controlled the strength of electric shocks via electrodes wired to the tails of semirestrained rats. Those receiving electric shocks preceded by a signal so that they could learn the discrimination of when it was dangerous and when it was safe had only one-fifth as many stomach lesions as those who received unsignalled shocks and hence could not learn such a discrimination (Weiss 1970). Rats who had the opportunity to learn a simple coping response of rotating a squirrel-cage wheel that allowed them to escape the shock had fewer stomach lesions than their yoked partners who received exactly the same shocks but had no opportunity to control them (Weiss 1968). But if the coping response was conflict-inducing, so that the rats had to take a shock to escape a longer train of shocks, the results were exactly reversed: those who controlled the situation developed considerably more stomach lesions than their helpless partners (Weiss 1971). In these experiments, the conditions that produced the most stomach lesions also produced the highest level of plasma corticosterone, the greatest depletion of brain norepinephrine, and the most fear measured by the CER. The logic of an interpretation in terms of fear is discussed by Miller (1982a). Since in each case the strength of the physical stressor, electric shock, was held equal, the large differences found in these experiments demonstrate the importance of a purely psychological variable: discrimination, coping, or conflict.

Procedures similar to those in the experiments by Weiss and his associates could profitably be used to analyze the effects of various psychological variables on cardiovascular pathology and on the immune response. Would each of the psychological factors have an effect in the same direction on each organ's system, or might some of these variables spare one system at the expense of another (Miller 1972, 1982a)?

Miller (1960) has shown that animals can be trained to persist in the face of fear and has raised the question as to whether such training reduces the physiological effect of fear or merely causes the subject to persist at a greater physiological cost. Subsequently, he has participated in experiments showing that, under some circumstances, repeated exposures to a stressor can elicit biochemical changes that reduce the depletion of brain norepinephrine, increase the effectiveness of that neurotransmitter at the synapse, reduce the elevation of plasma corticosterone (which would be expected to reduce suppression of the immune system), and reduce depressive effects on subsequent behavior (Glazer et al 1975, Weiss et al 1975). Finally, rats handled daily from birth through weaning have been found to have subsequently a greater antibody response to inoculation of flagellin than rats not subjected to this form of stress (Solomon et al 1968). Additional research should be profitable, aimed at determining the conditions under which prior exposures to stress leave the individual more vulnerable and those that have the opposite effect of immunizing or toughening the individual or teaching him to cope so that he is less susceptible to subsequent stressors.

Other Effects of Emotion on Health

In addition to the direct effects of emotions that we have been discussing, there are significant indirect effects. For example, some people respond to stressors by increased smoking, drinking, eating, or drug abuse. One of the effects of frustration and of unpredictable, uncontrollable stressors is mental depression. A minor depression can lead to some neglect of hygienic behavior, and severe depression can lead to catastrophic neglect or suicide. There are certain patients who, when told that they have inoperable cancer, turn their faces to the wall and die in a few days from no ascertainable physical cause (Lewis Thomas, personal communication). Conversely, hope can facilitate hygienic behavior, and the will to live is generally thought to be an important factor in recovery from illness.

Stress and other Psychological Problems of Physical Disease and Injury

Cousins (1979) has given a vivid description of some of the stressful features of hospital routines that are arranged for the efficiency of the overworked staff rather than for the convenience of the patients. As an example of one of the stressors, Järvinen (1955) found that patients with myocardial infarction were five times as likely to experience sudden death when unfamiliar staff were making ward rounds than would be expected in any other comparable time.

The anticipation of major surgery and the aftereffects that the patient did not anticipate and does not understand can be extremely frightening. The nausea produced by cancer chemotherapy causes some patients to feel overwhelming fear on entering the hospital so that they do not return for treatments even when these may have a high probability of saving them from otherwise certain early death. Drastic injuries, such as paralyzing high lesions of the spinal cord, create extremely difficult problems of adjustment. Dialysis for kidney failure, epilepsy, hemophilia, and diabetes, especially in childhood, pose severe problems of compliance, of feeling stigmatized, and of adjustment to a changed life style. Old age can involve a wide variety of difficult adjustments. The manifold behavioral problems posed by conditions such as the foregoing and the variety of contributions that psychology and other behavioral sciences are making toward ameliorating some of these problems are summarized elsewhere (Rodin & Langer 1977, Cohen & Lazarus 1979, Gugel 1979, Melamed & Siegel 1980, Lindemann 1981).

A study by Cromwell et al (1977), however, illustrates the complexity of the problem and the need for empirical research. In an experiment on the effects of different approaches after myocardial infarction, they used a 2 X 2 X 2 design with high vs low levels of medical information, diversion, and active participation in treatment. When the patients had a high level of participation in their treatment, a high level of information improved their recovery, apparently because they had an opportunity to do something about the information. But with a minimum level of participation, a high level of information had the opposite effect of impairing the recovery. Another main finding was that high information improved the recovery of anxious patients but had the opposite effect on nonanxious ones. This study illustrates that designing optimal psychological conditions for recovery is not simple; pilot studies are essential to provide empirical evidence that recommended procedures, no matter how plausible they may seem, actually are achieving the desired effects.

Health Effects of Positive Emotions

In contrast with the considerable amount of work on the adverse effects of stress, there is a conspicuous lack of empirical studies of the effects of positive emotions on preventing or healing illness. Such effects may be involved in the benefits of social support, but their role in such benefits has not been isolated. They may be a component of the powerful placebo effect, something that has not been adequately studied, and may also involve elements of a coping response and of the fear reduction produced when an infant clings to its mother or an individual is supported by a group (Miller 1980a). Norman Cousins (1979) has suggested that laughter may have a powerful healing effect, but no solid empirical studies are cited.

Experimental evidence does show that a rewarding situation can counteract at least some of the effects of pain. Pavlov (1927) describes counterconditioning, the inhibition of physiological reactions to pain when it is used as the signal for a strongly rewarding stimulus, such as presenting food to a very hungry animal. He says:

> Subjected to the very closest scrutiny, not even the tiniest and most subtle objective phenomenon usually exhibited by animals under the influence of strong injurious stimuli can be observed in these dogs. No appreciable changes in the pulse or in the respiration occur in these animals, whereas such changes are always most prominent when the nocuous stimulus has not been converted into an alimentary-conditioned stimulus (p. 30).

Ball (1967) found that electrical stimulation that functioned as a reward in certain areas of the rat's brain also inhibited evoked potentials in the trigeminal nucleus to painful stimulation of the face. Beecher (1956) reported that soldiers for whom a severe wound means escape from harrowing combat often show astonishingly few signs of pain and do not request morphine. In the light of such observations, it should be eminently worthwhile to investigate counterconditioning more thoroughly with the vastly improved techniques that are available today for measuring effects on physiology, pathology, and the immune system.

Hennessy & Levine (1979) summarize experiments showing that performing a variety of consummatory responses (i.e. achieving a variety of goals) reduces the plasma level of corticosteroids, which are hormones that are released during stress. Compared with rats shocked without any opportunity to attack, ones shocked in a situation where they can attack each other have less secretion of ACTH (and hence presumably less corticosteroid) (Conner et al 1971) and a smaller amount of stomach lesions (Weiss et al 1976).

Pleasant and unpleasant situations are not simple opposites, however. A bingo game rigged so that everyone was winning caused subjects to be extremely happy, but Frankenhaeuser (1976) found that it produced as large an elevation in metabolites of norepinephrine and epinephrine in the urine as did aversive situations that she had studied earlier.

There are many questions to be answered. To what extent do laughter, beauty, love, affection, success, or even of being able to express anger counteract the effects of stressors, and to what extent do they have an independent positive effect on health?

Brain Mechanisms Affecting Health of Body

Another factor that has contributed to the development of behavioral medicine is increasing knowledge of mechanisms in the brain and its neurohumoral systems that are available to produce effects of behavioral factors on the health of the body. The brain is the supreme organ of integration of the body. By its nerves and hormones it regulates vital functions such as fluid and electrolyte balance, blood flow to different organs, temperature, heart rate, blood pressure, breathing, and digestion. It also is responsible for drives and emotions, for perceptions of inner states of the body and outer events in the world, for learning and memory, speech, and reasoning. These functions are all interrelated; thus, reasoning that leads one to expect a great danger may increase one's blood pressure and also interfere with digestion, while an upset stomach may interfere with a cheerful, optimistic view of the world.

The general picture is one in which reflexes and other regulatory mechanisms at a lower level can be altered by influences from a higher one. For example, increases in blood pressure stimulate sensory elements in the carotid sinus which elicit, via a lower center of the brain, reflex slowing of the heart rate and vasodilation of blood vessels which cause the blood pressure to return to normal. But under circumstances of strong arousal by anger or fear, these reflexes are inhibited by impulses from higher centers so that blood pressure is set free to rise. This type of effect means that one cannot investigate functional connections in the nervous system without taking account of the behavioral state of the organism.

It used to be thought that responses elicited via the autonomic nervous system, especially its sympathetic component, were quite general. Now we are learning that there are possibilities for a much greater variety of different sophisticated patterns of effects on different organs (Smith et al 1982).

An example of the types of knowledge that are being acquired comes from studies of the immune system (Levy 1982). It has been known for some time that corticosteroids, released during stress, have a suppressant effect on various aspects of the immune system: they cause the involution of lymphoid tissue, suppress gamma globulin formation, reduce the eosinophil count, and interfere with the action of white blood cells. But a considerable number of different cells are involved in just the cellular reactions of the immune system: macrophages, T cells, natural killer cells, helper cells, and suppressor cells. These cells have been found to have receptors for a number of different hormones and peptides under the control of the brain, not only the corticosteroids but also the catecholamines and growth hormone, and it is probable that receptors of other types will be found.

Under stress, the foregoing three hormones have different time courses with the catecholamines having the most rapid onset and decay, corticosteroids being slower, and growth hormone still slower. Thus it can be seen that while mechanisms are available for higher psychosocial functions of the brain to affect the immune system, the details of their action are quite complex, which is in line with the complexity of the experimental effects that have been observed.

A considerable number of other brain mechanisms are available to account for psychosocial effects relevant to health. Summaries are available elsewhere of how the brain can affect pain (Liebeskind & Paul 1977), cardiovascular pathophysiology (Herd 1981), the gastrointestinal system (Brooks & Evers 1977), and the immune system (Levy 1982). But the details of exactly which mechanisms produce which pathophysiological effects under what psychosocial circumstances remain to be discovered by further research. With the recent increasing availability of ever more powerful and sensitive techniques, significant progress should be possible. Again, virtually all of the research has been on mechanisms involved in responses to aversive situations. It seems likely that significant mechanisms remain to be discovered that operate in pleasant situations such as those eliciting hope, joy, and love.

Therapeutic Techniques for Reducing "Stress"

The development of behavioral techniques for alleviating physical symptoms is another of the factors that have contributed to the growth of behavioral medicine. Since behavioral therapies have been dealt with extensively elsewhere (Miller 1978, Pomerleau & Brady 1979, Ray et al 1979, Melamed & Siegel 1980), they will be discussed only briefly here.

The evidence that has been discussed on the manifold medically adverse effects of stress provides the rationale for a variety of behavioral therapies aimed primarily at reducing stress. In the 1930s, Jacobson (1938) devised a method of progressive relaxation in which the patient is taught to canvass systematically all the parts of his body, tensing and then relaxing the muscles, concentrating on the sensations produced by relaxation and learning to produce progressively deeper relaxation. Autogenic training adds to this procedure passive concentration on imagery of warmth and heaviness (Schultz & Luthe 1969). Transcendental meditation involves a passive state of concentration on regular deep breathing and on the monotonous repetition of a word called a "mantra." Benson's (1975) relaxation response involves a combination of all the foregoing, each of which he points out tends to be incompatible with the state of high arousal involved in Cannon's (1953) flight-or-fight response. Stroebel's (1979) quieting reflex is somewhat similar but emphasizes practicing to be able to produce the relaxed anti-stress state promptly.

Biofeedback has been used, either separately or in combination with one or more of the foregoing techniques, to help the patient to learn muscular relaxation and perhaps other antistress responses by providing them with moment-to-moment information from instruments that measure the electrical activity of the muscles, the warmth of the fingers, a decrease in the galvanic skin response, or occasionally other responses such as reduced heart rate or increased alpha waves (Miller 1978, Ray et al 1979). When the patient is trying to produce these responses, the knowledge that he is succeeding serves as a reward to produce learning. It also may have more complicated effects, such as helping the patient to select successful strategies or increasing his feeling of competence and control, and thus achieving some of the stress-reducing effects shown by experiments on coping responses. An attractive feature of all these techniques is that, instead of doing something to the patients, they teach them to do something for themselves. Books have been written on each of these techniques; no brief summary can do them justice.

As would be expected from some of the manifold effects of stress, there is considerable evidence suggesting that, provided the patient continues to practice conscientiously, the foregoing techniques can be useful as a treatment, or part of the treatment, of a considerable variety of physical ailments, such as headaches, Raynaud's disease, cardiac arrhythmias, and hypertension. Unfortunately, much of the evidence is of the case-history type, and most of the better, more recently emerging, rigorously controlled studies still involve rather small numbers of cases; cooperative studies on more patients would be highly desirable. Furthermore, there does not seem to be much evidence on the differential effects of different ones or combinations of these techniques, and such evidence as there is indicates that these effects are approximately equal, so that there seems to be a practical advantage in trying the simpler ones, at least as the first step in a step-care procedure. It should be borne in mind, however, that many forms of surgery and other traditional forms of medical treatment are not yet adequately evaluated.

Of course, various types of psychotherapy also can reduce stress. Perhaps this is one of the reasons why there is evidence that the availability of suitable brief psychotherapy in a clinic established to deal with physical disorders can reduce the total load of that clinic, including the time spent in psychotherapy (Rosen & Wiens 1979).

Extending the Role of Learning in Etiology and Therapy

One of the important functions of the brain, particularly the human brain, is learning. Learning unhealthful or healthful life styles, learning what is dangerous and what is safe, learning coping responses, counterconditioning, and learning to relax all have been discussed. But behavioral scientists are discovering that learning plays a greater role in the cause and cure of some apparently physical conditions than had previously been realized, and it seems probable that additional research will considerably expand this role (Miller 1981).

In 1950, Dollard & Miller advanced in detail the thesis that neurotic symptoms are learned and that psychotherapy is the process of learning more adaptive social and emotional behavior and hence falls naturally within the province of psychology. Two of the symptoms they dealt with that manifest themselves physically were hysterical paralyses and anesthesias. They also dealt with psychosomatic symptoms induced by learned fears and conflicts. Later, a number of investigators considerably extended the range of learned effects specifically to include a variety of visceral responses (Miller 1969, Kimmel 1974). Such effects can be indirect, via learned skeletal responses which in turn affect visceral ones, or more direct effects of learning of a centrally organized skeleto-visceral pattern, or apparently direct learning of a specific visceral response; all three can be etiologically and/or therapeutically significant (Miller & Dworkin 1977, Miller & Brucker 1979).

BIOFEEDBACK Experimental evidence that visceral responses and the EEG (brain waves) can be brought under learned control, and that subjects who are given information from the EMG on the performance of single motor units can learn to control them, led to clinical applications that have been called biofeedback (Kamiya 1969, Kimmel 1974, Basmajian 1977, Miller 1978). Some of the many applications of biofeedback already have been discussed. One of the most successful ones has been in the rehabilitation of patients with neuromuscular disorders, such as the hemiplegias produced by strokes. Many such patients, who apparently had reached their limit of improvement by conventional methods, have learned materially better control of their muscles when the EMG or other measuring instruments have been used to give them better information on small changes in the activity of specific muscles. This application would be an especially favorable one for a model study designed to evaluate cost-effectiveness, since enabling patients partially paralyzed in midlife to feed or clothe themselves or, in some cases, to return to gainful work represents an enormous saving over the expected lifetime. Additional promising applications have been to the treatment of fecal incontinence, the alleviation of certain cases of drug-resistant epilepsy, and other conditions described in extensive summaries (Miller 1978, Ray et al 1979, White & Tursky 1982).

BEHAVIOR THERAPY IN MEDICAL SETTINGS Behavior therapists have been extending their applications of experimentally derived principles of learning from the treatment of neuroses to the treatment of conditions usually considered to be in the area of physical medicine (Pomerleau & Brady 1979, Melamed & Siegel 1980). One of their key ideas is that when sickness behavior is more strongly reinforced than is wellness behavior, it will persist after the organic cause has disappeared. Some of the considerable variety of sickness behaviors are extreme dependence, asking for medication, fatigue, weakness, various complaints, wincing, limiting physical activity, and other signs of pain. For such patients, the treatment is to discover how sickness behavior is being reinforced, remove those reinforcements, and find ways of adding additional reinforcements for wellness behavior. The attention and sympathy of care-facility staff and of family members can be a powerful reinforcement. All too often "it is the squeaking wheel that gets the grease"; complaints, difficulties, and symptoms of suffering elicit the attention and sympathy. Other common reinforcements are relief from arduous duties and responsibilities, disability payments, and pain-killing or sleep-inducing medications. After organic causes have been ruled out, *and one must not make the mistake of neglecting those that can be corrected by purely medical treatment,* a sophisticated behavioral analysis must be made of the reinforcements that are effective for the individual patient. Then behavior therapy is indicated if reinforcement for the symptoms is evident, and it is practicable to withhold reinforcements for sickness behavior and provide adequate reinforcement for wellness behavior first in the health-care situation and then in the patient's normal environment.

The behavior-therapy approach has been successful in improving patients with a wide variety of conditions for which no adequate organic remaining cause could be found or in which patients were not achieving their maximum abilities to cope in spite of an organic problem. Impressive case histories have been presented for a variety of conditions in which the single-subject design was used with objective measures of performance before, during, and after the treatment to demonstrate that it was effective (Pomerleau & Brady 1979). What is lacking, unfortunately, in many cases is evidence on how exceptional or typical such remarkable cures are—on what percentage of patients with what diagnoses met which criteria for treatment, and on what percentage of them responded successfully. The best evidence comes from the treatment of pain in studies by Fordyce et al (1973) and by Roberts & Reinhardt (1980).

No brief summary can do justice to the variety of ingenious procedures that have been worked out by the behavior therapists to apply a number of additional principles of learning to the treatment of problems in physical medicine.

ADDICTIONS, APPETITE, AND HOMEOSTASIS   Other lines of research also are extending our knowledge of the role of learning to new types of medically significant phenomena. For example, clinical observations and experimental data summarized by Wikler (1980) led him to the hypothesis that learning plays a major role in addiction to heroin and in relapse after detoxification. A convincing series of experiments by Siegel et al (1982) has shown that learning plays a significant role in the habituation to repeated doses of opiates and in withdrawal symptoms. They also have experimentally confirmed the following predictions from principles of learning: (a) that after habituation has been achieved in one stimulus context, if a dose of the drug that would be innocuous in that context is administered in a radically different one, it can be lethal; and (b) that if addiction occurs in one stimulus context and if withdrawal until the absence of withdrawal symptoms is accomplished in a different stimulus context, return to the original context will reinstate the withdrawal symptoms. Neither of these outcomes would be expected from purely pharmacological effects. They seem to be in line with clinical experience, and the second one should be relevant to the treatment of drug addicts.

Booth et al (1976) have shown that learning to respond to specific tastes plays a significant role in the control of appetite. Miller (1981) has discussed new roles for learning in homeostasis. It seems highly probable that further research will show that learning is involved in additional types of medically significant phenomena.

Automation; Electronic Advances

One of the advantages of biofeedback is that its measuring instruments provide the therapist with better information than he could secure from his own sense organs. After initial training, the patient is able to use this information to guide his own practice, thus relieving the therapist from constant vigilance. Helped by this information, a patient often eventually learns to discriminate the sensations indicating the correctness of his responses and thus no longer needs the help of the measuring instrument. Psychologists have developed other ingenious approaches to use automation to extend the effectiveness of the therapist. For example, when a child must exercise a certain muscle group, he may be motivated to comply by equipment that keeps a cartoon show turned on as long as he is performing satisfactorily. Ingenious use of rapid advances in chip and microprocessor technology will allow such applications to be radically extended. They could greatly increase the cost-effectiveness of behavioral therapies, allow the patients to be given longer periods of practice, and in certain cases to continue that practice in the life situation, thus solving the problem of transfer from the clinic to everyday life (Miller & Dworkin 1982).

Conclusion

The examples that have been presented show how basic laboratory research on the neural and humoral systems controlled by the brain, on skeletal and visceral learning, and on the other aspects of behavior has led to practical applications of medical significance. Many of these advances would have been impossible without the use of experimental animals. Examples have also shown how clinical observations such as those of effects of "stress" on a variety of psychosomatic and other diseases have led to new lines of laboratory research on topics such as the effects of psychosocial factors on the immune and the cardiovascular systems and the effects on stomach lesions of the purely psychological variables of coping, discrimination, and conflict. As more psychologists come into contact with a greater variety of aspects of physical medicine, we may expect this to lead to many new interesting lines of laboratory research and also to new practical applications in prevention, diagnosis, and therapy. As our knowledge increases, we may be able to suggest modifications in the work place and in society that will lead to a more healthful environment (Frankenhaeuser 1976). But before any widespread applications of behavioral principles to medical problems are launched, they should be carefully evaluated by pilot studies.

Literature Cited

Ader, R. 1981. Behavioral influences on immune responses. See Weiss et al 1981, pp. 163–82. New York: Academic

Almy, T. P. 1951. Experimental studies on the irritable colon. *Am. J. Med.* 10: 60–67

Anderson, D. E. 1982. Behavioral hypertension mediated by salt intake. See Smith et al 1982

Bailit, H. L., Silversin, J. B. 1981. Introduction. *J. Behav. Med.* 4:243–46

Ball, G. G. 1967. Electrical self-stimulation of the brain and sensory inhibition. *Psychon. Sci.* 8:489–90

Basmajian, J. V. 1977. Learned control of single motor units. In *Biofeedback: Theory and Research*, ed. G. E. Schwartz, J. Beatty, pp. 415–31. New York: Academic

Beecher, H. K. 1956. Relationship of significance of wound to pain experienced. *J. Am. Med. Assoc.* 61:1609–13

Benson, H. 1975. *Relaxation Response.* New York: Morrow

Berkman, L. F., Syme, S. L. 1979. Social networks, host resistance, and mortality: A nine-year follow-up study of Alameda County residents. *Am. J. Epidemiol.* 109:186–204

Berry, R. E., Boland, J. P., Smart, C. N., Kanak, J. R. 1977. *The Economic Cost of Alcohol Abuse, 1975. Final Report.* Contract No. ADM 281–76–0016. Bethesda: Natl. Inst. Alcohol Abuse and Alcoholism

Booth, D. A., Lee, M., McAleavey, C. 1976. Acquired sensory control of satiation in man. *Br. J. Psychol.* 67:137–47

Brooks, F. P., Evers, P. W., eds. 1977. *Nerves and the Gut.* Thorofare, NJ: Slack

Cannon, W. B. 1953. *Bodily Changes in Pain, Hunger, Fear and Rage.* Boston: Branford. 2nd ed.

Cassel, J. 1973. The relation of the urban environment to health: Implications for prevention. *Mt. Sinai J. Med.* 40: 539–50

Center for Disease Control. 1980. *Ten Leading Causes of Death in the United States, 1977.* Washington DC: GPO

Cohen, F., Lazarus, R. S. 1979. Coping with the stresses of illness. In *Health Psychology: A Handbook*, ed. G. C. Stone, F. Cohen, N. E. Adler, pp. 217–54. San Francisco: Jossey-Bass

Conner, R. L., Vernikos-Danellis, J., Levine, S. 1971. Stress, fighting and neuroendocrine function. *Nature* 234:564–66

Cousins, N. 1979. *Anatomy of an Illness.* New York: Norton

Cromwell, R. L., Butterfield, E. C., Brayfield, F. M., Curry, J. C. 1977. *Acute Myocardial Infarction: Reaction and Recovery.* St. Louis: Mosby

Davis, M. S. 1966. Variations in patient's compliance with doctor's orders: Analysis of congruence between survey responses and results of empirical investigations. *J. Med. Educ.* 41:1037–48

Dembroski, T. M., Weiss, S. M., Shields, J. L., et al, eds. 1978. *Coronary-prone Behavior.* New York: Springer

Dollard, J., Miller, N. E. 1950. *Personality and Psychotherapy.* New York: McGraw-Hill

Eliot, R. S., Buell, J. C. 1981. Environmental and behavioral influences in the major cardiovascular disorders. See Weiss et al 1981b, pp. 25–39

Evans, R. I., Rozelle, R. M., Mittlemark, M. D., Hansen, W. B., Bane, A. L., Haris, J. 1978. Deterring the onset of smoking in children: Knowledge of immediate physiological effects and coping with peer pressure, media pressure, and parent modeling. *J. Appl. Soc. Psychol* 8:126–35

Fordyce, W. E., Fowler, R. S., Lehmann, J. F., DeLateur, B., Sand, P. L., Trieshmann, R. B. 1973. Operant conditioning in the treatment of chronic pain. *Arch. Phys. Med. Rehabil.* 54:399–408

Frankenhaeuser, M. 1976. The role of peripheral catecholamines in adaptation to understimulation and overstimulation. In *Psychopathology of Human Adaptation*, ed. G. Serban, pp. 173–91. New York: Plenum

Freeland, M., Calat, G., Schendler, C. E. 1980. Projection of natural health expenditures, 1980, 1985, and 1990. *Health Care Financ. Rev.* 1: 1-27

Friedman, R., Dahl, L. K. 1975. The effect of chronic conflict on the blood pressure of rats with a genetic susceptibility to experimental hypertension. *Psychosom. Med.* 37:402–16

Glass, D. 1977. *Behavior Patterns, Stress, and Coronary Disease.* Hillsdale, NJ: Erlbaum

Glass, D. 1981. Type A behavior: Mechanisms linking behavioral and pathophysiological processes. In *Myocardial Infarction and Psychosocial Risks*, ed. J. Siegrist, M. J. Halhuber. Berlin: Springer

Glazer, H. I., Weiss, J. M., Pohorecky, L. A., Miller, N. E. 1975. Monoamines as mediators of avoidance-escape behavior. *Psychosom. Med.* 37:535–43

Goldberg, J. R., Spealman, R. D., Goldberg, D. M. 1981. Persistent behavior at high rates maintained by intravenous self-administration of nicotine. *Science* 214:573–75

Gugel, R. N. 1979. The effects of group psychotherapy on orientation, memory, reasoning ability, social involvement, and depression of brain damaged and non-brain damaged aged patients exhibiting senile behavior. *Diss. Abstr. Int.* 60 (5), Order No. 7925268

Hamburg, D. 1974. Coping behavior in life-threatening circumstances. *Psychother. Psychosom.* 23:13–25

Hennessy, J. W., Levine, S. 1979. Stress, arousal, and the pituitary-adrenal system: A psychoendocrine hypothesis. *Prog. Psychobiol. Physiol. Psychol.* 8:133–78

Henry, J. P., Stephens, P. M. 1979. An animal model of neuropsychological factors in hypertension. In *Prophylactic Approach to Hypertensive Diseases,* ed. Y. Yamori, W. Lovenberg, W. Freis, pp. 299–307. New York: Raven

Herd, J. A. 1981. Behavioral factors in the physiological mechanisms of cardiovascular disease. See Weiss et al 1981, pp. 55–65

Hulley, S. B., Fortman, S. P. 1981. Clinical trials of changing behavior to prevent cardiovascular disease. See Weiss et al 1981, pp. 89–98

Hurd, P., Johnson, C. A., Pechacek, T., Bast, L. P., Jacobs, D. R., Luepker, R. V. 1980. Prevention of smoking in seventh grade students. *J. Behav. Med.* 3:15–28

Hypertension Detection and Follow-Up Program Cooperative Group. 1979. Five-year findings of the Hypertension and Follow-Up Program. I. Reduction in mortality of persons with high blood pressure, including mild hypertension. *J. Am. Med. Assoc.* 242:2562–71

Institute of Medicine. 1979. *Sleeping Pills, Insomnia, and Medical Practice.* Washington DC: Natl. Acad. Sci.

Institute of Medicine. 1980a. *Smoking and Behavior.* Washington DC: Natl. Acad. Sci.

Institute of Medicine. 1980b. *Alcoholism, Alcohol Abuse, and Related Problems: Opportunities for Research.* Washington DC: Natl. Acad. Sci.

Institute of Medicine. 1981. *Research on Stress and Human Health.* Washington DC: Natl. Acad. Press

Institute of Medicine. 1982. *Health and Behavior: A Research Agenda.* Washington DC: Nat. Acad. Press

Jacobson, E. 1938. *Progressive Relaxation.* Chicago: Univ. Chicago Press

Janis, I., ed. 1982. *Counseling on Personal Decision.* New Haven: Yale Univ. Press

Janis, I., Mann, L. 1977. *Decision-Making: A Psychological Analysis of Conflict, Choice, and Commitment.* New York: Free Press

Järvinen, K. A. J. 1955. Can ward rounds be a danger to patients with myocardial infarction? *Br. Med. J.* 1:318–20

Kamiya, J. 1969. Operant control of the EEG alpha rhythm and some of its reported effects on consciousness. In *Altered States of Consciousness,* ed. C. Tart, pp. 489–501. New York: Wiley

Keller, S. E., Weiss, J. M., Schleiffer, S. J., Miller, N. E., Stein, M. 1981. Suppression of immunity by stress: Effect of a graded series of stressors on lymphocyte stimulation in the rat. *Science* 213:1397–99

Kimmel, H. D. 1974. Instrumental conditioning of autonomically mediated responses in human beings. *Am. Psychol.* 29:325–35

Knowles, J. H., ed. 1977. *Doing Better and Feeling Worse.* New York: Norton 1979

Krasnegor, N. A., ed. 1979. *Cigarette Smoking as a Dependence Process* (Res. Monogr. #23). Washington DC: GPO. DHEW Publ. No. (ADM) 79–800

Lalonde, M. 1974. *A New Perspective on the Health of Canadians: A Working Document.* Ottawa: Gov. Canada

Levi, L., Andersson, L. 1975. *Psychosocial Stress—Population, Environment and Quality of Life.* New York: Spectrum

Levine, S., Ursin, H., eds. 1980. *Coping and Health.* NATO Conf. Ser. New York: Plenum

Levy, S. M., ed. 1982. *Biological Mediators of Behavior and Disease: Neoplasia.* New York: Elsevier Biomedical

Liebeskind, J. C., Paul, L. A. 1977. Psychological and physiological mechanisms of pain. *Ann. Rev. Psychol.* 28:41–60

Lindemann, J. E. 1981. *Psychological and Behavioral Aspects of Physical Disability.* New York: Plenum

Lown, B., Verrier, R., Corbalan, R. 1973. Psychologic stress and threshold for repetitive ventricular response. *Science* 182:834–36

Maccoby, N., Farquhar, J. W., Wood, P. D., Alexander, J. 1977. Reducing the risk of cardiovascular disease: Effects of a community-based campaign on knowledge and behavior. *J. Community Health* 3:100–14

Mahl, G. F. 1949. Effect of chronic fear on

the gastric secretion of HCl in dogs. *Psychosom. Med.* 11:30–44

Mahl, G. F. 1950. Anxiety, HCl secretion and peptic ulcer etiology. *Psychosom. Med.* 12:140–69

Mahl, G. F. 1952. Relationship between acute and chronic fear and the gastric acidity and blood-sugar levels in *Macaca mulatta* monkeys. *Psychosom. Med.* 14:182–210

Mahl, G. F., Karpe, R. 1953. Emotions and hydrochloric acid secretion during psychoanalytic hours. *Psychosom. Med.* 15:312–27

Matarazzo, J. D. 1982. Behavioral health's challenge to academic, scientific, and professional psychology. *Am. Psychol.* 37:1–14

McAlister, A. L., Perry, C., Maccoby, N. 1979. Adolescent smoking: Onset and prevention. *Pediatrics* 63:650–58

Melamed, B. G., Siegel, L. J. 1980. *Behavioral Medicine. Practical Applications in Health Care.* New York: Springer

Miller, N. E. 1948. Studies of fear as an acquirable drive: I. Fear as motivation and fear reduction as reinforcement in the learning of new responses. *J. Exp. Psychol.* 38:89–101

Miller, N. E. 1960. Learning resistance to pain and fear: Effects of overlearning, exposure and rewarded exposure in context. *J. Exp. Psychol.* 60:137–45

Miller, N. E. 1969. Learning of visceral and glandular responses. *Science* 163:434–45

Miller, N. E. 1972. A psychologist's perspective on neural and psychological mechanisms in cardiovascular disease. In *Neural and Psychological Mechanisms in Cardiovascular Disease*, ed. A. Zanchetti, pp. 345–60. Milano: Casa Editrice "Il Ponte"

Miller, N. E. 1974. Introduction: Current issues and key problems. In *Biofeedback and Self-Control 1973*, ed. N. E. Miller, T. X. Barber, L. V. DiCara, J. Kamiya, D. Shapiro, J. Stoyva, pp. xi–xx. Chicago: Aldine

Miller, N. E. 1978. Biofeedback and visceral learning. *Ann. Rev. Psychol.* 29:373–404

Miller, N. E. 1980a. A perspective on the effects of stress and coping on disease and health. See Levine & Ursin, pp. 323–53

Miller, N. E. 1980b. Effects of learning on physical symptoms produced by psychological stress. In *Selye's Gyide to Stress Research*, ed. H. Selye, pp. 131–67. New York: Van Nostrand Reinhold

Miller, N. E. 1981. Learning in the homeostatic regulation of visceral processes. In *Advances in Physiological Sciences*, Vol. 17, *Brain and Behavior*, ed. G. Ádam, I. Mészáros, É. I. Bányai, pp. 141–51. Budapest: Akad. Kiadó

Miller, N. E. 1982a. Motivation and psychological stress. In *The Physiological Mechanisms of Motivation*, ed. D. W. Pfaff, pp. 409–32. New York: Springer

Miller, N. E. 1982b. Some behavioral factors relevant to cancer. See Levy 1982, pp. 113–22

Miller, N. E. 1983. Understanding the use of animals in behavioral research: Some critical issues. In *The Role of Animals in Biomedical Research*, ed. J. Sechzer. New York: NY Acad. Sci. In press

Miller, N. E., Brucker, B. S. 1979. Learned large increases in blood pressure apparently independent of skeletal responses in patients paralyzed by spinal lesions. In *Biofeedback and Self-Regulation*, ed. N. Birbaumer, H. D. Kimmel, pp. 287–304. Hillsdale, NJ: Erlbaum

Miller, N. E., Dworkin, B. R. 1977. Critical issues in therapeutic applications of biofeedback. In *Biofeedback: Theory and Research*, ed. G. E. Schwartz, J. Beatty, pp. 129–62. New York: Academic

Miller, N. E., Dworkin, B. R. 1982. Potentialities of automation and of continuous recording and training in life. In *Behavioral Treatment of Disease*, ed. R. S. Surwit, R. B. Williams Jr., NATO Conf. Ser. New York: Plenum. In press

National Center of Health Statistics. 1979. *Advance Data from Vital and Health Statistics*, No. 54. Hyattville: Natl. Center Health Stat.

National Commission on Digestive Diseases. 1979. *Report to the Congress of the United States*, Vol. 1, *Digestive Diseases: Neglected Problems—Exciting Opportunities*. DHEW Publ. No. (NIH) 79–1878

Patel, C., North, W. R. S. 1975. Randomized controlled trial of Yoga and biofeedback in management of hypertension. *Lancet* 2:93

Patel, C. H., Marmot, M. G., Terry, D. J. 1981. Controlled trial of biofeedback-aided behavioral methods in reducing mild hypertension. *Br. Med. J.* 282:2005–8

Paton, W. 1983. Animal experiments in international perspective. See Miller 1983

Pavlov, I. P. 1927. *Conditioned Reflexes.* Transl. G. V. Anrep. London: Oxford Univ. Press

Pickering, T. G., Harshfield, G. A., Kleinert, H. D., Blank, D., Laragh, J. H. 1982. Blood pressure during normal daily activities, sleep, and exercise. *J. Am. Med. Assoc.* 247:992–96

Pomerleau, O. F. 1981. Underlying mechanisms in substance abuse: Examples from research on smoking. *Addict. Behav.* 6:187–96

Pomerleau, O. F., Brady, J. P., eds. 1979. *Behavioral Medicine: Theory and Practice.* Baltimore: Williams & Wilkins

Puska, P., Tuomilehto, J., Missiner, A., Salonen, J., Maki, J., Pallonen, U. 1980. Changing the cardiovascular risk in an entire community: The North Karelia project. In *Childhood Prevention of Atherosclerosis and Hypertension,* ed. R. M. Lauer, R. B. Shekelle, pp. 441–51. New York: Raven

Ray, W. J., Raczynski, J. M., Rogers, T., Kimball, W. H. 1979. *Evaluation of Clinical Biofeedback.* New York: Plenum

Rice, D. P., Kleinman, J. C. 1980. National health data for policy and planning. *Health Policy Educ.* 1:129–41

Rice, D. P., Feldman, J., White, K. 1976. *The Current Burden of Illness in the United States.* Washington DC: Natl. Acad. Sci.

Riley, V. 1981. Psychoneuroendoctrine influences on immunocompetence and neoplasia. *Science* 212:1100–9

Roberts, A. H., Reinhardt, L. 1980. The behavioral management of chronic pain: Long-term follow-up with comparison groups. *Pain* 8:151–62

Rodin, J., Langer, E. J. 1977. Long-term effect of a control-relevant intervention with the institutionalized aged. *J. Pers. Soc. Psychol.* 35:897–902

Rosen, J. C., Wiens, A. N. 1979. Changes in medical problems and use of medical services following psychological intervention. *Am. Psychol.* 34:420–31

Rosenman, R. H., Brand, R. J., Sholtz, R. I., Friedman, M. 1976. Multivariate prediction of coronary heart disease during 8.5 year follow-up in the Western Collaborative Group Study. *Am. J. Cardiol.* 37:902–10

Sackett, D. L., Haynes, R. 1976. *Compliance with Therapeutic Regimes.* Baltimore: Johns Hopkins Univ. Press

Sackett, D. L., Haynes, R. B., Gibson, E. S., Hackett, B. C., Taylor, D. W., et. al. 1975. Randomized clinical trial of strategies for improving medication compliance in primary hyptertension. *Lancet* 1:1205–7

Schramm, C. J. 1977. *Alcoholism and its Treatment in Industry.* Baltimore: Johns Hopkins Univ. Press

Schultz, J. H., Luthe, W. 1969. *Autogenic Therapy.* New York: Grune & Stratton

Schwartz, G. E., Weiss, S. M. 1978. Yale conference on behavioral medicine: A proposed definition and statement of goals. *J. Behav. Med.* 1:3–11

Shapiro, A. K. 1978. Placebo effects in medical and psychological therapies. In *Handbook of Psychotherapy and Behavior Change: An Empirical Analysis,* ed. S. L. Garfield, A. E. Bergen, pp. 369–410. New York: Wiley. 2nd ed.

Shapiro, A. P., Schwartz, G. E., Ferguson, D. C., Redmond, D. P., Weiss, S. M. 1977. Behavioral methods in the treatment of hypertension. I. Review of their clinical status. *Ann. Intern. Med.* 86:626–36

Siegel, S., Hinson, R. E., Krank, M. D., McCully, J. 1982. Heroin "overdose" death: Contribution of drug-associated environmental cues. *Science* 216:436–37

Skinner, J. E., Lie, J. T., Entman, M. L. 1975. Modification of ventricular fibrillation latency following coronary artery occlusion in the conscious pig: The effects of psychologic stress and beta-adrenergic blockade. *Circulation* 51:656–67

Smith, D. A., Galosy, R., Weiss, S. M., eds. 1982. *Circulation, Neurobiology, and Behavior.* New York: Elsevier North Holland. In press

Solomon, G. F., Levine, S., Kraft, J. K. 1968. Early experience and immunity. *Nature* 220:821–22

Stamler, J. 1974. The problem and the challenge. In *Hypertension Handbook.* Rahway, NJ: Merck, Sharp & Dohme

Stamler, J. 1981. The scientific foundation for prevention of coronary heart disease. *Am. J. Cardiol.* (March)

Stein, M., Schiavi, R. C., Camerino, M. 1976. Influence of brain and behavior on the immune system. *Science* 191:435–40

Stout, C., Morrow, J., Brandt, N., Wolfe, S. 1964. Unusually low incidence of death from myocardial infarction. *J. Am. Med. Assoc.* 188:845–55

Stroebel, C. 1979. *The Quieting Reflex.* New York: Guilford

Stunkard, A. J. 1976. *The Pain of Obesity.* Palo Alto: Bull Publ.

Stunkard, A. J., ed. 1980. *Obesity.* Philadelphia: Saunders

Surgeon General. 1979. *Healthy People.* Washington DC: GPO

Surgeon General. 1982. *Report.* Washington DC: GPO

Taylor, C. B., Ed. 1981. *Behav. Med. Abstr.* 2:1–199

Telch, M. J., Killen, J. D., McAlister, A. L., Perry, C. L., Maccoby, N. 1982. Long-term follow-up of a pilot project on smoking prevention with adolescents. *J. Behav. Med.* In press

United States Department of Health, Education, and Welfare. 1979. *Smoking and Health.* Washington DC: GPO. DHEW Publ. No. (PHS)79–50066

Van Itallie, T. B. 1979. Obesity: Adverse effects on health and longevity. *Am. J. Clin. Nutr.* 32:2723–33

Weiner, H., Thaler, M., Reiser, M. F., Mirsky, I. A. 1957. Etiology of duodenal ulcer. I. Relation of specific psychological characteristics to rate of gastric secretion (serum pepsinogen). *Psychosom. Med.* 19:1–10

Weiss, J. M. 1968. Effects of coping responses on stress. *J. Comp. Phsyiol. Psychol.* 65:251–60

Weiss, J. M. 1970. Somatic effects of predictable and unpredictable shock. *Psychosom. Med.* 32:397–408

Weiss, J. M. 1971. Effects of punishing the coping response (conflict) on stress pathology in rats. *J. Comp. Physiol. Psychol.* 77:14–21

Weiss, J. M., Glazer, H. I., Pohorecky, L. A., Brick, J., Miller, N. E. 1975. Effects of chronic exposure to stressors on avoidance-escape behavior and on brain norepinephrine. *Psychosom. Med.* 37:522–34

Weiss, J. M., Pohorecky, L. A., Salman, S., Gruenthal, M. 1976. Attenuation of gastric lesions by psychological aspects of aggression in rats. *J. Comp. Physiol. Psychol.* 90:252–59

Weiss, S. M., Cooper, T., Detre, T. 1981a. Coronary-prone behavior and coronary heart disease: A critical review. *Circulation* 63:1199–1215

Weiss, S. M., Herd, J. A., Fox, B. H. 1981b. *Perspectives on Behavioral Medicine.* New York: Academic

White, L., Tursky, B., eds. 1982. *Clinical Biofeedback: Efficacy and Mechanisms.* New York: Guilford

Wikler, A. 1980. *Opioid Dependence: Mechanisms and Treatment.* New York: Plenum

Williams, R. B. Jr., Haney, T., Blumenthal, J. A. 1981. Psychological and physiological correlates of Type A behavior pattern. See Weiss et al 1981, pp. 401–5

Wolf, S., Wolf, H. G. 1947. *Human Gastric Function: An Experimental Study of a Man and His Stomach.* New York: Oxford Univ. Press

Wynder, E. L., Hoffman, D. 1979. Tobacco and health. A societal challenge. *N. Engl. J. Med.* 300:894–903

Ann. Rev. Psychol. 1983. 34:33–61

ELECTROPHYSIOLOGY OF COGNITIVE PROCESSING

Steven A. Hillyard and Marta Kutas

Department of Neurosciences, University of California San Diego, La Jolla, California 92093

CONTENTS

INTRODUCTION

The "information processing" approach to human perception and cognition emerged during the 1950s as a revolutionary departure from previous conceptual frameworks (Haber 1974). Over the past 25 years or so, it has assumed considerable influence over the theories and research designs of most cognitive psychologists. Within this same time frame, computerized techniques have evolved for examining the processing of sensory information in the human brain at a physiological level. Small, phasic brain poten-

0066-4308/83/0201-0033$02.00

tials elicited in conjunction with sensory, cognitive, and motor events can be easily detected by means of noninvasive electrical recordings from the scalp. These "event-related potentials" (ERPs) are the far-field reflections of patterned neural activities associated with informational transactions in the brain. Much of the current research on ERPs has been directed toward identifying specific components of brain wave activity that signify the operation of information processing "stages" such as encoding, selecting, memorizing, decision making, etc, using experimental designs borrowed from the domain of cognitive psychology. This convergence of paradigms and conceptual frameworks between psychological and physiological research into human information processing is the subject matter of the present review.

The scalp-recorded ERPs elicited by sensory signals (also known as evoked potentials) may be described in terms of a series of positive and negative peaks or components that occur at characteristic times. Some of the short-latency components represent activity in the peripheral sensory pathways such as the auditory brainstem relay nuclei (Waves I-VI in Figure 1). Most of the earlier ERP components (occurring before 80 msec) vary as a function of physical stimulus parameters and are relatively insensitive to changes in information processing demands; hence, they have been termed "exogenous" or "stimulus bound." In contrast, some of the longer latency components only appear in conjunction with specific perceptual or cognitive processes and are considered to be "endogenous." Two of the most widely studied endogenous components are the "Nd" wave, elicited by auditory signals that belong to an attended source or channel of input, and the P3 or P300 wave, which follows signals that occur unexpectedly and provide task-relevant information (Figure 1).[1]

A major goal of the emerging field of "cognitive psychophysiology" (Donchin 1982) is to identify particular ERP components as markers of specific aspects or stages of information processing. This can be accomplished through painstaking determinations of the ERP's responsiveness to different task demands and its relationships with behavioral measures of the process in question. Once validated in this way, ERP measures can clarify the timing, ordering, and interactions of the intermediate processes that are engaged in specific cognitive activities and lead to inferences about the mechanisms of parallel, serial, or hierarchical processing. Used as "converging operations" with behavioral measures, ERP data can also assist in the classification of perceptual, cognitive, and linguistic processes. While

---

[1]Two different labeling systems for ERP components are in common use. The polarity of the component is designated by P or N, and this may be followed by a small number or letter (P3, Pa, etc) that specifies its ordinal position in some particular wave sequence, or by a larger number (P300, N156, etc) that refers to its mean latency of occurrence in milliseconds.

ONGOING EEG

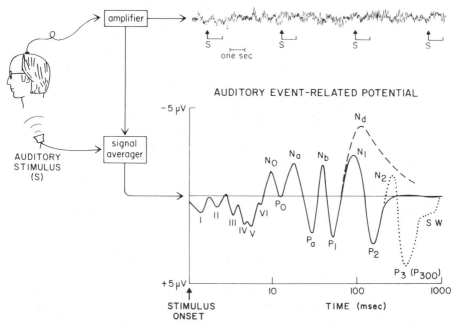

AUDITORY EVENT-RELATED POTENTIAL

Figure 1 Idealized waveform of the computer-averaged auditory event-related potential (ERP) to a brief sound. The ERP is generally too small to be detected in the ongoing EEG (top) and requires computer averaging over many stimulus presentations to achieve adequate signal/noise ratios. The logarithmic time display allows visualization of the early brainstem responses (Waves I-VI), the midlatency components (No, Po, Na, Pa, Nb), the "vertex potential" waves (P1, N1, P2), and task-related endogenous components (Nd, N2, P300, and slow wave).

qualitative differences in ERP patterns imply the operation of distinctive processing modes, an equivalence of ERP waveforms across tasks provides converging evidence for postulating a common stage of processing. Ultimately, as the physiological generators of the endogenous ERPs are identified through combined studies of humans and animals, we may be able to localize the brain systems that participate in specific cognitive activities (Galambos & Hillyard 1981).

The relationship of endogenous ERPs to cognitive processing has been examined thoroughly in several recent symposia (Callaway et al 1978, Otto 1978, Desmedt 1979, Begleiter 1979, Lehmann & Callaway 1979, Kornhuber & Deecke 1980, Galambos & Hillyard 1981, Donchin 1982). The present review concentrates on developments in this field subsequent to the coverage by Beck (1975) and John & Schwartz (1978) in the *Annual Review of Psychology.*

SELECTIVE ATTENTION

Theories of attention have traditionally been divided on the question of whether stimulus selections occur at an "early" or "late" stage of processing, or at both. Early selection theories assumed a rapid rejection of irrelevant stimuli based on a cursory examination of their physical properties by means of a hypothetical "filter" or "stimulus set" process (e.g. Broadbent 1971). Late selection models, in contrast, proposed that stimuli are analyzed in considerable detail before any selections take place (e.g. Norman 1968). This classic controversy still simmers, and evidence for both types of mechanisms is abundant (e.g. Keele & Neill 1978, Bookbinder & Osman 1979). There is now a large body of ERP evidence bearing on this "level of selection" issue. As described below, it appears that information about different stimulus features becomes available to attentional mechanisms at different times, depending upon stimulus and the task requirements.

Subcortical Gating

One possible mechanism for early stimulus selection involves the suppression or gating of irrelevant inputs at the peripheral levels of the sensory pathways (Hernandez-Peon 1966). A related proposal has implicated the modulation of sensory transmission at specific thalamic relay nuclei under the control of frontal cortex and midbrain reticular formation (Skinner & Yingling 1977). A number of animal investigations have supported the idea that selective gating of inputs to the cortex can occur as a function of stimulus relevance (Gabriel et al 1975, Olesen et al 1975, Oatman & Anderson 1977).

Since the earliest components of the scalp-recorded ERPs represent evoked neural activity in specific subcortical pathways (auditory) or primary cortical receiving areas (somatosensory), the possibility of subcortical gating during attention can be readily investigated in man. The click-evoked brainstem potentials reportedly remain invariant in the face of attentional shifts (Picton & Hillyard 1974, Picton et al 1971, Woods & Hillyard 1978), suggesting that peripheral modulation either was not operative or was not detectable in the tasks used. The midlatency click-evoked components between 10 and 50 msec were similarly insensitive to various attentional manipulations. More recently, however, Lukas (1980, 1981) has reported that components I (auditory nerve) and V (midbrain) of the tone-evoked potential from the brainstem were increased in amplitude and/or reduced in latency when the tones were attended. The modulation of auditory nerve activity was attributed to inhibitory influences on the hair cell receptors via the olivo-cochlear pathway under the control of higher centers. These promising results need to be followed up to determine the range of conditions under which subcortical modulation of auditory input may occur (e.g.

whether it occurs more readily with tones than with clicks) and whether it reflects an effective stimulus selection mechanism.

The primary cortical components of the somatosensory ERP were studied in an elegant experiment by Desmedt & Robertson (1977), wherein subjects switched attention between sequences of shocks applied to fingers of the two hands. The primary components with latencies between 20 and 40 msec were not sensitive to shifts of attention between the hands. Velasco et al (1980) similarly found that early cortical and subcortical (N20-P30) components, the latter recorded through depth probes, did not vary among conditions of attention (responding to evoking shocks), distraction (ignoring shocks), or inattention (responding to shocks on the opposite side). On the other hand, Lavine et al (1980) reported that the somatosensory P30 component was augmented during attention to a sequence of shocks in comparison with a distraction condition (mental arithmetic). Since their P30 measure was made with reference to an extended baseline or to the N70 peak, however, it is not clear whether attention-related modulation occurred in the primary cortical components themselves. By and large, present evidence does not seem conclusive on whether or not subcortical gating plays a substantive role in human selective attention.

Early Auditory Selection

A reliable ERP index of early selective attention has been reported under conditions where auditory stimuli were delivered in random order at rapid rates over two or more sensory channels[2] (Hillyard et al 1973, 1978). Under these "high load" conditions, auditory stimuli belonging to the attended channel elicited a broad negative ERP which began as early as 60–80 msec and increased the measured amplitude of the evoked N1 component. In most studies of this early ERP, attention was directed to one channel at a time by requiring subjects to detect "targets" that deviated slightly in some parameter (pitch, intensity, or duration etc) from the nontargets. The enhanced negativity was elicited by all stimuli, targets and nontargets alike, that shared the easily discriminable "channel cues" with the attended tones (Hink et al 1978c, Okita 1981, Donald & Little 1981). By presenting attended and unattended stimuli in random order and alternating attention between channels, this experimental design controlled for nonselective influences on the ERP due to global arousal or alertness factors (Naatanen 1975, Hillyard & Picton 1979).

Initially, this early attention effect was viewed as an augmentation of the evoked N1 wave to attended-channel stimuli (Hillyard et al 1973), but recent studies have made it clear that the negativity can extend well beyond

[2]The term "channel" is used here to designate the sensory cue characteristics that distinguish attended from unattended stimuli (e.g. ear of entry or tone frequency).

the normal time course of the N1 and is primarily endogenous in nature (Naatanen & Michie 1979, Okita 1979, Hansen & Hillyard 1980). This attention-related component, termed "processing negativity" by Naatanen and associates, can be readily visualized and quantified as the negative "difference wave" (Nd) between the ERP to stimuli in an attended channel minus the ERP to the same stimuli when they are not attended (that is, when another channel is attended, see Figure 2). The Nd has been resolved into two distinct phases; the second lasts up to several hundred milliseconds and is more frontally distributed than the first (Hansen & Hillyard 1980).

Because of its short latency of onset, the Nd effect was interpreted by Hillyard et al (1973) as a sign of an early mode of stimulus selection akin to the "stimulus set" or "filter" of Broadbent (1971) or the "input selection" of Treisman (1969). Naatanen (1982) has suggested that "a selective facilitation state in the sensory system" may provide the mechanism for stimulus

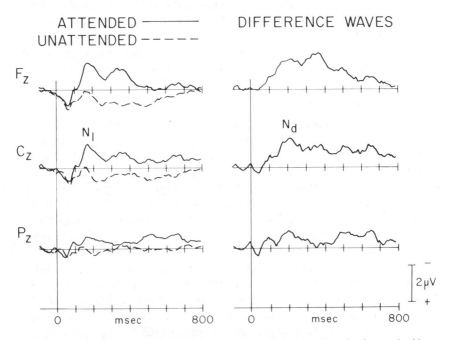

Figure 2   ERPs associated with selective attention to one of two channels of tones, in this case distinguished by frequency cues alone (300 Hz vs 700 Hz). High and low frequency tones were presented in random order at a rapid rate (about 3 per second). Subjects attended to one channel at a time, attempting to detect targets of longer duration therein. Attended-channel tones elicited a broad negative ERP, seen most clearly in the attended minus unattended difference waves (right). ERPs recorded from frontal (Fz), central (Cz), and parietal (Pz) scalp areas were averaged over several hundred stimulus presentations using a computer routine that extracts overlapping time epochs for stimulus presented at short intervals (Hansen & Hillyard 1982).

set. It is important to note in this connection that the *psychological* concept of a stimulus set or filter need not operate by means of a *physiological* gating or filtering mechanism (that is, by a simple modulation of exogenous activity) (Hillyard 1981a). Rather, a stimulus set implies that stimuli are selected rapidly and efficiently at an early stage of processing on the basis of some "distinct and conspicuous physical properties" (Keren 1976). This may be contrasted with a "response set" or "cognitive selection" whereby stimuli are distinguished by acquired categories of meaning, and hence must be analyzed more fully. Response set selections are associated with components later than the Nd, in many cases with the P300 component (Hillyard et al 1978).

Recent evidence has been generally supportive of the hypothesis that Nd is a neural sign of an early, stimulus set selection. This attention effect can be produced when channels are distinguished by a variety of physical cues (frequency, location, or intensity), and its latency of onset increases when the discrimination of the channel-cue is made more difficult (Hansen & Hillyard 1980). Okita (1979) has demonstrated nicely that the Nd effect appears when subjects attend to a moving channel of tones that shifts continuously in frequency and spatial location. Since a delayed Nd also can develop when the channels to be attended differ along more complex acoustic dimensions (e.g. the syllables "ba" vs "pa"), it appears that the speed of interchannel discrimination may be the limiting factor in allowing this attention effect to occur (Dickstein et al 1981).

If the Nd component reflects stimulus set selection, it follows that stimuli belonging to the rejected channel (and eliciting less early negativity) should not be processed to the same extent as those belonging to the attended channel. The consistent finding that target stimuli within the attended channel elicit much larger P300 components than do targets in the unattended channel has been taken to support such a hierarchical processing contingency (Hillyard et al 1978); stimuli that are rejected by the stimulus set do not reach the higher levels of analysis reflected in the P300. This conclusion must be tempered, however, by our incomplete understanding of the P300 wave, which is generally elicited by task-relevant stimuli that occur unexpectedly and require a motor response or cognitive decision. For instance, if the P300 is a sign of the "closure" of a decision process (Desmedt 1981) or a postdecisional updating of memory (Donchin et al 1978), then an absent P300 to targets in the unattended channel need not signify absence of perceptual processing of that channel.

Stronger evidence for an early perceptual selection has been obtained in a study where subjects listened selectively to one of four channels of tones, defined by two levels of frequency, each presented at two spatial locations (Hansen & Hillyard 1982). In some conditions, one of the two channel cues was made more difficult to discriminate than the other by moving the two frequencies or two spatial locations closer together. The ERPs to the tones in the attended channel and in the other channel that shared its easily discriminable attribute both showed an early Nd effect (at about 70 msec) in relation to tones in the channels that lacked the proper level of this attribute. About 100 msec later the attended channel ERP diverged from the ERP to tones that differed only along the less discriminable attribute. This ERP pattern suggests a hierarchical selection mechanism whereby tones are first selected (or rejected) on the basis of their easily discriminable attributes and then examined for more subtle cue characteristics. Most importantly, tones that were rejected for lacking the easily discriminable cue showed no ERP evidence of further analysis of their less discriminable attributes. This was taken as evidence against a single stage, late selection model.

There is general agreement that the Nd is a neural sign of some aspect of stimulus processing that follows the stimulus set selection, rather than the selection process itself (Naatanen & Michie 1979, Hillyard 1981a). Several proposals have been advanced: (a) Nd reflects the further analysis of attended-channel stimuli for their task relevant properties; (b) Nd is elicited to the extent that a stimulus matches or fulfills the cue specifications of the attended channel; and (c) Nd is associated with the maintenance and rehearsal of the cue characteristics of attended events in a short-term memory store (Picton et al 1978, Naatanen 1982).

In support of the "further analysis" hypothesis, Okita (1981) found that placing a target-defining pitch shift at the end of tone bursts in a two-channel attention task resulted in a delay of the buildup of Nd in relation to when the target information was provided at the onset of the tone. Moreover, the early phase of the Nd to standard tones was augmented when targets were presented more frequently (Donald & Little 1981) or when the tones were made more difficult to discriminate from a background noise (Schwent et al 1976). These results are difficult to account for under the "cue match" hypothesis. However, contrary to the predictions of the "further analysis" hypothesis, Parasuraman (1980) found that a moderate increase in the difficulty of the standard-target discrimination did not alter the Nd amplitude substantially in a two-channel selective attention task. Clearly, further work is needed to determine the precise role played by the Nd in selective auditory processing.

Early Somatosensory Selection

Desmedt & Robertson (1977) found that paying attention to shocks applied to one hand resulted in an early negative ERP to those stimuli, beginning at around 75 msec. This attention-related negativity augmented the amplitude of the N140 component and in some cases appeared to have an extended duration similar to the auditory Nd wave. The Nd to somatosensory stimuli was distinctive, however, in having an asymmetrical scalp distribution; it was larger over the sensory-motor cortex contralateral to the stimulated limb. At present it is not clear whether this negativity is entirely endogenous or includes some modulation of exogenous components.

Early Visual Selection

The relationship of visual ERPs to selective attention seems to be more complex than that in other modalities, with a variety of different components showing attention effects. The earliest visual changes identified so far occur during selective attention to spatial location, with subjects attending to flashing lights in one visual field while ignoring a concurrent sequence in the opposite field (Eason & Ritchie 1976, Van Voorhis & Hillyard 1977, Harter et al 1982). Attended-field flashes elicit ERPs with enlarged parieto-occipital components, including P1 (80–110 msec), N1 (160–180 msec), and P2 (200–250 msec) waves, together with a frontal-central N1 wave (150–170 msec) that lacks the prolonged duration of the auditory Nd component. Based on the polyphasic nature of the attention effect and its early onset, Eason & Richie suggested that it may arise from a gating of visual input at subcortical levels. The parieto-occipital components were largest over the hemisphere contralateral to the attended flashes. Hillyard (1981b) noted certain functional similarities between these ERPs in man and attention-related modulations of single unit discharge in the parietal lobe of trained monkeys.

Selective attention to other types of visual cues is manifested in specific configurations of ERP components. The cues (and the associated ERPs) that have been studied include the following: brightness (P200, Wastell & Kleinman 1980), color (N235, Harter et al 1982), spatial frequency (N160-350, Harter & Previc 1978), spatial orientation (N125, Harter et al 1979), contour (N150-235, Harter & Guido 1980), and alphanumeric characters (P250 and P450, Wastell & Kleinman 1980, Hillyard et al 1982). Since these attention-sensitive components differ in scalp distribution as well as in polarity and latency, they can be exploited to analyze the time course of the extraction of specific cue information from complex visual stimuli.

Multidimensional Stimulus Selection

There is current theoretical interest in the processing mechanisms that allow the separate attributes or dimensions of a compound stimulus to be integrated into a unified perceptual event (Miller 1978, Treisman & Gelade 1980). Do our attention mechanisms select the individual stimulus attributes of a multidimensional stimulus independently of one another or do we attend to the configuration of attributes (i.e. to the "object" itself)? It is possible to approach this question by recording ERPs to dual-attribute stimuli in a task where the attended events are defined as a conjunction of the attributes. The general design calls for presentation of randomized sequences of four stimuli, each having one of two levels of two attributes "A" and "B" (A1B1, A2B1, A1B2, and A2B2). When attention is directed toward each of these compound stimuli in turn, independent selection of the two attributes would be implied if the following relationship held among their ERPs:[3]

$$ERP\ (A^*B^*) - ERP\ (AB^*) = ERP\ (A^*B) - ERP\ (AB)$$

In other words, the ERP difference associated with selection of attribute A should not differ as a function of the level of attribute B. This type of equation has considerable generality for testing the independence of two processes using ERPs (Kutas & Hillyard 1980a).

This type of design was employed nicely by Harter and colleagues (1979). Subjects attended to one of four line gratings that were oriented either horizontally or vertically and had line widths of either 9 or 36 min. An early negative phase of the ERP obeyed the above equation, suggesting that selective attention resulted in independent analyses of the size and orientation features. Later components (beyond 250 msec), on the other hand, were specific to the attended conjunction (Harter 1982). It was concluded that selection takes place in two overlapping stages ("feature specific" and "conjunction specific"), and that the early selection may reflect modulation of activity in orientation-specific cortical channels.

A similarly structured experiment in the auditory modality revealed a different pattern of processing interactions. Hansen & Hillyard (1982) presented subjects with four channels of tone pips (high or low in frequency, at right and left locations), under instructions to detect occasional, longer duration tones in one channel at a time. When the two cues were highly discriminable, a large Nd was elicited only by tones in the attended channel (having the attended conjunction of frequency-location attributes). This ERP pattern argues against an independent feature selection mechanism for auditory frequency and localization. It was also found that delays in the onset latency of Nd brought about by reducing the discriminability of the channel-defining attributes were not paralleled by increases in either RT or

---

[3]A star beside a letter signifies that the ERP is recorded under a condition where that attribute is relevant. For example, A*B* refers to the attended stimulus compound, while A*B designates the ERP to the stimulus that shares attribute A but not B with the attended compound.

P300 latency to the longer duration targets. This was taken as supporting a "parallel contingent" model of cue selection (e.g. Hawkins 1969) wherein the duration attribute is processed in parallel with the channel attributes. A stimulus is rejected as soon as evidence accrues that any one of the attributes fails to match the target specifications.

ERP evidence has been used to reveal the ordering of cue selections to other types of stimuli as well. Harter & Guido (1980) found that the selection of linear grating patterns from diffuse flashes occurred in two distinct stages; an early ERP negativity (starting at 150 msec) registered the presence or absence of contour in the stimulus, while a later negativity (after 200 msec) was specific to the orientation of the attended grating. Recently, Harter et al (1982) have found that selection for location is manifest in the ERP prior to the selection for stimulus type (color and shape). They concluded that selection of relevant information is mediated by a hierarchical progression of temporally overlapping processes, with more complex stimulus features extracted at longer latencies.

Properties of Attentional Channels

The notion of a "channel" in sensory processing has been applied rather loosely to specific sources of stimuli in the environment, to circumscribed zones of receptor surface, or to sets of neurons that are selectively tuned to particular stimulus features. The concept of an "attentional channel," on the other hand, may be defined in terms of the set of stimuli that is processed more effectively when attention is directed toward a member of that set (Shiffrin et al 1976). Defining a channel as "that which is selected by attention" is not circular, but rather describes how narrowly stimulus selection is focused along a particular dimension.

The "bandwidth" of an attentional channel may be investigated with ERP techniques by measuring the progressive decline in amplitude of an attention-sensitive component as a function of distance from the attended locus. Harter & Previc (1978) have examined the properties of spatial frequency channels in the visual system. Subjects attended to a checkerboard having squares of a particular size (spatial frequency) presented among others of different sizes. A broad negative ERP (latency 150–300 msec) was elicited over the occipital scalp by the attended stimulus; its amplitude was reduced for spatial frequences that were increasingly disparate in size from the attended value. This attentional "tuning curve" became more sharply focused upon the attended locus at longer latencies. The authors suggested that selective attention modulated activity in spatial frequency-specific neural channels that were found to have a bandwidth similar to the attentional channels (about one octave).

The properties of attentional channels in other modalities have not been studied so systematically. In a study where tones were presented at five spatial locations with 45° separations between them, an Nd was elicited by the attended tones and by those at adjacent locations (Hink et al 1978a). While this suggests that the adjacent locations were included in the same attentional channel as the attended locus, the channel bandwidth for auditory spatial attention may well depend upon additional factors such as interstimulus interval (ISI), pitch cues, and task structure (cf Schwent & Hillyard 1975). For somatosensory attention, Desmedt & Robertson's (1977) data indicate that the attentional channel was broad enough to include at least two adjacent fingers, since shocks to either finger elicited equivalently enlarged N140 components when one was attended.

A central issue in the debate between early and late models of selective attention concerns the extent to which stimuli belonging to a presumably irrelevant or rejected channel are processed. While these early negative ERPs give some information on the breadth of an attentional channel, the P300 wave seems to be a particularly sensitive index of the degree of attention received by deviant stimuli in and out of the designated focus of attention. The P300 is generally largest for task-relevant stimuli, but deviant events within an attended sequence may elicit P300 waves even though they are not designated as task-relevant (Courchesne et al 1978, Roth et al 1978a). There is also evidence that deviant stimuli occurring on an irrelevant channel can elicit P300 waves if they are highly intrusive (e.g. N. K. Squires et al 1977), or if relevant and irrelevant channels are made less discriminable (Hansen & Hillyard 1982). Since the P300 waves to irrelevant stimuli habituate rapidly (Courchesne et al 1978) and correlate with behavioral measures of interference from the irrelevant events (N. K. Squires et al 1977), this ERP seems to index the extent to which attention is actively drawn to events outside the attended channel.

Infrequent stimuli that deviate from a repetitive auditory sequence elicit an earlier ERP complex that includes a negativity at about 200 msec (the N2, N200, or mismatch negativity) and a less consistent positivity at around 250 msec (the P3a) (N. K. Squires et al 1975, Snyder & Hillyard 1976, Ford et al 1976a,b, K. C. Squires 1977). Mismatch negativity is elicited by deviations in the pitch or intensity of tones in both attended and unattended channels (Naatanen et al 1980), and its amplitude appears to be determined primarily by the degree of deviation and stimulus probability. A somewhat earlier ERP (N140) is elicited by variations in the timing of repetitive sounds (Ford & Hillyard 1981). These mismatch negativities seem to reflect an automatic or preattentive registration of stimulus deviance from a steady-state background. This component may be a sign of the sensory template mismatch that has been postulated as a precursor to the orienting response (N. K. Squires et al 1975). If a deviant stimulus is processed further, either because it belongs to an attended channel or is salient enough to cause a redirection of attention, a P300 wave generally appears.

Temporal Dynamics of Attention

The speed with which attentional sets can be developed and switched has recently been evaluated using ERP measures. In a selective listening task, Donald & Young (1980) found that the Nd associated with selecting between tones in the two ears emerged almost immediately over the first few stimuli of each block. This contrasts with the slower buildup of attentional selectivity reported with dichotic verbal stimuli (Treisman et al 1974). A long-term habituation of the Nd, suggestive of a loss of interchannel selectivity with time on task, was also reported, but its generality is questionable (Hink et al 1978b).

The time course of the Nd may also reflect changes in selectivity as a function of ISI. At shorter ISIs, various measures of the Nd have been reported to increase in amplitude and decrease in latency (Parasuraman 1978, 1980, Naatanen et al 1982a). These effects may reflect an intensified selective set and/or a more rapid selection process invoked to deal with the increased information load. This improvement in ERP selectivity may result from the more frequent reinforcement of the memory representation of the attended cues at shorter ISIs (Hillyard 1981a, Naatanen 1982). These studies raise the possibility of using such ERP criteria to track attentional shifts on a moment to moment basis.

Resource Allocation

The selectivity of human information processing is often discussed in terms of the allocation of "attentional resources" to different tasks or classes of stimuli (Navon & Gopher 1979). Since these hypothetical resources are allocated from limited capacity "pools," improvement in performance of one task (benefits) may be associated with decrements in performance of other tasks (costs) that draw on the same resource pool. Allocations of attention among competing input channels are also reflected in ERP amplitudes. When subjects were required to detect targets in two channels simultaneously (divided attention), the amplitudes of the auditory Nd (or the visual N150) to each channel were intermediate between those elicited by the attended and rejected channels during focused attention (Hink et al 1977, Van Voorhis & Hillyard 1977, Parasuraman 1978, Okita 1979). Dividing attention also delayed the onset of Nd at high rates of stimulation (Parasuraman 1980). The total negativity elicited per unit time over both channels remained nearly constant, however, suggesting that these ERPs were indexing the allocation of processing resources from a limited pool.

Allocations of attention between two competing tasks have also been assessed through variations in the P300 elicited by task-related stimuli. Isreal et al (1980a, b) recorded the P300 in a "secondary" tone detection task performed concurrently with "primary" tasks such as tracking a visual target with a joystick or detecting shifts in target trajectories. P300 amplitudes were attenuated when the perceptual demands of the primary task were increased (e.g. more elements to be tracked), but not when the response demands became more severe (increases in tracking dimensionality or bandwidth). This result was consistent with a large body of evidence indicating that P300 indexes the processing resources involved with stimulus recognition and classification rather than response selection and execution (see below). Since reaction time (RT) data failed to differentiate increases in perceptual load from response load, the ERP measure was critical for the demonstration of multiple resources drawn from functionally distinct pools. Recent experiments along these lines have demonstrated a reciprocal relationship between the P300s elicited by primary and secondary task stimuli as the difficulty of one task was manipulated (Kramer et al 1981). The nature of these processing interactions, however, seems to depend on the subjects' level of practice and the specific tasks involved.

DETECTION AND RECOGNITION

Signal Detection Experiments

The ERP elicited by a threshold level acoustic signal provides a sensitive index of whether or not the sound was correctly detected. Early experiments showed that a large P300 component was elicited by correctly detected signals (Hits) but not by signals that were "missed." Moreover, the amplitude of P300 on Hits increased when the detections were made with greater accuracy or with a stricter decision criterion (Paul & Sutton 1972, K. C. Squires et al 1973). Mistaken reports of signal presence (False Alarms) on trials where no signal was present were also associated with a large P300 wave as long as the decision was made with a high degree of confidence and was time-locked to the averaging epoch (K. C. Squires et al 1975). Correct reports of signal absence (correct rejections) also elicited a P300 to the extent that decisions had a low probability of occurrence and adequate time-locking (see also Kerkhof 1978).

These experiments indicate that equivalent types of decisions are associated with equivalent endogenous ERPs, regardless of the actual physical stimulus. Whether the decision was based on signal presence or absence, P300 amplitudes were enlarged for more confident decisions and for less expected outcomes. Accordingly, Ruchkin & Sutton (1978) proposed that

P300 amplitude is related to the amount of prior uncertainty resolved by a stimulus; in communication theory terms, P300 is increased to the extent that the "equivocation" in the message is reduced.

The auditory N1 and the P300 components show parallel increases in amplitude and decreases in latency as a function of rated confidence of signal detections (K. C. Squires et al 1973, Parasuraman et al 1982). This suggests that the N1 component might be an index of the amount of signal information received by the detecting system (the "sensory magnitude" parameter of signal detection theory), while the P300 reflects some aspect of the decision process which utilizes that information. C. R. Chapman et al (1981) similarly found that variations in the somatosensory N1-P2 (N157-P237) components closely paralleled signal detection measures of pain discrimination. The authors suggested that this ERP also modeled the "sensory event" of detection theory and reflected the magnitude of the discharge of neural populations concerned with the perception of painful dental stimulation.

Parasuraman et al (1982) found a close correspondence between N1 and P300 amplitudes when subjects were required both to detect and identify tones of different frequencies. The N1 and P300 waves increased in amplitude with confidence of detection, but the P300 and a late slow wave were additionally sensitive to whether or not the signal was correctly identified. The authors concluded that stimulus detection and recognition were based on the same buildup of neural information, with detection beginning prior to recognition. However, the ERP and behavioral data suggested that detection and recognition could be dissociated and represented partially independent, overlapping processes in perception.

An interesting property of the threshold-detection P300 is its very short recovery or refractory period (Woods et al 1980). Unlike the long-latency exogenous components, the P300 showed little amplitude decrement in response to multiple signals presented at rates of two or three per second. This implies that the P300 reflects endogenous neural processes that are reactivated fully for each perceptual decision. The rapid recovery of the P300 closely parallels the speed with which sensory decisions can be executed (the psychological refractory period), indicating that P300 is generated by a neural system that shares the refractory properties of the decision process itself.

The P300 appears to represent a common, modality nonspecific process in these experiments, having a similar scalp distribution for detections of threshold level signals in auditory, visual, and somatic modalities (Snyder et al 1980); visual signals elicited the largest P300 amplitudes under conditions of modality uncertainty, perhaps reflecting an attentional bias toward vision. The detection of realistic visual targets (vehicles) in a simulated natural terrain is associated with especially large P300s that are visible on single trials (Cooper et al 1977).

Using a principal components analysis, Ruchkin et al (1980) showed that the ERP to detected threshold level tones could be dissected into overlapping P300 and slow wave components, which are confounded in conventional peak amplitude measures. While the P300 increased monotonically as a function of signal detectability, the slow wave showed the inverse relationship, suggesting that the slow wave may depend upon the level of task demands. Wilkinson & Seales (1978) warned that the P300 to detected tones also may be confounded with the positive-going offset of a prior contingent negative variation (CNV) component; reductions in the anticipatory CNV over a longer session may account for apparent reductions in the P300 with time on task. This thorny problem of how to disentangle multiple overlapping components is of increasing concern to investigators who wish to associate individual ERP configurations with specific aspects of information processing (Tueting 1978, Picton & Stuss 1980).

Recognition and Memory Matching

In the "oddball" type of experiment where subjects discriminate an infrequent "target" from a series of similar stimuli (e.g. Kutas et al 1977, Courchesne et al 1978), the elicitation of P300 is obviously contingent upon the recognition of the target. The appearance of P300 (and associated waves) thus depends upon those perceptual and mnemonic processes that underly stimulus recognition and classification. While the P300 is generally increased by assigning a task that makes a given class of stimuli relevant, there is evidence that P300 waves may be elicited by pictures (persons, places, paintings, etc) recognized by subjects given no task instructions other than to watch the "slide show" (Neville et al 1982c). This type of P300 clearly depends upon the subject's long-term memory for these familiar pictures and not upon performance of an assigned task to make differential responses.

Late positive ERPs are also elicited in tasks where a test stimulus must be compared with the short-term memory trace of a preceding stimulus (Posner et al 1973, Thatcher 1977, Sanquist et al 1980). In a classic series of experiments, Chapman and associates presented subjects with a randomized sequence of two numbers and two letters, with either numbers or letters designated as relevant (R. M. Chapman 1973, R. M. Chapman et al 1979, 1981). The second member of the relevant pair, which had to be compared with the first, elicited the largest P300 component. This would be expected if the P300 was triggered upon the recognition of stimulus relevance. The first relevant stimulus of the pair elicited a P250 component that correlated with behavioral measures of recall and was interpreted as a sign of storage in short-term memory. Friedman et al (1981) also found that the ERPs to numbers in a task that required the memory-matching of successive stimuli contained several late positive components, some of which were correlated with the requirement for short-term memory storage and others with target recognition. It is becoming clear that several late positive components are elicited in the 300–600 msec range during recognition and decision tasks (e.g. Friedman et al 1978), and that current concepts of the psychological correlates of "the P300" may have to be refined accordingly.

ERPs IN CHILDREN   Specific configurations of late ERPs are also associated with stimulus recognition and classification in children and infants. In 6- to 8-year-olds, the recognition of an assigned letter is followed by a series of late waves including Nc (400 msec), P3 (700 msec) and Pc (950 msec) components (Courchesne 1978). With maturation there is a progressive diminution of the Nc and Pc waves, leaving the P300 as the most prominent component in the adult ERP to infrequent target stimuli. Courchesne suggested that the Nc was associated with the perception of "attention getting" events. In a color discrimination task, a late positive component at about 400 msec was found to characterize the target ERP of 5- to 8-year-old children (Kurtzberg et al 1979); this wave showed changes in laterality which were ascribed to the maturation of parietal association areas involved in nonverbal processing.

The frontally distributed Nc component was also found to be a reliable measure of visual discrimination in 4- to 7-month-old infants (Courchesne et al 1981). When a random sequence of photographs of two faces was shown to alert infants, the less frequently presented face elicited a much larger Nc wave. In a similar design with 3-month-old infants, Hofmann et al (1981) found that the more infrequent of two striped patterns elicited a larger late positivity (300–600 msec) over the posterior scalp. This type of paradigm where differential ERPs are recorded to frequent/infrequent or familar/unfamiliar stimuli offers a powerful approach for analyzing perceptual and cognitive development in both normal and mentally deficient children.

ERPS AND MENTAL CHRONOMETRY

Belying its name, the P300 component associated with the detection of task-relevant stimuli has been found to vary in latency from less than 300 to nearly 1000 msec poststimulus; its latency is systematically lengthened as a function of increasing task difficulty or complexity of stimulus evaluation (Donchin et al 1978). While many of the same factors that influence behavioral measures of processing time also alter P300 latencies, these two metrics are dissociable and often display noncommensurate changes (e.g. N. K. Squires et al 1977).

Kutas et al (1977) manipulated the RT-P300 latency relationship by requiring subjects to perform simple or complex semantic categorizations in order to detect target stimuli during different response regimes. They found that under instructions stressing "speeded" responses the P300 latency-RT correlation was relatively low, whereas under "accuracy" instructions it was significantly elevated. It was proposed that P300 latency and RT are indices of the timing of different aspects of processing: while RT encompasses all the processes leading to a cognitive decision and behavioral response, the P300 latency is a pure measure of the duration of stimulus evaluation processes (encoding, recognition, and classification), independent of response selection and execution.

A direct test of this hypothesis was carried out by McCarthy & Donchin (1981). Stimulus evaluation time was manipulated by embedding a target word either in a matrix of # signs or within a confusable background of letters, while response selection was manipulated by changing the compatibility between the target word ("right" or "left") and the responding hand. The results showed that both visual "noise" and stimulus-response incompatibility increased RT to the target words, but only the presence of the "noisy" stimulus background had a significant effect on P300 latency.

Several researchers have taken advantage of this established relationship between P300 latency and stimulus evaluation time to assess alternative theories of perceptual processing. Duncan-Johnson & Donchin (1980) investigated the well-known reduction in RT that is seen for more highly expected events. Based on their finding that P300 latency and RT covaried as a function of target probability, they concluded that stimulus expectancy in choice RT situations influences both stimulus evaluation and response mobilization times. A similar approach has been employed to pinpoint the locus of interference in the Stroop color word test (Warren & Marsh 1979, Duncan-Johnson & Kopell 1981). In a standard Stroop task, RTs showed the usual interference effect between hue and word meaning. While the latency of the P300 remained invariant. This suggested that the Stroop effect was mainly attributable to response incompatibility rather than perceptual interference.

ERP investigations using the Sternberg memory matching paradigm have also revealed nonequivalent changes in P300 latency and RT, this time as a function of memory set size (Marsh 1975, Gomer et al 1976, Adam & Collins 1978, Roth et al 1978b). Both P300 latency and RT increased linearly with greater short-term memory load, but the slope of the function was steeper for RT (about 40 msec per item) than for P300 latency (about 25 msec per item). Given the close correspondence between P300 latency and stimulus evaluation time, there is every reason to believe that the P300 latency is a better measure of memory scanning than is RT (R. M. Chapman et al 1981).

Ford and colleagues (1979) used the pattern of P300 latency-RT covariation in a Sternberg-type task to compare the speed of short-term memory processes in young and elderly persons. They found that the elderly were much slower in responding to a probe stimulus in or out of the memorized set and displayed a steeper slope of increasing RT as a function of memory set size. However, their P300 latencies were only slightly longer than those of the younger subjects and showed identical slopes as a function of set size, indicating that both groups evaluated the probe against items in memory at the same rate. Accordingly, the longer response times of elderly subjects were almost entirely attributable to delays in response mobilization rather than to slower speeds of short-term memory processes.

The P300 generally occurs as part of an endogenous complex of components in which it is preceded by a negative peak (the N2 or N200) and followed by a long-lasting slow wave. Unlike the P300, the N200 is modality specific, being largest over preoccipital areas for visual stimuli and over the vertex for auditory stimuli (Simson et al 1977). Its earlier onset and modality specificity have led to the suggestion that the N200 may well be even more closely coupled to stimulus evaluation processes than the P300. Ritter et al (1979) found that increasing the difficulty of target detections produced approximately equivalent increases in RT, P300 latency, and N200 latency, but the correlation between N200 latency and RT was greater than that between P300 and RT. Towey et al (1980) obtained similar delays in the N200 with increasing difficulty of an auditory intensity discrimination that required mental counting. The latencies of the N200 and P300 were also found to increase in close correspondence with one another when the relevant cue for decision was systematically delayed (Hammond et al 1979). These findings suggest that the discriminative processing indexed by N200 gives rise to the P300, which reflects the next phase of memory updating or decision closure.

Renault et al (1982) have distinguished two types of "N200" components in a visual RT task, one related to modality-specific processing (N220) and the other to an "orienting" response (N256). The interrelationships between ERP and RT measures were taken to be consistent with "parallel contingent" or "cascade" models of information processing. Naatanen et al (1982b) have similarly distinguished an early "mismatch negativity" (N2a), which registers modality-specific stimulus deviations, and a later N2b which occurs as part of the endogenous ERP complex (that includes the P300) associated with the shifting of attention toward a deviant stimulus.

LANGUAGE PROCESSING

Linguistic Categories

Several recent investigations have been aimed at identifying ERP signs of specific levels of language processing ranging from the phonetic to the semantic. Sometime ago, Wood and colleagues reported that the auditory ERP recorded from the left hemisphere differed as a function of whether the eliciting CV syllable had been analyzed for phonetic or acoustic (fundamental frequency) cues (see Wood 1975). Grabow et al (1980) failed to replicate these findings, although they did note that the ERPs to CV syllables were consistently smaller over the left than the right temporal recording sites. Molfese (1978, 1980) also recorded ERPs to CV syllables, vowels, and nonspeech sounds and reported that some of the systematic variability in the ERPs reflected the presence or absence of formant transitions while a different component varied with formant bandwidth.

The search for ERP manifestations of meaning has taken several distinctly different tacks. R. M. Chapman et al (1980) have studied the ERPs associated with Osgood's orthogonal dimensions of connotative meaning—evaluative, potency, and activity. From their analysis, Chapman et al concluded that ERPs contain information about connotative meanings that is independent of any particular word. Semantic content was evident in a combination of ERP components, with the evaluative dimension showing the strongest correlations.

Brown and associates (1976, 1980) have also compared the ERPs to words with different meanings. Their approach, however, was to compare homophones invested with different meanings either by a sentence context or by instructions that predisposed a particular interpretation. Consistent ERP differences were found between the noun and verb forms of homophones, with the largest waveform differences localized to the left anterior scalp regions. A detailed examination of the topography of the scalp field potentials revealed that the noun forms of the homophones elicited greater positivity anteriorly and greater negativity posteriorly than did the verb forms. This ERP effect was fairly consistent across languages, modalities, and individuals. At present it is not known whether these ERP differences are specific to the semantic or syntactic aspects of the homophones.

There are indications that ERPs reflect the division of the lexicon into "open class" or content words, such as nouns, verbs, and adjectives, and "closed class" or function words that include members of the minor lexical categories (prepositions, conjunctions, auxiliaries, articles, etc). Kutas & Hillyard (1982a) reported differences in scalp distribution between the ERPs elicited by words belonging to these two vocabulary classes in two different experiments. The ERPs associated with open class words were characterized by a larger sustained positivity between 200–700 msec post-stimulus and by a greater left-right asymmetry in the 400 to 700 msec region than were the ERPs associated with the closed class words.

Effects of Context and Expectancy

Specific ERP components have been associated with the development and violation of semantic expectancies during reading. Kutas & Hillyard (1980a,b) reported that the ERPs to semantically anomalous words in otherwise meaningful sentences were marked by an enhanced centro-parietal negativity between 300 and 600 msec poststimulus (N400). The authors proposed that this N400 may be an electrophysiological sign of the interruption of sentence processing by a semantically inappropriate word and the attempt to reinterpret that information. Control experiments showed that nonlinguistic deviations in visually presented sentences did not elicit N400 components; for example, semantically appropriate words unpredictably presented in oversize boldface print were associated with ERPs characterized by a triphasic, late positivity.

Violations of grammatical structure that did not involve semantic incongruity were not associated with N400 waves (Kutas & Hillyard 1982a). Unpredictable grammatical errors such as incorrect noun-verb number correspondence or incorrect verb tense occurring in prose passages did not elicit clear N400 waves like those that followed semantic anomalies. These results indicate that the N400 component is not a general response to aberrant words in a sentence or prose passage but appears to be contingent on some aspect of semantic analysis. Unlike the P300 response to other surprising classes of stimuli, the N400 is relatively insensitive to manipulations of probability of occurrence of semantic anomalies and shows a slight but consistent right hemispheric predominance in amplitude and duration (Kutas & Hillyard 1982b).

We have recently undertaken a parametric evaluation of the relation between the N400 and word expectancy for terminal words in a group of sentences of which none were semantically anomalous. We borrowed 320 sentences for which Bloom & Fischler (1980) had established the degree of expectancy (Cloze probability) for alternative terminal words. The amplitude of the ERP in the 300 to 600 msec region to final words was highly correlated with the Cloze probability of those words, particularly for recordings taken over the posterior right hemisphere (r above 0.90 over 14 subjects). This suggests that the N400 effect is not contingent upon semantic incongruity but is instead a more general phenomenon that provides a graded measure of semantic expectancy in sentence contexts. These results link the N400 measure with a number of verbal processing phenomena that depend upon expectancy (semantic priming, lexical decision making, word recognition, etc).

The enhancement of a negative component at around 400 msec has been observed in a number of other experiments where subjects were required to read, name, or make a decision about a word based on its semantic attributes. In a study where subjects judged pairs of words to be the same or different by a semantic criterion (Sanquist et al 1980), the ERPs to the semantic mismatches displayed an increased negativity at around 400 msec. Boddy & Weinberg (1981) also showed ERP waveforms having larger N400 components to words that did not belong to a previously named category. Similar results were obtained by Polich et al (1981) in experiments involving semantic category judgments; they concluded that a late negativity (300–500 msec) was elicited by stimuli that did not belong to the category expected by the subject.

Late negative ERPs in the 400 msec range have also been reported in response to single words that were read orally or pictures that were named out loud. Stuss et al (1982) found that both pictures and words elicited a double-peaked negativity that was similar in morphology to the N400 associated with "semantic incongruity," but it had a more frontal scalp distribution. In this experiment, the stimuli were not semantically anomalous but were unpredictable as to content. Thus, the associated late negativity might reflect some aspect of the semantic activations triggered by unexpected words and other meaningful stimuli.

Neville and colleagues (1982a) found a negative component peaking at 410 msec in response to visually presented words which subjects had to identify in writing. The N410 was largest over anterior temporal regions and differed markedly from the late negativities described above in its scalp asymmetry, being larger over the left than the right hemisphere. This asymmetry was largest for words in the right visual field, which also showed the largest behavioral asymmetry for recognition. This pattern of asymmetries was not evident in the ERPs recorded from congenitally deaf subjects under the same conditions, suggesting differences in hemispheric specialization for linguistic functions in persons with abnormal language experience (Neville et al 1982b).

The exact relationship of these late negativities to various aspects of semantic processing has yet to be established. Nonetheless, the sensitivity with which these ERPs reflect verbal contexts and expectancies suggests that they will prove useful for analyzing the mechanisms by which word meanings are accessed during reading. Converging studies of ERPs and eye fixation patterns during reading (Just & Carpenter 1980) should make it possible to measure the intake of semantic information on a word-by-word basis with minimal disruption of natural modes of language usage.

CONCLUSION

The recording of ERPs from the scalp makes it possible to study cognitive and linguistic processes with greater precision than can be achieved with behavioral techniques alone. By providing a "second window" into the information processing activities of the human brain, ERP data have proven helpful in teasing apart stimulus evaluation from response mobilization factors, in identifying hierarchical levels of stimulus selection, and in distinguishing serial from parallel stimulus analyses. In the area of linguistics, specific ERP configurations are associated with fundamental theoretical categories such as function/content words and semantic/syntactic levels of analysis. However, we should not be too surprised or disconcerted by occasional dissociations between observed ERP patterns and those expected on theoretical grounds. Indeed, it is unlikely that the physiological signs of information processing will always bear a one-to-one correspondence with the constructs inferred from behavioral data (Donchin 1979). Such dissociations should not be cause for despair, but rather serve as an impetus to formulate new hypotheses regarding the processing events in question.

As ERP components continue to be validated as markers of specific cognitive and linguistic processes, they will have increasing utility for evaluating clinical syndromes. Latency measurements of exogenous ERPs have already become standardized diagnostic tests for neurological diseases affecting the integrity of the sensory pathways (Starr 1978). On the other hand, some of the endogenous ERPs seem particularly well suited for evaluating syndromes that involve deficits of selective attention such as hyperactivity (Loiselle et al 1980) and schizophrenia (Hink & Hillyard 1978). Tests of memory function derived from P300 latency measures are being applied to conditions where deficiencies of recognition and storage have been implicated (e.g. Goodin et al 1978, Ford et al 1979). Severe forms of psychopathology such as autism are reportedly associated with unusual late ERP configurations (Novick et al 1980). The recent observations of ERPs specific to semantic processing open the way for electrophysiological assessment of reading disorders and other forms of language deficiency. Finally, there are indications that endogenous ERPs can assess the impact of altered early environments upon later cognitive and linguistic development (Neville et al 1982a,b).

The ERP methodology can also play a significant role in the search for neural substrates of cognition. The enormous gulf that separates the realm of cellular neurophysiology from the domain of behavior and cognition has made it exceedingly difficult to conceptualize the electrochemical bases of thought and action. Since ERPs reflect patterns of neuronal activity at the physiological level and are correlated with perceptual and cognitive acts at the psychological level, they may provide a means for bridging this gap. A research strategy to this end would involve, first, identifying ERPs in animals that are homologous to those associated with known cognitive activities in man, and, second, characterizing their neuronal generators through invasive recording and lesioning techniques (Galambos & Hillyard 1981). This approach, supplemented by such evidence as is available from human patient ERP recordings and studies of localized cerebral metabolism (Lassen et al 1978), should yield new insights into the nature of the elusive connections between mind and body.

ACKNOWLEDGMENTS

This work was supported by grants from NIMH #1 R01 MH25594, NSF #BNS80-05525, Sloan Foundation #B1980. M. Kutas is supported by a Research Scientist Development Award, NIH #1K02MH00322. Thanks to H. J. Neville for her editorial suggestions.

Literature Cited

Adam, N., Collins, G. I. 1978. Late components of the visual evoked potential to search in short-term memory. *Electroencephalogr. Clin. Neurophysiol.* 44: 147–56

Beck, E. C. 1975. Electrophysiology and behavior. *Ann. Rev. Psychol.* 26:233–62

Begleiter, H., ed. 1979. *Evoked Brain Potentials and Behavior.* New York: Plenum

Bloom, P. A., Fischler, I. 1980. Completion norms for 329 sentence contexts. *Mem. Cognit.* 8:631–42

Boddy, J., Weinberg, H. 1981. Brain potentials, perceptual mechanism and semantic categorization. *Biol. Psychol.* 12: 43–61

Bookbinder, J., Osman, E. 1979. Attentional strategies in dichotic listening. *Mem. Cognit.* 7:511–20

Broadbent, D. E. 1971. *Decision and Stress.* New York: Academic

Brown, W. S., Lehmann, D., Marsh, J. T. 1980. Linguistic meaning-related differences in evoked potential topography: English, Swiss-German, and imagined. *Brain Lang.* 11:340–53

Brown, W. S., Marsh, J. T., Smith, J. C. 1976. Evoked potential waveform differences produced by the perception of different meanings of an ambiguous phrase. *Electroencephalogr. Clin. Neurophysiol.* 41: 113–23

Callaway, E., Tueting, P., Koslow, S., eds. 1978. *Event-Related Brain Potentials in Man.* New York: Academic

Chapman, C. R., Chen, A. C. N., Colpitts, Y. M., Martin, R. W. 1981. Sensory decision theory describes evoked potentials in pain discrimination. *Psychophysiology* 18:114–20

Chapman, R. M. 1973. Evoked potentials of the brain related to thinking. In *The Psychophysiology of Thinking,* ed. F. J. McGuigan. New York: Academic

Chapman, R. M., McCrary, J. W., Bragdon, H. R., Chapman, J. A. 1979. Latent components of event-related potentials functionally related to information processing. See Desmedt 1979, pp. 80–105

Chapman, R. M., McCrary, J. W., Chapman, J. A. 1981. Memory processes and evoked potentials. *Can. J. Psychol.* 35:201–12

Chapman, R. M., McCrary, J. W., Chapman, J. A., Martin, J. K. 1980. Behavioral and neural analyses of connotative meaning: Word classes and rating scales. *Brain Lang.* 11:319–39

Cooper, R., McCallum, W. C., Newton, P., Papakostopoulos, D., Pocock, P. V., Warren, W. J. 1977. Cortical potentials associated with the detection of visual events. *Science* 196:74–77

Courchesne, E. 1978. Neurophysiological correlates of cognitive development: Changes in long-latency event-related potentials from childhood to adulthood. *Electroencephalogr. Clin. Neurophysiol.* 45:468–82

Courchesne, E., Courchesne, R. Y., Hillyard, S. A. 1978. The effect of stimulus deviation on P3 waves to easily recognized stimuli. *Neuropsychologia* 16:189–99

Courchesne, E., Ganz, L., Norcia, A. M. 1981. Event-related brain potentials to human faces in infants. *Child Dev.* 52:804–11

Desmedt, J. E., ed. 1979. Cognitive components in cerebral event-related potentials and selective attention. In *Progress in Clinical Neurophysiology*, Vol. 6. Karger: Basel. 319 pp.

Desmedt, J. E. 1981. Scalp-recorded cerebral event-related potentials in man as point of entry into the analysis of cognitive processing. In *The Organization of the Cerebral Cortex*, ed. F. O. Schmitt, F. G. Worden, G. Adelman, S. D. Dennis, 19:441–73. Cambridge, Mass: MIT Press

Desmedt, J. E., Robertson, D. 1977. Differential enhancement of early and late components of the cerebral somatosensory evoked potentials during forced-paced cognitive tasks in man. *J. Physiol.* 271:761–82

Dickstein, P. W., Hansen, J. C., Berka, C., Hillyard, S. A. 1981. Electrophysiological correlates of selective attention to speech sounds. *Soc. Neurosci.* 7:452 (Abstr.)

Donald, M. W., Little, R. 1981. The analysis of stimulus probability inside and outside the focus of attention, as reflected by the auditory N1 and P3 components. *Can. J. Psychol.* 35:175–87

Donald, M. W., Young, M. 1980. Habituation and rate decrements in the auditory vertex potential during selective listening. See Kornhuber & Deecke 1980, pp. 331–66

Donchin, E. 1979. Event-related brain potentials: A tool in the study of human information processing. In *Evoked Brain Potentials and Behavior*, ed. H. Begleiter, pp. 13–88. New York: Plenum

Donchin, E., ed. 1982. *Cognitive Psychophysiology*. Hillsdale, NJ: Erlbaum

Donchin, E., Ritter, W., McCallum, W. C. 1978. Cognitive psychophysiology: The endogenous components of the ERP. See Callaway et al 1978, pp. 349–441

Duncan-Johnson, C. C., Donchin, E. 1980. The relation of P300 latency to reaction time as a function of expectancy. See Kornhuber & Deecke, pp. 717–22

Duncan-Johnson, C. C., Kopell, B. S. 1981. The Stroop effect: Brain potentials localize the source of interference. *Science* 214:938–40

Eason, R. G., Ritchie, G. 1976. *Effects of stimulus set on early and late compo-*

nents of visually evoked potentials. Presented at Psychon. Soc., St. Louis

Ford, J. M., Hillyard, S. A. 1981. ERPs to interruptions of a steady rhythm. *Psychophysiology* 18:322–30

Ford, J. M., Roth, W. T., Kopell, B. S. 1976a. Auditory evoked potentials to unpredictable shifts in pitch. *Psychophysiology* 13:32–39

Ford, J. M., Roth, W. T., Kopell, B. S. 1976b. Attention effects on auditory evoked potentials to infrequent events. *Biol. Psychol.* 7:65–77

Ford, J. M., Roth, W. T., Mohs, R. C., Hopkins, W. F., Kopell, B. S. 1979. Event-related potentials recorded from young and old adults during a memory retrieval task. *Electroencephalogr. Clin. Neurophysiol.* 47:450–59

Friedman, D., Vaughan, H. G. Jr., Erlenmeyer-Kimling, L. 1978. Stimulus and response related components of the late positive complex in visual discrimination tasks. *Electroencephalogr. Clin. Neurophysiol.* 45:319–30

Friedman, D., Vaughan, H. G. Jr., Erlenmeyer-Kimling, L. 1981. Multiple late positive potentials in two visual discrimination tasks. *Psychophysiology* 18:635–49

Gabriel, M., Saltwick, S. E., Miller, J. D. 1975. Conditioning and reversal of short-latency multiple-unit responses in the rabbit medial geniculate nucleus. *Science* 189:1108–9

Galambos, R., Hillyard, S. A. 1981. Electrophysiological approaches to human cognitive processing. *Neurosci. Res. Program Bull.* 20:141–265

Goodin, D. S., Squires, K. C., Starr, A. 1978. Long latency event-related components of the auditory evoked potentials in dementia. *Brain* 101:635–48

Gomer, F. E., Spicuzza, R. J., O'Donnell, R. D. 1976. Evoked potential correlates of visual item recognition during memory-scanning tasks. *Physiol. Psychol.* 4: 61–65

Grabow, J. D., Aronson, A. E., Offord, K. P., Rose, D. E., Greene, K. L. 1980. Hemispheric potentials evoked by speech sounds during discrimination tasks. *Electroencephalogr. Clin. Neurophysiol.* 49:48–58

Haber, R. N. 1974. Information processing. In *Handbook of Perception*, ed. E. C. Carterette, M. P. Friedman, 1:313–34. New York: Academic

Hammond, E. J., Silva, D. A., Klein, A. J., Teas, D. C. 1979. A technique for separating endogenous from exogenous human cortical potentials. *Electroencephalogr. Clin. Neurophysiol.* 46:482–85

Hansen, J. C., Hillyard, S. A. 1980. Endogenous brain potentials associated with selective auditory attention. *Electroencephalogr. Clin. Neurophysiol.* 49: 277–90

Hansen, J. C., Hillyard, S. A. 1982. Selective attention to multidimensional auditory stimuli in man. *J. Exp. Psychol: Hum. Percept. Perform.* In press

Harter, M. R. 1982. Discussion on selective attention. See Donchin 1982

Harter, M. R., Aine, C., Schroeder, C. 1982. Hemispheric differences in ERP measures of selective attention. See Stuss et al 1982

Harter, M. R., Guido, W. 1980. Attention to pattern orientation: Negative cortical potentials, reaction time, and the selection process. *Electroencephalogr. Clin. Neurophysiol.* 49:461–75

Harter, M. R., Previc, F. H. 1978. Size-specific information channels and selective attention: Visual evoked potential and behavioral measures. *Electroencephalogr. Clin. Neurophysiol.* 45: 628–40

Harter, M. R., Previc, F. H., Towle, V. L. 1979. Evoked potential indicants of size- and orientation-specific information processing: Feature-specific sensory channels and attention. See Lehmann & Callaway 1979, pp. 169–84

Hawkins, H. L. 1969. Parallel processing in complex visual discrimination. *Percept. Psychophys.* 5:56–64

Hernandez-Peon, R. 1966. Physiological mechanisms in attention. In *Frontiers in Physiological Psychology*, ed. R. W. Russell. New York: Academic

Hillyard, S. A. 1981a. Selective auditory attention and early event-related potentials: A rejoinder. *Can. J. Psychol.* 35:159–74

Hillyard, S. A. 1981b. Visual selective attention. See Galambos & Hillyard 1981, pp. 240–42

Hillyard, S. A., Hink, R. F., Schwent, V. L., Picton, T. W. 1973. Electrical signs of selective attention in the human brain. *Science* 182:177–80

Hillyard, S. A., Picton, T. W. 1979. Event-related brain potentials and selective information processing in man. See Desmedt 1979, pp. 1–50

Hillyard, S. A., Picton, T. W., Regan, D. M. 1978. Sensation, perception and attention: Analysis using ERPs. See Callaway et al 1978, pp. 223–322

Hillyard, S. A., Squires, K. C., Squires, N. K. 1982. The psychophysiology of attention. In *Attention: Theory, Brain Function, and Clinical Applications*, ed. D. Sheer. Hillsdale, NJ: Erlbaum. In press

Hink, R. F., Fenton, W. H. Jr., Pfefferbaum, A., Tinklenberg, J. R., Kopell, B. S. 1978a. The distribution of attention across auditory input channels: An assessment using the human evoked potential. *Psychophysiology* 15:466–73

Hink, R. F., Fenton, W. H. Jr., Tinklenberg, J. R., Pfefferbaum, A., Kopell, B. S. 1978b. Vigilance and human attention under conditions of methylphenidate and secobarbital intoxication: An assessment using brain potentials. *Psychophysiology* 15:116–25

Hink, R. F., Hillyard, S. A., Benson, P. J. 1978c. Event-related brain potentials and selective attention to acoustic and phonetic cues. *Biol. Psychol.* 6:1–16

Hink, R. F., Hillyard, S. A. 1978. Electrophysiological measures of attentional processes in man as related to the study of schizophrenia. *J. Psychiatr. Res.* 14:155–65

Hink, R. F., Van Voorhis, S. T., Hillyard, S. A., Smith, T. S. 1977. The division of attention and the human auditory evoked potential. *Neuropsychologia* 15: 597–605

Hofmann, M. J., Salapatek, P., Kuskowski, M. 1981. Evidence for visual memory in the averaged and single evoked potentials of human infants. *Infant Behav. Dev.* 4:401–21

Isreal, J. B., Chesney, G. L., Wickens, C. D., Donchin, E. 1980a. P300 and tracking difficulty: Evidence for multiple resources in dual-task performance. *Psychophysiology* 17:259–73

Isreal, J. B., Wickens, C. D., Chesney, G. L., Donchin, E. 1980b. The event-related brain potential as an index of display-monitoring workload. *Hum. Factors* 22:211–24

John, E. R., Schwartz, E. L. 1978. The neurophysiology of information processing and cognition. *Ann. Rev. Psychol.* 29: 1-29

Just, M. A., Carpenter, P. A. 1980. A theory of reading: From eye fixations to comprehension. *Psychol. Rev.* 87:329–54

Keele, S. W., Neill, W. T. 1978. Mechanisms of attention. In *Handbook of Perception*, ed. E. C. Carterette, M. P. Friedman, 9:1–47. New York: Academic

Keren, G. 1976. Some considerations of two alleged kinds of selective attention. *J. Exp. Psychol: Gen.* 105:349–74

Kerkhof, G. A. 1978. Decision latency: The P3 component in auditory signal detection. *Neurosci. Lett.* 8:289–94

Kornhuber, H. H., Deecke, L., eds. 1980. *Motivation, Motor and Sensory Processes of the Brain: Electrical Potentials, Behavior and Clinical Use. Prog. Brain Res.*, Vol. 54. Amsterdam: Elsevier/-North Holland

Kramer, A., Wickens, C., Vanasse, L., Heffley, E., Donchin, E. 1981. Primary and secondary task analysis of step tracking: An event-related potentials approach. *Proc. Hum. Factors Soc., 25th Ann. Meet., Rochester, NY*

Kurtzberg, D., Vaughan, H. G. Jr., Kreuzer, J. 1979. Task-related cortical potentials in children. See Desmedt 1979, 6: 216–23

Kutas, M., Hillyard, S. A. 1980a. Event-related brain potentials to semantically inappropriate and surprisingly large words. *Biol. Psychol.* 11:99–116

Kutas, M., Hillyard, S. A. 1980b. Reading senseless sentences: Brain potentials reflect semantic incongruity. *Science* 207:203–5

Kutas, M., Hillyard, S. A. 1982a. Event-related brain potentials and cognitive science. In *Cognitive Neuroscience*, ed. M. Gazzaniga. New York: Plenum. In press

Kutas, M., Hillyard, S. A. 1982b. The lateral distribution of event-related potentials during sentence processing. *Neuropsychologia*. In press

Kutas, M., McCarthy, G., Donchin, E. 1977. Augmenting mental chronometry: The P300 as a measure of stimulus evaluation time. *Science* 197:792–95

Lassen, N. A., Ingvar, D. H., Skinhoj, E. 1978. Brain function and blood flow. *Sci. Am.* 239:62–71

Lavine, R. A., Buchsbaum, M. S., Schechter, G. 1980. Human somatosensory evoked responses: Effects of attention and distraction on early components. *Physiol. Psychol.* 8:405–8

Lehmann, D., Callaway, E., eds. 1979. *Human Evoked Potentials: Applications and Problems*. New York: Plenum

Loiselle, D. L., Stamm, J. A., Maitinsky, S., Whipple, S. C. 1980. Evoked potential and behavioral signs of attentive dysfunctions in hyperactive boys. *Psychophysiology* 17:193–201

Lukas, J. H. 1980. Human attention: The olivo-cochlear bundle may function as a peripheral filter. *Psychophysiology* 17: 444–52

Lukas, J. H. 1981. The role of efferent inhibition in human auditory attention: An examination of the auditory brainstem potentials. *Int. J. Neurosci.* 12:137–45

Marsh, G. R. 1975. Age differences in evoked potential correlates of a memory scanning process. *Exp. Aging Res.* 1:3–16

McCarthy, G., Donchin, E. 1981. A metric for thought: A comparison of P300 latency and reaction time. *Science* 211:77–80

Miller, J. 1978. Multidimensional same-different judgements: Evidence against independent comparisons of dimensions. *J. Exp. Psychol: Hum. Percept. Perform.* 4:411–22

Molfese, D. L. 1978. Left and right hemisphere involvement in speech perception: Electrophysiological correlates. *Percept. Psychophys.* 23:237–43

Molfese, D. L. 1980. The phoneme and the engram: Electrophysiological evidence for the acoustic invariant in stop consonants. *Brain Lang.* 9:372–76

Naatanen, R. 1975. Selective attention and evoked potentials in humans—A critical review. *Biol. Psychol.* 2:237–307

Naatanen, R. 1982. Processing negativity-evoked potential reflection of selective attention. *Psychol. Bull.* In press

Naatanen, R., Gaillard, A. W. K., Mantysalo, S. 1980. Brain potentials correlates of voluntary and involuntary attention. See Kornhuber & Deecke 1980, pp. 343–48

Naatanen, R., Gaillard, A. W. K., Varey, C. A. 1982a. Attention effects on auditory EPs as a function of inter-stimulus interval. *Biol. Psychol.* 13:173–87

Naatanen, R., Michie, P. T. 1979. Early selective attention effects on the evoked potential. A critical review and reinterpretation. *Biol. Psychol.* 8:81–136

Naatanen, R., Simpson, M., Loveless N. E. 1982b. Stimulus deviance and event-related brain potentials. *Biol. Psychol.* In press

Navon, D., Gopher, D. 1979. On the economy of the human processing system. *Psychol. Rev.* 86:214–55

Neville, H. J., Kutas, M., Schmidt, A. 1982a. Event-related potential studies of cerebral specialization during reading. I. Studies of normal adults. *Brain Lang.* 16:300–15

Neville, H. J., Kutas, M., Schmidt, A. 1982b. Event-related potential studies of cerebral specialization during reading. II. Studies of congenitally deaf adults. *Brain Lang.* 16:316–37

Neville, H. J., Snyder, E., Woods, D. L., Galambos, R. 1982c. Recognition and surprise alter the human visual evoked response. *Proc. Natl. Acad. Sci. USA* 79:2121–23

Norman, D. A. 1968. Toward a theory of memory and attention. *Psychol. Rev.* 75:522–36

Novick, B., Vaughan, H. G. Jr., Kurtzberg, D., Simson, R. 1980. An electrophysiologic indication of auditory processing defects in autism. *Psychiatry Res.* 3:107–14

Oatman, L. C., Anderson, B. W. 1977. Effects of visual attention on tone burst evoked auditory potentials. *Exp. Neurol.* 57:200–11

Okita, T. 1979. Event-related potentials and selective attention to auditory stimuli varying in pitch localization. *Biol. Psychol.* 9:271–84

Okita, T. 1981. Slow negative shifts of the human event-related potential associated with selective information processing. *Biol. Psychol.* 12:63–75

Olesen, T. D., Ashe, J. H., Weinberger, N. M. 1975. Modification of auditory and somatosensory system activity during pupillary conditioning in the paralyzed cat. *J. Neurophysiol.* 38:1114–39

Otto, D., ed. 1978. *Multidisciplinary Perspectives in Event-Related Brain Potential Research.* EPA 600/9–77–043. Washington DC: GPO

Parasuraman, R. 1978. Auditory evoked potentials and divided attention. *Psychophysiology* 15:460–65

Parasuraman, R. 1980. Effects of information processing demands on slow negative shift latencies and N100 amplitude in selective and divided attention. *Biol. Psychol.* 11:217–33

Parasuraman, R., Richer, F., Beatty, J. 1982. Detection and recognition: Concurrent processes in perception. *Percept. Psychophys.* 31:1–12

Paul, D. D., Sutton, S. 1972. Evoked potential correlates of response criterion in auditory signal detection. *Science* 177:362–64

Picton, T. W., Campbell, K. B., Baribeau-Braun, J., Proulx, G. B. 1978. The neurophysiology of human attention: A tutorial review. In *Attention and Performance*, ed. J. Requin, 6:429–67. Hillsdale, NJ: Erlbaum

Picton, T. W., Hillyard, S. A. 1974. Human auditory evoked potentials. II. Effects of attention. *Electroencephalogr. Clin. Neurophysiol.* 36:191–200

Picton, T. W., Hillyard, S. A., Galambos, R., Schiff, M. 1971. Human auditory attention: A central or peripheral process? *Science* 173:351–53

Picton, T. W., Stuss, D. T. 1980. The component structure of the human event-related potentials. See Kornhuber & Deecke 1980, pp. 17–49

Polich, J., Vanasse, L., Donchin, E. 1981. Category expectancy and the N200. *Psychophysiology* 18:142

Posner, M. I., Klein, R., Summers, J., Buggie, S. 1973. On the selection of signals. *Mem. Cognit.* 1:2–12

Renault, B., Ragot, R., Lesevre, N., Remond, A. 1982. Onset and offset of brain events as indices of mental chronometry. *Science* 215:1413–15

Ritter, W., Vaughan, H. G. Jr., Friedman, D. 1979. A brain event related to the making of a sensory discrimination. *Science* 203:1358–61

Roth, W. T., Ford, J. M., Kopell, B. S. 1978a. Long-latency evoked potentials and reaction time. *Psychophysiology* 15:17–23

Roth, W. T., Rothbart, R. M., Kopell, B. S. 1978b. The timing of CNV resolution in a memory retrieval task. *Biol. Psychol.* 6:39–49

Ruchkin, D. S., Sutton, S. 1978. Equivocation and P300 amplitude. See Otto 1978, pp. 175–77

Ruchkin, D. S., Sutton, S., Kietzman, M. L., Silver, K. 1980. Slow wave and P300 in signal detection. *Electroencephalogr. Clin. Neurophysiol.* 50:35–47

Sanquist, T. F., Rohrbaugh, J. W., Syndulko, K., Lindsley, D. B. 1980. Electrocortical signs of levels of processing: Perceptual analysis and recognition memory. *Psychophysiology* 17:568–76

Schwent, V. L., Hillyard, S. A. 1975. Auditory evoked potentials and multi-channel selective attention. *Electroencephalogr. Clin. Neurophysiol.* 38:131–38

Schwent, V. L., Hillyard, S. A., Galambos, R. 1976. Selective attention and the auditory vertex potential. II: Effects of signal intensity and masking noise. *Electroencephalogr. Clin. Neurophysiol.* 40:615–22

Shiffrin, R. M., McKay, D. P., Shaffer, W. O. 1976. Attending to forty-nine spatial positions at once. *J. Exp. Psychol: Hum. Percept. Perform.* 2:14–22

Simson, R., Vaughan, H. G. Jr., Ritter, W. 1977. The scalp topography of potentials in auditory and visual discrimination tasks. *Electroencephalogr. Clin. Neurophysiol.* 42:528–35

Skinner, J. E., Yingling, C. D. 1977. Central gating mechanisms that regulate event-related potentials and behavior. In *Attention, Voluntary Contraction and Event-Related Cerebral Potentials. Prog. Clin. Neurophysiol.*, ed. J. E. Desmedt, 1:30–69

Snyder, E., Hillyard, S. A. 1976. Long-latency evoked potentials to irrelevant deviant stimuli. *Behav. Biol.* 16:319–31
Snyder, E., Hillyard, S. A., Galambos, R. 1980. Similarities and differences among the P3 waves to detected signals in three modalities. *Psychophysiology* 17:112–22
Squires, K. C., Donchin, E., Herning, R. I., McCarthy, G. 1977. On the influence of task relevance and stimulus probability on event-related potential components. *Electroencephalogr. Clin. Neurophysiol.* 42:1–14
Squires, K. C., Hillyard, S. A., Lindsay, P. L. 1973. Vertex potentials evoked during auditory signal detection: Relation to decision criteria. *Percept. Psychophys.* 14:265–72
Squires, K. C., Squires, N. K., Hillyard, S. A. 1975. Decision-related cortical potentials during an auditory signal detection task with cued observation intervals. *J. Exp. Psychol: Hum. Percept. Perform.* 104:268–79
Squires, N. K., Donchin, E., Squires, K. C., Grossberg, S. 1977. Bisensory stimulation: Inferring decision-related processes from the P300 component. *J. Exp. Psychol: Hum. Percept. Perform.* 3:299–315
Squires, N. K., Squires, K. C., Hillyard, S. A. 1975. Two varieties of long-latency positive waves evoked by unpredictable auditory stimuli. *Electroencephalogr. Clin. Neurophysiol.* 38:387–401
Starr, A. 1978. Sensory evoked potentials in clinical disorders of the nervous system. *Ann. Rev. Neurosci.* 1:103–27
Stuss, D. T., Sarazin, F., Leech, E., Picton, T. W. 1982. Evoked potentials during naming. In *Event-Related Potentials in Man,* ed. R. Karrer, P. Tueting, J. Cohen. New York: NY Acad. Sci. In press
Thatcher, R. W. 1977. Evoked potential correlates of hemispheric lateralization during semantic information processing. In *Lateralization of the Nervous System,* ed. S. Harnad, R. W. Doty, L. Goldstein, J. Jaynes, G. Krauthamer, pp. 429–48. New York: Academic

Towey, J., Rist, F., Hakerem, G., Ruchkin, D. S., Sutton, S. 1980. N250 Latency and decision time. *Bull. Psychon. Soc.* 15:365–68
Treisman, A. M. 1969. Strategies and models of selective attention. *Psychol. Rev.* 76:282–99
Treisman, A. M., Gelade, G. 1980. A feature-integration theory of attention. *Cogn. Psychol.* 12:97–136
Treisman, A., Squire, R., Green, J. 1974. Semantic processing in dichotic listening? A replication. *Mem. Cognit.* 2:641–46
Tueting, P. 1978. Event-related potentials, cognitive events, and information processing. See Otto 1978, pp. 159–69
Van Voorhis, S. T., Hillyard, S. A. 1977. Visual evoked potentials and selective attention to points in space. *Percept. Psychophys.* 22:54–62
Velasco, M., Velasco, F., Olvera, A. 1980. Effect of task relevance and selective attention on components of cortical and subcortical evoked potentials in man. *Electroencephalogr. Clin. Neurophysiol.* 48:377–86
Warren, L. R., Marsh, G. R. 1979. Changes in event related potentials during processing of Stroop stimuli. *Int. J. Neurosci.* 9:217–23
Wastell, D. G., Kleinman, D. 1980. Evoked potential correlates of visual selective attention. *Acta Psychol.* 46:129–40
Wilkinson, R. T., Seales, D. M. 1978. EEG, event-related potentials and signal detection. *Biol. Psychol.* 7:13–28
Wood, C. C. 1975. Auditory and phonetic levels of processing in speech perception: Neurophysiological and information-processing analysis. *J. Exp. Psychol.* 104:3–20
Woods, D. L., Courchesne, E., Hillyard, S. A., Galambos, R. 1980. Recovery cycles of event-related potentials in multiple detection tasks. *Electroencephalogr. Clin. Neurophysiol.* 50:335–47
Woods, D. L., Hillyard, S. A. 1978. Attention at the cocktail party: Brainstem evoked responses reveal no peripheral gating. See Otto 1978, pp. 230–33

Ann. Rev. Psychol. 1983. 34:63-94
Copyright © 1983 by Annual Reviews Inc. All rights reserved

ETHOLOGY, COMPARATIVE PSYCHOLOGY, AND ANIMAL BEHAVIOR

Charles T. Snowdon

Department of Psychology, University of Wisconsin, Madison, Wisconsin 53706

CONTENTS

INTRODUCTION

In the 7 years since William Mason and Dale Lott (1976) wrote the last review of Ethology and Comparative Psychology for the *Annual Review of Psychology* there have been many important developments. The most important was the publication of E. O. Wilson's *Sociobiology* (1975). This highly influential book has inspired many popular books, interpreting sociobiology to the general public (Dawkins 1976, Wilson 1978, Alcock 1979, Barash 1979, 1982, Gould 1982), and reflecting tremendous interest in the

63

0066-4308/83/0201-0063$02.00

study of animals, both within the scientific community and in the population at large. Unfortunately, it has also produced a retreat from the synthesis between ethology and comparative psychology that Mason & Lott (1976) had proclaimed was at hand.

Wilson (1975, p. 5) displayed a conjectural time course for the contributions of various disciplines to the study of behavioral biology. In 1950, he showed equal contributions of both comparative psychology and ethology. By 1975, as he was writing, he reduced the relative importance of ethology and had eliminated completely the role of comparative psychology. By 2000 he predicted that ethology and physiological psychology would have only a minor input to behavioral biology compared to the input of neurophysiology and sociobiology.

In 1981, as if to make Wilson's prophecy of the death of comparative psychology self-fulfilling, the American Psychological Association briefly terminated any publication outlet for work in comparative psychology. The venerable *Journal of Comparative and Physiological Psychology,* which began its life as the *Journal of Animal Behavior,* was to become the *Journal of Behavioral Neuroscience.* Only a concerted effort by comparative psychologists and animal behaviorists convinced the APA Board of Publications and Communications to produce a new *Journal of Comparative Psychology,* but on a 3-year trial basis.

What are the factors that have led to such a rapid ascendence of sociobiology and such a rapid demise of comparative psychology? The first main part of this review will deal with this question. It illustrates the strengths of sociobiology and the contributions it has made in general to animal behavior. On the other hand, sociobiology's assumptions are challenged by alternative hypotheses and data. It is argued that psychologists can be very useful in suggesting alternative hypotheses and testing them under controlled conditions.

The second part of the review will focus on comparative psychology, arguing that some of its perceived faults are illusory and that the techniques and methods of comparative psychology are still valuable. The studies of language training in chimpanzees will be presented to illustrate some of the enduring problems of comparative psychology.

The third part will review several topics of recent interest: (a) the effects of social behavior on physiological functioning; (b) new studies on dominance, including the roles of coalitions and reconciliations in aggressive behavior; (c) the psycholinguistic application to the understanding of animal communication.

The final part of the review will deal with the utility of studying animal behavior. Recent years have seen an erosion of government research support for behavioral research in general and for animal research in particular.

It is appropriate for us to consider what value the study of animal behavior has for the general welfare of human beings. There are several areas of application: (a) The behavioral variability of different species and different populations of animals can suggest to us possible ranges of behavioral solutions to problems of our own. (b) Animals can be used as models when considerations of ethics and of adequacy of control would preclude experimentation with human beings. (c) Naturalistic observational techniques are increasingly used for observing and understanding the behavior of human beings, both children and adults. (d) Many animal species are threatened or endangered, and the variability which they represent can be preserved only through the development of limited nature preserves or through captive breeding. Knowledge of behavior is crucial to the success of maintaining endangered species. (e) Pets play an important role in the lives of many human beings. Veterinarians are only slowly beginning to acknowledge psychological variables in understanding animals, and there is some evidence that pets are therapeutic to human beings (f) Working animals have been used for centuries but we are only now learning of their behavioral differences and suitable training techniques.

THE SYNTHESIS BETWEEN ETHOLOGY AND COMPARATIVE PSYCHOLOGY

As a prelude to the analysis of sociobiology and of comparative psychology, we need to review briefly the nature of the synthesis between ethology and comparative psychology that seemed so close at hand in 1976. The basis for a consensus was the acceptance by psychologists of the organic theory of evolution: it is assumed that organisms are subjected to natural selection which favors those individuals whose genes interact with the environment in such a way as to produce successful phenotypes, defined in terms of reproductive success. Throughout the 1960s and 1970s, psychologists began to accept this theory as applicable to the behavior of animals and also to accept a broader definition of environment as all of those factors with which an animal must interact over the course of its lifetime. Psychologists became more tolerant of descriptive natural history studies and of field work. Many psychologists went into the field themselves, and in a few departments ethologists trained as zoologists were hired to provide psychologists direct colleagueship with evolutionary biologists. At the same time, ethologists became more interested in controlled experimentation and in understanding the development of behavior within the individual. Many zoologists considered problems of behavioral development and of learning. Many devised seminaturalistic environments to provide a compromise between the naturalness of a field setting and the controlled environment of the laboratory.

Tinbergen (1951) organized his book, *The Study of Instinct,* around four basic biological questions relevant to the understanding of behavior: 1. Causation—What is the mechanism of behavior? 2. Ontogeny—How does a particular behavior develop within an individual? 3. Function—How does the behavior benefit the survival of an individual and his/her offspring? 4. Evolution—How has the behavior developed over the course of phylogeny?

Although all four questions are necessary to a total understanding of behavior, in reality a given scientist cannot study them all. Historically, comparative psychologists argued that the only important questions were causation and ontogeny, while the ethologists argued that the only important questions were function and evolution. Each set of questions requires different methods of study—causation and ontogeny require specified, controllable environments and direct experimenter manipulations; function and evolution require observations in natural environments with minimal intervention by the observer. As long as each group remained focused on its own particular set of questions and methods, it was inevitable that they would disagree seriously on the interpretation of behavior, on the problems considered to be of interest, and on their methods of study.

The consensus that developed in the mid-1970s was simply based on the recognition that all four questions were equally valuable. A synthesis developed through the comparative psychologist's acceptance of function and evolution along with naturalistic methods of observation and the ethologist's acceptance of the study of causation and ontogeny along with experimental manipulation in controlled environments. Rather than retain the old labels of ethology and comparative psychology with their associated connotations, I prefer to use the label of animal behavior, which implies an acceptance of the validity of all four questions.

SOCIOBIOLOGY

Let us examine the contributions and the drawbacks of sociobiology. Its main contribution was to develop a theoretical basis for the evolution of social behavior that was consistent with the principles of natural selection. Social behavior (especially cooperative or altruistic behavior) had proved to be difficult to explain. Why should an organism sacrifice some of its own future reproductive success by behaving to increase some other individual's reproductive success? Wynne Edwards (1962) had suggested that a theory of group selection was necessary to account for cooperation and altruism —simply put, individuals made sacrifices for the good of their population or their species. This type of argument is unsatisfactory as an evolutionary explanation. Natural selection is generally thought to act on individuals (rather than on groups, populations, or species).

Kinship

Sociobiology provided explanations for cooperative and altruistic behavior on an individual basis. One important concept was the notion of kin selection (Hamilton 1964, 1972). Inclusive fitness was defined as the sum of one's personal fitness plus all of the effects that the individual has on the fitness of his/her relatives. Thus, one might sacrifice one's personal fitness by behaving altruistically if in so doing one increased the fitness of one's relatives by a sufficient amount. The degree to which the fitness of one's relatives would compensate the loss of one's own fitness is proportional to the degree of relatedness or the average number of genes shared in common. Since one shares ½ of one's genes with a sibling, ¼ with a nephew or niece and ⅛ with a first cousin, one could sacrifice one's fitness if by so doing he were increasing by a comparable amount the fitness of two brothers or sisters, four nephews and nieces, or eight cousins or any combination equal to or greater than one. Individual selection of cooperation or of altruism is comprehensible if the behavior benefits a sufficient number of relatives.

A second mechanism for accounting for the evolution of altruistic behavior is the theory of reciprocal altruism (Trivers 1971). It might be adaptive to sacrifice my fitness to help you today, if I can reasonably expect that you will perform a similar act to help me sometime in the future. We can take a minor risk to help each other based on the expectation of reciprocity. This mechanism is fine in societies where altruistic acts, the actors, and the beneficiaries can be remembered well, but it is susceptible to cheating. You could use my help today, but fail to reciprocate when I need your help in the future. You would gain in fitness and I would lose. If cheating were extensive or it there were no safeguards against cheating, this form of altruism would quickly disappear. Wilson (1975) argues that reciprocal altruism exists only in humans, never in animals. Thus, sociobiology has essentially redefined apparently helpful or altruistic behaviors in terms of personal gain [or at least to the personal gain of one's genes (Dawkins 1976)]. There is no need to invoke any principles other than those of natural selection to explain altruism.

This focus on kin selection and its role in altruism has produced some exciting field studies. Several populations of animals are now known where detailed genealogical records cover several years and where specific predictions about kin selection and altruistic behavior can be tested. As one example, for more than 10 years Sherman (1977, 1980) has been studying a population of Beldings ground squirrels in California where animals have been marked at nest emergence. Thus, mothers and their offspring are known with precision and genealogies can be easily constructed. Related females tend to codefend a territory that is both larger and better defended than the territories of unrelated or distantly related females. Related females fight much less among themselves than do unrelated females, and warning calls at the sight of a predator are given more frequently by females when a close relative is nearby than when only unrelated animals are near.

A second population with well-known genealogies over many years are the Japanese macaques, whose population data have been maintained since the early 1950s. Closely related animals such as mothers and offspring or siblings and half-siblings are more tolerant of each other in feeding together than with unrelated animals; related animals display less aggressive behavior than do unrelated animals; and related animals groom each other more than do unrelated animals.

Genealogies also have been carefully documented over many years with the Florida scrub jay. Woolfenden (1975) has shown that more experienced jays are more successful at rearing young than are inexperienced birds, and that experienced birds with helpers present are the most successful at rearing young. The question arises: why should other birds serve as helpers rather than reproducing on their own? Initially, it appeared that most helpers were related to the reproducing pair whom they helped; helping was another form of kin selection. However, more recent data (Woolfenden & Fitzpatrick 1978) shows that there are individual benefits to the helpers. New territories become available to scrub jays only upon the death or disappearance of former territory holders. Helpers have a much greater probability of inheriting a territory than do other animals. Hence, the only way in which helpers might ever get to breed themselves is through associating with an already breeding pair. Furthermore, since experienced birds are more successful than inexperienced birds in rearing offspring, the experience of helping other birds care for their young might make a helper more parentally competent. This might explain why Woolfenden has found a small percentage of the helpers to be definitely unrelated to either of the mated animals which they are helping. Therefore, while kinship is important, it is not the only mechanism which makes helping adaptive.

In each of the above examples, the kin-related behavior does not appear with kin more distant than grandparents or grandchildren. Thus, behavior that is correlated with kinship does not extend beyond a relatedness coefficient of 0.25. One problem that animals face is being able to recognize kin. There has been only one study demonstrating that animals can recognize kin, equating such variables as time spent with animals. Wu et al (1980) tested pigtailed macaques separated from their mothers at birth and nursery reared. These isolate reared monkeys significantly preferred those monkeys to which they were related as half-sibs, even though they had never seen these animals before. There is no explanation for the recognition mechanism. In most other cases animals probably prefer those animals with whom they spend the most time. In mammals and altricial birds, these other animals with whom one spends most time are likely to be close relatives, with the degree of propinquity being directly proportional to the degree of relatedness. Thus, many of the activities that appear to be kin selected, may in fact be due to mere exposure or familiarity. Only with studies that vary kinship and propinquity independently or with cross-fostering studies can it be concluded whether or not kin selection is a useful explanatory principle.

Despite the possible confounds of relatedness with other variables, the study of populations where all kinship relations are known is of great scientific value, and such studies are much more likely since the advent of sociobiology.

Courtship, Mating, and Parenting

A second major contribution of sociobiology has been in describing the selfish interests involved in courtship, mating, and parental behavior. Males and females have different interests in reproduction that are determined by their relative parental investment. Parental investment (Trivers 1972) is "any investment by the parent in an individual offspring that increases the offspring's chance of surviving (and hence reproductive success) at the cost of the parent's ability to invest in subsequent offspring." Part of this investment is in gamete production (eggs and sperm), but for all species in which parental care is involved, the cost of gamete production is small compared to the subsequent investment in parental care. Since the size of sperm are quite small compared to the size of eggs, and since in mammals at least there is a long period of gestation of the fetus inside the female's uterus, the degree of parental investment is unequal, with females investing much more than males. What are the consequences of this unequal investment? We will consider only the case for mammals.

Since a female has invested so much through gamete production and gestation, she has already made a greater investment in an infant at birth than has a male. To ignore the infant at that point would mean the loss of the considerable investment made by the female. To preserve her investment she should continue to provide extensive parental care postnatally. The male, on the other hand, has made a relatively small investment in gamete production and little investment during gestation. His reproductive strategy is maximized if he inseminates additional females, since he can be confident that a female would care for her infants rather than risk the loss of her investment in them. Thus, males should naturally show less parental care than females. Parental care should be predominantly a female activity.

It is to the female's advantage to be quite choosy, mating only with the fittest male. In this way she insures her offspring have the greatest likelihood of reproductive success. Thus, while males should be willing to mate with any willing female, females should be selective about which males they will accept.

In mammals at least, only the female can be certain of maternity of her offspring, since she carries them in her uterus through gestation. No male can ever be certain that an infant is his unless he has guarded the female constantly. These differences in parental certainty also influence the parental behavior of animals. Since males cannot be certain of paternity, it will not aid their fitness to invest in infant care. Where males do show parental care, they should have a fear of cuckoldry, since any reduction in their paternal certainty makes their parental behavior less adaptive.

Some otherwise puzzling data may be explained by these observations. It has been reported both for monkeys (Mohnot 1971, Hrdy 1977, 1979), and for lions (Bertram 1975) that a new male taking over a harem of females frequently kills the infants. This bizarre-seeming behavior can be explained as follows. A new male taking over a harem can be certain of nonpaternity. None of the infants are his. There is nothing to gain by investing in the care of these infants and everything to gain by investing in infants of his own. The killing of the current infants removes the need to invest in unrelated animals. It has the secondary effect of stopping lactation in the mothers and thus bringing them into estrus sooner than would have been the case were the infants alive. The male can invest in his own offspring sooner than would otherwise have been possible by engaging in infanticide. What is unusual about this phenomenon is not that the males engage in infanticide, but why the females do not band together to defend their current infants. An alternative explanation for infanticide in monkeys has been proposed by Dolhinow (1977), who notes that infanticide has never been observed in groups of monkeys undisturbed by human intervention and whose population densities are low. The troops with infanticide are in areas of dense monkey and human habitation. The infanticide may be better viewed as an adaptation to overcrowding and social pathology rather than a normal adaptation.

If males are better off investing in new offspring than caring for their present offspring, and if males have little certainty of paternity, why should male parental care appear at all? Different mating systems lead to different degrees of parental certainty. For example, monogamous animals should have a great degree of certainty of parentage if they defend the monogamous bond against intrusion by others. Harem breeding animals should also be relatively certain of paternity, at least in those species where the guarding is said to be so complete that no outside males can breed with females (Kummer 1968). Finally, parental certainty should be least among males in promiscuous breeding systems. Several recent reviews have attempted to evaluate the parental certainty explanation of the presence or absence of paternal care in primates. Bales (1980) argued that paternal behavior could be directly related to the degree of parental certainty. He argued that paternal care was found in monogamous rather than in promiscuous monkeys. However, the correlation is not exact. Kleiman & Malcolm (1981) surveyed 70 species of mammals and found 76% of the monogamous species displayed paternal care. Surprisingly, however, 51% of the polygamous species also showed paternal care. Snowdon & Suomi (1982), reviewing the primate literature, found many exceptions to the expectations of the parental certainty explanation. While most monogamous primates are involved in parental care, the timing and degree of care varies from almost total infant care by male marmosets and tamarins, to interest and care of infants only after weaning in gibbons and siamangs, to virtual indifference toward infants by De Brazza's monkeys. Among promiscuous species there was a similar range of paternal behavior. In the rhesus macaque, paternal care is virtually nonexistent, while in baboons, males associate closely with females and their infants (Altmann 1980). The males associated with infants are likely to have been the biological fathers, but in some cases they were definitely not the fathers.

Additional evidence suggests that primates have to learn parental care skills and that males may be more interested in infants than can be normally observed. Marmosets and tamarins, both males and females, must have extensive prior infant care experience before they can become competent parents themselves. The infant mortality rate is very low if both parents have had previous parenting experience; it becomes higher if only one parent has had prior experience, and extremely high when neither parent has had experience with infants (Epple 1978). Recent work has shown that tamarins must have experience in interacting with at least two sets of infants. Juvenile animals interact with the next set of offspring primarily in play. Subadult animals share with the father most of the infant carrying duties (J. Cleveland and C. T. Snowdon, in preparation). In this case parenting is not instinctive but is acquired through experience.

Macaques, which rarely display paternal care in the wild, display adequate parental behavior under certain conditions. Redican (1978) presented male rhesus monkeys with infants and found that they were quite interested in the infants and took adequate care of the infants. Curtin (1980) and Berman (1982) have both demonstrated that male monkeys adopt orphaned infants and care for them appropriately. Gibber (1981) attempted to show differences in the responses of male and female adolescent monkeys to young infants. Much to her surprise, there were no sex differences. Males and females behaved identically toward infants when tested separately. However, when she put a male and a female together with an infant, the female always took charge of the infant, excluding the male from any participation. Much of the apparent lack of interest in infants by male monkeys may be due to female exclusion which prevents the male from learning to care for infants. These data indicate that the presence of a Y chromosome does not immunize an animal against being interested in infant care. Rather, individual experience seems to determine the presence or absence of paternal care at least as much as parental investment.

Caring for infants can be considered in economic terms as an alternative to the paternal certainty hypothesis. In the monogamous primates with the greatest paternal care, marmosets and tamarins, the female delivers twins which have a combined birthweight of 25–30% of the female's body weight. The female either has an immediate postpartum estrus or else estrus is delayed two months, so the female is still nursing one set of infants while pregnant with the next twins. Add to the female's chores the burden of carrying two growing monkeys, and the need for helpers becomes clear. Not only the fathers, but other siblings in the group share the job of carrying the infants, leaving the female free to cope with her substantial nutritional needs (J. Cleveland and C. T. Snowdon, in preparation). In the gibbons, infants are quite small relative to the mother, they are born singly, and subsequent pregnancies are delayed until after the infant is weaned. The male is not as necessary as a helper, and he does not display as much interest in infants as a male marmoset.

Age Structure and Demography

A third contribution of sociobiology has been the introduction of principles of population biology. Not only does this lead to the notions of kin selection discussed earlier, but it also focuses on problems of demography, in particular to the age structure of a population. Most psychologists prior to sociobiology used age of an animal as a variable in developmental research, but they would not have considered the age structure of a group as an important variable. As Rowell (1979) points out, the social organization of a group is highly dependent upon the age and sex structure of the population. A population consisting of many old adults and few new offspring will behave differently from a population with only a few adults and many young. A group with many juvenile and subadult males has a different social organization than a group with many juvenile and subadult females.

Wilson (1975) has also raised a question of reproductive value. How much is an individual worth in terms of how many offspring it contributes to the next generation The age of the individual becomes very important. An old animal that has already done most of its reproduction will have little effect on the next generation if it is lost, unless it also serves as a source of leadership or of knowledge for the social group. A very young animal also has little reproductive value since infant mortality is generally high and the average infant has little value. Animals that are just getting ready to breed have the greatest reproductive value since they have survived infancy and have their entire reproductive lives ahead of them. This argument suggests that predators, if they wish to maximize the number of prey available to them, should prey selectively on those animals with the least reproductive value. Thus, predators should specialize in very young or very old animals and avoid choosing prey of intermediate age. The literature on carnivores is quite conclusive in demonstrating the apparent "prudence" of predators. However, those animals that have the least reproductive value are also the ones that are most feeble and easiest to catch. It is not clear whether a predator is playing the evolutionary odds and being prudent or whether it is just catching prey in the easiest way it can.

In another perspective, Gadgil (1981) has used age structure in combination with the idea that older animals are most able to give help and younger animals (infants) are most in need of help to argue that helping behavior should be found most frequently between age groups with younger animals as the recipients. He posits that animals of the same age benefit little from either giving or receiving help to one another, hence cooperation or altruism should be least and competition greatest among animals of the same age level. Adolescence appears to be an interesting period; the adolescent cannot give help as effectively as an older animal, but it is no longer in need of help for itself. Thus, adolescents are the most independent of the social processes of the group, and it is adolescents whose behavior is most subjected to the effects of natural selection. Adolescents have the greatest freedom from the social constraints that are necessary for the functioning of the social group and thus can be most involved in experimentation. Since they have the highest reproductive value, if they experiment by colonizing a new habitat (Wilson 1975) or by eating new foods (such as the food washing of Japanese macaques) and are successful, they will leave behind many more offspring. If they fail, they will leave behind fewer offspring than animals of other ages. In general, the predictions do seem to be upheld that new colonies and new behaviors come primarily from adolescent and sub-adult animals.

The introduction of age structure and its attendant constructs suggests for animal behavior a whole new set of hypotheses about behavior development within a social group. Little work in this area has been done so far, so the adequacy of this part of sociobiology has yet to be tested.

Heritability

A final influence of sociobiology has been the reintroduction of nativist thinking to research on animal behavior. Implicit in all of the arguments of Wilson and his popularizers is that behavior is determined through the actions of natural selection acting to preserve certain genes while leading to the elimination of other genes. The only interaction envisioned with environment is that in different environments there will be different selective pressures leading to differential preservation or extinction of certain genes.

There are three points to consider concerning natural selection and behavior. First, is social behavior heritable? Wilson (1975) argues that "high degrees of heritability have been documented in many familiar elements of social behavior: group size and dispersion, the openness of groups to strangers, ... the readiness to explore newly opened space, aggressiveness, fighting ability, the tendency to assume high or low rank in dominance hierarchies, song learning (in birds) ... and others" (pp. 69–70). The well-informed animal psychologist will be quite puzzled by many of the items on this list. Although many of these behaviors show a high correlation between parent and offspring, evidence for genetic transmission exists for only a limited number of cases. Let us look at two examples. Marler (1970a) has shown that white-crowned sparrows must have experience early in life in order to learn their song, but that there are also species-specific constraints on the kinds of songs that can be learned. There is a mixture of genetic transmission and environmental influence on this song. On the other hand, there are many species of birds such as goldfinches, mockingbirds, and mynahs where song is apparently totally learned and subjected to modification throughout a bird's life. In this latter case, genetic transmission of the specific song is minimal.

In a second example, considerable evidence shows that dominance status is learned during a monkey's early infancy and is produced by the behavior of the mother toward her infant. Subordinate mothers tend to restrict the movements of their infants, depriving them of play and other social interactions, whereas more dominant mothers let their infants explore more at an earlier age and reinforce their infant's behavior by asserting their own dominance when the infant gets into trouble (French 1981, Altmann 1980). The strong correlation between the dominance of mothers and offspring and high heritability is due to an experiential not a genetic mechanism.

Barnett (1981) has written a lucid discussion of the concept of heritability and its misuse by sociobiologists and others that should be read by all animal behaviorists. Heritability is defined as the ratio of variance due to genes divided by the sum of the variance due to genes and the variance due to environment. If environmental variance approaches zero, heritability approaches 100%. As environmental variance increases, heritability decreases. The calculation of heritability and the value it attains is totally dependent upon the environment. The more similar the environments are in which a trait is evaluated, the higher will be the apparent heritability. If a similar learning process is applied to all animals at a certain time in development, then the learned behavior will have a high heritability coefficient even though the genetic transmission of that trait will be zero. Furthermore, heritability estimates for economically important traits in domestic animals are quite low (.2) (Hailman 1982). Hence there is little real evidence for the value of the heritability construct.

A second point concerns whether natural selection is operating at the level of behavior or indeed whether natural selection is operative at all. Hailman (1982) has argued that behavior is fundamentally different from morphology—the traditional focus of evolutionary biology. Behavior is not as easily and precisely measured as a morphological trait; behavior leaves behind no fossil record; and behavior in contrast to morphology can be transmitted culturally. Hailman goes on to argue that there is no evidence of selection at a genetic level of a behavioral trait within a single stable population. Comparison of behavioral differences between two different populations does not prove that genetic selection for those behaviors has occurred. The only cases that Hailman can find of selection of a behavioral trait within a stable, single population indicate that the trait is culturally transmitted [e.g. the food preparation habits developed in various groups of Japanese macaques (Kawai 1965)]. Hailman concludes that all of the phenomena of evolution can be generated without recourse to a mechanism of selection. The absence of selection ought to be taken as the null hypothesis against which notions of individual or kin selection should be tested.

It is interesting that Wilson (1975) stresses in his early chapters that his theory is hypothetico-deductive (it requires the formulation of testable hypotheses which must then be evaluated), but that the most basic assumption of his theory, namely that of genetic selection of all traits including those of social behavior, is never subjected to the rigor of hypothesis testing.

The third point concerning natural selection is that it assumes that there is a good fit between the behavior of animals (as evolved through natural selection) and the environment in which an animal lives. An animal's behavior is considered to be adaptive. Several recent papers have raised questions concerning the validity of the notion of adaptiveness of behavior. Hailman (1982) in his iconoclastic view challenges the evidence that behavior has evolved within an environment in such a way as to promote a close animal : environment match. Rowell (1979) also has questioned our ability to know that social behavior is adaptive. She describes many demographic variables that could affect the social behavior of a group independent of the adaptiveness of that behavior to a particular environment. As mentioned before, a group that happens to have many young males will behave differently than a group that by chance has a number of older females and very few young animals. These are differences due to demography, not to selection or adaptation (Altmann & Altmann 1979). In fact, we need to consider as a null hypothesis the idea that a behavior that we are observing is not adaptive.

The genetic characteristics of a population may change through chance, just as its demography could change through chance. Since we often cannot sample populations over long enough periods of time or sample enough different populations, we may mistakenly attribute as adaptive a behavior which arose purely by chance and which may be adaptive, maladaptive, or neutral. In most of the species that we observe we can never be sure that a behavior is adaptive. Finally, correlations between behavior and environment may exist but may not be genetically coded. Southwick (1967) has observed that monkeys show different behaviors in response to the size of their living space. Gartlan & Brain (1968) found that vervet monkeys in different habitats had different patterns of social organization. Edwards & Snowdon (1980) found very high levels of social behavior in a group of captive orangutans, indicating that the reports of their solitary behavior in the wild may simply represent an extreme end of a continuum of social flexibility which these animals are capable of showing. In each of these examples there have not been enough generations for genetic selection to have operated between one environment and another.

In summary, sociobiology has been very useful in suggesting to animal behaviorists a variety of new topics for study. Interest in social behavior has increased since Wilson's book appeared. More careful attention has been paid to the identification of kinship relations between animals within a group; and hypotheses concerning the different interests of males and females have led to interesting studies on courtship, sexual, and parental behavior. However, alternative explanations exist for each of these points, and there has been little criticism of the fundamental assumptions of the theory—namely that behavior is subject to natural selection at a genetic level just as morphology appears to be. As we have seen, there is little substantive evidence for this point though the genetic theory of natural selection remains an important heuristic for our work.

Comparative psychology should make clear the need to study the development of behavior within an individual, to point out the fallacy of the heritability argument, and to focus attention on the need for formulating truly testable hypotheses under conditions where competing hypotheses can be excluded. To date much of the value of sociobiology has been to stimulate new thinking and to point out new directions for research. If it is to be of further scientific value, its proponents must foster the rigorous testing of alternatives, including the assumptions that behavior is genetically selected. This type of testing is well within the traditional domain of psychologists.

COMPARATIVE PSYCHOLOGY

Several reasons have been given for the demise of comparative psychology; some are valid, others are not. One early criticism made by Beach (1950) was that comparative psychologists tended to study only white rats. Each decade brings a renewed criticism of animal psychologists on the same grounds (Dukes 1960, Lockard 1971, Porter et al 1981). Porter et al surveyed eight journals of comparative and physiological psychology and found an even greater proportion of studies on rats than in Beach's survey. However, most of the journals they selected were primarily animal learning or physiological journals. If one surveys *Animal Behaviour,* the major journal used by both psychologists and zoologists, one finds a much greater species diversity, even among the subset of authors who identify themselves as psychologists. Many animal behaviorists within psychology cover a wide array of species, many of them being truly comparative in their studies; however, they are publishing in journals other than traditional, establishment psychology journals. The criticism that comparative psychologists look mainly at white rats can be refuted.

Another commonly raised criticism is that comparative psychology is concerned mainly with experimental control and studies phenomena that are irrelevant for an animal's behavior and ignore the naturalistic environment. This criticism is not easily refuted. Psychologists have avoided naturalistic studies to their detriment. For example, although we now revere the studies of Garcia on taste aversion learning in rats as an example of one trial learning with long delays of reinforcement resistant to extinction, similar studies have been available in the zoological literature for much longer periods. There is an extensive literature on mimicry showing that predators learn to avoid noxious prey, that this learning occurs in essentially one trial, and that the learned response is very resistant to extinction (Brower 1958). Tinbergen & Kruyt (1938) showed that solitary wasps are able to demonstrate complex concept learning in a single trial in total violation of scala naturae arguments which relegated concept formation to a late evolutionary stage (Bitterman 1965, Dethier & Stellar 1970). A great familiarity with what our colleagues in zoology were doing might have saved us much time, effort, and controversy.

Miller (1977) proposed five roles that naturalistic studies could play for comparative psychology. 1. Naturalistic research is important for its own sake. It is valuable to understand how an animal species behaves in its natural environment. There is no reason why psychologists should be less fit than zoologists to do such naturalistic studies. 2. Naturalistic observations can serve as a starting point from which to develop a program of laboratory research. Many phenomena that have been studied in the laboratory had their origin in field observations. Studies of imprinting began with field observations and subsequently laboratory studies of imprinting became common. 3. Natural observations can validate or lend substance to previous laboratory findings. For example, after years of studying imprinting in the laboratory, Hess (1973) studied the natural process of imprinting and found, not surprisingly, that real mothers were more potent imprinting stimuli than arbitrary objects and that the notion of critical period had to be greatly redefined. 4. Natural observations can increase the efficiency of laboratory studies by pointing out species variables or biological constraints. For example, certain frogs respond to species-specific mating calls but are essentially deaf to all other sounds (Capranica 1966, Frischkopf et al 1968). A laboratory study of responsiveness to sounds in these frogs would be of little value if naturalistic stimuli were not used. 5. The field can be a natural laboratory in which hypotheses can be tested. Snowdon & Hodun (1981) found three variants of contact trills used by pygmy marmosets that seemed to have the same function in a laboratory setting. However, each variant had different sound localization properties. In the field, they showed that monkeys selectively used the most locatable calls when they were far away from other members of their group and used the least locatable call only at close distances.

A variety of benefits can accrue to an animal behaviorist from naturalistic studies that should complement the benefits from observations in controlled laboratory conditions. Although field conditions can't be controlled to the same degree as in the laboratory, there are some strict methodological principles (Altmann 1974) that can make observational studies just as rigorous as traditional experiments. It is only with greater knowledge of the natural behavior of animals that comparative psychologists will be able to shake off the accusation that their work is not relevant.

Perhaps the most widely known studies done by comparative psychologists over the past decade are those of language training in chimpanzees. A closer discussion of these studies and the critiques of them can illustrate both the contributions and the pitfalls of comparative psychology. A long history of attempts to get chimpanzees and other animals to imitate aspects of speech and language (Bierens de Haan 1929, Kellogg 1968) ended in failure. It took Beatrice Gardner (a student of Tinbergen's) to have the insight that chimpanzees use gestures to communicate; hence language training might be more successful through the use of sign language (Gardner & Gardner 1969). At the same time, Premack (1970) devised an artificial language based on arbitrary symbols with which he tested a chimpanzee's mastery of a variety of syntactic and semantic skills. Rumbaugh (1977) began a project using arbitrary lexigrams with a computer-controlled keyboard to test linguistic skills in a chimpanzee. In the early years with the first blush of success, each of the investigators wrote about the remarkable similarities of the linguistic skills of their chimpanzees and those of human beings. Chimpanzees learned to use signs or symbols in a grammatical fashion; they could coin intelligible new expressions; they were using sentences, learning symbolic referents, in short, using a rudimentary language. Their development of linguistic skills appeared to parallel the developmental sequence of human children (Gardner & Gardner 1978). Several popular books pointed to these studies as at last proving that there is no fundamental difference between apes and human beings (Linden 1974, Desmond 1979).

Two types of criticism soon appeared—methodological and conceptual. The Premack and Rumbaugh paradigms were accused of showing just chain or rote learning (Gardner & Gardner 1978). Pigeons were claimed to be able to converse by pecking at labeled colored lights (Epstein et al 1980). A second critique was that the fundamental creativity of language could not be demonstrated through fixed symbol sets and computer control.

Other methodological critiques were directed toward the sign language approaches. The trainers were accused of committing the Clever Hans fallacy (Sebeok & Rosenthal 1981). Terrace et al (1979) attempted to train a chimpanzee with sign language but found that apparently grammatical sequences of signs were often cued inadvertently by the actions of the trainer. Interpretations of one and two-word utterances were said to be overly elaborate. Thus, the coining of "water-bird" by a chimpanzee upon seeing a duck might not be a neologism for "duck" but a comment that the chimp was observing both water and a bird. Although elaborate interpretations of children's one- and two-word utterances are acceptable (R. Brown 1973), apparently they are not acceptable with chimpanzees.

The conceptual critiques focused first on the basic issue of the innateness of human language. Chomsky (1965) and Lenneberg (1967) argued that human brain structure, ease of learning language, and unique form of grammar made any attempts to demonstrate language in other species doomed to failure. Bronowski & Bellugi (1970) raised a number of criteria for language that the first report of Washoe did not demonstrate: use of signs in a fixed grammatical sequence, questions, negatives, the ability to communicate about concepts that could not be reified through sensory experience. All but the last point have been demonstrated subsequently. Despite all of the training techniques and the years of effort to date, chimpanzees communicate only instrumentally. That is, they do not seem to be using their language analogues for the fun of communicating, for the interchange of ideas, or for reflection; they use their "language" to get food, attention, to get in or out. In this they are quite different from human beings.

Another critique is that no study has considered the normal ecological and social environment of chimpanzees. An artificial system is imposed on them which (except for signing) bears no relationship to their natural signals. They are not housed in social conditions even remotely approaching those of the wild. And the training process has been much more intensive than the training given to human children. Because of these problems the chimpanzee studies cannot inform us how language evolved. Biologically, the most interesting continuities are not those that we impose on animals, but are those continuities that we can find in the natural individual and phylogenetic history of animals. Hill (1974) has argued that theories of continuity of language evolution can be developed by focusing on the function of communication within an ecological context. One does not have to compare human language with the skills of our closest relatives, the chimpanzees, but we can look at how other more vocal species such as forest primates or birds solve their communication problems and learn whether these solutions are similar to human language in any way.

In contrast, the chimpanzee studies have been useful in quite a different way. Rumbaugh (1981) notes that the keyboard he developed for use with chimpanzees has been quite successful when used with retarded children who could not speak. Through the keyboard technique, some retarded humans are now able to communicate (Parkel & Smith 1979). Other studies have used Premack's symbols (Carrier 1979) or have used signing (Kahn 1977) to develop the communicative skills in retarded human beings. The ape language studies have contributed directly to human welfare. In addition, they have provided us with information about the minds of chimpanzees. Essock (1977) observed that a chimpanzee names colors with the same color boundaries as human beings. Dooley & Gill (1977) demonstrated rudimentary counting abilities in a chimpanzee. Premack & Woodruff (1978) have shown through a variety of interesting tests an understanding of the chimpanzee mind.

What are the messages to animal behavior from the chimpanzee studies? First, we cannot expect that with sufficient training we can get an animal to perform whatever we want it to. There are limitations on what animals can do. It would be naive to expect a chimpanzee to become fluent in English or in an analogue. Second, although the use of sign language showed an excellent understanding of a natural communication modality of chimpanzees, we need to be even more biological in our approaches. We must understand that the evolution of a behavior can be understood only in its ecological and social context, and that when these contexts are greatly distorted we can no longer learn about the evolution of that behavior. Finally, we must also realize that the study of animal behavior may have some unexpected advantages, that human communication and the understanding of animal mental processes may be improved even if the original goal of showing that apes could use our language is not ultimately reached.

SEX, AGGRESSION, AND COMMUNICATION

Sociobiology and the demise of comparative psychology have not been the total concerns of animal behaviorists over the last few years. Interesting research has been done that is independent of the major theoretical issues discussed above. I will select three topics: the role of social behavior in influencing physiological functioning; new conceptions of dominance and aggressive behavior; and the use of linguistic and psycholinguistic models to better understand animal communication.

Social Behavior Influences Physiology

We are often impressed by reductionist arguments that physiology causes behavior. It is not the case that the effect of physiology on behavior is a unidirectional influence. There is now considerable evidence that physiology is affected by the social behavior of animals.

Reproductive physiology is severely altered by social behavior. McClintock (1971) demonstrated menstrual synchrony among college women living together. She subsequently found that female rats living together show a synchrony of ovulation and that isolated females exposed to the odors of cycling female rats develop an estrous synchrony with those other females (McClintock 1978). Thus, group living in rodents and human beings produces a synchrony of ovulation, and in rats, at least, this synchrony is produced by some olfactory cue (McClintock 1981).

A different phenomenon has been documented in some monogamous species. Abbott & Hearn (1978) found that young common marmosets living with their mothers showed normal estrus cycles, but when five young females were placed together in a peer group, all but the most dominant female ceased ovulation. J. A. French and C. T. Snowdon (in preparation) have found that cotton-top tamarin females display ovulatory suppression whenever they are subordinate (living in a peer group or in their natal group). When females are removed from more dominant females and given a male of their own they can ovulate within two weeks. The ovulation can be reversed by placing a female back in a social situation where she is subordinate to another female. Scent gland morphology also changes as a function of social status with glandular structure becoming larger with greater secretions as the female becomes dominant. A similar finding has been reported in gerbils (Swanson & Payman 1978), where females remaining with their parents had inactive scent glands and at autopsy displayed atrophic ovaries and uteri. Thus, in both monogamous rodents and monogamous primates social status of a female has an important influence on reproductive physiology and scent gland morphology.

Social behavior also influences male physiology. Bernstein et al (1977) have shown that the testosterone levels of male macaques increased when they were introduced to females, with the increase greatest in the breeding season. Vandenbergh & Drickamer (1974) brought two female rhesus monkeys into estrus during the nonbreeding season. This stimulated the males into increased sexual behavior and sex skin changes much earlier than normally would have occurred. They in turn apparently stimulated the untreated females into an earlier estrus, since the untreated females in the group delivered infants one month earlier than females in the control group of monkeys did. Thus, the social behavior of animals can lead to important physiological changes in both males and females. Behavior can affect physiology as physiology affects behavior.

Dominance and Aggression

The concept of dominance was initially used as a major explanatory concept for the social behavior of a group of animals. All groups were thought to be organized in a strict linear hierarchy with one animal at the top controlling the behavior of all others. This notion has fallen into disrepute both because various measures of dominance hierarchies within a group failed to correlate well with one another and because observations of the actual behavior of animals suggested that dominance behavior was rarely observed (Gartlan 1968, Rowell 1974). Rowell argued that the behavior of subordinate animals is more obvious than that of dominants and that if a term is needed to deal with the nonreciprocal relationships between animals it should be subordinacy not dominance. More recently, various writers have pointed out that dominance has two logically different meanings (Hinde 1978, Bernstein 1981). Dominance can be used to refer to the nonreciprocal behavior in the interactions between two animals within a group, or it can refer to the structure of the entire group in which each animal can be assigned a ranking. Both Hinde and Bernstein argue that the first meaning of dominance is the more useful one; one can make meaningful predictions about the interactions to occur between two individuals by knowing their relative dominance to one another. However, one cannot extrapolate from these to group rankings that will be useful in predicting the group's behavior.

In an empirical study of the effects of dominance rank on reproductive success among free-ranging female vervet monkeys, Cheney et al (1981) found that there was no correlation between rank and success. High-ranking animals survived no better than low-ranking animals. Death among low-ranking animals was due primarily to illness most likely due to restricted access to food and water, whereas deaths among high-ranking animals were due to predation. Animals of different ranks played different roles. High-ranking females gave more alarm calls and were more aggressive in intergroup encounters, while low-ranking females interacted in a friendly way with strange groups. Cheney et al suggest that different animals within the same group confront different selective pressures. Rank may be a reflection of different personality styles rather than an index of fitness as is more commonly assumed.

De Waal and his colleagues have recently reported on the aggressive behavior of chimpanzees. They studied a social group of 20 chimpanzees and defined three forms of dominance according to a cluster analysis of behaviors. Two types—agonistic and bluff dominance—occurred primarily among the males that occupied the top places in the hierarchy based on these types of dominance. The third form—nonagonistic competitive dominance—consisted primarily of supplantings, avoiding contacts, and vocal threats. This hierarchy was dominated by the females (Noe et al 1980). The behaviors of this last type are similar to those that led Rowell (1974) to speak of subordinacy rather than dominance. Male chimpanzees formed coalitions as one male recruited others to assist him in toppling the most dominant male. Bluffing and agonistic interactions were fairly frequent among males, but were almost always followed by a distinct period of reconciliation where the animals embraced, touched, hugged, and kissed each other (De Waal & van Roosmalen 1979). Among females overt fighting was rare as was reconciliation following a fight. Reconciliation may serve a socially homeostatic function restoring the cohesion of a group after an agonistic interaction.

Dominance relations are much more complex than we had previously thought. Dominance rank per se appears not to be adaptive, but the different social roles as expressed between individuals are. The importance of reconciliation among chimpanzees suggests that we should pay attention to the mechanisms in both animals and human beings for restoring the social status quo after aggressive interactions. Reconciliation would seem to preserve the cohesion of a social group and minimize the likelihood of injuries following aggression. It remains to be seen in how many other species reconciliation appears.

Linguistic and Psycholinguistic Approaches to Animal Communication

Marler (1970b) was the first to argue that the use of information from linguistics and psycholinguistics might be useful in the study of animal communication. Marler demonstrated the close parallels between the ontogeny of bird song and the ontogeny of human speech. Since then, there have been many other successful applications of models from human language to animal vocalizations. I will focus my discussion on new developments in primate communication.

First, data indicate that the vocabulary size of primate vocal repertoires is much larger than previously expected. Green (1975a) showed that Japanese macaques had a class of calls, "coos," that were separable into seven different variants, each of which was highly correlated with a specific situation. Others have reported similar findings in other species: Gautier (1974) in talapoin monkeys; Pola & Snowdon (1975) in the contact trills of pygmy marmosets; Lillehei & Snowdon (1978) in the "coo" vocalizations of stumptail macaques; Cleveland & Snowdon (1982) in the chirp vocalizations of cotton-top tamarins; Snowdon et al (1982) in the long calls of cotton-top tamarins; and Cheney & Seyfarth (1982) in the grunt calls of vervets. Thus, monkeys appear to have much larger repertoires than has been assumed.

Second, recent evidence suggests that monkeys use calls to indicate complex referents. Seyfarth et al (1980) showed that the three different forms of alarm calls given by vervet monkeys were specific to each of the three major predators. There was one call for snakes, another for leopards, and a third for eagles. Playback experiments showed that in the absence of the real predator, monkeys hearing the call responded as though the predator were present. Seyfarth et al argue that these data indicate the existence of symbolic communication in monkeys.

Smith et al (1982) have analyzed the chuck call of squirrel monkeys which they found was given only by females and only between females that were closely affiliated with each other. Thus, the chuck call seems to function to comment about the nature of the relationship between females, possibly a candidate for a metacommunicative signal.

Third, current research has explored the psychophysics of transmission of communication signals. Brown et al (1979) showed that frequency modulation was an important cue to sound localization in monkey vocalizations. Rhesus monkeys showed a great increase in their ability to localize a call when as little as 400 Hz of frequency modulation was added. Subsequent work (C. H. Brown 1982) has shown that the frequency modulation must be increased to at least 2000 Hz in order to effect an increase in locatability in a three-dimensional localization task. Snowdon & Hodun (1981) utilized these data to show in a field study on pygmy marmosets that monkeys used the most locatable calls when they were far apart from each other and the least locatable calls only when animals were close together. Thus, there is emerging a close interaction of laboratory studies of psychophysics with field research on the design features of communication signals.

Fourth, researchers have focused on how monkeys perceive their own vocalizations. Snowdon & Pola (1978) constructed a synthesizer to produce the various trills of the pygmy marmoset and acoustic intermediates between trill types. They found that monkeys produced categorical labeling functions, treating as equivalent synthesized calls that were quite variable, but showing sharp dividing lines on the dimensions that separated different call types. This is akin to the categorical perception of speech found in human beings (Liberman et al 1967).

Zoloth et al (1979) subsequently showed that Japanese macaques could discriminate between different forms of coo vocalizations that differed in the location of the peak frequency, while other species of monkeys learned the discrimination only with difficulty. Petersen et al (1978) showed that this discrimination was performed more successfully by the left hemisphere in Japanese macaques, while there was no hemispheric difference in the responses of other species. These studies indicate that some species have a species-specific perceptual system for their calls and that this mechanism is located in the left hemisphere as are the centers for speech in human beings.

Fifth, evidence for syntax in the calls of some monkeys has been demonstrated. Robinson (1979) showed that there was a fixed sequence of calls in the titi monkey with each sequence having a different meaning. Subsequently, he rearranged the sequences and found that monkeys showed a "disturbance" reaction to the rearranged syntax. Cleveland & Snowdon (1982) have reported several sequences in the calls of cotton-top tamarins.

Finally, the ontogeny of primate communication is being studied. Much of the data on ontogeny are very different from those of human infants. The preponderance of evidence so far argues for vocalizations being innate. Newman & Symmes (1974) found that socially isolated rhesus monkeys developed abnormalities on only one of their call types, while Talmage-Riggs et al (1972) found no deficits in deafened squirrel monkeys. Symmes et al (1979) showed that individual and dialect features in the isolation peep of squirrel monkeys appeared on the first day of birth and remained stable over the first year of life. Some evidence exists for dialects that might be learned. Green (1975b) described a possible dialect system among different groups of Japanese macaques, and Hodun et al (1981) have found dialectic differences among saddle-back tamarins. Both studies suggest the possibility that the dialects might be learned, although there is yet no evidence that learning plays an important role in acquisition of vocal behavior.

Seyfarth & Cheney (1982) have described the ontogeny of alarm calling in vervet monkeys. Young monkeys give alarms to a wide variety of stimuli, more or less appropriately. Thus, eagle alarm calls are given to a wide variety of birds, to falling leaves, etc, while snake alarms are given to a variety of sinuous objects on the ground. As animals get older they become more precise in their use of alarm calls, eventually restricting them to just the specific species that prey upon vervets. Seyfarth and Cheney hypothesize that imitation of adult behavior combined with selective reinforcement of calls given to appropriate objects is the mechanism by which the proper use of calls is learned.

APPLICATIONS OF ANIMAL BEHAVIOR RESEARCH

There are six important areas in which recent research in animal behavior has had important applications.

1. Variability of behavior: Perhaps the most important application of animal research is the least understood by the general public. Documenting the variability among different animal species has proved to be of great value in biomedical research. For example, the cotton-top tamarin is susceptible to spontaneous colonic cancer (Lushbaugh et al 1978). The mustached tamarin is the only species in which antibodies to hepatitis can be induced, leading to promising breakthroughs for a human vaccine for hepatitis (Ebert et al 1978). The behavioral variability displayed by different species of animals can be of similar value to understanding and modifying human behavior.

One striking example of this occurs in the different responses of infants of two different, but closely related, macaque species to infant separation. Pigtail macaque infants show high levels of behavior pathology when separated from their mothers, while infant bonnet macaques show very little evidence of disturbance. One cause of these behavioral differences arises in the nature of maternal behavior. Bonnet macaque mothers allow their infants to be very independent and to interact freely with other members of the group, while pigtail macaque mothers are very restrictive of their infants, tolerating no interaction with the infant by other group members (Kaufman & Rosenblum 1969). These findings could be translated to a testable hypothesis that would be useful to working human mothers. Allowing infants to experience a variety of caretakers from a very early age should make them more accepting of separation when the mother goes back to work. In contrast, infants whose mothers spend the early postnatal months as the almost exclusive caretaker are likely to experience distress when the mothers return to work.

The discussion of parental care above reflects the benefits of studying the behavioral variability of animals. Given that few male mammals participate in the care of their offspring, some sociobiologists have advised that the traditional human role division of females caring for infants has a biological basis. This is not true. There is a wide variety of parental care patterns, but the animals that have been studied most have been ones where paternal care has been minimal. Recent data on monogamous primates have shown that males and older siblings play an almost exclusive role in postnatal infant care. Furthermore, it has been shown that paternal care in primates must be learned through experience with infants. Finally, we have seen that in rhesus macaques where paternal behavior has rarely been seen in the wild, males do become interested in and care adequately for infants when there are no females around. Thus, the study of paternal care in a wide variety of species illustrates the wide variety of choices that human beings can make. We are not biologically constrained to persist in what have been traditional behavioral patterns.

2. Animal models of human behavior disorders: The most widely regarded application of animal behavior research has been in the development of models of various human pathological behaviors. One can carry out experiments with animals that would be impossible with human beings for either ethical or experimental reasons. Not all approaches to modeling psychopathology have been valid or useful. Abramson & Seligman (1977) reviewed the early literature on animal models and concluded that most of these attempts failed to be valid models of human disorders. Either the phenomena were not truly analogous to the human phenomena they claimed to represent or the methods of induction or treatment were grossly different from those known to be involved in the corresponding human disorder. Suomi & Harlow (1977) have discussed the need to evaluate both the validity of animal models and also the utility of the models. Not all models are useful; some mimic such a limited range of disorders that they are of little value. Suomi and Harlow categorize their own research on total isolation of monkeys during the first months of life as being of quite limited utility.

Despite these criticisms, there is much in current animal model research that has applicability to human disorders. This is most apparent in various models of depression. Seligman's (1975) formulation of learned helplessness has led to an active interaction of research between animal models and human beings. Although the initial formulation is recognized as inadequate (Abramson et al 1978), it still has been very important. The research on early infant separation in monkeys (Kaufman & Rosenblum 1969, Hinde & Spencer-Booth 1971, McKinney et al 1971) has led to a good understanding of separation-induced depression in young humans and has developed a model against which various possible treatments can be evaluated.

3. Application of ethological techniques to human behavior: Numerous studies have made use of ethological ideas to understand human behavior. These techniques have been widely applied, with considerable success, to the study of the play and aggressive behavior of young children (Blurton-Jones 1972, Freedman 1974) and to adult human nonverbal communication, territorial behavior, social attachment, intergroup and intragroup social behaviors, and social development (von Cranach et al 1980).

Ethological techniques have also been utilized in psychiatry. Evolutionary biology and ethology have been used to provide a functional classification of behavior and to describe the behavioral changes that occur with psychiatric disorders (McGuire & Essock-Vitale 1981, McGuire et al 1981). John Bowlby's writings (1969, 1973, 1980) have made an excellent synthesis between the findings of ethology and psychoanalysis in describing attachment, separation, and loss. Finally, one of the founders of ethology, Niko Tinbergen (see Tinbergen & Tinbergen 1972), has analyzed childhood autism in terms of ethological motivational conflicts and has applied ethological reasoning to prescribe the behavior for interacting with autistic children. He has reported success in dealing with these children who usually defy interaction with other human beings. Ethology has contributed to the description and analysis of normal social interactions of human beings and has increasing impact on the way in which psychiatrists deal with behavioral pathologies.

4. Protection and breeding of endangered species: In order to preserve the variability represented in different species, it is necessary to ensure that animals are available for future study. Many animal species are threatened or endangered. Efforts to preserve species' diversity in the face of extinction focus on the creation of natural reserves and on captive breeding. The understanding of behavior is crucial in both of these efforts. To maintain a natural reserve of adequate size and complexity for preservation of a species we need to know the ranging patterns of the animals, their reproductive and social patterns, their food needs, predator defense requirements, their interactions with other conspecific groups and with other species. It is also important to document the effects that humans have on the behavior of wild animals (Bishop et al 1981).

Knowledge of behavior is also important for captive breeding programs. For example, several species of marmosets and tamarins are threatened or endangered. It was not until behaviorists became involved in captive breeding programs that it was discovered that parental competence must be learned. Traditional animal production methods of pulling animals from their parents at weaning produced no successful reproduction among captive-born animals. Only when behaviorists insisted that young animals be kept with their parents to assist with successive infants did captive breeding become successful (Epple 1978, Kleiman 1978).

Behaviorists have designed optimal captive environments. Markowitz (1979) has reported a variety of ingenious innovations that he has made in caging design which improve the behavior and health of animals in captivity. Future success at preserving the species variability that may some day be of great importance to human welfare can come only with the active involvement of animal behaviorists.

5. Care of pets and pets as therapists: Pets are pervasive in society as companions of human beings, yet there are few data on their behavior and treatment of their behavioral disorders and even less data on the effects of pets on human behavior. Recently veterinarians have begun to realize the importance of behavior in the diagnosis and treatment of animals (Houpt & Wolski 1982).

Nonthreatening animate objects have been shown to have an important therapeutic effect on other animals. Novak & Harlow (1975) found that rhesus monkeys that had been isolated for several months from birth could be rehabilitated successfully by exposing them to monkeys which were three months younger. Whereas isolate-reared monkeys would behave fearfully in the presence of normally reared monkeys their own age, they accepted and learned to socialize with the younger monkeys. Mason & Kenney (1974) showed that isolate-reared monkeys could be rehabilitated through exposure to pet dogs. The monkeys developed close attachments to the dogs and showed considerable improvement in behavior. Corson et al (1977) used pet dogs with psychiatric patients and found that patients given pet dogs showed an increase of nonverbal and social responses first to the pets, then to the therapists who brought the pets, and eventually to other patients and medical staff. Corson et al posit that the pet is a nonthreatening organism that gives the patients a feeling of safety from which they can then develop more positive social relations with other people. Thus pets appear to be therapeutic for both disturbed animals and disturbed human beings.

6. Working animals: There are many examples of the human use of working animals yet little data on the selection and training of these working animals. Coppinger & Coppinger (1982) have reported interesting behavioral differences between livestock-guarding versus livestock-herding dogs. Both types of dogs are used with sheep but have very different behaviors and very different effects. One type of herding dog (the border collie) is used in areas without major predators. These dogs can move sheep around by acting like predators; they stalk sheep, moving them to whatever location the shepherd desires (P. B. McConnell and J. R. Baylis, in preparation). However, in areas of Europe where sheep predators are common, there are breeds of guarding dogs which look and act like sheep, showing no predatory behaviors toward sheep. They also attack predators. The Coppingers have shown that these guarding dogs can be very effective in keeping predators like coyotes from killing sheep in Western ranges. The importation of the breeds of guarding dogs and an understanding of how

they behave in controlling predation can have important economic benefits to sheep ranchers.

CONCLUSION

Despite the prediction of the demise of comparative psychology by sociobiologists, and the attempts to kill the field within psychology, animal behavior has become increasingly exciting over the past few years. Psychologists can and should play a major role in challenging some of the assumptions of sociobiology. However, we should be careful in making challenges that we do not lose sight of the importance of naturalistic studies and evolutionary mechanisms in the understanding of animal behavior. The contributions made primarily by psychologists in applying the results of animal behavior research to the better understanding of human behavior and its pathologies, and the economic contributions that can be made through better use of animals are important. Although animal behavior is under severe attack from some members of our own profession, from some government funding agencies, and from animal rights organizations, we should feel considerable pride in our accomplishments to date and in the potential of what we can accomplish in the future.

ACKNOWLEDGMENTS

Preparation of this manuscript was supported by a Research Scientist Development Award from the National Institute of Mental Health. I am grateful to Jeffrey French for information and discussions on social behavior and physiology, to Patricia McConnell for information and discussions concerning the applications of animal behavior research, and to Alexandra Hodun for critical comments on the manuscript.

Literature Cited

Abbott, D. H., Hearn, J. P. 1978. Physical, hormonal and behavioural aspects of sexual development in the marmoset monkey, *Callithrix jacchus. J. Reprod. Fertil.* 53:155–66

Abramson, L. Y., Seligman, M. E. P. 1977. Modeling psychopathology in the laboratory: history and rationale. In *Psychopathology: Experimental Methods,* ed. J. Mazur, M. E. P. Seligman, pp. 1–26. San Francisco: Freeman

Abramson, L. Y., Seligman, M. E. P., Teasdale, J. D. 1978. Learned helplessness in humans: critique and reformulation. *J. Abnorm. Psychol.* 87:49–74

Alcock, J. 1979. *Animal Behavior.* Sunderland, Mass: Sinauer. 2nd ed.

Altmann, J. 1974. Observational study of behavior: sampling methods. *Behaviour* 49:227–65

Altmann, J. 1980. *Baboon Mothers and Infants.* Cambridge: Harvard Univ. Press

Altmann, S. A., Altmann, J. 1979. Demographic constraints on behavior and social organization. In *Primate Ecology and Human Origins,* ed. I. Bernstein, E. O. Smith, pp. 47–63. New York: Garland STPM

Bales, K. B. 1980. Cumulative scaling of paternalistic behavior in primates. *Am. Nat.* 11:454–61

Barash, D. P. 1979. *The Whisperings Within: Evolution and the Origin of Human Nature.* New York: Harper & Row

Barash, D. P. 1982. *Sociobiology and Behavior.* New York: Elsevier. 2nd ed.

Barnett, S. A. 1981. *Modern Ethology: The Science of Animal Behavior.* New York: Oxford Univ. Press

Beach, F. A. 1950. The snark was a boojum. *Am. Psychol.* 5:115–24

Berman, C. M. 1982. The social development of an orphaned rhesus infant on Cayo Santiago: Male care, foster mother-orphan interaction and peer interaction. *Am. J. Primatol.* In press

Bernstein, I. S. 1981. Dominance: the baby and the bathwater. *Behav. Brain Sci.* 4:419–57

Bernstein, I. S., Rose, R. M., Gordon, T. P. 1977. Behavioural and hormonal responses of male rhesus monkeys introduced to females in the breeding and non-breeding seasons. *Anim. Behav.* 25:609–16

Bertram, B. C. R. 1975. Social factors influencing reproduction in wild lions. *J. Zool.* 177:463–82

Bierens de Haan, J. A. 1929. Animal language and its relation to that of man. *Biol. Rev. Cambridge Philos. Soc.* 4: 249–68

Bishop, N., Hrdy, S. B., Teas, J., Moore, J. 1981. Measures of human influence in habitats of South Asian monkeys. *Int. J. Primatol.* 2:153–67

Bitterman, M. E. 1965. Phyletic differences in learning. *Am. Psychol.* 20:396–410

Blurton-Jones, N. 1972. *Ethological Studies of Child Behaviour.* Cambridge: Cambridge Univ. Press

Bowlby, J. 1969. *Attachment.* New York: Basic Books

Bowlby, J. 1973. *Separation.* New York: Basic Books

Bowlby, J. 1980. *Loss.* New York: Basic Books

Bronowski, J., Bellugi, U. 1970. Language, name and concept. *Science* 168:669–73

Brower, J. V. Z. 1958. Experimental studies of mimicry in some North American butterflies: Part 1: The monarch, *Danaus plexippus,* and viceroy, *Limenitis a. archippus. Evolution* 12:32–47

Brown, C. H. 1982. Auditory localization and primate vocal behavior. In *Primate Communication,* ed. C. T. Snowdon, C. H. Brown, M. R. Petersen. New York: Cambridge Univ. Press.

Brown, C. H., Beecher, M. D., Moody, D. B., Stebbins, W. C. 1979. Locatability of vocal signals in old world monkeys: design features for the communication of position. *J. Comp. Physiol. Psychol.* 93:806–19

Brown, R. 1973. *A First Language.* Cambridge: Harvard Univ. Press

Capranica, R. R. 1966. Vocal response of the bullfrog to natural and synthetic mating calls. *J. Acoust. Soc. Am.* 40:1131–39

Carrier, J. K. Jr. 1979. Application of functional analysis and a nonspeech response mode to teaching language. In *Language Intervention from Ape to Child,* ed. R. L. Schiefelbusch, J. H. Hollis, pp. 363–418. Baltimore: Univ. Park Press

Cheney, D. L., Lee, P. C., Seyfarth, R. M. 1981. Behavioral correlates of non-random mortality among free-ranging female vervet monkeys. *Behav. Ecol. Sociobiol.* 9:153–61

Cheney, D. L., Seyfarth, R. M. 1982. How vervet monkeys perceive their grunts: Field playback experiments. *Anim. Behav.* In press

Chomsky, N. 1965. *Aspects of the Theory of Syntax.* Cambridge: MIT Press

Cleveland, J., Snowdon, C. T. 1982. The complex vocal repertoire of the adult cotton-top tamarin, *Saguinus oedipus oedipus. Z. Tierpsychol.* 58:231–70

Coppinger, L., Coppinger, R. 1982. Livestock guarding dogs that wear sheep's clothing. *Smithsonian* 13:65–73

Corson, S. A., Corson, E. O. L., Gwynne, P., Arnold, L. E. 1977. Pet dogs as nonverbal communication links in hospital psychiatry. *Compr. Psychiatry* 18:61–72

Curtin, S. H. 1980. Dusky and banded leaf monkeys. In *Malayan Forest Primates,* ed. D. J. Chivers, pp. 107–45. New York: Plenum

Dawkins, R. 1976. *The Selfish Gene.* New York: Oxford Univ. Press

Desmond, A. J. 1979. *The Ape's Reflexion.* New York: Dial Press/James Wade

Dethier, V. G., Stellar, E. 1970. *Animal Behavior.* Englewood Cliffs, NJ: Prentice Hall. 3rd ed.

de Waal, F. B. M., van Roosmalen, A. 1979. Reconciliation and consolation among chimpanzees. *Behav. Ecol. Sociobiol.* 5:55–66

Dolhinow, P. 1977. Normal monkeys? *Am. Sci.* 65:266

Dooley, G. B., Gill, T. V. 1977. Acquisition and use of mathematical skills by a linguistic chimpanzee. See Rumbaugh 1977, pp. 247–60

Dukes, W. F. 1960. The snark revisited. *Am. Psychol.* 15:157

Ebert, J. W., Maynard, J. E., Bradley, D. W., Lorenze, D., Krushak, D. H. 1978. Experimental infection of marmosets with hepatitis A virus. *Primates Med.* 10: 296–99

Edwards, S. D., Snowdon, C. T. 1980. Social

behavior of captive, group-living orangutans. *Int. J. Primatol.* 1:39–62

Epple, G. 1978. Reproductive and social behavior of marmosets with special reference to captive breeding. *Primates Med.* 10:50–62

Epstein, R. R., Lanza, R. P., Skinner, B. F. 1980. Symbolic communication between two pigeons, (*Columba livia domestica*). *Science* 207:543–45

Essock, S. M. 1977. Color perception and color classification. See Rumbaugh 1977, pp. 207–24

Freedman, D. X. 1974. *Human Infancy: An Evolutionary Perspective.* Hillsdale, NJ: Erlbaum

French, J. A. 1981. Individual differences in play in *Macaca fuscata:* The role of maternal status and proximity. *Int. J. Primatol.* 2:237–46

Frischkopf, L. S., Capranica, R. R., Goldstein, M. H. 1968. Neural coding in the bullfrog's auditory system—a teleological approach. *Proc. IEEE* 56:969–80

Gadgil, M. 1981. *Changes with age in the strategy of social behavior.* Presented at 17th Int. Ethol. Conf., Oxford

Gardner, R. A., Gardner, B. T. 1969. Teaching sign language to a chimpanzee. *Science* 165:664–72

Gardner, R. A., Gardner, B. T. 1978. Comparative psychology and language acquisition. *Ann. NY Acad. Sci.* 309:37–76

Gartlan, J. S. 1968. Structure and function in primate society. *Folia Primatol.* 8:89–120

Gartlan, J. S., Brain, C. K. 1968. Ecology and social variability in *Cercopithecus aethiops* and *C. mitis.* In *Primates: Studies in Adaptation and Variability,* ed. P. Jay, pp. 253–92. New York: Holt, Rinehart & Winston

Gautier, J.-P. 1974. Field and laboratory studies on the vocalizations of talapoin monkeys (*Miopithecus talapoin*). *Behaviour* 51:209–73

Gibber, J. R. 1981. *Infant-directed behaviors in male and female rhesus monkeys.* PhD thesis. Univ. Wis., Madison

Gould, J. L. 1982. *Ethology.* New York: Norton

Green, S. 1975a. Variations of vocal pattern with social situation in the Japanese monkey (*Macaca fuscata*): A field study. In *Primate Behavior: Developments in Laboratory and Field Research,* ed. L. A. Rosenblum, 4:1–102. New York: Academic

Green, S. 1975b. Dialects in Japanese monkeys: vocal learning and cultural transmission of locale specific behavior. *Z. Tierpsychol.* 38:304–14

Hailman, J. P. 1982. Evolution and behavior: an iconoclastic view. In *Learning Development and Culture: Essays in Evolutionary Epistemology,* ed. H. C. Plotkin, pp. 205–54. London: Wiley

Hamilton, W. D. 1964. The genetical evolution of social behavior. *J. Theor. Biol.* 7:1–52

Hamilton, W. D. 1972. Altruism and related behavior mainly in social insects. *Ann. Rev. Ecol. Syst.* 3:193–232

Hess, E. H. 1973. *Imprinting.* New York: Van Nostrand Reinhold

Hill, J. H. 1974. Possible continuity theories of language. *Language* 50:134–50

Hinde, R. A. 1978. Dominance and role—two concepts with dual meanings. *J. Soc. Biol. Struct.* 1:27–38

Hinde, R. A., Spencer-Booth, Y. 1971. Effects of brief separations from mothers on rhesus monkeys. *Science* 173:111–18

Hodun, A., Snowdon, C. T., Soini, P. 1981. Subspecific variation in the long calls of the tamarin, *Saguinus fuscicollis.* *Z. Tierpsychol.* 57:97–110

Houpt, K. A., Wolski, T. R. 1982. *Domestic Animal Behavior for Veterinarians and Animal Scientists.* Ames: Iowa State Univ. Press

Hrdy, S. B. 1977. Infanticide as a primate reproductive strategy. *Am. Sci.* 65:40–49

Hrdy, S. B. 1979. Infanticide among animals. *Ethol. Sociobiol.* 1:13–40

Kahn, J. V. 1977. A comparison of manual and oral language training with mute retarded children. *Ment. Retard.* 15:21–23

Kaufman, I. C., Rosenblum, L. A. 1969. Effects of separation from mother on the emotional behavior of infant monkeys. *Ann. NY Acad. Sci.* 159:689–95

Kawai, M. 1965. Newly acquired protocultural behavior of the natural troop of Japanese monkeys on Koshima islet. *Primates* 6:1–30

Kellogg, W. N. 1968. Communication and language in the home-raised chimpanzee. *Science* 162:423–27

Kleiman, D. G. 1978. *The Biology and Conservation of the Callitrichidae.* Washington: Smithsonian Inst. Press

Kleiman, D. G., Malcolm, J. R. 1981. The evolution of male parental investment in mammals. In *Parental Care in Mammals,* ed. D. J. Gubernick, P. H. Klopfer, pp. 347–87. New York: Plenum

Kummer, H. 1968. *Social Organization of Hamadryas Baboons.* Chicago: Univ. Chicago Press

Lenneberg, E. 1967. *Biological Foundations of Language.* New York: Wiley

Liberman, A., Cooper, F., Shankweiler, D., Studdert-Kennedy, M. 1967. Perception of the speech code. *Psychol. Rev.* 74:431–61

Lillehei, R. A., Snowdon, C. T. 1978. Individual and situational differences in the vocalizations of young stumptail macaques. *Behaviour* 65:270–81

Linden, E. 1974. *Apes, Men and Language.* New York: Dutton

Lockard, R. B. 1971. Reflections on the fall of comparative psychology: is there a message for us all? *Am. Psychol.* 26: 168–79

Lushbaugh, C. C., Humason, G. L., Schwartzendruber, D. C., Richter, C. B., Gengozian, N. 1978. Spontaneous colonic adenocarcinoma in marmosets. *Primates Med.* 10:119–34

Markowitz, H. 1979. Environmental enrichment and behavioral engineering for captive primates. In *Captivity and Behavior*, ed. J. Erwin, T. L. Maple, G. Mitchell, pp. 217–38. New York: Van Nostrand-Reinhold

Marler, P. 1970a. A comparative approach to vocal learning: Song development in white-crowned sparrows. *J. Comp. Physiol. Psychol. Monogr. Suppl.* 71:1–25

Marler, P. 1970b. Birdsong and speech development: Could there be parallels? *Am. Sci.* 58:669–73

Mason, W. A., Kenney, M. D. 1974. Redirection of filial attachments in rhesus monkeys: Dogs as mother surrogates. *Science* 182:1209–11

Mason, W. A., Lott, D. F. 1976. Ethology and comparative psychology. *Ann. Rev. Psychol.* 27:129–54

McClintock, M. K. 1971. Menstrual synchrony and suppression. *Nature* 229: 244–45

McClintock, M. K. 1978. Estrous synchrony and its mediation by airborne chemical communication (*Rattus norvegicus*). *Horm. Behav.* 10:264–76

McClintock, M. K. 1981. Social control of the ovarian cycle and the function of estrus synchrony. *Am. Zool.* 21:243–56

McGuire, M. T., Essock-Vitale, S. M. 1981. Psychiatric disorders in the context of evolutionary biology. A functional classification of behavior. *J. Nerv. Ment. Dis.* 169:672–86

McGuire, M. T., Essock-Vitale, S. M., Polsky, R. H. 1981. Psychiatric disorders in the context of evolutionary biology. An ethological model of behavioral changes associated with psychiatric disorders. *J. Nerv. Ment. Dis.* 169: 687–704

McKinney, W. T., Suomi, S. J., Harlow, H. F. 1971. Depression in primates. *Am. J. Psychiatry* 127:1313–20

Miller, D. B. 1977. Roles of naturalistic observation in comparative psychology. *Am. Psychol.* 32:211–19

Mohnot, S. M. 1971. Some aspects of social change and infant killing in the Hanuman langur, *Presbytis entellus* (Primates: Cercopithecae) in Western India. *Mammalia* 35:175–98

Newman, J. D., Symmes, D. 1974. Vocal pathology in socially-deprived monkeys. *Dev. Psychobiol.* 7:351–58

Noe, R., de Waal, F. B. M., van Hooff, J. A. R. A. M. 1980. Types of dominance in a chimpanzee colony. *Folia Primatol.* 34:90–110

Novak, M. A., Harlow, H. F. 1975. Social recovery of monkeys isolated for the first year of life: I. Rehabilitation and therapy. *Dev Psychol.* 11:453–65

Parkel, D. A., Smith, S. T. Jr. 1979. Application of computer-assisted language designs. See Carrier 1979, pp. 441–64

Petersen, M. R., Beecher, M. D., Zoloth, S. R., Moody, D. B., Stebbins, W. C. 1978. Neural lateralization of species-specific vocalizations by Japanese macaques (*Macaca fuscata*). *Science* 202:324–27

Pola, Y. V., Snowdon, C. T. 1975. The vocalizations of the pygmy marmoset, *Cebuella pygmaea. Anim. Behav.* 23: 826–42

Porter, J. H., Johnson, S. B., Granger, R. G. 1981. The snark is still a boojum. *Comp. Psychol. Newsl.* 1(5):1–3

Premack, D. 1970. Language in chimpanzee? *Science* 172: 808–22

Premack, D., Woodruff, G. 1978. Does the chimpanzee have a theory of mind? *Behav. Brain Sci.* 1:515–26

Redican, W. K. 1978. Adult male-infant relations in captive rhesus monkeys. In *Recent Advances in Primatology*, ed. D. Chivers, J. Herbert, 1:165–67. New York: Academic

Robinson, J. G. 1979. An analysis of the organization of vocal communication in the titi monkey, *Callicebus moloch. Z. Tierpsychol.* 49:381–405

Rowell, T. E. 1974. The concept of social dominance. *Behav. Biol.* 11:131–54

Rowell, T. E. 1979. How would we know if social organization were not adaptive? See Altmann & Altmann 1979, pp. 1–22

Rumbaugh, D. M. 1977. *Language Learning in a Chimpanzee.* New York: Academic

Rumbaugh, D. M. 1981. Who feeds Clever Hans? *Ann. NY Acad. Sci.* 364: 26–34

Sebeok, T. A., Rosenthal, R. 1981. The Clever Hans Phenomenon: Communication with horses, whales, apes and people. *Ann. NY Acad. Sci.* 364:1–311

Seligman, M. E. P. 1975. *Helplessness.* San Francisco: Freeman

Seyfarth, R. M., Cheney, D. L. 1982. How monkeys see the world: A review of recent research on East African vervet monkeys. See Brown 1982

Seyfarth, R. M., Cheney, D. L., Marler, P. 1980. Vervet monkey alarm calls: semantic communication in a free-ranging primate. *Anim. Behav.* 28:1070–94

Sherman, P. 1977. Nepotism and the evolution of alarm calls. *Science* 197:1246–53

Sherman, P. 1980. The limits of ground squirrel nepotism. In *Sociobiology: Beyond Nature:Nurture,* ed. G. Barlow, J. Silverberg, pp. 505–44. Boulder, Colo: Westview

Smith, H. J., Newman, J. D., Symmes, D. 1982. Vocal concomitants of affiliative behavior in squirrel monkeys. See Brown 1982

Snowdon, C. T., Cleveland, J., French, J. A. 1982. Responses to context- and individual-specific cues in cotton-top tamarin long calls. *Anim. Behav.* In press

Snowdon, C. T., Hodun, A. 1981. Acoustic adaptations in pygmy marmoset contact calls: Locational cues vary with distances between conspecifics. *Behav. Ecol. Sociobiol.* 9:295–300

Snowdon, C. T., Pola, Y. V. 1978. Interspecific and intraspecific responses to synthesized marmoset vocalizations. *Anim. Behav.* 26:192–206

Snowdon, C. T., Suomi, S. J. 1982. Paternal care in primates. In *Child Nurturance,* ed. H. E. Fitzgerald, J. A. Mullins, P. Gage, Vol. 3. New York: Plenum

Southwick, C. H. 1967. An experimental study of intragroup agonistic behaviour in rhesus monkeys (*Macaca mulatta*). *Behaviour* 28:182–209

Suomi, S. J., Harlow, H. F. 1977. Production and alleviation of depressive behaviors in monkeys. See Abramson & Seligman 1977, pp. 131–73

Swanson, H. H., Payman, B. C. 1978. Social and spatial influences on puberty in the female mongolian gerbil. In *Hormones and Brain Development,* ed. G. Dorner, M. Kawakami, pp. 375–80. New York: Elsevier

Symmes, D., Newman, J. D., Talmage-Riggs, G., Katz-Lieblich, A. 1979. Individuality and stability of isolation peeps in squirrel monkeys. *Anim. Behav.* 27:1142–52

Talmage-Riggs, G., Winter, P., Ploog, D., Mayer, W. 1972. Effect of deafening on the vocal behavior of the squirrel monkey (*Saimiri scurieus*). *Folia Primatol.* 17:404–20

Terrace, H. S., Petitto, L. A., Sanders, R. J., Bever, T. G. 1979. Can an ape create a sentence? *Science* 206:891–902

Tinbergen, N. 1951. *The Study of Instinct.* Oxford: Oxford Univ. Press

Tinbergen, N., Kruyt, W. 1938. Über die orientierung des Bienenwolfes (*Philanthus triangulum*). III. Die Bevorzugung bestimmter Wegmarken. *Z. Vergl. Physiol.* 25:292–334

Tinbergen, N., Tinbergen, E. A. 1972. Early childhood autism—a hypothesis. *Z. Tierpsychol. Suppl.* 10:1–53

Trivers, R. L. 1971. The evolution of reciprocal altruism. *Q. Rev. Biol.* 46:343–51

Trivers, R. L. 1972. Parental investment and sexual selection. In *Sexual Selection and the Descent of Man, 1871–1971,* ed. B. Campbell, pp. 136–79. Chicago: Aldine

Vandenbergh, J. G., Drickamer, L. C. 1974. Reproductive coordination among free-ranging rhesus monkeys. *Physiol. Behav.* 13:373–76

von Cranach, M., Foppa, K., Lepenies, W., Ploog, D. 1980. *Human Ethology.* Cambridge: Cambridge Univ. Press

Wilson, E. O. 1975. *Sociobiology: The New Synthesis.* Cambridge: Harvard Univ. Press

Wilson, E. O. 1978. *On Human Nature.* Cambridge: Harvard Univ. Press

Woolfenden, G. E. 1975. Florida scrub jay helpers at the nest. *Auk* 92:1–15

Woolfenden, G. E., Fitzpatrick, J. 1978. The inheritance of territory in group-breeding birds. *Bioscience* 28:104–8

Wu, H. M. H., Holmes, W. G., Medina, S. R., Sackett, G. P. 1980. Kin preference in infant *Macaca nemestrina. Nature* 285:225–27

Wynne Edwards, V. C. 1962. *Animal Dispersion in Relation to Social Behavior.* New York: Hafner

Zoloth, S. R., Petersen, M. R., Beecher, M. D., Green, S., Marler, P., Moody, D. B., Stebbins, W. C. 1979. Species-specific perceptual processing of vocal sounds by monkeys. *Science* 204:870–72

Ann. Rev. Psychol. 1983. 34:95–128

AUDITION: Some Relations Between Normal and Pathological Hearing

Dennis McFadden

Department of Psychology, University of Texas, Austin, Texas 78712

Frederic L. Wightman

Northwestern University Auditory Research Laboratory, Evanston, Illinois 60201

CONTENTS

95

0066-4308/83/0201-0095$02.00

INTRODUCTION

Our intent for this chapter was to examine one primary theme—the research lying at the interface between normal and pathological hearing. Specifically, we were interested in the various attempts to apply established procedures and paradigms, initially used for basic research on normal auditory systems, to the study of pathological systems. One reason for our choice of this topic is a long-standing, shared belief that the study of pathologies has not advanced our knowledge of the auditory system to the same degree that it has our knowledge of other sensory systems—witness the contributions of color blindness, night blindness, cataracts, amblyopia, and strabismus to knowledge about the normal visual system. Second, we believe that various scientific and practical factors are now producing increasing interest in auditory pathologies among scientists previously content to study normal listeners, and if we are correct about this trend, it warrants notice in this series. Not the least of our reasons for focusing on this topic is the fact that a number of interesting and exciting discoveries have been made in the area; some of these offer insight into pathology, some into normal function, and some into both. Our hope is that basic scientists reading this review will learn a few interesting facts about pathological conditions, and that clinicians and applied scientists will come to see certain pathological conditions from a new perspective.

As narrow as this topic may appear, further arbitrariness became necessary as the project developed. The explosion of activity in the area of acoustic emissions led us into a full coverage of that topic, even though some of the material was not directly related to our initial theme, and that coverage required the regrettable omission of several interesting and important topics related to our theme, such as recent work on the neurophysiological underpinnings of temporary and permanent threshold shift (e.g. Lonsbury-Martin & Meikle 1978, Robertson & Johnstone 1980) and on the effects of reverberation on intelligibility (Nabelek & Robinette 1978). We hope the reader appreciates that space was an ever-present constraint upon our desire to examine our chosen theme exhaustively.

MEASURING AUDITORY PATHOLOGY

Psychophysical research on auditory pathology began more than 40 years ago with the birth of the field of audiology. The focus of the early work was development of effective tools for diagnosis of hearing impairments. From the beginning, the most widely used diagnostic tool has been the pure-tone audiogram, a description of an individual's loss in pure-tone sensitivity at a number of frequencies. As this and more sophisticated diagnostic tools were developed and refined, researchers in the area contributed greatly to our understanding not only of auditory pathology but also of normal auditory processes.

Now, more and more researchers are using the results of experiments on damaged auditory systems to draw inferences about normal auditory function. In the last 5 years there has been a dramatic increase in studies of the basic auditory abilities of hearing-impaired individuals. Unfortunately, the results of these studies have not been particularly revealing. In spite of the use of sophisticated techniques, well-practiced listeners, carefully controlled stimuli, etc, the results have yet to provide integrative new insights. The problem seems to be variability. While data from individual subjects are usually reliable, subjects with apparently similar pathology often produce very different results. Since nearly all the research thus far has been of the "hypothesis-testing" sort, it follows that large intersubject variability will preclude meaningful conclusions.

Very recently a small number of research groups has been studying the interrelations among the various auditory abilities in both normal and hearing-impaired listeners. The results of their experiments, which we call "test-battery" studies, are expressed in terms of correlations among the various measures. Rather than being restricted by it, this approach exploits the large intersubject variability encountered in work with the hearing impaired. Only a few preliminary results of these test-battery studies have been published, so it is too early to assess the potential of this new approach. However, to the extent that auditory pathology affects the interactions among hearing functions, the test-battery approach may be the *only* reasonable way to study the patterns of interactions.

In the sections that follow we will review some of the recent studies of the impact of pathology on individual auditory functions and then describe the new test-battery studies and their preliminary findings. The experiments we will review have focused on pathology of presumed cochlear origin, and in general appear to have been motivated by the desire to explain the difficulty which many cochlear-impaired individuals have in understanding speech in noisy backgrounds.

Frequency Analysis

Many believe that loss of the ability to understand speech is largely the result of a decrease in auditory frequency-resolving power. Frequency analysis is one of the ear's most salient properties, and there can be little doubt that it is involved in the complex process of decoding an incoming speech waveform. Research on frequency analysis in normal listeners has for the most part consisted of masking experiments which assess the extent to which one stimulus, the "masker," interferes with the detection of another stimulus, the "signal." The results have led quite naturally to the development of several measures of the "precision" of auditory frequency analysis. The width of the so-called "critical band" is a good example (see Scharf 1970 for a review of the extensive work on this topic). In the past few years the most popular measures of frequency-resolving power have been the psychophysical tuning curve or PTC (Small 1959, Zwicker 1974, Moore 1978) and "auditory filter" shape (Patterson 1974, Houtgast 1977, Pick 1980). When these measurements have been obtained from listeners with cochlear pathology, the results suggest a reasonably strong relationship between degree of hearing loss (as measured by loss of pure-tone sensitivity) and loss of frequency-resolving power. Measurements of the width of the PTC (inversely related to frequency-resolving power) are the most consistent; nearly every study concludes that one consequence of cochlear pathology is reduced frequency resolution (Scharf & Hellman 1966, Hoekstra & Ritsma 1977, Leshowitz & Lindstrom 1977, Wightman et al 1977, Zwicker & Schorn 1978, Florentine et al 1980, Nelson & Turner 1980, Feth et al 1980, Ritsma et al 1980, Tyler et al 1982). However, it is clear that the relationship is not a simple one. For example, both Leshowitz & Lindstrom (1977) and Hoekstra & Ritsma (1977) reported that in some cases of a loss of more than 40 dB the PTC takes on a strange "W" shape, in addition to becoming generally broader (an effect also seen in the neurophysiological measures of Dallos & Harris 1978). Moreover, the Northwestern group (Wightman et al 1977, McGee 1978) described a few cases with a loss of less than 40 dB in which the PTC was near normal. To further complicate the picture, both Bonding (1973) and de Boer & Bouwmeester (1974) reported that several individuals with cochlear pathology demonstrated normal frequency resolution, at least as indicated by critical bandwidths. In a similar vein, Margolis & Goldberg (1980) presented results suggesting that some listeners with cochlear pathology (in their case presbycusis) may demonstrate normal frequency selectivity in some tasks and abnormal selectivity in others.

In some ways the most direct indication of the precision of auditory frequency analysis may come from classical frequency-discrimination experiments in which listeners try to detect a frequency difference between two sinusoids presented in succession. The normal just-noticeable-difference (jnd) in frequency is about 1–2 Hz at 1000 Hz (Wier et al 1977). The influence of cochlear pathology on the frequency jnd has been measured in relatively few studies. The usual finding is that in most, but not all, cases of cochlear impairment, the jnd for frequency is abnormally large (Butler & Albrite 1956, Konig 1957, Ross et al 1965, Gengel 1973, Hoekstra & Ritsma 1977). The most recent measurements are from the Northwestern group (Wightman 1982), and while only two listeners were involved, the results are provocative. Even though the two listeners were carefully matched on audiometric variables (profile of loss, probable etiology, etc), their frequency jnds were different by almost an order of magnitude; one of the listeners demonstrated nearly normal frequency jnds.

Several investigators have argued that the precision of auditory frequency selectivity is determined in part by cochlear nonlinearities of the sort responsible for the phenomenon known as lateral suppression (Houtgast 1972). Thus it is conceivable that the degradation of frequency selectivity caused by cochlear pathology may be a result of, or may be correlated with, abnormal nonlinear effects in impaired ears. The few data on this relationship that have appeared (Leshowitz & Lindstrom 1977, Wightman et al 1977) do suggest that the nonlinear mechanism responsible for lateral suppression is vulnerable to cochlear pathology. Whether this mechanism is connected in any way with the precision of frequency analysis is very much open to question.

Temporal Analysis

Rapid changes in parameters of a speech waveform (e.g. its formants) carry important information, and thus accurate speech understanding requires the ability to detect and process these rapid changes. The hypothesis that impaired speech understanding is a result of degraded temporal resolution has motivated several experiments on temporal processing by hearing-impaired listeners. The early studies measured the limits of temporal integration, the process by which the auditory system integrates incoming acoustic power to lower detection thresholds or to increase loudness. While the results are inconsistent, it seems reasonable to conclude that cochlear pathology can lead to abnormally shallow temporal integration functions, suggesting an impairment of the "integrating" mechanism (Miskolczy-Fodor 1953, Sanders & Honig 1967, Wright 1968, Gengel & Watson 1971, Stelmachowicz & Seewald 1977). One modern study provides data that support this point of view (Tyler & Summerfield 1980).

Most of the recent work on temporal processing by hearing-impaired listeners has focused on temporal acuity rather than on temporal integration. In normal listeners the limits of temporal acuity—defined as the minimum separation between two brief stimuli required for a determination of their temporal order, or by the minimum detectable silent gap in a long-duration stimulus—is about 2–3 msec (Green 1971, Abel 1972). The temporal acuity of impaired ears has been measured in three recent experiments. Jesteadt et al (1976), in what was basically a temporal order experiment, reported that eight of their ten listeners with sensorineural hearing loss actually demonstrated better-than-normal temporal acuity in some conditions. In contrast, Irwin et al (1981) and Fitzgibbons & Wightman (1982) studied the minimum detectable silent gap in a burst of noise and came to the opposite conclusion. It should be noted that in addition to the obvious differences in experimental paradigm, intersubject variability in all three experiments was very large, so firm conclusions are unwarranted.

Another indication of temporal resolution is the rate of decay of masking following termination of a masking stimulus. In these terms, cochlear pathology seems to result in degraded temporal resolution. Both Elliott (1975) and Nelson & Turner (1980) have shown that masking decays much more slowly in the impaired ear. Once again, however, the variability in the results is so large as to preclude all but the most general conclusions.

Binaural Analysis

The effectiveness with which an individual deals with his auditory environment is dependent upon his ability to organize it, and this in turn is dependent upon the interactions between the neural signals originating at the two ears (binaural analysis). The impact of cochlear pathology on binaural analysis is not well understood in spite of a substantial number of research efforts during the last several decades. Scharf (1978a) and Durlach et al (1981) have recently provided excellent, detailed reviews of research in this area; the interested reader is referred to them for details. For our purpose here it will be sufficient to note that Durlach et al were unwilling to draw any "... firm, incisive conclusions ... concerning the effects of hearing impairments on binaural interactions" (p. 206). Among the problems they faced were: (a) the experiments and resulting data did not allow determination of whether performance deficits reflected reduced sensitivity (resolving power) or abnormal response processes, and (b) most of the experiments measured performance on only one task. As Durlach et al noted, "... the failure to examine performance on a variety of tasks, and to explore the correlations between the different results, seriously limits the value of the study." Both of these problems are characteristic of nearly all but the most recent work on hearing-impaired listeners.

Understanding Speech

It is generally accepted that one consequence of sensorineural hearing impairment is a loss of the ability to comprehend speech. Given the obvious importance of speech comprehension for everyday existence, it is surprising that so little research has been directed at a better understanding of the nature of the speech perception deficit suffered by the hearing impaired. Speech comprehension ability is typically assessed in the clinic by measuring the percentage of isolated monosyllabic words correctly recognized (repeated back to the tester). Thus, it is not surprising that most of the research on speech comprehension by the hearing impaired has focused on word-recognition scores and the effects on them of various distortions, testing conditions, list composition, etc. The only general finding that has come from these studies is that speech recognition scores (as measured by the conventional monosyllable tests) do not appear to be correlated with audiometric data.

Several studies reported in the last decade have attempted a more detailed examination of the nature of speech processing deficits by analyzing patterns of errors made by hearing-impaired listeners. Studies of patterns of consonant confusions are the most numerous. While there are some areas of agreement (e.g. errors of "place of articulation" predominate), inconsistencies are common. The studies are most divided over the relationships among a listener's pure-tone audiogram, the "type" of impairment, and his pattern of errors. For example, Bilger & Wang (1976), describing the results of a study using CV and VC nonsense syllables, write "scaling . . . resulted in consistent classification of subjects according to audiometric configuration . . ." Owens et al (1972) seem to agree with Bilger and Wang, thus summarizing their analysis of phoneme errors on standard monosyllable tests: "Probability of error for individual phonemes seemed to be more closely related to pure-tone configuration than to kinds of hearing impairment." But the generally confused state of research in this area is well exemplified by Owens' own statement in a later report of a similar study (1978) conducted on 550 (!) sensorineural hearing-impaired listeners ". . . in only a few instances would the pure-tone configuration of a given patient be of any special help in predicting those consonants particularly difficult to recognize."

Summary

The renewal of interest in the consequences of auditory pathology has stimulated a great deal of research. Most of the recent experiments have used the same well-controlled psychophysical paradigms that have produced stable data from normal listeners for nearly two decades. Unfortunately, as the foregoing review suggests, the results of these experiments have been highly variable, frequently inconsistent, and not particularly enlightening with regard to the underlying pathology. There are many possible reasons for this. For one thing, it could be argued that experiments on hearing-impaired listeners are simply more difficult to do well. Potentially important factors such as subject age and motivation are nearly impossible to control. In addition, it is frequently difficult to know exactly how to compare performance of hearing-impaired listeners to so-called "normal" performance. For example, consider the simple issue of stimulus level. Since hearing-impaired listeners are often tested at higher sound-pressure levels than normals, should comparison be made at equal SPLs or equal SLs (sensation levels)? Sensible arguments could be offered for each point of view, and the issue has stimulated several experiments on, for example, the influence of level on measures of frequency resolution (Pick 1980, Green et al 1981, Wightman 1982).

Perhaps the most important reason for the inconclusive nature of research on the hearing-impaired concerns the possible interrelations among auditory abilities and the fact that most experiments to date have ignored this possibility (a point mentioned by Durlach et al 1981). As an example, suppose that normal performance on a frequency discrimination test is dependent upon a number of factors not obviously related to frequency discrimination—for example, temporal processing and intensity processing. Now if abnormal performance is observed on the frequency discrimination test and frequency discrimination is the only ability tested, it is obviously not possible to determine whether the deficit was a result of impaired frequency discrimination, impaired temporal processing, or impaired intensity processing. The various impairments could have produced very different patterns of abnormality in the frequency discrimination results, and thus would greatly complicate interpretation of the data. In testing normal listeners the interrelations are probably hidden; normal performance on a given test in most cases would imply that all the component processes were normal.

Experiments specifically designed to reveal the interrelations among auditory abilities are just now being considered as a possible approach to the study of hearing impairment. We turn now to the results of some of these experiments.

The Multivariate Approach

The multivariate or "test-battery" approach to the study of basic auditory abilities is not new. Over 40 years ago, Karlin (1942) reported a study intended to identify basic auditory "factors," or patterns of results from a battery of auditory tests given to normal listeners. Karlin's factor analysis was inconclusive. No clear auditory factor emerged, indicating that the tests were more or less independent. Given that the intersubject variability on most auditory measures is quite small with normal listeners, Karlin's result was not unexpected. Meaningful correlations between measures can be obtained only if intersubject variability is much larger than intrasubject variability. For this reason, the test-battery approach may be ideally suited to studies of the perceptual consequences of hearing impairment. The large intersubject variability which has confounded interpretation of results from single-test studies may actually be advantageous in a test-battery study. Unfortunately, very little research of this type has yet been published.

Nearly all of the published test-battery studies of normal listeners appear to have suffered from this "problem" of low intersubject variability. The large-scale study reported by Elliott et al (1966) is a good example. Six auditory discrimination measures were obtained from a random sample of 400 normal-hearing, high school sophomores. Other than the fact that listeners who scored well on one test tended to score well on all of them (this factor accounted for 34% of the common variance), the data produced no clear patterns. The investigators concluded that ". . . various discrimination tests tend to be relatively independent of each other." It is possible that the Elliott et al finding was a result of high intrasubject variability (the subjects were untrained). However, in a recent study in which training variables were under better control, Festen & Plomp (1981) administered 12 tests to 50 subjects and obtained very few meaningful correlations. The low correlations were not due to poor test reliability.

While no large test-battery studies of hearing-impaired listeners have yet appeared, there are a few published experiments with the same motivation but a more limited scope. All of these have attempted to relate performance on one or more tests of basic auditory abilities with loss of speech comprehension. The results are mixed. For example, Noble (1973), after reviewing the published work in the area, concluded ". . . efforts to relate performance-tests to each other . . . have had disappointing results." A few years later, de Boer & Bouwmeester (1974) reported no relation between speech discrimination scores and reduced frequency resolution in a group of 23 hearing-impaired children. In his review of research up to 1977, Scharf (1978b) concluded that while the evidence is not conclusive, it does suggest a relation between speech comprehension ability and frequency resolution in impaired ears. The recent research has been somewhat more definitive. For example, Dreschler & Plomp (1980) describe an exciting study of the relations between basic auditory function and speech perception in the hearing-impaired. In this experiment speech perception was assessed separately in quiet and in noise by means of an SRT (speech reception threshold) for sentence test. The speech measures were then related to measures of sensitivity loss, frequency resolving power, and vowel perceptions. The SRT measured in quiet was rather independent of the other measures, but the SRT in noise was strongly correlated with several of the other measures. This result seems consistent with the common report of hearing-impaired individuals that understanding speech in noise is their most frustrating problem. Tyler et al (1982) conducted a study specifically aimed at the relation between frequency resolution and speech comprehension in the hearing-impaired. Their major conclusions were basically the same as those of Dreschler & Plomp (1980).

The main reasons for the current lack of large test-battery studies of hearing-impaired listeners are that (a) there are many difficulties associated with testing hearing-impaired listeners, and (b) a test-battery study requires a large number of subjects (subject-to-variable ratio should be at least 5 in order to obtain reliable intertest correlations). However, we are aware of at least three laboratories actively engaged with this multivariate approach, so the next few years should bring new developments in this promising area.

TINNITUS

As a research area, tinnitus has been with us for decades, continually emitting new information at a low, irregular rate, but rarely becoming a detectable signal out of the background of activity in auditory science. Recently, however, this area has undergone a dramatic change of state, and in the process, several glimmers of precious light have already been given off. This change of state was brought about by nearly simultaneous, but independent, developments on several fronts—the masking of tinnitus was seriously undertaken as a method of treatment, several drugs effective against tinnitus were discovered, direct electrical stimulation of the cochlea was noted to affect tinnitus, and (for a time at least) it appeared that an objective acoustic basis for some tinnitus had been discovered emanating from the cochlea. We will touch on all of these developments in what follows. Additional information is available in three proceedings volumes (Ciba Foundation 1981, Shulman 1981, McFadden 1982).

By way of background, the reader should know certain basic facts about tinnitus. Most importantly, tinnitus is a *symptom* of many different underlying anomalies located in the auditory or other systems—that is, it is not a single entity in etiology, phenomenology, magnitude, annoyance, etc. Obviously then, no one treatment could be expected to be effective against all forms of tinnitus. No matter, however, because for years there has been no real treatment offered to sufferers from severe tinnitus. The typical procedure has been for a hearing professional to assure the sufferer that tinnitus is not uncommon, that it is typically not a harbinger of an imminent auditory, neurological, or psychological crisis, that there is basically nothing that can be done about tinnitus, and thus that the patient will simply have to learn to live with it. For many, such knowledge was helpful, if not fully assuring; for others, it was decidedly inadequate because of the severity of their symptoms and of the accompanying debilitation.

A recent British survey indicates that between 0.5–1.0% of the population suffers at times from tinnitus of sufficient severity to be nearly totally debilitating (Institute of Hearing Research 1981). Were this estimate accurate for the U.S. population, it would correspond to approximately 1.1–2.2 million people. Clearly, this is a major health problem which has been essentially ignored until very recently.

Some tinnitus has as its basis an acoustic source located in the head or neck regions of the sufferer—anomalies of vasculature, musculature, etc. Some truly extraordinary cases of such so-called objective tinnitus have been reported in man (Glanville et al 1971, Huizing & Spoor 1973) and other animals (Decker & Fritsch 1982). The vast majority of tinnitus cases, however, are characterized as subjective, indicating that they have no (as yet discovered) acoustic or objective concomitants, but presumably arise from an anomaly in some neural element(s) in the auditory chain. In order to encompass both objective and subjective forms, the best definition of tinnitus appears to be: the perception of a sound that originates in the head of its owner.

Contrary to intuition, perhaps, the subjective characteristics and qualities of tinnitus appear so far to be generally *not* informative as to the origin of the tinnitus. Patients' descriptions of tinnitus can vary from the simple ("steady, tonal, and at the same frequency") to the complex, possibly depending more upon the patient's vocabulary and powers of description than anything else. But so far at least, no mapping of experience to origin has proved successful. The low-frequency roaring associated with Meniere's Disease and otosclerosis are the primary exceptions.

Hazell (1981) has attempted to obtain more objective characterizations of tinnitus than are provided by verbal reports or by simple pitch matches. Hazell uses a commercial music synthesizer that he and the patient gradually adjust until the best match is obtained. The process can take hours, and the resulting waveforms are often very complex. Typically there are one or more relatively narrow bands with one or more pure-tone components imposed upon them. These synthesized waveforms are much appreciated by the patients because they provide a previously unavailable means for demonstrating to relatives and friends exactly what is being experienced day in and day out.

Masking and Tinnitus

For at least 50 years (Jones & Knudsen 1928) it has been realized that masking sounds can provide some tinnitus sufferers with a measure of relief. [The question of why tinnitus sufferers accept and/or prefer one continuous (external) sound over another continuous (internal) sound is discussed by McFadden 1982.] Not until recently, however, has anyone tried to capitalize on this fact for treatment purposes. Since the late 1970s a group at the Oregon Medical Center has been spearheading a movement to treat selected tinnitus sufferers with masking. The masking sound is typically supplied by a device mounted in a standard hearing-aid chassis (with or without the hearing aid circuitry removed). A selection of masking waveforms is available, but as yet none is particularly narrowband, so the choice of brand and model still involves difficult compromises; however, there is no reason for digital technology not to improve this situation eventually.

What evidence exists indicates that masking is an effective treatment for severe tinnitus in about 40–80% of the cases (depending upon how "success" is calculated; see Schleuning et al 1980, McFadden 1982), and refinement of diagnostic procedures and technological improvements in the devices prescribed promise even higher success rates. Our interest here, however, is not in the purely clinical side of the tinnitus issue.

To the basic scientist new to tinnitus probably its most interesting—and most perplexing—characteristics will be those surrounding its various responses to masking sound. By one estimate (Feldmann 1971), tinnitus *cannot* be masked by any sound in about 11% of the seriously afflicted. In contrast, the tinnitus in about 32% of this sample could be masked by presenting nearly *any* weak sound. Obviously, in neither instance is the tinnitus behaving like an external sound. But there's more. In some patients professing a purely monaural tinnitus, a sound delivered to the contralateral ear can be an effective masker [McFadden (1982) discusses some difficulties underlying a simple interpretation of this outcome]. And perhaps most interesting is the fact that for some patients the tinnitus does not return immediately upon termination of an effective masker; rather, it returns gradually over the course of seconds or even minutes. This effect was first noted by Feldmann (1971) and has since been named residual inhibition (Vernon 1977). It is perhaps the strongest argument that "masking" of tinnitus is not masking in the usual sense of the word. About three-quarters of the patients seen by the Oregon group experience full or partial residual inhibition. In a standard procedure adopted there (Vernon et al 1980), a masker is presented at 10 dB SL for one minute, and the typical subject experiencing residual inhibition reports a return of tinnitus to full strength within 30–60 seconds. An early hope of the Oregon group was that the period of residual inhibition might be extendable, and thus might become a source of relief for some tinnitus sufferers (Vernon et al 1980). This hope was fueled by some instances of apparently permanent cures following minimal use of a tinnitus masking unit. But while such cures are apparently real, they are very infrequent, and to date little progress has been made in extending residual inhibition.[1] A final curious feature of tinnitus masking is mentioned at the end of the next section.

---

[1]The reader interested in residual inhibition, but not afflicted with tinnitus, might consider inducing tinnitus with high doses of aspirin (begin with about 4 grams/day); in the experience of D.M. this type of tinnitus is subject to residual inhibition from both ipsilateral and contralateral tones of low intensity.

Annoyance of Tinnitus

To the nonsufferer, perhaps the most striking characteristic of tinnitus is the apparent discrepancy between its loudness and its annoyance. Nearly all tinnitus is matched in loudness to sounds of 20 dB SL or less (Fowler 1942, 1943, Graham 1960, Reed 1960, Vernon 1976), yet many sufferers regard their tinnitus to be highly annoying. At the outset, it must be noted that discrepancies between loudness and annoyance are well known to scientists concerned with traffic and airport noise (Fidell 1978, Schultz 1978), and everyone has surely experienced high annoyance from a buzzing fly or a crinkling cellophane wrapper even though the sound levels were low. But while loudness and annoyance are known to be poorly correlated, their dissociation in severe tinnitus has been attributed to a number of physiological and psychological mechanisms.

A proposal that has much intuitive appeal is that a form of recruitment is operating to render the tinnitus louder than an uncritical examination of the loudness matches might indicate. Recruitment is defined as an abnormally rapid rate of growth of loudness with increasing stimulus intensity, and it is a commonly observed effect with various auditory pathologies. In so-called complete recruitment, hearing can be essentially normal at high intensities, even though absolute sensitivity is considerably reduced. As is true of much in the clinic, loudness matches to tinnitus are typically expressed in units of sensation level—i.e. decibels above absolute sensitivity in that frequency region. Since severe tinnitus is often accompanied by hearing loss, a small number of decibels SL can correspond to a much larger number of decibels SPL. Consequently, a recurring suggestion about tinnitus is that it may be subject to a recruitment-like mechanism which renders its loudness appropriate for (or even greater than) a sound having the corresponding SPL. For a number of reasons, unfortunately little is known about the SPLs necessary to mask or to match the loudness of common tinnitus, so this intuitive explanation is not presently testable, but Goodwin & Johnson (1980) compared binaural and monaural estimates of tinnitus magnitude and concluded that recruitment was a significant factor in the annoyance of tinnitus.

A fascinating characteristic of tinnitus that possibly contributes to its high annoyance was discovered by Penner (1980, 1982). She worked only with subjects having a presbycusic or noise-trauma pattern of hearing loss; by one estimate, such people constitute about one-third of the sufferers from severe tinnitus (Feldmann 1971). The tinnitus of such people is typically fairly narrowband and located in the sharp transition region (the "edge") between normal and abnormal hearing. Using a high-pass/low-pass, band-narrowing procedure, Penner determined the limits of a relatively narrow band of noise capable of masking the tinnitus. Subjects were then asked to continuously adjust the intensity of this noise band in order to achieve masking of the tinnitus. The surprising outcome was that as time passed every subject gradually required greater and greater masker intensity in order to keep the tinnitus masked; the average change in masker intensity across a 30 minute test period was 30 dB and some subjects required 45 dB. As a control, the same subjects were asked to perform the same task using an external tone as the signal to be masked, and as expected, in this case the masker intensities did not vary across the test interval. One interpretation of this outcome is that tinnitus is immune to whatever processes of "adaptation" external sounds are subject to, but whatever its physiological basis, this is an important finding that may help explain the high annoyance reported by many tinnitus sufferers.

Electrical Stimulation

Over the years, there have been repeated reports of electrical stimulation to the head and body having effects on tinnitus (e.g. Field 1893, Hatton et al 1960, Ciba Foundation 1981, p. 226). In his comprehensive study of cochlear-implant patients, Bilger (1977) noted in passing that for some patients, activation of the prosthesis exacerbated the tinnitus, while for others, activation reduced or eliminated the tinnitus. Brackmann (1981) has confirmed the latter effect and implies that some implant patients also experience residual inhibition following use of their devices.

These reports recently have been put on a firmer experimental basis by studies conducted in the laboratory of J.-M. Aran. In the course of developing a screening test battery for patients likely to profit from cochlear implants and other therapies, Cazals et al (1978) delivered electrical stimulation of various sorts to the promontory or round window via a transtympanic electrode. All of the subjects were categorized as severely or profoundly deaf, but were otherwise not homogeneous. In a typical procedure, the reference electrode is attached to the earlobe, and the active electrode is attached to either the round window or promontory. Stimuli are electrical pulses whose duration, frequency (rate), intensity, and polarity can be varied.

When the pulse polarity was set to deliver "negative current" to the active electrode, the majority of the patients reported auditory sensations of some sort for some combinations of stimulus values. Presumably this is just a transtympanic version of the effect upon which hope for a cochlear-implant prosthesis is based. In contrast, when the polarity of the pulses at the active electrode was positive, auditory sensations were only rarely reported, but a majority of the tinnitus sufferers experienced a suppression of their tinnitus throughout the course of the stimulation. (Contrary to intuition, perhaps, tinnitus is frequently severe and highly annoying in the profoundly deaf.) Of course, for different subjects different stimulus intensities were required to achieve suppression, but stimulus frequency (pulse rate) was not critical as long as it exceeded some lower value which also varied across subjects. While no constant clinical feature(s) appeared to discriminate those patients experiencing tinnitus suppression from those who did not, the authors implied that tinnitus of peripheral origin may succumb to electrical stimulation whereas tinnitus of central origin may not. More specifically, they suggested that the positive current flow produces a tinnitus-cancelling hyperpolarization at some (peripheral) location in the auditory chain. A quibble with this explanation is that diminished auditory sensitivity might be an expected concomitant of the electrical stimulation, yet Aran has never noted any observable interference with hearing from the stimulation in those few patients studied having some residual hearing.

In a second paper (Portmann et al 1979), a few additional patients were reported, and it was noted that hour-long electrical stimulation did not lose its power to suppress tinnitus, nor could electrical stimulation suppress tinnitus "localized centrally" or at the other ear. In the most complete report yet published (Aran & Cazals 1981), 106 patients of widely varying hearing competence were studied. About 60% of those with tinnitus experienced its total elimination with ipsilateral electrical stimulation to the round window, and about 43% experienced at least some suppression when the stimulation was delivered to the promontory. Some patients were studied with both placements, and the round window electrode was always more effective than the promontory electrode. Aran has observed an occasional instance of suppression outlasting the duration of the electrical stimulation, but they are very rare. Unfortunately, identification of clinical signs definitively predictive of successful tinnitus suppression has yet to be achieved.

The Aran demonstrations produce a vision that previously would have been dismissed as science fiction—the prospect that severe tinnitus might some day be treated by implanting electrodes in the middle ear and driving them remotely with the appropriate waveforms.

The Melanin Connection

A topic of active study in the past few years has been drugs capable of reducing or eliminating severe tinnitus. Without going into the details of these studies, we can note that lidocaine, carbamazepine, tocainide, and sodium amylobarbitone, among others, all appear to have some power against tinnitus (see Goodey 1981, McFadden 1982). All of these particular drugs have drawbacks serious enough to prevent their widespread use against tinnitus, but they do offer hope that eventually treatment by drugs will be an option open to the tinnitus sufferer refractory to other treatment.

The topic is mentioned here because it raises an issue relevant to our examination of the interface between basic and applied psychoacoustics.

The relevant action(s) of those drugs effective against tinnitus are not yet known. Certain reports are suggestive in this regard, however. Englesson et al (1976) and Lyttkens et al (1979) noted that lidocaine—perhaps the most effective drug against tinnitus yet discovered—binds to melanin present in the inner ear. The experiments involved autoradiography following intravenous injections of ^{14}C-labeled lidocaine into pigmented rats. The label did not bind to the melanin in the stria vascularis, but it did to melanin in the modiolus. This outcome is of interest in part because several highly ototoxic drugs such as kanamycin, streptomycin, and quinine are also known to bind to inner-ear melanin (Lindquist 1973), and in part because a melanin connection is implicated in studies of temporary and permanent threshold shift (TTS and PTS, respectively).

In man, melanocytes can be found throughout the labyrinth, except in the semicircular canals. They are most numerous in the cochlea, with the greatest density appearing along the bony wall of the modiolus and the bony spiral lamina. Laferriere et al (1974) demonstrated that overall melanin density in the human inner ear varies directly with skin pigmentation, and for some years there have been hints that skin and/or eye color may co-vary with noise-induced hearing loss (Bunch & Raiford 1931, Post 1964, Shepherd et al 1964, Karsai et al 1972; see Royster et al 1980 for a review.) Thus, by implication, inner-ear melanin, skin and/or eye color, and noise-induced hearing loss may all be related. The direction of the effect is toward less hearing loss in the dark-skinned and/or dark-eyed population than in the fair-skinned, light-eyed population, a fact that may be related to the famous reports about the lack of hearing loss with age in the Mabaans (Rosen et al 1962) and the Todas (Kapur & Patt 1967). Royster et al (1980) studied the hearing records of approximately 30,000 employees from more than 20 different industries in North Carolina and confirmed the earlier findings of less hearing loss in black than in white employees; further, for the blacks there was less change in hearing with additional exposure. Both of these effects were most marked at frequencies above 2 kHz, where they were often 20–30 dB. Such outcomes obviously have important, but as yet not addressed, implications for the establishment and implementation of damage-risk criteria.

It is common to see similar relationships in PTS and TTS data, but attempts to duplicate the skin-color/PTS effect in TTS experiments have been mixed. In an early report, Tota & Bocci (1967) noted markedly less TTS in male subjects with light- and dark-brown irises than in those with blue irises. However, Karlovich (1975) was unable to discern even a trend toward greater TTS in his blue-eyed subjects, male or female. Inevitably, there were differences in procedure in the two experiments, and Hood et al (1976) believe that one of these is responsible for the discrepancy. Hood et al used both continuous and pulsed tones to monitor sensitivity during the postexposure period. With the pulsed-tone procedure—also used by Karlovich—the Karlovich outcome of no relation between TTS and eye color was obtained. With the continuous-tone procedure—used by Tota & Bocci —the subjects with light- and dark-brown eyes did manifest less TTS than did those with blue (and green-gray) eyes. This latter effect was small in the Hood et al experiment for exposure intensities of 80–100 dB, but grew to a difference of more than 20 dB for exposures of 110 and 120 dB.

There appears to be converging evidence that some fundamental aspect(s) of the operation of the peripheral auditory system may involve the melanin located in the inner ear. The mechanisms are not yet understood, but their study offers promise of a better understanding of such phenomena as the ototoxicity and tinnitus-suppressing capabilities of various drugs, the bases for temporary and permanent exposure-induced hearing loss, individual differences in susceptibility to exposure-induced hearing loss, etc.

ACOUSTIC EMISSIONS FROM THE COCHLEA

If any recent discovery about the auditory system qualifies as a bombshell —comparable to the brain-stem evoked response, psychophysical tuning curve, lateral suppression, and the second filter of the mid-1970s—it is the so-called acoustic emissions discovered by Kemp (1978). In the discussion that follows, the thread running through this review is stretched thin in places, but we hope there is not a complete break with the theme of eventually understanding pathology. To date, emissions of at least three types have been seen.

Cochlear Echoes

In 1978 Kemp reported detecting an acoustic signal in the outer ear canal that appeared to "echo" from the cochlea following acoustic stimulation. Others, interested in the response characteristics of the middle ear, had previously studied acoustic activity in the ear canal for the first few milliseconds following stimulus termination, but the emissions detected by Kemp had escaped notice, probably because they are weak and thus difficult to detect without sealing a miniature microphone into the ear canal and using averaging techniques. Further, these emissions appear with a time delay much longer than that shown by the middle-ear response. Thus, it had previously been known that following the presentation of a brief click, there exists in the ear canal a damped oscillatory response that rapidly decays to zero within about 6 msec (the impulse response of the middle ear). But what Kemp showed was that at about 6 msec another signal (the emission) begins to emerge; it grows in amplitude until about 10–15 msec and then slowly declines and disappears over a period of about 50–60 msec.

The emitted waveform evidences frequency dispersion, with the highest frequency components having the shortest latency and the successively lower components having successively longer latencies. Often, particular frequency components will appear repeatedly at apparently regular intervals following the stimulus; we shall return to this issue of multiple emissions below. Typically, it is the frequency components from about 500 Hz to 4000 Hz that are most prominent in the emission—presumably due to the attenuation characteristic of the middle ear. (Echoes recorded in the ear canal necessarily represent sounds that have passed through the middle ear system twice.) The emissions show a nonlinear growth in amplitude with increasing stimulus intensity. A typical relation is about 3 dB of growth in the emission for every 10 dB of increase in the stimulus (Kemp 1982). As stimulus intensity is increased beyond about 50–60 dB SPL, the emission becomes nearly totally obscured by the much larger middle-ear response. The maximum levels of the emissions are typically 15–20 dB SPL as measured in the sealed meatus.

The evidence that the emissions do in fact originate from the cochlea are:

1. Following stimulation by a click, a normal auditory system and an appropriately damped acoustic cavity both produce initial decaying impulse responses that are very similar, yet the acoustic cavity does not produce the additional, longer-latency responses generated by the normal ear.
2. Pathological ears of various sorts produce altered or no emissions.
3. The emissions observed are not characteristic of a single resonator, say, a highly resonant cavity located somewhere in the head.
4. Emissions of muscular origin would presumably not be able to follow the high stimulation rates that can be used to induce emissions (up to 80 Hz), nor would they be expected to show the phase inversion seen in the emissions when click polarity is reversed, nor would the middle-ear musculature be activated by the weak stimuli that can induce emissions.
5. Particular frequency components in the emission can be suppressed using steady tones, and the shapes and extents of these narrow suppression regions are reminiscent of the suppression regions mapped physiologically and psychophysically.
6. Stimulation with intense sounds can alter the frequency makeup of the emission in a way similar to that seen physiologically and psychophysically.
7. Manipulations known to affect cochlear structures and fluids also affect the emissions.

The exact mechanism(s) underlying acoustic emissions will surely be a matter of experimental and theoretical attention for some time to come, but Kemp has supplied an explanatory overview that is instructive and useful for our discussion (Kemp 1978, 1980b, Kemp & Chum 1980). The presence of echoes in the ear canal many milliseconds following stimulus offset implies that mechanical energy can be transferred in a retrograde direction (apical to basal) within the cochlea. The fact that the emission evidences frequency dispersion implies that the point of origin of this reflected mechanical energy is different for different frequency components in the acoustic stimulus—with the lower frequency components propagating further along the cochlear partition than the higher frequency components before a reflection is initiated. Partly on the basis of some of the evidence mentioned above, Kemp (e.g. see Kemp & Chum 1980) believes that the acoustic emissions originate from an array of linear, narrowband filters (hair cells?) driven in parallel by the acoustic stimulus. He believes that the observed nonlinearity and suppression effects arise in a compressively nonlinear stage located at the outputs of each of these linear, narrowband filters. The relationship between these filters and the so-called second filter has been discussed (Anderson 1980, Kemp 1980b, Siegel & Kim 1982a, Wilson 1980c). Some appreciation for the challenges emissions pose for the modelers can be obtained from de Boer (1980).

There are individual differences in the echoes recorded from different people (e.g. Kemp & Chum 1980, Rutten 1980a, b, Wit & Ritsma 1980b), but these are primarily minor matters of degree (slightly different latencies or magnitudes for particular frequency components, etc). The differences are much greater, however, when pathological ears are compared with normal ones. Kemp (1978) studied about two dozen people with auditory pathologies of various sorts. Following the damped, 5 msec response of the middle ear system, he observed essentially no emissions as long as the hearing loss exceeded about 30 dB. Rutten (1980a) confirmed and refined this observation. He showed that a seemingly normal echo can be obtained as long as the hearing loss does not exceed about 15 dB, and further, that extreme losses at high frequencies do not prevent the appearance of normal echoes at low frequencies, as long as the hearing is within 15 dB of normal there. Electrocochleography done on selected patients confirmed the cochlear origin of the hearing losses. It must be noted in this regard that nominally normal ears can also possess localized frequency regions that are devoid of echoes. These echoless regions are surrounded by normal echo regions (Kemp 1982); whether they are related to the microstructure of the audiogram (see below) is not clear.

The implication that near-normal absolute sensitivity is necessary for cochlear echoes to exist is interesting to contemplate relative to the issue of the two hair-cell populations. For some years evidence has been accumulating that when the normal complement of outer hair cells (OHCs) is reduced through controlled application of ototoxic drugs or exposure to intense sounds, there are parallel behavioral and physiological changes that are highly predictable (for a review see Dallos 1981). Primary among these is a change in absolute sensitivity. The absence of cochlear echoes in pathological ears that, by inference, are deficient in OHCs raises the question whether the OHCs are the source of these emissions. Kemp (1980b, 1982) and Anderson & Kemp (1979) have considered the possible role of the hair-cell stereocilia in the emission process, but the discussions have been understandably cautious. It will be interesting to watch future developments on the twin issues of the two hair-cell populations and the absence of cochlear echoes in ears with sensorineural hearing loss.

SUPPRESSION OF THE ECHO   As noted above, the acoustic emission to a click can be altered by introduction of a second acoustic stimulus. Kemp has shown that the intensity, spectral characteristics, and timing of this second stimulus are all relevant to this suppression effect. Kemp has used two basic suppression stimuli in his studies—clicks and tones. By varying the presentation time of the suppressor click relative to the stimulus click, Kemp & Chum (1980) showed that suppression does not begin immediately —as would be expected if the generator of the emission interacted directly with the input—but instead requires 7–10 msec to appear. Further, the suppression persists for at least 30 msec. With the suppressor click 10 dB more intense than the stimulus click, greatest suppression (about 20 dB) occurs with a simultaneous presentation of suppressor and stimulus, but suppression exceeds 3 dB over the range of –6 to +3 msec. With other intensity ratios between the suppressor and stimulus clicks, there was little difference in suppression when the suppressor preceded the stimulus, but when it followed the stimulus click, small increases in suppressor intensity produced large increases in suppression. This effect is attributed to a second type of nonlinearity.

The use of a continuous, tonal suppressor has revealed that suppression is localized to the frequency region of the suppressor. From experiments using tonal suppressors and click stimuli, Kemp has derived estimates of the bandwidths and rejection rates of the filters he believes generate acoustic emissions (Kemp & Chum 1980). From data on one ear he estimated a half-power bandwidth of about 18 Hz at 1250 Hz, with rejection rates of about 160 and 280 dB/octave on the low- and high-frequency sides, respectively. At different points across the usable spectrum he has derived bandwidths of 18–100 Hz, with a mean of 68 Hz; while it is not clear from Kemp's report, it appears that these values do not show a regular change with center frequency. Wit & Ritsma (1979) and Wilson (1980a) used tones for both stimulus and suppressor and also obtained rather narrow "suppression tuning curves" for the cochlear echo. We know of no systematic attempt to relate the extent of these suppression regions to those found psychophysically or physiologically.

The narrowness of these estimated bandwidths is responsible in part for Kemp's suggesting that the long latencies seen in the acoustic emission (10–15 msec poststimulus offset until the maximum response is reached, and several tens of milliseconds until the response dies out) might be largely or wholly attributable to the response times of these narrow filters (e.g. Kemp 1979b, Kemp & Chum 1980). That is, the long latencies observed may not be in contradiction with established estimates of (comparably much more rapid) propagation velocities for traveling waves along the cochlear partition. [Also see the discussions of Anderson (1980) and Kemp (1980a) and the data of Wit & Ritsma (1980a, b).]

Exposure to an intense tone can also diminish the magnitude and alter the frequency content of the cochlear echo. The process of recovery and the frequency pattern of effect are said to be similar to those seen behaviorally in experiments on temporary threshold shift (Kemp 1982), implying that this may be a valuable new tool for use in studying auditory fatigue. Kemp (1982) has also noted some postexposure changes in emissions that he feels may be related to postexposure tinnitus.

COCHLEAR ECHOES IN NONHUMANS   There are obviously many aspects of stimulated cochlear emissions that could better be studied in animals other than humans, but unfortunately, echoes have been difficult to find in nonhumans. Wit & Ritsma (1980a) looked in guinea pigs and Schmiedt & Adams (1981) in Mongolian gerbils with no success. Wit & Ritsma suggested that perhaps the shorter basilar membranes, and consequently shorter travel times (forward and backward), in such animals caused the echoes to be obscured by the final segment of the acoustic stimulus. Schmiedt & Adams attempted a test of this suggestion by stimulating electrically through a bipolar electrode coupled to the round window. This produced a briefer acoustic pulse than was possible with the acoustic driver, and it did lead to an N_1 response, but cochlear echoes were still not detected. Schmiedt & Adams (1981) offered several explanations for the apparent absence of echoes in these species, but their belief seems to be that the echoes *are* absent, not just undetected. Dancer & Franke (1980) detected what appeared to be an echo in a guinea pig, but Schmiedt & Adams (1981) pointed out that the apparent echo has a latency less than that of CM, and thus this is likely to be an encounter with an unidentified fallacious object of extra-cochlear origin. Not so easily explained is the report by

Zwicker & Manley (1981), who claimed to have detected cochlear echoes in about half the guinea pigs' ears they studied. They used stimuli different from the standard brief click—namely, single cycles of pure tones. These emissions behaved in accord with expectations in some regards: they had short latencies, grew nonlinearly with stimulus intensity, and were reduced by hypoxia. But in certain other ways these emissions were unusual: they were much less intense than expected, they did not show frequency dispersion, but were basically single-frequency echoes, and they could be suppressed even with tones quite different in frequency from the stimulus (compare above).

While echoes in rodent ears remain controversial, the existence of echoes becomes less controversial as one climbs the phylogenetic tree. Wilson (1980b) found stimulated echoes in several cats; they were of short latency, demonstrated frequency dispersion, and were apparently very similar to the echoes recorded from humans. The same was found in two species of monkey (Anderson & Kemp 1979).

Emitted Distortion Products

It is essential that what we have been calling cochlear echoes be distinguished from another form of acoustic emission. To this point we have been concerned only with those cochlear emissions that are observed following stimulation with brief acoustic signals. Emissions can also be detected with certain *continuous* signals, and while at first these were regarded to be only slightly different manifestations of the same basic phenomenon, evidence is accumulating that they may have different substrates. Specifically, it is possible to detect acoustic energy in the ear canal at the frequencies $F_2 - F_1$ and $2F_1 - F_2$ during continuous stimulation with the two primaries F_1 and F_2 (see, for example, Mountain 1980, Kim et al 1980, Schmiedt & Adams 1981, Wilson 1980c). Like the cochlear echo, these emitted distortion products grow nonlinearly with stimulus intensity and are susceptible to hypoxia, acoustic fatigue, and ototoxic drugs (e.g. Kim 1980a). Unlike the cochlear echo, however, they are routinely found emanating from non-human ears, even those rodent ears so stingy with their echoes (Kim 1980a, Schmiedt & Adams 1981).

In an interesting set of experiments, it has been shown that the emitted distortion products $F_2 - F_1$ and $2F_1 - F_2$ measured in the ear canal can be altered by electrical stimulation of the crossed olivocochlear bundle (COCB). Mountain (1980) first showed this for $F_2 - F_1$ in guinea pigs, and Siegel & Kim (1982a, b) showed it for both $F_2 - F_1$ and $2F_1 - F_2$ in the chinchilla. The data are not in perfect accord—Mountain saw only decreases in the distortion product with COCB stimulation, and Siegel and Kim saw both decreases and increases—but as Siegel & Kim (1982b) point out, there were numerous procedural differences between the experiments. Since the preponderance of the fibers of the COCB synapse directly onto OCHs (Warr 1978), these results seem to further implicate the OHCs in the generation of acoustic emissions. One of the important findings of Siegel & Kim (1982b) is that perfusion of curare through scala tympani eliminates the control that COCB stimulation otherwise has over the acoustic distortion products. Curare acts at neuromuscular junctions by blocking acetylcholine receptors on the postsynaptic surface; by analogy, curare is believed to block the effects of the COCB post-synaptically—that is, on the OHC surface. In accord with this view, following administration of curare, COCB stimulation no longer affects CM and N_1, and now Siegel & Kim have added the acoustic distortion products to this list.[2]

It is important, of course, to determine if the two effects—cochlear echoes and emitted distortion products—originate from different structures and/or through different mechanisms; in the meantime, nonexperts are well advised to maintain a mental distinction for the two stimulus conditions. A question worthy of study is whether pathological human ears that show diminished or no cochlear echoes to brief stimuli also show diminished acoustic distortion products to continuous stimuli.

If the differences between transient and steady-state emissions hold following further study, it will raise an extremely important issue for students of the auditory system. Until now there has been reasonably general agreement that all mammalian auditory systems are basically the same, and thus, that what is learned from one species will generalize to the others. Now, however, we are faced with the possibility that some very well-studied rodent systems may differ in an apparently important way from the cat, monkey, and human systems. Perhaps this change of view was inevitable eventually, but one's expectation might have been that the differences would be minor matters of degree, not differences in fundamentals like the sources and loci of inherent nonlinearities.

Microstructure of the Audiogram

A delayed, retrograde transfer of energy along the cochlea naturally raises several questions: about possible subsequent reflections, about the possibility of standing waves, and about the possibility of self-excitations. As indicated above, multiple emissions of the same frequency component are

---

[2]To our knowledge, no attempt has been made to determine whether the stimulated emissions seen following click stimuli are also affected by stimulation of the COCB. Further, it would be worthwhile to see if a spontaneous emission (see below) could be altered by efferent activity. This might be done with electrical stimulation of the COCB in one of those rare animals having a spontaneous emission, or perhaps by delivering an appropriate sound to the contralateral ear of a human with a spontaneous emission.

often seen following stimulation with a click, and these presumably result from multiple forward and backward transfers of energy (Kemp 1980b). The existence of such intracochlear reflections has been used to explain two interesting effects—microstructure in the audiogram and spontaneous emissions.

For some time it has been known that careful exploration can reveal marked fluctuations in auditory sensitivity with very small changes in test frequency (see Cohen 1982 for a literature review). Local differences of 12–14 dB are not uncommon, and the differences can be highly reliable across time (Elliott 1958, Kemp 1981; but see Cohen 1982). Kemp (1979a, b, 1980b) has argued that such microstructure in the audiogram is an expected concomitant of intracochlear reflections and sharp cochlear resonances. In his view, partial reflection of the forward traveling wave occurs at the place along the basilar membrane where the mechanical impedance is rapidly changing for that frequency (i.e. on the basal side of the point at which maximal displacement occurs); the resulting retrograde traveling wave returns to the basal end where it is partially reflected, thereby producing another forward traveling wave, and so on. This process of multiple reflections results in multiple emissions for click stimulation and in a series of standing-wave resonances for longer signals. Kemp believes each resonance is responsible for a local peak in the audiogram, but his model offers no explanation of why individual ears differ in their patterns of resonance across frequency (Kemp 1979b). In support of his view, Kemp has demonstrated that measures of acoustic impedance also undergo marked fluctuations with small changes in test frequency, and further, that these fluctuations are in excellent accord with the psychophysical microstructure (Kemp 1979b). Using a special "masking" procedure, Kemp (1981) obtained an estimate of the so-called recirculation loop time of the human cochlea. Its value is close to 8 msec, which leads to an expectation of a pattern of resonances (and antiresonances) at 125-Hz intervals along the length of the cochlear partition, which he feels is in reasonable accord with the psychophysical data (Kemp 1981). The data of Cohen (1982) do not appear to support the idea of regular patterns in the microstructure of the audiogram, but important psychophysical details were different in the two experiments, and the discrepancy may be easily resolved. [Wilson has offered an explanation of the microstructure that appeals to interference between cochlear reflections (see Kemp 1979b.)]

COMMENTS   In passing it should be noted that the discovery of multiple emissions extending for tens of milliseconds following presentation of a brief acoustic stimulus offers a possible explanation of the Pfeiffer & Kim (1972) report that about 7% of the primary auditory fibers they studied showed a cyclic response pattern that persisted far longer than normal after the click stimulus. Possibly these cells were serving segments of the basilar membrane that were being periodically reexcited by multiple reflections within the cochlea (Kim 1980b). A problem with this interpretation is that Pfeiffer & Kim (1972) claimed to have found normal and aberrant cells having similar characteristic frequencies in the same animals (but compare Kim 1980a).

The existence of multiple emissions following a click stimulus naturally raises the question of whether they ever have been, or could be, detected psychophysically. Clicks are popular stimuli, particularly in binaural experiments, and one might expect that multiple emissions might have been heard, or might have contributed to (perhaps aberrant) data even though unheard. In the past, unsuspecting psychophysicists may have escaped difficulty by using relatively intense clicks; now there is a reason to try weak clicks on good introspectors.

Spontaneous Emissions

Now, if there were metabolically dependent sources of reflection in the cochlea, might it be possible for one or more of them to malfunction in such a way as to drive the system into oscillation at some frequency? If so, one might expect to observe in the ear canal a continuous, spectrally constrained emission that requires no external stimulus to activate. Indeed, such "spontaneous" emissions have been observed (Kemp 1979a) and by one count at least (Zurek 1981), this third type of emission is very common, existing in as many as two-thirds of nominally "normal" ears.

The procedures for recording spontaneous emissions are similar to those used for studying stimulated emissions. The primary difference is that it is not necessary to introduce an acoustic stimulus in order to observe a spontaneous emission. Kemp believes that the energy source for spontaneous emissions is the background noise in the cochlea attributable to Brownian motion and the physiological noise of the body. Spontaneous emissions are typically very narrowband [1.2 to 4.7 Hz using a 0.16-Hz filter (Kemp 1981)], are highly stable across time (Kemp 1981, Zurek 1981), and are typically between 5 and 20 dB SPL as measured in the sealed ear canal. To date, they have been found predominantly in the region below about 3000 Hz (Zurek 1981), but the apparent rarity of spontaneous emissions at high frequencies may be due to the increasing difficulty of detecting them that is imposed by the high-frequency attenuation characteristic of the middle-ear system.

RELATION TO TINNITUS   Understandably, the discovery of spontaneous, nearly tonal emissions from the cochlea produced considerable optimism in some investigators that an important concomitant of problem tinnitus had been discovered. Wilson & Sutton (1981) studied about a dozen people, some of whom answered newspaper ads soliciting tinnitus sufferers. Four of these people had a spontaneous emission corresponding to their tinnitus (they and the other people studied also had additional, unheard emissions). A set of demonstrations made it highly likely that the spontaneous emission was the source of the perceived tinnitus for these four people. For example, contralateral pitch matching to the tinnitus yielded a frequency in good accord with the center frequency of the spontaneous emission. Second, introducing air-pressure changes in the outer ear could sometimes shift the frequency of the spontaneous emission, and when it did, the pitch of the tinnitus changed in the same direction. Third, Wilson (1980a) had reported that apparently normal fluctuations in magnitude of the emission were correlated with fluctuations in tinnitus magnitude. Finally, those spontaneous emissions that are heard are typically described as noisy, not tonal, and this is in accord with Kemp's (1981) report that emissions are noise bands 1.2–4.7 Hz in width.

But while this array of associations momentarily aroused the hopes of some that an objective basis for problem tinnitus had been found, contrary evidence has since punctured the hope. Balanced against the approximately half-dozen cases of people who do experience a tinnitus apparently corresponding to a spontaneous emission (Kemp, 1981, Wilson & Sutton 1981, Zurek 1981), there now stand at least 200 cases of spontaneous emissions having no corresponding tinnitus. Some of this work is not yet published (R. S. Tyler and P. M. Zurek, personal communications), but Zurek (1981) did describe nearly three dozen subjects, collectively having more than 20 spontaneous emissions without a single report of a concomitant tinnitus. Conversely, Zurek (unpublished) studied 16 patients with severe tinnitus of various sorts and found no concomitant spontaneous emissions. Also important to note is that, while the subjective experiences reported by those people who do hear their spontaneous emissions may technically satisfy the definition of tinnitus, they differ in a fundamental way from the experiences reported by true tinnitus sufferers. Namely, they are *not* a source of annoyance or distress (Wilson & Sutton 1981, Zurek 1981); the emission-related experiences are apparently quite faint and unobtrusive.

The status of things, then, is that spontaneous acoustic emissions are commonly observed objectively, but only infrequently observed subjectively. Thus, they should not be expected to be found underlying cases of severe tinnitus. In passing we should note that when it comes to tinnitus, all logically possible combinations exist: there is (subjective) tinnitus that can be perceived only by its owner, there is (objective) tinnitus that has an acoustic basis and thus can also be perceived by others (with or without the aid of special devices), and there are objectively detected, acoustic signals emitted by the cochlea that pass unheard by their owners.

Exactly why spontaneous emissions of 5–20 dB SPL pass unheard by their owners is not yet known. Wilson (1980a) and Wilson & Sutton (1981) imply that the microstructure of the audiogram may be involved. Another (not necessarily mutually exclusive) possibility is that the continuous stimulation provided by the spontaneous emission has produced an "adaptation" at some point(s) in the neural chain—an "adaptation" that is either permanent, like those seen in the visual system following early selective deprivation, or is reversible, as in perstimulatory fatigue.

SUPPRESSION, BEATS, AND DIPLACUSIS   Just as stimulated emissions can be partially or fully suppressed by introducing additional external sounds, spontaneous emissions can also be suppressed. Zurek (1981) demonstrated that the intensity necessary for a fixed amount of suppression varies across suppressor frequency in a pattern remarkably similar to that seen when determining a psychophysical tuning curve, and he argued that this is additional strong evidence for the spontaneous emission being a product of the cochlea, as opposed (say) to its being vascular in origin. The suppression patterns found by Zurek were very similar to the "suppression tuning curves" obtained for the cochlear echo by Wit & Ritsma (1979) and Kemp & Chum (1980). Wilson (1980a) and Wilson & Sutton (1981) have confirmed these observations by Zurek.

Zurek (1981), Wilson (1980a), and Wilson & Sutton (1981) have shown that several different types of interaction besides suppression can occur between a spontaneous emission and an external tone of similar frequency. For example, Wilson (1980a) reported subjective abolition (cancellation) of a heard spontaneous emission in two subjects following careful adjustment of frequency and level of the external tone (it is unclear whether objective measures were also made in these cases). In addition, if a continuous external tone is brought close in frequency to a spontaneous emission, the emission can be "pulled in" by the external tone and can remain locked to it for some time. As the intensity of the external tone is increased by 30 dB, the frequency band over which this synchronization occurs increases from about 15 Hz to about 130 Hz (Wilson & Sutton 1981, Figure 3). [It is also possible to synchronize a spontaneous emission using a click stimulus presented at an appropriate rate (Wilson 1980a.)]

Occasionally, Zurek's and Wilson's subjects reported hearing a slow beat when a single external tone was presented. This experience may be due to a regular acquisition and loss of frequency locking between the spontaneous emission and an external tone slightly too different in frequency to allow prolonged locking. This is an interesting effect, for it offers a possible explanation for a number of peculiar reports appearing over the years. For example, the issue of beats against a tonal tinnitus has been controversial for more than 50 years. Wegel (1931) claimed to be able to hear an irregular, "mushy" beat in his tinnitus when certain single tones were presented, and while it is clear from his remarks that he appreciated how different his experience was from true beats (he sometimes heard "complete silence"), his readers have sometimes not, and this report has been widely (mis-)cited. In their studies of monaural diplacusis, Flottorp (1953) and Ward (1955) encountered situations in which a single external tone would appear to fluctuate in level (there was no tinnitus). These reports, and that of Wegel, come to have a remarkably similar flavor when it is recalled that spontaneous emissions can be either heard (Wegel?) or unheard (Flottorp and Ward?), and can be partially synchronized and sometimes cancelled by external tones of the correct frequency. This issue is discussed by Zurek (1981), but it is well worth the interested student's time to read the Flottorp and Ward papers to see how amazingly modern are their discussions of what was clearly a very peculiar phenomenon. Buffs of the history of auditory science are also strongly encouraged to read Gold's (1948) prescient comments about what are now called stimulated and spontaneous acoustic emissions.

SPONTANEOUS EMISSIONS IN NONHUMANS   To date, spontaneous emissions have been found only infrequently in nonhumans, a problem that has retarded complete physiological study of the phenomenon. A cat producing a clearly audible, tonal sound has been mentioned (Ciba Foundation 1981, p. 133), but not fully described. Decker & Fritsch (1982) have described a dog which emitted an audible narrow band of noise that was continuous and centered at about 10.3 kHz, but since the dog was a pet, it was not fully studied physiologically. Without more detailed information, it cannot be known if these are two instances of spontaneous emissions in nonhumans. However, many of the pawmarks are present.

Evans et al (1981) discovered an elderly, but apparently healthy guinea pig having a low-frequency spontaneous emission. Observations confirming the cochlear origin of this emission included: it was not affected by either paralysis of the middle-ear muscles or by sectioning of their tendons; it was abolished under hypoxia and returned following restoration of a normal oxygen suppply; it was suppressed by external tones of the appropriate frequency and intensity; and it responded to changes in middle-ear air pressure in the same way as do spontaneous emissions in humans (Kemp 1979b, Wilson 1980a, Wilson & Sutton 1981). [Intravenous curare did not affect this spontaneous emission (compare Siegel & Kim 1982b.)]

Zurek & Clark (1981) looked for spontaneous emissions in the ears of about two dozen chinchillas that were raised in a low-noise environment and found none. Some of these animals were subsequently exposed to intense sounds and examined again for emissions. Two emissions were detected in noise-exposed animals. Curiously, these emissions were not particularly stable in frequency; rather, they drifted slowly over a relatively narrow frequency range and they occasionally shifted suddenly into a frequency region several hundred Hertz away. Further, these emissions were all quite high in frequency (about 4600–6600 Hz) even though the exposure was an octave band centered at 500 Hz. To our knowledge, there have been no other attempts to produce emissions in emission-free ears.

Summary and Comments

Since this final section has diverged somewhat from the previous two and from the stated goal of this review, it appears worthwhile to emphasize the ties between acoustic emissions and auditory pathologies. Spontaneous emissions do appear to result from abnormal or atypical conditions in the cochlea, but their prevalence and apparent innocuousness makes it unclear whether "pathology" is an appropriate characterization of them. The audiogram is such an integral part of our thinking about auditory pathology that the relation between its microstructure and multiple intracochlear reflections must necessarily be of interest to all auditory specialists. Finally, the fact that pathological ears that, by inference, are lacking outer hair cells do not support cochlear echoes raises the prospect of modified diagnostic routines for establishing site of lesion. Whether acoustic emissions will acquire unanticipated diagnostic powers, as has the brain-stem response, only time can tell, but the potential appears high.

As Kim (1980a) points out, the excitement surrounding Kemp's discovery is attributable in large part to the link it provides to physiological and psychophysical evidence of nonlinearity in the peripheral auditory system. Until recently, all direct measures of basilar membrane activity have necessarily been taken at relatively high sound-pressure levels, yet numerous eighth-nerve and psychophysical studies made it clear that certain nonlinearities are present at low SPLs, and the implication was that the cochlear partition was the source of these nonlinearities. Kemp's demonstration of stimulated emissions is viewed as the first unambiguous demonstration of a mechanical nonlinearity in the cochlea at low SPLs. It is to be hoped that evidence obtained from measurements of emissions will eventually be bolstered by direct measures of the cochlear partition under low levels of stimulation; perhaps the new technique based upon laser interferometry developed by Khanna & Leonard (1982) will provide a first step.

FINAL COMMENT

In this review we have touched upon a number of major and minor topics lying at the interface between normal and pathological hearing. Naturally, our initial goal involved much wider coverage and deeper analyses than we have achieved, but if goals and accomplishments were ever to match, there would be nothing left to do. Fortunately, our work, and yours, can continue.

ACKNOWLEDGMENTS

The preparation of this review was supported in part by NINCDS grants NS08754 and NS15895 awarded to D. M. F. L. W. was responsible for the section entitled MEASURING AUDITORY PATHOLOGY and D. M. for the rest. We are indebted to Lanier Bayliss for her assistance in preparing the manuscript.

Literature Cited

Abel, S. M. 1972. Discrimination of temporal g. ps. *J. Acoust. Soc. Am.* 52:519–24
Ander on, S. D. 1980. Some ECMR properties in relation to other signals from the auditory periphery. *Hear. Res.* 2: 273–96
Anderson, S. D., Kemp, D. T. 1979. The evoked cochlear mechanical response in laboratory primates. *Arch. Otorhinolaryngol.* 224:47–54
Aran, J.-M., Cazals, Y. 1981. Electrical suppression of tinnitus. In *Tinnitus,* Ciba Found. Symp. 85, pp. 217–24. London: Pitman
Bilger, R. C. 1977. Evaluation of subjects presently fitted with implanted auditory prostheses. *Ann. Otol. Rhinol. & Laryngol.* Suppl. 38
Bilger, R. C., Wang, M. D. 1976. Consonant confusions in patients with sensorineural hearing loss. *J. Speech Hear. Res.* 19:718–48
Bonding, P. 1973. Critical bandwidth in loudness summation in sensorineural hearing loss. *J. Speech Hear. Res.* 13: 23–30
Brackmann, D. E. 1981. Reduction of tinnitus in cochlear-implant patients. See Shulman 1981, pp. 163–65
Bunch, C. C., Raiford, T. S. 1931. Race and sex variations in auditory acuity. *Arch. Otolaryngol.* 13:423–24
Butler, R. A., Albrite, J. P. 1956. The pitch-discrimination function of the pathological ear. *Arch. Otolaryngol.* 63:411
Cazals, Y., Negrevergne, M., Aran, J.-M. 1978. Electrical stimulation of the cochlea in man; hearing induction and tin-

nitus suppression. *J. Am. Audiol. Soc.* 3:200–13
Ciba Foundation Symposium 85. 1981. *Tinnitus.* London: Pitman
Cohen, M. F. 1982. Detection threshold microstructure and its effect on temporal integration data. *J. Acoust. Soc. Am.* 71:405–9
Dallos, P. 1981. Cochlear physiology. *Ann. Rev. Psychol.* 32:153–90
Dallos, P., Harris, D. 1978. Properties of auditory nerve responses in absence of outer hair cells. *J. Neurophysiol.* 41: 365–83
Dancer, A., Franke, R. 1980. Intracochlear sound pressure measurements in guinea pigs. *Hear. Res.* 2:191–205
de Boer, E. 1980. Nonlinear interactions and the 'Kemp echo'. *Hear. Res.* 2:519–26
de Boer, E., Bouwmeester, J. 1974. Critical bands and sensorineural hearing loss. *Audiology* 13:236–59
Decker, T. N., Fritsch, J. H. 1982. Objective tinnitus in the dog. *Am. Vet. Med. J.* 180:74
Dreschler, W. A., Plomp, R. 1980. Relation between psychophysical data and speech perception for hearing-impaired subjects. *J. Acoust. Soc. Am.* 68: 1608–15
Durlach, N. I., Thompson, C. L., Colburn, H. S. 1981. Binaural interaction in impaired listeners—a review of past research. *Audiology* 20:181–211
Elliott, D. N., Riach, W. D., Sheposh, J. P., Trahiotis, C. 1966. Discrimination performance of high school sophomores on

a battery of auditory tests. *Acta Otolaryngol.* Suppl. 216, pp. 1–59

Elliott, E. 1958. A ripple effect in the audiogram. *Nature* 181:1076

Elliott, L. L. 1975. Temporal and masking phenomena in persons with sensorineural hearing loss. *Audiology* 14:336–53

Englesson, S., Larsson, B., Lindquist, N. G., Lyttkens, L., Stahle, J. 1976. Accumulation of ¹⁴C-lidocaine in the inner ear. *Acta Otolaryngol.* 82:297–300

Evans, E. F., Wilson, J. P., Borerwe, T. A. 1981. Animal models of tinnitus. In *Tinnitus,* Ciba Found. Symp. 85, pp. 108–28. London: Pitman

Feldmann, H. 1971. Homolateral and contralateral masking of tinnitus by noisebands and by pure tones. *Audiology* 10:138–44

Festen, J. M., Plomp, R. 1981. Relations between auditory functions in normal hearing. *J. Acoust. Soc. Am.* 70:356–69

Feth, L., Burns, E. M., Kidd, G., Mason, C. R. 1980. Effects of noise exposure on frequency selectivity in normal and hearing-impaired listeners. In *Psychophysical, Physiological, and Behavioural Studies in Hearing,* ed. G. van den Brink, F. Bilsen, pp. 149–52. Delft, The Netherlands: Delft Univ. Press

Fidell, S. 1978. Nationwide urban noise survey. *J. Acoust. Soc. Am.* 64:198–206

Field, G. P. 1893. *A Manual of Diseases of the Ear.* London: Balliere, Tindell & Cox

Fitzgibbons, P., Wightman, F. L. 1982. Temporal resolution in listeners with sensorineural hearing loss. *J. Acoust. Soc. Am.* In press

Florentine, M., Buus, S., Scharf, B., Zwicker, E. 1980. Frequency selectivity in normally-hearing and hearing-impaired observers. *J. Speech Hear. Res.* 23:646–69

Flottorp, G. 1953. Pure-tone tinnitus evoked by acoustic stimulation: the idiophonic effect. *Acta Otolaryngol.* 43:396–415

Fowler, E. P. 1942. The 'illusion of loudness' of tinnitus: its etiology and treatment. *Laryngoscope* 52:275–85

Fowler, E. P. 1943. Control of head noises: their illusions of loudness and of timbre. *Arch. Otolaryngol.* 37:391–98

Gengel, R. W. 1973. Temporal effects in frequency discrimination by hearing-impaired subjects. *J. Acoust. Soc. Am.* 54:11–15

Gengel, R. W., Watson, C. S. 1971. Temporal integration: I. Clinical implications of a laboratory study. II. Additional data from hearing-impaired subjects. *J. Speech Hear. Disord.* 36:213–24

Glanville, J. D., Coles, R. R. A., Sullivan, B. M. 1971. A family with high-tonal ob-

jective tinnitus. *J. Laryngol. Otol.* 85:1–10

Gold, T. 1947/1948. Hearing. II. The physical basis of the action of the cochlea, *Proc. R. Soc. London Ser. B* 135:492–98

Goodey, R. J. 1981. Drugs in the treatment of tinnitus. In *Tinnitus,* Ciba Found. Symp. 85, pp. 263–73. London: Pitman

Goodwin, P. E., Johnson, R. M. 1980. The loudness of tinnitus. *Acta Otolaryngol.* 90:353–59

Graham, J. T. 1960. *An analysis of certain psychophysical parameters of tinnitus aurium.* PhD thesis. Stanford Univ. Stanford, Calif. Unpublished

Green, D. M. 1971. Temporal auditory acuity. *Psychol. Rev.* 78:540–51

Green, D. M., Shelton, B. R., Picardi, M. C., Hafter, E. R. 1981. Psychophysical tuning curves independent of signal level. *J. Acoust. Soc. Am.* 69:1758–62

Hatton, D. S., Erulkar, S. D., Rosenberg, P. E. 1960. Some preliminary observations on the effect of galvanic current on tinnitus aurium. *Laryngoscope* 70:123–30

Hazell, J. W. P. 1981. A tinnitus synthesiser: physiological considerations. See Shulman 1981, pp. 187–95

Hoekstra, A., Ritsma, R. J. 1977. Perceptive hearing loss and frequency selectivity. In *Psychophysics and Physiology of Hearing,* ed. E. F. Evans, J. P. Wilson, pp. 263–72. London: Academic

Hood, J. D., Poole, J. P., Freedman, L. 1976. Eye color and susceptibility to TTS. *J. Acoust. Soc. Am.* 59:706–7

Houtgast, T. 1972. Psychophysical evidence for lateral inhibition in hearing. *J. Acoust. Soc. Am.* 51:1885–94

Houtgast, T. 1977. Auditory filter characteristics derived from direct-masking data and pulsation-threshold data with a rippled-noise masker. *J. Acoust. Soc. Am.* 62:409–15

Huizing, E. H., Spoor, A. 1973. An unusual type of tinnitus. *Arch. Otolaryngol.* 98:134–36

Institute of Hearing Research. 1981. Epidemiology of tinnitus. *In Tinnitus,* Ciba Found. Symp. 85, pp. 16–25. London: Pitman

Irwin, R. J., Hinchcliff, L. K., Kemp, S. 1981. Temporal acuity in normal and hearing-impaired listeners. *Audiology* 20:234–43

Jesteadt, W., Bilger, R. C., Green, D. M., Patterson, J. H. 1976. Temporal acuity in listeners with sensorineural hearing loss. *J. Speech Hear. Res.* 19:357–70

Jones, I. H., Knudsen, V. O. 1928. Certain aspects of tinnitus, particularly treatment. *Laryngoscope* 38:597–611

Kapur, Y. P., Patt, A. J. 1967. Hearing in Todas of South India. *Arch. Otolaryngol.* 85:74–80

Karlin, J. E. 1942. A factorial study of auditory function. *Psychometrika* 7:251–79

Karlovich, R. S. 1975. Comments on the relations between auditory fatigue and iris pigmentation. *Audiology* 14:238–43

Karsai, L. K., Bergman, M., Choo, Y. B. 1972. Hearing in ethnically different longshoremen. *Arch. Otolaryngol.* 96: 499–504

Kemp, D. T. 1978. Stimulated acoustic emissions from within the human auditory system. *J. Acoust. Soc. Am.* 65:1386–91

Kemp, D. T. 1979a. Evidence of mechanical nonlinearity and frequency selective wave amplification in the cochlea. *Arch. Otorhinolaryngol.* 224:37–45

Kemp, D. T. 1979b. The evoked cochlear mechanical response and the auditory microstructure. In *Models of the Auditory System and Related Signal Processing Techniques*, ed. M. Hoke, E. de Boer, pp. 36–47. *Scand. Audiol.* special issue

Kemp, D. T. 1980a. Comment. See Feth et al 1980, pp. 75–76

Kemp, D. T. 1980b. Towards a model for the origin of cochlear echoes. *Hear. Res.* 2:533–48

Kemp, D. T. 1981. Physiologically active cochlear micromechanics: one source of tinnitus. In *Tinnitus,* Ciba Found. Symp. pp. 54–81. London: Pitman

Kemp, D. T. 1982. Cochlear echoes: implications for noise-induced hearing loss. In *New Perspectives in Noise-Induced Hearing Loss,* ed. R. P. Hamernik, D. Henderson, R. Salvi, pp. 189–207. New York: Raven

Kemp, D. T., Chum, R. 1980. Properties of the generator of stimulated acoustic emissions. *Hear. Res.* 2:213–32

Khanna, S. M., Leonard, D. G. 1982. Basilar membrane tuning in the cat cochlea. *Science* 215:305–6

Kim, D. O. 1980a. Cochlear mechanics: implications of electrophysiological and acoustical observations. *Hear. Res.* 2: 297–317

Kim, D. O. 1980b. Transcript of the mid-symposium discussion period. *Hear. Res.* 2:581–87

Kim, D. O., Molnar, C. E., Matthews, J. W. 1980. Cochlear mechanics: nonlinear behavior in two-tone responses as reflected in cochlear-nerve-fiber responses and in ear-canal sound pressure. *J. Acoust. Soc. Am.* 67:1704–19

Konig, E. 1957. Pitch discrimination and age. *Acta Otolaryngol.* 48:251–79

LaFerriere, K. A., Arenberg, I. K., Hawkins, J. E., Johnsson, L.-G. 1974. Melanocytes of the vestibular labyrinth and their relationship to the microvasculature. *Ann. Otol.* 83:685–94

Leshowitz, B., Lindstrom, R. 1977. Measurement of nonlinearities in listeners with sensorineural hearing loss. See Hoekstra & Ritsma 1977, pp. 283–92

Lindquist, N. G. 1973. Accumulation of drugs on melanin. *Acta Radiol.* 325: 5–92 (Suppl.)

Lonsbury-Martin, B. L., Meikle, M. B. 1978. Neural correlates of auditory fatigue: frequency-dependent changes in activity of single cochlear nerve fibers. *J. Neurophysiol.* 41:987–1006

Lyttkens, L., Larsson, B., Goller, H., Englesson, S., Stahle, J. 1979. Melanin capacity to accumulate drugs in the internal ear. *Acta Otolaryngol.* 88:61–73

Margolis, R. H., Goldberg, S. M. 1980. Auditory frequency selectivity in normal and presbyacusic subjects. *J. Speech Hear. Res.* 23:603–13

McFadden, D. 1982. *Tinnitus: Facts, Theories, and Treatments.* Washington DC: Natl. Acad. Sci. Press

McGee, T. 1978. *Psychophysical tuning curves from hearing-impaired listeners.* PhD thesis. Northwestern Univ., Evanston, Ill.

Miskolczy-Fodor, F. 1953. Monaural loudness-balance test and determination of recruitment-degree with short sound-impulses. *Acta Otolaryngol.* 43:573–95

Moore, B. C. J. 1978. Psychophysical tuning curves measured in simultaneous and forward masking. *J. Acoust. Soc. Am.* 63:524–32

Mountain, D. C. 1980. Changes in endolymphatic potential and crossed olivocochlear bundle stimulation alter cochlear mechanics. *Science* 210:71–72

Nabelek, A. K., Robinette, L. 1978. Influence of the precedence effect on word identification by normally hearing and hearing-impaired subjects. *J. Acoust. Soc. Am.* 63:187–94

Nelson, D., Turner, C. W. 1980. Decay of masking and frequency resolution in sensorineural hearing-impaired listeners. See Feth et al 1980, pp. 175–82

Noble, W. G. 1973. Pure-tone acuity, speech-hearing ability and deafness in acoustic trauma—a review of the literature. *Audiology* 12:291–315

Owens, E. 1978. Consonant errors and remediation in sensorineural hearing loss. *J. Speech Hear. Disord.* 43:331–47

Owens, E., Benedict, M., Schubert, E. D. 1972. Consonant phonemic error associated with pure tone configuration and certain kinds of hearing impairment. *J. Speech Hear. Res.* 15:308–22

Patterson, R. D. 1974. Auditory filter shape. *J. Acoust. Soc. Am.* 55:802–9

Penner, M. J. 1980. Two-tone forward masking patterns and tinnitus. *J. Speech Hear. Res.* 23:779–86

Penner, M. J. 1982. The annoyance of tinnitus. *Hear. Instrum.* 33:19–20

Pfeiffer, R. R., Kim, D. O. 1972. Response patterns of single cochlear nerve fibers to click stimuli: descriptions for cat. *J. Acoust. Soc. Am.* 52:1669–77

Pick, G. F. 1980. Level dependence of psychophysical frequency resolution and auditory filter shape. *J. Acoust. Soc. Am.* 68:1085–95

Portmann, M., Cazals, Y., Negrevergne, M., Aran, J.-M. 1979. Temporary tinnitus suppression in man through electrical stimulation of the cochlea. *Acta Otolaryngol.* 87:294–99

Post, R. H. 1964. Hearing acuity variation among Negroes and Whites. *Eugen. Q.* 11:65–81

Reed, G. F. 1960. An audiometric study of two hundred cases of subjective tinnitus. *Arch. Otolaryngol.* 71:94–104

Ritsma, R. J., Wit, H. P., Van der Lans, W. P. 1980. Relations between hearing loss, maximal word discrimination score and width of psychophysical tuning curves. See Feth et al 1980, pp. 472–76

Robertson, D., Johnstone, B. M. 1980. Acoustic trauma in the guinea pig cochlea: early changes in ultrastructure and neural threshold. *Hear. Res.* 3:167–79

Rosen, S., Bergman, M., Plester, D., El-Mofty, A., Satti, M. H. 1962. Presbycusis study of a relatively noise-free population in the Sudan. *Ann. Otol. Rhinol. Laryngol.* 71:727–43

Ross, M., Huntington, D. A., Newley, H. A., Dixon, R. 1965. Speech discrimination of hearing-impaired individuals in noise. *J. Aud. Res.* 5:47–72

Royster, L. H., Royster, J. D., Thomas, W. G. 1980. Representative hearing levels by race and sex in North Carolina industry. *J. Acoust. Soc. Am.* 68:551–66

Rutten, W. L. C. 1980a. Evoked acoustic emissions from within normal and abnormal human ears: comparison with audiometric and electrocochleographic findings. *Hear. Res.* 2:263–71

Rutten, W. L. C. 1980b. Latencies of stimulated acoustic emissions in normal human ears. See Feth et al 1980, pp. 68–76

Sanders, J., Honig, E. 1967. Brief tone audiometry: results in normal and impaired ears. *Arch. Otolaryngol.* 85:640–47

Scharf, B. 1970. Critical bands. In *Foundations of Modern Auditory Theory*, ed. J. V. Tobias, pp. 157–98. New York: Academic

Scharf, B. 1978a. Comparison of normal and impaired hearing I. Loudness, localization. In *Sensorineural Hearing Impairment and Hearing Aids*, ed. C. Ludvigsen, J. Barfod. *Scand. Audiol. Suppl.* 6:49–76

Scharf, B. 1978b. Comparison of normal and impaired hearing II. Frequency analysis, speech perception. See Scharf 1978a, 6:81–106

Scharf, B., Hellman, R. P. 1966. Model of loudness summation applied to impaired ears. *J. Acoust. Soc. Am.* 40:71–78

Schleuning, A. M., Johnson, R. M., Vernon, J. A. 1980. Evaluation of a tinnitus masking program: a follow-up study of 598 patients. *Ear Hear.* 1:71–74

Schmiedt, R. A., Adams, J. C. 1981. Stimulated acoustic emissions in the ear canal of the gerbil. *Hear. Res.* 5:295–305

Schultz, T. J. 1978. Synthesis of social surveys on noise annoyance. *J. Acoust. Soc. Am.* 64:377–405

Shepherd, D. C., Goldstein, R., Rosenblut, B. 1964. Race differences in auditory sensitivity. *J. Speech Hear. Res.* 7:389–97

Shulman, A., Chairman. 1981. *Tinnitus: Proc. 1st Int. Tinnitus Semin. J. Laryngol. Otol.* Suppl. 4

Siegel, J. H., Kim, D. O. 1982a. Cochlear biomechanics: vulnerability to acoustic trauma and other alterations as seen in neural responses and ear-canal sound pressure. See Kemp 1982, pp. 137–51

Siegel, J. H., Kim, D. O. 1982b. Efferent neural control of cochlear mechanics? Olivocochlear bundle stimulation affects cochlear biomechanical nonlinearity. *Hear. Res.* 6:171–82

Small, A. M. 1959. Pure-tone masking. *J. Acoust. Soc. Am.* 31:1619–25

Stelmachowicz, P., Seewald, R. C. 1977. Threshold and suprathreshold temporal integration function in normal and cochlear-impaired subjects. *Audiology* 16:94–101

Tota, G., Bocci, G. 1967. The importance of the color of the iris in the evaluation of resistance to auditory fatigue. *Oto-Neuro-Oftalmologica* 42:183–92

Tyler, R. S., Summerfield, A. Q. 1980. Psychoacoustical and phonetic measures of temporal processing in normal and hearing-impaired listerners. See Feth et al 1980, pp. 458–65

Tyler, R. S., Wood, E. J., Fernandez, M. 1982. Frequency resolution and hearing loss. *Br. J. Audiol.* 16:45–63

Vernon, J. 1976. The loudness (?) of tinnitus. *Hear. Speech Action* 44:17–19

Vernon, J. 1977. Attempts to relieve tinnitus. *J. Am. Audiol. Soc.* 2:124–31

Vernon, J., Johnson, R., Schleuning, A., Mitchell, C. 1980. Masking and tinnitus. *Audiol. Hear. Res.* 6:5–9

Ward, W. D. 1955. Tonal monaural diplacusis. *J. Acoust. Soc. Am.* 27: 365–72

Warr, W. B. 1978. The olivocohlear bundle: its origins and terminations in the cat. In *Evoked Electrical Activity in the Auditory Nervous System*, ed. R. F. Naunton, C. Fernandez, pp. 43–65. New York: Academic

Wegel, R. L. 1931. A study of tinnitus. *Arch. Otolaryngol.* 14:158–65

Wier, C. C., Jesteadt, W., Green, D. M. 1977. Frequency discrimination as a function of frequency and sensation level. *J. Acoust. Soc. Am.* 61:178–84

Wightman, F. L. 1982. Psychoacoustic correlates of hearing loss. See Kemp 1982, pp. 375–94

Wightman, F. L., McGee, T., Kramer, M. 1977. Factors influencing frequency selectivity in normal and hearing-impaired listeners. See Hoekstra & Ritsma 1977, pp. 295–306

Wilson, J. P. 1980a. Evidence for a cochlear origin for acoustic reemissions, threshold fine-structure and tonal tinnitus. *Hear. Res.* 2:233–52

Wilson, J. P. 1980b. Model for cochlear echoes and tinnitus based on an observed electrical correlate. *Hear. Res.* 2:527–32

Wilson, J. P. 1980c. The combination tone, $2f_1 - f_2$, in psychophysics and ear-canal recording. See Feth et al 1980, pp. 43–49

Wilson, J. P., Sutton, G. J. 1981. Acoustic correlates of tonal tinnitus. In *Tinnitus,* Ciba Found. Symp. 85, pp. 82–100. London:Pitman

Wit, H. P., Ritsma, R. J. 1979. Stimulated acoustic emissions from the human ear. *J. Acoust. Soc. Am.* 66:911–13

Wit, H. P., Ritsma, R. J. 1980a. Evoked acoustical responses from the human ear: some experimental results. *Hear. Res.* 2:253–61

Wit, H. P., Ritsma, R. J. 1980b. On the mechanism of the evoked cochlear mechanical response. See Feth et al 1980, pp. 53–63

Wright, H. 1968. The effect of sensorineural hearing loss on threshold-duration functions. *J. Speech Hear. Res.* 11: 842–52

Zurek, P. M. 1981. Spontaneous narrowband acoustic signals emitted by human ears. *J. Acoust. Soc. Am.* 69:514–23

Zurek, P. M., Clark, W. W. 1981. Narrowband acoustic signals emitted by chinchilla ears after noise exposure. *J. Acoust. Soc. Am.* 70:446–50

Zwicker, E. 1974. On a psychoacoustical equivalent of a tuning curve. In *Facts and Models in Hearing*, ed. E. Zwicker, E. Terhardt, pp. 132–41. New York: Springer

Zwicker, E., Manley, G. 1981. Acoustical responses and suppression-period patterns in guinea pigs. *Hear. Res.* 4:43–52

Zwicker, E., Schorn, K. 1978. Psychoacoustical tuning curves in audiology. *Audiology* 17:120–40

Ann. Rev. Psychol. 1983. 34:129–66
Copyright © 1983 by Annual Reviews Inc. All rights reserved

PERCEPTION AND REPRESENTATION

Paul A. Kolers

Department of Psychology, University of Toronto, Toronto, Ontario,
Canada M5S 1A1

CONTENTS

INTRODUCTION

The topic of visual perception traditionally covers the subjects space and
form, sometimes temporal phenomena such as flicker, rarely motion perception, almost never art or other such cognitive objects. The emphasis has
been upon the more realistic functions, the close mapping of stimulus and

experience. Over the past two decades, however, considerable interest has developed among some investigators in perceptual experiences less realistic than those of the traditional topics. I have in mind not art but phenomena associated with persistence of vision, inhibition, supplementation, and imagination. Not always studied with the rigor that they require or that is often the mark of investigations in traditional topics, these four provide a ground on which rigorous experimentation can exercise itself on complex processes. Some movement in that direction is already perceptible.

The terms refer to phenomena also called iconic memory, backward masking, apparent motion, and imagery. I had intended to review all four but as space limitations supervened, I have left out apparent motion. The other three challenge our best understanding of visual perceptual processes. After their review I will also mention some topics in the study of representation, and will end with a few comments on practical problems associated with possible hazards from viewing CRTs.

The very good news for 1981 to students of perception was the award of the Nobel Prize to Roger Sperry for his monumental work on brain functions, including perceptual experiences, and to David Hubel and Torsten Wiesel for their analyses of cerebral components of visual functions. Sperry may now be best known for the development of the split brain technique for the study of localization phenomena; his earlier work on regeneration of neural tracts after surgery, and his challenge to the notion that perception is a matter of contours moving across the cortical surface, were also golden. The work of Hubel and Wiesel in recording from single cells traced the transformation of light into coded object through various levels of visual system. Their earlier work proposed a strictly serial model of processing; later work has applied to the visual system and elaborated the notion of columnar organization of cortex. The relation of single-cell recording to perceptual experience has of course still to be worked out; Sperry (1976) among others has speculated on some of the relations of experience and consciousness.

An interesting professional development has been the rich number of textbooks over the past few years. There was a period from the mid-1960s on when almost nothing new appeared; and now several are available. They range from the selective, beautiful, and probably misguided monograph of Frisby (1980) to the detailed, more thorough, and more physiologically oriented books of Brown & Defenbacher (1979) or Levine & Shefner (1981), to an engineering-oriented monograph by Caelli (1981). Goldstein (1980) has written a less technical but useful text for the first course in perception. The dominant quality across the range of texts is their lack of a fixed focus. Frisby has sold his soul to a machine analogy; Levine and Shefner write as if perception were identifiable with the conduction of impulses in the nerve fibers; Caelli is all networks, convolutions, and MTFs. Eye movements are of continuing interest: Fisher et al (1981) have edited the third volume in a series [Levy-Schoen & O'Regan (1979) and Rayner (1978) summarized the state of the art in respect to reading]; Carpenter (1977) has described the eye movement system in great detail. Uttal (1981) continues his synoptic account of visual processes with the third volume of a projected five. Art has not been neglected: Hagen (1980) edited two volumes, and Kim (1981) has revealed an extraordinary ability to create graphic symmetries.

In the bad news for 1981 the untimely death of two distinguished investigators is prominent. David Marr had a radical, reorganizational influence on the study of machine vision. Trained in biology and artificial intelligence, he moved the field away from the increasingly unfruitful metaphor that sought a language of vision in shapes and rules for combining them and toward the analysis of local regions of stimulation. Startling successes marked the developments of only a few years' work, reviewed sympathetically by Stent (1981). Frank Restle, the other grievous loss, was a psychologist with a broad range of interests. He contributed creatively to many subjects in the study of perception and cognition, and capped his career as editor of the *Journal of Experimental Psychology: Human Perception and Performance.* He tried to extend the reach of the discipline and edited as if he thought that authors should be helped to say more clearly what they were trying to say, rather than insisting on the rightness of his own theoretical perspective or technical prejudice. Memorial funds have been established to commemorate both of these gifted investigators.

ICONS

Some experiments 20 years ago demonstrated afresh that people can describe various features of letters and digits that were presented briefly but were no longer present to view (Averbach & Coriell 1961, Sperling 1960, 1967, 1970). Sperling's technique was to signal with a tone whether the observer was to report the contents of a top, middle, or bottom row of characters, the tone presented *after* the offset of the display. Unsignaled, the observer reported about 4.5 characters from a brief display of 12 or more. When a tone followed the display immediately, the person could report 3 of the characters, on average, from any haphazardly chosen row of 4, for a nominal availability in memory of 9 of the 12 characters. Likelihood of correct report of characters declined in a regular way with the interval between target offset and tone, an interval of about 300 msec yielding results equal to the unsignaled report. The signaled procedure is called partial report, in contrast to the normal full report.

The effect acquired great interest among cognitive psychologists, especially following Neisser's (1967) naming it "iconic memory" and arguing for it as the first stage in a process of information extraction in perception. The notion was that the visual system is limited in its processing of stimuli and that long-term memory and interpretation were carried out on the linguistic labels mind attached to the visual displays. Whatever was not tagged or labeled in the brief interval between the occurrence of a flash and its decay was lost to a person irretrievably on this theory. Iconic memory was alleged to contain a "precategorical, large capacity, rapidly fading stimulus trace . . . following the offset of a brief stimulus display" (Long 1980, p. 787) on which the tagging was carried out. The "precategorical" component is of importance (actually precategorial is meant); sometimes the terms "literal" or "unrecoded" are used to indicate "that the internal representation of a stimulus shares many of the properties of the stimulus itself" (Coltheart 1980, p. 184), that is, is a "true copy" of aspects of the stimulus. As the icon was thought to contain raw sense data, therefore, discrimination or readout from the icon was said to be possible only for the "physical" properties of the stimuli but not for "categorical" (cognitive) properties. Coltheart (1980) has again reviewed much of the literature on these effects, which were given the greatest importance in certain theories of perceptual processing. Sakitt (1976) and her occasional collaborator Long (1980) have reinterpreted them.

Icons as Afterimages

From time to time the claim was heard that the icon was nothing more than a species of afterimage, associated with the afterdischarge that characterizes most sensory events. Sakitt (1976) carried out several experiments to explore that idea and found evidence "that a significant part, or possibly all, of iconic storage is due to persistence of photoreceptor activity after a brief visual stimulus has been extinguished. . . . icons are weak afterimages stored in the retina" (p. 273). The claim was not designed to calm; it was subsequently modified to allow for separate shorter-lived, color sensitive cone icons and longer-lived, contrast sensitive rod icons (Sakitt & Long 1979). Coltheart (1980), however, distinguishes neural persistence, visible persistence, and iconic memory and so claims differences among phenomena that are sometimes treated as one. Long (1980), in contrast, after reminding readers of the rich history on persistence of vision (Allen 1926), criticized a number of studies as confounding stimuli, processes, or interpretations, and supported Sakitt's unitarian view. In more recent empirical work, Long & Sakitt (1981) have pursued the argument that different investigators may unwittingly have measured different visual events, but that iconic memory (as they define it) has its basis in the afterdischarge of the photoreceptors.

The contrast between Long's and Coltheart's reviews is marked. Coltheart discusses issues in the study of iconic memory that are especially relevant to the perception of printed words, particularly the notion of the icon as a precategorial store or postcategorial store. Coltheart has been dedicated to the cognitive information processing view of mind and, without supporting it wholeheartedly, writes in favor of the view that

> Iconic memory consists of the tagging of each of these entries with information about the physical manifestation of the word corresponding to that entry. This physical information decays away rapidly unless "lexically stabilized" by a "lexical monitor" of limited capacity. Lexical excitation itself also decays (though more slowly), and so also may require lexical stabilization. Backward masking can interfere with lexical stabilization by claiming the attention of the lexical monitor: this is how "perception without awareness" occurs (p. 225).

The unsupported invocation of mechanisms is notable: *tagging, entries, information, lexical stabilization, lexical monitor* are a few of Coltheart's operationally unidentified notions. Limited understanding of process and impatient ambition to know combine to produce such notions, but they show little trace of evolutionary history or adaptability, and they yield no gain in understanding of process. Long (1980), in contrast, seems to go out of his way to relate the special effects discovered in iconic memory experiments to a well-documented and long-standing field of research in perceptual processes, particularly to the older persistence of vision studies (Allen 1926).

Coltheart argued for a distinction between iconic memory and visible persistence partly on the basis of a claim that the two have different outcomes when stimulus energy is manipulated. The role of energy, particularly of stimulus duration, has long been equivocal in this area (Dick 1974); the rightness of Long's claim for a unitarian view is still therefore to be determined, particularly with experiments that avoid what he considers to be contaminating influences in the older literature. He is, it must be said, rather quick to claim artifact in the data that are otherwise disagreeable to his view. Recent work by Banks & Barber (1980) and Adelson & Jonides (1980) meet his requirements, yet seem inconsistent with the receptor-based account of Sakitt and Long.

Other Accounts

One important limitation to the afterimage view is its relative indifference to the content of the flashes. In one technique, a scene is flashed briefly, then a "related" scene is flashed after some pause. Long (1980) calls this the Successive-Field Procedure. A variant exploited by Di Lollo (1980) presents some number of dots fewer than 24 in one flash and the remainder in a second. The observer's task is to say which one of the cells in a 5 X 5 matrix was not filled by the two flashes. Di Lollo (p. 80), consistent with Sakitt and Long's claims, argues that "visual persistence is an attribute of each individual dot rather than of the overall configuration"; and that the relevant temporal dimension is the time elapsed from the beginning of the first flash, "exposure duration of local detail" (p. 81). However, he also argues that, not a passive reservoir sort of memory, but some active operation on the stimulus is the source of the icon, a claim echoing Erwin's (1976) argument for active processing rather than passive visual copy. Wilson (1981) showed that persistence was characteristic of both onset and offset.

Merikle (1980) also raised some issues at a categorial level. Recall that the claim had been made that the poststimulus cue was not effective for all categories of stimulation, only for "physical" or "literal" ones. It was said, therefore, that the visual system could not be cued to select only digits or only letters from a mixed display of letters and digits, because that is a distinction due to category, not to "raw stimulation." However, a haphazard arrangement of letters and numerals, lacking other organization, could oblige the perceiver to evaluate them only one after the other. Thus, to discriminate letters from numerals would require the person to survey all three rows of the display—in effect, to carry out a full report. The failure to obtain an advantage to partial report in such circumstances would depend, not on the difference between "physical" and "categorial" discriminations, but on the way the person carried out the task. Merikle's (1980) view of the problem favored this idea. In a series of experiments he varied the spacing and format of the display and found that cuing was as effective for categorial as for physical attributes of the stimuli (as those terms are used). He argued against the notion of a special stage or memory in the acquisition of visual information, and suggested that different categories of information about a stimulus, such as its location and identity, probably develop at different speeds in the nervous system.

Assumptions and Implications

The basis or controlling mechanism of iconic memory is not always the topic of greatest interest, however. Among psychologists who take primarily an inflow theory of perception, iconic memory was often construed as a buffer store or holding tank into which a linguistic operator delved to assign linguistic permanence to ephemeral visual stimulation. An important component in the interest that many investigators have held in iconic memory is therefore the claim that it provides evidence of and information about precategorial storage, and that the person's report of the contents of the icon reveals the features of the physical world that can be known directly rather than only in recoded form.

UNBIASED REPORTER   It was never exactly clear how reports of the unrecoded information could be made, however. To claim them implies an Unbiased Reporter: a reporter of mental events that can accurately reveal the contents of an operation without influencing it or being influenced by it.

The assumption of the Unbiased Reporter is similar to the assumption made by the advocates of analytical introspectionism as the model technique of cognitive psychology (Titchener 1902, Humphrey 1951), and is subject to the same complaints. The introspectionists sought the sensory elements of experience, the first stage in the mind's acquisition of information from physical objects. In doing so, they assumed that the remainder of mind could be disconnected from its "front end" that responded to sensory stimuli, and that an Unbiased Reporter could report selectively on the features processed there; in a word, that mind could monitor its own workings and indeed that its workings were selectively visible to an Unbiased Reporter. The Introspectionists did not always appreciate that what they experienced as sensations were the result of extensive processing by mind, not some initial stage. Many students of cognition now seem to miss the same point—that what can be reported as a perceptual event is the result of extensive operations carried out by the visual mechanisms, and not some selected content or stage.

It is difficult to understand why an Unbiased Reporter, having free access to monitor any stage of operation, would report fewer or more characters, or report more slowly from one display than another (Merikle 1980). It is unclear why an Unbiased Reporter would report differently according as it was required to speak or write its report (Von Wright 1972). The notion of an Unbiased Reporter that is able to be placed at and report fully and accurately on any specifiable point in a processing sequence seems to be present in much theorizing; the notion needs serious analysis. It may not be justified.

SKILLS AND TRAINING   The phenomenon of visual persistence seems to have recovered a substantial explanatory purchase on effects that for the past 20 years have been attributed to other mechanisms. Those implicated a particular theory of perception, if not of mind, and they, along with coordinated notions of strict serial processing, seem to be fading. Nonetheless it would not be wholly right to say that iconic memory is only an afterimage. A light can be flashed at a cat and its afterimage studied, either biochemically or electrophysiologically. A light can be flashed at a person to achieve the same end. But if the light flashed at the person spelled a word in a known language, its report would involve substantially more than the report of the same light flashed at the cat. Systematically enriching a stimulus might illuminate expansions in its processing, and perhaps Sperling's ingenious technique could be applied to that end. Whether iconic memory can be exploited or trained for any good purpose of mind seems not to have been studied in the long series of investigations directed at it; perhaps it should be so studied.

To say that a person selectively reporting the contents of an afterimage is "only" experiencing an afterimage would be to caricature a complex event as surely as did the first and popular accounts of the phenomena. The source of the stimulus may indeed be an afterdischarge of the photoreceptors; the experience and report of the event surely are not. A person must know a great deal about his or her own mind to know how to report selectively about a stimulus no longer present to view regarding its duration, color, location, size, brightness, or name.

VISUAL MASKING

Icons are phenomena of persistence; their existence violates naive expectation by revealing that perceptions continue although external stimulation has ceased. More violative of naive expectation is backward masking, an event later in time interfering with the perception of an earlier one.

Although the eyes of the normal awake person are in frequent movement, most of the changes are fairly small when a person is looking at another person, a picture, or is reading a text; and most of the larger movements are to accomplish the logistical task of getting the eyes pointed to a new target to be examined. The relative fixity of gaze on an object long seduced students of visual perception into treating visual scenes as constants and as acquired much as still photographs. During the last 20 years, techniques developed to present stimuli for controlled durations within single fixations have revealed a wealth of new phenomena and have radically affected descriptions of perceptual processing: away from laws regarding geometric or luminance relations of stimuli in favor of the mechanisms that must underlie the coherence of visual scenes that former approaches often took for granted. Backward masking has played an important role in these investigations.

Two lines of research have studied the effects, one the psychophysical investigation of detection of flashes of light, the second concerned more with the perception of form. Different procedures, different sorts of measurement, and different interests have marked the two approaches, with a corresponding confusion of terminology. I will use the term masking in a general sense to describe alteration of perception due to sequential presentation of stimuli.

The principal observation is that stimulus event M occurring after event T nevertheless affects the perception of T. The phenomenon is counterintuitive to the extent that we think of events as monolithic and think of causation in terms of time's arrow. Early efforts to explain the effects were therefore stated in terms of some process associated with M catching up to and interfering with a process associated with T (Fry 1934, Piéron 1935); this was plausible as M was usually larger or more intense than T, and so had a shorter latency and a conduction advantage in the nervous system. Appeal to this form of the catching up account was presumably eliminated by finding that masking occurred even when M was less energetic than T (Kolers & Rosner 1960, Boynton 1961). No conduction advantage could be associated with M in these cases. Another finding was that sometimes the interference followed a U-shaped curve when it was plotted against the time interval separating the flashes and sometimes it was monotonic. The stimulus conditions required for the two results—called Type B and Type A curves, respectively (Kolers 1962, Fox 1978)—have been established approximately.

Subsequent approaches regarded the stimuli as composite rather than as monolithic, and fractionated their effects along lines suggested by the discovery of lateral inhibitory networks in *Limulus* (Hartline et al 1956; see also Ratliff 1974). The strategy worked for flashes of light presented to the dark-adapted eye, but failed for black shapes flashed to the light-adapted eye (Kolers & Rosner 1960) even though the data were complementary in form. [It often happens in visual studies that complementary or symmetrical data are obtained from flashes of light or white and flashes of black (*mutatis mutandis*) with deep significance for theory. Models of masking based on lateral inhibition (Bridgeman & Leff 1979) or on related processes (Breitmeyer 1980, Felsten & Wasserman 1980) often improperly ignore the dissimilarities in prediction for light and black as stimuli.]

Basis of Evaluation

When the time interval separating the two flashes is appropriately brief, the two stimuli tend to be seen as a single object. As the interval increases, T is seen less distinctly; later still, during the recovery stage, they are often seen as two temporally distinct objects. Not only was the "backward" aspect of masking counterintuitive, the fact that visibility of T first decreased and then recovered as time between T and M increased violated many assumptions about visual perception; particularly, it violated the assumption that perceptions were coded immediately and were realistically faithful to stimulus events. The nonmonotonicity of masking has been especially troublesome to some investigators (Eriksen 1980, Eriksen & Collins 1965, Eriksen & Marshall 1969). The alternative claim for masking has been that the interference was actually monotonic, and could be accounted for in terms of the summation of luminances and reduction of contrast in the region in which the masking form replaced the target. This view was affirmed even though masking was shown to occur at temporal separations that exceeded the intervals for luminance integration in human vision (Battersby & Defabaugh 1969, Kolers & Rosner 1960), facts which rendered the proposal somewhat specious.

Felsten & Wasserman (1980) have reviewed some of the masking literature anew and have proposed a resolution to what is seen as a conflict of theories. The notion of luminance summation in masking assumes a cooption, amalgamation, or fusing of the two stimuli into a single processed object. An alternative, called interruption theory, supposes that the arrival of the second stimulus interferes with, attenuates, or interrupts the processing of the first, either directly by overtaking, or by the sudden arrival of M affecting procedures normally directed at T (Kolers 1968). Different sorts of processes are thought to characterize the two notions, integrative theories being energy-dependent, and interruptive theories based on time-dependent mechanisms. In their densely argued paper, Felsten and Wasserman propose that masking occurs at many different levels of the visual system, that the interruption that is alleged to occur is due to attenuation of response from the receptor site, not to attenuated operation of a "processor," and that different aspects of an encoding are based on different aspects of the sensory signal. (They caution investigators who use a mask to "erase" or "stop" the processing of a prior stimulus that their models may be faulted if it should turn out that interruption, so defined, is not a likely alternative.) Their paper is something of a tour de force in accounting for a number of outcomes by the phased operation of a single process. They write: "The sensory code for stimulus detection is the amplitude of the response to the stimulus; the sensory code for perceived duration is the duration of the response that remains above a criterion potential; the sensory code for stimulus identification is the integral of the neural response to the stimulus" (p. 349).

An important virtue of this approach is the notion that different aspects of a perceptual experience may be based, not on different receptors, but on different features of fundamentally the same response. Nevertheless, it is difficult to know how far to follow this analysis, partly because the authors restrict it to conditions in which the stimuli are thought to share receptors, partly because the authors are not always careful enough in their claims (as in the last clause of the quotation above), and partly because their claims are sometimes inaccurate. For one point in contrast, a disk has an edge and an interior which, to revert to an old report (Kolers 1962), seem to subscribe to different aspects of perceptual processing. For a second point, detectability of a target disk follows a U-shaped masking curve when an aftercoming black masking disk is only slightly larger than the target, but follows a monotonic masking curve when the diameter of M is still larger. A black disk masked by a black ring might be said to suffer contrast reduction, but there is no apparent way for that explanation to be true of a black disk masked by a following black disk; moreover, the account by contrast reduction does not specify why the distance between the borders of the two disks should be so critical to the outcome, which is the case. Felsten and Wasserman argue usefully that a multiplicity of events follow stimulation; but attributing all of them to the operation of a single process such as reaction to luminance at the receptor surface carries parsimony to the point of deprivation.

Other models treat the phenomena as composed of a quick process and a slow one (Breitmeyer & Ganz 1976, Breitmeyer 1980); or conceptualize edge and interior in terms of spatial frequency discriminations, for sensitivity to masking varies somewhat with spatial frequency of the target and mask (Green 1981, Growney 1978, Legge 1978, White & Lorber 1976). Sharp perceptual definition of an edge requires a higher spatial frequency analysis, whereas a homogeneous interior can be detected with less resolving power.

FOVEAL STIMULATION   Some reports deny that masking occurs in the human fovea, others affirm it, and others suggest that it is merely hard to find. Ventura (1980) studied the question both experimentally and by detailed examination of the published reports; he makes two important points. One is that amount of practice is important in establishing whether people can detect luminance changes in foveal stimulation; the implication is that increase in practice may sometimes result in decrease in alertness, motivation, sensitivity, or other related conditions. The second point is that some observers report a biphasic change in the brightness of a white stimulus against a black ground, and may at different times use different aspects of the perceived target as the object judged. (Not different aspects of the receptor response, of course, but different aspects of the perceptual experience.) These considerations have considerable importance for theories of masking, as Ventura points out. Consistent with one of his claims, Lyon et al (1981) reported foveal masking when the stimuli were small enough. Bridgeman & Leff (1979) studied the interaction of size, spatial separation, and retinal location; they also found robust foveal masking, and challenged the sustained-transient model of Breitmeyer & Ganz (1976) with their results. Meanwhile, Bowen & Markell (1980) found substantial differences in people's ability to integrate luminous energy in a simple brightness matching experiment; Bowen et al (1981) confirmed the finding of systematic individual differences in judgments of brightness but found it had little generality to other perceptual tasks. They suggest that the results are better attributed to stylistic or strategic differences among subjects in their choice of perceptual criteria than to fundamental differences in the underlying neurophysiology, a point Ventura (1980) also made.

OTHER FEATURES   Lehmkuhle & Fox (1980) described masking in stereoscopic displays. Both target and mask were created out of random dot patterns so that both existed only as perceived, or cyclopean, but not as physical objects. (Of course the dots out of which the perception was synthesized existed as physical objects.) They report that stereoscopic masking shares some features with masking by physical contours but differs in others; in particular, asymmetries related to perceptual space were found, and these cannot be assigned to variations in receptor response. Other experiments that demonstrate interactions in color (Reeves 1981a), apparent duration (Petry 1978), location (Lowe 1975), and retinal locus (Walsh et al 1978) support the observation that stimuli are compositions of features, and perception of any feature of the stimulus apparently can be interfered with by the appropriate masking stimulus.

X-Y THEORIES Presumably a number of interactions occur when the stimuli are complex, perhaps with different latencies and different time course. Breitmeyer & Ganz (1976) based their model on the interaction of two classes of neural mechanisms, Y and X, sometimes associated with types of cells (transient and sustained, edge and interior, location and identity—many such dichotomies have been proposed), an approach others have also followed (Breitmeyer et al 1981, Brooks et al 1981). Suppose, however, that the retinal location of a stimulus triggered a fast response whereas information about identity traveled more slowly; and suppose too that the former could interfere with the latter (MacLeod 1978). Is the outcome due to differential velocity of the neural signals or to the kind of information transmitted? A system can make do with much less detailed information to determine an objects's location than to determine its identity, hence location would be established more rapidly than identity. Perhaps both the type of signal and the determination are involved—low frequency responses establishing location traveling more rapidly and being interpreted more quickly than high frequency responses establishing identity. Information about an aftercoming ring could presumably catch up to and interfere with information about the identity of a prior disk (Breitmeyer & Ganz 1976). On this account the reverse should equally be true. The location of an aftercoming disk should equally interfere with the identity of a prior ring. In fact, an aftercoming disk interferes with a prior ring far less than an aftercoming ring interferes with a prior disk (Kolers & Rosner 1960). Moreover, as Werner (1935) showed with shapes, and as Taylor & Chabot (1978) confirmed with letters, details of geometric structure (identity) affect the degree of interference measured. Many more attributes of a stimulus can be identified than can be associated with its spatial frequency, and far more complexity characterizes the neural reaction than is accounted for by two cell types. Rodieck (1979), in fact, lists more than a dozen cell types; Kolb et al (1981) enrich aspects of the description. That richness has not been exploited in theories of masking.

The interactions, moreover, presumably occur in a network; not only would X and Y influence each other, but many events would affect and be affected by others. Moreover, different sorts of processes might be operative, some based on the interaction of receptors themselves (Foster 1978, 1979), others due to the inability of a particular operator to handle stimuli arriving in too rapid succession (Kolers 1968); and still others, due to figural or dimensional properties of the perception (Lehmkuhle & Fox 1980). Rodieck (1979) actually cautions against identifying any perceptual experience with the operation of any neural detector, the relations being too complex to support straightforward mapping.

Nomenclature

What sometimes seems like unnecessary confusion is due to the naming of the phenomena. Stigler (1910) used *metacontrast* to describe an induced change in brightness of one flash, presented before but due to another. *Masking* was used, in turn, to describe the interference in the perception of forms or contours, similarly induced (Kolers & Rosner 1960). Both terms refer to an inhibition in seeing. Different stimulus configurations were used in different experiments, however, and at present a number of authors identify the phenomena by placement of the stimuli. The term metacontrast is applied on this convention when T and M stimulate separated retinal regions, and the term masking otherwise (Felsten & Wasserman 1980, Fox 1978). This may not be a reliable criterion. Usually we name things according to their similarity in appearance to other named things, according to some similarity of process common to them, or according to a task a person is required to perform in respect to them. Placement of stimuli abides by none of these criteria and may actually be a misleading criterion compared, say, to the task the person must perform. For example, if the inner diameter of the aftercoming ring is smaller than the diameter of the disk, two different discriminations are possible, depending on timing (Kolers 1962). Where disk and ring overlap, an increase in blackness occurs but nothing is seen in the hole of the ring; or a dark shape is seen in the hole of the ring but with no change in blackness in the region of overlap. Different time courses characterize the two perceptions, one monotonic, the other U-shaped; one a matter of summation of blackness, the other a matter of discrimination of form; "masking" in one discrimination, "metacontrast" in the other, with no change in stimulus placement.

The term masking might be used to describe *any* interference in the perceptibility of one stimulus attributable to the presence of another; the term metacontrast might be reserved to judgment of brightness, as implied in the *contrast* component. This may not be wholly appropriate either, however, since stimuli whose spatial frequency is due to sine wave modulation of brightness are frequently described in terms of their form characteristics. A coherent nomenclature or coding system for visual stimuli is badly needed.

Letters and Words

The study of masking has not been restricted to the psychophysics of form and brightness. Students of information processing have been interested in the discriminability or processing of shapes, some geometric, but some linguistic. In their experiments the mask sometimes both precedes and follows the stimulus, as in Dodge's (1907) experiments on perceptibility of letters and words; in others the target may be a letter, word, or pseudoword, and the mask may be a flash of light, other letters, words, pseudowords, or a random pattern. The principal inquiries in these studies are into the effects of time on processing and into the effects of the various masking flashes on perception of the target.

Hellige et al (1979) presented curvilinear letters as target and either curvilinear or rectilinear masks; they also varied adaptation, presenting stimuli sometimes to the dark-adapted and sometimes to the light-adapted eye. The customary U-shaped curves described detectability of the target as a function of the interval between target and mask, and the time course varied with the geometry of the characters and with extent of adaptation. Massaro & Klitzke (1979) presented letters, words, or pseudowords and masked them with line segments. One point of the test was to trade off the effects of orthographic structure against time separating target and mask. The findings were that words were recognized better at short temporal separations, but single letters were recognized better at longer separations. Massaro and Klitzke supposed that at short separations little masking has occurred and, because enough of the other letters are visible, the subject can make a good guess at the word, but that at longer separations the subject can at best recover only individual letters. Their model explicitly assumes that the mask stops the processing of the previous stimulus.

Taylor & Chabot (1978) also masked letters and words with flashes, letters, and words, with results only somewhat like Massaro and Klitzke's. With letters or words as target, the power of a mask to impair perception increased as the mask was changed from a blank flash to letter segments to words. The results suggest that the effect of orthographic structure was to enhance report of words, and that words as masking forms inhibit other words better than pseudowords do. This concern with structure was expressed also in a study by McClelland & Miller (1979), and, in a different sort of paradigm, by Mewhort & Campbell (1980).

Generality

The studies of masking described in the perception literature have been concerned with the influence of variables such as intensity, geometry, spatial arrangement, and the like. The perceiver's knowledge, as represented by sensitivity to the difference between a string of letters that spell a word or that do not, has not been an independent variable until now, but with increasing technical control of stimulus displays and increasing interest in cognitive processes, knowledge is likely to become a variable. The question then becomes the "level" at which masking is conceptualized; or whether, to put it differently, masking is more general a process than is dreamed of by current models of lateral inhibition, luminance summation, or the interaction of X and Y cells.

Many conditions induce masking: light, pattern, depth, among visual factors; part of speech and language-like approximation of the stimuli among others. The fact that so large a range of conditions may all induce some impairment in perception or memory suggests that all are similar expressions of process, however differently different aspects may run off. The underlying theme is disruption in processing of one stimulus due to the insistence or salience or intensity of demand of a second. Suppose that a ringing telephone followed by a brief conversation interrupts an ongoing conversation. It is not uncommon, on finishing the telephone conversation, to find oneself temporarily lost as to the subject of the prior conversation; dealing with the telephone displaces a prior line of activity. Suppose that one is doing some one other thing and a pistol shot or a fire alarm or any other disruptive stimulus occurs; again, very often, perceptual contact with the antecedent task is lost, especially when the task was in process rather than completed. The generality of mechanism need be no more extensive than that an intrusive later event interferes with an ongoing one; the specific means of the interference can differ according to the stimulus and its location on a sensory surface. This is not to claim that a single "processor" is responsible for all the outcomes, but rather that a similar simple principle of displacement of one operation by another is carried out independently in different perceptual domains.

IMAGERY

Imagery has an old but confused status in the study of mind; for many philosophers it was both the carrier of information from the environment to mind and mind's expression of that information (Blanc-Garin 1974). Kosslyn (1980) gives the flavor of some of the variety by means of a string of citations from Aristotle forward. Renewed interest in the study of perceptual aspects of imagining has made it almost an industry in modern psychology, so extensive and varied are the publications. The new *Journal of Mental Imagery* deals specifically with the topic although often from a social and clinical perspective. Even within academic disciplines the range of investigation is substantial, from the definition of spatial properties of the mental image (Kosslyn 1980), to the useful role of imagery in memory (Richardson 1980) and in creativity (Perkins 1981). Blanc-Garin (1974) also pointed out the different status of and the different treatment accorded the notion of imagery among French, Russian, and North American investigators of mind. For convenience in description, I restrict what follows to studies carried out by workers in the last-named tradition.

New exploration of this topic has occurred largely in the 20-odd years since Miller et al (1960) noted the report that bizarre imagery could aid memory for imaged items. The first extensive work was then undertaken with lists of words that referred to concrete objects or to abstractions, many experiments summarized by Paivio (1971), who put them forward in the context of a "dual code theory"—the notion that we utilize two different but redundant coding systems to represent the world, a pictorial system and a linguistic system. [The contrast is often put as between visual and verbal, but that is misleading; written language is both visual and verbal, for example. Goodman's (1968) distinction of pictorial and linguistic seems to capture the important difference better.]

The study of a pictorial representational system created considerable difficulty for many investigators working in the then-current tradition of brief visual icons translated into longer term linguistic representations; they had no clear way for such perceptions (or music, or tastes, or smells, for that matter) to be stored and retrieved except by linguistic mediation. Paivio's (1971, 1978) solution seemed actually to propose pictures in the mind, and many investigators still work in the tradition of visual imagery as a distinctively pictorial or spatial representation of events in mind. Some difficulties for theorists were brought out in Pylyshyn's (1973) spirited attack on the notion of pictorial mental representations. Two camps were very soon discerned, one affirming a fundamentally pictorial mental representation (also called analog, or spatial, or visual), the other affirming a fundamentally language-like representation (also called symbolic, or propositional, or list-like). At issue were both the nature of imagery and the proper description of perceptual experience and of mind.

Ontological Status

The principal argument has been over the issue of status—whether a mental image of an event is a picture in the mind, whether it is better described by a list of statements, or whether still something else is the case. Pylyshyn's

(1973) argument distinguished pictorialists from propositionalists—those who argued for the fundamentally pictorial or spatial or "analog" representation of objects in mind versus those who argued that all mental events were best captured in a list of statements something like those of a computer program. The arguments have continued, with thrust for propositionalization (Pylyshyn 1979, 1981) and counterthrust for pictorialization (Kosslyn & Pomerantz 1977, Kosslyn 1980, 1981, Finke 1980). Some of the arguers seem to be able to repeat themselves often, without fatigue.

Anderson (1978) made some observations critical of propositional and pictorial theorists alike; he claimed that some of the issues were undecidable in principle, and concluded by recasting his former commitment to propositional theory into a vote for Paivio's (1971) dual code theory. Kolers & Smythe (1979), surveying the field, pointed out some misconceptions regarding symbolization due to both pictorialists and propositionalists, and proposed an alternative account of this basic process. Keenan & Moore (1979) claimed that the issues Anderson thought undecidable were in fact decidable; and Anderson's assertions about the logical structure of psychological theory were said to be at a level of abstraction that did not make contact with the psychological issues (Shepard 1981). Throughout the debate the notion of symbol has fluttered, claimed by the propositionalists but avoided by the pictorialists. The contrast is sometimes put, in fact, as between *pictorial* mental representations and *symbolic* representations, the latter identified with mathematical or similarly language-like symbolization. This, it is important to show, is an erroneous contrast.

SYMBOLIZATION   Kolers & Smythe (1979) discussed the issues in the context of Goodman's (1968) theory of reference. Goodman takes as a symbol anything that stands for or represents anything else, by denoting, depicting, or exemplifying it, and discusses the characteristics of various kinds of symbol system and their respective abilities and limitations. All symbols abide by some syntactic or structural requirements, and some referential or semantic requirements. Goodman identified five features of diagnostic value. When a system of symbols abides by all five it is notational, whereas different departures from subscription to all five criteria limit a set of symbols so far as accuracy of reference and consistency of interpretation are concerned. Words characteristically are the symbols of denotation; but other forms, such as diagrams or graphs, staff notation in music, some dance notations, also denote. Pictures are of particular interest in contrast; whereas, classically, a distinction has been drawn between pictures and words as the two main communicative media, Goodman shows that it is not pictures versus words that is distinctively important for representation, but articulateness versus density of symbols. Words are syntactically disjoint, articulate, and separable each from the other, thereby meeting syntactic requirements on notationality; certain pictures, and many other perceivable objects, are syntactically dense symbols.

One of the keys to understanding the issue is to ask which aspects of a symbol can be changed without changing its communication to a knowledgeable recipient. Language and pictures illustrate one contrast. Printed language is an allographic medium; a printed work can be factored into the parts constitutive of the work and the parts that are incidental or contingent. The constitutive component of a textual work is its spelling. As long as all of the alphanumeric characters are present in the right order and with the right spacing, the copy of the text is genuine. Style of the type, its size, or the color of the paper are irrelevant so far as fidelity to an original text is concerned. Painting is an autographic medium; a painting cannot be factored, for everything about a painting is part of it—design, coloration, brush stroke, texture, and so on. A painting is unrepeatable in the strict sense of the term. Of course its texture or brush stroke can be described as a feature of a painting; but rules for using a particular texture or a particular brushstroke or the like are not so readily formalized, nor can these features be varied without varying the painting as a whole. This is not a matter of specification of features. With fine enough sampling and enough dimensions a plausible copy, even a very good copy, of a painting could be created, and yet the copy would still not be true. In fact, a photographic print is also unrepeatable exactly inasmuch as its characteristics depend upon a multitude of physicochemical reactions which cannot be duplicated exactly.

Changing the typeface or the color of ink does not change the accuracy of reproduction of the text of a printed sentence; changing the color or other such feature of a dense symbol like a painting does change it. Thus, only some symbols are discrete, factorable, and able to conform to rules for combining their features; other symbols are made of inseparable or unfactorable constituents, but are symbols nevertheless. The greater part of contemporary argument over the symbolic nature of mind supposes that only the discrete or language-like object is properly a symbol; Pylyshyn (1980, 1981) particularly makes this arbitrary assumption, but he is not alone in the error (Newell 1980). The participants in the imagery debate have not usually appreciated that pictures are also symbols or that symbols and symbol systems can be sorted into kinds.

SEMANTIC ASPECTS   Goodman (1968) shows that there are semantic requirements along with the syntactic requirements for symbols to be notational. The semantic requirements are that a symbol have only a single reference or interpretation and that objects referred to be assignable to a particular symbol. Necessarily confusing therefore is the structure of natural language; polysemy, multiple interpretations assignable to a single word, makes natural language nonnotational. (*Cleave,* for example, means to separate and to join; *scan* means to glance at and to study deeply. *Box, bear, paint* are a few other words of varied reference. On the other point, a single person may be assignable to several symbol classes, as the person may be a male, a parent, a doctor, a computer scientist, a Hindu, etc. The contrast is to imagine that *5* may be interpretable as two or five and that *3* may equally instance three, seven, multiply, and square root. Clearly one could not do even arithmetic with such conditions.) Extralinguistic factors are used to make ordinary discourse commonly interpretable, such as frequent redefinition ("No, no; I mean the one on the fridge"), appeal to gesture, intonation, and the like. Subsets of natural language can be constrained to function notationally; good textbook or technical writers strive for that clarity as do also some analysts in philosophy, psychology, or other disciplines. Natural language vocabulary requires careful definition and circumspect usage to acquire notationality, and these do not come easily. Several unseemly consequences flow from the difficulty.

Theories of Imagery and Mind

Two debates in the imagery literature are concerned with the way mind represents imagery and the way that a theory may represent mind. As mentioned earlier, the argument separates propositionalists from pictorialists, the latter advocating pictorial or spatial representation as the mind's way of reporting or constructing imagery, and the former advocating lists of statements similar in structure to a computer program.

The issues are even more complicated, as the following three views reveal. Kosslyn (1980, p. 91) places one foot in each camp in affirming that the experience of imagery or the images themselves "are functional, quasi-pictorial representations" while supposing that the generative or long-term structure of the imagery is propositional; his epiphanic analogy was the TV set, whose output is a picture, but whose mechanisms for generating the picture are expressed in the discrete symbols of electronics. Shepard (1981), a long-term, articulate member of the pictorialist group, also, curiously, separates the pictorial experience from some propositional underlying generator and seeks to represent imagery, along with many other mental events, in a geometrical "deep structure." Pylyshyn (1980, 1981) meanwhile introduced the notion of cognitive penetrability of a process, by which he means to divide mind into a hard-wired component for processing the physical world that is alike in all people, and a software component representing modifications through experience. Processes that can be influenced by thoughts, expectations, knowledge, and the like are said to be cognitively penetrable, in contrast to processes so predetermined by structure as to be beyond influence. The latter might be thought to have a fixed biological substrate whereas the former are based on a separate language-like organization of acquired knowledge and belief.

All three of these views adopt a contrast between an experience and its controlling mechanism by positing a superficial and a deep structure or, as Pylyshyn does, by positing two kinds of mental event. Many perceptual events, however, some yielding the richest sorts of experience or memory, do not lend themselves to analysis beyond the experience itself. Smell and taste are notable examples. Their perceptual experience is often described only by referring to substances with which a smell or taste is identified, and the underlying mechanisms of smell are not even known; there is no secure way to factor these experiences. As for two kinds of mental event, there seems to be good reason to think that learning actually modifies biological structure (Greenough 1975, 1978, Freeman 1979), making a division such as Pylyshyn proposes very difficult to maintain, if not vacuous. (The occurrence of psychosomatic conditions also demonstrates an influence of affect and thought upon "wired-in" connections.) The basic contrast of wired-in and modifiable mental events may accurately describe the computer better than it does people. Computers characteristically come with a small program wired in which, once activated, allows the computer to load other programs. It is not necessarily the case, however, that Nature followed that same path in solving the learning problem that occurred to Pylyshyn.

Claims and Counterclaims

The question of interest to some investigators is whether an imagined event represents the same sort of information and is created by the same sort of process as perception in response to a physical stimulus, or whether the image depends principally upon a person's store of knowledge.

The titles of some of the papers convey their arguments: "Visual images preserve metric spatial information" (Kosslyn et al 1978); "Measuring the size of mental images" (Weber & Malmstrom 1979); "Symbolic comparisons of objects on color attributes" (Paivio & te Linde 1980); "Mental measurement of line length" (Hartley 1981); "Mapping the visual field in mental imagery" (Finke & Kurtzman 1981a); "Emergent two-dimensional patterns in images rotated in depth" (Pinker & Finke 1980); "Mental imagery and the third dimension" (Pinker 1980). In addition, a few papers claim that what had been taken to be sense-dependent phenomena can be obtained also by imagination: sensitivity to wavelength is said to be affected by imagining an appropriate color, and imagining a masking form is said to affect the perceptibility of a target (Reeves 1980, 1981b). A little earlier, Finke & Schmidt (1977) had reported color-contingent aftereffects (McCollough effects) in imagination.

Finke (1980) is particularly concerned with the notion of functional equivalence, a weakened version of the claim that visual imagery and visual perception utilize fundamentally the same processes (Shepard & Podgorny 1978) or at least processes that are in "functional correspondence" (Podgorny & Shepard 1978). The notion of equivalence was extended to the motor domain, as between imagination and motor adjustment (Finke 1979). Finke & Kosslyn (1980) measured "acuity" for visual imagery in various parts of the peripheral mind's eye, and Finke & Kurtzman (1981b) measured perceptual resolution for physically present and imagined circular patterns. In both cases considerable similarity was found for presented and imagined targets, supporting the claim of equivalence of process.

The other side has also been heard from. The report of imagined color aftereffects is not universally accepted. Broerse & Crassini (1980) question their occurrence and, in rebuttal to Finke (1981), Broerse & Crassini (1981) and Kunen & May (1981) report differences in the conditions in which visually induced and imaginary McCollough effects are found and differences in their mental manipulability. Intons-Peterson & White (1981) describe a number of problems with imagery research, and report that they could not measure some of the effects claimed to occur, perhaps because of strategic differences in the subjects' options, demand characteristics of the experiments, or knowledge applied by the subjects either consciously or unconsciously. Richman et al (1979) also suggest that strategic options may come into play according to demand characteristics of the experiment. Intons-Peterson (1981) supports her claim with a demonstration that familiar objects are imaged more successfully than unfamiliar or bizarre ones. She also points out that some features of an object may occur optionally in an image but are perceived obligatorily in the corresponding physical stimulus (Intons-Peterson 1980). Keenan & Moore (1979) note the important role that instructions play in imagery experiments. In these many studies knowledge is clearly implicated as a factor independent of imaging, yet operating upon the imagery.

People can compare their size, scan across or turn imagined objects, and in other ways manipulate the positions of the mind's eye or of the object imagined. It is often claimed that estimation of distances or comparison of objects in imagination yield functions of time to compare versus magnitude compared that are similar to the functions obtained with objects or distances present to view. Some of these results are called the *symbolic distance effect,* to capture the similarity of outcome for imagined objects and presented objects. Banks (1977) pointed out that comparative judgments can be made on linguistic or similarly nonpictorial stimuli and thus questioned the interpretation of the symbolic distance effect as necessarily pictorial; Baum & Jonides (1979) reported that distance estimates were in fact carried out differently for perceived and imagined distances. Dependence of some of the results on strategy or knowledge was brought out by Pringle & Cowan (1978), who found that complexity of the imagined object influenced performance, and that assumed rather than physical characteristics of the stimuli affected rate of imagined rotation. These are all instances of nonvisual factors affecting the visualized experience.

Finke & Kurtzman (1981c) reported that they were able to replicate their own questioned findings. Finke (1980) also proposed that some operations might be carried out identically for imagined and physically presented objects and others differently, but was not specific as to kind. Various conjectures about level or complexity of processing were also put forward by these authors.

It is useful to point out also that the greater number of investigations of imagery have concerned visual experience and visual imagery principally; yet people who write or who anticipate speaking publicly will often try out, imagine, or think about phrases, sentences, even topics of discourse; a gourmet will try to anticipate or taste imaginatively how different foods will go together at a meal or which wines would best complement them; a stage director will usually imagine beforehand the placement of actors or the sense of their movement across a stage, and so on. These are only some of the uses of imagination in cognition. In addition to its expression in visual perception, imagery may function as anticipatory action or refer to events realizable in other symbol systems.

Perceptual Equivalence

It is remarkable that in the debate over functional equivalence of perception and imagination no one has addressed the issue of net gain in understanding due to the claims. It is not clear what is won by insisting that "mental images can stimulate visual processing mechanisms directly" (Finke 1980, p. 130), or that "neural mechanisms that are activated when objects are imagined at particular locations in the visual field are like those activated when objects are observed at particular locations in the visual field" (Finke & Kosslyn 1980, p. 138), and the like.

The fact is that a large number of investigators have reported similar effects when people respond to an object physically present and when they imagine the event. At issue is the reason for the similarity: because similar distinctively visual mechanisms are involved in both instances; or because processes external to vision are influencing the visualized image, such as general knowledge, inference, practice, assumptions, and the like.

Imagery is driven by self-instruction, often triggered by a linguistic system of symbols. The experimenter requests a person, in words, to imagine something or the person instructs himself or herself to do so. Perceiving the environment does not typically require such support from or have such dependence upon language. Imagery must thus require some interaction between linguistic and pictorial symbol systems, and in this respect at least involve processes different from those required for spontaneous perception of the visible environment. Moreover, perceiving an object requires an object to be perceived, whereas imagining creates its object. This too is a fundamental difference in perceiving imagined and physically presented objects. Finke & Kurtzman (1981a) argue that "common sense" should show that if similar data are obtained for measurements of physically presented and imagined stimuli, then common mechanisms must be inculpated. However, as it is in the nature of "similarity" that at some level of description any two events can be shown to be similar, little would seem to be gained from this application of common sense, especially if the very foundations of the system of measurement are under inquiry.

Goodman (1972) shows that to say things are similar is first to have an assumption or theory of the features or properties in respect to which the similarity relation is to be judged. Similarity is thus more a property of judgment than of the objects judged, and so it can be assessed as to shape, position, color, density, means of fabrication, history, or any other distinguishable feature. Hence, to say of two things that they are similar is actually to say very little about them; claiming similarity among things is often little more than a linguistic or descriptive convenience. Quine (1969) has even argued that to state that objects are similar represents modest failure in more accurate description of or sensitivity to differences among things; everything, in the limiting case, is different from everything else. Establishing the degree of correlation between processes can illuminate features of their occurrence. Insisting that processes are fundamentally similar because they are similar in some features hinders fuller understanding.

Serial Models

It is useful to realize that assertions of equivalence implicate a structure to perceptual processing—typically, of modular components or centers arranged hierarchically. In Finke's application, the modularity implies that an appropriate signal can be inserted into a processing network and all outcomes thereafter be indistinguishable to the skilled scrutinizer. The kind of signal that would "pass" in this way would of course depend upon the level of the system at which it was inserted. Hierarchical arrangements seem to be particularly attractive to information-processing psychologists; Deutsch & Feroe (1981), among many writers, appeal to one. The models simplify description, although how faithful they are to actual psychological processing is another matter. Even computer scientists, once among the most committed of hierarchical modelers, moved first to heterarchic programming, in which control can be passed laterally, and more recently have forgone even those structures in favor of local or cooperative computation.

Notions of hierarchical organization derive from the formerly popular serial processing views in which visual experience was thought to be built up through a series of transformations, each level of the system altering by refinement the input that it turned into output (Chung 1968). Although conceptually powerful, such models have not survived the demonstration that different features of a percept are processed interactively, and apparently at local levels. For example, processing of form affects processing of color, and color was found to be sensitive to processing of movement (Kolers & von Grunau 1976). In a study of illusory depth derived from the stereoptical organization of correlated dot patterns, sometimes the depth dimension depended upon the processing of pattern, sometimes the pattern depended upon perceived depth (Lehmkuhle & Fox 1980). Similar contingent relations have been found for shape and depth (Hochberg 1982) and lightness and form (Gilchrist 1980, Rock & Smith 1981), and Shepard (1981) showed that judgments of size can depend on assumed orientation. Local contingencies play a marked role in the processing or construction of perceptual experience, whereas in a hierarchical serial system there is no obvious way that a kind of information coded later could influence the processing of an attribute coded earlier. It seems rather that everything affects everything else all the time; hence, discussion of levels or hierarchies is more an arbitrary convenience than an accurate description of perceptual processing. In the general scheme of things aspects of serial processing hold true: the flash precedes its perception, the book precedes its reading, and today precedes tomorrow. Individual events within that broad scheme seem less amenable to accurate description and dissection in terms of serial stages than was once thought to be the case. Although the appearance of an imagined object and one physically present may be very similar, therefore, the reasons for the similarity may be remote and not assignable to a model of mind; asseverations of equivalence in the various perceptual experiences do not seem to have increased understanding of any process.

Remaining Issues

The number of possible contaminants of measurements of imagery is large: tacit knowledge, past experience, method of measurement, attention, demand characteristics, as Pylyshyn (1981) and Banks (1981) especially have claimed. Kosslyn, Finke, and Pinker have plausible counterarguments for each of the critical contentions taken individually. Rebutting arguments individually rarely allays the disquiet underlying the arguments, however. Pylyshyn and the other propositionalists, in turn, misconstrue symbolization. Neither the propositionalists nor the pictorialists seem to be able finally to persuade the other, for good reason; and in fact the arguments have begun to assume a stereotypy and predictability that no longer illuminates issues. The arguments sometimes seem like those of Medieval Scholastics debating the attributes of imagined Powers, and this aspect of the debate has taken on some of the inutility of the earlier one that led to the rejection of imagery by the Behaviorists. How the imaging is achieved, whether it can be inculcated, how it depends upon the person's history and whether it may go beyond it, what processes and mechanisms it depends upon, what uses imaging can be put to—these and like questions seem to me to be somewhat more interesting than discussion of whether imagery (and mind) are better described as propositional or pictorial, or than blanket assertions that imagery uses the same mechanisms as visual perception. The pragmatic rather than the ontological status of imagery may be the richer road for the study of perception and mind.

Cognitive Maps

One use to which imagery and its study have been put is called cognitive maps. The notions of place learning versus response learning relate the topic to the disputes among animal psychologists of some years ago. The more cognitive students of learning, such as Krechevsky (1932) and Tolman (1948), argued for intelligence in rats and an ability to relate to an environment, whereas the more reinforcement-oriented theoreticians argued for acquisition of habituated responses (Spence 1951). Do people acquire detailed habits, responses, or do they develop a sense of place, an implicit environment in which to move? And what is the reference for their skill, lists of language-like statements or schematic geometric layouts?

Some of the issues were studied in connection with mobility and representation by the blind. The blind typically form tunnels in space, as it were, fixed paths rather than spatial layouts in mind. Armstrong (1978) found that by proper instruction the tunnels could be expanded into larger-scale, more map-like representations. Vincent (1980) devised an instructional technique that enables the blind to make remarkably accurate two-dimensional pictures of three-dimensional objects that they had experienced theretofore only by touch. The implication seems clear that the congenitally blind can imagine three-dimensional space, and configurations within the space, in the absence of visual support or visual experience. Since many visual functions are known to deteriorate at the physiological level with disuse (Freeman 1979), it is not clear what aspects of visual function other than the symbolic would be activated by these techniques.

The simple assumption about cognitive maps is that they are wholistic spatial representations of an environment, great plans of space. This has been shown to oversimplify; mental maps seem to have at least some reference points or familiar landmarks (Oatley 1974, Sadalla et al 1980), and Sherman et al (1980, p. 561) suggest that "An unnecessarily restrictive implication of the term 'map' is an image-like format with attendant analog principles governing the retrieval and use of spatial information." A sense of orientation and assumptions about space affect map use (Sholl & Egeth 1980), as do assumptions about the interpretation to be assigned to symbols used in drawing maps (Underwood 1980). Skill is important: Eley (1981) found that geographers' mental maps were principally spatial, whereas Hintzman et al (1981) suggest that among college students mental maps are not singular objects but are composed from linguistically based information. Foos (1980) reports that the order in which information about a locale was supplied critically affected the success of a symbolic construction, and suggested that the construction was largely the linguistic representation of spatial relations. Sherman et al (1979) confirmed that a person's pattern of travel through an environment will affect the cognitive representation of its structure, and Thorndyke & Stasz (1980) found that methods and procedures directed at map reading greatly influenced the information people were able to retrieve from maps. Most of the information was delivered, however, in a linguistically controlled way. Ward & Russell (1981) suggest that a person's relation to an environment encompasses many experiential dimensions.

Consensus and reason suggest that maps are created in mind and are used in partial, not wholistic ways; a person imagines regions or sections, not wholes. Use of these regions seems to be based on a mix of a sense of spatial layout supplemented by language-like commentary. In this respect the findings should be interpreted as suggesting not that mental maps are principally spatial or principally linguistic, but rather that in appropriate coordination, linguistic and pictorial symbols can supplement and enhance each other. Language and pictures seem to convey different kinds of information, and convey it in different ways (Goodman 1968, Gonzales & Kolers 1982). Ways of presenting information and the kinds of information different media readily represent are only beginning to be studied (Bertin 1980).

Individual differences seem to be quite marked in imagery (Cooper 1982). One wonders whether people who grow up in large cities are more likely to code their movements in terms of language-based instructions whereas people who grow up in rural environments are more likely to code the environment spatially or by compass. Illustrating the fact of individuality, Shepard's (1981) description of mind makes it principally spatial and geometric; Newell's (1980) account makes it linguistic and algebraic. Even this seems restrictive. Some people may prefer to represent pictorially, others linguistically, but some by movement, others still in sound masses, still others by affective "feel," and some perhaps by smells. Indeed, some people may use a number of representational procedures to code their perceptual experiences in different circumstances, and these need not all reduce to a common descriptor. It may be a bit soon to affirm with too much vigor that all the capabilities of mind are usefully captured by any single formalism.

REPRESENTATION

Perhaps one of the most difficult problems for the student of perception is to devise a means for representing what is fundamentally a private experience. The objects perceived are external to the observer and so are consensually reportable; their perception is internal and private. Moreover, it is not the objects of the world that are internalized but only some representation of them. Perceptions are symbols that stand for or represent external objects or events; symbols moreover that are experienced by each person privately. The problem is to find a way of correlating these symbols in personal experience with the objects attributed to the world external to the perceiver.

Some Views

Many approaches to this formidable problem have been tried, for the questions have a long history in the study of mind. Modern approaches range from the view that there is no problem because evolution has aided us to see the world as it really is (Shaw & Turvey 1981), to the view that mind has acquired suitable transformational operations for modeling the world, either in geometry (Shepard 1981) or in algebra (Anderson 1976, Newell 1980), to claims that rather than perception or mind modeling the world, worlds are created by mind and perception (Goodman 1978, Wheeler 1979).

At a more elementary level is the issue of the proper description of forms and of ways of representing them. Perceptual experience is of discrete objects moving in space; the compelling question is how the continuous flux of stimulation falling on sensory surfaces is translated into that experience. Earlier approaches sought the answer in matching operations (templates), or analytical operations (feature analysis, contour tracing), or grammars of vision (reviewed in Kolers & Eden 1968, Uhr 1973, Watanabe 1972). Standard notions of template do not seem to appeal to psychologists, many of whom believe that the mind works on abstractions of experience rather than its instances. Workers in Scene Analysis, the branch of artificial intelligence concerned with machine recognition of visible objects, sought a visual grammar, a description in terms of elements that were combined according to rule, much as the transformational grammarians approached the problem of analyzing sentences into syntactic structures. More recent efforts, stimulated in large measure by the work of the late David Marr and his associates (summarized in Frisby 1980, Marr 1980, Stent 1981) take a bottom-up view of processing, and with the aid of more powerful computers try to arrive at an identified object through successive stages of analysis and integration of the light input. Strong claims are made in some of this work for its relevance to human vision; the claims are often too strong.

The notion that the visual system writes descriptions of what it sees was proposed by Clowes (1971) and Sutherland (1968) and, in a variation, is now considered by Rock and his associates (Rock & Smith 1981, Rock & Gutman 1981). It is not clear how such descriptions could be derived from a continuous stimulus flux, however. A description requires elements for its composition, and it is just their identity that is unknown and is sought in the study of perception. Other sorts of hypothesis-testing or top-down approaches had varied success (Kasvand 1972). Marr suggested that knowledge-based processes be avoided in favor of conceptually simpler operations carried out on the incident stimulus itself. His untimely death has slowed an interesting approach to vision, albeit one whose application to the human condition seemed limited. In a discussion of motion perception from that perspective (Ullman 1979), for example, mathematical elegance or computational convenience were often given precedence over perceptual or experimental facts.

Coding

Topics related to representation have been revived in several volumes from their long slumber. It should not surprise the reader that first efforts are remarkably inclusive formalisms. The propositionalists are not content only to model imagery with sets of propositions; there seems to be a dread among them of allowing for experience, and memory for events in terms of experience, and they try to model all knowledge and all of mind's operations in lists of statements. Their procedure is to analyze observables into classes of features and then to propose rules for their combination. This makes for mathematical and manipulative convenience but with uncertain consequences for proper understanding of psychological processes. The level of abstraction at which the arguments are carried forward, moreover, may not even be appropriate to the phenomena or likely mechanisms that produce them. A concern with, say, whether the propositional or the predicate calculus is the proper tool for representing perception and memory for sentences (Anderson 1976) may be construed, at least, as somewhat premature, especially as there is still sufficient argument over the mechanisms of remembering (Cermak & Craik 1979).

Palmer (1978) tried to cope with representation by describing types; the relation between a world of objects (he calls this a represented world) and schemes for ordering or arranging the objects (a representing world). In describing these relations, Palmer begs the question of object identification, however; his analysis is merely a description of alternate ways of coding or categorizing objects, but does not deal with the basic problem of how objects are first created perceptually out of their continuous physical enviroment. Like many other workers in the higher reaches of cognition, Palmer takes for granted that the eyes or the ears do their work of presenting to consciousness well-formed objects, which consciousness is then able to operate on according to specifiable rule. How that work is carried out, and whether the way it is carried out limits the application of rules as descriptors, are among the many difficult questions that tend to be ignored by these workers. [As two samples of the difficulty of the problem of identifying constituents, Beck et al (1982) conclude their series of experiments with the observation that object perception is based on local conditions rather than on the global statistics of displays, whereas Harvey & Gervais (1981) hold that forms can be built up out of spatial frequencies. Barlow (1981) meanwhile surveyed some of the features of the representational problem from a neurophysiological and operational perspective.]

A related kind of oversimplification of issues is found in recent work on perception of alphabetic characters. McClelland & Rumelhart (1981) utilized a set of alphabetic characters composed from a small number of geometric features and found weights that described the contribution of the constituents to recognition. In the natural task, people recognize characters in many different type faces, however, apparently utilizing different features, perhaps even different strategies, for the different faces (Kolers 1969, Shimron & Navon 1981), and the transfer from practice on one face to performance on another often inculpates transformational operations that are not visible in either the training or test faces (Kolers et al 1980). Building into one's stimuli features on whose use a "theory" is formalized, as McClelland and Rumelhart have done, may reveal more about the authors' tactics in research than about their subjects' tactics in perception.

It may also be noted that many experiments propose that the perception of pictures or of the words that name them can be referred to a common mental representation (Snodgrass & Vanderwart 1980, among others). The experiments seem to be misconceived, however, for no questions regarding pictorial features of the drawings (or of the words) are usually asked of the subjects. Questions regarding characteristics of the medium are appropriate to test for pictorial features—color, shape, position on the page, for example. Instead, the subjects are tested for the name of the drawn object or are tested to see whether the drawing influenced the perception or memory of the words. In such experiments the drawings are not used as pictorial objects; they are used only pictographically, as alternate ways of writing the names that are realized also in the words. The experiment is roughly equivalent to testing whether presenting a numeral such as *5* would influence the recall of the word *five* or vice versa. This is hardly a proper test of whether words and pictures, once perceived, are stored in a common abstract way. Calis & Leeuwenberg (1981), Collard & Leeuwenberg (1981), and van Tuijl & Leeuwenberg (1979), in turn, continued efforts to devise a notational system for shape, but without much surety that the code matches a psychological process.

The input to the human visual system is undifferentiated light which, through mechanisms, skill, and practice, the person comes to segregate into the experience of objects and events, personal symbols. The human experience is based on scene-sampling, on overlapped inputs derived from eyes that move about approximately three times per second. The stability of human perception of objects is thus based on neurophysiological processing by unknown numbers of cells responding to varieties of stimulation in an eye moving about at a variable rate. If we accept the fact that the universe is constant change, recognition of any object is actually a matter of assigning an identity relation across disparate instances; it is not a matter of matching identical copies. Further, it is difficult to believe that all minds operate preferentially with the same geometric or linguistic formalism to capture all their competences. Recent work on perception and use of language is pertinent to this point. There it is claimed that although some children and adults learn rules and regularities, others are better described as instance learners or situation learners (Peters 1977, Snow & Hoefnagel-Hoehle 1979). The difference seems to be a fundamental discriminator and suggests, as Brooks (1978) did also, that many behaviors are described better as situational than as rule-governed. [Actually, the very notion of rule is ambiguous, as Howard (1980) brings out.] Old contrasts distinguish "analytic" and "synthetic" people, wholists and analysts, people who think in pictures and people who think in words. The relation of symbol manipulation to skills in processing is suggested in books by Howard (1982) and Sudnow (1978), who comment deeply on perception from the perspective of skilled performance in the arts. Goodman (1982) suggests that, rather than in words or pictures only, people can think in all of the ways in which they have manipulable systems of symbols. A general increase in interest in the problems of symbolization is apparent, as in Bates et al (1979) among others, especially in an effort to trace skills in symbolization to the history of personal activity.

Perceptual Organization

An interesting collection of essays on the problems of perceptual organization has been edited by Kubovy & Pomerantz (1981). The papers were presented at a conference in 1977 and subsequently were updated; they vary from reviews of research programs to elaborations of points of view, and span the field. To mention just a few, Julesz reviews his long-term search for an accounting of object perception out of the statistics of the study of random dot patterns; Hochberg discusses some aspects of motion perception and appeals to a Helmholtzian sort of mental supplementation; Shepard proposes that the mind models the world through development of a geometric "deep structure"; and Shaw and Turvey propose that there may not be a mind, and there certainly is not a model. The volume also contains a useful tutorial essay on spatial frequency channels (Norma Graham), two essays on auditory processing (Kubovy and A. Bregman), essays on wholistic processing (Pomerantz, W. Garner, I. Biederman), on attention (D. Kahneman and A. Henik), and brief commentary by F. Attneave. Summary and synthesizing chapters by the editors add to the structure of the volume.

Machine Vision

Activity is increasing greatly among computer scientists interested in implementing vision in machines, particularly in such topics as motion, depth, and object (reviewed in Barrow & Tenenbaum 1981, Flinchbaugh & Chandrasekaran 1981, Tsotsos et al 1980); a contrast of alternate views is found in a volume of proceedings (Beck & Rosenfeld 1982). It is especially interesting to note an increased effort to model systems in parallel, both biological systems (Lennie 1980) and machine systems (Feldman & Ballard 1982). This contrasts with the previous wholesale commitment to serial processing that dominated the psychological modeling of the past two decades. A particular feature of the computationalist approach, however, is that it often begins with the objects of perception, much as Palmer did, with the nameable or discernible features that are already the products or outputs of human perceptual processing. To put it another way, the computer scientist takes, say, discernible movement of objects in space as the event to be modeled, whereas the psychologist is often more interested in modeling the means by which object and movement are created perceptually.

Perception is based on personal symbols; on the results of psychological work carried out in the argot of a person's particular experience of a stimulus. In contrast, the details the machine is to respond to and the mode of its operation are built in and assigned by the programmer and hardware specialist. The features that a human responds to are not fully known, the features that the machine is to respond to are predetermined. In this sense, the symbol system appropriate to description of human and machine performance may share little, the one based on a system of personal symbols, the other based on a system of symbols consensually arrived at. It would seem to be important not to confuse the objects of experience with the procedures for creating them. The contents of consciousness may provide a programmer a starting point for designing an artificial vision system; the means by which his or her own visual system created the experience of those objects cannot be identified with straightforward computations such as the vision system might carry out. Although the study of human perceiving may continue to inform the study of machine vision, it remains to be seen whether students of computer vision will teach us much about human perceiving. A pessimistic projection would be that the interaction of students of machine vision and human vision may be no more illuminating than the relation of any pair of people, one of whom wonders about the structure of his or her own experience or why things happen as they do, while the other tries mainly to get a machine to work.

Visual Fatigue

A topic of practical importance to many students of perception is the human's reaction to viewing CRTs or related electronic screens. It is estimated that 10 million CRTs are in use now, and recent publicity has encouraged the belief that numerous hazards attend their use; complaints have been reported from 35% to 100% of users in various studies. The principal complaints mentioned are fear of radiation from the screen of the display unit and stresses induced in the users, including muscle strain and visual fatigue. Newspaper reports have listed complaints that vary from eyestrain and headache to defects among the offspring of pregnant users. Issues such as luminance and contrast of the displays (Stone et at 1980) are important to performance; and such features, along with the design of the workplace, room lighting, position of the monitor, and the like seem to be of great significance (Cakir 1980). Radiation levels, however, seem to be indistinguishable from background noise. Dainoff et al (1981) surveyed some of the worker complaints; Matula (1981) prepared a bibliography on the subject; both of these papers are included in two special issues of the journal *Human Factors* devoted to aspects of viewing CRTs (Bhise & Rinalducci 1981). The complexity of the issue of "visual fatigue" is brought out anew with efforts to model it as a direct process (Malmstrom et al 1981) or to assign it to conditions that cause discomfort, such as poor design of a workplace, glare, muscular tension, and the like. The weight of evidence at the present time suggests that the hazards of viewing CRTs are related more to ergonomic factors associated with the work environment than to radiation. In fact, greater hazards may be associated with the use of ophthalmic instruments used to examine the interior of the eye (Sperling 1980) than with the use of CRTs.

Acknowledgment

Preparation of this report was supported in part by Grant A7655 from National Science and Engineering Research Council Canada.

Literature Cited

Adelson, E. H., Jonides, J. 1980. The psychophysics of iconic storage. *J. Exp. Psychol: Hum. Percept. Perform.* 6: 486–93

Allen, F. 1926. The persistence of vision. *Am. J. Physiol. Optics* 7:439–57

Anderson, J. R. 1976. *Language, Memory, and Thought.* Hillsdale, NJ: Erlbaum. 546 pp.

Anderson, J. R. 1978. Arguments concerning representations for mental imagery. *Psychol. Rev.* 85:249–77

Armstrong, J. D. 1978. The development of tactual maps for the visually handicapped. In *Active Touch,* ed. G. Gordon, pp. 249–61. Oxford: Pergamon

Averbach, E., Coriell, E. 1961. Short-term memory in vision. *Bell Syst. Tech. J.* 40:309–28

Banks, W. P. 1977. Encoding and processing of symbolic information in comparative judgments. In *The Psychology of Learning and Motivation,* ed. G. Bower, 11:101–59. New York: Academic

Banks, W. P. 1981. Assessing relations between imagery and perception. *J. Exp. Psychol: Hum. Percept. Perform.* 7: 844–47

Banks, W. P., Barber, G. 1980. Normal iconic memory for stimuli invisible to the rods. *Percept. Psychophys.* 27: 581–84

Barlow, H. B. 1981. Critical limiting factors in the design of the eye and visual cortex. *Proc. R. Soc. London Ser. B* 212: 1–34

Barrow, H. G., Tenenbaum. J. M. 1981. Computational vision. *Proc. IEEE* 69: 572–95

Bates, E., Benigni, L., Bretherton, I., Camaioni, L., Volterra, V., and collaborators. 1979. *The Emergence of Symbols: Cognition and Communication in Infancy.* New York: Academic. 381 pp.

Battersby, W. S., Defabaugh, G. L. 1969. Neural limitations of visual excitability: After-effects of subliminal stimulation. *Vision Res.* 9:757–68

Baum, D. R., Jonides, J. 1979. Cognitive maps: Analysis of comparative judgments of distance. *Mem. Cognit.* 7: 462–68

Beck, J., Prazdny, S., Rosenfeld, A. 1982. A theory of textural segmentation. See Beck & Rosenfeld 1982

Beck, J., Rosenfeld, A., eds. 1982. *Human and Machine Vision.* New York: Academic. In press

Bertin, J. 1980. The basic test of the graph: A matrix theory of graph construction and cartography. In *Processing of Visible Language* ed. P. A. Kolers, M. E.

Wrolstad, H. Bouma, 2:585–604. New York: Plenum. 616 pp.

Bhise, V. D., Rinalducci, E. J., eds. 1981. CRT Viewing I, II. *Hum. Factors.* 23(4, 5)

Blanc-Garin, J. 1974. Recherches récentes sur les images mentales: Leur rôle dans les processus de traitement perceptif et cognitif. *Année Psychol.* 74:533–64

Bowen, R. W., Markell, K. A. 1980. Temporal brightness enhancement studied with a large sample of observers: Evidence for individual differences in brightness perception. *Percept. Psychophys.* 27:465–76

Bowen, R.W., Sekuler, R., Owsley, C.J., Markell, K. A. 1981. Individual differences in pulse brightness perception. *Percept. Psychophys.* 30:587–93

Boynton, R. M. 1961. Some temporal factors in vision. In *Sensory Communication,* ed. W. A. Rosenblith, pp. 739–56. Cambridge, Mass: MIT Press

Breitmeyer, B. G. 1980. Unmasking visual masking: A look at the "Why" behind the veil of the "How". *Psychol. Rev.* 87: 52–69

Breitmeyer, B. G., Ganz, L. 1976. Implications of sustained and transient channels for theories of visual pattern masking, saccadic suppression, and information processing. *Psychol. Rev.* 83: 1–36

Breitmeyer, B. G., Rudd, M., Dunn, K. 1981. Metacontrast investigations of sustained-transient channel inhibitory interactions. *J. Exp. Psychol: Hum. Percept. Perform.* 7:770–79

Bridgeman, B., Leff, S. 1979. Interaction of stimulus size and retinal eccentricity in metacontrast masking. *J. Exp. Psychol: Hum. Percept. Perform.* 5:101–09

Broerse, J., Crassini, B. 1980. The influence of imagery ability on color aftereffects produced by physically present and imagined induction stimuli. *Percept. Psychophys.* 28:560–68

Broerse, J., Crassini, B. 1981. Misinterpretations of imagery-induced McCollough effects: A reply to Finke. *Percept. Psychophys.* 30:96–98

Brooks, B. A., Impelman, D. M., Lum, J. T. 1981. Backward and forward masking associated with saccadic eye movement. *Percept. Psychophys.* 30:62–70

Brooks, L. 1978. Nonanalytic concept formation and memory for instances. In *Cognition and Categorization,* ed. E. Rosch, B. B. Lloyd, pp. 172–211. Hillsdale, NJ: Erlbaum

Brown, E. L., Deffenbacher, K. 1979. *Percep-*

tion and the Senses. New York: Oxford Univ. Press. 520 pp.

Caelli, T. 1981. *Visual Perception: Theory and Practice.* Oxford: Pergamon. 197 pp.

Cakir, A. 1980. Human factors and VDT design. See Bertin 1980, pp. 481–95

Calis, G., Leeuwenberg, E. 1981. Grounding the figure. *J. Exp. Psychol: Hum. Percept. Perform.* 7:1386–97

Carpenter, R. H. S. 1977. *Movements of the Eyes.* London: Pion. 420 pp.

Cermak, L. S., Craik, F. I. M., eds. 1979. *Levels of Processing in Human Memory.* Hillsdale, NJ: Erlbaum. 479 pp.

Chung, S. -H. 1968. Neurophysiology of the visual system. See Kolers & Eden 1968, 3:82–103

Clowes, M. B. 1971. On seeing things. *Artif. Intell.* 2:79–116

Collard, D., Leeuwenberg, E. 1981. Judged temporal order and spatial context. *Can. J. Psychol.* 35:323–29

Coltheart, M. 1980. Iconic memory and visible persistence. *Percept. Psychophys.* 27:183–228

Cooper, L. A. 1982. Strategies for visual comparison and representation: Individual differences. In *Advances in the Psychology of Human Intelligence,* ed. R. J. Sternberg, Vol. 1. Hillsdale, NJ: Erlbaum

Dainoff, M. J., Happ, A., Crane, P. 1981. Visual fatigue and occupational stress in VDT operators. *Hum. Factors* 23:421–38

Deutsch, D., Feroe, J. 1981. The internal representation of pitch sequences in tonal music. *Psychol. Rev.* 88:503–22

Dick, A. O. 1974. Iconic memory and its relation to perceptual processing and other memory mechanisms. *Percept. Psychophys.* 16:575–96

Di Lollo, V. 1980. Temporal integration in visual memory. *J. Exp. Psychol: Gen.* 109:75–97

Dodge, R. 1907. An experimental study of visual fixation. *Psychol. Rev. Monogr. Suppl.* 8:whole No. 35

Eley, M. G. 1981. Imagery processing in the verification of topographical cross-sections. *Educ. Psychol.* 1:39–48

Eriksen, C. W. 1980. The use of a visual mask may seriously confound your experiment. *Percept. Psychophys.* 28:89–92

Eriksen, C. W., Collins, J. F. 1965. Reinterpretation of one form of backward and forward masking in visual perception. *J. Exp. Psychol.* 70:343–51

Eriksen, C. W., Marshall, P. H. 1969. Failure to replicate a reported U-shaped visual masking function. *Psychon. Sci.* 15:195–96

Erwin, D. E. 1976. The extraction of information from visual persistence. *Am. J. Psychol.* 89:659–67

Feldman, J. A., Ballard, D. H. 1982. Connectionist models and their properties. *Cogn. Sci.* In press

Felsten, G., Wasserman, G. S. 1980. Visual masking: Mechanisms and theories. *Psychol. Bull.* 88:329–53

Finke, R. A. 1979. The functional equivalence of mental images and errors of movement. *Cogn. Psychol.* 11:235–64

Finke, R. A. 1980. Levels of equivalence in imagery and perception. *Psychol. Rev.* 87:113–32

Finke, R. A. 1981. Interpretations of imagery-induced McCollough effects. *Percept. Psychophys.* 30:94–95

Finke, R. A., Kosslyn, S. M. 1980. Mental imagery acuity in the peripheral visual field. *J. Exp. Psychol: Hum. Percept. Perform.* 6:126–39

Finke, R. A., Kurtzman, H. S. 1981a. Mapping the visual field in mental imagery. *J. Exp. Psychol: Gen.* 110:501–17

Finke, R. A., Kurtzman, H. S. 1981b. Area and contrast effects upon perceptual and imagery acuity. *J. Exp. Psychol: Hum. Percept. Perform.* 7:825–32

Finke, R. A., Kurtzman, H. S. 1981c. Methodological considerations in experiments on imagery acuity. *J. Exp. Psychol: Hum. Percept. Perform.* 7:848–54

Finke, R. A., Schmidt, M. J. 1977. Orientation specific color after-effects following imagination. *J. Exp. Psychol: Hum. Percept. Perform.* 3:599–606

Fisher, D. F., Monty, R. A., Senders J. W., eds. 1981. *Eye Movements: Cognition and Visual Perception.* Hillsdale, NJ: Erlbaum. 360 pp.

Flinchbaugh, B. E., Chandrasekaran, B. 1981. A theory of spatio-temporal aggregation for vision. *Artif. Intell.* 17:387–408

Foos, P. W. 1980. Constructing cognitive maps from sentences. *J. Exp. Psychol: Hum. Learn. Mem.* 6:25–38

Foster, D. H. 1978. Action of red-sensitive color mechanism on blue-sensitive color mechanism in visual masking. *Opt. Acta* 25:1001–4

Foster, D. H. 1979. Interactions between blue- and red-sensitive color mechanisms in metacontrast masking. *Vision Res.* 19:921–31

Fox, R. 1978. Visual masking. In *Handbook of Sensory Physiology.* Vol. 8: *Perception,* ed. R. Held, H. W. Leibowitz, H.-L. Teuber 20:629–53. Berlin: Springer

Freeman, R. D., ed. 1979. *Developmental Neurobiology of Vision.* New York: Plenum. 446 pp.

Frisby, J. P. 1980. *Seeing: Illusion, Brain and Mind.* Oxford: Oxford Univ. Press. 160 pp.

Fry, G. A. 1934. Depression of the activity aroused by a flash of light by applying a second flash immediately afterwards to adjacent areas of the retina. *Am. J. Physiol.* 108:701–7

Gilchrist, A. L. 1980. When does perceived lightness depend on perceived spatial arrangement?. *Percept. Psychophys.* 28:527–38

Goldstein, E. B. 1980. *Sensation and Perception.* Belmont, Calif: Wadsworth. 492 pp.

Gonzalez, E. G., Kolers, P. A. 1982. Words and pictures as representations. *J. Biocommun.* 9(2):22–27

Goodman, N. 1968. *Languages of Art.* Indianapolis: Bobbs-Merrill. 2nd ed., 1976, Indianapolis: Hackett. 277 pp.

Goodman, N. 1972. Seven strictures on similarity. In *Problems and Projects* 9:437–47. Indianapolis: Bobbs-Merrill. 462 pp.

Goodman, N. 1978. *Ways of Worldmaking.* Indianapolis: Hackett

Goodman, N. 1982. On thoughts without words. *Cognition* 10: In press

Green, M. 1981. Spatial frequency effects in masking by light. *Vision Res.* 21:861–66

Greenough, W. T. 1975. Experiential modification of the developing brain. *Am. Sci.* 63:37–46

Greenough, W. T. 1978. Development and memory: The synaptic connection. In *Brain and Learning,* ed. T. Teyler. Stamford, Conn: Greylock

Growney, R. 1978. Metacontrast as a function of the spatial frequency composition of the target and mask. *Vision Res.* 18:1117–23

Hagen, M. A., ed. 1980. *The Perception of Pictures,* Vols. 1, 2. New York: Academic. 293 pp., 356 pp.

Hartley, A. A. 1981. Mental measurement of line length: The role of the standard. *J. Exp. Psychol: Hum. Percept. Perform.* 7:309–17

Hartline, H. K., Wagner, H. G., Ratliff, F. 1956. Inhibition in the eye of *Limulus. J. Gen. Physiol.* 39:651–73

Harvey, L. O., Gervais, M. J. 1981. Internal representation of visual texture as the basis for the judgment of similarity. *J. Exp. Psychol: Hum. Percept. Perform.* 7:741–53

Hellige, J. B., Walsh, D. A., Lawrence, V. W., Prasse, M. 1979. Figural relationship effects and mechanisms of visual masking. *J. Exp. Psychol: Hum. Percept. Perform.* 5:88–100

Hintzman, D. L., O'Dell, C. S., Arndt, D. R. 1981. Orientation in cognitive maps. *Cogn. Psychol.* 13:149–206

Hochberg, J. 1982. How big is a stimulus? In *Organization and Representation in Perception,* ed. J. Beck, pp. 191–217. Hillsdale, NJ: Erlbaum

Howard, V. A. 1980. Theory of representation: Three questions. See Bertin 1980, pp. 501–15

Howard, V. A. 1982. *Artistry: The Work of Artists.* Indianapolis: Hackett. 212 pp.

Humphrey, G. 1951. *Thinking.* London: Methuen. 331 pp.

Intons-Peterson, M. J. 1980. The role of loudness in auditory imagery. *Mem. Cognit.* 8:385–93

Intons-Peterson, M. J. 1981. Constructing and using unusual and common images. *J. Exp. Psychol: Hum. Learn. Mem.* 7:133–44

Intons-Peterson, M. J., White, A. R. 1981. Experimenter naivete and imaginal judgments. *J. Exp. Psychol: Hum. Percept. Perform.* 7:833–43

Kasvand, T. 1972. Experiments with an on-line picture language. See Watanabe 1972, pp. 223–64

Keenan, J. M., Moore, R. E. 1979. Memory for images of concealed objects: A reexamination of Neisser and Kerr. *J. Exp. Psychol: Hum. Learn. Mem.* 5:374–85

Kim, S. 1981. *Inversions.* Peterborough, NH: BYTE/McGraw-Hill. 122 pp.

Kolb, H., Nelson, R., Mariani, A. 1981. Amacrine cells, bipolar cells, and ganglion cells of the cat retina: A Golgi study. *Vision Res.* 21:1081–1114

Kolers, P. A. 1962. Intensity and contour effects in visual masking. *Vision Res.* 2:277–94

Kolers, P. A. 1968. Some psychological aspects of pattern recognition. See Kolers & Eden 1968, 1:4–63

Kolers, P. A. 1969. Clues to a letter's recognition: Implications for the design of characters. *J. Typogr. Res.* 3:145–67 (now *Visible Language*)

Kolers, P. A., Eden, M., eds. 1968. *Recognizing Patterns: Studies in Living and Automatic Systems.* Cambridge, Mass: MIT Press. 237 pp.

Kolers, P. A., Palef, S. R., Stelmach, L. B. 1980. Graphemic analysis underlying literacy. *Mem. Cognit.* 8:322–28

Kolers, P. A., Rosner, B. S. 1960. On visual masking (metacontrast): Dichoptic observation. *Am. J. Psychol.* 73:2–21

Kolers, P. A., Smythe, W. E. 1979. Images,

symbols, and skills. *Can. J. Psychol.* 33:158–84

Kolers, P. A., von Grunau, M. 1976. Shape and color in apparent motion. *Vision Res.* 16:329–35

Kosslyn, S. M. 1980. *Image and Mind.* Cambridge, Mass: Harvard Univ. Press

Kosslyn, S. M. 1981. The medium and the message in mental imagery: A theory. *Psychol. Rev.* 88:46–66

Kosslyn, S. M., Ball, T. M., Reiser, B. J. 1978. Visual images preserve metric spatial information: Evidence from studies of image scanning. *J. Exp. Psychol: Hum. Percept. Perform.* 4:47–60

Kosslyn, S. M., Pomerantz, J. R. 1977. Imagery, propositions, and the form of internal representations. *Cogn. Psychol.* 9:52–76

Krechevsky, I. 1932. "Hypotheses" in rats. *Psychol. Rev.* 39:516–32

Kubovy, M., Pomerantz, J. R., eds. 1981. *Perceptual Organization.* Hillsdale, NJ: Erlbaum. 506 pp.

Kunen, S., May, J. G. 1981. Imagery-induced McCollough effects: Real or imagined? *Percept. Psychophys.* 30:99–100

Legge, G. E. 1978. Sustained and transient mechanisms in human vision: Temporal and spatial properties. *Vision Res.* 18:69–81

Lehmkuhle, S., Fox, R. 1980. Effect of depth separation on metacontrast masking. *J. Exp. Psychol: Hum. Percept. Perform.* 6:605–21

Lennie, P. 1980. Parallel visual pathways: A review. *Vision Res.* 20:561–94

Levine, M. W., Shefner, J. M. 1981. *Fundamentals of Sensation and Perception.* Reading, Mass: Addison-Wesley. 516 pp.

Lévy-Schoen, A., O'Regan, K. 1979. The control of eye movements in reading. In *Processing of Visible Language,* ed. P. A. Kolers, M. E. Wrolstad, H. Bouma, 1:7–36. New York: Plenum. 537 pp.

Long, G. M. 1980. Iconic memory: A review and critique of the study of short-term visual storage. *Psychol. Bull.* 88:785–820

Long, G. M., Sakitt, B. 1981. Differences between flicker and non-flicker persistence tasks: The effects of luminance and the number of cycles in a grating target. *Vision Res.* 21:1387–93

Lowe, D. G. 1975. Processing of information about location in brief visual displays. *Percept. Psychophys.* 18:309–16

Lyon, J. E., Matteson, H. M., Marx, M. S. 1981. Metacontrast in the fovea. *Vision Res.* 21:297–99

MacLeod, D. I. A. 1978. Visual sensitivity. *Ann. Rev. Psychol.* 29:613–45

Malmstrom, F. V., Randle, R. J., Murphy, M. R., Reed, L. E., Weber, R. J. 1981. Visual fatigue: The need for an integrated model. *Bull. Psychon. Soc.* 17:183–86

Marr, D. 1980. Visual information processing: The structure and creation of visual representations. *Philos. Trans. R. Soc. London Ser. B.* 290:199–218

Massaro, D. W., Klitzke, D. 1979. The role of lateral masking and orthographic structure in letter and word recognition. *Acta Psychol.* 43:413–26

Matula, R. A. 1981. Effects of visual display units on the eyes: A bibliography (1972–1980). *Hum. Factors* 23:581–86

McClelland, J. L., Miller, J. 1979. Structural factors in figure perception. *Percept. Psychophys.* 26:221–29

McClelland, J. L., Rumelhart, D. E. 1981. An interactive activation model of context effects in letter perception: Part 1. An account of basic findings. *Psychol. Rev.* 88:375–407

Merikle, P. M. 1980. Selection from visual persistence by perceptual groups and category membership. *J. Exp. Psychol: Gen.* 109:279–95

Mewhort, D. J. K., Campbell, A. J. 1980. The rate of word integration and the overprinting paradigm. *Mem. Cognit.* 8:15–25

Miller, G. A., Galanter, E., Pribram, K. H. 1960. *Plans and the Structure of Behavior.* New York: Holt. 226 pp.

Neisser, U. 1967. *Cognitive Psychology.* New York: Appleton-Century-Crofts. 351 pp.

Newell, A. 1980. Physical symbol systems. *Cogn. Sci.* 4:135–83

Oatley, K. 1974. Mental maps for navigation. *New Sci.* 64:863–66

Paivio, A. 1971. *Imagery and Verbal Processes.* Toronto: Holt, Rinehart & Winston. 596 pp.

Paivio, A. 1978. The relationship between verbal and perceptual codes. In *Handbook of Perception,* Vol. 8: *Perceptual Coding,* ed. E. C. Carterette, M. P. Friedman, 11:375–97. New York: Academic. 417 pp.

Paivio, A., te Linde, J. 1980. Symbolic comparisons of objects on color attributes. *J. Exp. Psychol: Hum. Percept. Perform.* 6:652–61

Palmer, S. E. 1978. Fundamental aspects of cognitive representation. See Brooks 1978, pp. 262–303

Perkins, D. N. 1981. *The Mind's Best Work.* Cambridge, Mass: Harvard Univ. Press. 314 pp.

Peters, A. M. 1977. Language learning strategies: Does the whole equal the sum of the parts? *Language* 53:560–73

Petry, S. 1978. Perceptual changes during metacontrast. *Vision Res.* 18:1337–41

Piéron, H. 1935. Le processus du metacontraste. *J. Psychol. Normet Pathol.* 32: 5–24

Pinker, S. 1980. Mental imagery and the third dimension. *J. Exp. Psychol: Gen.* 109:354–71

Pinker, S., Finke, R. A. 1980. Emergent two-dimensional patterns in images rotated in depth. *J. Exp. Psychol: Hum. Percept. Perform.* 6:244–64

Podgorny, P., Shepard, R. N. 1978. Functional representations common to visual perception and imagination. *J. Exp. Psychol: Hum. Percept. Perform.* 4: 21–35

Pringle, R., Cowan, T. M. 1978. Mental rotation of possible and impossible four-cornered toruses. *Percept. Psychophys.* 24: 84–92

Pylyshyn, Z. W. 1973. What the mind's eye tells the mind's brain: A critique of mental imagery. *Psychol. Bull.* 80:1–24

Pylyshyn, Z. W. 1979. Validating computational models: A critique of Anderson's indeterminacy of representation claim. *Psychol. Rev.* 86:383–94

Pylyshyn, Z. W. 1980. Computation and cognition: Issues in the foundations of cognitive science. *Behav. Brain Sci.* 3: 111–69

Pylyshyn, Z. W. 1981. The imagery debate: Analogue media versus tacit knowledge. *Psychol. Rev.* 88:16–45

Quine, W. V. 1969. Natural kinds. In *Ontological Relativity and Other Essays.* New York: Columbia Univ. Press

Ratliff, F., ed. 1974. *Studies on Excitation and Inhibition in the Retina.* New York: Rockefeller Univ. Press. 668 pp.

Rayner, K. 1978. Eye movements in reading and information processing. *Psychol. Bull.* 85:618–60

Reeves, A. 1980. Visual imagery in backward masking. *Percept. Psychophys.* 28: 118–24

Reeves, A. 1981a. Metacontrast in hue substitution. *Vision Res.* 21:907–12

Reeves, A. 1981b. Visual imagery lowers sensitivity to hue-varying, but not to luminance-varying, visual stimuli. *Percept. Psychophys.* 29:247–50

Richardson, J. T. E. 1980. *Mental Imagery and Human Memory.* New York: St. Martin's

Richman, C. L., Mitchell, D. B., Reznick, J. S. 1979. Mental travel: Some reservations. *J. Exp. Psychol: Hum. Percept. Perform.* 5:13–18

Rock, I., Gutman, D. 1981. The effect of inattention on form perception. *J. Exp. Psychol: Hum. Percept. Perform.* 7: 275–85

Rock, I., Smith, D. 1981. Alternative solutions to kinetic stimulus transformations. *J. Exp. Psychol: Hum. Percept. Perform.* 7:19–29

Rodieck, R. W. 1979. Visual pathways. *Ann. Rev. Neurosci.* 2:193–225

Sadalla, E. K., Burroughs, W. J., Staplin, L. J. 1980. Reference points in spatial cognition. *J. Exp. Psychol: Hum. Learn. Mem.* 6:516–28

Sakitt, B. 1976. Iconic memory. *Psychol. Rev.* 83:257–76

Sakitt, B., Long, G. M. 1979. Spare the rod and spoil the icon. *J. Exp. Psychol: Hum. Percept. Perform.* 5:19–30

Shaw, R., Turvey, M. T., 1981. Coalitions as models for ecosystems: A realist perspective on perceptual organization. See Kubovy & Pomerantz 1981, pp. 343–416

Shepard, R. N. 1981. Psychological complementarity. See Kubovy & Pomerantz 1981, pp. 279–342

Shepard, R. N., Podgorny, P. 1978. Cognitive processes that resemble perceptual processes. In *Handbook of Learning and Cognitive Processes,* Vol. 5: *Human Information Processing,* ed. W. K. Estes, 5:189–237. Hillsdale, NJ: Erlbaum. 337 pp.

Sherman, R. C., Croxton, J., Smith, M. 1979. Movement and structure as determinants of spatial representations. *J. Nonverb. Behav.* 4:27–39

Sherman, R. C., Oliver, C., Titus, W. 1980. Verifying environmental relationships. *Mem. Cognit.* 8:555–62

Shimron, J., Navon, D. 1981. The distribution of information within letters. *Percept. Psychophys.* 30:483–91

Sholl, M. J., Egeth, H. E. 1980. Interpreting direction from graphic displays: Spatial frames of reference. See Bertin 1980, pp. 315–30

Snodgrass, J. G., Vanderwart, M. 1980. A standardized set of 260 pictures: Norms for name agreement, image agreement, familiarity, and visual complexity. *J. Exp. Psychol: Hum. Learn. Mem.* 6: 174–215

Snow, C. E., Hoefnagel-Hoehle, H. 1979. Individual differences in second language ability: A factor analytic study. *Lang. Speech* 22:151–62

Spence, K. W. 1951. Theoretical interpretations of learning. In *Handbook of Ex-*

perimental Psychology, ed. S. S. Stevens, 18:690–729. New York: Wiley. 1436 pp.

Sperling, G. 1960. The information available in brief visual presentations. Psychol. Monogr. 74:whole No. 498

Sperling, G. 1967. Successive approximations to a model for short-term memory. Acta Psychol. 27:285–92

Sperling, G. 1970. Short-term memory, long-term memory, and scanning in the processing of visual information. In Early Experience and Visual Information Processing in Perceptual and Reading Disorders, ed. F. A. Young, D. B. Lindsley, pp. 198–218. Washington: Nat. Acad. Sci. 533 pp.

Sperling, H. G., ed. 1980. Intense light hazards in ophthalmic diagnosis and treatment. Vision Res. 20:whole No. 12

Sperry, R. W. 1976. Mental phenomena as causal determinants in brain function. In Consciousness and the Brain, ed. G. G. Globus, G. Maxwell, I. Savodnik. New York: Plenum

Stent, G. S. 1981. Cerebral hermeneutics. J. Soc. Biol. Struct. 4:107–24

Stigler, R. 1910. Chronophotische Studien ueber den Umgebungskontrast. Pfluegers Arch. Ges. Physiol. 134:365–435

Stone, P. T., Clarke, A. M., Slater, A. I. 1980. The effect of task contrast on visual performance and visual fatigue at a constant illuminance. Light Res. Technol. 12:144–59

Sudnow, D. 1978. Ways of the Hand: The Organization of Improvised Conduct. Cambridge, Mass: Harvard Univ. Press

Sutherland, N. S. 1968. Outlines of a theory of visual pattern recognition in animals and man. Proc. R. Soc. London Ser. B 171:297–317

Taylor, G. A., Chabot, R. J. 1978. Differential backward masking of words and letters by masks of varying orthographic structure. Mem. Cognit. 6:629–35

Thorndyke, P. W., Stasz, C. 1980. Individual differences in procedures for knowledge acquisition from maps. Cogn. Psychol. 12:137–75

Titchener, E. B. 1902. An Outline of Psychology. New York: Macmillan

Tolman, E. C. 1948. Cognitive maps in rats and men. Psychol. Rev. 55:189–208

Tsotsos, J., Mylopoulos, J., Covvey, D., Zucker, S. 1980. A framework for visual motion understanding. IEEE Trans. Pattern Anal. Machine Intell. 2:563–73

Uhr, L. 1973. Pattern Recognition, Learning, and Thought. Englewood Cliffs, NJ: Prentice-Hall. 506 pp.

Ullman, S. 1979. The Interpretation of Visual Motion. Cambridge, Mass: MIT Press. 229 pp.

Underwood, J. D. M. 1980. The influence of texture gradients on relief interpretation from isopleth maps. See Bertin 1980, pp. 279–90

Uttal, W. R. 1981. A Taxonomy of Visual Processes. Hillsdale, NJ: Erlbaum. 1097 pp.

Van Tuijl, H. F. J. M., Leeuwenberg, E. L. J. 1979. Neon color spreading and structural information measures. Percept. Psychophys. 24:269–84

Ventura, J. 1980. Foveal metacontrast: I. Criterion content and practice effects. J. Exp. Psychol: Hum. Percept. Perform. 6:473–85

Vincent, C. N. 1980. Pictorial recognition and teaching the blind to draw. See Bertin 1980, pp. 459–71

Von Wright, J. M. 1972. On the problem of selection in iconic memory. Scand. J. Psychol. 13:159–71

Walsh, D. A., Till, R. E., Williams, M. V. 1978. Age differences in peripheral perceptual processing: A monoptic backward masking investigation. J. Exp. Psychol: Hum. Percept. Perform. 4: 232–43

Ward, L. M., Russell, J. A. 1981. The psychological representation of molar physical environments. J. Exp. Psychol: Gen. 110:121–52

Watanabe, S., ed. 1972. Frontiers of Pattern Recognition. New York: Academic

Weber, R. J., Malmstrom, F. V. 1979. Measuring the size of mental images. J. Exp. Psychol: Hum. Percept. Perform. 5:1–12

Werner, H. 1935. Studies on contour: I. Qualitative analyses. Am. J. Psychol. 47: 40–64

Wheeler, J. A. 1979. Frontiers of time. In Problems in the Foundations of Physics, Rendiconti della Scuola Internazionale di Fisica 'Enrico Fermi', ed. N. Toraldo di Francia, 72:395–497. Amsterdam: North-Holland

White, C. W., Lorber, C. M. 1976. Spatial-frequency specificity in visual masking. Percept. Psychophys. 19:281–84

Wilson, J. T. L. 1981. Visual persistence at both onset and offset of stimulation. Percept. Psychophys. 30:353–56

Ann. Rev. Psychol. 1983. 34:167–93
Copyright © 1983 by Annual Reviews Inc. All rights reserved

DIAGNOSIS AND CLINICAL ASSESSMENT: THE DSM-III

H. J. Eysenck

Institute of Psychiatry, University of London, London, SE5 8AF, England

James A. Wakefield, Jr.

Department of Psychology, California State College, Stanislaus, Turlock, California 95380

Alan F. Friedman

Del Mar Psychiatric Clinic, 240 9th Street, Del Mar, California 92014

CONTENTS

INTRODUCTION

The problems raised by the elaboration and use of methods of diagnosis and clinical assessment are basically theoretical; yet in surveys such as this the emphasis is of necessity on psychometric niceties and questions of test construction, reliability, etc. In concentrating our discussion on topics related to DSM-III, we have tried not only to look at the factual material

167

available, but also to raise some fundamental questions. Others we have been unable to deal with because of space limitation. The quantitative and test-construction related training of the psychologist has led to the creation of many devices which are meant to aid in diagnosis and clinical assessment; yet psychologists have been reluctant to question the truly important assumptions on which much of their work is based. Is it really sensible to work with tests designed for the purpose of assigning individuals to psychiatric categories when these categories are largely arbitrary, have no scientific status, cannot be reliably assessed, and contradict in their very conception the strong evidence pointing in the direction of a dimensional rather than a categorical system of measurement (Eysenck 1970)? Should we not, as independent scientists, work out a system of classification based on empirical evidence, psychological theory, and experimental support, rather than accept more or less blindly a medical system whose only virtue (if that be the right term) seems to be that it is based on some form of consensus? Can any system be acceptable to workers trained in scientific method where diagnosis (e.g. of schizophrenia) depends far more on the nationality of the person making the diagnosis than on any behavior shown by the patient (Cooper et al 1972)? Does the unreliability of psychiatric diagnosis perhaps indicate not so much a failure in the methods of clinical assessment used, but rather a fundamental fault in the whole conception of "mental disease"? These are the sorts of questions which readers should constantly have in mind when reading the evidence available on DSM-III. The system may be acceptable to psychiatrists, but in our view it is not acceptable in principle to psychologists, and no tinkering with it will solve the basic faults inherent in the general model constructed by generations of psychiatrists.

RESEARCH AND CONCERNS LEADING TO DSM-III

The DSM-II (APA 1968) included definitions of 10 general areas of mental disorders. For each of the specific diagnoses, descriptive definitions were presented along with occasional examples of situations in which the diagnosis would or would not be appropriate. The DSM-II was designed to correspond with the ICD-8 (WHO 1968), although a few ICD-8 diagnoses were not included and several other ICD-8 diagnoses were split into more specific categories. The DSM-II also attempted to avoid implying causes in the names of the diagnoses unless the cause was critical to the diagnosis. For example, "Schizophrenic reaction" in the DSM-I was changed to "schizophrenia" in the DSM-II. Without specific criteria, diagnosis on the basis of DSM-II depended heavily on the judgement of the clinician. Neither reliability nor validity studies were reported in the manual.

Jackson (1970) criticized the DSM-II shortly after it was published. Problems with the DSM-II were lack of definition of terms such as symptom and syndrome, classification of neurosis as a disease, and an inadequate section on childhood disorders. These criticisms have been addressed by the DSM-III, although not to the satisfaction of all critics.

Tarter et al (1975) evaluated the reliability of diagnosis using the DSM-II. Overall agreement between two of five experienced psychiatrists' diagnoses of 256 patients was 48%. The agreement for organic disorders was 72%, functional psychoses 55%, neuroses 46%, and personality disorders 48%. Depressive neurosis (Klerman et al 1979) was a particularly vague, unreliable, and overused category. This and similar neurotic categories were excluded from DSM-III.

McGuire (1973) reviewed the percentage agreements on diagnostic categories among psychiatrists in studies performed between 1949 and 1964. The modal percentage agreements for broad categories were in the 70s, and in the 50s for specific categories. These figures do not differ greatly from those presented in the DSM-III (APA 1980a).

Spitzer et al (1975) suggested the use of formal inclusion and exclusion criteria to improve the reliability of psychiatric diagnosis. Strauss (1975) considered a multivariable approach to diagnosis as another improvement over the simple typological system then in use in the DSM-II. The five variables he suggested are similar but not identical to the five axes finally adopted in DSM-III.

A problem with the DSM-II was that it included "borderline schizophrenia" in the category of schizophrenia, latent type (Spitzer et al 1979), while there was a large literature on borderline conditions. In an attempt to include all diagnoses that clinicians believe are of clinical importance and that can be reliably defined, criteria were developed for the categories Borderline Personality Disorder and Schizotypal Personality Disorder which discriminated these patients from a control sample of moderately or severely ill psychiatric patients with diagnoses other than psychosis or borderline categories.

Consensus of opinion among psychiatrists has been of central importance in determining whether any particular category was included in the DSM. An example of the difficulties presented when consensus was not achieved is shown by Stoller et al (1973) over the issue of including homosexuality. Professional consensus is still a critical criterion for inclusion of diagnostic categories in DSM-III (APA 1980a).

THE DIAGNOSTIC AND STATISTICAL MANUAL OF MENTAL DISORDERS (DSM-III)

Two major systematic classifications in the USA antedate the development of the DSM-III. The DSM-I was published in 1952 and replaced the outdated mental illness section of the Standard Classified Nomenclature of

Diseases, the military and Veterans Administration's systems (Webb et al 1981a). The DSM-II was published in the USA in 1968 and was based on the mental disorder section of the International Classification of Diseases Eighth Edition (ICD-8). The DSM-II revision was based mainly on the systems of psychiatrists and was not field tested for reliability of diagnostic accuracy. The development of the DSM-III represents the efforts of a task force assembled in 1974 by the American Psychiatric Association (APA) to develop an improved psychiatric classification system. Besides general user dissatisfaction with the DSM-II, additional impetus for developing DSM-III was generated by plans of the World Health Organization (WHO) to create a revised International Classification of Disease (ICD-9) system. The ICD is a classification system containing numerous disease entities and is published for worldwide use in general by the WHO. Because the mental disorders section of the ICD-9 was unacceptable to many clinicians, it was modified to make it more compatible for use with the DSM-III in this country (Webb et al 1981a). This change resulted in ICD-9-CM (a clinical modification), which has been in effect since 1979. Some of the ICD-9-CM categories are not listed in DSM-III, but all DSM-III categories are listed in ICD-9-CM.

The major goals of the DSM-III task force in revising the psychiatric nomenclature revolved around the general existing aim to reflect the many advances in the knowledge of psychopathology. Specifically, the task force focused on creating meaningful diagnostic categories that would allow treatment and management decisions in varied settings, reliable diagnostic categories, acceptability to clinicians and researchers of varying theoretical orientations, and consistency with research data bearing on the validity of diagnostic categories (DSM-III, APA 1980a). A number of rough drafts were constructed and examined in field studies using actual patients before the final manual was published. These numerous field studies were conducted to identify various problems with the system and to explore alternatives that were more satisfactory. According to Spitzer (APA 1980a, p. 5) "12,667 patients were evaluated by approximately 550 clinicians, 474 of whom were in 212 different facilities, using successive drafts on DSM—III." According to Spitzer, the majority of participants responded favorably to DSM-III.

The DSM-III (APA 1980a) is published in the form of a 494-page text that consists of an introduction, 3 chapters, 5 appendixes, and an index. The first chapter is simply a listing of the various diagnostic categories with concomitant code numbers. Chapter 2 describes how to use the DSM-III system. There is a detailed description of how to make use of the multiaxial system that serves as the system's foundation, and useful clinical examples are presented. The third chapter describes the psychiatric syndromes as well as conditions not attributable to a mental disorder that are a focus of treatment or attention. The chapter also explains how to specify whether there is insufficient information to make a diagnosis. Each of the listed mental disorder categories in the chapter contains information about associated features, typical age at onset, course of illness, level of impairment, various complications, predisposing factors, prevalence, sex ratio, familial pattern, and differential diagnosis.

While the DSM-III manual contains lengthy information about the various disorders, it should be noted that the abbreviated 267-page pocket edition of the manual called the "Quick Reference" (APA 1980b) eliminates the lengthy discourses and provides the user with the vital information for making use of the system (e.g. decision trees for differential diagnosis, diagnostic criteria for the disorders). It has been recommended that the quick reference be employed for daily clinical use, with the manual used as a reference text (Webb et al 1981a). It is also suggested that the interested reader consult the DSM-III training guide (Webb et al 1981a), which is designed as a self-instructional guide in the use of the DSM-III system and can be used as an adjunctive aide in teaching and preparing professionals in the use of the DSM-III system. Additional training aides (e.g. videotape, slides) are available to assist educators in preparing professionals in the application of the new classification system. The training guide is concise (158 pages) and is divided into four sections with a total of 24 chapters. Section I describes the history and development of DSM-III, explains the rationale for the system, contrasts the gross differences between DSM-II and DSM-III, and outlines the relationship between the mental disorders sections of ICD-9-CM and DSM-III. Section II focuses primarily on the diagnostic criteria and describes the major classifications on their respective axes. Section III looks at specific disorders in some detail with case vignettes included to illustrate the various classifications. Section III is designed to present case examples and instructs the reader in the use of coding procedures. The authors state that the training guide could be used in conjunction with the DSM-III manual to "assist the clinician in accurately applying the new classification system to the diagnosis of patients and clients" (page xv, Webb et al 1981a). It should be noted, however, that the codes are not listed for each of the categories of DSM-III, so the "training guide" cannot be used exclusively in lieu of the DSM-III manual. Additional case material is presented by Spitzer et al (1981).

The DSM-III is described as atheoretical in nature in that the various diagnostic categories are descriptive and do not imply an etiological basis in the disorders. The nonetiological, atheoretical, and descriptive nature of the DSM was intentional so as not to alienate potential users from diverse theoretical orientations. The more than 200 disorders and conditions included in DSM-III have been grouped into 18 distinguishable groups. These various groups or disorders are categorized on 2 of 5 axes used in the DSM-III system. Basically the 5 axes each represent a different class of information. Axis I represents the clinical psychiatric syndrome that is the focus of treatment or attention. Axis II represents the personality disorders which may be ascribed to adults, adolescents, or children, as well as specific developmental disorders for children and adolescents, and, in some cases, adults. Axis III is reserved for physical disorders that are relevant to either or both of the first two axes. Axis IV represents a coding of the severity of stressors judged to be precipitating or contributing to a disorder noted on either axis I or II. A basic 7-point continuum is used for deciding the severity level and is dependent upon the clinician's judgment. Axis V represents the highest level of adaptive functioning of the individual within a year of his/her presenting complaints and is used primarily for making a prognosis. Adaptive functioning refers to social relations, occupational functioning, and use of leisure time. Similar to Axis IV, a 7-point continuum is used on Axis V for ascertaining the premorbid functioning level of the individual.

The first two axes include the entire set of categories relevant to making a psychiatric diagnosis (including conditions which are not considered mental disorders but which are a focus of attention or treatment). The following 16 disorders or conditions are coded on Axis I:

1. Disorders Usually First Evident in Infancy, Childhood, or Adolescence
2. Substance Use Disorders
3. Organic Mental Disorders
4. Schizophrenic Disorders
5. Psychotic Disorders not elsewhere classified
6. Paranoid Disorders
7. Affective Disorders
8. Anxiety Disorders
9. Dissociative Disorders
10. Somatoform Disorders
11. Factitious Disorders
12. Psychosexual Disorders
13. Disorders of Impulse Control not elsewhere classified
14. Adjustment Disorders
15. Psychological Factors Affecting Physical Condition
16. Codes for Conditions Not Attributable to a Mental Disorder

The following two disorders are noted on Axis II: Personality Disorders and Specific Developmental Disorders. This listing does not follow the exact sequence of disorders as listed in DSM-III, but rather follows the schema as Webb et al have it mapped out in their training guide. Webb et al state that "there is no simple, perfect flow in this sequence, but, in general, the classification begins with disorders arising in early years, then disorders with some organic element, then major (psychotic) disorders, followed by more and more minor classes of disorders and the two Axis II disorders." The following brief synopsis (taken in large part from Webb et al 1981a) of important features within each of the 18 listed major categories should help familiarize the reader with the major changes between DSM-III and DSM-II.

Disorders Usually First Evident in Infancy, Childhood, or Adolescence: Although diagnoses for children should first be checked in this section, it is possible that an adult diagnosis may be applicable. A childhood diagnosis may also apply to an adult (e.g. anorexia nervosa). The disorders in this section cover 5 general areas reflecting the basic area of disturbance. These five areas are: Intellectual, Behavioral, Emotional, Physical, and Developmental. The categories covered in these 5 areas are: Mental Retardation, Attention Deficit Disorder, Conduct Disorder, Anxiety Disorders of Childhood or Adolescence, Other Disorders of Infancy, Childhood or Adolescence (reactive attachment disorder of infancy, schizoid disorder of childhood or adolescence, elective mutism, oppositional disorder, identity disorder) eating disorders, stereotyped movement disorders, other disorders with physical manifestations, pervasive developmental disorders, and specific developmental disorders (which are coded on Axis II). This DSM-III category represents extensive modifications in classification that are beyond the scope of this paper, and the interested reader should consult the manual.

The *Substance Use Disorders* classification refers to the abnormal consumption of alcohol, drugs, and tobacco. A substance is identified and then the degree of use (abuse or dependence) is noted, followed by the pattern of intake (e.g. continuous, episodic). The DSM-II drug dependence category did not include tobacco and alcohol (coded separately), whereas the DSM-III subsumes them under the Substance Use Disorders.

Organic Mental Disorders replaces the DSM-II category title of Organic brain syndromes. In DSM-II Organic brain syndrome was essentially viewed as one syndrome with a specified number of manifestations; OBS was either classified as psychotic or nonpsychotic. This distinction is dropped in DSM-III as is the chronic vs acute classification. The DSM-III system includes 9 different organic brain syndromes: intoxication, withdrawal, delirium, dementia, amnestic syndrome, delusional syndrome, hallucinosis, affective syndrome, and personality syndrome.

The *Schizophrenic Disorders* category represents a refinement over the usually inconveniently used DSM-II concept of schizophrenia. Among the many changes in DSM-III regarding this category is the dropping of the nonpsychotic type schizophrenias which have been labeled previously as latent schizophrenia, simple schizophrenia, and pseudoneurotic schizophrenia. A personality disorder diagnosis must now be made for such cases.

The restrictive criteria specified made schizophrenia a very serious illness, including aberration in a variety of mental functions. The use of inclusive and exclusive criteria for this disorder purportedly enables the clinician to identify a group that is more similar in regard to differential response to somatic therapy, familial pattern, a tendency toward onset in early adult life, recurrence, and severe functional impairment.

Psychotic Disorders not elsewhere classified covers the following four categories: Brief Reactive Psychosis, Schizophreniform Disorder, Schizoaffective Disorder, and Atypical Psychosis. What was termed in DSM-II as "acute schizophrenic episode" now covers the first two above-mentioned disorders. In Brief Reactive Psychosis, symptoms appear after a recognizable psychosocial stressor and last less than 2 weeks. Schizophreniform Disorder meets all of the criteria for schizophrenia but lasts more than 2 weeks less than 6 months. When a clinician is unable to differentiate between affective disorder and either schizophrenia or schizophreniform disorder, the category Schizoaffective Disorder is used. Atypical Psychosis is a residual category for cases in which there are psychotic symptoms that do not meet the criteria for any specific mental disorder (e.g. psychoses with mixed clinical features which do not permit a more specific diagnosis).

The *Paranoid Disorders* are psychotic states characterized by an organized delusional system in an otherwise well functioning individual. The four disorders within this classification are Paranoia, Acute Paranoid Disorder, Shared Paranoid Disorder, and Atypical Paranoid Disorder. Duration is the main differential defining feature between Acute Paranoid Disorder and Paranoia. Shared paranoid disorder is reserved for someone who has a relationship with someone who has a paranoid psychotic state of any class and through the relationship adopts the delusions of the paranoid person. In the past this has been traditionally labeled *Folie à deux*. Atypical Paranoid Disorder is a residual category for paranoid disorders not classified in any of the specific categories. While the paranoia classification is similar to the DSM-II category of paranoia, the other categories in this area represent new defining features in DSM-III.

The *Affective Disorders* category is reserved for disturbances in mood and is divided into three subclasses: 1. Major Affective Disorders: includes bipolar disorder and major depression. The major distinguishing features include a full affective syndrome and the presence or absence of any history of a manic episode. 2. Other Specific Affective Disorders: includes cyclothymic and dysthmic disorders and is described by a partial affective syndrome of at least 2 years duration. 3. Atypical Affective Disorders: includes atypical bipolar disorder and atypical depression, both of which are residual categories for individuals who cannot be classified in the above-mentioned categories. It should be noted that the new criteria for affective disorders enlarges the boundary definition for this condition and makes the diagnosis of Schizophrenic Disorders somewhat more restrictive than in the past.

Anxiety Disorders is characterized by those conditions whereby the individual directly experiences felt anxiety. In the DSM-II the concept of neurosis included conditions where anxiety was directly and indirectly experienced (e.g. hysterical neurosis, conversion type). Many of the DSM-II neurotic conditions are now under new separate headings. Some have been completely eliminated (e.g. hysterical neurosis) with multiple meanings of the term included within new categories (e.g. Somatoform and Dissociative Disorders). The DSM-III Anxiety Disorders are: Phobic Disorders (formerly phobic neuroses), Anxiety States (formerly anxiety neuroses) and Post-traumatic Stress Disorder.

Dissociative Disorders (formerly labeled hysterical neuroses, dissociative type in DSM-II) include the following subclasses: psychosis amnesia, psychogenic fugue, multiple personality, depersonalization disorder, and atypical dissociative disorder. Sleepwalking disorder is listed in the section "disorders usually first evident in infancy, childhood, or adolescence" and is defined as a disturbance of a particular stage of sleep.

Somatoform Disorders essentially represent somatic complaints without demonstrable organic findings or known physiological findings and the symptoms are not under voluntary control. This category includes somatization disorder, conversion disorder (formerly hysterical neurosis, conversion type), psychogenic pain disorder, hypochondriasis (formerly hypochondriacal neurosis), and atypical somatoform disorder.

Factitious Disorders is a new classification in DSM-III and is characterized by physical or psychological symptoms that are either self-inflicted or faked by the individual as a deliberate sham and are under voluntary control. Factitious Disorders with psychological symptoms has been previously referred to as Ganser syndrome, pseudo-psychosis, and pseudodementia. Chronic factitious disorders with physical symptoms involve the presentation of physical symptoms that are under voluntary control and include a history of multiple hospitalizations. This disorder has also been referred to as Munchausen syndrome, hospital hoboes, and hospital addiction. Atypical factitious disorder with physical symptoms is another residual category for those cases which do not conform to the specified criteria.

Psychosexual Disorders includes only those disorders in which psychological factors exert a major role; organic causes for physical dysfunction are not included here. They would be noted on Axis III. The psychosexual disorders are: gender identity disorders, paraphilias, psychosexual dysfunctions, ego-dystonic homosexuality, and other psychosexual disorders not elsewhere classified (a residual category). This DSM-III category includes many new categories and terms not included in DSM-II.

Disorders of Impulse Control not elsewhere classified means exactly what is implied. That is, this is another residual category that includes disorders of impulse control which are not found in other categories. The six categories in this classification are: pathological gambling, kleptomania, pyromania, intermittent explosive disorder, isolated explosive disorder, and atypical impulse control disorder. This is another new category in the DSM-III.

The *Adjustment Disorders* category in DSM-III is more encompassing than its DSM-II predecessor. This category is reserved for those maladaptive reactions that are precipitated by a psychosocial stressor and which do not meet the criteria for another specific disorder such as anxiety or affective disorder. This category replaces the DSM-II classification of "transient situational disturbances." It also excludes transient reactions of psychotic proportions since they are classified elsewhere. The adjustment disorders are subtyped by the predominant symptomatology rather than by developmental stage as in DSM-II. It was thought that the symptom picture would be important in treatment planning. The various types of symptoms associated with adjustment disorders that represent distinct subcategories are: depressed mood, anxious mood, mixed emotional features, disturbance of conduct, mixed disturbance of emotions and conduct, work or academic inhibition, withdrawal, and atypical features.

Psychological Factors Affecting Physical Condition is a new category for the DSM-III and is reserved for those complex situations where there is a bona fide organic disease but psychological factors are thought to be significant in initiating, exacerbating, or maintaining the condition.

Codes for Conditions Not Attributable to a Mental Disorder that are a focus of attention or treatment is different than its DSM-II counterpart which was limited to "individuals who are psychiatrically normal but who nevertheless have severe enough problems to warrant examination by a psychiatrist." DSM-II was remiss in not defining normality. The following DSM-III categories can be applied to individuals with mental disorders as long as the condition itself is not attributable to a mental disorder: malingering, borderline intellectual functioning, adult antisocial behavior, childhood or adolescent antisocial behavior, academic problem, occupational problem, uncomplicated bereavement, noncompliance with medical treatment, phase of life or other life circumstance problem, marital problem, parent-child problem, other specified family circumstances, and other interpersonal problem.

The following personality disorders are coded on Axis II: paranoid, schizoid, schizotypal, histrionic, narcissistic, antisocial, borderline, avoidant, dependent, compulsive, passive-aggressive, and atypical, mixed, or other personality disorder. One of these personality disorders is assigned to an individual when personality traits become maladaptive, cause subjective distress, and result in significant impairment in social or occupational functioning. Whereas DSM-II permitted the clinician to find only one appropriate personality disorder to describe the individual, DSM-III allows for multiple diagnoses if an individual meets the criteria for more than one. New terms and concepts are introduced in the DSM-III regarding personality disorders (e.g. histrionic personality disorder and borderline personality disorder) and the interested reader is referred to Millon (1981) for further study.

RESEARCH EVALUATING DSM-III

Research conducted during the development of the DSM-III was mostly concerned with the reliability of diagnosis and the acceptability of the proposed categories to clinicians. Reliability studies continue to be performed, along with studies on the effects of clinical experience and the use of formal interview schedules on the reliability of diagnosis. A few validity studies have also been done. These dealt with differential diagnosis of schizophrenia and other psychotic disorders, children's categories, and response to treatment and prognosis. One study compared DSM-III categories with MMPI codetypes.

Reliability

The interrater reliabilities reported in the DSM-III field trials were generally higher than previously achieved (Spitzer et al 1979, Spitzer & Forman 1979). For Axis I diagnoses, the overall Kappa coefficient was .78 for joint interviews and .66 for separate interviews. For Axis II—personality disorders and specific developmental disorders—the kappas were .61 (joint) and .54 (separate). For Axis IV—severity of psychosocial stressors—the kappas were .62 (joint) and .58 (separate). For Axis V—highest level of adaptive functioning in the past year—coefficients of .80 (joint) and .69 (separate) were reported. Reliabilities for Axis III—physical conditions—were not reported. The DSM-III also produced an overall kappa of .74 for the diagnoses of 95 adolescent inpatients (Strober et al 1981).

A study (Pfohl 1980) on the effects of clinical experience on rating DSM-III symptoms of schizophrenia compared the interrater reliabilities of 11 psychiatry staff physicians, 11 resident physicians, and 11 medical students. After watching interviews of two patients by an experienced psychiatrist, the three groups were asked to rate symptoms from the DSM-III criteria for schizophrenia. None of the three groups produced significant interrater reliabilities on the symptoms. Webb et al (1981b), however, reported an overall 74% agreement between workshop participants and clinical faculty for diagnoses on a series of videotaped case vignettes.

Morey (1980) presented DSM-III symptoms of schizophrenia, mania, and dementia to 15 psychologists and 15 psychiatrists. The clinicians were asked to sort the symptoms according to their importance in reaching each of the three diagnoses. The median correlation among clinicians for these ratings was .55. There were only a chance number of significant differences between the psychologists and psychiatrists in their ratings of the symptoms.

Robins et al (1981) have presented a diagnostic interview schedule that permits lay interviewers or clinicians to make diagnoses according to DSM-III. All concordances between lay interviewers' and psychiatrists' diagnoses were greater than .4 and all but one were greater than .5. Raskin & Hall (1979) used DSM-III criteria to construct an 80-item inventory defining narcissistic personality disorder.

Validity

Diagnosis of schizophrenia using DSM-III requires 6 months of illness. While this requirement is restrictive, one study (Helzer et al 1981) found that of 125 subjects diagnosed as schizophrenic by the DSM-III, none showed a change in diagosis over time.

Using DSM-III criteria, information from interviews with the families of acutely psychotic patients influenced the differential diagnosis of schizophrenia and mania (Braden, et al 1980). Symptoms of mania were reported by the family more frequently than by the patient. Sole reliance on interviews with the patient may lead to underdiagnosis of mania and overdiagnosis of schizophrenia. However, using DSM-III criteria altered the ratio of diagnosed schizophrenia to diagnosed manic-depressives from 12:1 to approximately 1:1 (Keisling 1981).

The DSM-III identifies persecutory and jealousy delusions with paranoid disorders and all other delusions (in the absence of an affective disorder) with schizophrenia. Kendler (1980) points out that several reviews of empirical evidence do not support this distinction.

The presence and number of schizophrenic symptoms from DSM-III in manic patients were unrelated to a variety of demographic, clinical, historical, laboratory, and familial variables (Abrams & Taylor 1981). Schizophrenic symptoms do not play an important role in patients who satisfy diagnostic criteria for mania.

Evans & Elliott (1981) focused on the confusion about schizophrenia in deaf patients. Using a symptom checklist from DSM-III, six symptoms were identified as usual in psychotic and nonpsychotic deaf patients while nine symptoms were identified as useful for screening for schizophrenia in deaf patients.

Attention deficit disorder without hyperactivity as defined in the DSM-III characterized 17% of patients aged 7 to 14 seen in a child psychiatry service (Maurer & Stewart 1980). Of these, 80% had other psychiatric disorders. Attention deficit disorder without hyperactivity appears not to be an independent syndrome as suggested by the DSM-III.

A comparison of the description of the children's diagnostic categories in the DSM-III with first-order factors from several studies of children's behavior indicated that generally DSM-III categories are more specific than factors derived from behavior instruments (Dreger 1981). Of course, with the higher-order factors, the DSM-III categories had to be collapsed substantially to produce any correspondence with the empirical behavioral factors. This author notes that factor analytic work has apparently influenced the classification of children's disorders more than that of the adult disorders in the DSM-III. A comparison of adult behavioral factors and DSM-III categories would probably produce even less agreement than was the case for children.

Four studies published together consider the use of the DSM-III with childhood psychiatric disorders. The average rater agreement of 20 psychiatrists with the diagnosis the authors considered most appropriate was less than 50% (Cantwell et al 1979b). Average interrater agreement of DSM-III Axis I was about the same (but slightly lower) than that for DSM-II (54 vs 57%) (Mattison et al 1979). The multiaxial system of DSM-III produced more complete diagnoses for complex cases (Russell et al 1979) and is generally preferred over DSM-II (Cantwell et al 1979a).

While DSM-III does not use response to therapy in its system, this information actually is used to aid in diagnosis. Of 31 patients diagnosed as schizophrenic by DSM-III criteria, almost one-third (9) responded to a 2-week lithium trial (Herschowitz et al 1980). Most of the responders fit the criteria for schizophreniform disorder and for good prognosis schizophrenia. The response of these patients to lithium suggests that they should be considered cases of affective disorders with atypical schizophrenic-like features.

The DSM-III melancholia criteria correctly identified 77% of a sample of 123 inpatients into those with an autonomous syndrome and those who responded to psychosocial intervention without drug treatment (Nelson et al 1981). The melancholia criteria were more selective than were the primary affective disorder criteria.

Suicide attempts, mostly not serious, occurred in most (28 of 39) patients diagnosed as antisocial personality disorder (Garvey & Spoden 1980). These authors suggest that previous suicide attempts be considered as a potential addition to DSM-III criteria.

The DSM-III provides categories of stress response syndromes that were not included in DSM-II (Horowitz et al 1980). Intrusive ideas and feelings are prevalent in these patients.

Winters, Weintraub & Neale (1981) investigated the relationships between codetypes from the Mini-Mult [71 items from the MMPI (Kincannon 1968)] and diagnoses from DSM-II and DSM-III. For DSM-II depression, DSM-III unipolar depression, and DSM-III bipolar depression, concordances of greater than 70% between codetypes (Marks et al 1974) and diagnoses were obtained. The concordances were not significantly different from each other. The concordance between DSM-II schizophrenia and schizophrenic codetypes was 68%, while the concordance between these codetypes and DSM-III schizophrenia was only 37%.

THEORETICAL ASPECTS OF DSM-III

The DSM-III was intended to be atheoretical and useful for clinicans who hold a variety of theories of psychopathology. Judging from several of the critical responses to the DSM-III, the committee of (mostly) psychiatrists who developed it allowed theoretical assumptions to influence their work, although not as much as other critics would have liked. Most reactions to the DSM-III focused on the "medical model" or categorical approach to mental disorders. The DSM-III was criticized by behavior therapists, dynamic therapists, and clinicans concerned with several specific categories.

On the positive side, Spitzer, Williams & Skodol (1980) discuss the major achievements of the DSM-III and compare it to the DSM-II. The process of developing the DSM-III took 5 years and included representation from various professional groups. Consensus was achieved on most controversial diagnostic categories. A definition of mental disorder that stresses the presence of either distress or disability was offered. Operational diagnostic criteria were included. Diagnostic reliability was generally improved over DSM-II. Finally, the DSM-III represents a multiaxial system of evaluation. The first three axes constitute the official diagnostic assessment, and the last two are available for research for special clinical purposes.

The DSM-III includes the category of ego dystonic homosexuality (Spitzer 1981a). This category avoids the issue of whether homosexuality is abnormal, which became highly publicized during the revision of DSM-

II. In the DSM-III, homosexuality is a disorder if the patient is distressed about it and not a disorder otherwise.

Murphy (1980) lists nine features of DSM-III and concludes that it is superior to its predecessors as a manual for community research. On a more critical note, Skinner (1981) considered the DSM-III simultaneously as a scientific theory that should be open to empirical falsification and as a diagnostic system that should be subjected to standards similar to those required of a psychological test. The different axes of the DSM-III imply different classification models. Both Axes I (clinical psychiatric syndrom) and II (personality or developmental disorder) have implicit hierarchical structures, mixing quantitative distinctions (levels of mental retardation) with clearly qualitative distinctions (sleepwalking vs eating disorder). Axes IV (psychosocial stressors) and V (level of adaptive functioning in past year) are quantitative ratings of severity of impairment. With regard to internal properties, particularly interrater reliability, the DSM-III appears to be a substantial improvement over earlier systems of diagnosis. The validity of DSM-III, on the other hand, seems to have been ignored, although it is far more researchable than its predecessors.

Cantor et al (1980) consider psychiatric diagnoses made with the DSM-III as examples of prototype categorization which they distinguish from classical categorization. Prototypes consist of larger sets of correlated features rather than selected defining features as in the classical. "Messy" aspects of diagnosis from a classical perspective, such as heterogeneity of category membership, borderline cases, and imperfect reliability, are seen as fundamental properties of the system from the prototype viewpoint. DSM-III diagnoses are more similar to prototype classifications than were DSM-II diagnoses. Depending on correlated features, prototype diagnoses are more similar to psychometric and factor analytic dimensions than to medical categories.

Woods (1979) sees the revision of the DSM as an opportunity to examine assumptions underlying classification systems. The change from listing typical features of classes as in DSM-II (e.g. class X has features A, B, C, and sometimes D) to presenting criteria in DSM-III (e.g. to diagnose X, A and B *must* be present and at least two of C, D, E, F, G) makes the boundaries between diagnostic classes clearer. Since disagreements among clinicians usually involve boundary or borderline cases rather than disagreements over the nature of the categories, agreement should be higher with the DSM-III. An additional axis for rating the environment is suggested.

McReynolds (1979) objects to the extension of the "medical model" to many new behavioral disturbances in the DSM-III. A similar criticism in the area of childhood disorders is presented by Garmezy (1978). The emphasis of the DSM-III on the medical model, closed categories, and artificial classifications will prevent it from being a standard research tool, although certain features of the DSM-III may improve clinical practice (Zubin 1977–78).

Schacht & Nathan (1977) focus on the potential negative consequences for psychologists of DSM-III. DSM-III considers mental disorders as a subset of medical disorders and requires a statement about nonmental medical disorders on Axis III to complete a diagnostic evaluation. These characteristics greatly enlarge the domain of psychiatry and diminish the domain of other mental health workers. Legislators and insurers may use the adoption of DSM-III to require that mental disorders be first diagnosed by physicians who would then decide whether psychologists would treat them.

Foltz (1980) presented the wary reaction of the Board of Directors of the American Psychological Association to the DSM-III. The DSM-III extended the definition of mental illness into areas not previously claimed by psychiatry. The weakest area of DSM-III was in child and adolescent disorders where a psychological system might be constructed to compete with DSM-III. The categories in DSM-III were said to be "created or deleted based on committee vote rather than on hard data." The DSM-III was also criticized for using a categorical rather than a dimensional model.

In an article defending the DSM-III against criticism from psychologists, Spitzer (1981b) pointed out that the motivation for DSM-III was not to establish psychiatric hegemony over the mental health professions but simply to coincide with the revision of the World Health Organization's International Classification of Diseases (ICD). He denies that the DSM-III is based on the "medical model" since this term is vague. Any expansion of the concept of mental disorders in DSM-III is in terms of specificity, not to increase the scope of mental disorders. He also suggests that psychologists might construct their own classification system that might supplement or compete with DSM-III. It will be difficult, however, for psychologists simply to ignore DSM-III.

In an article dealing with teaching the DSM-III system to clinicians, Skodal, Spitzer & Williams (1981) list the following as areas of ambiguity and controversy. Is assessing *dimensions* more useful than choosing diagnostic *categories*? Should psychodynamic material concerning the development of psychopathology be included in the system? How valid are the discriminations among the categories?

Although the DSM-III is intended to be atheoretical, it has been criticized from a psychodynamic orientation for attempting to draw a sharp and artificial line between classification and explanation (Frances & Cooper 1981). Descriptive categories in the DSM-III and psychodynamic explanation overlap and are dependent on each other. Also from a psychodynamic viewpoint, Karasu & Skodol (1980) criticize the DSM-III for failing to make diagnostic discriminations needed to plan psychotherapy treatments. They recommend the inclusion of a treatment-oriented sixth axis for the DSM-III.

McLemore & Benjamin (1979) argue that functional mental disorders are implicitly diagnosed on the basis of interpersonal behavior. They hypothesize that an approach based formally on interpersonal diagnosis could compare favorably with the DSM-III.

Harris (1979) discussed the implications of DSM-III for children in the context of behavior therapy. The DSM-III is more detailed than the DSM-II, and the greater detail should contribute to the reliability of the system. Also, DSM-III avoids psychodynamic assumptions and focuses more on observable behavior. The two strongest reservations about DSM-III are that response to treatment and treatment recommendations are not included in the system and that previously nonmedical problems falling into the domains of speech therapists, educators, and counselors have been now defined as psychiatric/medical disorders.

Fox (1981) compares the DSM-II and DSM-III concepts of schizophrenia. The question of the appropriate classification of schizoaffective disorders is problematic for clinicians. The same seems to be true for nonclinicians (North & Cadoret 1981). All five popular published accounts of "schizophrenia" reviewed failed to meet the DSM-III criteria for schizophrenia. They usually met the criteria for affective disorders or a naturally remitting condition such as depression. Support for "cures" based on these accounts is misleading.

Lieberman (1979) criticizes the treatment of "schizoaffective" illness in DSM-III. These patients defy the validity of the schizophrenic-affective dichotomy on which current models of diagnosis are based.

On the other hand, Strauss (1979) discusses his view of the appropriate treatment of schizophrenia using the five axes of DSM-III. New DSM-III criteria and definitions of organic mental disorders should stimulate research on these neglected categories (Lipowski 1980a). Akiskal (1980) proposes that biological techniques be used to validate DSM-III diagnoses particularly in the area of affective disorders. Additional biological criteria might improve diagnostic accuracy in this area.

The DSM-III had been criticized (Tu 1980) for failing to include epilepsy in the nosological system while including 21 subcategories of sexual disorders.

Lipowski (1980b) considered the diagnosis of delirium using the DSM-III criteria. The criteria were criticized for including the vague terms "clouding of consciousness" and "speech that is at times incoherent" while leaving out any reference to abnormal thinking and failing to require laboratory evidence of disordered cerebral function such as EEG slowing.

Frances (1980) discusses the low reliability of the personality disorders section of the DSM-III as compared with the other major sections. A problem with personality diagnosis is that continuous and correlated personality differences do not fit easily into a categorical system. Although the DSM-III does allow for multiple and mixed diagnoses and provides "schizotypal" and "borderline" categories, a dimensional rather than categorical system should receive increasing attention in the future.

In what appears to be a compromise between the dimensional nature of personality differences and practical pressures to state categorical diagnoses, Millon (1981) has discussed the personality disorders on Axis II. He views these as basically dimensional and shows how the categories on Axis II fit his dimensional view. Millon considers the relevance of Axis II information to Axis I diagnoses. He also provides recommendations for treatment which are completely excluded from DSM-III.

TOWARD DSM-IV

What are the pressures that will shape DSM-IV? A tentative answer to this question may be found by examining the pressures that led to DSM-III. First, it should be recognized that DSM-III is primarily a *professional* manual and only secondarily, if at all, a *scientific* manual. The strong pressures influencing the revision of the DSM are the practical concerns of communication within the profession and defining the legitimate boundaries of the profession. These concerns are best dealt with through consensus. The DSM-IV must be in at least general agreement with the next revision of the ICD. Consensus within the profession must be obtained even if it means voting on the abnormality of homosexuality. The willingness of government, patients, and especially third party payers to accept the manual must be respected, even if it means defining some conditions as normal because insurance companies might refuse to pay for them (Spitzer 1981b).

What about the influence of scientific research on the revision of the DSM? Scientific research cannot be completely ignored. Considerable effort went into demonstrating a marginal improvement in reliability for DSM-III. Nevertheless, some diagnoses were included simply because they were made by some group of psychiatrists. From reading DSM-II and DSM-III, one might think that less is known about etiology now than was known earlier. However, the absence of causal implications in diagnostic labels (e.g. reaction) does not come from empirical research but from an attempt to achieve professional consensus. Likewise, the absence of treatment recommendations is an attempt to achieve consensus among the various "schools," whose members would certainly object if a competitor's treatment were recommended over their own.

Unfortunately, the route from scientific finding to professional application is long, taking perhaps 50 years (Eysenck & Eysenck 1979). This is certainly true of the relationship between scientific psychological research and professional application in a psychiatric setting. Diagnostic categories, for example, are a scientific anachronism, but professional consensus among psychiatrists and their need to justify themselves to other physicans as practicing a proper medical speciality treating categorical disease entities demand categories. The attacks of Szasz (1974) and Laing (1976) from within psychiatry intensify this "reaction."

Given these pressures, it should probably be recognized that recommendations from scientific research will have only gradual and belated impact on future revisions of the DSM. Nevertheless, some recommendations are offered.

First, categorical diagnosis must be replaced with dimensional assessment (Lang, 1978). Linnaean taxonomic systems (Rome 1979) are apparently appropriate for classifying different species when quantitative differences between them become relatively large. Large differences and adaptation to different environmental circumstances result in different noninterbreeding populations. "Borderline" cases between species are rare or nonexistent. Medical categorical diagnosis may be appropriate in those specialities in which each diagnosis can be matched with a specific causal species of pathogen. In other specialties involving specific causes that are not species of microorganism, such as major gene defects and specific dietary deficiencies, a categorical approach is useful.

Psychological problems, however, are not generally analogous to these medical specialties. (Of course, major gene defects such as Down's syndrome and the psychological consequences of infectious diseases such as syphillis are exceptions.) They are usually more extreme examples of behavior shown by unquestionably "normal" persons every day. The identification of certain behaviors as abnormal depends in some part on their infrequency. Since these infrequent behaviors form continua with more frequent "normal" behavior, any cutoff between normal and abnormal will necessarily produce more "borderline" cases than clearly abnormal cases. The necessity of large "borderline" categories in DSM-III attests to the inadequacy of a categorical approach to psychopathology.

The alternative to categorical diagnosis is dimensional assessment. The degree of a certain type of behavioral deficiency can be (and for most of this century, in the case of intelligence, has been) measured along a scale with known reliabilities and validities and communicated clearly. Even with intelligence, which is the best established behavioral dimension, the DSM-

III continues to provide several heterogeneous and arbitrarily defined categories when the single score on the intelligence dimension provides much clearer information. Even when adaptive behavior, which allows the cutoffs to be adjusted five points in either direction, is considered, simply communicating these two scores would provide clearer information than would the category label "mild retardation."

For the present, the candidates for behavioral dimensions for assessment include intelligence (Eysenck 1979) and its subfactors and the personality dimensions of extraversion, neuroticism, and psychoticism (Eysenck 1976, 1981). The literature on causes (Eaves & Eysenck 1975, Eysenck 1979, Fulker 1981) and consequences of these dimensions has expanded greatly during the last few years and promises to continue growing.

The second recommendation is that psychological assessments must be considered in interaction with treatment options (Cronbach & Snow 1977). Psychological research is still characterized by two parallel empirical approaches, one that predicts behavior and one that changes behavior. The separation of these two "disciplines" prolongs the time that we spend administering possibly effective treatments to inappropriate subjects. Some research has been done that attempts to match the right treatment with the right person to maximize treatment outcome for adults in counseling (DiLoreto 1971) and for children in educational settings (McCord & Wakefield 1981). An interaction between type of treatment (drug vs psychotherapy) and psychoticism has also been suggested for neurotic patients (Rahman & Eysenck 1978). A few manuals for employing empirical and theoretical interactions in treatment have become available (Goldstein 1976, Wakefield 1979, Wakefield & Goad 1982). Much more interactional research is required.

A third recommendation—that assessments be based on observable behavior rather than on subjective impressions of the clinicians—is, for the most part, no longer needed. Although several ambiguous criteria remain in the DSM-III, it is much more objective than was DSM-II and should be commended for this. Further improvements in this direction are encouraged in future revisions.

Another set of negative recommendations for future assessment practice involves ways in which assessment should not change. Several recommendations for future assessment practice have been made by psychologists representing fairly restricted viewpoints. Each of these viewpoints has something to offer assessment but has been presented as a replacement for current assessment procedures rather than as a supplement to them.

The first negative recommendation is not to replace assessment of a person's behavior with assessment of the person's situation (Mischel 1968). This approach has been found wanting (Eysenck and Eysenck 1980). Even in cases in which situational variables have initiated or maintained problem behaviors, the behaviors themselves are the problems and assessment of the situation is assessment one step removed from the problem. Of course, appropriate analysis of situational variables can add a great deal to the effectiveness of treatment by allowing interactions between behavioral and situational variables to be studied and exploited. Research that identifies environmental factors and their interactions with behavioral factors is more promising than the current arbitrary task analysis approach. Unfortunately, factor analytic work with environments is more difficult.

A related concern is "committed" environmentalism. Certainly environmental effects on behavior—either direct or through interactions—should be included in treatment planning. However, environmentalist propaganda serves no useful purpose and tends to cloud issues that might be seen clearly. For example, the term "medical model" has become so widely used as a derogatory term for psychiatric diagnoses that it has lost its clear meaning (Spitzer 1981b). Referring to categorical diagnoses, this term usefully indicates a severe conceptual problem with psychiatric labels. Used by committed environmentalists, this term includes the use of physiological or genetic information in assessment, as well as the use of dimensional systems of behavioral differences that suggest any limitations on environmental control. A biological basis for individual differences, however, does not require categorical diagnosis, as can be seen in the theoretical paper by Hendrickson & Hendrickson (1980).

Another unproductive suggestion has arisen from marriage counseling. This suggestion, in various forms, is that dyads, couples, families, or systems should be the unit for assessment. The marriage literature (e.g. Gottman 1979) has called for assessing and treating the couple or family as a unit. At least one large study (Eysenck & Wakefield 1981) calls this approach into question. Effects of one spouse on the other and effects of the couple as a unit which were not completely explained by their individual additive effects were small, while overall individual contributions of personality, attitudes, and especially sexual behavior on marital satisfaction were large. Even in marriage therapy, the appropriate unit for assessment is the individual person rather than some larger unit.

OTHER DEVELOPMENTS IN CLINICAL ASSESSMENT

For assessment to have any clinical usefulness, there must be some theory linking the results of assessment to possible treatment options. The most clearly stated and widely researched theory is the model consisting of extraversion, neuroticism, psychoticism, and intelligence (Eysenck 1976,

1981). The variables in this model and their interactions with and prediction of learning (M. W. Eysenck 1981, Levey & Martin 1981), social behavior (Wilson 1981), and achievement variables (Wakefield 1979, McCord & Wakefield 1981) have been studied extensively. The underlying genetic (Eysenck 1979, Fulker 1981) and physiological determinants (Gray 1981, Powell 1981, Stelmack 1981) have been studied. Cultural factors have also been considered extensively (Al-Issa 1982). Several studies have focused on the relationship between this theory and the atheoretical MMPI (Wakefield et al 1974, 1975, Friedman et al 1982).

In the assessment of intelligence, Sattler's (1982) book on children's intelligence and abilities provides a counterpart for Matarazzo's (1972) book on adult intelligence. The heredity-environment debate (Eysenck & Kamin 1981) continues and has become the central paradigm of research in this area. Despite the premature claims of the death of this issue, the primary alternative, interactionism, appears not to be consistent with the data on intelligence (Eysenck 1979), although in personality assessment (Eysenck 1981) this approach is far more promising (Henderson 1982). In the year of Wechsler's death, the *Wechsler Adult Intelligence Scale* (Wechsler 1981) was revised. This revision consisted of fairly minor modifications in the content of the scale. The norms give IQs that are about eight points lower than before.

Neuropsychology has been the focus of considerable research recently. A particularly interesting development has been research on Luria's front-to-rear organization of abilities (Das et al 1979) and the practical measurement of abilities in this framework (Golden et al 1980, Golden 1981). Integration of this approach with the more widely publicized left-right organization has also received some attention (Golden 1981). Evidence that assessment generally aids treatment has also been forthcoming (Bradley et al 1979).

During the 1970s, a substantial literature developed around the term behavioral assessment (Hersen & Bellack 1976, Ciminero et al 1977, Haynes & Wilson 1979). The term behavioral assessment was used to distinguish treatment-related assessment procedures in behavior therapy from "traditional" assessment procedures. Behavioral assessment has been used variously to exclude only projective instruments or to exclude virtually all trait measures from the field. As it becomes more widely recognized that behavioral assessment is not exempt from properly demonstrated reliability and validity (Hartmann 1977, Lewin & Wakefield 1979, Wakefield 1980), behavioral assessment is gradually coming to terms with stable behavior traits (Eysenck & Eysenck 1980). Trait-like dimensions such as assertiveness, social skills, and fears have been (re)discovered in the behavioral assessment literature (Haynes & Wilson 1979). Older personality and intellectual traits are also frequently incorporated in behavioral assessment (Ciminero et al 1977). Projective devices, such as the Rorschach, are still firmly excluded, although higher reliabilities for the Rorschach have been reported using Exner's (1978, Wiener-Levy & Exner 1981) scoring system than have been reported in the past.

CONCLUSION

Our survey of the available evidence on the DSM-III leaves us with the impression that while an improvement on previous schedules, this new scheme is based on foundations so insecure, so lacking in scientific support, and so contrary to well-established facts that its use can only be justified in terms of social need. Psychologists may have to use the system because of social pressures of various kinds, but this should not blind them to the fundamental weaknesses of any such scheme based on democratic voting procedures rather than on scientific evidence. The fact that the categories of the scheme can be diagnosed only in a manner which results in unacceptably low reliabilities, thus giving us a criterion for test construction which hardly invites confidence, is only one of many indications of the weakness of current psychiatric theorizing, but it is not the most important. Psychologists tend to contrast in their minds the unreliability of psychiatric diagnosis with the supposititious accuracy of other types of medical diagnosis; this is wishful thinking. Medical diagnoses are extremely unreliable in all fields; when diagnoses of cause of death are compared with autopsy results, accuracy varies from 45% (Heasman & Lipworth 1966) and 47.5% (Waldron & Vickerstaff 1977) to a magnificent high of 61% (Cameron & McGoogan 1981a,b)! This is hardly better than psychiatric diagnoses! It is the absence of any indication of validity which is far more critical, as is the absence of any appreciation of the importance of scientific proof for schemes of this kind.

DSM-III includes many behaviors which have little or no medical relevance and belong properly in the province of the psychologist, e.g. gambling, malingering, antisocial behavior, academic and occupational problems, parent-child problems, marital problems, and the curious "substance use disorders," which apparently would bring almost any kind of behavior within the compass of psychiatry—drinking coffee, having sex, eating wiener schnitzel. Psychiatry has always been ill defined as a specialty (Eysenck 1975), but this is going well beyond the pale. It is the mixture of unlimited aspiration and practical failure to reach scientifically meaningful conclusions which has characterized so much psychiatric work in the past; DSM-III suggests that the aspirations have grown, if anything, while the performance of the scientific tasks implied by the scheme has badly lagged behind. Until the basic causes of this mismatch are attacked more energetically than they have been in the past, we are unlikely to see any real advance in this field.

Literature Cited

Abrams, R., Taylor, M. A. 1981. Importance of schizophrenic symptoms in the diagnosis of mania. *Am. J. Psychiatry* 138:658–61

Akiskal, H. S. 1980. External validating criteria for psychiatric diagnosis: their application in affective disorders. *J. Clin. Psychiatry* 41 (12):6–15

Al-Issa, I. 1982. *Culture and Psychopathology.* Baltimore: Univ. Park Press

American Psychiatric Association. 1968. *Diagnostic and Statistical Manual of Mental Disorders.* Washington DC: APA. 2nd ed.

American Psychiatric Association. 1980a. *Diagnostic and Statistical Manual of Mental Disorders.* Washington DC: APA. 3rd ed.

American Psychiatric Association. 1980b. *Quick Reference to the Diagnostic Criteria from DSM-III.* Washington DC: APA.

Braden, W., Bannasch, P. R., Fink, E. B. 1980. Diagnosing mania: the use of family informants. *J. Clin. Psychiatry* 41:226–28

Bradley, P. E., Battin, R. R., Sutter, E. F. 1979. Effects of individual diagnosis and remediation for the treatment of learning disabilities. *Clin. Neuropsychol.* 1 (2):25–32

Cameron, H. M., McGoogan, E. 1981a. A prospective study of 1152 hospital autopsies: I. Inaccuracies in death certification. *J. Pathol.* 133:273–83

Cameron, H. M., McGoogan, E. 1981b. A prospective study of 1152 hospital autopsies: II. Analysis of inaccuracies in clinical diagnoses and their significance. *J. Pathol.* 133:285–300

Cantor, N., Smith, E. E., French, R. D., Mezzieh, J. 1980. Psychiatric diagnosis as prototype categorization. *J. Abnorm. Psychol.* 89:181–93

Cantwell, D. P., Mattison, R., Russell, A. T., Will, L. 1979a. A comparison of DSM-II and DSM-III in the diagnosis of childhood psychiatric disorders: IV. Difficulties in use, global comparison, and conclusions. *Arch. Gen. Psychiatry* 36:1227–28

Cantwell, D. P., Russell, A. T., Mattison, R., Will, L. 1979b. A comparison of DSM-II and DSM-III in the diagnosis of childhood psychiatric disorders: I. Agreement with expected diagnosis. *Arch. Gen. Psychiatry* 36:1208–13

Ciminero, A. R., Calhoun, K. S., Adams, H. E., eds. 1977. *Handbook of Behavioral Assessment.* New York: Wiley

Cooper, J. E., Kendell, R. E., Gurland, B. J., Sharpe, L., Copeland, J. R. M., Simon, R. 1972. *Psychiatric Diagnosis in New York and London.* London: Oxford Univ. Press

Cronbach, L. J., Snow, R. E. 1977. *Aptitudes and Instructional Methods.* New York: Wiley

Das, J. P., Kirby, J. R., Jarmin, R. F. 1979. *Simultaneous and Successive Cognitive Processes.* New York: Academic

DiLoreto, A. O. 1971. *Comparative Psychotherapy.* New York: Aldine-Atherton

Dreger, R. M. 1981. First, second, and third-order factors from the children's behavioral classification project instrument and an attempt at rapprochement. *J. Abnorm. Psychol.* 90:242–60

Eaves, L., Eysenck, H. J. 1975. The nature of extraversion: a genetical analysis. *J. Pers. Soc. Psychol.* 32:102–12

Evans, J. W., Elliott, H. 1981. Screening criteria for the diagnosis of schizophrenia in deaf patients. *Arch. Gen. Psychiatry* 38:787–90

Exner, J. E. 1978. *The Rorschach: A Comprehensive System.* New York: Wiley

Eysenck, H. J. 1970. A dimensional system of psychodiagnostics. In *New Approaches to Personality Classification,* ed. A. R. Mahrer, pp. 169–208. London: Columbia Univ. Press

Eysenck, H. J. 1975. *The Future of Psychiatry.* London: Methuen

Eysenck, H. J. 1976. *The Measurement of Personality.* Baltimore: Univ. Park Press

Eysenck, H. J. 1979. *The Structure and Measurement of Intelligence.* Berlin: Springer

Eysenck, H. J. 1981. *A Model for Personality.* Berlin: Springer

Eysenck, H. J., Eysenck, S. B. G. 1979. Introduction. See Wakefield 1979

Eysenck, H. J., vs. Kamin, L. 1981. *The Intelligence Controversy.* New York: Wiley

Eysenck, H. J., Wakefield, J. A. Jr. 1981. Psychological factors as predictors of marital satisfaction. *Adv. Behav. Res. Ther.* 3:151–92

Eysenck, M. W. 1981. Learning, memory, and personality. See H. J. Eysenck 1981, pp. 169–209

Eysenck, M. W., Eysenck, H. J. 1980. Mischel and the concept of personality. *Br. J. Psychol.* 71:191–204

Foltz, D. 1980. Judgment withheld on DSM-III, new child classification pushed. *APA Monitor* 11(1):1, 33

Fox, H. A. 1981. The DSM-III concept of schizophrenia. *Br. J. Psychiatry* 138: 60–63

Frances, A. 1980. The DSM-III personality disorders section: a commentary. *Am. J. Psychiatry* 37:1050–54

Frances, A., Cooper, A. M. 1981. Descriptive and dynamic psychiatry: a perspective on DSM-III. *Am. J. Psychiatry* 138: 1198–1202

Friedman, A. F., Gleser, G. C., Smeltzer, D. J., Wakefield, J. A. Jr., Schwartz, M. S. 1982. MMPI overlap item scales for differentiating psychotics, neurotics, and nonpsychiatric groups. *J. Consult. Clin. Psychol.* In press

Fulker, D. W. 1981. The genetic and environmental architecture of psychoticism, extraversion, and neuroticism. See H. J. Eysenck 1981, pp. 88–122

Garmezy, N. 1978. DSM-III: never mind the psychologists—is it good for the children? *Clin. Psychol.* 31 (3–4):1, 4–6

Garvey, M. J., Spoden, F. 1980. Suicide attempts in antisocial personality disorder. *Compr. Psychiatry* 21:146–49

Golden, C. J. 1981. The Luria-Nebraska Neuropsychological Battery: theory and research. In *Advances in Psychological Assessment*, ed. P. McReynolds, 5:191–235. San Francisco: Jossey-Bass

Golden, C. J., Hammeke, T. A., Purisch, A. D. 1980. *The Luria-Nebraska Neuropsychological Battery.* Los Angeles: West. Psychol. Serv.

Goldstein, A. P. 1976. *Prescriptive Psychotherapies.* New York: Pergamon

Gottman, J. M. 1979. *Marital Interaction: Experimental Investigations.* New York: Academic

Gray, J. A. 1981. A critique of Eysenck's theory of personality. See H. J. Eysenck 1981, pp. 246–76

Harris, S. L. 1979. DSM-III—Its implications for children. *Child Behav. Ther.* 1:37–46

Hartmann, D. P. 1977. Considerations in the choice of interobserver reliability estimates. *J. Appl. Behav. Anal.* 10:103–16

Haynes, S. N., Wilson, C. C. 1979. *Behavioral Assessment.* San Francisco: Jossey-Bass

Heasman, M. A., Lipworth, L. 1966. *Accuracy of Certification of Cause of Death.* London: H.M.S.O.

Helzer, J. E., Brockington, I. F., Kendall, R. E. 1981. Predictive validity of DSM-III and Feighner definitions of schizophrenia: a comparison with research diagnostic criteria and CATEGO. *Arch. Gen. Psychiatry* 38:791–97

Henderson, N. D. 1982. Human behavior genetics. *Ann. Rev. Psychol.* 33:403–40

Hendrickson, D. E., Hendrickson, A. E. 1980. The biological basis of individual differences in intelligence. *Pers. Individ. Differ.* 1:3–33

Herschowitz, J., Casper, R., Garver, D. L., Chang, S. 1980. Lithium response in good prognosis schizophrenia. *Am. J. Psychiatry* 137:916–20

Hersen, M., Bellack, A. S., eds. 1976. *Behavioral Assessment: A Practical Handbook.* Oxford: Pergamon

Horowitz, M. J., Wilner, N., Kaltreider, N., Alvarez, W. 1980. Signs and symptoms of posttraumatic stress disorder. *Arch. Gen. Psychiatry* 37:85–92

Jackson, B. 1970. The revised *Diagnostic and Statistical Manual of the American Psychiatric Association. Am. J. Psychiatry* 127:65–73

Karasu, T. B., Skodol, A. E. 1980. VIth axis for DSM-III; psychodynamic evaluation. *Am. J. Psychiatry* 137:607–13

Keisling, R. 1981. Underdiagnosis of manicdepressive illness in a hospital unit. *Am. J. Psychiatry* 138:672–73

Kendler, K. S. 1980. Are there delusions specific for paranoid disorders vs. schizophrenia? *Schizophr. Bull.* 6:1–3

Kincannon, J. C. 1968. Prediction of the standard MMPI scale scores from 71 items: the Mini-Mult. *J. Consult. Clin. Psychol.* 32:319–25

Klerman, G. L., Endicott, J., Spitzer, R., Hirschfeld, R. M. A. 1979. Neurotic depressions: A systematic analysis of multiple criteria and meanings. *Am. J. Psychiatry* 136:57–61

Laing, R. D. 1976. *The Facts of Life.* New York: Pantheon

Lang, R. J. 1978. Multivariate classification of day-care patients: personality as a dimensional continuum. *J. Consult. Clin. Psychol.* 46:1212–26

Levey, A. B., Martin, I. 1981. Personality and conditioning. See H. J. Eysenck 1981, pp. 123–68

Lewin, L. M., Wakefield, J. A. Jr. 1979. Percentage agreement and phi: a conversion table. *J. Appl. Behav. Anal.* 12:299–301

Lieberman, C. 1979. Schizoaffective illness defies the dichotomy . . . and keeps the DSM-III pondering. *Schizophr. Bull.* 5:436–40

Lipowski, Z. J. 1980a. A new look at organic brain syndromes. *Am. J. Psychiatry* 137:674–78

Lipowski, Z. J. 1980b. Delirium updated. *Compr. Psychiatry* 21:190–96

Marks, P. A., Seeman, W., Haller, D. 1974. *The Actuarial Use of the MMPI with*

Adolescents and Adults. Baltimore: Williams & Wilkins

Matarazzo, J. D. 1972. *Wechsler's Measurement and Appraisal of Adult Intelligence.* Baltimore: Williams & Wilkins. 5th ed.

Mattison, R., Cantwell, D. P., Russell, A. T., Will, L. 1979. A comparison of the DSM-II and DSM-III in the diagnosis of childhood psychiatric disorders: II. Interrater agreement. *Arch. Gen. Psychiatry* 36:1217–22

Maurer, R. G., Stewart, M. A. 1980. Attention deficit without hyperactivity in a child psychiatry clinic. *J. Clin. Psychiatry* 41:232–33

McCord, R. R., Wakefield, J. A. Jr. 1981. Arithmetic achievement as a function of introversion-extraversion and teacher-presented reward and punishment. *Pers. Individ. Differ.* 2:145–52

McGuire, R. J. 1973. Classification and the problem of diagnosis. In *Handbook of Abnormal Psychology,* ed. H. J. Eysenck, pp. 3–33. San Diego: EdITS

McLemore, C. W., Benjamin, L. S. 1979. Whatever happened to interpersonal diagnosis? A psychosocial alternative to DSM-III. *Am. Psychol.* 34:17–34

McReynolds, W. T. 1979. DSM-III and the future of applied social science. *Prof. Psychol.* 10:123–32

Millon, T. 1981. *Disorders of Personality: DSM-III, Axis II.* New York: Wiley

Mischel, W. 1968. *Personality and Assessment.* London: Wiley

Morey, L. C. 1980. Differences between psychologists and psychiatrists in the use of the DSM-III. *Am. J. Psychiatry* 137:1123–24

Murphy, J. M. 1980. Continuities in community-based psychiatric epidemiology. *Arch. Gen. Psychiatry* 37:1215–23

Nelson, J. C., Charney, D. S., Quinlan, D. M. 1981. Evaluation of the DSM-III criteria for melancholia. *Arch. Gen. Psychiatry* 38:555–59

North, C., Cadoret, R. 1981. Diagnostic discrepancy in personal accounts of patients with 'schizophrenia.' *Arch. Gen. Psychiatry* 38:133–37

Pfohl, B. 1980. Effects of clinical experience on rating DSM-III symptoms of schizophrenia. *Compr. Psychiatry* 21:233–35

Powell, G. E. 1981. A survey of the effects of brain lesions upon personality. See H. J. Eysenck 1981, pp. 65–87

Rahman, M. A., Eysenck, S. B. G. 1978. Psychoticism and response to treatment in neurotic patients. *Behav. Res. Ther.* 16:183–89

Raskin, R. N., Hall, C. S. 1979. A narcissistic personality inventory. *Psychol. Rep.* 45:590

Robins, L. N., Helzer, J. E., Croughan, J., Ratcliff, K. S. 1981. National Institute of Mental Health diagnostic interview schedule: its history, characteristics, and validity. *Arch. Gen. Psychiatry* 38:381–89

Rome, H. P. 1979. The classifications of schizophrenia: a historical review *Psychiatr. Ann.* 9:5–13

Russell, A. T., Cantwell, D. P., Mattison, R. Will, L. 1979. A comparison of the DSM-II and DSM-III in the diagnosis of childhood psychiatric disorders: III. Multiaxial features. *Arch. Gen. Psychiatry* 36:1223–26

Sattler, J. M. 1982. *Assessment of Children's Intelligence and Special Abilities* Boston: Allyn & Bacon. 2nd ed.

Schacht, T., Nathan, P. E. 1977. But is it good for the psychologists? Appraisal and status of DSM-III. *Am. Psychol.* 32:1017–25

Skinner, H. A. 1981. Toward the integration of classification theory and methods. *J. Abnorm. Psychol.* 90:68–87

Skodal, A. E., Spitzer, R. L., Williams, J. B. W. 1981. Teaching and learning DSM-III. *Am. J. Psychiatry* 138:1581–86

Spitzer, R. L. 1981a. The diagnostic status of homosexuality in DSM-III: A reformulation of the issues. *Am. J. Psychiatry* 138:210–15

Spitzer, R. L. 1981b. Nonmedical myths and the DSM-III. *APA Monitor* 12(10):3, 33

Spitzer, R. L., Endicott, J., Gibbon, M. 1979. Crossing the border into borderline personality and borderline schizophrenia. *Arch. Gen. Psychiatry* 36:17–24

Spitzer, R. L., Endicott, J., Robins, E. 1975. Clinical criteria for psychiatric diagnosis and the DSM-III. *Am. J. Psychiatry* 132:1187–92

Spitzer, R. L., Forman, J. B. W. 1979. DSM-III field trials: II. initial experience with the multiaxial system. *Am. J. Psychiatry* 136:818–20

Spitzer, R. L., Forman, J. B. W., Nee, J. 1979. DSM-III field trials: I. initial interrater diagnostic reliability. *Am. J. Psychiatry* 136:815–17

Spitzer, R. L., Skodal, A. E., Gibbon, M., Williams, J. B. W. 1981. *DSM-III Case Book.* Washington DC: Am. Psychiatr. Assoc.

Spitzer, R. L., Williams, J. B. W., Skodal, A. E. 1980. DSM-III: the major achievements and an overview. *Am. J. Psychiatry* 137:151–64

Stelmack, R. M. 1981. The psychophysiology of extraversion and neuroticism. See H. J. Eysenck 1981, pp. 38–64

Stoller, R.J., et al. 1973. A symposium: Should homosexuality be in the APA nomenclature? *Am. J. Psychiatry* 130: 1207–16

Strauss, J. S. 1975. A comprehensive approach to psychiatric diagnosis. *Am. J. Psychiatry* 132:1193–97

Strauss, J. S. 1979. Developing a comprehensive treatment for schizophrenia. *J. Natl. Assoc. Priv. Psychiatr. Hosp.* 10: 75–79

Strober, M., Green, J., Carlson, G. 1981. Reliability of psychiatric diagnosis in hospitalized adolescents. *Arch. Gen. Psychiatry* 38:141–45

Szasz, T. S. 1974. *The Myth of Mental Illness.* New York: Harper & Row

Tarter, R. E., Templer, D. I., Hardy, C. 1975. Reliability of the psychiatric diagnosis. *Dis. Nerv. Syst.* 36:30–31

Tu, J. B. 1980. Epilepsy, psychiatry, and DSM-III. *Biol. Psychiatry* 15:515–16

Wakefield, J. A. Jr. 1979 *Using Personality to Individualize Instruction.* San Diego: EdITS

Wakefield, J. A. Jr. 1980. Relationship between two expressions of reliability: percentage agreement and phi. *Educ. Psychol. Meas.* 40:593–97

Wakefield, J. A. Jr., Bradley, P. E., Doughtie, E. B., Kraft, I. A. 1975. Influence of overlapping and nonoverlapping items on the theoretical interrelationships of MMPI scales. *J. Consult. Clin. Psychol.* 43:851–57

Wakefield, J. A. Jr., Goad, N. A. 1982. *Psychological Differences: Causes, Consequences, and Uses in Education and Guidance.* San Diego: EdITS

Wakefield, J. A. Jr., Yom, B. H. L., Bradley, P. E., Doughtie, E. B., Cox, J. A., Kraft, I. A. 1974. Eysenck's personality dimensions: a model for the MMPI. *Br. J. Soc. Clin. Psychol.* 13:413–20

Waldron, H. A., Vickerstaff, L. 1977. *Intimations of Quality.* London: Nuffield Provincial Hospitals Trust

Webb, L. J., DiClemente, C. C., Johnstone, E. E., Sanders, J. L., Perley, R. A. 1981a. *DSM-III Training Guide: For Use with the American Psychiatric Association's Diagnostic and Statistical Manual of Mental Disorders.* New York: Brunner/Mazel. 3rd ed.

Webb, L. J., Gold, R. S., Johnstone, E. E., DiClemente, C. C. 1981b. Accuracy of DSM-III diagnoses following a training program. *Am. J. Psychiatry* 138:376–78

Wechsler, D. 1981. *Manual for the Wechsler Adult Intelligence Scale-Revised.* New York: Psychol. Corp.

Wiener-Levy, D., Exner, J. E. Jr. 1981. The Rorschach comprehensive system: an overview. In *Advances in Psychological Assessment,* ed. P. McReynolds, 5:236–93. San Francisco: Jossey-Bass

Wilson, G. D. 1981. Personality and social behaviour. See H. J. Eysenck 1981, pp. 210–45

Winters, K. C., Weintraub, S., Neale, J. M. 1981. Validity of MMPI codetypes in identifying DSM-III schizophrenics, unipolars, and bipolars. *J. Consult. Clin. Psychol.* 49:486–87

Woods, D. J. 1979. Carving nature at its joints? Observations on a revised psychiatric nomenclature. *J. Clin. Psychol.* 35:912–20

World Health Organization. 1968. *International Classification of Diseases.* Geneva: WHO. 8th ed.

Zubin, J. 1977–78. But is it good for science? *Clin. Psychol.* 31(2):1, 5–7

Ann. Rev. Psychol. 1983. 34:195–222
Copyright © 1983 by Annual Reviews Inc. All rights reserved

PERSONALITY: STAGES, TRAITS, AND THE SELF

Jane Loevinger

Social Science Institute, Washington University, St. Louis, Missouri 63130

Elizabeth Knoll

Committee on the Conceptual Foundations of Science, University of Chicago, Chicago, Illinois 60637

CONTENTS

Given "personality" as our purview, we have chosen to emphasize cognitive-developmental stage theories, partly because of a spate of new publications, partly because previous coverage in the *Annual Review of Psychology* has been brief. Having chosen that topic, complementary topics were added: alternative stage theories and alternatives to stage-theory approaches to similar topics. Personality has been taken in its broadest, most encompassing sense, which we arbitrarily construe to include morality, the self, empathy, and related topics. Morality could be taken to be part of social psychology, and stages are developmental psychology. Including them within the field of personality implies that moral stages trace a dimension

195

0066-4308/83/0201-0195$02.00

of individual differences in adult life, which we take to be central to personality.

For all its flaws, the editorial review process is a necessary part of science, as Ziman (1971) has argued. This chapter will therefore include only books and reviewed articles. Unpublished manuscripts and theses, however worthy, are arbitrarily excluded, though many are reviewed in books and articles mentioned. Preference has been given to books rather than articles. Personality theory rarely advances by single discoveries reported in primary research journals, however significant statistically (Meehl 1978). Only when a series of research articles is restated in book or review-article form does it have major impact.

The Piagetian revolution has come to the field of personality, where its cognitive-developmental theory now competes with social learning theory, behaviorism, and psychoanalysis. One salient feature of the Piagetian view is the concept of qualitatively distinct stages of development. Each equilibrated stage has an inner logic, and there is an inevitable logic to the sequence of stages. Each stage is constructed anew by the child; social interaction facilitates development but does not dictate its content. Rewards and punishments are irrelevant; imitation is not mentioned. Trait theories are rival hypotheses, since they reduce qualitative differences to quantitative ones, whereas the Piagetian discerns the qualitative within the apparently quantitative changes. That cognitive developmentalism opposes social learning theory, behaviorism, and trait theory is insisted on by each side; psychoanalysis, however, may be compatible with it. At any rate, many authors have independently volunteered to reconcile psychoanalysis with Piagetian psychology (Rosenblatt & Thickstun 1977, Weiner 1979, Malerstein & Ahern 1982).

The leading figure in the cognitive-developmental school is Kohlberg, whose adaptation of Piaget's device of presenting subjects with a moral dilemma, followed by a probing interview, is known even to readers of airline magazines. Many of Kohlberg's former students and associates have developed their own tests, experiments, or systems of stages, lately culminating in a series of books, each with its unique purview and emphasis. Kohlberg is both the most popular theorist in this school and the favorite target of critics, inhouse and outside.

Moral development is where the Piagetian personologists first staked out a claim, though they have now invaded many other fields. Other approaches to moral development are also actively cultivated under such headings as prosocial behavior (Staub 1978), altruism (Rushton & Sorrentino 1981, Hoffman 1981), socialization (Staub 1979), and empathy.

Age does not wither nor custom stale interest in consistency of personality, despite its infinite variety. If there is no consistency in behavior, as some behaviorists and social learning theorists were insisting a few years ago, then the field of personality should disappear and be entirely replaced by social psychology, concerned as the latter is with the effect of situation on behavior. Those who belittled consistency have not ceased to write about personality and shifted to social psychology—perhaps they did not want to demonstrate the consistency they denied. Meanwhile, personality has been defended by those who see consistency over time (Block 1977, Sroufe 1979) and over situations (Epstein 1980b, McClelland 1981) as well as consistent interactions between traits and situations (Endler 1981), or among traits, situations, beliefs, and desires (Hirschberg 1978).

Interest in the self, far from being taboo, as it once was, is now chic. Development of the self is one of the domains covered by several more or less Piagetian approaches. The term used in some cases is "ego development," but the topic is development of the self, as that term is usually used. Among psychoanalysts, a school founded by Kohut (1971, 1977) has taken the self as its centerpiece and appropriated the term "psychology of the self," as a previous generation of psychoanalysts appropriated the term "ego psychology." (The niceties of distinctions between ego, self, and personhood, though not without substance, will not be our topic.) Even social learning theorists now claim the self as part of their turf (Bandura 1978), though to do so they involve themselves in logical difficulties (Secord 1977, Kuhn 1978).

Despite the heralded demise of psychoanalysis a few years ago, Freud continues to provide employment for personality theorists as well as clinicians; rereading Freud is a growth industry. The variety of rereadings is astonishing and, as all of the scholarly ones have some foundation, chastening for those who think they understand psychoanalysis or Freud's writings. Contrary to the assertion in most psychology texts that "orthodox" psychoanalysis purges all dissenters, some of the most radical new readings are by members of the psychoanalytic establishment (Schafer 1978, Gedo 1979).

STAGES

Moral Development: Kohlberg and Some Critics

Kohlberg's first two books cover a general survey of the development and validation of his test (1981b) and the philosophical aspects of his theory on the development of moral judgment, or, as he sometimes puts it, the moralization of judgment (1981a). The latter, first of three volumes, reprints his major essays from 1967 through 1979 and shows their relation to his grand plan. Volume 2 will present his psychological writings and Volume 3 the writings concerned with applications. Semipopular expositions of his theory have appeared as books (Galbraith & Jones 1976, Hersh et al 1979, Rosen

1980). The long-promised, often-revised scoring manual for his Moral Judgment Instrument (MJI) has been completed (Colby et al 1983a), as has the longitudinal study on which it is based (Colby et al 1983b).

Kohlberg's main contribution remains the formulation of the six stages, two each at the preconventional, the conventional, and the principled levels. He has toyed with adding a seventh stage (1981a, Chap. 9); he uses substages and transitional stages, and the latest manual drops Stage 6, but he does not see these forays as compromising his fundamental notion of logically discrete stages.

The central issue for Kohlberg in validating the stage conception is the question of sequentiality: each stage must be traversed in order, that order is never reversed, and no stage can be skipped. On the whole, evidence supports sequentiality (Davison et al 1978, White et al 1978, Colby et al 1983b), particularly for the early stages. Stages and substages at the postconventional, principled level do not always appear in the postulated order (J. M. Murphy & Gilligan 1980). Earlier results showing regression from Stage 4 to Stage 2 in some college students were handled by postulating an optional Stage 4½, a compromise of a strict stage conception but consistent with the later progression of most of the students to Stage 5. With improvements in scoring rules, this device is no longer needed (Colby et al 1983b).

The claim that each stage is a "structured whole" is evaluated in terms of the variability of scores on issues within a protocol. By current rules, most protocols have all scores at one or at two adjacent stages. However, any measure of intraprotocol variability is somewhat arbitrary because there are arbitrary steps in the scoring algorithm, e.g. lower stage remarks are disregarded if they occur in context of a higher stage elaboration of the same idea.

Murphy & Gilligan (1980), who also found apparent regression in college students studied longitudinally, rescored their protocols according to Perry's (1970) scheme, which traces intellectual-ethical development in college from dualistic thinking to multiplicity, to contextual relativistic thinking, to commitment. The relativistic thinking which an early Kohlberg manual scored as Stage 2 is, according to Perry's scheme, a sophisticated, late stage; they find the absence of a distinction between multiplicity and relativity a problem even in the current manual.

Other evidence for validity of the Colby et al manual comes from attempts to accelerate development (Faust & Arbuthnot 1978, Berkowitz et al 1980). Kuhn et al (1977) found that some achievement of Piagetian formal operations was prerequisite to achievement of principled moral reasoning; in their data holding mental age constant did not significantly decrease the relation between formal operations and moral reasoning. Estimates of reliability of the manual are high for those trained by the Harvard group (Colby et al 1983b).

Questions have been raised particularly about the principled stages. Those stages demand the kind of ratiocination congenial to intellectual males living in a technical society (E. V. Sullivan 1977, Haan 1978), hence lack the implied universal applicability (Edwards 1981). Gibbs (1979) considers them philosophical elaborations of Stage 4 thinking rather than new stages.

Basing her work on studies of women, including ones who faced real-life dilemmas, Gilligan (1982) traces the development of an ethic of care and responsibility corresponding to Kohlberg's ethic of justice in men. Theories of development by men such as Kohlberg and Erikson tend to define maturity in terms of autonomy and achievement; in that framework, women's lifelong concern with relationships appears as a weakness rather than as a strength. Gilligan traces an alternative course for women's moral development: In the first stage, concern is primarily for survival; in the second, concern is for responsibility and not hurting others; in the third, the woman sees herself as meriting care equally with others. The midlife concern for the problem of intimacy found in recent studies of men (e.g. Vaillant 1977) would appear as delayed maturity if measured against a scale where women were taken to define the norm.

Arguing that the central issue in moral judgment is moral action and that Kohlberg's system favors a typically male, intellectualized denial of situational detail in forming moral judgments, Haan (1978) presents an alternative model of "interpersonal morality," based on interpersonal "moral balance," oriented toward action. In games requiring cooperation or competition, teenagers' levels of moral judgment as assessed by interviews predicted their behavior poorly, but they used more interpersonal than formal (Kohlbergian) moral reasoning. Coping and defensive ego processes (Haan 1977) were more frequently associated with interpersonal than with formal morality. After a series of games, measures of both kinds of moral reasoning showed significant gains compared to a control group.

Because Kohlberg's MJI is notoriously difficult to administer and score, Rest (1979) developed an objective test, the Defining Issues Test, applicable to Kohlberg's conception. The test is based on Rest's finding that persons understand reasoning of stages lower than their own spontaneous moral level, but reasoning of higher stages less often. It presents moral dilemmas, including three of Kohlberg's, and asks the subject to choose a course of action. Then he is given a list of 12 issues that may have influenced his choice and asked to rate each as to how important it was. Finally, he selects the four most important issues and ranks them in order of importance. Scoring algorithms are based on the ranking or the ratings of issues. For Rest, moral maturity involves gradually increasing use of principled moral reasoning. Thus he argues for a fundamentally continuous variable, as opposed to discrete stages, which Kohlberg upholds in principle (although

Kohlberg also uses scoring algorithms that vary continuously). Because it is the only objectively scored test in this domain, the Defining Issues Test has been widely used. By virtue of being objective, however, the test taps a slightly different strand than does Kohlberg's, Defining Issues being a recognition task, the MJI a production task. Scores on Rest's test are related to but not reducible to pure measures of intelligence. Cross-sectional, longitudinal, experimental, and psychometric validational studies are summarized by Rest, including many conducted outside his own group.

Another attempt to solve some of the psychometric difficulties of Kohlberg's MJI is Gibbs's Sociomoral Reflection Measure (Gibbs et al 1982). It uses the Kohlberg dilemmas followed by standard probe questions. Responses are written; the test is intended for group administration. The rationale for scoring follows that of the MJI, and the test is being validated against the MJI.

Kohlberg's ideas may be more influential outside psychology than within it. He has been especially interested in application to education (Galbraith & Jones 1976, Hersh et al 1979, Kohlberg 1981b) and to correctional institutions (Hickey & Scharf 1980) via the creation of "just communities," i.e. democratically governed institutions run according to a constitution, replacing traditional institutions.

Criticisms of Kohlberg's theory prior to those reviewed above are discussed by H. Rosen (1980) and others (Lickona 1976).

Other Cognitive-Developmental Sequences

Selman (1980) has evolved a method based on that of Kohlberg for investigating "interpersonal perspective-taking," which he sees as more fundamental than moral reasoning. While Kohlberg's test is used chiefly with adolescents and adults, Selman's has a form for school-age children and another for adolescents; age-appropriate stories are read to children or presented as filmstrips, followed by a probing interview. At Stage 0, undifferentiated egocentric perspective-taking, the individual is perceived only as a physical entity and interpersonal connections are a matter of physical proximity. Progress occurs through increasing intentionality, cognitive complexity, reciprocity, and awareness of existence over time. At Stage 4, in-depth social perspective-taking, individuals are conceived as complex systems and interpersonal relations as forms of balanced tensions, with friendship seen as autonomous interdependence and peer groups as pluralistic organizations. Décalage takes the form that Individual conceptions of a stage emerge before its Friendship conceptions, which are followed by conceptions of group relations. Selman presents his theory and normative, longitudinal, and clinical research, but excerpts from rather than a complete scoring manual. A small clinical sample showed retardation of social perspective-taking relative to the child's age and intellectual potential. Youniss (1980), combining insights from H. S. Sullivan with those from Piaget, has studied similar topics.

Disagreeing with Piaget and Kohlberg, who assume that young children do not distinguish violations of conventions from immorality, Turiel (1978) sees social convention as a separate domain. Though much research on moral behavior, such as the forbidden-toy technique of the social learning theorists, confuses actions bad in themselves with those bad because forbidden, even 6-year-olds distinguish violations of moral principle from those of conventional rules and judge them differently (Nucci & Turiel 1978). Hitting another child is bad, whether or not there is a rule against it, whereas leaving toys on the floor tends to be bad only if there is a rule against it (Weston & Turiel 1980). There are three domains, the moral, the societal, and the personal, the last being acts which are contrary to social norms but affect only the actor, such as wearing long hair in defiance of a school's dress code. A significant number of children from the second grade through college ranked moral transgressions the worst and violations of rules in the personal domain the least bad (Nucci 1981). The relation between these domains is one of "informational exchange rather than structural interdependence" (Turiel 1978, p. 102).

Damon's (1977) chief concern is issues of justice and fairness, and his hallmark is contrasting behavior in two situations. In one, a hypothetical dilemma is presented to the child for judgment; in the other, a parallel situation is created experimentally to see how he will behave in a real situation. Suppose children have to distribute unequal rewards, such as five candy bars for four children. The youngest (about age 4) confuse justice with their own wishes. Next, some arbitrary characteristic, such as size or sex, is invoked as justification for the child's wishful choice. The next level opts for strict equality, then follows an idea of reciprocity. By age 8 children usually understand that people have different but equally valid claims, which must be compromised. The sequence is identical for real and hypothetical situations; however, children are usually farther advanced in reasoning about hypothetical ones, which Damon accounts for by the intrusion of self-interest in the real situation.

Broughton (1980), drawing ideas from J. M. Baldwin and Piaget, has explored the development of natural or commonsense epistemologies from preschool age to maturity. His interviews concern the mind-body distinction, sense of self, knowledge, and reality. At the earliest stage (4 to 7 years) the self is the self-evident bodily self. Next, the child sees himself as an individual and as agent. The third stage, the divided self of adolescence, has particularly interested Broughton (1981a). His highest stage, Stage 7, is dialectical materialistic, seeing self in historical context. On the basis of several experiments, however, Johnson & Wellman (1982) challenge Broughton's description of the preschool child's confusion of mind and brain.

Development of Ego or Self

Beginning with the interpersonal integration stages of C. Sullivan, M. Q. Grant & J. D. Grant (1957), who based their conception as much on the interpersonal psychiatry of H. S. Sullivan as on Piaget, Loevinger (1976a, 1979c) has used data from a sentence completion test to delineate a scale of ego development (Loevinger et al 1970). (Whereas Kohlberg's research originally involved males only, Loevinger's originally involved females only. Both have long since expanded their data base, but possibly Loevinger's conception reflects a sexual bias, as Kohlberg's has been accused of doing.) Currently, ten stages or transitional levels mark the sequence from egocentric impulsivity, through rule-bound conformity, to a self-aware orientation that fulfills its self-chosen responsibilities, to value for individuality and acceptance of inner conflict. Construct validity studies have shown several kinds of evidence for sequentiality: cross-sectional and longitudinal gains with age, correlations over long time spans, and better comprehension of lower levels than higher. Theoretical descriptions of stages are supported by correlations with tests of related stage conceptions, with appropriate behaviors at lower levels, and with appropriate attitudes at higher levels (Loevinger 1979a).

A shortened form of the sentence completion test has been used in a large-scale national research conducted by the Yankelovich Opinion Survey group (Holt 1980). Among 18- to 25-year-olds in the United States, the modal level is the Conscientious-Conformist stage (or transitional level), characterized by self-awareness, awareness of exceptions to general rules, aspiration to sincerity as opposed to simply good behavior, and conscious flexibility rather than blind application of group norms. This personality type has received little attention in previous accounts of development, perhaps because it is ubiquitous. Nationally, women rate slightly higher than men and college students somewhat higher than the noncollege population of the same age.

Tamashiro (1979) has traced stages in adolescents' concepts of marriage and related them to ego development as measured by the sentence completion test. Children begin with a magical view of marriage as eternal happiness through fusion and move through idealized conventionality which focuses on social codes, an individualistic stage in which the aim of marriage is to foster the growth of the individual, to an "affirmational" stage in which marriage is seen as a relation in which conflicts and changes are confronted.

Stages in the development of faith are traced by Fowler (1981), beginning with the undifferentiated faith of infancy. In intuitive-projective faith, typical for ages 3 to 7, faith is embodied in fluid and imaginative fantasies. In mythic-literal faith, typical for school age and a few adults, there is primitive reciprocity with God and literal adoption of the family beliefs. Synthetic-conventional faith, typical for adolescents and many adults, is a conformist stage. Change can be mediated by a major event such as leaving home, by a clash between authorities, or by a change in authorities themselves. In individuative-reflective faith, typical for late adolescence and adult life, the person takes responsibility for his or her commitments and life-style and frames a self-conscious world view but ignores unconscious factors. Fowler finds it hard to put Stages 5 and 6 into words, and we shall not try.

Moral development and development of the self are united in the problem of responsibility, which A. Blasi (1982) has studied. Posing a dilemma that pits altruistic helping against a rule or law, Blasi found three stages. At the lowest, predominant in the first grade, children have little distance from their wants. Contrary to what one might expect on the basis of Kohlberg's lowest stage, called Punishment and Obedience Orientation, first-graders more often choose the altruistic course of action than the obedient course; helping others is experienced as a spontaneous desire but not an obligation. In the sixth grade, children most often choose obedience as the course but in the context of reasons for obeying. None reckon the child as being blameworthy for not having chosen the altruistic course, even the few who say he should choose it. Thus at this stage there are two moralities, a private one, which may be altruistic, and a public one of obedience, to which alone blame and responsibility can be attached. By the eleventh grade a few children recognize that one might be blamed for not having chosen the altruistic course, and the person is responsible not only for what he does but for what kind of person he is. Only at this stage is integrity recognized as a virtue.

Kegan (1982) has an analysis of ego or self development that is akin to Loevinger's in its delineation of stages but seeks the "deep structure" of the ego in terms of subject-object relations. The subject of each stage is the object of the next one. At the Impulsive Stage the self is its impulses and perceptions. At the Imperial Stage impulses and perceptions become objects, with the self, or subject, being needs, interests, and wishes. At the Interpersonal Stage needs, interests, and wishes become object to interpersonal mutuality as subject, and so on through the Institutional and Interindividual Stages. Kegan adds clinical vignettes to enrich his conception. Unlike most stage theorists, whose primary interest is description of the (postulated) equilibrated stages, Kegan's primary interest is the (equally hypothetical) process of transition between stages.

The California Youth Authority has had for many years a Community Treatment Program based on the C. Sullivan et al (1957) conception of ego development, elaborated in the lower and middle stages in terms of subtypes pertinent to delinquent behavior. Those subtypes have been widely used as a basis for differential treatment programs (e.g. Warren 1979). Warren (1982) has compared several theories of delinquency in terms of how well the assumptions of each theory fit a small sample of female delinquents from each of five subtypes. The "social control," i. e. situational, theory fit several subtypes of delinquent girls better than other theories, but the psychodynamic theory fit the most numerous subtypes the best.

Structural Models

Thus we face stages-in-the-development-of: moral judgment, interpersonal morality, interpersonal perspective-taking, fairness, conventions, epistemology, several versions of ego development, responsibility, faith, the concept of marriage, conceptions of society (Furth 1980), and no doubt other things, each sequence referring to a hypothetical mental structure. These mental structures are too much alike to be completely independent and too different to be mutually assimilated. If each topic requires a new structure, what's a structure for? And should the definition of stages be logical or empirical? Presumably all hands agree that ultimately it must be both, but different parties approach that goal from different directions.

Kohlberg and other strict Piagetians construct their sequences so that in principle each stage is a logically coherent ensemble of ideas, the succession of stages is logically necessary, and the higher stages are more inclusive and better than lower stages. As to the profusion of structures, Kohlberg sees the several structures as correlated but asymmetrically related. Attaining Selman's fourth stage is prerequisite to attaining Kohlberg's fourth stage (Kohlberg 1981b). However, the evidence cited is fragmentary, and it is not obvious how one decides which stages in the two sequences match. Of those starting with Kohlberg's scheme, only Rest has adopted a probabilistic approach.

In contrast, Loevinger's method of measuring ego development is stochastic. In constructing the scoring manual of the sentence completion test (Loevinger et al 1970), the primary consideration was psychometric, predicting total protocol score from item responses, with theoretical justification secondary. While no glaring theoretical inconsistencies result, many responses that are prima facie ambiguous or unrelated to ego development are assigned a stage empirically. The method has resulted in new theoretical insights that would be foreclosed to a logically consistent stage model (Loevinger 1979c). As to the profusion of sequences, Loevinger (1976a) sees all the foregoing sequences as aspects of a partly ineffable unity; her term ego development stands not for its conventional psychoanalytic meaning but rather for the diversity of manifestations of the central core of personality.

Damon (1977) has a complex model for social development. The child has, appropriately, separate concepts for such areas as adult authority, social regulation, positive justice, and peer authority. Relations between different concepts result from common environmental factors as well as from "informative and supportive conceptual relations between concepts" (p. 327). Thus Damon does not search for a single "deep-structural" entity. He postulates a necessary but not sufficient relation between certain achievements in the logical domain and matched ones in the social domain, but he does not predict or find direct, strong confirmation in data, since no single test indexes the entire logical domain. While his voice is the voice of a structuralist, Damon's model is indistinguishable from a stochastic one.

Bickhard (1978) and Feldman (1980) have modified structural models. Bickhard sees each stage as "knowing" the preceding one but not the succeeding one; he plays down structure within a stage. His model applies to Kegan's (1982) stages. Feldman found that three child prodigies (two chess players and a composer) achieved formal operations in their own fields long before they achieved them elsewhere, thus documenting a kind of décalage long suspected.

Loevinger's scheme has been criticized for its lack of logical consistency, particularly its confusion of structure with content (Habermas 1979, Kohlberg 1981b). However, Colby (1978) acknowledges that the history of Kohlberg's scoring manual is one of progressive redefinition of the structure-content distinction; thus the distinction is not absolute. Levine (1979) criticizes Kohlberg's use of that distinction as ambiguous; he would apply the distinction only to social influences. And of course the logic of the Piagetian sequences is the logic of the researchers, not their subjects, whose inevitable inconsistencies are papered over with the euphemism, *décalage.*

Given the imperfections of all current measuring devices, the ghostly battle between the structural-rationalists and the stochastic-empiricists can continue with neither side risking final defeat.

Cross-Cultural Applicability

The foregoing sequences are more or less Piagetian ones; they are drawn with some degree of abstractness (despite the fact that several authors confound stage and age in their research design), and thus are potential candidates for cultural universality. There are other, non-Piagetian stage conceptions, such as Levinson's (1978) stages of life for adult men, closely tied to age and to specific life tasks in our culture, such as choosing a career, becoming established in a profession, and so on. Presumably such culturally specific sequences make no claim to cultural universality. Levinson writes of structure-building at each stage, but the connotations appear different from the hierarchical structures of the cognitive developmentalists.

A considerable amount of cross-cultural research has been published using some version of Kohlberg's test (Weinreich 1977, Bar-Yam et al 1980, others reviewed by Edwards 1981) and the sentence completion test (Kusatsu 1977, Snarey & J. Blasi 1980, Rosén & Nordquist 1980). The interest in these lines of research in other countries (e.g. Döbert et al 1977, Limoges & Paul 1981) further testifies to some cross-cultural applicability.

Cross-cultural applicability has, however, been questioned (Smith 1978). Empirical as well as philosophical considerations suggest that the development from impulsivity to conventionality may be a more or less universal shift required by any form of socialization, but the postconformist stages described by the foregoing authors may be peculiar to individualistic, future-oriented, liberal "modernity" (Suzman 1977, Edwards 1981, Broughton 1981b).

TRAITS

Trait Approaches to Morality

Rest (1983) identifies four components in morality: interpreting situations in terms of how one's actions affect others, determining what action best fulfills moral ideals, deciding what to do, and doing it. His review is devoted mainly to the second, cognitive element and covers the work of the Piagetian school. Other personality theorists turn away from a cognitive emphasis toward less rational affective elements of morality.

Hogan (Hogan et al 1978) sees moral development in terms of three largely independent traits: rule attunement or socialization, social sensitivity or empathy, and autonomy, which he equates with self-awareness. Hogan et al no longer emphasize moral knowledge, which everyone has, nor the "ethics of conscience vs the ethics of responsibility," which, they now say, comes to liberalism vs conservatism. The three traits mature in three periods, but these are not defined by qualitatively distinct modes of thought. Development is a continual process of adapting to environmental demands.

Hoffman (1981, 1982) emphasizes socialization and empathy as sources of altruism. He connects altruism in maturity with the parents' use of induction (i.e. sweet reason?) as a disciplinary technique in preference to punishment or withdrawal of love. Empathy for the victim is an important element in his explanation of altruistic actions, as well as his theory of the evolution of guilt. (But contrast the theory of conscience development in Loevinger 1976b.) Lewis (1981) reinterprets the literature on the effect of socialization on children's behavior. If induction appears to account for favorable outcomes in child-rearing, that may be because tractable children can be reasoned with, rather than because reasoning with children makes them tractable (or altruistic).

Thus empathy is often nominated either as a constituent of morality or as a major mediating factor though not intrinsically moral (Coke et al 1978, Staub 1978, Hoffman 1981, Feshbach 1982). Empathy has both cognitive and affective components. For Feshbach (1978) there are two cognitive components: ability to discriminate the affects of other people and the ability to take their perspective. Emotional capacity and responsiveness are the crucial third element. For her, empathy is measured in terms of match between affect of subject and object. Cognitive elements are most amenable to measurement, but the affective elements are the most essential. Smither (1977) warns that researchers must guard against inferring empathy from pseudo-empathic projection or generalization of the subject's own experience. Empathy always requires making sense of an entire situation, and emotions are partly constituted by cognitive appraisal. The cognitive element implies that empathy develops.

Hoffman (1982) distinguishes four sociocognitive stages, with a different form of empathy characteristic of each. When infants do not distinguish self from the other, they are capable only of global empathy. When they have acquired person permanence, they experience egocentric empathy. When children begin to be aware of others as having their own inner states, they are capable of empathy for another's feelings. When they realize others have identities and experiences beyond the immediate situation, they become capable of empathy for someone's general life condition. However, one form of empathy does not necessarily replace earlier ones. For Hoffman the degree of match between the feelings of subject and object is not definitive for empathy. Selman (1980) delineates in depth Hoffman's third and fourth stages.

Some years ago the predominant view in psychoanalysis, behaviorism, and social learning theory seemed to be that children were born more or less antisocial and needed to be socialized. The work on empathy and other prosocial behavior has led many (Staub 1978, Hoffman 1981) to turn that around. Prosocial, altruistic behavior is also natural and inborn. Recent work (Feshbach 1982) on empathy reveals complications. For girls, who tend to be more empathic than boys, the correlates of empathy are, as expected, a positive self-concept, prosocial behavior, low aggression, and low antisocial behavior. For boys, a more complex situation seems to obtain, depending on the intensity of the experience and whether the affects aroused are euphoric or dysphoric. Such interaction effects call for confirmation and theoretical explanation.

Despite the convincing argument and the investment in empathy as a constituent or predecessor of morality (see also Hoffman 1977), a meta-analysis of numerous studies by Underwood & Moore (1982) fails to confirm any substantial correlation between measures of altruism and those of empathy; such relation as is found holds only for adults. By contrast, their meta-analysis of Piagetian and Kohlbergian moral maturity scores shows for both a reliable though not high relation to prosocial behavior.

Consistency of Personality

The problem of the consistency of personality is usually framed as the relative importance of traits versus situations in determining behavior, which has been discussed in earlier issues of the *Annual Review of Psychology* (Helson & Mitchell 1978, Sundberg et al 1978, Jackson & Paunonen 1980). By now all hands agree that interaction of trait with situation is most important; still personologists represent each other as upholding the importance of traits only, or situations only, or psychodynamics only, or "traits-states," or the like. There is agreement that everyone is more or less adaptable to situations, that too little adaptability is, by definition, maladjustment, and too much bespeaks dependence or psychopathy. People do tend to perceive stable traits where they do not in fact exist, which social psychologists class under the "fundamental attribution error" (Jones 1979), but making attributions to situations can be just as fundamental an error (Harvey et al 1981).

The hope that trait-situation interaction effects could be measured by interaction terms in analysis of variance designs flared only briefly. The "mechanical" or additive ANOVA model contrasts with the dynamic-interactive model of psychological theory (Buss 1977)—same word, different meaning. However, the use of moderator variables to find subgroups consistent with respect to particular traits succeeds. Kenrick & Stringfield (1980) used self-ratings of consistency as a way of picking the trait most relevant for each subject from their list of 16. On those traits, particularly the ones self-rated as publicly visible, the agreement between self-ratings and ratings of peers and parents was high.

Moss & Susman (1980), reviewing longitudinal studies of personality throughout the life-span, found greatest stability in socially valued traits. Using data from several extensive longitudinal studies, J. Block (1977) showed that data derived from observers' ratings of natural behavior and from self-report questionnaires displayed consistency over long time spans. Only data from objective, artificial test or laboratory situations did not show much predictability. W. Mischel (1977), against whose denigration of trait theory much of Block's article was aimed, replied that ratings are just perceptions, whereas the tests that Block admitted are not predictable are real behavior. Pervin (1977) called attention to Brunswik's principle of ecologically representative design in this context. The careful ratings of everyday behavior utilized in the studies Block quoted would appear to be more ecologically valid than artificial laboratory tasks. Whether ratings are linguistic artifacts with little relevance to personality continues to be debated (Block et al 1979, Shweder & D'Andrade 1979).

Interactions, besides not being easily replicated, are too numerous to be investigated easily (Epstein 1980b). Inferring trait status from adequate aggregates of specific behaviors and samples of occasions is more feasible. When sufficiently broad measures are thus defined, stable traits are shown (Epstein 1980b, Block et al 1981); objective measures and measures of performance on laboratory tasks are predictable (Epstein 1979) even at preschool ages (J. H. Block & J. Block 1980).

Hirschberg (1978) pointed out that beliefs and desires interact with dispositions to determine behavior in specific situations. Making a similar point, McClelland (1981) added that responses may be thought samples or actions and may be respondent or operant. Tests, particularly objective tests, are at the respondent extreme, whereas consistency is more likely for operant behavior. Respondent behavior is by definition situationally responsive.

Trait theory is more impressive—and more interesting—when it displays not literal consistency from one situation to another but predictability or coherence in what appear to be different behaviors, a point made in various ways by Bowers (1977), Magnusson & Endler (1977), Kagan (1980), and McClelland (1981). The search for continuity in personality is somewhat at variance with the search for stages, since it is characteristic of stage conceptions to find the continuity in apparently different manifestations. The differences between stages may be so great that it is not at all apparent that there is a connection between them (L. B. Murphy 1981).

As an example of the continuity paradox, Sroufe (1979) found that the kind and degree of maternal attachment is relatively consistent from 12 months to 18 months; however, the specific behaviors by which the kind of attachment is shown change radically in that time. Thus the naive behaviorist might conclude that behavior is inconsistent, whereas a more inferential approach demonstrates consistency.

There is an entirely different sense in which one may speak of personal consistency, namely, the consistency between moral judgment and moral action. Relating this topic to the polarization between cognitive developmentalists and social learning theorists, A. Blasi (1980) reviewed empirical studies of the issue. His analysis showed a clear trend toward a positive relation in most areas researched. That correlation is not simply another prediction, he pointed out; the concordance is what is called integrity.

SELF AND EGO

Recent symposia on the self (T. Mischel 1977, Whiteley 1979, Lynch et al 1981) include contributions by psychologists, psychoanalysts, philosophers, sociologists, educators, and counselors. Many discussions call for investigating development of the self; that is occurring, sometimes under other headings, in the cognitive-developmental school (Damon & Hart 1982).

Moral choices are crucial indicators of the person as an active agent (Alston 1977, McCall 1977, Taylor 1977, Toulmin 1977). Everyone admits that people exercise self-control, but how? They may do so by rewarding and punishing themselves (W. & H. N. Mischel 1977). However, people change not only their actions but also their motivations. There are higher and lower motives. Ordinarily lower ones prevail, but they can be overruled by higher level motives (Alston 1977). This is not simply a matter of radical choice, for that implies there is no reason or motive. Rather, it is a matter of articulating and confirming one's identity, one's sense of self, the kind of person one thinks of oneself as being (Taylor 1977).

Logically, any system that has operant behaviorism as its core cannot accommodate self-control; according to Skinner, contingencies can only be identified by their effects on the probability of response, so self-reinforcement is a logical contradiction (Secord 1977). Social learning theory has a similar problem, seeing behavior as controlled both by external stimuli and the person's own self-regulatory system (Kuhn 1978). Thus, behavior therapists use contingencies of reinforcement with respect to target behaviors, but common sense or an anthropomorphic view in relation to the client as an autonomous person who plans and makes choices.

Day (1977), an avowed Skinnerian, believes there is no such thing as self; self-deception is simply absence of knowledge about oneself; and moral responsibility reduces to group membership and social needs. Similarily, Gergen (1977, 1981) finds that by introspection the properties of the self-concept are an empty set; there is nothing to know. Self-esteem, at least for college students, appears to depend on immediate past and present experiences, hence the self-concept is a social construction, not an enduring disposition. It follows that therapists might simply devote their attention to ways of renegotiating self-concepts. Fitts (1981), however, asks whether changing a person's self-concept from Type X to Type K will make the client more like a Type K person and less like a Type X person.

The self is sometimes defined in terms of information processing and internal organizational structures, screening and selecting from experience to maintain structural equilibrium (Markus 1977, Greenwald 1980, Mancuso & Ceely 1980). Toulmin (1977) differentiates self- used as prefix (self-knowledge, self-control), self as a hypothetical entity or intervening variable (which we believe is the straw-man opponent of those who deny the existence of the self), and self as used in clinical and everyday description. Development of integration and autonomy from childhood to adult life involves the first and third meanings. The reflexive form is, however, different in Greek, German, French, and Italian from its form in English. Languages without the equivalent of our self- prefix put less emphasis on the self as entity, Toulmin shows. Harré (1977), who is examining the relation between the reflexive form and the theory of the person in Japanese culture, carries the point further: Responsibility arises simply as a grammatical requirement in accounting for the meaning and justification of actions; it need not be construed as raising the ontological problem of the "mysterious self."

Hamlyn (1977), contrary to Day, says that self-knowledge is not information-getting. Self-knowledge requires a view of one's practical self, of one's past and future life, and some involvement in them to the extent that division from oneself is ruled out. One cannot view oneself as one does another person. Hamlyn interprets his thesis as opposed to that of Freud; the importance of transference, he says, implies that self-knowledge cannot be the goal of psychoanalysis.

Loewald (1978), however, brings together transference, moral responsibility, and self-knowledge. Psychoanalysis, in making the unconscious conscious and having the ego come into being where id was, implies a view of the person's moral nature. The process promotes taking responsibility for oneself, for one's past history and for the history being made now, even for the past that took place without one's awareness. The past includes not only experiences but also an archaic mode of thinking, as in dreams and in modern art. So today one adds: "Where ego is, there id shall come into being again to renew the life of the ego and of reason" (Loewald 1978, p. 16). Transference reveals the historical dimension of love life and the erotic dimension of becoming a self. In its nonpathological meaning, as the dynamic of psychological development, transference reveals our historical continuity despite changes.

Epstein (1980a) whose theory of the self is an elaboration of Sullivan's anxiety-gating theory (cf Loevinger 1976a, Chap. 12), points out that some theorists speak of a need to maintain and enhance the self, but this is a logical contradiction, pitting stability against change. Evidence suggests that people with low self-esteem are less happy with positive evaluations than those with high self-esteem. Epstein finds a general factor of self-esteem, reasonably stable over time, having many relations with other cognitive and emotional variables. Confirming his Sullivanian theory, he finds a syndrome of low self-esteem, high anxiety, and proneness to disorganization. Block (1982) arrives at a similarly Sullivanian view of the relation of anxiety to personality stage change, beginning with a logical analysis of Piaget's concepts of assimilation, accommodation, and equilibration. Greenwald (1980) compares the self to an authoritarian regime, suppressing unflattering news about itself. However, he does not argue for personal unity; the person's verbal system and nonverbal or physical system are only partly encompassed in the self (1982). Golding (1978) also has a Sullivanian theory of personality.

Any psychologist investigating the self-concept must start with Wylie's (1979) massive compendium, now updated. However, as McGuire & McGuire (1981) point out, about 90% of the studies refer to a single aspect, self-esteem. Most studies ask subjects to respond in terms of the psychologist's frame of reference rather than their own. When people are asked simply, "Tell me about yourself," only about 7% of the material is self-evaluative.

Turner & Gordon (1981) have asked subjects to recall occasions that express their true or genuine self and why those occasions did so, then to recall occasions that betrayed their true self and why. For some, the true self involves ambition, morality, etc, hence is rooted in institutional structure. For others, unpremeditated impulse felt more authentic; hence their self was anchored in self-conscious separation from institutional structure. Inauthenticity was often related to family and early life, authenticity to peers and current life. There is a customary or usual self that lies between the true and spurious self; hence they are boundaries of self.

Marcia's (1976) account of the achievement of ego identity, adapted from Erikson's description of late adolescence, provides another perspective on the self. The four identity statuses—diffusion, foreclosure, moratorium, and achievement (their presumed developmental order)—may be seen as personality types, as stages, as alternative pathways, or as some combination. A variety of studies relating Marcia's interview and test to other variables can be construed as giving support to the construct validity of the measures, but neither the test nor the interview directly assess ego synthesis, sense of temporal continuity, nor role stability (Bourne 1978). The four statuses may be multidimensional rather than unitary, and the interview, which concentrates on occupation, religion, and politics for men, may not include all the major components for achieving identity status (Bourne 1978). The women's interview includes questions on premarital sex. When that topic is included on interviews for men women are more likely than men to have experienced a reflective crisis in the area of sexual ideology, while men are more likely to be foreclosed (Waterman & Nevid 1977).

Shrauger & Schoeneman (1979) reviewed more than 60 studies germane to the symbolic interactionist conception of the "looking-glass self," that self-concept reflects one's perceptions of how one appears to others. Concordance between self-concept and how people think others perceive them is consistently high in most studies. Concordance between self-concept and how others actually perceive the person tends to be lower and is often not even significantly positive. Perhaps the symbolic interactionists have reversed cause and effect.

Complementary to the self-concept as reflecting others' opinions is the view of social behavior as essentially self-presentation, an attempt to convey information to others about oneself (Baumeister 1982). Self-presentation may be motivated by the desire to please a particular audience or by the desire to construct a public self like one's ideal self. A wide range of social behaviors can be explained in these terms, including altruistic and aggressive behaviors, conformity and reactance.

In conclusion, the concept of self is a chimera (Day 1977, Gergen 1977). Or perhaps it is constructed by social experience and maintained by social role requirements (Hogan et al 1978), or by the use of shared systems of meaning (Smith 1980), or by social reinforcements (Bandura 1978). Or the self is the cognitive structure which gives meaning and organization to one's experience. Or the self is the person's own construction, the core of one's responsibility and one's moral being (Loewald 1978, Blasi 1980). In any case, the concept of self and associated concepts such as ego identity have generated interesting empirical research.

PSYCHOANALYTIC PERSONALITY THEORY

In the enormous literature of psychoanalysis, a recent group of books begins by acknowledging that there are many contradictory strains in Freud's writings and then reinterprets his main ideas as consistent with a previously underestimated strand (Gedo & Goldberg 1973, Izenberg 1976, Loewald 1978, Sulloway 1979). In some, the reappraisal hinges on flaws in translation (Kaufmann 1981, Bettelheim 1982). A slightly different approach discards what are admittedly some of Freud's favorite ideas in order to create a more logically consistent psychoanalytic theory (Schafer 1976, Rosenblatt & Thickstun 1977, Loevinger 1979b, Breger 1981b). Schafer, in particular, is not so much rereading Freud as rewriting psychoanalysis. Finally, there are primarily clinical approaches that also imply altered conception of normal personality (Kernberg 1975, Horowitz 1977, Kohut 1977, Wishnie 1977).

Ever since Freud proposed the so-called structural model of ego, superego, and id, psychoanalysts have discussed its relation to the earlier topographic model of conscious, unconscious, and preconscious systems; they argued for dispensing with one or the other or for various ways of combining them. Gedo & Goldberg (1973) point out that there was still another model of mind, the reflex-arc model, in the final chapter of *Interpre-*

tation of Dreams. They propose a hierarchical superordinate model into which the others fit as a developmental series. The reflex-arc model characterizes the neonatal period. The tripartite ego-superego-id model characterizes the post-Oedipal period. (They prefer the term "tripartite" to "structural," since all models refer to structures.) The topographic model characterizes adult life. Between the primitive reflex-arc model and the tripartite one there is an immense gap, covering the period of the construction and consolidation of the sense of self. Taking indications from the writings of Freud and other analysts, they propose to fill the gap by a model first of part-selves related to part-objects, or self-nuclei related to object-nuclei, then one of whole self related to whole object. They object to terms such as "ego-nuclei" and "superego-nuclei," which import terms from a later model into description of an earlier one. Later models replace earlier ones, they do not grow out of them, any more than a car grows out of a bicycle. Each of their models of mind thus constitutes a developmental stage.

Sulloway (1979) argues that the clue to Freud's personality theory is to be found in the discarded *Project for a Scientific Psychology,* which was based on his biological training and attempted to create a reductionistic (physiological-mechanical or biological-developmental or both) model of mental functioning. Freud lost interest in the *Project* because he found he could not explain repression without postulating an observing ego, but that negated the reductionism. Thus the attempt was a failure.

What Sulloway depicts as the biological core of Freud's theories comprises the elements that modern psychoanalytic theorists find dispensable because they are outdated, erroneous biology and because they are inconsistent with the psychological core of the theory as embodied in therapy (Breger 1981a). Breger's (1981b) rereading of Freud also begins with Freud's biological-scientific-reductionistic background, but he broadens the picture to include the conservative social milieu: male domination, devaluation of what was culturally described as "feminine," and overvaluation of work as opposed to pleasure. In the nineteenth century sex was a dark and dangerous force, masturbation the presumed source of physical and mental illness. These are among the views that psychoanalysis, with its implied social criticism, has liberated us from, yet in Freud's writings they persist, hardly disguised. In the early writings, masturbation was said to cause a specific kind of neurosis, and other sexual practices were similarly stigmatized. Even the latter-day Freud, turning to ego psychology, kept the idea of the sexual instinct as a dangerous and hostile force in the form of the id. Throughout, both strains of thought persist, the nineteenth century conservative world view and the new, socially critical view which psychoanalysis, perhaps more than anything else, has made the twentieth century view, the latter prominent in later works. The essential strain of Freud's thought is not, Breger asserts, instinct theory but the symbolic transformation of experience, which is the stuff of psychoanalysis as therapy and as a human enterprise.

For Bettelheim (1982), who, like Kaufmann, spoke German before English, the scientific-reductionistic tone of Freud's writings is largely due to mistranslation, a reflection of the influence of American technocratic ethos. Freud purposely chose words from common speech and is misrepresented by learned terms such as ego (*das Ich*), id (*das Es*), cathexis (*Besetzung*), and even mind (*Seele*).

Freud's first great discovery, psychic determinism, was based on a fundamental assumption of the unity of nature (Loevinger 1979b). This fundamental assumption has often been left unexplained or erroneously attributed to Brücke and the Helmholtz School, whose members were materialistic and reductionistic in science; hence, says Kaufmann (1981), they were opposite to Freud in this respect. Freud said more than once that it was hearing a reading of Goethe's essay on nature that was responsible for his choice of medicine as a profession, a remark most biographers do not connect with his theories. Kaufmann (1981) translated and reprinted the essay; it illustrates, he says, how Goethe's writings were the source of Freud's assumption of the unity of nature. Kaufmann attributes to Goethe the idea of development, including personality development, and particularly the growth of autonomy in adult life, a central aspect of maturity (Shapiro 1981), contrary to the usual emphasis on Darwin as Freud's source for the idea of development. Finally, contrary to the usual gloss of psychoanalytic interpretation as unmasking the "real person," Kaufmann credits Freud with adopting Goethe's view that a person is his deeds; the meanings interpreted in psychoanalysis come from symptoms, dreams, "mischievements," jokes, and so on, all deeds.

Schafer's (1976, 1978) action language for psychoanalysis is an extended argument for essentially the last point, namely, that psychoanalytic descriptions of people can be couched entirely in terms of deeds, with a gain in clarity and insight as compared with current psychoanalytic language with its many hypothesized entities. Schafer would eliminate technical nouns from the psychoanalytic vocabulary, not only cathexis (psychic energy), which has fallen into disrepute among a growing group of psychoanalysts and analytic psychologists (Gill & Holzman 1976), but also superego, id, ego, ego ideal, self, and so on. For example, Schafer says one does not need to reify the unconscious; it suffices to say that the person is doing something unconsciously.

A loose category of cognitive-dynamic theorists can be discerned, most of them drawing some of their insights from Piaget as well as from psychoanalysis. They do not, however, constitute a school in the sense of referring to each other's work.

Gedo (1979), the least Piagetian of the group, finds formative and even pathogenic influences on his patients not just in traumatic events, drives, and drive-derivatives, but especially in both consciously held and disavowed values and goals. An important place in his therapy is occupied by recognition and discussion of the values of the patient and of the people in the patient's past and current environment. Drive theory and object-relations theory should be replaced, he believes, by the theory of self-organization, his term for the hierarchy of aims. Unlike Klein's (1976) self-schema, which is purely cognitive, Gedo's self-organization does not separate cognitive from affective aspects.

Malerstein & Ahern (1982) are the most explicitly Piagetian in approach. They discern three types of character structure, named after and taking form from three intellectual stages defined by Piaget, the symbolic (ages 2–4), the intuitive (ages 5–7), and the (concrete) operational (ages 8–11). The symbolic type needs attachments to other people to have a secure identity; the intuitive needs other people for narcissistic supplies; the operational is achievement oriented and has more mature relationships. Everyone falls into one of those types.

Another type of cognitive-dynamic approach consists of a diagramatic representation of the mental processes of patients. Wishnie (1977) has accomplished this for the impulsive characters he has treated, mostly addicts and delinquent men. In his treatment the patient and the therapist together work out the preconscious ideas that precede and constitute the symptomatic outbursts.

Horowitz (1977, 1979) has several schematics that assist in visualizing cognitive-dynamic processes. One schematic (1979) is similar to Wishnie's in showing how a particular mental state predictably provokes another particular one. Another kind of diagram (1977) depicts the several "selves," roughly, internalized versions of members of the patient's family of origin, among which a patient's self-image is divided. Another diagram (1977) depicts psychoanalytic psychotherapy in terms of a Piagetian process of revision of primitive schemes to accommodate more mature insights.

The detractors and admirers of the radical proposals of Schafer, Gedo, and others generate a lively dialogue in psychoanalytic literature.

CONCLUSION

Could one write a chapter such as this for a volume on "Advances in . . ."? How much has been an advance? Many recent trends, such as interactionism, were anticipated by pioneers such as Gardner Murphy and Henry

Murray (Magnusson & Endler 1977, Maddi 1980, L. B. Murphy 1981). Empathy, too, is an old topic. The topic of self and the rereadings of Freud are in such disarray (however much we may have our preferred readings) that one cannot yet speak of advance. Psychologists, psychoanalysts, and philosophers often do not profit from each others' work; the Balkanization of research exists even within psychology, with its proliferation of stage sequences.

For all its conceptual and methodological problems, we consider the topic of stages to be a genuine advance. The understanding of children's personality development has been deepened and enriched by stage theories, even if the details need to be amended; the same theories quicken our understanding of individual differences in adult life. Admittedly, the cognitive developmentalists have a theoretical reach that exceeds their empirical or methodological grasp. Some, like most psychoanalysts, afford their readers no more glimpse of their data than charming quotations or case vignettes. And the highest stage described by a theorist may be an *apologia pro vita sua*. Intrinsic difficulties beset validational studies, however. Any given setting is likely to yield people with minimal stage variability, thus rendering moot the question of relations with other variables. Raising stage variability by combining subsamples from different settings, usually different ages or educational levels, introduces confounding variables and makes resulting correlations higher but uninterpretable.

Like Maddi (1980), we consider theory building important, yet we also are inclined to "acknowledge the possibility that there is never going to be a really impressive theory in personality or social psychology" (Meehl 1978, p. 829). But to Meehl's five "noble traditions"—descriptive clinical psychiatry, psychometric assessment, behavior genetics, behavior modification, and psychodynamics—we nominate a sixth: cognitive-developmental stage theories.

We have omitted some major trends, particularly sex roles and gender differences, but the topics touched on do reflect current trends. As to psychologists' approaches to morality—Kohlberg's ratiocination, Hogan's rule-conformity, Gilligan's caring responsibility, Hoffman's altruism, Haan's interpersonal balance, Blasi's responsibility—none of them (except Fowler's faith) much resembles or allows for some prominent religious trends among young people, the charismatic and evangelical sects, return to fundamentalism, or the laid-back, quasi-religious, narcissistic morality of groups such as est (Tipton 1982). One can relegate such trends to some low level, as perhaps all of the foregoing psychologists would. Or perhaps psychologists are out of touch with real-world morality. Or perhaps psychologists with renewed interest in "inner life" are, in their own way, being carried along by the same tide as those turning to religious renewal.

ACKNOWLEDGMENTS

Preparation of this chapter was assisted by a grant from the Spencer Foundation. We thank Augusto Blasi and Anne Colby for suggestions.

Literature Cited

Alston, W. P. 1977. Self-intervention and the structure of motivation. See T. Mischel 1977, pp. 65–102
Bandura, A. 1978. The self system in reciprocal determinism. *Am. Psychol.* 33: 344–58
Bar-Yam, M., Kohlberg, L., Naame, A. 1980. Moral reasoning of students in different cultural, social, and educational settings. *Am. J. Educ.* 88:345–62
Baumeister, R. F. 1982. A self-presentational view of social phenomena. *Psychol. Bull.* 91:3–26
Berkowitz, M. W., Gibbs, J. C., Broughton, J. M. 1980. The relation of moral judgment stage disparity to developmental effects of peer dialogues. *Merrill-Palmer Q.* 26:341-57
Bettelheim, B. 1982. Reflections: Freud and the soul. *New Yorker* 58:52–93
Bickhard, M. H. 1978. The nature of developmental stages. *Hum. Dev.* 21:217–33
Blasi, A. 1980. Bridging moral cognition and moral action: A critical review of the literature. *Psychol. Bull.* 88:1–45
Blasi, A. 1982. Autonomy in obedience: The development of distancing in socialized action. In *Contemporary Approaches to Social Cognition,* ed. W. Edelstein. Frankfurt: Suhrkamp. In press
Block, J. 1977. Advancing the psychology of personality: Paradigmatic shift or improving the quality of research? See Magnusson & Endler 1977, pp. 37–63
Block, J. 1982. Assimilation, accommodation, and the dynamics of personality development. *Child Dev.* 53:281–95
Block, J., Buss, D. M., Block, J. H., Gjerde, P. F. 1981. The cognitive style of breadth of categorization: Longitudinal consistency of personality correlates. *J. Pers. Soc. Psychol.* 40:770–79
Block, J., Weiss, D. S., Thorne, A. 1979. How relevant is a semantic similarity interpretation of personality ratings? *J. Pers. Soc. Psychol.* 37:1055–74
Block, J. H., Block, J. 1980. The role of ego-control and ego-resiliency in the organization of behavior. In *Development of Cognition, Affect, and Social Relations,* ed. W. A. Collins. *Minn. Symp. Child Psychol.* 13:39–101. Hillsdale, NJ: Erlbaum

Bourne, E. 1978. The state of research on ego identity: A review and appraisal. Parts I, II. *J. Youth Adolesc.* 7:223–51, 371–92
Bowers, K. S. 1977. There's more to Iago than meets the eye: A clinical account of personal consistency. See Magnusson & Endler 1977, pp. 65–81
Breger, L. 1981a. Freud conventionalized. *J. Am. Acad. Psychoanal.* 9:459–72
Breger, L. 1981b. *Freud's Unfinished Journey.* London: Routledge & Kegan Paul. 145 pp.
Broughton, J. M. 1980. Genetic metaphysics: The developmental psychology of mind-body concepts. In *Body and Mind,* ed. R. W. Rieber, pp. 177–221. New York: Academic. 261 pp.
Broughton, J. M. 1981a. The divided self in adolescence. *Hum. Dev.* 24:13–32
Broughton, J. M. 1981b. Piaget's structural developmental psychology. V. Ideology-critique and the possibility of a critical developmental theory. *Hum. Dev.* 24:382–411
Buss, A. R. 1977. The trait-situation controversy and the concept of interaction. *Pers. Soc. Psychol. Bull.* 3:196–201
Coke, J. S., Batson, C. D., McDavis, K. 1978. Empathic mediation of helping: A two-stage model. *J. Pers. Soc. Psychol.* 36:752–66
Colby, A. 1978. Evolution of a moral-developmental theory. *New Dir. Child Dev.* 2:89–104
Colby, A., Kohlberg, L., Gibbs, J. C., Candee, D., Speicher-Dubin, B., et al. 1983a. *Measuring Moral Development: Standard Issue Scoring Manual.* New York: Cambridge Univ. Press. In press
Colby, A., Kohlberg, L., Gibbs, J. C., Lieberman, M. 1983b. A longitudinal study of moral judgment. *Monogr. Soc. Res. Child Dev.* In press
Damon, W. 1977. *The Social World of the Child.* San Francisco: Jossey-Bass. 361 pp.
Damon, W., Hart, D. 1982. The development of self-understanding from infancy through adolescence. *Child Dev.* In press
Davison, M. L., Robbins, S., Swanson, D. B. 1978. Stage structure in objective moral judgments. *Dev. Psychol.* 14:137–46

Day, W. F. Jr. 1977. On the behavioral analysis of self-deception and self-development. See T. Mischel 1977, pp. 224–49

Döbert, R., Habermas, J., Nunner-Winkler, G., eds. 1977. *Entwicklung des Ichs.* Cologne: Kiepenheuer & Witsch. 360 pp.

Edwards, C. P. 1981. The comparative study of the development of moral judgment and reasoning. In *Handbook of Cross-cultural Human Development,* ed. R. H. Munroe, R. L. Munroe, B. B. Whiting, pp. 501–28. New York: Garland. 888 pp.

Endler, N. S. 1981. Persons, situations, and their interactions. In *Further Explorations in Personality,* ed. A. I. Rabin, J. Aronoff, A. M. Barclay, R. A. Zucker, pp. 114–51. New York: Wiley. 281 pp.

Epstein, S. 1979. The stability of behavior. I. On predicting most of the people much of the time. *J. Pers. Soc. Psychol.* 37:1097–1126

Epstein, S. 1980a. The self-concept: A review and the proposal of an integrated theory of personality. In *Personality: Basic Aspects and Current Research,* ed. E. Staub, pp. 81–132. Englewood Cliffs, NJ: Prentice-Hall. 386 pp.

Epstein, S. 1980b. The stability of behavior. II. Implications for psychological research. *Am. Psychol.* 35:790–806

Faust, D., Arbuthnot, J. 1978. Relationship between moral and Piagetian reasoning and the effectiveness of moral education. *Dev. Psychol.* 14:435–36

Feldman, D. H. 1980. *Beyond Universals in Cognitive Development.* Norwood, NJ: Ablex. 204 pp.

Feshbach, N. D. 1978. Studies of empathic behavior in children. *Prog. Exp. Pers. Res.* 8:1–47

Feshbach, N. D. 1982. Sex differences in empathy and social behavior in children. In *The Development of Pro-Social Behavior,* ed. N. Eisenberg-Berg, pp. 315–38. New York: Academic

Fitts, W. H. 1981. Issues regarding self-concept change. See Lynch et al 1981, pp. 261–72

Fowler, J. W. 1981. *Stages of Faith.* San Francisco: Harper & Row. 332 pp.

Furth, H. 1980. *The World of Grown-Ups.* New York: Elsevier. 221 pp.

Galbraith, R. E., Jones, T. M. 1976. *Moral Reasoning: A Teaching Handbook for Adapting Kohlberg to the Classroom.* Anoka, Minn: Greenhaven. 209 pp.

Gedo, J. E. 1979. *Beyond Interpretation.* New York: Int. Univ. Press. 280 pp.

Gedo, J. E., Goldberg, A. 1973. *Models of the Mind.* Chicago: Univ. Chicago Press. 220 pp.

Gergen, K. J. 1977. The social construction of self-knowledge. See T. Mischel 1977, pp. 139–69

Gergen, K. J. 1981. The functions and foibles of negotiating self-conception. See Lynch et al 1981, pp. 59–73

Gibbs, J. C. 1979. Kohlberg's moral stage theory: A Piagetian revision. *Hum. Dev.* 22:89–112

Gibbs, J. C., Widaman, K., Colby, A. 1982. *Social Intelligence: Measuring the Development of Sociomoral Reflection.* Englewood Cliffs, NJ: Prentice-Hall. 271 pp.

Gill, M. M., Holzman, P. S., eds. 1976. Psychology versus metapsychology: Psychoanalytic essays in memory of G. S. Klein. *Psychol. Issues* 9(4):1–376

Gilligan, C. 1982. *In a Different Voice: Psychological Theory and Women's Development.* Cambridge: Harvard Univ. Press. 180 pp.

Golding, S. L. 1978. Toward a more adequate theory of personality: Psychological organizing principles. In *Personality: A New Look at Metatheories,* ed. H. London, pp. 69–95. Somerset, NJ: Halsted

Greenwald, A. G. 1980. The totalitarian ego: Fabrication and revision of personal history. *Am. Psychol.* 35:603–18

Greenwald, A. G. 1982. Is anyone in charge? Personalysis versus the principle of personal unity. In *Psychological Perspectives on the Self,* ed. J. Suls. 1:151–81. Hillsdale, NJ: Erlbaum.

Haan, N. 1977. *Coping and Defending.* New York: Academic. 368 pp.

Haan, N. 1978. Two moralities in action contexts: Relationships to thought, ego regulation, and development. *J. Pers. Soc. Psychol.* 36:286–305

Habermas, J. 1979. Moral development and ego identity. In *Communication and the Evolution of Society,* ed. J. Habermas, pp. 69–94. Boston: Beacon. 239 pp.

Hamlyn, D. W. 1977. Self-knowledge. See T. Mischel 1977, pp. 170–200

Harré, R. 1977. The self in monodrama. See T. Mischel 1977, pp. 318–48

Harvey, J. H., Town, J. P., Yarkin, K. L. 1981. How fundamental is the "fundamental attribution error"? *J. Pers. Soc. Psychol.* 40:346–49

Helson, R., Mitchell, V. 1978. Personality. *Ann. Rev. Psychol.* 29:555–85

Hersh, R. H., Paolitto, D. P., Reimer, J. 1979. *Promoting Moral Growth.* New York: Longman. 270 pp.

Hickey, J. E., Scharf, P. L. 1980. *Toward a*

Just Correctional System. San Francisco: Jossey-Bass. 202 pp.

Hirschberg, N. 1978. A correct treatment of traits. See Golding 1978, pp. 45–68

Hoffman, M. L. 1977. Personality and social development. *Ann. Rev. Psychol.* 28: 295–321

Hoffman, M. L. 1981. Is altruism part of human nature? *J. Pers. Soc. Psychol.* 40:121–37

Hoffman, M. L. 1982. Development of prosocial motivation: Empathy and guilt. See Feshbach 1982, pp. 281–313

Hogan, R., Johnson, J. A., Emler, N. P. 1978. A socioanalytic theory of moral development. See Colby 1978, 2:1–18

Holt, R. R. 1980. Loevinger's measure of ego development: Reliability and national norms for male and female short forms. *J. Pers. Soc. Psychol.* 39:909–20

Horowitz, M. J. 1977. Structure and the processes of change. In *Hysterical Personality,* ed. M. J. Horowitz, pp. 329–99. New York: Aronson. 441 pp.

Horowitz, M. J. 1979. *States of Mind.* New York: Plenum. 282 pp.

Izenberg, G. 1976. *The Existentialist Critique of Freud.* Princeton: Princeton Univ. Press

Jackson, D. N., Paunonen, S. V. 1980. Personality structure and assessment. *Ann. Rev. Psychol.* 31:503–51

Johnson, C. N., Wellman, H. M. 1982. Children's developing conceptions of mind and brain. *Child Dev.* 53:222–34

Jones, E. E. 1979. The rocky road from acts to dispositions. *Am. Psychol.* 34:107–17

Kagan, J. 1980. Perspectives on continuity. In *Constancy and Change in Human Development,* ed. O. G. Brim Jr., J. Kagan, pp. 26–74. Cambridge, Mass: Harvard Univ. Press. 754 pp.

Kaufmann, W. 1981. *Discovering the Mind. Vol. 3. Freud versus Adler and Jung.* New York: McGraw-Hill. 494 pp.

Kegan, R. 1982. *The Evolving Self.* Cambridge: Harvard Univ. Press. 307 pp.

Kenrick, D. T., Stringfield, D. O. 1980. Personality traits and the eye of the beholder: Crossing some traditional philosophical boundaries in the search for consistency in all of the people. *Psychol. Rev.* 87:88–104

Kernberg, O. F. 1975. *Borderline Conditions and Pathological Narcissism.* New York: Aronson. 361 pp.

Klein, G. S. 1976. *Psychoanalytic Theory: An Exploration of Essentials.* New York: Int. Univ. Press. 330 pp.

Kohlberg, L. 1981a. *Essays on Moral Development.* Vol. 1. *The Philosophy of Moral Development.* San Francisco: Harper, Row. 441 pp.

Kohlberg, L. 1981b. *The Meaning and Measurement of Moral Development.* Worcester, Mass: Clark Univ. Press. 56 pp.

Kohut, H. 1971. The analysis of the self. *Monogr., Psychoanal. Study Child* No. 4. 368 pp.

Kohut, H. 1977. *The Restoration of the Self.* New York: Int. Univ. Press. 345 pp.

Kuhn, D. 1978. Mechanisms of cognitive and social development: One psychology or two? *Hum. Dev.* 21:92–118

Kuhn, D., Langer, J., Kohlberg, L., Haan, N. S. 1977. The development of formal operations in logical and moral judgment. *Genet. Psychol. Monogr.* 95:97–188

Kusatsu, O. 1977. Ego development and socio-cultural process in Japan. I, II. *Keizagaku-Kiyo (Journal of Economics)* 3(1):41–109; 3(2):74–128

Levine, C. G. 1979. The form-content distinction in moral development research. *Hum. Dev.* 22:225–34

Levinson, D. 1978. *The Seasons of a Man's Life.* New York: Knopf. 363 pp.

Lewis, C. C. 1981. The effects of parental firm control: A reinterpretation of findings. *Psychol. Bull.* 90:547–63

Lickona, T., ed. 1976. *Moral Development and Behavior.* New York: Holt, Rinehart & Winston. 430 pp.

Limoges, J., Paul, D. 1981. *Le Développement du Moi.* Longueuil, Quebec: Editions Prolingua. 131 pp.

Loevinger, J. 1976a. *Ego Development.* San Francisco: Jossey-Bass. 504 pp.

Loevinger, J. 1976b. Origins of conscience. See Gill & Holzman 1976, pp. 265–97

Loevinger, J. 1979a. Construct validity of the sentence completion test of ego development. *Appl. Psychol. Meas.* 3:281–311

Loevinger, J. 1979b. Psychoanalysis as a quasi-scientific paradigm. In *Scientific Ways in the Study of Ego Development,* ed. J. Loevinger, pp. 25–59. Worcester, Mass.: Clark Univ. Press. 59 pp.

Loevinger, J. 1979c. Theory and data in the measurement of ego development. See Loevinger 1979b, pp. 1–24

Loevinger, J., Wessler, R., Redmore, C. 1970. *Measuring Ego Development,* Vols. 1, 2. San Francisco: Jossey-Bass. 245 pp., 457 pp.

Loewald, H. W. 1978. *Psychoanalysis and the History of the Individual.* New Haven: Yale Univ. Press. 77 pp.

Lynch, M. D., Norem-Hebeisen, A. A., Gergen, K. J., eds. 1981. *Self-Concept: Advances in Theory and Research.* Cambridge, Mass: Ballinger. 367 pp.

Maddi, S. R. 1980. The uses of theorizing in personology. See Epstein 1980a, pp. 333–75

Magnusson, D., Endler, N. S. 1977. Interactional psychology: Present status and future prospects. In *Personality at the Crossroads,* ed. D. Magnusson, N. S. Endler, pp. 3–31. Hillsdale, NJ: Erlbaum. 454 pp.

Malerstein, A. J., Ahern, M. 1982. *A Piagetian Model of Character Structure.* New York: Human Sciences Press. 252 pp.

Mancuso, J. C., Ceely, S. G. 1980. The self as memory processing. *Cogn. Ther. Res.* 4:1–25

Marcia, J. E. 1976. Identity six years after: A follow-up study. *J. Youth Adolesc.* 5:145–60

Markus, H. 1977. Self-schemata and processing information about the self. *J. Pers. Soc. Psychol.* 35:63–78

McCall, G. J. 1977. The social looking-glass: A sociological perspective on self-development. See T. Mischel 1977, pp. 274–87

McClelland, D. C. 1981. Is personality consistent? See Endler 1981, pp. 87–113

McGuire, W. J., McGuire, C. V. 1981. The spontaneous self-concept as affected by personal distinctiveness. See Lynch et al 1981, pp. 147–71

Meehl, P. E. 1978. Theoretical risks and tabular asterisks: Sir Karl, Sir Ronald, and the slow progress of soft psychology. *J. Consult. Clin. Psychol.* 46:806–34

Mischel, T., ed. 1977. *The Self: Psychological and Philosophical Issues.* Totowa, NJ: Rowman, Littlefield. 359 pp.

Mischel, W. 1977. The interaction of person and situation. See Magnusson & Endler 1977, pp. 333–52

Mischel, W., Mischel, H. N. 1977. Self-control and the self. See T. Mischel 1977, pp. 31–64

Moss, H. A., Susman, E. J. 1980. Longitudinal study of personality development. See Kagan 1980, pp. 530–95

Murphy, J. M., Gilligan, C. 1980. Moral development in late adolescence and adulthood: A critique and reconstruction of Kohlberg's theory. *Hum. Dev.* 23:77–104

Murphy, L. B. 1981. Explorations in child personality. See Endler 1981, pp. 161–95

Nucci, L. P. 1981. The development of conceptions of personal issues: A domain distinct from moral or societal concepts. *Child Dev.* 52:114–21

Nucci, L. P., Turiel, E. 1978. Social interactions and the development of social concepts in preschool children. *Child Dev.* 49:400–7

Perry, W. G. Jr. 1970. *Forms of Intellectual and Ethical Development in the College Years.* New York: Holt, Rinehart & Winston. 256 pp.

Pervin, L. A. 1977. The representative design of person-situation research. See Magnusson & Endler 1977, pp. 371–84

Rest, J. R. 1979. *Development in Judging Moral Issues.* Minneapolis: Univ. Minn. Press. 305 pp.

Rest, J. R. 1983. Morality. In *Carmichael's Manual of Child Psychology,* ed. P. Mussen. 4th ed. In press

Rosén, A.-S., Nordquist, T. A. 1980. Ego developmental level and values in a yogic community. *J. Pers. Soc. Psychol.* 39:1152–60

Rosen, H. 1980. *The Development of Sociomoral Knowledge.* New York: Columbia Univ. Press. 197 pp.

Rosenblatt, A. D., Thickstun, J. T. 1977. Modern psychoanalytic concepts in a general psychology. *Psychol. Issues* 11(2–3):3–348

Rushton, J. P., Sorrentino, R. M., eds. 1981. *Altruism and Helping Behavior.* Hillsdale, NJ: Erlbaum

Schafer, R. 1976. *A New Language for Psychoanalysis.* New Haven: Yale Univ. Press. 394 pp.

Schafer, R. 1978. *Language and Insight.* New Haven: Yale Univ. Press. 208 pp.

Secord, P. F. 1977. Making oneself behave: A critique of the behavioral paradigm and an alternative conceptualization. See T. Mischel 1977, pp. 250–73

Selman, R. L. 1980. *The Growth of Interpersonal Understanding.* New York: Academic. 343 pp.

Shapiro, D. 1981. *Autonomy and Rigid Character.* New York: Basic Books. 179 pp.

Shrauger, J. S., Schoeneman, T. J. 1979. Symbolic interactionist view of self-concept: through the looking glass darkly. *Psychol. Bull.* 86:549–73

Shweder, R. A., D'Andrade, R. G. 1979. Accurate reflection or systematic distortion? A reply to Block, Weiss, and Thorne. *J. Pers. Soc. Psychol.* 37:1075–84

Smith, M. B. 1978. Psychology and values. *J. Soc. Issues* 34:181–99

Smith, M. B. 1980. Attitudes, values, and selfhood. In *Nebr. Symp. Motiv.* 27:305–50

Smither, S. 1977. A reconsideration of the developmental study of empathy. *Hum. Dev.* 20:253–76

Snarey, J. R., Blasi, J. R. 1980. Ego development among adult kibbutzniks: A cross-cultural application of Loevinger's theory. *Genet. Psychol. Monogr.* 102: 117–57

Sroufe, L. A. 1979. The coherence of individual development: Early care, attachment, and subsequent developmental issues. *Am. Psychol.* 34:834–41

Staub, E. 1978. *Positive Social Behavior and Morality*, Vol. 1. *Social and Personal Influences.* New York: Academic. 490 pp.

Staub, E. 1979. *Positive Social Behavior and Morality*, Vol. 2. *Socialization and Development.* New York: Academic. 317 pp.

Sullivan, C., Grant, M. Q., Grant, J. D. 1957. The development of interpersonal maturity: Applications to delinquency. *Psychiatry* 20:373–85

Sullivan, E. V. 1977. A study of Kohlberg's structural theory of moral development: A critique of liberal social science ideology. *Hum. Dev.* 20:352–76

Sulloway, F. J. 1979. *Freud: Biologist of the Mind.* New York: Basic Books. 612 pp.

Sundberg, N. D., Snowden, L. R., Reynolds, W. M. 1978. Toward assessment of personal competence and incompetence in life situations. *Ann. Rev. Psychol.* 29:179–221

Suzman, R. M. 1977. Social change in America and the modernization of personality. In *We, the People: American Character and Social Change*, ed. G. J. DiRenzo, pp. 40–81. Westport, Conn: Greenwood

Tamashiro, R. T. 1979. Adolescents' concepts of marriage: A structural-developmental analysis. *J. Youth Adoles.* 8:443–52

Taylor, C. 1977. What is human agency? See T. Mischel 1977, pp. 103–35

Tipton, S. M. 1982. The moral logic of alternative religions. *Daedalus* 111:185–213

Toulmin, S. E. 1977. Self-knowledge and knowledge of the "self." See T. Mischel 1977, pp. 291–317

Turiel, E. 1978. Distinct conceptual and developmental domains: Social convention and morality. *Neb. Symp. Motiv.* 25:77–116

Turner, R. H., Gordon, S. 1981. The boundaries of the self: The relationship of authenticity in self-conception. See Lynch et al 1981, pp. 39–57

Underwood, B., Moore, B. 1982. Perspective-taking and altruism. *Psychol. Bull.* 91:143–73

Vaillant, G. E. 1977. *Adaptation to Life.* Boston: Little, Brown. 396 pp.

Warren, M. Q. 1979. The female offender. In *Psychology of Crime and Criminal Justice*, ed. H. Toch, pp. 444–69. New York: Holt, Rinehart & Winston

Warren, M. Q. 1982. Delinquency causation in female offenders. In *Judge, Lawyer, Victim, Thief: Women, Sex Roles and the Criminal Justice System*, ed. N. H. Rafter, E. A. Stanko. Boston: Northeastern Univ. Press. In press

Waterman, C. K., Nevid, J. S. 1977. Sex differences in the resolution of the identity crisis. *J. Youth Adolesc.* 6:337–42

Weiner, M. L. 1979. A Freudian and Piagetian rapprochement in psychotherapy. *Bull. Menninger Clinic* 43:443–62

Weinreich, H. 1977. Some consequences of replicating Kohlberg's original moral development study on a British sample. *J. Moral Educ.* 7:32–39

Weston, D. R., Turiel, E. 1980. Act-rule relations: Children's concepts of social rules. *Dev. Psychol.* 16:417–24

White, C. B., Bushnell, N., Regnemur, J. L. 1978. Moral development in Bahamian school children: A 3-year examination of Kohlberg's stages of moral development. *Dev. Psychol.* 14:58–65

Whiteley, J. M., ed. 1979. Ego and self. *Couns. Psychol.* 8:2–40

Wishnie, H. 1977. *The Impulsive Personality.* New York: Plenum. 208 pp.

Wylie, R. C. 1979. *The Self-Concept*, Vols. 1, 2. Lincoln: Univ. Nebraska Press. Rev. ed.

Youniss, J. 1980. *Parents and Peers in Social Development.* Chicago: Univ. Chicago Press. 301 pp.

Ziman, J. M. 1971. Information, communication, knowledge. *Am. Psychol.* 26: 338–45

Ann. Rev. Psychol. 1983. 34:223–60
Copyright © 1983 by Annual Reviews Inc. All rights reserved

EVALUATION RESEARCH: A METHODOLOGICAL PERSPECTIVE

Paul M. Wortman

School of Public Health and Institute for Social Research, P.O. Box 1248, University of Michigan, Ann Arbor, Michigan 48106

CONTENTS

INTRODUCTION

According to Mosteller (1981), the earliest known evaluation study was a nutrition quasi-experiment conducted by Daniel, Shadrach, Meshach, and Abednego. The results, reported in the Old Testament, showed a vegetarian diet to be equally as effective as one containing meat. Despite its roots in antiquity, evaluation research is a relatively young field. This is only the third chapter on the topic to appear in the *Annual Review of Psychology* (Perloff et al 1976, Glass & Ellett 1980). The two earlier reports focused on defining the area and providing an overview of the activities that comprise evaluation research. Such broad perspectives are no longer possible, nor even desirable, in a short review. In the past few years the efforts of the early evaluation researchers have flourished and the field is literally ablaze with activity. There are now three major evaluation journals, two national evalu-

223

0066-4308/83/0201-0223$02.00

ation organizations, and dozens of books on all aspects of the evaluation enterprise.

Since the last report on evaluation research the field has been especially productive in the number and quality of the volumes that have appeared. This period has witnessed a successor to the classic work of Campbell & Stanley (1966) on quasi-experimental design (Cook & Campbell 1979); a major treatise by Glass and his associates (1981) on meta-analysis; and a long sermon on the proper conduct of the evaluation enterprise (Cronbach et al 1980). In addition, there have been volumes on other important topics in evaluation research such as secondary analysis (Boruch et al 1981b), cost-benefit analysis (Thompson 1980), and structural equations modeling (Kenny 1979), as well as a number of textbooks (Posavac & Carey 1980, Saxe & Fine 1981, Rossi & Freeman 1982).

Evaluation research is an applied, largely (and unfortunately) atheoretic, multidisciplinary activity spanning the social sciences and including education, health, and social work as well. While it shares with all these fields the common goal of assessing or evaluating innovative social programs aimed at improving human welfare, one might despair at discerning any other common threads that unite these disparate activities and weave them into a shared destiny. Indeed, it is the very question of how to synthesize such a diverse set of activities and facts that contains, as the ancient Chinese proverb claims, the seeds of its own answer. Evaluators have been grappling with this very problem. They have been asking: "How do I get the facts necessary to evaluate a program?" "And once I have them, how do I combine them into a comprehensive evaluation?" While the questions are almost philosophical in nature, they represent to the evaluator pragmatic concerns over the choice of appropriate scientific research methods.

It is a shared need for useful evaluation methods that cuts across the disciplinary fiefdoms and unites the evaluation community. This does not mean that there is peace and calm in the choice of appropriate methods. To the contrary, there have been religious crusades, minor vendettas, and the numerous scholarly bloodbaths that one would expect when different disciplines converge on an activity. These clashes are the inevitable growing pains of a young profession. The examination of some of these evaluative methods and the debate surrounding them is the subject of this chapter. The perspective is historical in that it briefly examines the predominant methodological school of thought from the "early days," then considers a topic of recent development and present concern, and concludes with an examination of an evaluative method that looms increasingly important in the near future of the field. The first method, social experimentation, deals with the question of how to obtain the facts; the later two—meta-analysis and cost-effectiveness analysis, respectively—are concerned with the synthesis of that information. Each method, and its associated controversy, increases the scope of evaluation activities toward the ultimate end of fulfilling their primary goal to provide useful, policy-relevant information.

SOCIAL EXPERIMENTATION

The evaluation of a social program is a difficult, time-consuming, and expensive activity. While the ultimate scientific test of any claimed fact is its replicability, these high resource costs provide infrequent opportunities for this in evaluation. For this reason among others, many evaluation methodologists have urged that the most unequivocal procedure or design be used in assessing an innovative program. In particular, they have advocated the use of randomized social experiments or their equivalent. In the health area, where a similar debate has raged (Gehan & Freireich 1974, Byar et al 1976), the concept is referred to as the randomized, clinical trial or RCT. (In the following discussion both terms will be used where appropriate.) When randomization is impossible, proponents argue for strong quasi-experiments such as regression discontinuity or time-series designs (Riecken et al 1974). The volume by Riecken and his associates was the first to emerge from the battles over the proper interpretation of the early evaluations of the Great Society programs that carried this message. They claimed, "the general stance of this volume is to endorse experimentation as a superior means of getting dependable knowledge about social interventions . . ." This approach represents the application of the experimental model, common in psychology, to the applied field settings that characterize evaluation research.

Validity

The foundation of social experimentation was laid by Campbell & Stanley (1966) in their monograph describing a conceptual framework for assessing the quality of various research methods. To do this, they borrowed a concept developed in the field of tests and measurement known as "validity." They applied this concept to experimental design to indicate the equivocality or validity of the findings. Originally, the world was divided into two types of validity—"internal" and "external." The former refers to the credibility of the causal relationship between treatment program and outcome while the latter is concerned with the generalizability of that relationship to other persons, locations, programs, and outcome measures. Each of these two validity types, in turn, contained a set of phenomena that could account for the observed results and thus cloud the interpretation of the experiment. These were called "threats" to validity or "plausible rival hypotheses." For internal validity there were eight such threats (i.e. testing, history, instrumentation, selection, maturation, experimental mortality, statistical regression, and selection-maturation and other interactions) easily remembered by the mnemonic THIS MESS (J. Polka, personal communication). There were only four threats to external validity: reactive effect of testing, selection-treatment program interaction, reactive effects of the experiment, and multiple program or treatment interference.

In the more recent reformulation by Cook & Campbell (1979), the conceptual framework has swollen significantly. The number of validity categories has doubled from two to four while the total number of specific threats to validity has nearly tripled, jumping from 12 to 33. Five new threats were added to internal validity and two were added to external validity. For example, four of the new threats to internal validity deal with factors that could affect the performance of the control group (i.e. "diffusion" of the program, "compensatory equalization," and "rivalry," and "resentful demoralization"). The titles are nearly self-explanatory. Thus the diffusion or "imitation" of the program refers to the situation where the control group has access to and uses a comparable program. Similarly, for external validity the interaction of the treatment program with either location (or "setting") or time (or "history") have been added to the interaction with persons or "selection."

Each of these original categories, in turn, spawned a new type of validity. Internal validity produced "statistical conclusion validity," and "construct validity" was split off from external validity. The former contained seven totally new threats to validity, while the latter was composed of ten threats of which four stemmed from the original Campbell and Stanley typology. The remainder of this section briefly describes these two new validity categories.

STATISTICAL CONCLUSION VALIDITY   The threats to validity involving the data analytic procedures used to determine if the threatment program has a causal impact were called statistical conclusion validity. Most of these are obvious and well-known factors such as inadequate statistical power (Cohen 1977), violation of important assumptions for the statistical procedure, multiple tests of significance (Tukey 1977), and variability produced by the outcome measures (i.e. "reliability"), program setting, or participants. All of these can affect the results adversely, with the majority making it difficult to reject the null hypothesis of no program impact. For example, McSweeny & Wortman (1979) uncovered a number of threats to statistical conclusion validity in their reanalysis of a major study evaluating a community-based mental health treatment facility. One problem they found—not included in the Cook and Campbell list of threats—involved errors in coding and recording the data. As Chalmers and his co-workers note (1981), if researchers are not "blind" to the source of the data, systematic errors can occur at this step in the research process.

There is no question that statistical issues play an obvious and critical role in research. Perhaps that accounts for their omission by Campbell and Stanley. It was only in the succeeding years that evaluators fully realized the statistical quagmire posed by some commonly used quasi-experiments. The debate over the appropriate analysis of (or adjustments for) statistical regression artifacts resulting from measurement error or unreliability is indicative of the learning that occurred (e.g. Campbell & Erlebacher 1970, Wortman et al 1979). In light of this, one may question the decision of Cook and Campbell not to move statistical regression from internal validity into this new category of essentially statistical problems.

One threat, "the reliability of treatment implementation," is a bit more problematic. While it is true that variability in treatment implementation has the effect of reducing the statistical power of the analyses (Boruch & Gomez 1977), it is more likely that this results from a change in program definition. This could occur for two reasons: normal adaptation to local resources such as skills of personnel, funds, and available facilities, or the natural development of the program over time—the so-called "moving target" problem (Wagner 1979). These changes in what Sechrest and his associates (1979) call the "integrity" of the program are viewed by them and others (cf Judd & Kenny 1981) as more appropriately categorized as a threat to construct validity.

CONSTRUCT VALIDITY That part of the evaluative research process dealing with theoretical or hypothetical constructs (e.g. desegregation) and their proper translation (or operationalization) in programs and outcome measures is the domain of construct validity. As Sechrest et al (1979) note, "it refers to our interpretation of treatments, not to the treatments themselves." Cook and Campbell indicate that researchers typically refer to this as "confounding." Confounding can occur when there is a simple disagreement over the definition or label attached to the program—"inadequate preoperational explication of constructs" according to Cook and Campbell. However, it is more likely to result over a dispute about which of the multiple elements that comprise most social programs (i.e. "confounding constructs and levels of constructs") actually produced the observed effects.

Two other confounds in construct validity were derived from Campbell and Stanley's threat to external validity called "reactive effects of experimental arrangements"—"evaluation apprehension" and "experimenter expectancies." These refer to the desire of participants in experiments to please the researcher and the biases transmitted to them by the experimenter, respectively. In the health area, RCTs containing placebo controls and double-blind procedures are often employed to remove these annoying excess constructs. However, in most evaluations it is not possible to blind participants to the programs they are receiving.

Another threat to validity appears to have changed names in the revision of the Campbell and Stanley scheme. "Multiple-treatment interference" was rechristened "interaction of different treatments" during its metamorphosis from external to construct validity. Cook and Campbell claim that the receipt of multiple programs is "quite rare in field settings." However, Albritton (1978) describes an evaluative study where there were similar competing state and federal vaccination programs. In light of the large array of social service programs, it is likely that this threat will be more common in evaluation than Cook and Campbell indicate.

SUMMARY   The validity approach was revised by Cook and Campbell for "convenience" and because it was "practical" in viewing the research process. The four categories of validity have great heuristic value in sorting through the complex issues that inevitably surround any program evaluation (cf Wortman & St. Pierre 1977, McSweeny & Wortman 1979). They are even useful in gaining a perspective on other evaluative methodologies, as will be demonstrated in the discussion below on meta-analysis. At the level of specific threats to validity, however, the sheer number is both overwhelming and somewhat confusing. Some threats seem a bit esoteric, especially for evaluators (e.g. "ambiguity about the direction of casual influence" and "hypothesis-guessing within experimental conditions," for example); some seem to differ only in small degree ("compensatory rivalry by respondents receiving less desirable treatments" and "resentful demoralization of respondents receiving less desirable treatments," for example); and still others (noted above) seem to be miscategorized, thereby blurring the differences among the major validity types. In addition, some of these threats are relevant during the design and planning for an evaluative study while others are more appropriate to the management and conduct of the study (e.g. multiple statistical testing, program implementation, diffusion, etc). Perhaps some consolidation is needed to make the whole structure less cumbersome and "threatening."

Some evaluators disagree with the major validity categories themselves, the priority attached to them, or the faithfulness of the adherents to this approach. For example, Judd & Kenny (1981) define external validity solely as the generalizability to other theoretical constructs, a part of Cook and Campbell's definition of construct validity. Their justification seems a bit strained, and it only confuses those trying to understand this new typology. Another related issue that also has not gone unquestioned is Cook and Campbell's advocacy of "the primacy of internal validity." Finally, two other threats to construct validity represent frequent complaints about the "fairness" of the evaluation enterprise. These concern the use of a single, primary outcome measure (i.e. "mono-operation bias") or a single evaluative method (i.e. "mono-method bias"). These issues will be addressed in the following section dealing with critical reactions to the experimental, validity-based approach to program evaluation.

Reactions and Controversies

The validity framework provides an almost inexorable logic that has been used to justify higher-quality evaluation of program outcome or impact. The trend toward impact assessments using strong research methods, particularly randomized experiments, has not gone unchallenged, however. The thesis advocated most strongly by social psychologists like Campbell and his associates has, as would be expected, generated a number of "antitheses." Some of these reactions have been quite specific, such as the following one (of 95) by Cronbach and associates (1980): "Much that is written on evaluation recommends some one 'scientifically rigorous' plan. Evaluations should, however, take many forms, and less rigorous approaches have value in many circumstances" (p. 7). The authors attribute their strong Reformational counterattack to what they term "recent propaganda." Later in the volume they elaborate that they are "only restoring a balance that the evaluative commandments overturned." Much of the argument hinges on a few vivid case studies using quasi-experiments that obtain larger effects. Cognitive psychologists (Tversky & Kahneman 1974, Nisbett & Ross 1980) have warned about the judgmental bias in using such data. Moreover, the "big bang" notion harks back to the specious expectations of the early days of program evaluation (cf Boruch & Wortman 1979) when large effects were claimed in part to muster political support for a new social program. Other arguments based on costs, external validity, and politics are equally flawed and lacking in persuasion.

Cronbach and his colleagues (1980) claim, for example, "Internal validity, however, is not of salient importance in an evaluation. What counts is external validity." Even such sympathetic reviewers as House & Mathison (1981) have commented that "the case against internal validity may be overstated." Cronbach et al feel that such "tight designs" compromise political relevance and that the "policy shaping community" or "PSC," as they call it, "always reaches beyond the data." The problems in generalizing from incorrect causal inferences or estimates of effect (see below) have been all too amply demonstrated by the earliest evaluation efforts. There are few who would prefer to return to those quarrelsome times. However, a larger dilemma is revealed by the recommendation, and its associated political pressure, for the priority of external validity. This concerns the ability to evaluate program impact at all.

EFFICACY   The debate over the relative importance of external and internal validity reflects a certain amount of disciplinary myopia stemming from the very origins of evaluation in education. In the area of health evaluation a different conceptual perspective prevails that sheds some light on this issue. The Office of Technology Assessment (OTA) has clarified and defined the two relevant concepts—"efficacy" and "effectiveness"—in a recent report (1978). Translating OTA's concepts into a more common evaluation vernacular, efficacy is defined as: "The . . . benefit to individuals in a defined population from a [social program] applied for a given . . . problem under *ideal conditions of use*" (emphasis added).

In health, efficacy evaluations are often achieved through large, cooperative, multicenter RCTs. These studies are expensive, complex, long-term undertakings. Nevertheless, there are many notable RCTs in health evaluating the efficacy of innovative medical treatments (e.g. tests of drug therapy for hypertension and coronary-artery bypass surgery for ischemic heart disease); and there has been a modest trend for an increasing number of such trials (Fletcher & Fletcher 1979). Indeed, the FDA requires new drugs to be evaluated by RCTs.

Effectiveness, on the other hand, is identical to efficacy in definition, except that it refers to "average conditions of use." Thus efficacy involves determining whether a program *can* have an impact while effectiveness is concerned with whether it *does* have an impact. The majority of evaluations have been conducted in less than "ideal" field settings and have thus been assessing effectiveness. The continued advocacy for the primacy of external validity will only perpetuate a situation where program impact is confounded with "conditions of use." In such circumstances it will be impossible to know how the program would have functioned under "ideal conditions."

Certain organizational and political constraints promote effectiveness evaluations in education and make efficacy assessments even more difficult to achieve. Education is a public monopoly that is part of the political environment. Moreover, federal policymakers often advocate the widest possible test of a new program to generate the necessary political support for funding the program. This means that ideal conditions will generally not be available. Campbell (1979a) as well as Boruch et al (1981a) have recommended more focused experiments. One way this could be accomplished is to solicit willing and organizationally exemplary school districts to be part of a social experiment within the large diffusion of the program. Even here, care in site selection will be necessary since benefits, especially outside funds, are often the primary motive for participation in such studies (cf Wortman & St. Pierre 1977). In these cases, program implementation is likely to be inadequate.

This is not meant to imply that the experimental approach is without legitimate limitations and criticisms. These have been raised by House (1980) and others in education and by Horwitz & Feinstein (1981) and others in health. The former have been concerned with understanding process rather than outcome. In education, evaluators have discovered that the effects are typically small and cumulative and, as a consequence, much attention has been focused on program implementation including its strength and integrity (Williams 1976, Boruch & Gomez 1977, Sechrest et al 1979). Given the inherent complexity of most educational programs, careful attention to these process issues is warranted. Faulty implementation has often been discovered as the root cause of finding no effects.

QUALITATIVE METHODS   In response to earlier criticisms of his advocacy of a rigorous experimental approach to program evaluation, Campbell (1979a) labeled this as a "controversy between 'qualitative' vs. 'quantitative' modes of knowing." He noted that this debate which is characteristic of the social sciences has "spilled over into evaluation research." One way of viewing this dispute is as a fight for methodological evaluation turf. Given the multidisciplinary nature of evaluation research, it is not surprising to find social scientists advocating the legitimacy of the methods in their disciplines as suitable for conducting program evaluations. Thus those with a background in social anthropology feel that enthnographic case studies are appropriate, while those in sociology think participant observation studies are also useful. The debate surrounding these and other similar methods (e.g. interviews, document analysis, etc) has recently reached a crescendo where qualitative methods are viewed as comprising a Kuhnian "paradigm shift" (Partlett & Hamilton 1976, Patton 1978). The proponents of these methods feel that there is a "methodological status hierarchy . . . that denigrates those who employ qualitative methodology" (Patton 1978), but that the dominant quantitative paradigm is "inadequate for elucidating the complex problem areas they confront" (Partlett & Hamilton 1976).

Another way of viewing the dispute is that it represents a useful critique of current, mainstream (primarily experimental) approaches to conducting an evaluation. The qualitative methodologists have claimed that quantitative methods are not comprehensive. They feel such methods force the evaluator to examine a limited, and often biased, set of outcomes that usually do not include the views, reactions, and feelings of program participants. Moreover, they believe the quantitative approach is unrealistic and unworkable. The experimental approach assumes strict control over a stable program—both questionable assumptions, according to qualitative proponents. They view programs as complex interventions that not only vary from site to site, but also develop and change over time. As McLaughlin stated (in Davis 1982), "Experimental methods, at their best, can describe what happened, but they cannot explore crucial contextual and process issues of *how* and *why.*" Thus qualitative methods are believed to be essential in expanding the evaluator's repertoire of skills and ability to answer different questions.

Patton (1978) has elaborated on the characteristics that differentiate the two paradigms. He identifies eight dimensions that separate the two approaches. In addition to the qualitative-quantitative distinction just discussed, others include "objectivity" or "subjectivity" of the measures, the perspective (i.e. "holistic" or "component") and "distance" of the evaluator (i.e. "closeness" or far). Patton feels that the "subjective" observations of a trained scientist are valid and essential for a true "understanding" of a program's impact. They bring the evaluator closer to the phenomena of the program and provide a broader view of it. Campbell (1979a), while acknowledging the truth of such criticisms as "measurement rigidity," finds them not totally compelling. Although Partlett & Hamilton (1976) claim that the third stage of their qualitative approach called "illuminative evaluation" is to "delineate cycles of cause and effect," Campbell maintains that, "naturalistic observation of events is an intrinsically equivocal arena for causal inference . . . because of the ubiquitous confounding of selection and treatment." He does not see causal inference as being achieved by the "substitution of qualitative clairvoyance." Moreover, Campbell's associates (Reichardt & Cook 1979) contend that there really is not an alternative, qualitative paradigm at all. In examining the various distinguishing features proposed by Patton and others, they conclude that "the attributes of a paradigm are not inherently linked to either qualitative or quantitative methods."

While paradigms may be an inappropriate level of the debate, what are the implications of the claims for methodological diversity in evaluation research? On this score there seems to be an emergent consensus: both approaches are valid and useful. McLaughlin (Davis 1982) calls for "ways to combine the strengths of the methodological tools available—quantitative assessment of outcomes and qualitative examination of [process]." Despite his pique at Reichardt and Cook's analysis, Patton (1980) also shares this view. Campbell (1979b) advocates a "sensible joint use of models" and has, upon reflection, granted that qualitative, case study approaches can in some cases provide "a kind of pattern matching" to test theories. Moreover, qualitative methods can be used with either quantitative or other qualitative methods to "triangulate" on a phenomenon and remove observer or instrument bias. Similarly, Reichardt & Cook (1979) advise the evaluator "to use whatever methods are best-suited to their research needs" even if that entails "a combination of qualitative and quantitative methods." They see such a combination as not only extending the scope of the evaluation, but also yielding new insights not accessible by either method alone. Their only concerns are the expense, time, and skills needed to conduct such evaluative studies which leaves them "not optimistic" that such multimethod evaluations will become widespread.

Finally, there is one other important benefit to be gained from combining the two methods and avoiding what Campbell (1979a) called the "all or none flip-flop." This concerns the utilization of the evaluation—a topic of great concern to evaluators over the past few years (Weiss 1977, Alkin et al 1979). Qualitative case study information is likely to be more persuasive and memorable than numerous tables containing the results of quantitative analyses. Nisbett & Ross (1980) reviewed a number of studies demonstrating that a "single, vivid instance" can affect social attitudes when "pallid statistics of far greater evidential value do not." The information used in these studies was similar to that obtained by qualitative methods. It is vivid in that it has concrete, imagerial, and emotional properties. It is just such information that is easily learned and recalled. As Tversky & Kahneman (1974) note, it is more "available." Thus qualitative data may play an essential role in making evaluative findings more utilizable by providing memorable and powerful images that illustrate major points and findings.

TIMING   An important issue embedded in the debate over randomized social experiments concerns the appropriate time when an evaluation should be conducted. Given the controversy that surrounded the early evaluations of the Great Society social programs, it seems clear that most field settings are inappropriate locations for evaluations. As McLaughlin noted in her debate with Boruch (Davis 1982), such evaluations are susceptible to problems in "participant motivation, the quality of technical assistance, and the level of institutional support." In other words, these are assessments of effectiveness and not efficacy. While McLaughlin was arguing against "an experimental paradigm" that includes randomized studies, she did not address the efficacy/effectiveness issue. This is due in part to the absence (until recently) of the concept in educational evaluation and in part to the limited opportunities for such evaluations. According to Cronbach and associates (1980), only programs or innovations that have completed their initial stage of development and moved onto the second, so-called "superrealization," stage of innovational maturity are ready for an efficacy assessment. Unfortunately, Cronbach et al note: "Superrealizations are not often set up for social programs, because impatient policy makers are quick to put an appealing idea into practice on a substantial scale" (p. 150). Later, they elaborate by observing that education and social service programs, unlike health, are not based on well-defined theory so that "there is less interest in what is ideally possible." The point being made is a subtle one: there is a time for evaluating a program's efficacy (i.e. at the superrealization stage), but that point may be skipped in the hasty development of most social programs.

Contrary to the belief of Cronbach and his co-workers, the situation in health is not much better. Chalmers (1981) and his associates (1972), in commenting on the low rate of RCTs, have observed, "The uncontrolled pilot study . . . often leads to ethical arguments against a definitive clinical trial." Again, there is a tendency to skip an efficacy assessment and move from what McKinlay (1981) calls a "promising report" to a stage of rapid diffusion that permits only effectiveness studies. Knox (1980), in commenting on heart transplants, observed: "There has never been a mechanism in this country to regulate the diffusion of new medical technology once past the strictly investigational stage, other than the skepticism or enthusiasm of the doctors involved." Chalmers has taken the almost radical position that, "The only way to circumvent this impasse is to begin randomization with the first patient." He claims that for ethical reasons randomization should begin early since many innovations turn out to be either harmful or ineffective (e.g. due to low dosage or toxic side effects).

Innovators, on the other hand, claim that this would be unfair since they need time to develop the program or technology (i.e. they are at the initial or "breadboard" stage as Cronbach et al call it). However, Chalmers feels that this approach itself is unethical since it often denies the patient the knowledge and choice of other more established treatments. Moreover, determinations of the proper dosage or treatment strength (Sechrest et al 1979) are, he claims, areas where randomization is useful. Often innovation is spurred by desperate patients (Warner 1975) who have exhausted all conventional approaches in combating a life-threatening illness. Even here, Chalmers believes randomized studies should be conducted. Such patients often have other complications that place them at even greater risk for the negative side effects of the innovative treatment. Mosteller (1981) adds that from a societal perspective the results of such studies will benefit future patients and generations, including one's family and friends. If such studies are not conducted or certain patients decline to participate, then the results may be unavailable or biased.

It is clear that important, policy-relevant randomized studies have been conducted (cf Boruch et al 1978), but that they are only a small fragment of the total (cf Wortman 1981b). Should program evaluators follow Chalmers' advice, or is it both infeasible and incorrect? Costs are certainly a problem. Randomized studies are more complicated and expensive to conduct. Most researchers do not have the fiscal and organizational resources to mount such investigations. Even where there is support, the number of available subjects may be too small, thus necessitating yet more complex interinstitutional arrangements such as cooperative trials. All these are formidable obstacles that may daunt the most entrepreneurial evaluator. Chalmers feels the rewards are worth the effort. However, evaluation research is primarily a government administered and subsidized activity. Funds are limited, although in some areas more are being urged (Office of Technology Assessment 1982). Moreover, political demands for prototypes in geographically diverse locations make efficacy evaluations problematic. Clearly, more support is needed for the basic research that must precede any significant innovation (Comroe 1978), and time is needed to perform small-scale or "focal-local" evaluations (Campbell 1976) under "ideal conditions." In this sense, Cronbach and associates are correct; the PSC does control the process. Evaluators must convince themselves that efficacy is worth the effort and then persuade the funding agencies that comprise the PSC as well.

Is this the correct course? Mosteller (1981) and his co-workers (Gilbert et al 1975, 1977) have conducted two studies examining program evaluations and surgical innovations. In both cases only half the innovations were judged "successful." Given the high failure rate, Mosteller concludes that, "This suggests strongly that social or medical innovations *do* need to be evaluated." Boruch (in Davis 1982) views high-quality, primarily randomized, studies as a cost-effective activity since, "We will not have to do real experiments after bad quasi-experiments in an effort to justify programs." This, he claims, will provide policymakers with "the gradual accumulation of decent information on how well ideas work and their costs." The work in these latter two areas—the accumulation of evidence and costs—is discussed in the following two sections.

META-ANALYSIS

The past few years have seen the development, application, and widespread adoption of a new statistical technique for aggregating the results from many research studies. This method has been called "meta-analysis" or the "analysis of analyses" by its originator (Glass 1976). Although other similar statistical procedures have been developed and applied (Rosenthal 1978, Cooper 1979), the term and method promulgated by Glass and his associates have been the most utilized by far. In fact, the rapidity of its diffusion is somewhat of a methodological phenomenon in its own right. In their recent book discussing the meta-analysis procedure, Glass and his associates (1981) cite over 40 different applications in nearly as many areas of research in the 5 year period since its introduction. Many of these applications have been in psychology, and the trend is growing, as indicated by the recent spate of articles in *Psychological Bulletin* (cf Burger 1981, Johnson et al 1981, Strube & Garcia 1981)—the major review journal for the discipline. While the majority of these examples involve the synthesis of basic research, the method is applicable, relevant, and useful in applied areas as well (e.g. Smith & Glass 1977). In particular, there are many evaluative areas with sufficient studies to warrant meta-analysis.

In its simplest form, meta-analysis involves the computation of the average effect size (ES or, more recently, Δ in the Glass et al notation) for a group of studies. The effect size measure used by Glass is the standard score obtained by subtracting the mean of the control group from that of the treatment group (i.e. $T - C$) and dividing this difference by the standard deviation of the control group (SD_C). An effect size can be calculated for each relevant outcome or dependent variable in a study. In such situations, the unit of analysis becomes the effect size rather than the study (see below). The effect sizes are then summed and divided (by the total number of effects) to obtain a single quantitative number, the average effect size. Then, assuming that the results are normally distributed, a Z-table can be consulted to determine the percentile rank of the average person, as indicated by the average effect size, in the treated group. A positive effect size would usually indicate a beneficial treatment while a negative value would indicate that the treatment was ineffective or even harmful.

Social scientists are used to dealing with small effects, and Cohen (1962) has even gone so far as to provide rules of thumb for categorizing effects as "small," "medium," or "large," depending on their absolute value. Nevertheless, Glass et al (1981) exhort their readers to cease from such labeling, claiming that there is "no wisdom whatsoever" in this practice. Sechrest & Yeaton (1981) agree that it is inappropriate to use absolute values to interpret an effect size. They note that small effects may be "deceptively worthwhile" while effects that seem large may be considered "trivial." Sechrest and Yeaton discuss two ways of classifying an effect-size estimate which they call "judgmental" and "normative" approaches.

The judgmental approach involves an assessment by a relevant individual such as a policymaker or "expert." Sechrest and Yeaton feel that experts are especially suited to make such judgments since experts probably share a common "experiential background" and, therefore, a similar, implicit metric. They briefly discuss two small studies where they found that experts were able to predict the size of effects found in experimental treatments. It is also likely that such experts share a common scientific body of knowledge. For that reason groups of experts might produce even better estimates than individuals, given the pooled knowledge and experience that would be available. On a more informal basis, such "consensus" activities are currently being conducted by the National Institutes of Health to assess the scientific evidence bearing on new medical technologies (Wortman 1981a).

The second or normative procedure for interpreting the magnitude of an effect involves the use of comparative rather than "absolute" standards. This approach would compare an effect with the prevailing norm derived from previous studies. Thus, if a new effect is larger than any previously found, it would be judged as (comparatively) a significant finding. Sechrest and Yeaton feel this is a more common occurrence. Such a use of effect sizes has been recommended by Posavac (1980) in a meta-analysis of patient education programs.

Glass (1977) has advocated meta-analysis as a replacement for the traditional way of summarizing the research literature—the review article. The method apparently delivers an objective result borne of a straightforward statistical procedure. Moreover, the resulting effect-size estimate has both direction and magnitude—an improvement over the subjective judgment that comprises most literature reviews. In synthesizing the literature the reviewer is asked to perform an almost impossible cognitive task: combining the results from dozens of studies using different research designs and outcome measures that may vary in both quality and appropriateness. It is not surprising that such reviews typically call for more definitive research or rely on the small minority of studies that are relatively spotless scientifically. Statistical methods for research synthesis like Glass's meta-analysis avoid cognitive overload and much of the subjective bias it entails. It thus allows a single, objective summary finding to emerge that may not have been apparent in the single study or review.

A dramatic example of the potential benefits of such data integration methods is provided by a recent article in the medical literature (Baum et al 1981). These authors performed a formal synthesis of all RCTs using no-treatment controls to assess the effectiveness of antibiotics as a prophylactic in colorectal surgery. Effectiveness was determined by examining both abdominal wound infection and mortality rates. They located 26 studies published between 1965 and 1980 and in 22 of them found that antibiotics produced a lower rate of infection. The temporal pattern of the effect sizes was displayed graphically (see Figure 1). Overall, the infection rate was reduced by about 20 percent for those patients treated prophylactically with antibiotics. The mortality rate also indicated a consistent benefit for those treated by antibiotics with the average rate about 6 percent lower or about 60 percent fewer deaths than in the control group.

The investigators did not directly calculate a standardized effect size. Instead, they only report the 95 percent confidence intervals for mean

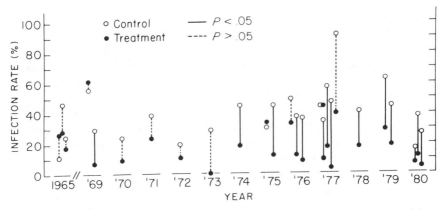

Figure 1   Infection rates for both the treatment and control regimens for the individual trials by year reported, with statistical significance noted. Reprinted by permission of *The New England Journal of Medicine,* 1981, 305:796.

differences, also using another interesting graph to reveal the temporal pattern of the cumulative findings (see Figure 2). In both cases this interval does not contain zero, thus indicating a statistically significant effect for antibiotics. As Figure 2 indicates, the 95 percent confidence interval for infection rates excluded zero by 1969 (after only five studies). Glass et al (1981) recommend using a probit transformation to obtain an effect size

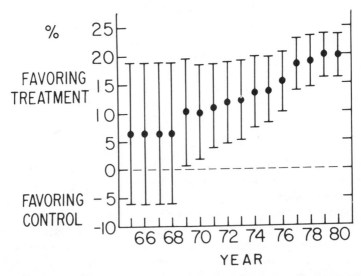

Figure 2   The 95 percent confidence intervals on the true difference in infection rates, calculated over time. Reprinted by permission of *The New England Journal of Medicine,* 1981, 305:796.

estimate for such data. The differences noted above correspond to effect sizes of approximately .6 and .4 standard deviation units for infection and mortality rates, respectively.

Baum and associates demonstrate a major advantage of research synthesis by showing that the cumulative findings from these research studies yielded a statistically reliable positive effect for antibiotic prophylaxis as early as 1975. At that time, only 9 of 12 studies indicated a lower postoperative infection rate, in which only 3 had statistically significant results. Moreover, the synthesis provides enough cases for the analysis of mortality data—something that was not possible for any single study because there were too few outcomes. Finally, the authors claim that the results of these studies indicate that the continued use of no-treatment control groups is inappropriate. They recommend instead that future studies employ a "previously proved standard of comparison," even though they realize that this leads to a "scientific dilemma," since it will be much more difficult to demonstrate additional gains in effectiveness for new treatments. For example, using one of the effective drugs as a control in a new RCT would require over 1000 patients to demonstrate a reduction in infection by another 50 percent. Thus it would be prohibitively expensive to demonstrate similar gains in mortality.

Validity

Although they were developed to assess the quality of individual studies, the validity categories discussed above are relevant to the discussion that has surrounded the introduction and application of meta-analysis. They provide a useful approach to organizing these comments and examining the limitations of the method. In this section the four types of validity developed by Campbell and his associates (Campbell & Stanley 1966, Cook & Campbell 1979) will be applied to a critical examination of meta-analysis.

EXTERNAL VALIDITY   One of the major objections to meta-analysis is that it mixes "apples and oranges" (Gallo 1978, Presby 1978). For example, these critics of Smith & Glass's (1977) meta-analysis of psychotherapy have claimed that it is inappropriate to cluster or stratify different kinds of therapy into a single category. This is listed as "Criticism #1" by Glass et al (1981) in their discussion of the meta-analysis method. They are not persuaded by this criticism and even find it "inconsistent." They claim that subjects within a study are as different as those between studies.

Elashoff (1978), in commenting on whether to aggregate the results of several studies, addresses this external validity issue. Specifically, she recommends against synthesis when the results are not "homogeneous across different patient populations." She cites as examples the differential effects of steroid therapy for alcoholic hepatitis found in males and females, and the improved efficacy of cimetidine in treating duodenal ulcer as a function of duration of therapy.

There are statistical procedures for determining the homogeneity of the results (Gilbert et al 1977, Hunter et al 1982). Elashoff applied the procedure recommended by Gilbert and associates to the two reviews noted above (i.e. steroid therapy for alcoholic hepatitis and cimetidine for duodenal ulcer) and found it appropriate to combine the results of the cimetidine studies, but not those from the steroid therapy studies. For the latter, the standard deviation for the percentage differences in mortality was 27, of which only 7 percentage points could be expected from sampling variation alone.

Hunter and coworkers (1982) have addressed the issue from another perspective. These investigators ask whether the variability in the effect sizes can be accounted for by sampling alone. If not, other variables need to be entered into the analysis. In other words, apples and oranges may be included in the latter situation by appropriate blocking or stratifying variables that separate the "fruits of one's analysis." These techniques thus reduce the debate over external validity to a statistical test of the homogeneity of variance. Baum et al (1981) used this procedure before "pooling" the results of the studies on antibiotic prophylaxis in colon surgery.

CONSTRUCT VALIDITY   The "apples and oranges" problem is to a large extent an issue in construct validity. The determination of the study's scope is probably the first question asked. This is a critical issue for it sets the boundary on what studies should or should not be included in the meta-analysis. As Glass et al (1981) acknowledge, the solution "depends entirely on the exact form of the question being addressed." If studies are testing the same hypothesis, then aggregation would be appropriate. However, critics contend that the operationalization of the theoretical construct (i.e. the independent variable) presents the problem. Thus, for example, should behavior modification be treated as equivalent to rational-emotive therapy (Presby 1978)? Again, the answer appears to follow from the question posed, as Glass et al contend. If a policy decision to reimburse clinical psychologists for psychotherapy is being considered, then a general question concerning the effectiveness of all therapies seems appropriate. Similarly, the Baum et al (1981) study did not ask which specific antibiotic was most effective in preventing adverse consequences of colorectal surgery. If one finds heterogeneous results, using the above methods, it may be that too broad a theoretical construct (or "construct of causes") is being investigated. Fortunately, this is an empirical question that can be easily addressed.

Where there is faulty operationalization it may be necessary to exclude studies. For example, DeSilva and his coworkers (1981) found it appropriate to aggregate only 6 of 15 RCTs in determining the effectiveness of lignocaine (or lidocaine) in preventing irregular heartbeats in patients who had suffered a heart attack. The excluded studies used "subtherapeutic concentrations of lignocaine," either an improper initial dose or an incorrect injection. These are both violations of construct validity.

A related construct validity issue concerns the appropriateness of the measures (or dependent variables) employed in the various studies. Berk & Chalmers (1981) attempted to integrate the research literature dealing with the cost-effectiveness of ambulatory care. They found that only 4 of 78 studies used an appropriate measure of costs. In such situations, studies may have to be excluded, even if that jeopardizes the ability to conduct the meta-analysis. There is considerable room for judgment here, and the research investigator should explicitly state the construct being investigated and the studies actually excluded on these grounds.

In evaluation research, standardized measures are typically employed. Then the decision to include these studies involves the quality of the measures and their similarity. Although standardized achievement tests have been shown to vary in the skills they assess (Porter et al 1978), most researchers would agree that such tests are similar enough to be used to integrate study findings. In evaluation research, the debate is more often on the comprehensiveness or "fairness" of these measures in assessing the variety of programmatic objectives (House et al 1978, House 1980).

INTERNAL VALIDITY   The role of internal validity considerations in the proper conduct of meta-analysis has, as might be expected, figured prominently in the discussion of this new method. What is unexpected is the heated nature of the debate and the accompanying level of invective. Such words and phrases as "simplistic," "tendentious diatribes," "astute dismantling of [author's name] myth," and "abandonment of scholarship" have littered the verbal landscape of the exchanges between Glass and his critics. The reader may wonder what provoked such emotional reactions and whether the criticisms are, in fact, legitimate.

The major controversy concerns whether design quality (i.e. internal validity) affects the results (Mansfield & Busse 1977, Eysenck 1978, Jackson 1980, Marshall 1980). Critics such as Mansfield & Busse (1977) maintain that studies with more threats to internal validity (i.e. "poorly designed") are more likely to report large effects than those with few plausible threats to internal validity (i.e. "well-designed"). Instead, they recommend a triage strategy: throw out those studies wtih significant methodological problems and divide the remainder into well-designed and less well designed categories. Separate meta-analyses can then be performed to see if there is convergence in the results. If there is not, then the results from the well-designed group are more credible. There is considerable empirical evidence to support the contention that design quality is inversely related to effect size in other areas such as health (e.g. Gilbert et al 1977, Wortman 1981), and even Glass's own work (Glass & Smith 1979) in education has shown that quality can affect the results.

For his part, Glass (1977, 1978) and his associates (Glass and Smith 1978, Glass et al 1981) have steadfastly maintained that, "It's bad advice to eliminate virtually any studies on strictly methodological grounds." They contend that the effect of design quality can be detected *"a posteriori"* without excluding any studies that may, in the final analysis, have comparable effects to those deemed better. Glass consistently cites the results of his meta-analysis of psychotherapy (Smith & Glass 1977) where design quality had "virtually no correlation with study findings." If this is not the case, as in the Glass & Smith (1979) study, then "the sensible course was elected" and the results of the well-controlled studies were emphasized. They attribute the need to control for design quality to the small effects found in that meta-analysis. Glass et al (1981) acknowledge that research quality is a "central concern in meta-analysis" but maintain that it is an "empirical matter." They offer as additional evidence the results of 12 other meta-analyses where there is little variation in results attributable to internal validity. They conclude that this should be "an effective antidote to rampant a priorism" that seeks to exclude studies from the meta-analysis.

A number of points can be made in rebuttal, however. First, the majority of the studies in the Smith & Glass (1977) meta-analysis of psychotherapy —65 percent according to a recent reanalysis (Landman & Dawes 1982)— were well controlled. In fact, the quality of the studies, as a whole, was quite high. Thus the correlation between quality and effect size would be expected to be low since the range (of internal validity) was restricted. Second, Glass et al (1981) categorized studies as "high," "medium" or "low" in internal validity. They do not define the coding procedure, but it is apparently somewhat subjective. Recently there have been some published reports on procedures for grading and coding study quality (Mosteller et al 1980, Chalmers et al 1981). These methods require attention to a large variety of methodological detail (i.e. over 30 study characteristics in the Chalmers et al system) that is not captured in the broad categories used by Glass et al. Moreover, ratio scales can be constructed to assess internal validity from the Chalmers et al system; these are likely to be more sensitive than the nominal scales used by Glass and his associates. In addition, the Chalmers et al procedure incorporates most of the threats to validity described by Cook & Campbell (1979) along with other design features and allows direct comparisons with other research syntheses (e.g. Baum et al 1981).

Finally, many studies may have to be excluded from the meta-analysis because they lack the appropriate statistical information to calculate an effect size. Despite the ingenious, and even heroic, methods that Glass (1977) and his collaborators (Glass et al 1981) have developed for salvaging this information, it may not be possible to obtain an estimate of the effect size. Often these studies are the worst ones from a methodological standpoint and thus would not be available for the correlational analyses performed by Glass et al (1981). In work examining the school desegregation literature (Wortman et al 1982), 79 percent of the studies had to be excluded largely for this reason.

From the perspective of internal validity, there do appear to be a number of (what one critic has called) "logical considerations" that must be handled a priori. The type of control group used—whether no-treatment, placebo, or existing standard—is just as essential to the estimate of effect size as the type of treatments were from an external validity perspective. The estimate of effect size is likely to decrease as one moves from a no-treatment control group to one composed of the existing standard. This was one of the major criticisms cited by Landman & Dawes (1982) for their reanalysis of the Smith & Glass (1977) meta-analysis of psychotherapy. Landman and Dawes, therefore, confined their secondary analysis to RCTs having no-treatment controls. They also performed a separate analysis for those studies including placebo controls. Their results are in substantial agreement with those of Smith and Glass. This is not surprising given the high quality of the studies in the original analyses, but it does avoid the methodological controversy noted above. Moreover, the type of control group does affect the results. Landman and Dawes report an effect size reduced by nearly one-third when a placebo control is employed.

The type of design can also affect the results of a meta-analysis. One of the major threats to the internal validity of nonrandomized studies is differential selection. If subjects systematically differ along a crucial dimension of concern to the study's hypothesis, then the results will be biased. Moreover, the effect-size estimate used by Glass implicitly assumes a randomized study. For quasi-experiments, a second term in the equation is needed to remove the pre-existing difference or initial effect size due to improper selection. (This term would have an expected value of zero for RCTs.) Since most evaluation studies are quasi-experiments, it is important to remove the pretest differences between the treatment and control groups. When such a pretest-adjusted meta-analysis was conducted for the predominantly quasi-experimental literature dealing with the effects of school desegregation on minority achievement, statistically significant differences were found (Wortman et al 1982). The results are displayed in Table 1. Those studies that were judged a priori not to have a selection problem had a

Table 1 Adjusted and unadjusted methods for the meta-analysis of quasi-experiments

Meta-analysis method	Overall mean ES	Selection problems[a]	No selection problems
Unadjusted	0.42 (n = 32)	0.57 (n = 20)	0.20 (n = 10)
Pretest adjusted	0.16 (n = 32)	0.16 (n = 20)	0.20 (n = 10)
Pairwise t-value	t_{62} = 2.73, p < .02	t_{38} = 2.94, p < .01	t_{18} = 0, n.s.

[a] In two cases it was not possible to determine whether or not there were selection problems.

negligible effect size difference at pretest, while those judged to have a selection problem had a pretest difference of nearly 0.6. The overall, average effect size was 0.42 using the Glass method and 0.16 when adjusted for pretest differences. Thus the bias introduced by threats to internal validity can be both substantial and systematic.

Glass (1978) has even gone so far as to lament that the weaker pretest-posttest quasi-experimental design studies were not included in the meta-analysis of psychotherapy. In addition to the selection problems noted above, the results would also be confounded by maturation and statistical regression. All of these threats to internal validity would probably increase the estimate of effect size. As a consequence, studies using such designs should probably be excluded from the meta-analysis. Without other evidence it would be impossible to correct for the bias introduced by those validity problems.

In conclusion, differences in the type of control group and design can affect the result of a meta-analysis. As Jackson (1980) has noted, it is likely that there will be "incongruencies in the findings," and then one needs some well-designed studies to determine whether internal validity is a source of the variation. A simple solution is to perform separate analyses on the relevant categories (i.e. no-treatment and placebo control, randomized or quasi-experiment). One cannot assume that these threats will be either self-cancelling, small, or sparse. In particular, adjustments to eliminate preexisting group differences should be considered in meta-analyses of quasi-experiments. Alternatively, where there are sufficient studies, one can confine the analysis to RCTs with no-treatment control groups as was done by Baum et al (1981).

STATISTICAL CONCLUSION VALIDITY The final validity issue concerns the appropriateness of the statistical methods employed. A number of related concerns such as testing for homogeneity and adjusting for pretest differences in quasi-experiments have already been noted. The most consistent statistical comment has focused on the practice of combining multiple results from a single study. Landman & Dawes (1982) noted five different kinds of nonindependence of measures (e.g. multiple measures from the same subject, at multiple points in time, etc). Glass et al (1981) consider this technical criticism to be the most "cogent." Their stated position is that: "The simple (but risky) solution is to regard each finding as independent of the others. The assumption is untrue, but practical." (p. 200).

Landman & Dawes (1982) followed the practice employed by other investigators and used the study as the unit of analysis by pooling the multiple effect size estimates in each report to produce an average effect size. Glass et al (1981) claim this is a "facile solution" that is "likely to obscure many important questions" that could be answered by the multiple measures. They recommend more esoteric procedures such as Tukey's jackknife method to handle interdependent data. However, most meta-analysts, including Smith & Glass (1977), have taken the "simple" path. Landman and Dawes found that there was "no consistent impact" on the results when the study was the unit of analysis. Such a cautious approach, however, seems reasonable given the uncertainty in resolving this issue. An analogy from analysis of variance methodology may be appropriate here: test for main effects before looking for simple effects and interactions.

Summary

There is no doubt that formal methods for synthesizing research results from many studies represent a significant methodological innovation. The meta-analysis procedure, in particular, is illustrative of these statistical methods—their utility and limitations. These techniques can often burn through the haze of uncertainty that surrounds any one study and clearly reveal effects only dimly perceived before. On the other hand, the allure of such apparently simple statistical magic can blind the potential user to the limitations of these methods.

For all its computational simplicity, such methods are usually quite laborious. They require a scouring of the literature for all potential studies. This is followed by a sequence of judgmental steps that are all open to various threats to validity. These involve the selection of studies addressing the topic or hypothesis and using comparable measures (i.e. construct validity), the use of stratifying or moderating variables (i.e. external validity), the exclusion of studies with weak designs or inappropriate control groups (i.e. internal validity), and the appropriate unit of analysis (i.e. statistical conclusion validity). As with any new innovation, there is a period of development and adjustment. Meta-analysis, and other similar research synthesis methods, are clearly in this early stage of "trial-and-error" learning despite their widespread diffusion. The validity concepts developed for assessing the quality of individual evaluative studies provide a useful framework for examining these data aggregation approaches. There are, however, other limitations involving coding of the studies, the type of inferences that can be made, and problems in using regression analyses (see Jackson 1980 for a discussion). It is important that the methodological consumer of these new evaluation techniques be aware of their potential problems as well as their strengths.

COST-EFFECTIVENESS ANALYSIS

Evaluation researchers, especially psychologists, have been largely concerned with determining the effectiveness of innovative social programs. The last decade has witnessed tremendous progress in developing research methods for accomplishing this goal, as the preceding discussion has indicated. However, as the recent debate over federal policy for mental health services has indicated (Kiesler 1980, 1982, Saxe 1982), the demonstration of program effectiveness is not sufficient to affect decision and other policymakers. The next step after the evaluation of program effectiveness is the determination of whether the programs are efficient in their use of scarce economic resources (McKinlay 1981). The methods involved in making this determination are called cost-benefit and cost-effectiveness analysis. Although an earlier *Annual Review of Psychology* chapter (Perloff et al 1976) contained a brief section on "benefit-cost analysis," the methods have undergone such rapid development in both conception and importance as to warrant a second, more detailed, discussion.

In a seminal paper appearing in the first major treatise on evaluation research, Levin (1975) described the rationale and general approach in conducting a cost analysis. Levin noted that the evaluator's excitement in discovering significant effects for a program may be "misleading" since it ignores cost considerations. Levin demonstrated the cogency of this comment by an actual example drawn from the evaluation of an innovative educational program using computer-aided instruction (CAI). While the CAI program was able to produce mathematics gains for elementary school children, it did so at a cost of about $150 per year. Using data from the control group, Levin found that the same gains could be achieved by adding approximately a half hour of additional instruction at a cost of only $35 per year. Thus, the statistically significant findings demonstrating the effectiveness of the CAI program cost four times as much as a simple alternative involving only a small increase in teaching.

Definitions

Current practitioners view the methods of cost-effectiveness and cost-benefit analysis as being similar and complementary processes (Warner & Luce 1982). For this reason, recent reports (Office of Technology Assessment 1980) have referred to them by their initials as CEA/CBA, respectively. CEA/CBA is viewed as a dicision-making tool for allocating public funds to programs that are more efficient.

The terms CBA and CEA are defined as: "formal analytical techniques for comparing the positive and negative consequences of alternative ways to allocate resources" (OTA 1980). The results of research studies and other applied findings are often used in conjunction with elaborate mathematical and other models to determine or compare the costs and benefits of the program under consideration. A wide variety of techniques can be used in conducting a CBA and CEA.

The principal difference between these two approaches lies in the "valuation" of benefits. In CBA all benefits as well as all costs are valued in monetary terms. This permits the decision maker to compare projects or programs of different kinds (such as mental hospitals with drug addiction treatment programs). On the other hand, CEA does not value benefits in terms of monetary value but measures them in some other unit (such as quality of life-years or years of life gained). As a consequence, CEA does not result in a net monetary value (that is, of benefits minus costs), but instead the amount of dollars or costs involved in achieving some desired effect. Therefore, CEA only allows a decision maker to compare programs that have similar objectives.

Principles

Despite this difference, the methods are considered as generally similar in both "concept and purpose." CEA is now viewed as an important adjunct to CBA. Moreover, analysts have become more sophisticated and this has allowed them to combine the two. For example, monetary benefits are also included in a CEA by transforming them into negative costs. This allows one to compute "the *net* cost per unit of effectiveness." While there is no standard method, OTA (1980) did find "general agreement on a set of 10 principles of analysis that could be used to guide the conduct, evaluation, or use of CEA/CBA studies." These principles, listed in Table 2, are consistent with the description of other authors (Thompson 1980, Warner & Luce 1982) and are discussed briefly below.

Table 2 Ten general principles of analysis (for CEA/CBA methodology)[a]

1. Define problem	6. Differentiate perspective of analysis
2. State objectives	7. Perform discounting
3. Identify alternatives	8. Analyze uncertainties
4. Analyze benefits/effects	9. Address ethical issues
5. Analyze costs	10. Interpret results

[a] Reprinted with permission from the Office of Technology Assessment (1980).

PROBLEM DEFINITION   The first step in the conduct of a cost analysis (#1) involves the specification of the problem including its scope. For example, if one is concerned with the anguish and suffering of those who are mentally ill, then it is appropriate to consider alternative forms of treatment such as the most effective psychotherapeutic procedures. On the other hand, if one takes a broader perspective that includes future mental illness, then prevention becomes a relevant concern and a larger set of alternatives should be considered.

Evaluation research, however, has been program, rather than problem, focused. The perspective is admittedly a narrow and limited one. In these situations, evaluators have been primarily concerned with either program operation (or process) or program outcome (or impact). A CEA/CBA would focus on whether these outcomes are achieved "efficiently." While most CEA/CBAs have been, in fact, program or technology focused in the past few years, they run the risk, according to Warner & Luce (1982), of "missing the forest for the trees." That is, analytical rigor may be achieved at the price of ignoring the broader perspective involving a comparison with alternative programs. However, in evaluation research this is often not possible for there are seldom alternative programs available for comparison except in a prospective way. While CEA/CBA is appropriate for analyzing prospective programs, it places a greater burden on the analyst in estimating future costs and outcomes.

OBJECTIVES   Once the problem has been specified, the next task (#2) is to define concrete objectives. This also poses many problems. The major one concerns measurement. It may simply be impossible to measure or even specify the objectives that are of major interest. For example, psychotherapy may have as its major objective diminished mental anguish or, alternatively, improved mental health. Thus, the alleviation of pain, suffering, and incapacity may have many associated variables that are difficult, if not impossible, to quantify. A useful outcome measure might be an increase in the number of additional high quality years of life, but as yet there are few measures available to provide quality of life indices for mental illness prevention and treatment.

More commonly there will be multiple objectives and these should be noted. It is important that they represent the most important dimensions of the problem and capture the impacts of the program. This should include "non-measurable goals and outcomes." Currently, CEA/CBA analysts tend to ignore such difficult problems and focus instead on the quantifiable objectives. This means that the difficult problems are not getting appropriate consideration. On the other hand, it may not be worthwhile to invest considerable resources in quantifying such objectives. In some cases it may be possible to achieve a meaningful analysis using secondary measures. For example, the cost of maintaining mental patients in noninstitutionalized settings may be cheaper than the old mental hospital, and it may be agreed that the quality of patients' lives is definitely as great, if not greater, than when they were institutionalized. In this case the deinstitutionalization program would be seen as cost-effective.

IDENTIFICATION OF ALTERNATIVES When considering this issue (#3), analysts typically are thinking of "explicit programs with budgets, organization, inputs, and outputs." However, as noted above, in evaluation there are often no alternative programs to be considered. One also should keep in mind "nonprogrammatic" alternatives that may not be amenable to CEA/CBA since their costs and benefits may be difficult to assess. For broadly defined problems, the analyst may be forced to reduce the number of alternatives considered. In this case, he or she should select a variety of programs that are considered to be "potentially cost-effective." If possible, these should be representative of the various possible alternatives. When choosing among similar alternatives, one should select the program that is most effective.

MEASUREMENT AND ANALYSIS OF BENEFITS AND COSTS The next steps (#4 and 5) involve the description of what is called a "production function." The production function is used to relate economic resources or "inputs" to benefits or outcomes (sometimes called "outputs"). This is often a mathematical procedure involving techniques such as linear programing, Markov processes, and computer simulations. For example, in perhaps the first reported cost-benefit analysis (Guess 1981), Bernoulli in 1760 employed a differential equations model to determine the effectiveness of smallpox vaccine on mortality. More recently, Albritton (1978) performed an interrupted time-series analysis to estimate the impact of a federally sponsored measles vaccination program (i.e. the "number of cases averted").

Schoenbaum et al (1976) used the Delphi technique to obtain several estimates needed to determine the likely effectiveness of the swine flu vaccine program on various subgroups of the population. According to Warner & Luce (1982), this is "one of the most technically challenging aspects of analysis." In many cases an analyst can borrow from comparable programs in other locations to determine the relationships. A variety of external validity factors should be considered, including the scale of the program, whether the technology or program has changed, whether the program being used as a model is really efficient, and whether it has some unique resources that cannot be duplicated in the program under consideration.

Once this is accomplished the next step is the "identification, measurement, and evaluation of the costs and benefits associated with the production process" (Warner & Luce 1982). As noted above, in CEA cost savings are included not as a benefit but as a negative cost. This allows one to examine net cost changes compared to "all net health benefit changes measured in some non-monetary units." There are both direct and "indirect" costs that must be taken into account in calculating the CBA/CEA. The direct costs refer to actual resources used in producing outcomes while indirect costs involve resources not directly affecting the outcomes; for example, the value of a patient's time that may be used in other productive activities rather than waiting for services to be delivered. These so-called "opportunity costs" should follow directly from the specification of the production function.

Once the resources involved have been identified, their cost or "valuation" must be determined. This, too, is generally a straightforward procedure when one uses current wage rates and other monetary expenditures. However, caution is recommended in using the actual, rather than the billed, charges for costs, for in many cases these charges are adjusted to subsidize other unprofitable activities in the organization.

A similar process occurs on the benefits or effectiveness side involving the outputs of the process. First, one identifies the potential objectives or the benefits that one wants to attain and then assigns a dollar value to them if one is dealing in a cost-benefit approach. Otherwise, for CEA the process ends at this identification step. The benefits involve personal, institutional, and societal outcomes. For example, this could include reduced days of illness, decreased days in institutions, and increased work as a result of better health. Also one has to take into account the "intangible," "nonquantitative" benefits such as reduced pain and suffering.

According to Warner & Luce (1982), one of the major problems for CBA in the areas of health and mental illness concerns the assessment of benefits involving "the value of human life"—specifically such benefits as "the avoidance of premature mortality or unnecessary morbidity." The traditional way of handling this in CBA has been to use a procedure called the "human capital approach." Briefly, this involves using labor market values such as work productivity or earnings as the measure for such benefits. This approach has been criticized for being too restrictive in omitting values of personal enjoyment and quality of life above and beyond the economic rewards of work. Moreover, wage measures can be biased in that white males are likely to be given a higher value than females or minorities. Despite these criticisms and recent developments using other procedures, the human capital approach still is the most widely used method for CBA.

CEA has provided a useful alternative procedure to dealing with this problem. It can include the "nonmarket value of life," using such quantitative measures as "deaths averted" or "life-years saved." However, CEA does not entirely avoid the issue of the value of human life; for once money is allocated to a program, it is possible to derive a minimum or maximum value of life. Thus Warner & Luce (1982) observe that there is not as large a "conceptual difference" between CBA and CEA as may appear. The former explicitly places values on life while the latter allows decision makers to accomplish this implicitly and perhaps avoids the ethical problems associated with valuing life (Kelman 1981).

Weinstein & Stason (1977) have recommended the use of "quality-adjusted life years" as a more sensitive measure of effectiveness than the more traditional improvements in mortality and morbidity. Mosteller (1981) concurs that "we need to assess the quality of life" since many treatment innovations have this as their major goal. One approach to deriving such measures involves the use of health-status indexes (Stewart et al 1981). The index acts as a "weighting scheme" to adjust changes in mortality (i.e. increased life expectancy) for the quality of life during that time.

PERSPECTIVE   Most CEA/CBAs in program evaluation would be conducted from a governmental perspective. It is important to note this (#6) because perspective effects the resources considered in the analysis. If the program were run by a charity, certain costs, reimbursed or exempted by state and federal governments, may not have to be considered, for example. Fischhoff (1977) also warns that the perspective of the analyst could affect the fairness of the results. In particular, care must be taken to ensure that a societal perspective is not subverted by a special interest.

DISCOUNTING   Since all costs and benefits do not occur at the same time, the analyst must devise a method of converting them into a common metric (#7). This procedure is called "discounting" and is based on the assumption that "current and future dollars are not the same." In fact, a preference for present dollars over future dollars is presumed, since they can be invested to yield a profit. The procedures for discounting are straightforward. However, the results of a CEA/CBA may be sensitive to the actual discount rate used.

Warner & Luce (1982) note that while there is agreement that discounting should be employed, there is "less consensus" on the exact rate. The importance of small changes in the rate should not be ignored or underestimated. The authors provide an example where one program that is superior (in net benefits) to another at 0% and 2% discount rates, becomes inferior at a 4% rate. Such reversals are likely when large benefits are delayed many years, as they often are in screening and other preventive programs (e.g. Head Start).

SENSITIVITY ANALYSIS   Since the choice of a discount rate and other assumptions made in CEA/CBA make the results somewhat uncertain and open to criticism, analysts have developed a technique known as "sensitivity analysis" to test the robustness of their findings (#8). The procedure, in brief, allows the analyst to determine whether different assumptions yield different results. Thus, for example, do changes in the value of human life, different personnel configurations, costs of tests, or the discount rate used to assess the value of future benefits and costs affect the result? One approach is to perform a so-called "worst case" analysis, employing values for those variables that will most bias the results against the findings obtained.

Another approach is known as "break even analysis." In this procedure the analyst compares alternatives involving nonmonetary measures of effect. For example, a program that costs a million dollars could be compared to another program that costs only $900,000 but saves 10 lives. In this case a life would be have to be valued at $10,000 to make the two programs equal in cost. Since most would agree that that is a relatively low value for human life, the second program would be viewed as preferable. Thus, sensitivity analyses allow the investigator to determine whether the results are dependent upon a particular assumption, for what range of values for a particular variable the program is cost effective, and also to identify issues needing further research.

ETHICAL ISSUES   It is important that ethical issues be included, or at least noted, in the analysis (#9). These include not only problems in valuing human life, but issues concerning the potential harmful side effects of a program, the deprivation in withholding services, and "equity" issues in providing services. The OTA report (1980) notes that CEA is efficiency oriented and thus may not take such ethical issues as equity into account. It is possible, for example, that cost-effective decisions could systematically favor the well-to-do. The OTA report candidly acknowledges that

"CEA/CBA is weak in the areas of equity and other ethical considerations."

This is essentially an external validity issue, and Levin (1975) has made a cogent recommendation for handling it. He suggests that the analysis be broken down by subpopulation. If equity is a relevant concern, then different weights can be used so that, for example, the effects for low-income people are counted more heavily than those for the more affluent. This would yield an "effectiveness index."

RESULTS   The final step in the process (#10) is the presentation and interpretation of findings. The analyst should indicate the key variables and assumptions, including the limitations of the analysis and sensitivity analyses if they have been performed. In particular, Warner & Luce (1982) note that a "very popular misconception" is that a cost-benefit ratio is an adequate measure or index of a program's performance. In fact, they recommend that a CBA should report net benefits, not the ratio, since the latter can sometimes be misleading. They cite as an example a program that produces $4000 worth of benefits from $2000 in costs, as opposed to a program that produces $3 million in benefits for $2 million dollars in cost. In the former case the ratio is 2 and in the latter 1.5. However, the former program only produces $2000 in net benefits as opposed to $1 million in the latter. Assuming that resources were available and that programs cannot be expanded or contracted in the same cycle, then the latter program is clearly preferable to the former even though it has a smaller benefit-cost ratio. Moreover, they note that these ratios are also sensitive to whether economic benefits are treated as negative costs. On the other hand, CEA, lacking an economic measure of benefits, does report a cost-effectiveness ratio as an index of program performance. However, the authors warn that this measure should not be accepted uncritically for often one can save more lives with an increase in cost that is not considered inappropriate.

In some cases it may not be possible to report the analysis in terms of a single measure of effectiveness or dollars for either CEA or CBA. In such cases analysts recommend that multiple outcomes be presented. For example, such measures of effectiveness as "quality-adjusted life years," morbidity days saved, and disability days may represent a set of measures that cannot be combined. When alternative programs differ in both cost and benefits, it is impossible to arrive at an objective ranking. However, when the costs are the same, some comparisons are possible, particularly in those cases where one alternative clearly dominates another; that is, it has larger or smaller benefits than another alternative. In some cases, the analyst will be required to use subjective judgments to determine whether slight differences in benefits are superior and thus allow one program to be ranked higher than another.

Levin (1975) notes that there are at least three measures of CEA: "total cost for achieving a certain level of effectiveness; average cost per unit of effectiveness; and marginal cost for additional units of effectiveness." Total costs are appropriate when equal levels of effectiveness are achieved. When this is not the case, average cost per unit effectiveness, as noted earlier, is appropriate. There is, however, one serious problem with this measure. It does not take into account the scale of the program and thus assumes that these results can be extrapolated, an assumption that may or may not be true. For example, if a program has a large amount of costs that are fixed, it will show a high average cost when, in fact, one could enlarge it at small costs and get more benefits. In these cases, the marginal costs are the appropriate measures to be used. For program evaluators, this is calculated by subtracting the effects for the control group from the results of the experimental programs and then dividing that number (e.g. number of people returning to work, number of people cured by therapy, etc) into the additional costs in mounting these alternative programs (obtained by subtracting the cost of the control program from these alternative programs).

The Potential Application of CEA/CBA to Psychotherapy

Saxe (1980) maintains that CEA/CBA can be "potentially" useful to decision makers in allocating scarce fiscal resources for mental health services. He illustrates how this approach could be applied to assessing psychotherapy. The discussion reveals the difficulty of using these methods. Major obstacles for CEA/CBA occur in identifying and measuring benefits and finding useful empirical estimates. As Boruch (1982) has recently noted: "The absence of formal cost-benefit analyses of evaluations, including experiments, is remarkable. Part of the problem lies in defining benefits." These problems are briefly reviewed in the remainder of this section.

BENEFITS   According to Saxe, "The unique problems of CEA/CBA of psychotherapy have to do with the difficulty of comprehensively assessing and valuing the effects of psychotherapy" (e.g. "reduction of pain and suffering," "improved well-being"). He notes that the identification process, itself, is problematic. It is often difficult to determine which effects or benefits are attributable to psychotherapy. This requires having good research data, but such information is often "inadequate." This is due to either poor research designs or the absence of appropriate measures (see below). Similar problems beset the assignment of benefits to those associated with patients, such as families, friends, employers, and even society. Generally either "willingness to pay" or earnings are used as proxies for such benefits as reduced unemployment payments and increased productivity. However, the former is somewhat controversial since sick patients may not be able to make such cost decisions (Kelman 1981). Benefits, thus, are the most problematic component in the analysis. One may either not fully identify all benefits that should be considered or underestimate their value when they are properly identified.

EMPIRICAL EVIDENCE   Saxe briefly reviews the few empirical studies dealing with the impact of psychotherapy on the utilization of medical services. Nine studies (including one review of 25 studies) are referenced and briefly discussed; all show that psychotherapy lowers the utilization of medical services. This has led Kiesler (1980) to claim that, "We know that adding the option of psychological services to an existing physical health care system is cost-effective and reduces the use of the physical health system." While this evidence is provocative, it is apparently not as conclusive as Kiesler's remark indicates.

There are a number of serious methodological problems that characterize these studies that necessarily add caution to their interpretation. The most critical are those affecting internal validity. As Saxe notes, many of the studies did not include "appropriate control group conditions." In others, patients who were high utilizers of services were studied, introducing the possibility of statistical regression artifacts. Another major problem stems from construct validity concerns. The timing of the psychotherapeutic intervention usually occurred after an initial period of high utilization and thus is potentially confounded with the normal temporal pattern of service utilization. As is customary with such reviews, it concludes by calling for "additional research."

Utility of CEA/CBA

Despite the problems noted above, Saxe (1980) concludes that psychotherapy is "scientifically assessable" using CEA/CBA in combination with other rigorous research methods. In this he is in agreement with Kiesler's (1980) analysis of the research needed to provide a strong mental health policy analysis. However, this does not mean that definitive CEA/CBA studies can be conducted that will be the sole basis for the policy. At present, the OTA report (1980) notes that most CEA/CBA studies are "academic exercises" of little policy relevance.

The OTA report concluded that CEA/CBA has "too many methodological and other limitations" to be used as the only evidence for decision-making. Mosteller (1981) has also observed that health-care goals often conflict. For example, in minimizing lives lost and days hospitalized for an appendectomy, many unnecessary surgeries are required for the former and some deaths in the latter. Mosteller notes that this is an instance of "the classical mathematical dilemma that we cannot expect to maximize two functions at the same time." For such reasons OTA recommended that the CEA/CBA techniques be used to "structure" the problem, to obtain the information, and then to present or "array" the data elements that would be included in making a decision. Such caution has also been urged by others (cf Roid 1982) including the American Public Health Association (1981).

In conclusion, knowledge and use of CEA/CBA may be essential for the very survival of evaluation research. The decade of the 1970s witnessed the rapid development of methods for assessing the effectiveness of innovative social programs. This was an area that psychologists felt most comfortable with since it required only moderate extensions and refinements of skills basic to the profession. Issues concerning costs and policy analysis have been foreign to the training and experience of psychologists/evaluators. Given the recent fiscal and political climate, cost considerations may be essential in the current decade for appropriate and useful evaluation. Such analyses represent a logical step in the development of methods for evaluation research. In some quarters the debate on establishing formal organizations to gather cost-effectiveness data has already begun (Relman 1982, Bunker et al 1982).

CONCLUSION

Evaluation research is a multidisciplinary activity that is united by its concern for sound methods that can be used to obtain valid information. It is appropriate to consider the role of psychology in this young field. Psychologists have played a central role in the development and creative adaptation of rigorous experimental and quasi-experimental designs for evaluating innovative social programs. They have made their evaluation colleagues aware of the problems posed by the improper conduct and analysis of evaluative studies. In doing so, they have provided a critical logic along with the statistical skills needed to refine other methods of potential use in evaluating programs. Despite these accomplishments, there remains important work to be done. The repertoire of methods should be expanded to include more qualitative methods that can illuminate and corroborate the statistical findings. The search for better outcome measures of program benefits focusing on quality-of-life and other, primarily psychological, outcomes must continue. The initial development of methods for synthesizing the expanding varieties of information into a coherent assessment must be completed. Finally, psychologists must learn that they cannot do it all themselves. There must be a greater spirit of social science ecumenism in their evaluation approaches and staffs.

ACKNOWLEDGMENTS

The author thanks Fred Bryant, Judy Garrard, Leonard Saxe, William Shadish, and Bill Yeaton for their careful reading and thoughtful comments on earlier drafts of this chapter. Thanks are also in order for Rita Page for her conscientious and patient typing of the many drafts and revisions. The work on this chapter was supported by grants from the National Institute of Education (NIE-G-79-0128) and the National Center for Health Services Research (HS 04849-01).

Literature Cited

Albritton, R. B. 1978. Cost-benefit of measles eradication: Effects of a federal intervention. *Policy Anal.* 4:1–22

Alkin, M. C., Daillak, R., White, P. 1979. *Using Evaluations: Does Evaluation Make a Difference?* Beverly Hills/London: Sage. 269 pp.

American Public Health Association. 1981. Use of cost-benefit analysis in public health regulation. *Nation's Health* 11(9):3

Baum, M. L., Anish, D. S., Chalmers, T. C., Sacks, H. S., Smith, H., Fagerstrom, R. M. 1981. A survey of clinical trials of antibiotic prophylaxis in colon surgery: Evidence against further use of no-treatment controls. *N. Engl. J. Med* 305:795–99

Berk, A. A., Chalmers, T. C. 1981. Cost and efficacy of the substitution of ambulatory for inpatient care. *N. Engl. J. Med.* 304:393–97

Boruch, R. F. 1982. Experimental tests in education: Recommendations from the Holtzman report. *Am. Stat.* 36:1–8

Boruch, R. F., Cordray, D. S., Pion, G., Leviton, L. 1981a. A mandated appraisal of evaluation practices: Digest of recommendations to the Congress and the Department of Education. *Educ. Res.* 10:10–13, 31

Boruch, R. F., Gomez, H. 1977. Sensitivity, bias, and theory in impact evaluations. *Prof. Psychol.* 8:411–34

Boruch, R. F., McSweeny, A. J., Soderstrom, E. J. 1978. Randomized field experiments for program planning, development, and evaluation: An illustrative bibliography. *Eval. Q.* 2:655–95

Boruch, R. F., Wortman, P. M. 1979. Implications of educational evaluation for evaluation policy. In *Review of Research in Education,* ed. D. C. Berliner, 7:309–61. Washington DC: Am. Educ. Res. Assoc.

Boruch, R. F., Wortman, P. M., Cordray, D. S., et al. 1981b. *Reanalyzing Program Evaluations.* San Francisco: Jossey-Bass. 403 pp.

Bunker, J. P., Fowles, J., Schaffarzick, R. 1982. Evaluation of medical-technology strategies: Part II. Proposal for an Institute for Health-Care Evaluation. *N. Engl. J. Med.* 306:687–92

Burger, J. M. 1981. Motivational biases in the attribution of responsibility for an accident: A meta-analysis of the defensive-attribution hypothesis. *Psychol. Bull.* 90:496–512

Byar, D. P., Simon, R. M., Friedewald, W. T., Schlesselman, J. J., DeMets, D. L. et al. 1976. Randomized clinical trials: Perspective on some recent ideas. *N. Engl. J. Med.* 295:74–80

Campbell, D. T. 1979a. Assessing the impact of planned social change. *Eval. Program Plann.* 2:67–90

Campbell, D. T. 1979b. "Degrees of freedom" and the case study. In *Qualitative and Quantitative Methods in Evaluation Research,* ed. T. D. Cook, C. S. Reichardt, 1:49–67. Beverly Hills/London: Sage (Res. Prog. Ser. Eval.). 160 pp.

Campbell, D. T. 1976. Focal local indicators for social program evaluation. *Soc. Ind. Res.* 3:237–56

Campbell, D. T., Erlebacher, A. 1970. How regression artifacts in quasi-experimental evaluations can mistakenly make compensatory education look harmful. In *Compensatory Education: A National Debate,* ed. J. Hellmuth, 3:185–210. New York: Bruner/Mazel. 225 pp.

Campbell, D. T., Stanley, J. C. 1966. *Experimental and Quasi-experimental Designs for Research.* Chicago: Rand McNally. 84 pp.

Chalmers, T. C. 1981. The clinical trial. *Milbank Mem. Fund Q.* 59:324–39

Chalmers, T. C., Block, J. B., Lee, S. 1972. Controlled studies in clinical cancer research. *N. Engl. J. Med.* 287:75–78

Chalmers, T. C., Smith, H., Blackburn, B., Silverman, B., Schroeder, B., et al. 1981. A method for assessing the quality of a randomized control trial. *Controlled Clin. Trials* 2:31–49

Cohen, J. 1962. The statistical power of abnormal-social psychological research: A review. *J. Abnorm. Soc. Psychol.* 65:145–153

Cohen, J. 1977. *Statistical Power Analysis for the Behavioral Sciences.* New York: Academic. 474 pp. Rev. ed.

Comroe, J. H. Jr. 1978. The road from research to new diagnosis and therapy. *Science* 200:931–37

Cook, T. D., Campbell, D. T. 1979. *Quasi-experimentation: Design & Analysis Issues for Field Settings.* Chicago: Rand McNally. 405 pp.

Cooper, H. M. 1979. Statistically combining independent studies: A meta-analysis of sex differences in conformity research. *J. Pers. Soc. Psychol.* 37:131–46

Cronbach, L. J., Ambron, S. R., Dornbusch, S. M., Hess, R. D., Hornik, R. C., et al. 1980. *Toward Reform of Program Evaluation: Aims, Methods, and Institutional Arrangements.* San Francisco: Jossey-Bass. 438 pp.

Davis, B. G., ed. 1982. Boruch and McLaughlin debate. *Eval. News* 3:11–20

DeSilva, R. A., Hennekens, C. H., Lown, B., Casscells, W. 1981. Lignocaine prophylaxis in acute myocardial infarction: An evaluation of randomized trials. *Lancet* ii:855–58

Elashoff, J. D. 1978. Combining results of clinical trials. *Gastroenterology* 75:1170–72

Eysenck, H. J. 1978. An exercise in mega-silliness. *Am. Psychol.* 33:517

Fischhoff, B. 1977. Cost benefit analysis and the art of motorcycle maintenance. *Policy Sci.* 8:177–202

Fletcher, R. H., Fletcher, S. W. 1979. Clinical research in general medical journals: A 30-year perspective. *N. Engl. J. Med.* 301:180–83

Gallo, P. S. Jr. 1978. Meta-analysis—A mixed meta-phor? *Am. Psychol.* 33: 515–17

Gehan, E. A., Freireich, E. J. 1974. Nonrandomized controls in cancer clinical trials. *N. Engl. J. Med.* 290:198–206

Gilbert, J. P., Light, R. J., Mosteller, F. 1975. Assessing social innovations: An empirical base for policy. In *Evaluation and Experiment: Some Critical Issues in Assessing Social Programs,* ed. C. A. Bennett, A. A. Lumsdaine, pp. 39–193. New York: Academic. 553 pp.

Gilbert, J. P., McPeek, B., Mosteller, F. 1977. Progress in surgery and anesthesia: Benefits and risks of innovative therapy. In *Costs, Risks, and Benefits of Surgery,* ed. J. P. Bunker, B. A. Barnes, F. Mosteller, pp. 124–69. New York: Oxford Univ. Press. 401 pp.

Glass, G. V. 1976. Primary, secondary, and meta-analysis of research. *Educ. Res.* 5:3–8

Glass, G. V. 1977. Integrating findings: The meta-analysis of research. In *Review of Research in Education,* ed. L. S. Shulman, 5:351–79. Itasca, Ill: Peacock. 399 pp.

Glass, G. V. 1978. Reply to Mansfield and Busse. *Educ. Res.* 7:3

Glass, G. V., Ellett, F. S. Jr. 1980. Evaluation research. *Ann. Rev. Psychol.* 31:211–28

Glass, G. V., McGaw, B., Smith, M. L. 1981. *Meta-analysis in Social Research.* Beverly Hills/London: Sage. 279 pp.

Glass, G. V., Smith, M. L. 1978. Reply to Eysenck, *Am. Psychol.* 33:517

Glass, G. V., Smith, M. L. 1979. Meta-analysis of research on class size and achievement. *Educ. Eval. Policy Anal.* 1:2–16

Guess, H. A. 1981. Bernoulli's cost-benefit analysis of smallpox immunization. *N. Engl. J. Med.* 305:347

Horwitz, R. I., Feinstein, A. R. 1981. Improved observational method for studying therapeutic efficacy. *J. Am. Med. Assoc.* 246:2455–59

House, E. R. 1980. *Evaluating with Validity.* Beverly Hills/London: Sage. 295 pp.

House, E. R., Glass, G. V., McLean, L. D., Walker, D. F. 1978. No simple answer: Critique of the Follow Through evaluation. *Harvard Educ. Rev.* 48:128–60

House, E. R., Mathison, S. 1981. Book review of *Toward Reform of Program Evaluation. Eval. News.* 2:314–20

Hunter, J. E., Schmidt, F. L., Jackson, G. 1982. *Meta-analysis: Cumulating Research Findings Across Studies.* Beverly Hills/London: Sage. In press

Jackson, G. B. 1980. Methods for integrative reviews. *Rev. Educ. Res.* 50:438–60

Johnson, D. W., Maruyama, G., Johnson, R., Nelson, D., Skon, L. 1981. Effects of cooperative, competitive, and individualistic goal structures on achievement: A meta-analysis. *Psychol. Bull.* 89: 47–62

Judd, C. M., Kenny, D. A. 1981. *Estimating the Effects of Social Interventions.* Cambridge/London: Cambridge Univ. Press. 243 pp.

Kelman, S. 1981. Cost-benefit analysis: An ethical critique. *Regulation* Jan/Feb: 33–40

Kenny, D. A. 1979. *Correlation and Causality.* New York: Wiley. 277 pp.

Kiesler, C. A. 1980. Mental health policy as a field of inquiry for psychology. *Am. Psychol.* 35:1066–80

Kiesler, C. A. 1982. On cost effectiveness. *Am. Psychol.* 37:95–96

Knox, R. A. 1980. Heart transplants: To pay or not to pay. *Science* 209:570–75

Landman, J. T., Dawes, R. M. 1982. Psychotherapy outcome: Smith and Glass' conclusions stand up under scrutiny. *Am. Psychol.* 37:504–16

Levin, H. M. 1975. Cost-effectiveness analysis in evaluation research. In *Handbook of Evaluation Research,* ed. M. Guttentag, E. L. Struening, 2:89–122. Beverly Hills/London: Sage. 736 pp.

Mansfield, R. S., Busse, T. V. 1977. Meta-analysis of research: A rejoinder to Glass. *Educ. Res.* 6:3

Marshall, E. 1980. Psychotherapy works, but for whom? *Science* 207:506–8

McKinlay, J. B. 1981. From "promising report" to "standard procedure": Seven stages in the career of a medical innovation. *Milbank Mem. Fund Q.* 59:374–411

McSweeny, A. J., Wortman, P. M. 1979. Two regional mental health treatment facilities: A reanalysis of evaluation of services. *Eval. Q.* 3:537–56

Mosteller, F. 1981. Innovation and evaluation. *Science* 211:881–86

Mosteller, F., Gilbert, J. P., McPeek, B. 1980. Reporting standards and research strategies for controlled trials. *Controlled Clin. Trials* 1:37–58

Nisbett, R., Ross, L. 1980. *Human Inference: Strategies and Shortcomings of Social Judgment.* Englewood Cliffs, NJ: Prentice-Hall. 334 pp.

Office of Technology Assessment. 1978. *Assessing the Efficacy and Safety of Medical Technologies.* Washington DC: GPO (No. 052–003–00593–0). 133 pp.

Office of Technology Assessment. 1980. *The Implications of Coss-Effectiveness Analysis of Medical Technology.* Washington DC: GPO (Stock No. 052–003–00765–7). 219 pp.

Office of Technology Assessment. 1982. *Technology Transfer at the National Institutes of Health.* Washington DC: GPO. 188 pp.

Partlett, M., Hamilton, D. 1976. Evaluation as illumination: A new approach to the study of innovatory programs. In *Evaluation Studies Review Annual,* ed. G. V. Glass, 1:140–57. Beverly Hills/London: Sage. 672 pp.

Patton, M. Q. 1978. *Utilization-focused Evaluation.* Beverly Hills/London: Sage. 303 pp.

Patton, M. Q. 1980. Making methods choices. *Eval. Program Plann.* 3:219–28

Perloff, R., Perloff, E., Sussna, E. 1976. Program evaluation. *Ann. Rev. Psychol.* 27:569–94

Porter, A. C., Schmidt, W. H., Floden, R. E., Freeman, D. J. 1978. Practical significance in program evaluation. *Am. Educ. Res. J.* 15:529–39

Posavac, E. J. 1980. Evaluations of patient education programs: a meta-analysis. *Eval. Health Profs.* 3:47–62.

Posavac, E. J., Carey, R. G. 1980. *Program Evaluation: Methods and Case Studies.* Englewood Cliffs, NJ: Prentice-Hall. 350 pp.

Presby, S. 1978. Overly broad categories obscure important differences between therapies. *Am. Psychol.* 33:514–15

Reichardt, C. S., Cook, T. D. 1979. Beyond qualitative *versus* quantitative methods. See Campbell 1979b, 1:7–32

Relman, A. S. 1982. An institute for health-care evaluation. *N. Engl. J. Med.* 306:669–70

Riecken, H. W., Boruch, R. F., Campbell, D. T., Caplan, N., Glennan, T. K. Jr., et al, eds: 1974. *Social Experimentation: A Method for Planning and Evaluating Social Intervention.* New York: Academic. 339 pp.

Roid, G. H. 1982. Cost-effectiveness analysis in mental health policy. *Am. Psychol.* 37:94–95

Rosenthal, R. 1978. Combining results of independent studies. *Psychol. Bull.* 85: 185–93

Rossi, P. H., Freeman, H. E. 1982. *Evaluation: A Systematic Approach.* Beverly Hills/London: Sage. 352 pp. 2nd ed.

Saxe, L. 1980. *Background Paper #3: The Efficacy and Cost Effectiveness of Psychotherapy.* Washington DC: Off. Technol. Assess. (GPO Stock No. 052–003–007853–5). 93 pp.

Saxe, L. 1982. Public policy and psychotherapy: Can evaluative research play a role? *New Dir. Program Eval.* 14:73–86

Saxe, L., Fine, M. 1981. *Social Experiments.* Beverly Hills/London: Sage. 267 pp.

Schoenbaum, S. C., McNeil, B. J., Kavet, J. 1976. The swine-influenza decision. *N. Engl. J. Med.* 295:759–65

Sechrest, L., West, S. G., Phillips, M. A., Redner, R., Yeaton, W. 1979. Some neglected problems in evaluation research: Strength and integrity of treatments. In *Evaluation Studies Review Annual,* ed. L. Sechrest, S. G. West, M. A. Phillips, R. Redner, W. Yeaton, 4:15–35. Beverly Hills/London: Sage. 766 pp.

Sechrest, L., Yeaton, W. 1981. Assessing the effectiveness of social programs: Methodological and conceptual issues. *New Dir. Program Eval.* 9:41–56

Smith, M. L., Glass, G. V. 1977. Meta-analysis of psychotherapy outcome studies. *Am. Psychol.* 32:752–60

Stewart, A. L., Ware, J. E. Jr., Brook, R. H. 1981. Advances in the measurement of functional status: Construction of aggregate indexes. *Med. Care* 19:473–88

Strube, M. J., Garcia, J. E. 1981. A meta-analytic investigation of Fiedler's model of leadership effectiveness. *Psychol. Bull.* 90:307–21

Thompson, M. S. 1980. *Benefit-Cost Analysis for Program Evaluation.* Beverly Hills/London: Sage. 310 pp.

Tukey, J. W. 1977. Some thoughts on clinical trials, especially problems of multiplicity. *Science* 198:679–84

Tversky, A., Kahneman, D. 1974. Judgment under uncertainty: Heuristics and biases. *Science* 185:1124–31

Wagner, J. L. 1979. Toward a research agenda on medical technology. In *Medical Technology,* ed. J. L. Wagner, pp. 1–12. Washington DC: GPO (PHS-79-3254, NCHSR Res. Proc. Ser.) 120 pp.

Warner, K. E. 1975. A "desperation-reaction" model of medical diffusion. *Health Serv. Res.* 10:369–83

Warner, K. E. 1975. Luce, B. R. 1982. *Cost-Benefit and Cost-Effectiveness Analysis in Health Care: Principles, Practice, and Potential.* Ann Arbor: Health Admin. Press. 384 pp.

Weinstein, M. C., Stason, W. B. 1977. Foundations of cost-effectiveness analysis for health and medical practices. *N. Engl. J. Med.* 296:716–21

Weiss, C. H., ed. 1977. *Using Social Research in Public Policy Making.* Lexington, Mass: Heath. 256 pp.

Williams, W. 1976. Implementation problems in federally funded programs. In *Social Program Implementation,* ed. W. Williams, R. F. Elmore, pp. 15–40. New York: Academic. 299 pp.

Wortman, P. M. 1981a. Consensus development. In *Methods for Evaluating Health Services,* ed. P. M. Wortman, 8:9–22. Beverly Hills/London: Sage (Res. Prog. Ser. Eval.) 143 pp.

Wortman, P. M. 1981b. Randomized clinical trials. See 1981a, 8:41–60

Wortman, P. M., King, C. S., Bryant, F. B. 1982. Meta-analysis of quasi-experiments: School desegregation and black achievement, Part I—Retrieval and coding. Ann Arbor: Inst. Soc. Res. (tech. rep.) 22 pp.

Wortman, P. M., Reichardt, C. S., St. Pierre, R. G. The first year of the Education Voucher Demonstration: A secondary analysis of student achievement test scores. *Eval. Q.* 2:193–214

Wortman, P. M., St. Pierre, R. G. 1977. The educational voucher demonstration. *Educ. Urban Soc.* 9:471–92

Ann. Rev. Psychol. 1983. 34:261–95

INSTRUCTIONAL PSYCHOLOGY

Robert M. Gagné and Walter Dick

Department of Educational Research, Development and Foundations, Florida State University, Tallahassee, Florida 32306

CONTENTS

INTRODUCTION

The field of research encompassed by instructional psychology has become large, as noted by Resnick (1981), and has continued to grow during the 5 years prior to July 1981. Since one of us participated in preparing the original article with this title (Gagné & Rohwer 1969), he can state with

261

0066-4308/83/0201–0261$02.00

some assurance that the task of examining the current published work in the field cannot be approached with the techniques possible in that earlier time, nor with the same commitment to comprehensiveness. Resnick's remark that much of instructional psychology is now within the mainstream of cognitive psychology also recognizes a circumstance that must be taken into account in the preparation of an article such as the present one.

We attempt to report and reflect upon some of the major trends in the field, within an organization that intends to describe the major points of influence research may have upon instruction. Since the most recent article in the series on this topic (Resnick 1981) sought to review the research on instruction in particular school subjects, we have tried instead to pick up the threads of inquiry on more general psychologically oriented areas that cut across subject-matter categories.

Our review includes a section dealing with the growing number of instructional theories of recent vintage, and closes with examples of applications of some principles of instructional psychology. Within the confines of allotted space, we have not found it possible to give consideration to the many individual studies of learnable student characteristics and the instructional techniques which may be used to establish them. Naturally, we acknowledge these areas to be of substantial importance to instructional psychology, and trust that others will undertake to synthesize these works and their findings.

We begin our chapter by taking note of some *general works* which have contributed to the definition of the field of instructional psychology, the description of some of its historical roots, and the identification of its boundaries. A following section provides an account of *instructional theories* that have newly appeared or attained some prominence during the period of this review, and another deals with some *concepts of cognitive psychology* of recent origin that may be expected to influence instructional theory and practice. The body of research on *student characteristics and their interaction* (ATI) with modes of instruction is examined in terms of major trends. As a final section, we describe and consider critical issues in the *applications* of instructional psychology.

We made an attempt to gather a variety of information on applications, recognizing that there are many organizations whose business it is to carry out applied work in the design of instructional content and delivery. These organizations include specialized divisions of industrial concerns, military training agencies, independent research and development firms, and university centers. Our efforts in this direction were no more than minimally successful. Although we were able to verify a general awareness that instructional psychology has widespread applicability to concrete problems, the constraints of time made it impossible for us to follow up many of the suggestions we received. It is our impression that a descriptive account of instances of application would be a highly desirable product, and that something like 5 man-years of effort would be required to prepare it. For the present chapter, we are able only to include three clusters of projects which exemplify applications in as many areas.

GENERAL WORKS

Theoretically related concepts described by investigators who have decided to call themselves "cognitive psychologists" greatly enriched the domain of learning and memory psychology, from which many of the organizing ideas of instructional psychology must be drawn. Prominent among books which will doubtless serve as key references for a span of years are the series of handbooks edited by Estes (1975, 1976a,b, 1978a,b) and the fifth edition of *Theories of Learning* by Bower & Hilgard (1981). A theme-setting article by Simon (1980a) relates this field to cognitive science as a "science of the artificial." Other books of particular value in presenting and clarifying information-processing views of learning and memory, appearing in this time period, are by Bransford (1979), Glass, Holyoak & Santa (1979), Klatzky (1980), Lachman, Lachman & Butterfield (1979), and J. R. Anderson (1980). This listing is by no means exhaustive, nor does it include the many excellent edited volumes containing individual chapters, which have made equally valuable contributions to the field.

Works of historical and programmatic interest to instructional psychology are of several sorts. Many prominent investigators in the field contribute such articles to the *Educational Researcher.* An insightful article bringing the psychology of learning up to date was offered by Greeno (1980). Glaser has made several influential contributions serving to define the field of instructional psychology, including articles outlining varieties of research questions (1979, 1982), the first volume of a series of books containing contributed chapters (1978a), and a collection of essays relating research and development to school change (1978b), dedicated to Ralph Tyler. Another noteworthy publication of general interest is a book of case studies sponsored by the National Academy of Education, exemplifying the influence of research on education (Suppes 1978), which includes evaluative essays on mental mesurement and the contributions of E. L. Thorndike, Piaget, Freud, Skinner, and others. A recent book edited by Farley & Gordon (1981) offers up-to-date reviews of a number of areas of instructional psychology, including individual differences, intellectual development, learning and instruction. A new journal, *Journal of Instructional Development,* launched during this period by the Association for Educational Communications and Technology, appears to have achieved a favorable foothold, and frequently includes articles partaking of instructional psychology. Of particular interest to university instructors is the volume collection of outstanding articles on learning and instruction edited by Wittrock (1977).

Instructional psychology reaches into the fields of adult education and higher education. Cross (1976) reviews evidence of the effectiveness of various kinds of programs and instructional adaptations aimed at college students. These include remedial education, programs for individualizing instruction (including computer-based models), mastery learning and self-paced modules (PSI). A more recent work (Cross 1981) is devoted to problems of instruction with adult learners—who participates, why or why not, and some implications of increasing participation in lifelong learning. A variety of lines of research on adult learning are captured in a book edited by Howe (1977). Knox's (1977) book includes a thoughtful chapter on instructional techniques designed to facilitate adult learning. Despite the high quality of many of these efforts, one comes away from the books with the impression that some of the most important questions about adult learning have yet to be formulated.

INSTRUCTIONAL THEORIES

Theories of instruction attempt to relate specified events comprising instruction to learning processes and learning outcomes, drawing upon knowledge generated by learning research and theory. Often instructional theories are prescriptive in the sense that they attempt to identify conditions of instruction which will optimize learning, retention, and learning transfer. Originators of such theories sometimes refer to Simon's (1969) description of "sciences of the artificial" as characteristic of their efforts. To be classified as theories, these formulations may be expected, at a minimum, to provide a rational description of causal relationships between procedures used to teach and their behavioral consequences in enhanced human performance.

Different from instructional theories as so defined are models of instructional design. While naturally related, the latter have the purpose of identifying efficient procedures by means of which instruction may be designed. It is not necessary for an instructional design model to give a rational account of causal relations of instructional events to learning processes, although of course such relations are usually implicit and may be explicit. Typically, models of instructional design begin with needs assessment and specify a number of stages of design and development activities including tryout, evaluation, and costing. Medial stages such as "choosing instructional strategies," "selecting media," and "development of course materials" obviously depend upon one or more instructional theories, which in different models may be given more or less prominence. Examples of instructional design models which have seen publication during the period of this review are those by Briggs & Wager (1981), Dick & Carey (1978), and the *Instructional Systems Development* model described by Branson (1979). Two volumes edited by O'Neil (1979a,b) deal with procedures and issues in instructional system development. A critical review of 40 models of instructional design is given by Andrews & Goodson (1980).

Gagné-Briggs

The Gagné-Briggs (1979) theory of instruction, based in part upon the work of Gagné (1977b), begins with a taxonomic framework of learning outcomes considered essential for an understanding of human learning as it occurs in instructional settings. Learning outcomes, conceived as acquired capabilities of human learners, are classified as (a) verbal information, (b) intellectual skills, (c) cognitive strategies, (d) motor skills, and (e) attitudes. Although independently derived, these categories have an approximate correspondence with those of Bloom and his co-workers (Bloom 1956). The first three of these categories also correspond with those in the psychology of cognition and learning, named respectively (a) declarative knowledge, (b) procedural knowledge, and (c) cognitive strategies (J. R. Anderson 1980, Bower 1975).

In addressing the matter of instruction, the Gagné-Briggs theory proposes that each of the categories of learning outcome requires a different set of conditions for optimizing learning, retention, and transferability. Optimal conditions include external events in the learner's immediate environment, usually called "instruction," and internal conditions acting through the learner's working memory, which have their origins largely in previous instruction (Gagné 1977b). It is the contention of this theory that traditional factors in learning, such as contiguity, exercise, and reinforcement, while of undoubted relevance, are much too general in their applicability to be of particular use in the design of instruction. Instead, internal and external conditions must be specified separately for the learning of verbal information, for intellectual skills, and for each of the other categories of learned capabilities.

The processes of learning assumed by the Gagné-Briggs theory are those included in the information-processing model of learning and memory, as described by Atkinson & Shiffrin (1968) and employed in essential aspects by several other memory theorists (Greeno & Bjork 1973). Prominent among these processes are attention, selective (feature) perception, short-term memory, rehearsal, long-term memory storage, and retrieval. Externally, reinforcement via informative feedback is also assumed (Atkinson & Wickens 1971, Estes 1972). From these processes are derived both the internal and external events which make possible effective learning and retention. Instruction is defined as a set of events external to the learner which are designed to support the internal processes of learning (Gagné 1977c). Specifically, these events are conceived as taking place in an approximately ordered sequence as follows: (a) gaining attention, (b) informing learner of the objective, (c) stimulating recall of prerequisites, (d) presenting the stimulus material, (e) providing "learning guidance," (f) eliciting the performance, (g) providing feedback, (h) assessing the performance, and (i) enhancing retention and transfer. While all of these events are considered to be involved in each act of learning, it is noted that as novice learners become more experienced, the events tend to be more frequently provided by the learners themselves rather than by external agents. As factors influencing learning, many of these events are included in other instructional theories (Bloom 1976, Merrill et al 1979) and share with them evidences of their individual causal effects.

Several characteristics of this prescriptive instructional model make it distinctive from others. In the first place, it is based upon identified aspects of information-processing theories of learning (Bower & Hilgard 1981), including the human modeling concept of Bandura (1969). The model does not attempt to propose new theory pertaining to learning and memory, but only to use existing theory as a basis for the conceptualization of instruction. [A particulate exception is the theory of learning hierarchies (Gagné 1968, 1977b).] Secondly, the theory is comprehensive in the sense that it attempts to include all of the kinds of learning outcomes to which instruction is usually addressed. This is the basic significance of the theory's proposal of five kinds of learning outcomes, including attitudes and motor skills as well as cognitive capabilities. A third distinctive feature is the fact that the theory provides a rational basis for instruction as a set of events which interact with internal learning processes, and also with previously acquired contents retrieved from the learner's long-term memory. The inclusion of these characteristics makes it possible for this theory to deal with instruction of many forms in a great variety of settings.

Bloom

The model of instruction described as *mastery learning* (Block 1971, Bloom 1971, 1981) continues to receive research attention. Its rationale is derived in part from the model described by Carroll (1963), and includes these major variables: aptitude (time required to learn), quality of instruction, ability to understand instruction, perseverance (time the learner is willing to spend in learning), and opportunity (time allowed for learning). In more recent accounts (Bloom 1976) the theory has come to give primary emphasis to "alterable variables" for schooling, which are (a) cognitive entry behaviors, (b) affective entry characteristics of students, and (c) a number of specific factors making up the quality of instruction. Among the most prominent contributors to instructional quality are student participation and the corrective feedback which follows.

Emphasis on the study of alterable variables, as opposed to the relatively stable ones often called aptitudes or abilities, is likely to have a stimulating influence on instructional research. This strand of the theory is well developed and well documented with a considerable body of evidence (Bloom 1976), including some that has been more recently assembled by some of Bloom's students (MESA Seminar 1980). The "micro-level studies" referred to by Bloom constitute a substantial part of the corpus of instructional psychology, as reflected in this article and those that have preceded it. By this time there are massive amounts of research findings about the effects of cognitive prerequisites, distinctive cues, learner practice, and corrective feedback on learner achievement.

The second strand of Bloom's theory states a more radical hypothesis. It proposes that individual differences in achievement can be reduced in their amount of variation over time occupied by successive learning units. Such reduction in variability, it is stated, can occur as those students who are originally low achievers are given high quality instruction, including corrective feedback, and are then permitted to take more time to reach mastery. When this procedure is carried out over successive units of instruction, the theory says, the lower-achieving students will become more like the higher-achieving students. As this begins to happen, it is possible that as achievement improves (with quality of instruction), secondary effects will come from improvements in cognitive entry behaviors and in affective entry characteristics. L. W. Anderson's (1976) study showed that eighth grade low-achieving students in matrix arithmetic, when given quality instruction according to mastery learning methods, reduced their need for extra on-task time from an additional 66% on the first unit to 30% on the second, and to 5% on the third. Additional studies designed to test this variation-reduction hypothesis are awaited.

The investigation of alterable variables is obviously an effort of considerable potential value for education, through the promise it holds for the design of high-quality instruction. Variables included in the theory are derived from evidence concerning "what makes a difference" in the determination of instructional outcomes. Bloom's theory is thus an empirically based theory, of the sort that Carroll (1965) called "econometric." While each alterable variable is considered to have a causal effect on achievement, the theory puts forward no hypothetical learning processes, nor processes which seek to explain the action of instructional variables on learning and retention. In this respect it differs from a number of other theories.

Merrill

Merrill and his collaborators (Merrill et al 1977, 1979, Reigeluth et al 1978) have described a prescriptive theory aimed at instructional quality. To begin with, these authors consider that quality of instruction depends upon the adequacy and the consistency with which the purpose of instruction is represented in objectives, the consistency and adequacy with which these are represented by tests, and the consistency and adequacy with which these outcomes are represented in the instructional presentation. Dealing with the outcomes of (a) concepts, (b) principles, and (c) procedures, the theory holds that there are three levels for the representation of what has been learned and what is to be tested: remembering an instance, remembering a generality, and using a generality. A test-presentation consistency table indicates which "primary presentation form" should be used for each of these levels of test items. Thus, for example, for remembering a generality, the generality presentation form is appropriate, whereas the instance presentation form is not.

Within the confines of proper presentation forms, instructional presentation can be more or less adequate depending upon what strategies are used. For concepts, some strategies that are considered relevant are listed. They include the following: (a) providing immediate informative feedback; (b) isolating the presentation form by separating it from other material and clearly labeling it; (c) giving helps, such as mnemonic aids, attention focusing, algorithms; (d) providing an adequate sampling of instances; (e) indicating divergence (differences) of instances; (f) using a range of difficulty levels; (g) arranging instances so as to favor matching of common properties. Similar strategies are listed as applicable to the presentation of the other two categories encompassed by the theory, principles and procedures.

Some of the instructional strategies suggested by this theory have received empirical verification by such investigators as Tennyson et al (1975) and Markle & Tiemann (1974), among others. While all the suggestions appear to be soundly based when judged against known research findings, specific design of strategies for the three categories of outcome has not as yet been described. It would appear that such strategies may best be viewed as providing a basis for a checklist of points to keep in mind while designing instruction. The relation of instructional strategies to learning theory is not given. A prominent feature of this theory is actually an instructional design procedure, including its insistence on precise consistency in the sequence of instructional derivation: from goals to objectives to tests to instructional presentations.

Reigeluth

An Elaboration Theory of instruction has been described by Reigeluth and colleagues (Reigeluth 1979, Reigeluth et al 1978, Reigeluth & Rodgers 1980). This theory intends to deal primarily with "macro" strategies for organizing instruction, those that pertain to the sequencing and interrelating of topics within a course. Although its basic rationale is partly shared with Merrill's instructional theory (see the previous section), the latter is considered to deal with "micro" strategies for the design and presentation of material within a topic.

The kinds of instructional content with which Reigeluth's theory deals, aside from "rote facts," are concepts, principles, and procedures. The general theoretical conception of instruction is compared to viewing a scene with the use of a zoom lens. Beginning with a wide-angle view, one gradually increases the detail and complexity of parts by zooming in on them. Following this, one must again return to the wide view in order to integrate the specific information with the larger whole and to review previous instruction. Periodic review and synthesis are considered important aspects of the theory which have the effect of enhancing learning, retention, and transfer. The wide-angle view has the purpose of epitomizing the organizing content, which is given the meaning of "teaching a small number of concepts" by the use of applications.

When instructional sequences are being designed, the presentation of an epitome is followed by the teaching of an operation, and this in turn is followed by what is called the "expanded epitome." An instructional sequence designed in this manner would have the following steps (Reigeluth & Rodgers 1980): (*a*) select all the operations to be taught (by performing a task analysis); (*b*) decide which operation to teach first; (*c*) sequence all the remaining operations; (*d*) identify the supporting content; (*e*) allocate all content to lessons and sequence them; (*f*) sequence the instruction within each lesson; and (*g*) design instruction on each lesson and expanded epitome.

Obviously this theory incorporates a number of ideas that are common to other prescriptive models. It utilizes both information-processing task anslysis (P. F. Merrill 1976) and learning hierarchy (Gagné 1977a,b), and it claims to use to advantage the idea of subsumption (Ausubel et al 1978). It accepts the procedures of "micro-strategies" for component lessons, as involved in the theory of M. D. Merrill (previous section). The theory's outstanding novel contribution appears to be the prescription of frequent "zooming" from the most general view of the content to be learned, to selected specific details, making provision for the learning or recall of prerequisites, returning to the general view once more, with provision for review and practice. Repeated application of this sequence is proposed to make it possible for the learning to acquire an increasingly elaborate view of the subject. There appears to be some compatibility with the idea of the "spiral curriculum" (Bruner 1960) which included the proposal of periodic return to main concepts by review and elaboration. Ausubel's notion of progressive differentiation (Ausubel et al 1978) advocates beginning instruction with the larger, more general and unifying ideas before proceeding to detailed concrete ones. Gagné & Briggs (1979) place most weight on relevant prior learning as a basis for sequencing instruction. In all of these cases, differences from the sequencing prescription of the Elaboration Theory may be primarily matters of emphasis.

Case

A Neo-Piagetian theory of instruction has been proposed by Case (1978a,b,c). Instructional implications are derived from a theory of intellectual development which holds that the sequence of behavior that emerges during each of the major stages of intellectual development (Piaget 1970) depends upon the appearance of increasingly complex cognitive strategies ("executive strategies"). Two kinds of influences are considered to explain the succession of strategies within each stage. One is the acquiring of strategies through experience or through encounters with planned instruction. The second factor is a gradual increase in the size of working memory (sometimes called M-power). Case proposes that this increase in working memory results from automatization of the basic cognitive operations of which the learner is capable. Furthermore, the cognitive strategies available at each developmental stage must be assembled in working memory from components available at the previous stage. Such assembly is possible only when the operations of a previous stage have attained an appropriate degree of automaticity.

Implications for instruction of this developmental theory are phrased in terms of instructional design. A first step is to identify the goal of the task to be performed. Following this, a series of operations is mapped out by means of which the learner may reach the goal; it is suggested that personal introspection or "expert" protocols may be used. The next step is to compare this series with the performance (and reported thoughts) of skilled performers. A second phase of instructional design is to assess students' current level of functioning, discovering by clinical questioning or otherwise how the "novice" approaches the task. Instructional design is then undertaken, including exercises that demonstrate to the learner the inadequacies of his current strategy, and providing an explanation of why the "correct" strategy works better. This is followed by the presentation of additional examples using the new strategy, and practice with them. Throughout the process of developing instruction, careful attention is paid to minimizing cognitive complexity, in view of the learner's M-power as a limiting factor.

Considering the circumstance that this instructional theory has seen a gradual development from the fundamentals of Piaget's work, its departures from traditional interpretations of that work are remarkable. For one thing, it acknowledges that the Piagetian structural analysis of conventional academic tasks is virtually impossible and must be replaced by an analysis of executive strategies. Secondly, a definite distinction is drawn between theory which deals with development of intellectual competence and procedures which are concerned with adapting the content of instruction to the operational level of the learner. A distinctive feature of this instructional theory, one which retains the theme of the Piagetian tradition, is its proposal that existing cognitive strategies of uninstructed students be discovered, analyzed, and used as a basis for contrast with the more efficient executive procedures to be newly taught. A further characteristic to be noted, common to "developmental" theories, is its exclusive concern with the learning of cognitive strategies, with consequent inattention to other kinds of learning outcomes.

Collins

Collins (1977) describes a theory of Socratic Tutoring which he considers capable of teaching new knowledge and also the skills necessary for applying that knowledge to new problems and situations. The theory is conceived to be particularly useful in developing an intelligent CAI system (Collins et al 1975). The teaching dialogue of such a system is best characterized as a blend of diagnosis and correction strategies; the tutor probes the student's understanding and uses errors as clues to misconceptions. Applications of these ideas in conveying an understanding of such topics as evaporation, the weather system, and the effects of water and air currents on world climates are described by Stevens & Collins (1981).

In this tutoring system, the tutor's questions are guided by a number of rules, beginning with "ask about a known case, if it is the start of a dialogue, or if there is no other strategy available" (Collins 1977). Twenty-four such rules are described, 15 of which are "formulation rules" and the remainder "application rules." Collins illustrates their use in tutoring dialogues on growing grain, population density, and other topics. Analysis of these and other protocols indicates that students learn new information, make functional inferences, and learn to "reason" about the problems presented in the tutoring situation.

The Socratic Tutoring theory proposes that suitably designed CAI routines can make it possible for students to carry out problem-solving exercises in areas of knowledge that are initially unfamiliar to them. In so doing, such routines not only convey new organized knowledge, but also permit the student to practice reasoning strategies relevant to the new content being learned. While evidences of learning exist, it appears evident that additional research will be needed to illuminate many as yet unanswered questions about this promising theory. Two that suggest themselves immediately are: (*a*) what are the effects of student characteristics (age, intelligence, prior knowledge, etc) on the learning outcomes, and (*b*) what transferable strategies and skills result from this method of instruction?

Rothkopf

A theory of instruction proposed by Rothkopf (1981) emphasizes empirical variables such as those suggested by Carroll (1963), but in addition provides a theoretical rationale for their inclusion as factors which promote learning. The factors identified are considered to increase the probability of success in attaining a designated learning objective. First, there is *disparity* between the defined performance outcome and the instruction itself, whether the latter is verbal or in some other form. Disparity thus describes the kind of transformation the student must perform on the instruction in order to achieve a successful performance. This means specifically that the student must have the ability to engage in suitable *mathemagenic activities* (Rothkopf 1965, 1971). These activities depend on the learner, but can be modified by various instructional means such as the use of adjunct questions. A third set of factors consists of the *intellectual capabilities* of students. The difficulty of processing instructional information is reduced when the elements of these capabilities are familiar. Such familiarity, in turn, is derived from the previous instruction-relevant experience of the learner. Other resource limitations in this category are the capacity limits of the learner.

This instructional theory is discussed within a larger framework of what makes a difference in school instruction. In this context, factors such as frequency of instructional events (I), attendance-compliance (A-C), and retrievability (R) are added. Rothkopf states his purpose of describing a molar theory rather than a molecular one. Actually, one gains the impression of a somewhat mixed set of variables: the first three plus retrievability possess theoretical rationales relating instruction to learning, whereas those dealing with frequency and time are management factors that have confirmation in recent empirical studies (e.g. Denham & Lieberman 1980). The concepts of this theory are not differentially applied to different kinds of learning outcomes; otherwise, they show considerable resemblance to those of other instructional theories of the cognitive variety.

Markle & Tiemann

If the question is raised, "What has become of programmed instruction?" the answer is, it has lost an "m," but otherwise has been carefully nurtured and greatly elaborated by Markle & Tiemann (1974, Markle 1978). As an instructional theory, it is applied to a number of kinds of learning outcomes, categorized as psychomotor, simple cognitive, and complex cognitive. The last of these includes concepts, principles (rule application), and strategies. The theoretical concepts included in this theory are primarily three, familiar in this field of instructional design: (a) active responding, (b) "errorless" learning, and (c) immediate feedback. These principles are described in great detail, with many examples for the learning of concepts, rules, and procedural rules. Instruction for other outcomes such as verbal knowledge employs the same principles, and additional conceptualizations of learning processes appear to be considered unnecessary. For instruction in intellectual skills and problem solving, particularly when self-instructional materials are appropriate, both theory and design procedures are developed with remarkable thoroughness.

Scandura

Over a period of 15 years or more, and in many articles and books, Scandura (1977a,b, 1980) has described the various characteristics, predictions, and limitations of structural learning theory. This theory deals with intellectual competency. It proposes that competence underlying any particular problem domain can be represented in terms of finite sets of rules. As for the rules themselves, each is conceived as having the three features of (a) a domain, or set of conditions to be satisfied by inputs; (b) a range, or set of conditions characterizing the outputs the learner expects the rule to produce; and (c) an operation, or procedure, which, when applied to the contents of the domain, generates a unique output. Expanding upon this conceptual basis, structural learning theory proceeds to deal with the control process called "goal-switching" and its application to the utilization of rules and higher-order rules. When the learner fails to find the rules to achieve problem solution, the goal-switching process directs the search for higher-order rules which generate other potential solution rules. When applied, the newly generated rule is added to the set of available rules, and the search reverts to the next lower level.

Structural learning theory has particular implications for cognitive processing load and speed, for the analysis and assessment of individual learner competence, and accordingly for the systematic design of instruction aimed at establishing problem-solving capabilitiy (Scandura 1977a). Almost all of its examples and its predictions are couched in mathematical terms. It may best be viewed, therefore, as a theory of rule learning and rule application. While well developed in those domains, its scope does not appear to encompass the learning of such capabilities as foreign language, historical knowledge, a good tennis serve, or preference for abstract art.

Landa

Landa's (1976) second book expands upon the theory of algorithmization of instruction as originally described in his work (translated from the Russian) of 1964. Defining and using algorithms has the purpose of assuring instructional effectiveness and efficiency. The basic properties of algorithms are as follows: (*a*) specificity, which means that all actions of the user of an algorithm are unambiguously determined by statements of rules; (*b*) generality, implying that the algorithm is applicable to an entire set of problems belonging to a particular class; and (*c*) resultivity, indicating that the algorithm is always directed toward achieving the sought-after result. These characteristics appear clearly to equate algorithms with rules, or with rule systems embodied in procedures. Landa discusses the differences between algorithmic procedures and heuristics, and particularly the differences in mental operations which characterize creative behavior. In addition, he provides examples of algorithmic instruction in geometric problem-solving, in foreign language teaching, and in several other instructional areas.

In common with a number of other instructional theories, Landa's model of effective instruction calls for systematic analysis of the learning task, precise definition of the procedures (rules) to be taught, and the presentation and exemplification of these procedures to the student in the clearest and most direct possible manner. To Landa, algorithms are the "basic" aspects of instruction, which pave the way for heuristic learning and creative thinking.

Karplus, Lawson

It is noteworthy that investigators of education in scientific subjects continue the trends noted by Resnick (1981). Some of their theories and empirical findings are reported in the 1980 Yearbook of the Association for the Education of Teachers in Science (Lawson 1980). While continuing to be cognizant of evidence indicating the gradual nature of intellectual development (Karplus 1980), these researchers seek to interpret and apply evidence that will improve students' ability to think in ways related to the reasoning exhibited by scientists. Lawson & Lawson (1980) include in their instructional recommendations (*a*) testing the truth of categorical propositions, (*b*) testing hypothetical causal propositions, and (*c*) strategies of hypothetico-deductive reasoning. In general, most investigators in this tradition suggest the use of concrete problem-solving exercises representing particular kinds of reasoning to support the development of critical and creative thinking. As instructional theory, these ideas are narrowly oriented, although they are based in most instances upon solid evidences of student performance.

Suppes

Suppes (1978) discusses the idea of "global models" of instruction, so-called because they deal with such variables as students' mean rates of progress through a topic course. At the same time, such models ignore the details of responding that are traditionally of interest to the instructional psychologist. Findings of global studies may be used to indicate, for example, the proportion of time which should be devoted to the teaching of arithmetic at the fifth-grade level; or within an arithmetic course, how much time should be devoted to computation and how much to problem solving. The aim of such investigation is to permit use of the model for optimization of outcomes.

A set of axioms is stated as a basis for deriving the general equation of the theory, as follows: $y(t) = bt^k + c$. (The y variable refers to grade or course placement of the student; t is the student's time in the system; b, c, and k are parameters to be estimated for each student.) Trajectories of students in several schools for the deaf and one school for Indian children, in CAI in mathematics, reading, and language arts were used to test the fit of data to theoretical curves (Suppes et al 1975, 1978). Another test of the theory is provided by data from the Nicaragua Radio Mathematics Project (Searle et al 1976) relating to the problem of optimizing review exercises within each 25-minute radio lesson, and within the approximately 150 lessons per school year. It is noteworthy that the predictions made by global models are not restricted to subjects of the elementary school, as indicated by application of the trajectory model to a university-level course on introduction to logic (Larsen et al 1978). For investigators who seek to explore global predictions for optimizing various aspects of instruction and curriculum patterning, these models appear to have considerable usefulness.

CONTRIBUTIONS OF COGNITIVE PSYCHOLOGY

By this time it has become entirely customary for research questions about the psychology of instruction to be phrased in terms of the concepts of cognitive psychology (Bower & Hilgard 1981, Estes 1975, 1976a,b, 1978a,b). Accordingly, instructional procedures are often described in the language of cognitive psychology, such as short-term and long-term memory, semantic encoding, retrieval, and the like (cf Gagné 1977b, Merrill et al 1981). During the period covered by this article, certain concepts of cognitive psychology have become prominent which are of undoubted relevance to instruction.

Cognitive Strategies

During the period of this review, considerable research effort has been devoted to the investigation of cognitive strategies of learning and remembering. The effects of such strategies have been verified in connection with the learning of word pairs and lists (R. C. Anderson 1970, Bower 1970) as well as with prose learning (DiVesta et al 1973, Levin & Divine-Hawkins 1974). The technique of study skills described by Robinson (1946) called SQ3R has had remarkable durability, and appears in modified form in a recent text on cognitive psychology (J. R. Anderson 1980). In recent years, more ambitious research projects have been undertaken to design training programs with the specific intention of teaching learning strategies and evaluating their effectiveness. Some of these efforts are described in a book edited by O'Neil (1978).

Dansereau (1978) describes a program designed by him and his coworkers to teach college students cognitive strategies of learning and retention. Instruction was developed for the following categories called *primary strategies:* (*a*) comprehension and retention strategies consisting of paraphrase-imagery, networking, and analysis of key ideas; and (*b*) retrieval and utilization strategies using such techniques as breaking questions down into subqueries and employing contextual cues. Other components were called *support strategies,* which included (*a*) cultivating a positive learning attitude, (*b*) concentration (coping with distractions), and (*c*) monitoring the progress of learning.

A number of additional varieties of learning strategies have been suggested, some of which continue under active investigation. Among these are elaboration strategies (Weinstein 1978), anxiety reduction and self-monitoring skills (Richardson 1978), goal imaging (Singer 1978), inferring deep-structure trace from surface structure (J. S. Brown et al 1978), and several varieties of self-programming skills (Rigney 1978). The work being done in this field of "learning strategies" has surely accomplished the identification of strategies that are learnable. Much additional research is needed to assess their effectiveness as components of instruction in the learning of educationally realistic tasks in the outcome categories of verbal knowledge and intellectual skills. Learning strategies enhance the effectiveness of learning and remembering of material such as word lists primarily because they make possible meaningfully organized encoding. Effective strategies for the learning of material which is itself meaningfully organized may be more difficult to discover, and their influence may turn out to be inherently weaker.

PROBLEM SOLVING   By making an intensive analysis of an individual's solution of the Tower of Hanoi problem, Anzai & Simon (1979) provide an account of the "learning by doing" of successively more complex cognitive strategies. Initially a strategy of selective search was employed in avoiding bad moves. The problem solver was then able to develop a strategy of employing recursive subgoals. Still another useful strategy was the chunking of moves. And finally, a particular subgoal strategy (in this problem, called the "pyramid subgoal" strategy) was generated, making possible a particularly effective set of solution moves. In general, this account provides evidence that individuals are capable of transforming strategies, retrieving stored memories of strategies and problem procedures, and proceeding from looking ahead to looking backward.

Simon (1980b) reviews and comments on recent evidence regarding the learning of general problem-solving capabilities. While acknowledging the important role of accumulated knowledge, he disagrees with Goldstein & Papert (1977) in their assignment of primary importance to this factor. In addition, he states, there have to be processes for operating on that knowledge to solve problems and answer questions. Students need to acquire intellectual skills and to distinguish the learning of this kind of procedural knowledge from the learning of propositions (verbal knowledge). In addition, Simon sees the possibility that learners can acquire problem-solving strategies, including very general ones like means-end analysis, by practice with the working of examples and the explication of problem-solving principles.

Metacognition

In a series of articles, Flavell (1976, 1978, Flavell & Wellman 1977) has described and exemplified a domain of intellectual functioning called metacognition. Although originally concerned with metamemory (Flavell & Wellman 1977, A. L. Brown 1978), the ideas have been elaborated to include a greater range of cognitive phenomena. The categories of knowledge about one's own cognition, according to Flavell, include *sensitivity,* knowing what situations call for intentional cognitive activity; *person variables,* knowledge of those attributes that influence learning and memory; a *task* category, referring to characteristics of the intellectual task which influence performance; and procedures for solution, or *strategies.* These metacognitive phenomena make possible cognitive monitoring (Flavell 1978, 1981) which can influence both the course and the outcome of cognitive activity. A comprehensive review of metacognitive effects, particularly as they pertain to learning and remembering, is by A. L. Brown (1978). Evidence is included on the effects of knowing one's knowledge state, of prediction of intellectual performance, of planning ability, and of checking and monitoring cognitive activities. Results of studies of training metacognitive sensitivity and strategies are also summarized and interpreted.

Obviously the concept of metacognition raises the sights of research on cognition well beyond the scope of work on traditional memory tasks. Knowledge of the conditions that affect the acquisition and employment of knowledge may be obtained through experience or as a result of deliberately planned instruction. Such knowledge can be used, presumably, as a basis from which to originate the cognitive strategies which affect the processes involved in learning, remembering, and thinking. Presumably, experienced learners and thinkers are accustomed to engaging in cognitive monitoring and in the use of (meta) cognitive strategies. Young children and other inexperienced learners can be trained to employ these strategies to good advantage, as the work of such investigators as Campione & Brown (1977), Belmont & Butterfield (1977), Markman (1977) and others has shown. Future research may be expected to illuminate further the specific nature of effective metacognitive strategies.

Schemata

The views of several cognitive theorists converge in proposing that knowledge is represented in human memory as semantic networks called schemata. As a network of concepts or of propositions (Norman et al 1976), a schema makes possible interrelations of elements of information about a topic, represents important features, functions, rules for selection and use of the conceptual unit. A "functional" schema may in addition represent a set of conditions and the events of a procedure. Similar in conception is the description of schema provided by Rumelhart & Ortony (1977), which states that schemata are data structures for representing generic concepts, applicable to objects, situations, events, sequences of events, actions, and sequences of actions. While acknowledging the work of Bartlett (1932), these authors consider their notion of schema to resemble more closely that of Kant (1963). Schemata function in the storage of knowledge, in comprehension, in making inferences, and also in organizing action. J. R. Anderson (1980) considers a schema in its basic sense to be a "collection of feature sets," forming a category. Concepts are learned as the learner picks out correlations of features in the environment and develops categories around these correlations. Schemata may also be formed in more complex domains of cognition. Rumelhart & Norman (1978) propose that learning may take the form of accretion of instances to a schema, "restructuring" by the creation of a new schema, or "tuning," which refers to modification of the variables within a schema without changing its basic structure. In the work described by Schank & Abelson (1977), the educationally important idea of *understanding* is reflected in schemata that are distinguished as scripts, plans, and goals.

For instructional psychology, the implications of the schema conception would appear to be these: (*a*) Newly learned information is stored by being incorporated in one or more schemata, which have been formed by previous learning. (*b*) In general, as Bartlett's (1932) work showed, recall of previously learned verbal information is strongly influenced by schemata; remembering is a "constructive" act. (*c*) A schema not only helps retention of new material by providing a framework for its storage; it also alters the new information by making it "fit" the schema. (*d*) The schema, based as it is upon prior learning, makes it possible for the learner to make inferences which "fill the gaps" in stories or other expository prose. (*e*) Schemata are organized not only in terms of verbal (declarative) knowledge, but also as components of intellectual skills (procedural knowledge). (*f*) Learning how to evaluate and modify one's own schemata is a matter of considerable importance to the student; the instructional requirements of this activity are not yet well understood.

Knowledge Compilation and Optimization

In connection with their studies of problem solving in plane geometry, J. R. Anderson et al (1981) introduce some ideas which pertain to the consolidation, application, and generalization of knowledge. In other terms, they relate to the instructional event which Gagné (1977b,c) calls "enhancing retention and transfer." Anderson and his co-workers propose that students first encode intellectual skills as declarative information (verbal knowledge) within semantic networks. When such knowledge is used, general interpretive procedures apply it to the features of particular situations. As the knowledge is employed many times in a particular way, new procedures are developed which apply it directly without the interpretive step. This is the aspect of learning called *knowledge compilation,* and it consists of the two processes of *composition* and *proceduralization.* Composition reduces a series of intellectual skills to a single step. Proceduralization creates intellectual skills with knowledge formerly retrieved from long-term memory built into them, leading to their increased automatization (Neves & Anderson 1981).

When skills are proceduralized, this is not enough to guarantee successful solving of problems. Knowledge optimization implies other processes. Experienced problem solvers, in an activity such as generating plane geometry proofs, appear to be using heuristics of search which enable them to try the right inferences first. Such heuristics are acquired, it is hypothesized, by a process of generalization based on comparison of problems and their solutions; by the process of discrimination which places restrictions on the range of applicability of procedures; and by the process of composition, which leads to the formation of multiple-operator sequences.

Whether or not the initial stage of declarative encoding turns out to be a necessary phase of intellectual skill learning, these authors have directed attention to the processes of learning which occur subsequent to that event which may be called "initial acquisition." These additional learning processes, which presumably occur as the learner continues to practice with varied examples, are those which lead to heightened retention and to more highly probable transfer of skills to novel instances and situations. They appear to be of great importance to the understanding of instruction, and are obviously in need of increased research attention.

Automaticity of Cognitive Processes

It is a curious and somewhat ironic circumstance that the idea of automaticity, so clearly described in James's (1896) chapter on Habit, and so long proscribed as a phenomenon for investigation during the behaviorist era, should again come to prominence as a process of considerable importance to human cognitive activity. According to modern views (Spelke et al 1976, Schneider & Shiffrin 1977, Shiffrin & Schneider 1977, J. R. Anderson 1980), cognitive processes have two processing modes: controlled and automatic. Controlled processing demands much attentional capacity, is serial in nature, and is frequently conscious. Automatic processing demands little attention, is parallel in its operation, and difficult to alter or suppress. Automatic processing occurs not only in the early perceptual stages of cognition, but also in later stages, as exemplified by the automatization of well-practiced skills. A number of subjects of school learning may be influenced by automatization. Thus, facile reading is considered to be affected by the capability of automatic decoding (Lesgold & Perfetti 1981). Many of the operations of arithmetic would appear to depend upon certain "identity rules" which, if they are not automatized, greatly slow the processes of mathematical problem solving (cf Resnick 1981). The implications are that some part of instruction in the realm of intellectual skills must serve "bottom-up" needs. Some skills need to be practiced until they become automatic, if the learner is to make satisfactory progress in "higher-level" learning.

INSTRUCTION AND STUDENT CHARACTERISTICS

Of central importance to instructional psychology are questions about the manner in which the events of instruction are designed and delivered. Investigations have focused on such questions as the role of goals, objectives, and learning hierarchies in the design of instruction, the organization of content, the use of media, and the role of illustrations. Research studies show a current trend of interest in practice and feedback, including the use of adjunct questions, as factors causally related to achievement.

Instruction is expected to have an effect on the lasting capabilities or dispositions of students. Some student characteristics, such as the capacity of short-term memory, may be viewed as unalterable by means of instruction. Others are more or less stable, but their alterability through instruction or experience is questionable, or at least not firmly established (e.g. field dependence). Perhaps most interesting of all to instructional psychology are personal qualities that can be changed demonstrably by instruction or training, and which then serve as positive factors in their influence on achievement; examples would include accumulated knowledge and strategies of "how to learn."

Research continues its search for noninstructional correlates of academic achievement, including the familiar variables of measured intelligence, locus of control, anxiety, tolerance for ambiguity, field dependence-independence, and reflection-impulsivity, among others. Noteworthy reviews of some nonalterable variables affecting instructional outcomes are by Nuttall et al (1976), Fennema & Sherman (1977), Bar-Tal (1978), Cicirelli (1978), Banks & McQuater (1978), Seginer (1980), and Scarr & Yee (1980). For kindergarten and prekindergarten children, positive predictions of later academic achievement were found for a number of psychometric measures (Stevenson et al 1976a,b, Ernhart et al 1977) as well as for teachers ratings (Feshbach et al 1977), social competence (Perry et al 1979), self-esteem and achievement motivation (Bridgeman & Shipman 1978).

Beyond the satisfaction of investigator curiosity, it is difficult to surmise a purpose for many of the published investigations of student characteristics of the sort which are doubtfully alterable. For any instructional system there would appear to be three main courses of action possible with regard to the use of findings of correlations between any student characteristic and a desired educational outcome. First, students could be selected on the basis of a positively correlated trait. Although selection is undoubtedly done by schools, particularly by private ones, there does not appear to be much confidence that predictions of educational outcome can be raised worthwhile amounts beyond those already provided by measures of (a) general intelligence and (b) prior achievement.

As a second possibility, student characteristics which are more general than are implied by specific instructional content can be instilled in the learner by regimens of learning that range in duration from very short to very long. Characteristics of this sort are usually not viewed as traits but as *learned capabilities*. Specifically, they are intellectual skills, verbal knowledge, cognitive strategies, and attitudes. The importance to new learning of prior learning of these types of characteristics is an axiom of many instructional theories, as described in a previous section. If one is interested in systematic design of adaptive instruction, these are the student characteristics that can be depended upon. As yet, no other kinds of traits, whether alterable or not, have been shown to have an equal degree of usefulness to instructional design and practice.

A third intriguing idea is to the effect that measures of student characteristics could be employed to make possible a match between "aptitude" and "treatment," and thereby bring about a general rise in the measure of achievement (or other outcome). Studies of attribute-treatment interactions (ATI) are yielding positive evidence of interactions, particularly for such student characteristics as anxiety, locus of control, academic self-esteem, and the like, and such instructional modes as lecture versus individual tutoring. It appears, however, that the traits themselves are so relatively situation-specific and the instructional "treatments" so broadly structured that a truly systematic technology of adaptive instruction seems a remote possibility at best. The most feasible employment of ATI results to date would appear to lie in subtle and opportunistic adjustments of teacher strategies to individual students.

Attribute-Treatment Interactions

Following publication of the essential handbook by Cronbach & Snow (1977), interest in attribute-treatment interaction (ATI) studies continues to be high. Many studies explore the attribute variables suggested by Snow (1976): anxiety (A_x), achievement via independence (A_i), and achievement via conformity (A_c), which are expected to interact with instructional treatments characterized by different "structure" and "participation." The other set of variables mentioned by Snow are mental ability of the sort called crystallized intelligence (G_c, verbal achievement), fluid intelligence (G_f, analytic reasoning), and spatial visualization (G_v).

Significant interactions usually seem to be found between anxiety and a "structured" approach to instruction; that is, high-anxious students have better achievement in a teacher-centered approach, while low-anxious students do better in a student-centered approach. In Peterson's (1977) study of ninth graders in a social science course, stepwise regression analysis was used to reveal ATIs due to combinations of both structure and participation. Further results showed a complex Aptitude X Aptitude X Treatment interaction, in which high anxious–low ability students performed better in classes in which the teacher did not place high demands on them (low structure), whereas high anxious–high ability students did well in classes with high demands. Other studies exploring the interactions of anxiety and ability with instructional treatment are by Corno (1979), Peterson & Janicki

(1979), Janicki & Peterson (1981), and Corno et al (1981). Generally, the results are consistent with the notion that highly structured approaches are favorable for low-ability students, but that this relationship is also influenced by anxiety in the manner previously described.

Beginning with an article (1976) on achievement-treatment interactions, Tobias (1977a,b,c, 1979) has contributed a number of insightful reviews concerning anxiety and its interaction with instructional methods. He proposes a research model (1977c) which draws distinctions among the sites of influence of anxiety, during (*a*) preprocessing, (*b*) processing, and (*c*) after processing and before output. Tobias proposes that research seek out the relevant cognitive operations of these three stages; for example, at the processing stage, task difficulty, reliance on memory, and organization of the task. Tobias (1979) goes on to propose a research emphasis on the treatment of anxious individuals in test-anxiety reduction programs.

The long-term educational goal of attribute-treatment interaction studies is the development of systems of instruction which are adapted to individual learner differences (Cronbach 1967). The volume and variety of studies of ATI phenomena are extensive, and reviews devoted specifically to them are obviously of greater value to the researcher than a general review of this sort. Attribute variables have by no means "settled down," and new ones continue to appear, to compete with the more familiar variables of academic ability, self-concept, locus of control, achievement motivation, anxiety, and various "cognitive styles." Although feasible variations in instruction must surely be seen as part of the ATI problem, equally diverse variations in instructional modes and methods characterize studies in this area: lecture vs discussion, teacher-centered vs student-centered, programmed instruction vs reading, prescribed sequence vs learner control, and a number of others. The identification of learner processing variables affected by variations in instruction is also in a somewhat undeveloped state: such variables as task difficulty, content preference, attention and memory demands appear as initial tries in a domain of variables not yet well defined.

The ultimate applicability of ATI research is worthy of some consideration. If indeed the relevant kinds of individual differences continue to proliferate, and new varieties of approach to instruction continue to be suggested, the whole enterprise of systematic adaptive instruction may become impossibly complex for the classroom. Is this where the computer enters the picture? Perhaps so, but one should be reminded that there are some aspects of classroom instruction which computer-based instruction does not (and cannot) simulate, namely those centered around the interpersonal student-teacher interaction. How can these be included in a system of adaptive instruction which is simultaneously taking into account a great variety of personal traits of the learner?

Another precaution for the guidance of research is suggested by the results of many ATI studies. Interactions of treatments with those personal traits called "aptitudes" do not typically yield effects of great size. In the background of every investigator's experience is the well-established finding, which continues to appear, that the most powerful variables related to school achievement are (a) intellectual ability and (b) the accumulated effects of prior learning. Most investigators equate these factors with Cattell's (1971) fluid and crystallized intelligence. Whether or not the equivalence is seen, these two factors continue to exert the strongest effects on the outcomes of student learning. Instructional systems which can adapt to these two human characteristics (whether by computer or by human action) would appear to have some likelihood of success in assuring student achievement.

APPLICATIONS OF INSTRUCTIONAL PSYCHOLOGY

Projects which employ psychological principles to solve applied problems are described in this section. The problems examined include those of selecting and sequencing appropriate content for inclusion in specialized curricula; second, improving the effectiveness of operational computer-assisted instructional systems; and third, improving teacher skills through inservice instruction. Each description includes a statement of the problem, a rationale for the psychological principle(s) employed, and the outcome of the project to date. In none of these studies can the outcomes be attributed solely to the principle identified; many factors have contributed to the solution of each problem.

Applications of Hierarchical Analysis

How should one identify and sequence intellectual skills? This problem arises when instructional materials are to be developed in areas in which no instruction previously existed, or that which existed was unsatisfactory, or, as in the case that follows, a new medium of instruction is employed.

Since 1970 the Ontario Institute for Studies in Education has been involved with the schools and community colleges of Ontario in the cooperative development of computer-assisted instruction (CAI). In a recent report (Gershman & Sakamoto 1980), CAI instructional sequences were described for 30 of the most important topics in intermediate mathematics including arithmetic, algebra, probability, and measurement.

The development activities were conducted by joint teams consisting of OISE staff members and teachers from cooperating schools. Their basic approach was to cluster the skills to be taught into a terminal objective and one or more enabling objectives which represent skills that must be achieved in order to reach the terminal objective. The objectives form a hierarchical relationship in which subordinate skills must be achieved prior to the learning of superordinate skills (Gagné 1968).

This analytic approach was especially critical in this project because it provides not only the identification of skills and sequence for teaching them; it also provides a branching rationale for the CAI lessons. For example, in a typical lesson, students may be asked if they can perform the terminal objective. If they can, they are shown the subordinate skills and asked which is the most difficult one they can do. Students are then sequenced through the hierarchy based upon performance on tests embedded in the instruction. The hierarchy is also used as a major component of the sequential testing strategy. It is estimated that this technique reduces testing time by 50 percent.

The CAI mathematics curriculum which is based on the hierarchical analysis of each terminal objective was extensively evaluated during the 1979–80 academic year. From September to January over 2000 Ontario students in 18 schools spent an average of four hours to cover an average of seven topics. Great variability was found in the number of topics covered by the students. Pretest-posttest analyses indicate there were significant gains for both CAI and comparison non-CAI students in the same schools; however, the CAI students gained significantly more. Attitude questionnaire results showed that 94 percent of the students said CAI was "fun," "interesting," and 72 percent said they liked math better with CAI. Similar results have been reported for the other courses developed by the OISE staff.

The U.S. Navy also has found it useful to incorporate the use of hierarchical analysis into the curriculum development process. The need for added instruction in basic skills has resulted from the Navy's inability to attract personnel with aptitude scores high enough to qualify them for entry into initial job training programs. One response to the problem has been reported by Harding and his co-workers (1980). As contractors of the Navy Personnel Research and Development Center, they faced the task of identifying what basic skills should be taught to entering recruits in order to prepare them for the "A" (initial job training) Schools (JOBS program).

The research team's most successful approach to identifying needed skills was that of first identifying the major learning tasks in each of four A School curricula. Based on this analysis, tentative sets of skills were identified which appeared to be prerequisite to the skills that had to be learned in the A school. The types of skills that were tentatively identified were: find information in a table, add numbers, read a setting on a micrometer, comprehend a written passage, and solve word problems.

Hierarchical analysis procedures were used to identify subordinate basic skills which were prerequisite to those skills needed in the A Schools. The hierarchies served as the basic design component which resulted in the development of instructor guides, student guides, lesson summaries, practice exercises, overhead transparencies, and various evaluation instruments.

A preliminary evaluation of the JOBS program has been reported by Baker & Huff (1981). The performance of students entering the JOBS program was compared with that of those who chose not to enter it, and with students who were qualified directly to enter an A School. The students in the JOBS courses demonstrated gains of about 42 points from pre- to posttests, and 95 percent went on to complete the JOBS program successfully. Of the graduates of the program, 75 percent were able to graduate from A School. These percentages compare favorably with the qualified student graduation rate of 87 percent. Eight months after graduation, the qualified group had approximately three times as many fleet discharges as did the JOBS group. While the results are supportive of the JOBS program, an experimental study has not yet been conducted which includes JOBS-eligible students who do not get JOBS training but go directly to A School.

The OISE and JOBS projects are examples of two highly successful efforts which relied heavily on the hierarchical analysis of terminal objectives to identify the prerequisite subordinate skills and the appropriate sequence for those skills. Revisions of the hierarchies came about through the formative evaluation and revision of the instruction. The hierarchical approach, initially investigated as theory, appears to have served a very pragmatic role in these and many other instructional development projects.

Computer-Managed Instruction (CMI)

An area of increasing interest in recent years has been the use of computers in instruction. While research has been underway for over a decade (e.g. Dick & Gallagher 1972), there has been a resurgence of interest because of the use by military agencies of both large computer systems and microcomputers in nearly every education and training setting. Investigators were initially interested in computers as instructional delivery systems because they made possible the automation of many of the behavioral principles of learning. More recently, cognitive psychologists have used the computer as a device to represent their theories (Greeno 1978) or as a direct model of a problem-solving strategy (Alderman 1978). Meta-analysis of research on college level computer-based instruction by Kulik et al (1980) indicates a consistent positive effect on both learning outcomes and attitudes, as well as a substantial reduction in learning time.

Numerous computerized learning systems are currently in use. One of the largest is the Navy's CMI system. By 1980, it had approximately 9000 daily users from 10 different technical training schools. Various evaluations of the system have demonstrated its general effectiveness, but users and observers agree that further improvements can be made. A study by Van Matre (1980) documented these needs. It included observations of the system in operation and questionnaires and interviews with CMI managers, instructors, and students. The result of the study was the development of a list of priority projects which address student and system deficiencies and limitations.

A number of these projects have been conducted and the results of four of them have been reported. One dealt with the effect of altering student/instructor ratios, while another investigated the effect of different test item formats and procedures on student performance (see Van Matre et al 1981, Lockhart et al 1981). A third study by Hamovitch & Van Matre (1981) determined the feasibility of automating the testing of performance skills and knowledge, in comparison with the traditional manual testing and grading system. A fourth study, employing the direct application of previous findings of instructional psychology, attempted to increase the motivation of students who use the CMI system. It was observed that not all students progressed at their optimal pace through the individualized course. An experiment was conducted by Pennypacker et al (1980) which drew upon the first author's prior work on charting student progress as a means of enhancing motivation.

A CMI course in basic electronics and electricity, taught in Memphis, was used as the vehicle for the research study. Progress charts displayed the ratios of actual learning times to predicted learning times; in some groups they were shown periodically, in others when requested by the student. The outcomes of the study indicated no significant differences among groups on the final comprehensive examination. However, those students who were provided a progress chart only when they requested it required significantly less time to complete the course than the other groups. The ten percent time savings represents more than one full day of training. If this outcome were replicated across all the students who take the course in a year, there would be a savings of over 20,000 training days. Both students and instructors were extremely supportive of the charting procedures.

A related set of research studies have been conducted on the appropriate role of the instructor within a CMI system (McCombs & Dobrovolny 1980) and the application of learning (as opposed to teaching) strategies in a computer-based technical training system (McCombs 1981). These studies focused on the Air Force's Advanced Instructional System which is a large-scale individualized CMI system. The latter study is of particular importance because it focuses upon the learning difficulties of students who lack some of the basic skills and who also exhibit motivation and study skill deficiencies.

In the research reported by McCombs, it was found that these students had little interest in learning the course materials; experienced high anxiety about the course and tests; had poor logical reasoning, reading comprehension, and study skills; and tended to be the younger students having less educational experience.

A battery of measures was developed to be used on an ongoing basis to assess students' expectations and problems, and materials were designed to aid learners to be more effective in the CMI environment. For example, one set of materials describes the requirements of a self-paced, individualized, computer-managed instructional setting. Four other study skills modules emphasize reading comprehension, memorization, test taking, and concentration management. A third set of materials has been produced by McCombs to help students develop positive motivation and personal responsibility. All of the instruction appears in printed, self-instructional format. It is designed to be read easily with accompanying visuals, and it includes practice exercises. The modules vary in average learning time from 30 minutes to about 4 hours.

At this stage in the project the researchers are attempting to assess the facilitative effect of these specialized learning strategy materials in terms of learning outcomes, learning time, and attitudes. However, it will be extremely difficult to isolate the effects of any single module. Many observers would be required to determine changes in "process skills" which, in turn, result in outcome changes. There will be difficulty also in implementing an effective research design in an operational military training environment. The McCombs study exemplifies the application of instructional psychology principles to specific learning problems. In this case, deficient learning skills have been identified and instructional materials developed for students who are studying in a computer-based, individualized environment.

Teacher Inservice Training

The final application study to be described is concerned with the problem of providing teachers with research-based inservice training. After extensive efforts to bring research findings into the classroom, Huitt & Rim (1980) report that the "methods and materials used by researchers to describe from limited observations the conditions and processes that can be generalized to the school year likely are more complex and time-consuming than is necessary for practitioners concerned with what is happening now to make for a better year" (p. 47). This observation was based upon the experience of implementing the Research for Better Schools (RBS) four-phase Instructional Improvement Cycle—a process which links research findings with classroom practice.

RBS, an educational research, development, and service organization, worked out a process with local schools in which data are collected in classrooms on selected variables. These are equivalent to and compared with data from reported research studies. The teacher decides if improvements can be made in the classroom and, if so, what change goals should be established. After the commitment to change is made, the teacher studies an array of alternative strategies which might be employed and selects the one which seems most promising. The final cycle includes the implementation of the plan, another round of data collection, and further modification if the results warrant it.

In order to implement this process, RBS recognized the support role they would have to play. They began by conducting a rigorous examination of what is referred to as process/product research, i.e. the research that attempts to link specified teaching practices with successful learning outcomes. The most creditable reviews of this research were selected. These were used to identify areas of focus which appeared to have the greatest potential for instructional improvement in the classroom. The variables thus identified were: student engaged time, the overlap between content taught and content tested, and prior learning relevant to the task to be learned.

After these variables were identified, RBS developed instruments and procedures which could be employed by classroom teachers to determine the status of their classrooms on these variables. In addition, it was necessary to develop special reference materials to be used by teachers in comparing their data with those reported by researchers. The final component of the system is a set of strategies which suggest ways of implementing the various alternatives the teacher might select. RBS attempted to deal only with those strategies that had research support.

Initial results indicate that teachers can be taught to use the "engaged time" data collection system in less than 10 hours. Huitt & Rim (1980) report initial informal success from the implementation of the student-engaged time procedures in classrooms by the teachers. The total results of a formal evaluation are not yet available, but the researchers plan to combine engaged time training with training on instructional overlap and prior learning.

Summary

The studies reviewed in this section tend to lack the rigor of those reported in earlier sections. They are important because they provide an entirely different perspective on the field of instructional psychology. In each of these projects an instructional problem existed—how to identify and sequence content for intellectual skills, how to improve the effectiveness of a CMI system, or how to enhance the instructional effectiveness of teachers. In each project the investigators drew upon the existing research base in order to develop a solution. While not all instructional psychologists are likely to be concerned about the immediate application of their research findings, it is worth bearing in mind that application is the appropriate endpoint for the research cycle, and often the beginning of the next.

ACKNOWLEDGMENTS

This work has been supported in part by Contract #N6601-81C-0456 with the U.S. Navy Personnel Research and Development Center. We thank Felix Bongjoh, Dale Farland, Peggy Perkins, and Katherine Sink for assistance in location and review of items in the literature.

Literature Cited

Alderman D. L. 1978. Tree searching and student problem solving. *J. Educ. Psychol.* 70:209–17

Anderson, J. R. 1980. *Cognitive Psychology and Its Implications.* San Francisco: Freeman. 503 pp.

Anderson, J. R., Greeno, J. G., Line, P. J., Neves, D. M. 1981. Acquisition of problem-solving skill. In *Cognitive Skills and Their Acquisition,* ed. J. R. Anderson, pp. 191–230. Hillsdale, NJ: Erlbaum. 386 pp.

Anderson, L. W. 1976. An empirical investigation of individual differences in time to learn. *J. Educ. Psychol.* 68:226–33

Anderson, R. C. 1970. Control of student mediating processes during verbal learning and instruction. *Rev. Educ. Res.* 40:349–69

Andrews, D. H., Goodson, L. A. 1980. A comparative analysis of models of instructional design. *J. Instr. Dev.* 3:2–16

Anzai, Y., Simon, H. A. 1979. The theory of learning by doing. *Psychol. Rev.* 86: 124–40

Atkinson, R. C., Shiffrin, R. M. 1968. Human memory: A proposed system and its control processes. In *The Psychology of Learning and Motivation,* ed. K. W. Spence, J. T. Spence, 2:89–195. New York: Academic. 249 pp.

Atkinson, R. C., Wickens, T. D. 1971. Human memory and the concept of reinforcement. In *The Nature of Reinforcement,* ed. R. Glaser, pp. 66–120. New York: Academic. 379 pp.

Ausubel, D. P., Novak, J. D., Hanesian, H. 1978. *Educational Psychology: A Cognitive View.* New York: Holt, Rinehart & Winston. 733 pp. 2nd ed.

Baker, M., Huff, K. 1981. *The evaluation of a job-oriented basic skills training program—interim report.* Tech. Rep. 82–

14. San Diego: Navy Pers. Res. Dev. Cent. 25 pp.

Bandura, A. 1969. *Principles of Behavior Modification.* New York: Holt, Rinehart & Winston. 677 pp.

Banks, W. C., McQuater, G. V. 1978. Toward a reconceptualization of the social-cognitive bases of achievement orientations in blacks. *Rev. Educ. Res.* 48:381–97

Bar-Tal, D. 1978. Attributional analysis of achievement-related behavior. *Rev. Educ. Res.* 48:381–97

Bartlett, F. C. 1932. *Remembering: A Study in Experimental and Social Psychology.* Cambridge: Cambridge Univ. Press. 317 pp.

Belmont, J. M., Butterfield, E. C. 1977. The instructional approach to developmental cognitive research. In *Perspectives on the Development of Memory and Cognition,* ed. R. V. Kail, J. W. Hagen, pp. 437–81. Hillsdale, NJ: Erlbaum. 498 pp.

Block, J. H., ed. 1971. *Mastery Learning, Theory and Practice.* New York: Holt, Rinehart & Winston. 152 pp.

Bloom, B. S., ed. 1956. *Taxonomy of Educational Objectives. Handbook I. Cognitive Domain.* New York: McKay

Bloom, B. S. 1971. Learning for mastery. In *Handbook on Formative and Summative Evaluation of Student Learning,* ed. B. S. Bloom, J. T. Hastings, G. F. Madaus, pp. 43–57. New York: McGraw-Hill. 923 pp.

Bloom, B. S. 1976. *Human Characteristics and School Learning.* New York: McGraw-Hill. 284 pp.

Bloom, B. S. 1981. *All Our Children Learning.* New York: McGraw-Hill. 275 pp.

Bower, G. H. 1970. Analysis of a mnemonic device. *Am. Psychol.* 58:496–510

Bower, G. H. 1975. Cognitive psychology: An introduction. See Estes 1975, pp. 25–80

Bower, G. M., Hilgard, E. J. 1981. *Theories of Learning.* Englewood Cliffs, NJ: Prentice-Hall. 647 pp. 5th ed.

Bransford, J. D. 1979. *Human Cognition.* Belmont, Calif: Wadsworth. 300 pp.

Branson, R. K. 1979. Implementation issues in instructional systems development: Three case studies. See O'Neil 1979a, pp. 181–204

Bridgeman, B., Shipman, V. C. 1978. Preschool measures of self-esteem and achievement motivation as predictors of third-grade achievement. *J. Educ. Psychol.* 70:17–28

Briggs, L. J., Wager, W. 1981. *Handbook of Procedures for the Design of Instruction.* Englewood Cliffs, NJ: Educ. Technol. 261 pp. 2nd ed.

Brown, A. L. 1978. Knowing when, where, and how to remember: A problem of metacognition. See Glaser 1978a, pp. 77–165

Brown, J. S., Collins, A., Harris, G. 1978. Artificial intelligence and learning strategies. See O'Neil 1978, pp. 107–39

Bruner, J. S. 1960. *The Process of Education.* Cambridge, Mass: Harvard Univ. Press. 97 pp.

Campione, J. C., Brown, A. L. 1977. Memory and metamemory development in educable retarded children. See Belmont & Butterfield 1977, pp. 367–406

Carroll, J. B. 1963. A model of school learning. *Teach. Coll. Rec.* 64:723–33

Carroll, J. B. 1965. School learning over the long haul. In *Learning and the Educational Process,* ed. J. D. Krumboltz, pp. 249–69. Chicago: Rand McNally. 277 pp.

Case, R. 1978a. A developmentally based theory and technology of instruction. *Rev. Educ. Res.* 48:439–63

Case, R. 1978b. Intellectual development from birth to adulthood: A neo-Piagetian interpretation. In *Children's Thinking: What Develops?* ed. R. S. Siegler, pp. 37–71. Hillsdale, NJ: Erlbaum. 371 pp.

Case, R. 1978c. Piaget and beyond: Toward a developmentally based theory and technology of instruction. See Glaser 1978a, pp. 167–228

Cattell, R. B. 1971. *Abilities: Their Structure, Growth, and Action.* Boston: Houghton-Mifflin. 583 pp.

Cicirelli, V. G. 1978. The relationship of sibling structure to intellectual abilities and achievement. *Rev. Educ. Res.* 48: 365–79

Collins, A. 1977. Processes in acquiring knowledge. In *Schooling and the Acquisition of Knowledge,* ed. R. C. Anderson, R. Spiro, W. E. Montague, pp. 339–64. Hillsdale, NJ: Erlbaum. 448 pp.

Collins, A., Warnock, E. H., Aiello, N., Miller, M. L. 1975. Reasoning from incomplete knowledge. In *Representation and Understanding. Studies in Cognitive Science,* ed. D. C. Bobrow, A. Collins, pp. 383–415. New York: Academic. 427 pp.

Corno, L. 1979. A hierarchical analysis of selected naturally occurring aptitude-treatment interactions in the third grade. *Am. Educ. Res. J.* 16:391–409

Corno, L., Mitman, A., Hedges, L. 1981. The influence of direct instruction on student self-appraisals: A hierarchical analysis of treatment and aptitude-treatment interaction effects. *Am. Educ. Res. J.* 18:39–61

Cronbach, L. J. 1967. How can instruction be adapted to individual differences? In *Learning and Individual Differences,* ed. R. M. Gagné, pp. 23–39. Columbus, Ohio: Merrill. 265 pp.

Cronbach, L. J., Snow, R. E. 1977. *Aptitudes and Instructional Methods.* New York: Irvington. 574 pp.

Cross, K. P. 1976. *Accent on Learning.* San Francisco: Jossey-Bass. 291 pp.

Cross, K. P. 1981. *Adults as Learners.* San Francisco: Jossey-Bass. 300 pp.

Dansereau, D. 1978. The development of a learning strategies curriculum. See O'Neil 1978, pp. 1–29

Denham, C., Lieberman, A. 1980. *Time to Learn.* Washington DC: Natl. Inst. Educ. 246 pp.

Dick, W., Carey, L. 1978. *The Systematic Design of Instruction.* Chicago: Scott, Foresman. 216 pp.

Dick, W., Gallagher, P. D. 1972. Systems concepts and computer-managed instruction: An implementation and validation study. *Educ. Technol.* 12:33–39

DiVesta, F. J., Schultz, C. B., Dangel, I. R. 1973. Passage organization and imposed learning strategies in comprehension and recall of connected discourse. *Mem. Cognit.* 1:471–76

Ernhart, C. B., Spaner, S. D., Jordan, T. E. 1977. Validity of selected preschool screening tests. *Contemp. Educ. Psychol.* 2:78–89

Estes, W. K. 1972. Reinforcement in human behavior. *Am. Sci.* 60:723–29

Estes, W. K., ed. 1975. *Handbook of Learning and Cognitive Processes,* Vol. 1. *In-*

troduction to Concepts and Issues. Hillsdale, NJ: Erlbaum. 304 pp.

Estes, W. K., ed. 1976a. *Handbook of Learning and Cognitive Processes,* Vol. 3. *Approaches to Human Learning and Motivation.* Hillsdale, NJ: Erlbaum. 374 pp.

Estes, W. K., ed. 1976b. *Handbook of Learning and Cognitive Processes,* Vol. 4. *Attention and Memory.* Hillsdale, NJ: Erlbaum. 436 pp.

Estes, W. K., ed. 1978a. *Handbook of Learning and Cognitive Processes,* Vol. 5. *Human Information Processing.* Hillsdale, NJ: Erlbaum. 352 pp.

Estes, W. K., ed. 1978b. *Handbook of Learning and Cognitive Processes,* Vol. 6. *Linguistic Functions in Cognitive Theory.* Hillsdale, NJ: Erlbaum. 311 pp.

Farley, F. H., Gordon, N. J., eds. 1981. *Psychology and Education, The State of the Union.* Berkeley, Calif: McCutchan. 405 pp.

Fennema, E., Sherman, J. 1977. Sex-related differences in mathematics achievement, spatial visualization and affective factors. *Am. Educ. Res. J.* 14:51–71

Feshbach, A., Adelman, H., Fuller, W. 1977. Prediction of reading and related academic problems. *J. Educ. Psychol.* 69:299–308

Flavell, J. H. 1976. Metacognitive aspects of problem solving. In *The Nature of Intelligence,* ed. L. B. Resnick. Hillsdale, NJ: Erlbaum. 364 pp.

Flavell, J. H. 1978. Metacognitive development. In *Structural/Process Theories of Complex Human Behavior,* ed. J. M. Scandura, C. J. Brainerd, pp. 213–45. Alphen a.d. Rijn, The Netherlands: Sijthoff & Hoordhoff. 612 pp.

Flavell, J. H. 1981. Cognitive monitoring. In *Children's Oral Communication Skills,* pp. 35–60. New York: Academic. 364 pp.

Flavell, J. H., Wellman, H. M. 1977. Metamemory. See Belmont & Butterfield 1977, pp. 437–81

Gagné, R. M. 1968. Learning hierarchies. *Educ. Psychol.* 6:1–9

Gagné, R. M. 1977a. Analysis of objectives. In *Instructional Design,* ed. L. J. Briggs, pp. 115–45. Englewood Cliffs, NJ: Educ. Technol. 532 pp.

Gagné, R. M. 1977b. *The Conditions of Learning.* New York: Holt, Rinehart & Winston. 339 pp. 3rd ed.

Gagné, R. M. 1977c. Instructional programs. In *Fundamentals and Applications of Learning,* ed. M. H. Marx, M. E. Bunch, pp. 404–28. New York: Macmillan. 550 pp.

Gagné, R. M., Briggs, L. J. 1979. *Principles of Instructional Design.* New York: Holt, Rinehart & Winston. 321 pp. 2nd ed.

Gagné, R. M., Rohwer, W. D. Jr. 1969. Instructional psychology. *Ann. Rev. Psychol.* 20:381–418

Gershman, J. S., Sakamoto, E. J. 1980. *Intermediate mathematics: CARE Ontario Assessment Instrument Pool.* Final Rep., Contract No. 206. Toronto: Ontario Inst. Stud. Educ. 141 pp.

Glaser, R. 1978a. *Advances in Instructional Psychology,* Vol. 1. Hillsdale, NJ: Erlbaum. 304 pp.

Glaser, R., ed. 1978b. *Research and Development and School Change.* Hillsdale, NJ: Erlbaum. 109 pp.

Glaser, R. 1979. Trends and research questions in psychological research on learning and schooling. *Educ. Res.* 8:6–13

Glaser, R. 1982. Instructional psychology: Past, present, and future. *Am. Psychol.* 37:292–305

Glass, A. L., Holyoak, K. J., Santa, J. L. 1979. *Cognition.* Reading, Mass: Addison-Wesley. 521 pp.

Goldstein, I., Papert, S. 1977. Artificial intelligence, language, and the study of knowledge. *Cogn. Sci.* 1:84–124

Greeno, J. G. 1978. Natures of problem-solving abilities. See Estes 1978a, pp. 239–70

Greeno, J. G. 1980. Psychology of learning, 1960–1980. One participant's observations. *Am. Psychol.* 35:713–28

Greeno, J. G., Bjork, R. A. 1973. Mathematical learning theory and the new "mental forestry." *Ann. Rev. Psychol.* 24:81–116

Hamovitch, M., Van Matre, N. 1981. *CMI in the Navy: III. Automated performance testing in the radioman "A" school.* Rep. TR 81–7. San Diego: Navy Pers. Res. Dev. Cent. 19 pp.

Harding, S. R., Mogford, B., Melching, W. H., Showel, M. 1980. *The development of four job-oriented basic skills (JOBS) programs.* Final tech. rep., Northrop Services. San Diego: Navy Pers. Res. Dev. Cent. 57 pp.

Howe, M. J. A. 1977. *Adult Learning. Psychological Research and Applications.* London: Wiley. 291 pp.

Huitt, W. C., Rim, E. D. 1980. *A basic skills instructional improvement program. Utilizing research to improve classroom practice.* Presented at Ann. Meet. Am. Educ. Res. Assoc., Boston, Mass. 61 pp.

James, W. 1896. *Principles of Psychology,* Vol. 1. New York: Holt. 689 pp.

Janicki, T. C., Peterson, P. L. 1981. Aptitude-treatment interaction effects of variations in direct instruction. *Am. Educ. Res. J.* 18:63–82

Kant, I. 1963. *Critique of Pure Reason.* London: Macmillan. 681 pp.

Karplus, R. 1980. Teaching for the development of reasoning. See Lawson 1980, pp. 150–73

Klatzky, R. L. 1980. *Human Memory: Structures and Processes.* San Francisco: Freeman. 358 pp. 2nd ed.

Knox, A. B. 1977. *Adult Development and Learning.* San Francisco: Jossey-Bass. 679 pp.

Kulik, J. A., Kulik, C. C., Cohen, P. A. 1980. Effectiveness of computer-based college teaching: A meta-analysis of findings. *Rev. Educ. Res.* 50:525–44

Lachman, R., Lachman, J. L., Butterfield, E. C. 1979. *Cognitive Psychology and Information Processing: An Introduction.* Hillsdale, NJ: Erlbaum. 573 pp.

Landa, L. M. 1976. *Instructional Regulation and Control.* Englewood Cliffs, NJ: Educ. Technol. 496 pp.

Larsen, I., Markosian, L. Z., Suppes, P. 1978. Performance models of undergraduate students on computer-assisted instruction in elementary logic. *Instr. Sci.* 7: 15–35

Lawson, A. E. 1980. *The Psychology of Teaching for Thinking and Creativity* (1980 AETS Yearbook). Columbus: ERIC Clearinghouse Sci., Math., Environ. Educ. Ohio State Univ. 319 pp.

Lawson, A. E., Lawson, C. A. 1980. A theory of teaching for conceptual understanding, rational thought, and creativity. See Lawson 1980, pp. 104–49

Lesgold, A. M., Perfetti, C. A. 1981. *Interactive Processes in Reading.* Hillsdale, NJ: Erlbaum. 420 pp.

Levin, J. R., Divine-Hawkins, P. 1974. Visual imagery as a prose learning process. *J. Reading Behav.* 6:23–30

Lockhart, K. A., Sturges, P. T., Van Matre, N. H., Zachai, J. 1981. *CMI in the Navy: IV. The effects of test item format on learning and knowledge retention.* Rep. TR 81–8. San Diego: Navy Pers. Res. Dev. Cent. 48 pp.

Markle, S. M. 1978. *Designs for Instructional Designers.* Champaign, Ill: Stipes. 214 pp.

Markle, S. M., Tiemann, P. W. 1974. Some principles of instructional design at higher cognitive levels. In *Control of Human Behavior,* ed. R. Ulrich, T. Stachnik, T. Mabry, 13:312–23. Glenview, Ill: Scott-Foresman. 453 pp.

Markman, E. M. 1977. Realizing that you don't understand: A preliminary investigation. *Child Dev.* 48:986–92

McCombs, B. L. 1981. *Transitioning learning strategies research into practice: Focus on the student in technical training.* Presented at Ann. Meet. Am. Educ. Res. Assoc., Los Angeles. 28 pp.

McCombs, B. L., Dobrovolny, J. L. 1980. *Theoretical definition of instructor role in computer-managed instruction.* Tech. Note 80–10. San Diego: Navy Pers. Res. Dev. Cent. 39 pp.

Merrill, M. D., Kelety, J. C., Wilson, B. 1981. Elaboration theory and cognitive psychology. *Instr. Sci.* 10:217–37

Merrill, M. D., Reigeluth, C. M., Faust, G. W. 1979. The instructional quality profile: A curriculum evaluation and design tool. See O'Neil 1979b, pp. 165–204

Merrill, M. D., Richards, R. E., Schmidt, R. V., Wood, N. D. 1977. *The Instructional Strategy Diagnostic Profile Training Manual.* San Diego: Courseware. 232 pp.

Merrill, P. F. 1976. Task analysis—An information processing approach. *NSPI J.* 15:7–11

MESA Seminar 1980. *The State of Research on Selected Alterable Variables in Education.* Chicago: Dep. Educ., Univ. Chicago. 123 pp.

Neves, D. M., Anderson, J. R. 1981. Knowledge compilation: Mechanisms for the automatization of cognitive skills. See Anderson et al 1981, pp. 57–84

Norman, D., Gentner, D., Stevens, A. 1976. Comments on learning schemata and memory representation. In *Cognition and Instruction,* ed. D. Klahr, pp. 177–96. Hillsdale, NJ: Erlbaum. 361 pp.

Nuttall, E. V., Nuttall, R. L., Polit, D., Hunter, J. B. 1976. The effects of family size, birth order, sibling separation and crowding on the academic achievement of boys and girls. *Am. Educ. Res. J.* 13:217–23

O'Neil, H. F. Jr., ed. 1978. *Learning Strategies.* New York: Academic. 230 pp.

O'Neil, H. F. Jr., ed. 1979a. *Issues in Instructional Systems Development.* New York: Academic. 211 pp.

O'Neil, H. F. Jr., ed. 1979b. *Procedures for Instructional Systems Development.* New York: Academic. 321 pp.

Pennypacker, H. S., Van Matre, N., Hartman, W. H., Brett, B. E., Ward, L. S. 1980. *CMI in the Navy: I. The effects of charted feedback on rate of progress through a CMI course.* Report DIN 306-80-14. San Diego: Navy Pers. Res. Dev. Cent. 48 pp.

Perry, J. D., Guidubaldi, J., Kehle, T. J. 1979. Kindergarten competencies as predictors of third-grade classroom behavior and achievement. *J. Educ. Psychol.* 71:443–50

Peterson, P. L. 1977. Interactive effects of student anxiety, achievement orientation, and teacher behavior on student achievement and attitude. *J. Educ. Psychol.* 69:779–92

Peterson, P. L., Janicki, T. C. 1979. Individual characteristics and children's learning in large-group and small-group approaches. *J. Educ. Psychol.* 71:677–87

Piaget, J. 1970. Piaget's theory. In *Carmichael's Manual of Child Psychology*, ed. P. Mussen, 1:703–32. New York: Wiley. 1519 pp.

Reigeluth, C. M. 1979. In search of a better way to organize instruction: The elaboration theory. *J. Instr. Dev.* 2:8–15

Reigeluth, C. M., Merrill, M. D., Bunderson, C. V. 1978. The structure of subject matter content and its instructional design implications. *Instr. Sci.* 7:107–26

Reigeluth, C. M., Rodgers, C. A. 1980. The elaboration theory of instruction: Prescriptions for task analysis and design. *NSPI J.* 19:16–26

Resnick, L. B. 1981. Instructional psychology. *Ann. Rev. Psychol.* 32:659–704

Richardson, F. 1978. Behavior modification and learning strategies. See O'Neil 1978, pp. 57–78

Rigney, J. W. 1978. Learning strategies: A theoretical perspective. See O'Neil 1978, pp. 165–205

Robinson, F. P. 1946. *Effective Study.* New York: Harper. 365 pp.

Rothkopf, E. Z. 1965. Some theoretical and experimental approaches to problems in written instruction. See Carroll 1965, pp. 193–221

Rothkopf, E. Z. 1971. Experiments of mathemagenic behavior and the technology of written instruction. In *Verbal Learning Research and the Technology of Written Instruction,* ed. E. A. Rothkopf, P. E. Johnson, pp. 284–303. New York: Teach. Coll. 367 pp.

Rothkopf, E. Z. 1981. A macroscopic model of instruction and purposive learning: An overview. *Instr. Sci.* 10:105–22

Rumelhart, D. E., Norman, D. A. 1978. Accretion, tuning, and restructuring: Three modes of learning. In *Semantic Factors in Cognition,* ed. J. W. Cotton, R. L. Klatzky, pp. 37–53. Hillsdale, NJ: Erlbaum. 239 pp.

Rumelhart, D. E., Ortony, A. 1977. The representation of knowledge in memory. See Collins 1977, pp. 99–136

Scandura, J. M. 1977a. *Problem Solving: A Structural/Process Approach with Instructional Implications.* New York: Academic. 580 pp.

Scandura, J. M. 1977b. Structural approach to instructional problems. *Am. Psychol.* 32:33–53

Scandura, J. M. 1980. Theoretical foundations of instruction: A systems alternative to cognitive psychology. *J. Struct. Learn.* 6:347–93

Scarr, S., Yee, D. 1980. Heritability and educational policy: Genetic and environmental effects on IQ aptitude and achievement. *Educ. Psychol.* 15:1–22

Schank, R., Abelson, R. 1977. *Scripts, Plans, Goals and Understanding.* Hillsdale, NJ: Erlbaum. 248 pp.

Schneider, W., Shiffrin, R. M. 1977. Controlled and automatic human information processing: I. Detection, search, and attention. *Psychol. Rev.* 84:1–66

Searle, B., Friend, J., Suppes, P. 1976. *The Radio Mathematics Project: Nicaragua 1974–1975.* Stanford, Calif: Inst. Math. Stud. Soc. Sci., Stanford Univ. 261 pp.

Seginer, R. 1980. The effects of cognitive and affective variables on academic ability: A multivariate analysis. *Contemp. Educ. Psychol.* 5:266–75

Shiffrin, R. M., Schneider, W. 1977. Controlled and automatic human information processing: II. Perceptual learning, automatic attending, and a general theory. *Psychol. Rev.* 84:127–90

Simon, H. A. 1969. *The Sciences of the Artificial.* Cambridge, Mass: M.I.T. 123 pp.

Simon, H. A. 1980a. Cognitive science: The newest science of the artificial. *Cogn. Sci.* 4:33–46

Simon, H. A. 1980b. Problem solving and education. In *Problem Solving and Education,* ed. D. T. Tuma, F. Reif, pp. 81–96. Hillsdale, NJ: Erlbaum. 212 pp.

Singer, R. N. 1978. Motor skills and learning strategies. See O'Neil 1978, pp. 79–106

Snow, R. E. 1976. Research on aptitude for learning: A progress report. In *Review of Research in Education,* ed. L. S. Shulman, 4:50–105. Itasca, Ill: Peacock. 360 pp.

Spelke, E., Hirst, W., Neisser, U. 1976. Skills of divided attention. *Cognition* 4:215–30

Stevens, A. L., Collins, A. 1981. Multiple conceptual models of a complex system. In *Conference Proceedings: Aptitude, Learning, and Instruction. Vol. 2: Cognitive Process Analyses of Learning and Problem Solving,* ed. R. E. Snow, P. A. Frederico, W. E. Montague, pp. 177–97. San Diego, Calif/Arlington, Va: Navy Pers. Res. Dev. Cent. and Off. Naval Res. 336 pp.

Stevenson, H. W., Parker, T., Wilkinson, A., Hegion, A., Fish, E. 1976a. Longitudinal study of individual differences in cognitive development and scholastic achievement. *J. Educ. Psychol.* 68:377–400

Stevenson, H. W., Parker, T., Wilkinson, A., Hegion, A., Fish, E. 1976b. Predictive value of teachers' ratings of young children. *J. Educ. Psychol.* 68:507–17

Suppes, P., ed. 1978. *Impact of Research on Education: Some Case Studies.* Washington DC: Nat. Acad. Educ. 672 pp.

Suppes, P., Fletcher, J. D., Zanotti, M. 1975. Performance models of American Indian students on computer-assisted instruction in elementary mathematics. *Instr. Sci.* 4:303–13

Suppes, P., Macken, E., Zanotti, M. 1978. The role of global psychological models in instructional technology. See Glaser 1978, pp. 229–59

Tennyson, R. D., Steve, M. W., Boutwell, R. C. 1975. Instance sequence and analysis of instance attribute representation in concept acquisition. *J. Educ. Psychol.* 67:821–27

Tobias, S. 1976. Achievement treatment interactions. *Rev. Educ. Res.* 48:61–74

Tobias, S. 1977a. Anxiety and instructional methods: An introduction. In *Anxiety, Learning, and Instruction,* ed. J. E. Sieber, H. F. O'Neil Jr., S. Tobias, pp. 75–85. Hillsdale, NJ: Erlbaum. 262 pp.

Tobias, S. 1977b. Anxiety-treatment interaction: A review of research. See Tobias 1977a, pp. 86–116

Tobias, S. 1977c. A model for research on the effect of anxiety on instruction. See Tobias 1977a, pp. 223–40

Tobias, S. 1979. Anxiety research in educational psychology. *J. Educ. Psychol.* 71:573–82

Van Matre, N. 1980. *Computer-managed instruction in the Navy: I. Research background and status.* Spec. Rep. San Diego: Navy Pers. Res. Dev. Cent. 18 pp.

Van Matre, N., Hamovitch, M., Lockhart, K. A., Squire, L. 1981. *CMI in the Navy: II. A comparison of two student/instructor ratios in CMI learning centers.* Rep. TR 81–6. San Diego: Navy Pers. Res. Dev. Cent. 28 pp.

Weinstein, C. E. 1978. Elaboration skills as a learning strategy. See O'Neil 1978, pp. 30–55

Wittrock, M. C., ed. 1977. *Learning and Instruction.* Berkeley, Calif: McCutchan. 631 pp.

Ann. Rev. Psychol. 1983. 34:297–323
Copyright © 1983 by Annual Reviews Inc. All rights reserved

HORMONAL INFLUENCES ON MEMORY

James L. McGaugh

Department of Psychobiology, School of Biological Sciences, University of California, Irvine, California 92717

CONTENTS

INTRODUCTION

There is extensive evidence that learning experiences alter the electrical activity, structure, and chemistry of the brain (Rosenzweig & Bennett 1976, Dunn 1980, Shashoua 1982), and that learning and memory are influenced by a variety of treatments, including electrical stimulation, lesions, drugs, and hormones (McGaugh 1973, 1976, McGaugh & Gold 1976, Hunter et al 1977, Martinez et al 1981b, Squire & Davis 1981). It is generally thought that such treatments affect learning and memory through direct modulating influences on brain processes underlying the storage or consolidation of recently acquired information (McGaugh 1966, McGaugh & Herz 1972).

0066-4308/83/0201-0297$02.00

297

Experiences have many effects: Sensory systems, as well as nonspecific brain systems, are activated; motor activity usually results; and, as this chapter stresses, hormones are released. Consider the effects of hearing a nearby automobile backfire, seeing a flashing red light in the rearview mirror, or hearing a squeaky door when you are alone in a darkened house. Such experiences provide sensory information, they are arousing, they activate hormonal systems, and they may leave lasting memories.

There is much recent evidence to support the view (Kety 1972, Gold & McGaugh 1975) that the degree to which memories are lasting may be influenced by hormonal systems activated by experiences. That is, the physiology of memory storage may involve hormones as endogenous modulators of the neurobiological processes underlying memory storage.

This review examines recent studies of the effects on memory of hormones, as well as treatments affecting hormonal functioning. Also considered is the question of whether treatments known to modulate memory storage act through influences on hormones. This review focuses on adrenergic catecholamines (norepinephrine and epinephrine), pituitary peptides [adrenocorticotropic hormone (ACTH), vasopressin, and oxytocin], and opiate peptides (endorphin and enkephalin). (For other recent reviews see Dunn 1980 and Martinez et al 1981c.) This review also focuses on experiments in which the treatments are administered shortly after training. There are several reasons for this. First, treatments administered before training can influence many processes involved in the performance and acquisition of the learned response. With the use of posttraining treatments the results cannot readily be attributed simply to treatment influences on performance since the animal is not directly under the influence of the treatment during either training or treatment. Second, with posttraining treatments the influences are greatest at the time during which it is assumed memories are being stored or consolidated. Thus, there is maximal opportunity for influencing memory storage. Third, since hormonal systems are influenced by training experiences, the influence of posttraining treatments is greatest at the time when hormones would normally have an opportunity to act on memory storage processes (Gold & McGaugh 1975).

CATECHOLAMINES

Numerous studies have shown that learning and memory are affected by treatments that influence catecholamines (Gorelick et al 1975, Oei & King 1980). Learning and retention are enhanced by drugs such as amphetamine (McGaugh 1973) and impaired by drugs such as diethyldithiocarbamate (DDC) and reserpine that decrease levels of catecholamines (McGaugh et al 1975). Since these drugs readily enter the brain and affect central catecholamines, it would seem likely that their effects on memory are directly due to influences on the brain. There is evidence to support this conclusion. However, there is also much recent evidence suggesting that such drugs, as well as other treatments affecting memory, act at least in part through influences on peripheral catecholamines. Peripheral influences will be examined after a review of central effects.

Central Catecholamines

Numerous experiments have studied the effects on learning and retention of treatments that affect central catecholamines. Studies of the effects on learning and memory of lesions of the locus coeruleus or lesions of the dorsal noradrenergic bundle with neurotoxins (such as 6-OHDA) that severely deplete forebrain norepinephrine have yielded mixed results. Some studies report that learning is impaired (Ogren et al 1980) while others report finding no effects (Fibiger et al 1975). Most recent studies report that such treatments impair learning. Perhaps the most robust finding is that learning is impaired in animals with both locus coeruleus lesions and adrenalectomy (Ogren & Fuxe 1974, Roberts & Fibiger 1977, Wendlant & File 1979, Archer et al 1981). Ogren et al (1980) found that in rats active avoidance is impaired by a new neurotoxin DSP4, and they suggest that this drug is more effective than 6-OHDA in influencing learning because of more extensive depletion of norepinephrine throughout the brain and spinal cord. Leconte & Hennevin (1981) found that maze learning is impaired by 6-OHDA lesions of the dorsal adrenergic bundle. Since the lesions also blocked the increase in paradoxical (REM) sleep that has been reported to occur following training sessions (Bloch et al 1977), they suggested that the impairment of learning may be due to the effects of the 6-OHDA on posttraining REM sleep. Kasamatsu & Pettigrew (1976) reported that depletion of forebrain norepinephrine by 6-OHDA impairs cortical plasticity during visual development in kittens—a process that might be considered to be a form of learning. Ridley et al (1981) recently reported that problem solving in the marmoset is impaired by injection of an α-adrenergic antagonist (aceperone).

Recent studies have also shown that retention is impaired by central administration of drugs that interfere with the synthesis of catecholamines. In most of these studies the treatment was administered shortly before or after training in order to study the treatments' effects on memory storage processes. Jensen et al (1977) found that intracerebroventricular (i.c.v.) administration of DDC impaired rat's retention of an inhibitory avoidance response if administered either shortly before or shortly after training. In the doses used, norepinephrine levels were reduced to approximately 50% in various brain regions. Retention of a T-maze by mice is impaired by DDC as well as by α-methyl-p-tyrosine (AMPT) administered to specific brain regions after training (Flood et al 1980). DDC was effective when injected into the amygdala while AMPT was effective when administered to the caudate nucleus. Hippocampus and brain stem injections produced amnesia with both drugs. In view of the low doses used in this study and the regional specificity, it seems likely that the effects of the drugs on memory were initiated at or near the injection sites.

There is also evidence that retention is affected by central administration of catecholamine agonists and antagonists. Haycock et al (1977) reported that retention of inhibitory avoidance learning in mice is enhanced by posttraining i.c.v. administration of a low dose of norepinephrine. Further, Gallagher and her colleagues (Gallagher et al 1977, 1981, Gallagher & Kapp 1981b) found that retention of an inhibitory avoidance response is affected by posttraining administration of adrenergic antagonists to the amygdala. The β-adrenergic blockers dl-propranolol and dl-alprenolol produced retention impairment which was blocked by administration of l-norepinephrine. Administration of the α-antagonist phentolamine enhanced retention and blocked the impairing effect of propranolol. These findings are of interest in view of evidence that there are both α- and β-receptors within the amygdaloid complex (U'Prichard et al 1980). As will be discussed below, these findings are consistent with other evidence that memory is affected by treatments influencing the amygdala as well as by evidence suggesting that adrenergic influences on memory might involve activity of the amygdala.

Other recent findings indicate that the retention impairment produced by peripheral administration of DDC can be attenuated by i.c.v. administration of catecholamines. Stein et al (1975) and Meligeni et al (1978) administered DDC to rats prior to training on inhibitory avoidance and administered norepinephrine (i.c.v.) after training. The posttraining norepinephrine blocked the impairing effect of DDC on retention. These findings, considered alone, suggest that the norepinephrine blocked the retention deficit by replacing the brain norepinephrine depleted by DDC. However, additional evidence (Meligeni et al 1978, McGaugh et al 1979) indicated that the impairing effect of DDC on retention was also attenuated by subcutaneous (s.c.) administration of norepinephrine as well as epinephrine. Since norepinephrine and epinephrine do not readily pass the blood-brain barrier, these latter findings suggest that their effects on memory may work through peripheral influences. It is, of course, possible that the effects are due to the passage of minute amounts of norepinephrine and epinephrine into the brain. However, it should be noted that the greatest attenuation of DDC-induced amnesia was produced by low to moderate doses of peripherally administered epinephrine. Amnesia was not attenuated by the highest doses of epinephrine.

Peripheral Catecholamines

Many recent studies have provided additional evidence suggesting that memory is influenced by treatments that affect peripheral catecholamines (Walsh & Palfai 1979). Retention in rats is impaired by injections of reserpine and the peripherally acting reserpine-like compound syrosingopine as well as guanethidine (which blocks release in peripheral sympathetic nerves), if the drugs are injected prior to training. The retention deficits were blocked by peripheral injections of norepinephrine or dopamine (but not epinephrine) either before or shortly after training. While the reserpine depleted brain catecholamines, syrosingopine and guanethidine did not affect levels of brain catecholamines (Brown et al 1981). The findings clearly suggest that these drugs affect memory through influences on peripheral catecholamines. The finding that epinephrine was ineffective in attenuating the retention impairment is of interest since it does not fit with the finding that DDC amnesia is blocked by peripheral epinephrine. Thus, this finding suggests different bases for the amnestic influences of drugs affecting synthesis versus release of peripheral catecholamines. The findings are also of interest in view of evidence that amnesia produced by central injection of the protein synthesis inhibitor cycloheximide is attenuated by metaraminol, a peripherally acting noradrenergic receptor agonist (Serota et al 1972).

As I pointed out above, there is considerable evidence that retention is influenced by posttraining administration of amphetamine. Since amphetamine readily enters the brain when administered intraperitoneally (i.p.), it has been generally assumed that its effects on learning and memory are directly due to influences on central catecholamines. The findings of a series of recent studies suggest, however, that amphetamine effects on memory may be due at least in part to peripheral adrenergic influences. Martinez et al (1980a) compared the effects of i.p. and i.c.v. d-amphetamine on rat's retention of a one-trial inhibitory avoidance response. The injections were administered immediately after training and retention was tested 24 hours later. While retention was enhanced by i.p. injection, the i.c.v. injections, over a wide dose range, did not affect retention. The i.c.v. amphetamine did, however, produce dose-dependent effects on locomotor activity. Further, Martinez et al (1980b) found that retention is enhanced by posttraining i.p. administration of dl-4-OH-amphetamine, a metabolite of amphetamine that does not readily pass the blood-brain barrier. While this drug has some effects on central catecholamines, the effects are seen only in extremely high doses (Ishikawa et al 1981). The effects of d-amphetamine and dl-4-OH-amphetamine seem not to work through peripheral sympathetic neurons: Enhancing effects on memory were found with both drugs in animals given peripheral 6-OHDA 24 hours prior to training (Martinez et al 1980a). In fact, enhancement of retention was obtained with lower doses of both d-amphetamine and dl-4-OH-amphetamine in 6-OHDA-treated rats. The findings of other experiments strongly suggest that the effect of amphetamine on memory involves adrenal catecholamines. The enhancing effects of both d-amphetamine and dl-4-OH-amphetamine were attenuated in rats whose adrenal medullae were surgically removed prior to training (Martinez et al 1980b). Further, adrenal demedullation blocked the effect of amphetamine and 4-OH amphetamine on active avoidance as well as inhibitory avoidance tasks (Martinez et al 1981a).

The findings summarized above strongly suggest that amphetamine influences on memory involve peripheral catecholamines. Considered alone, such evidence does not provide any conclusion on whether peripheral catecholamines normally serve to influence memory storage processes. Evidence from several recent studies indicating that retention is influenced by posttraining peripheral administration of norepinephrine and epinephrine provides additional support to the view that catecholamines of the adrenal medulla may play a role as endogenous modulators of memory storage (Gold & McGaugh 1978, McGaugh et al 1980, 1982).

In a series of studies, Gold and his colleagues (e.g. Gold et al 1982) investigated the effects of posttraining peripherally administered adrenergic hormones on retention in rats and measured central and plasma catecholamines following training to determine whether retention is related to catecholamine levels. In an initial study (Gold & van Buskirk 1975), posttraining s.c. injections of epinephrine enhanced retention of an inhibitory avoidance response. The effect was time-dependent and dose-dependent. Immediate posttraining injections were the most effective. Injections administered 2 hours after training did not affect retention. Moderate doses (0.01 to 0.1 mg/kg) produced the greatest enhancement. A larger dose (0.5 mg/kg) appeared to impair retention. The optimal dose on the inverted-U dose-response curve depended upon the motivational conditions used for training: A dose found to enhance retention when a low footshock was used in training impaired retention when a high footshock was administered (Gold & van Buskirk 1976a). These results are similar to those found in the study of the effect of s.c. norepinephrine on DDC-treated rats (Meligeni et al 1978): The dose-response curve was an inverted U and the optimal dose varied with the training footshock. Further, as is noted below, comparable results have been found in studies of the effects of ACTH on memory (Gold & van Buskirk 1976b, Gold & Delanoy 1981). The dose-response effect of epinephrine on retention can also be shifted by adrenergic receptor blockers. Epinephrine enhancement of retention is blocked by the β-adrenergic receptor blocker propranolol, and epinephrine impairment of retention is blocked by the α-adrenergic receptor blocker phenoxybenzamine (Gold & van Buskirk 1978b).

These findings suggest that the effects of peripherally administered hormones interact with those resulting from the release of endogenous hormones following training. This view is supported by evidence from several studies indicating that training affects brain and plasma levels of catecholamines. It is well known that footshock increases plasma levels of norepinephrine and epinephrine (e.g. Natelson et al 1981). McCarty & Gold (1981) reported that plasma levels of epinephrine vary with the intensity of the footshock administered during inhibitory avoidance training. Further, a dose of epinephrine found to enhance retention produces plasma epinephrine levels comparable to those found after training with a high footshock. Several recent studies have reported that the level of norepinephrine in many brain regions is decreased following acute stress produced by footshock, tailshock, or immobilization (Nakagawa et al 1981, Iimori et al 1982, Tanaka et al 1982). Other recent studies have also confirmed and extended earlier evidence (Lewy & Seiden 1972) that training affects brain catecholamines. Kovács et al (1981b) trained rats in an inhibitory avoidance task, tested for retention 24 hours later, and measured brain catecholamine turnover two days later. In rats that displayed good retention, catecholamine turnover was higher in the dorsal hippocampus and amygdala. Everett & Roberge (1981) found that in cats, training on a discrimination task altered norepinephrine in several brain regions. Decreases in levels of norepinephrine in the piriform lobe (including the amygdala), mesencephalon, and thalamus were accompanied by increased dopamine-β-hydroxylase activity. Cats trained in a delayed response task showed greater changes in noradrenergic metabolism in the frontal cortex and amygdala (Vachon & Roberge 1981).

Gold & van Buskirk (1978a) found that a single high-intensity footshock like that used in inhibitory avoidance training produced a transient (20–30 min) 20% decrease in levels of brain norepinephrine and adrenal epinephrine. A low dose of epinephrine administered after a low footshock (a condition shown to enhance retention) resulted in a comparable decrease in brain norepinephrine and adrenal epinephrine. In rats given high footshock and a high dose of epinephrine (conditions resulting in poor retention performance), levels of brain norepinephrine and adrenal epinephrine were reduced by 30–40%. These findings indicate that retention performance is related to levels of brain norepinephrine and adrenal epinephrine following training and are generally consistent with the view that retention is influenced by training-initiated release of these catecholamines.

Adrenergic Involvement in Brain Treatments Affecting Memory

If, as the studies summarized above suggest, memory storage processes are modulated by influences of adrenergic responses to the training, then post-training treatments that alter retention might be expected to affect adrenergic responses. Further, it should be possible to alter the effects of memory-influencing treatments by administering adrenergic hormones and adrenergic antagonists. Both of these implications have been examined in recent experiments.

FRONTAL CORTEX STIMULATION EFFECTS ON MEMORY: ADRENERGIC INFLUENCES   Gold & Murphy (1980) reported that posttraining electrical stimulation of rat's frontal cortex, at an intensity that produces retrograde amnesia, resulted in a 30% decrease in forebrain norepinephrine 10 min after training. This decrease is greater than that produced by training alone (20%) and comparable to that produced by high doses of epinephrine which produced memory impairment (Gold & van Buskirk 1978a). However, frontal cortex stimulation following training does not seem to have much effect on the level of plasma epinephrine and norepinephrine measured immediately after training (Gold & McCarty 1981). The effect of footshock followed by cortical stimulation was not much greater than that of footshock alone. Thus, it would seem that the amnestic effect of frontal cortex stimulation is not based on plasma levels of epinephrine and norepinephrine following the treatment. Other recent findings indicate that the amnestic effect of frontal cortex stimulation is not attenuated by bretylium, which blocks the release of norepinephrine in sympathetic neurons (Sternberg et al 1982) or by adrenal demedullation prior to training (D. B. Sternberg, unpublished data). However, several recent studies have shown that the amnestic effects of a variety of treatments including electrical stimulation of the frontal cortex or amygdala, pentylenetetrazol, DDC, and cycloheximide are attenuated by adrenergic antagonists administered prior to training (Gold & Sternberg 1978). The attenuation has been found with both α- and β-antagonists, in a visual discrimination task as well as in an inhibitory avoidance task (Sternberg & Gold 1980, 1981b), and with retention enhancement as well as retention impairment produced by frontal cortex stimulation (Sternberg et al 1981). While it has been argued that such findings might be based on illness or some other nonspecific effect of the combination of an amnestic treatment and an adrenergic antagonist (Squire et al 1980), most of the evidence seems to support the view that the antagonists alter the adrenergic consequences of the modulating treatments.

Another recent finding suggests that adrenergic blockers attenuate the effects of memory-modulating treatments by interfering with peripheral adrenergic responses. Adrenergic antagonists did not attenuate retrograde amnesia produced by frontal cortex stimulation when the drugs were centrally (i.c.v.) administered (Sternberg & Gold 1981a).

These findings provide additional evidence that peripheral adrenergic responses can influence the modulating effects of central treatments. However, it is difficult to reconcile these results with the findings, cited above, that frontal cortex stimulation administered posttraining does not result in concentrations of plasma epinephrine and norepinephrine much greater than those found with footshock alone (Gold & McCarty 1981). Why, according to these findings, is the amnestic effect of cortical stimulation blocked by peripherally, but not centrally, administered adrenergic antagonists? Further, if memory modulation produced by cortical stimulation is blocked by adrenergic antagonists, why isn't the modulation also blocked by adrenal demedullation? While recent findings do not provide conclusive or convenient answers to these questions, some recent results cast the questions in a somewhat different light.

AMYGDALA STIMULATION EFFECTS ON MEMORY: INFLUENCE OF PERIPHERAL EPINEPHRINE   The findings of several recent experiments suggest that, at least under some conditions, centrally initiated modulation of memory, such as that produced by brain stimulation, is influenced by peripheral epinephrine. That is, although brain stimulation is known to affect central as well as adrenal epinephrine and norepinephrine (Gunne & Reis 1963, Gold & McCarty 1981), the effects of brain stimulation on memory may be due to influences of peripheral epinephrine on central systems underlying memory modulation rather than to the effects of stimulation on peripheral epinephrine.

The amygdaloid complex is one of the brain regions most extensively investigated in studies of the effects of electrical stimulation of the brain on memory. In rats, retention can be enhanced or impaired by posttraining electrical stimulation of the amygdala (McGaugh & Gold 1976, Berman & Kesner 1981, Kesner 1981). Further, as was noted above, retention is also modulated by adrenergic antagonists administered directly into the amygdala (Gallagher et al 1977, Gallagher & Kapp 1981b), and the amnestic effect of electrical stimulation of the amygdala is blocked by adrenergic antagonists administered prior to training (Sternberg & Gold 1981b). Several recent studies have shown that the effects of amygdala stimulation on retention are also altered by adrenal demedullation as well as by peripheral administration of epinephrine. In these studies (McGaugh et al 1982), rats were first implanted bilaterally with amygdala electrodes and then demedullated or denervated (by removing the adrenal glands from the splanchnic nerves and placing them in the fatty tissue around the kidney). The animals were then successively trained and tested for retention on inhibitory and active avoidance tasks. The same pattern of results was obtained with demedullated and denervated rats and with both active and inhibitory avoidance tasks (Brewton et al 1981). First, as was expected, posttraining amygdala stimulation impaired retention in sham-operated rats (i.e. rats with intact adrenal medullae). Second, retention was significantly impaired in implanted (but unstimulated) rats that were demedullated (or denervated). Third, posttraining amygdala stimulation did not impair retention in the demedullated and denervated rats. Rather, in these rats retention was enhanced: Their retention performance was comparable to that of unimplanted and implanted controls with intact adrenal medullae. The retention of demedullated and denervated rats was also enhanced by posttraining s.c. administration of epinephrine. Thus, removal of the adrenal medullae impairs retention (in rats with implanted electrodes) and alters the effects of posttraining amygdala stimulation on retention. The finding that amygdala stimulation enhanced retention in both demedullated and denervated animals argues against the interpretation that the amygdala stimulation effect on memory is mediated by release of peripheral epinephrine (Sternberg & Gold 1981b). It would seem more likely that the amygdala stimulation works through central effects that are influenced by adrenal epinephrine. This interpretation is supported by recent findings (Bennett et al 1982) that amygdala stimulation does impair retention in demedullated rats if the rats are given epinephrine s.c. immediately after training, just prior to the brain stimulation. The finding, cited above, that the memory-modulating influences of frontal cortex stimulation are blocked by peripherally administered adrenergic antagonists (Gold & Sternberg 1978, Sternberg et al 1981) is also consistent with the view that peripheral adrenergic influences alter the effect of brain stimulation on memory.

Thus, it seems that a critical factor in the effect of brain stimulation may be the release of peripheral epinephrine shortly before the brain is stimulated, rather than an increase in epinephrine following the stimulation. Recent findings by Gold & Reigel (1980) are consistent with this interpretation. Electrical stimulation of the cortex impaired rat's retention of an inhibitory avoidance response when administered one day or even one week following training in animals given epinephrine 30 seconds prior to the brain stimulation. The epinephrine was ineffective if given 10 minutes prior to training. In view of the findings of the effect of epinephrine on memory impairment produced by amygdala stimulation, it would be of interest to know whether the amnestic effect of cortical stimulation is potentiated by epinephrine administered after the brain stimulation. Another finding of Gold & Reigel (1980) should be noted in this context. Epinephrine did not potentiate the effect of cortical stimulation when injected 10 min prior to the brain stimulation. Since plasma epinephrine is increased for at least 40 min after s.c. injection of epinephrine (Gold & McCarty 1981), Gold & Reigel suggest that the onset of the increase in peripheral epinephrine, rather than the sustained level, may be the critical factor in potentiating the amnestic effect of cortical stimulation.

PERIPHERAL-CENTRAL INTERACTION   Considered together, these recent findings suggest that the modulating effects of brain stimulation on memory involve influences of peripheral epinephrine on central processes. It is not yet known, however, whether this is an effect unique to epinephrine or whether comparable effects can be produced by other hormones known to influence memory. Further, there is as yet little evidence to allow any conclusions concerning details of the involvement of central processes in the modulating influences of epinephrine on memory. The findings of a recent experiment suggest that endogenous modulation of memory may depend upon amygdala influences on the brain mediated by the stria terminalis, a major pathway of the amygdala. Effects of amygdala stimulation on retention are blocked by disruption of the stria terminalis (Liang & McGaugh 1981; K. C. Liang et al, in preparation). Further, lesions of the stria terminalis also block the enhancing effect of posttraining epinephrine on retention (Liang & McGaugh 1982).

According to these findings, it seems likely that epinephrine effects on memory as well as the effects of amygdala stimulation on memory involve influences via the stria terminalis. It will be important to determine whether the epinephrine effects on memory are due to influences on amygdala activity or whether epinephrine acts by affecting brain processes that are also influenced by amygdala activity. It is, of course, also essential to determine how epinephrine influences the brain. This is a puzzling issue since catecholamines do not readily pass the blood-brain barrier (Bertler et al 1966). This issue is further discussed below.

PITUITARY HORMONES

The release of pituitary hormones is a well-known and extensively studied consequence of stimulation. While stressful stimulation is typically used in studies of pituitary hormone release, it is clear that, like adrenal catecholamines, pituitary as well as adrenal hormones are released by relatively mild forms of stimulation such as those resulting from the training procedures used in learning tasks and, by inference, stimulation that results in memory of experiences.

ACTH

The possibility that learning might be influenced by pituitary hormones was first studied by de Wied almost two decades ago. De Wied found that active avoidance learning was impaired by removal of the anterior pituitary and that the deficit was attenuated by administration of ACTH (de Wied 1964). Subsequent studies showed that ACTH affects learning in many types of tasks, that the influences on acquisition and extinction are not mediated through influences on the adrenal cortex, and that effects on learning are also produced by analogs of ACTH which contain only peptide fragments of the ACTH molecule and do not influence the adrenal cortex (Rigter & van Riezen 1978, de Wied 1980).

The questions of interest here are whether ACTH affects memory storage and whether it is reasonable to conclude that ACTH released during learning is involved as an endogenous modulator of memory storage. These questions have been addressed in studies by Gold and his colleagues (for review see Gold & McGaugh 1978, Gold & Delanoy 1981). In rats, hypophysectomy impairs retention of a one-trial inhibitory avoidance response as well as a Y-maze discrimination task, and the impairment is attenuated by posttraining systemic administration of ACTH. Posttraining administration of ACTH also modulates retention in rats with intact pituitaries. The effect is dose-dependent (inverted-U) and varies with the intensity of footshock used in the training (Gold & van Buskirk 1976b). Doses of ACTH that enhance retention when low-intensity footshock is used in training impair retention when high footshock is used. As I noted, these results suggest that ACTH administered posttraining summates with endogenously released ACTH in influencing memory storage. These results are very much like the findings, summarized above, of the effects of posttrial epinephrine on retention (Gold et al 1982) and strongly suggest that ACTH plays a role in the endogenous modulation of memory.

Studies of the effects of ACTH analogs including $ACTH_{4-10}$ and $ACTH_{4-9}$ on retention have produced somewhat more mixed findings. Flood et al (1976) reported that posttraining administration of $ACTH_{4-10}$ in mice affected retention in both active and inhibitory avoidance tasks. Further, the effect depended on the isomer of the amino acid in the 7th position. $ACTH_{4-10}$ D-Phe-7 impaired retention, whereas $ACTH_{4-10}$ L-Phe-7 enhanced retention. Since these peptides do not affect the adrenal cortex, these findings suggest that ACTH influences on memory are not mediated by adrenal activity. However, studies of the effects of ACTH analogs have not provided consistent results (Soumireu-Mourat et al 1981,

Fekete & de Wied 1982). Effects on retention are generally found when the peptides are administered prior to training. Thus, it may be that such pretraining injections affect retention through influences on sensory, attentive, motivational, or performance processes during the training (Martinez et al 1979, Bohus & de Wied 1981). Thus, ACTH and ACTH analogs may have different behavioral effects and may affect learning and memory through different mechanisms. As Gold & Delanoy have pointed out (1981), experiments to date have not determined whether corticosterones released from the adrenal cortex are involved in the effect of posttraining ACTH on memory. Recent studies of the effects of ACTH on retention of a learned change in social behavior in mice indicate that corticosterone release is involved in the effect. ACTH administered after an attack results in increased submission on subsequent tests. Since comparable effects are produced by corticosterone, the effects of ACTH appear to be mediated, in this situation, by the influence of ACTH on the adrenal cortex (Leshner & Potlitch 1979, Leshner et al 1981).

A number of studies have shown that ACTH as well as ACTH analogs improve performance when administered prior to a retention test. A "retrieval" or "reminder" effect (Riccio & Concannon 1981) has been found with both appetitive and aversive tasks and with rats given posttraining amnestic treatments (Rigter & van Riezen 1978). However, under such conditions the enhanced retention appears to be transient (Rigter & van Riezen 1975, Mactutus et al 1980). It may be that the hormones act by providing an internal cue that serves to aid memory retrieval.

CENTRAL AND PERIPHERAL INFLUENCES OF ACTH   It is not known whether ACTH affects behavior through peripheral influences or through direct action on the brain. Large peptide molecules do not readily pass the blood-brain barrier. ACTH is found in a number of brain regions (Krieger & Liotta 1979), and it now seems likely that they are synthesized in the brain. Thus, ACTH of brain origin might be involved in influences on behavior. $ACTH_{4-10}$ affects learning when injected directly into the brain (Sagen & Routtenberg 1981). The effective i.c.v. dose is $1/100$ of the effective peripherally administered dose (de Wied et al 1978).

The effects of posttraining ACTH on retention are remarkably similar to the effects of epinephrine (Gold & Delanoy 1981). In view of this, McCarty & Gold (1981) examined the effect of ACTH on plasma epinephrine and norepinephrine. ACTH did not elevate plasma epinephrine or norepinephrine and did not influence the epinephrine response to footshock. Thus, it seems that ACTH does not affect memory through the release of these peripheral catecholamines. However, the effects of peripherally administered ACTH on brain norepinephrine are similar to those produced by peripheral epinephrine. ACTH administered after footshock training in an inhibitory avoidance task produces a 20–40% reduction in brain norepinephrine shortly after the treatment (Gold & McGaugh 1978). Thus, it is clear that peripherally administered ACTH influences brain functioning as well as behavior. It is not yet clear, however, whether the effects are due to entry of peripheral ACTH into the brain.

Vasopressin and Oxytocin

Vasopressin and oxytocin are peptide hormones secreted by the posterior pituitary. Vasopressin (also termed ADH-antidiuretic hormone) is known to influence the contraction of peripheral blood vessels and to regulate osmolarity and volume of body fluids. Oxytocin acts on the mammillary gland to regulate milk release and also influences parturition. Recent research has shown that these hormones also influence learning and retention in rats as well as humans (Weingartner et al 1981). In an early experiment, de Wied & Bohus (1966) found that a crude extract of posterior pituitary tissue containing vasopressin retarded extinction. Subsequent experiments have shown that vasopressin and analogs of vasopressin enhance learning and retention in a wide variety of learning tasks (Bohus 1977, van Wimersma Greidanus et al 1981, Bohus et al 1982, Alliot & Alexinsky 1982).

While there is some recent evidence suggesting that vasopressin influences motivational processes (Sahgal et al 1982), a number of studies have reported that vasopressin modulates memory storage. Posttraining i.c.v. administration of arginine-8-vasopressin in a very low dose (1.0 ng) enhances retention of an inhibitory avoidance response (Bohus et al 1978). Retention is impaired by i.c.v. administration of vasopressin antiserum within a few hours after training (van Wimersma Greidanus & de Wied 1976). The amnestic effect of centrally administered antiserum can be attenuated by systemic administration of vasopressin. Interestingly, retention is not affected by i.v. administration of extremely high doses of vasopressin antiserum.

The effects of oxytocin are generally opposite those of vasopressin. Posttraining i.c.v. administration impairs retention. Bohus et al (1982) and van Wimersma Greidanus et al (1981) suggest that oxytocin may be an endogenous amnestic peptide. Retention is also altered by microinjection of vasopressin and oxytocin into various brain regions. Retention is enhanced by posttraining injections of vasopressin in the hippocampal dentate gyri and dorsal raphe nucleus. Oxytocin injections impair retention. Neither peptide is effective when injected into the amygdala, locus coeruleus subiculum, or dorsal septal area (Bohus et al 1982).

Both vasopressin and oxytocin have been found to influence retention when the peptides are administered prior to retention testing in animals that have received posttraining amnestic treatments. Systemic injections of vasopressin attenuate the retention impairment produced by electroconvulsive shock (ECS) (Pfeiffer & Bookin 1978) and anisomycin (Judge & Quartermain 1982). Subcutaneous as well as i.c.v. administration of vasopressin attenuates the amnestic effects of pentylenetetrazol. Partial attenuation was produced by vasopressin injected into the amygdala and dentate gyrus of the hippocampus (Bohus et al 1982).

In view of evidence reviewed above concerning the involvement of peripheral epinephrine, central norepinephrine, and the amygdala in memory modulation, it is of interest to note that the effects of posttraining systemic vasopressin on retention are influenced by adrenalectomy and by s.c. injections of epinephrine (Borrell et al 1981) and that the effects of posttraining systemic (s.c.) injections of vasopressin on retention are blocked by 6-OHDA lesions of the dorsal adrenergic bundle (Bohus et al 1982). These findings suggest that the effects of vasopressin on memory may involve interaction with central norepinephrine. Further, vasopressin as well as $ACTH_{4-10}$ effects on avoidance behavior are blocked by lesions of the amygdala (van Wimersma Greidanus et al 1979).

While the findings of recent studies are not in complete agreement, most of the evidence supports the view that vasopressin and oxytocin affect memory storage and retrieval. It is not known how these peripherally administered peptides influence brain processes.

OPIOID PEPTIDES

The recent discovery of the endogenous opioid peptides, the endorphins and enkephalins, greatly stimulated interest in the influence of peptide hormones on behavior. Opioid peptides, like ACTH, vasopressin, and epinephrine, are known to be released when animals are stressed (Amir et al 1980, Bodnar et al 1980). These peptides are widely distributed in the brain (Krieger & Liotta 1979, Bloom & McGinty 1981). In rats, β-endorphin is released, together with ACTH, from the pituitary, and enkephalin appears to be released along with epinephrine from the adrenal medulla (Viveros et al 1980). Like other pituitary and adrenal hormones, endorphin and enkephalin have been found to have behavioral effects. In particular, many recent studies have shown that the endogenous peptides, as well as opiate agonists and antagonists, affect learning and memory (Martinez et al 1981c, Riley et al 1980).

Opiate Agonists and Antagonists

Several recent studies have reported that retention is enhanced by the opiate antagonist naloxone. Enhancement is found with a variety of tasks including inhibitory avoidance, active avoidance, and habituation, and with peripheral as well as central administration. Further, naloxone effects on retention are attenuated by morphine (Messing et al 1979, Izquierdo 1979, Jensen et al 1978). Gallagher and her colleagues (Gallagher & Kapp 1978, 1981a) found that in rats retention of inhibitory avoidance is enhanced by posttraining intra-amygdala injections of naloxone. Further, intra-amygdala administration of the opiate agonist levorphanol resulted in retention impairment which was blocked by concurrent administration of naloxone. Comparable effects were found in studies of the effects of levorphanol and naloxone on heart rate conditioning in rabbits. The findings of studies of morphine are less consistent. While recent evidence indicates that posttraining morphine impairs retention (Castellano 1975, Messing et al 1981), several studies have reported that posttraining i.c.v. or systemic administration of morphine enhances retention. The studies reporting enhancement have generally used high doses (Mondadori & Waser 1979, Belluzzi & Stein 1977, 1981). The effects of opiate agonists and antagonists depend upon the dose as well as the experimental conditions used (Messing et al 1981).

Endorphins and Enkephalins

Numerous recent studies have reported that learning is influenced by low doses of endorphin and enkephalin administered systemically prior to training (Kastin et al 1976, Riley et al 1980, Koob et al 1981, Kovács & de Wied 1981, Martinez et al 1981d, Luttinger et al 1982). In a series of studies, Rigter & Martinez and their colleagues (Rigter et al 1980a,b, Martinez 1982a, Martinez et al 1981d) found that active avoidance in rats is impaired by Leu-enkephalin and Met-enkephalin administered shortly before training. The effect of Met-enkephalin but not Leu-enkephalin was blocked by concurrent administration of naloxone. Further, the effects of both Leu- and Met-enkephalin were attenuated in adrenal-demedullated rats. Higher doses of Leu- but not Met-enkephalin restored the impairing effect of learning. These findings are consistent with evidence from a number of recent studies reviewed above, indicating that adrenal-demedullated rats are less responsive to many treatments, including drugs and electrical stimulation of the brain, as well as hormones that affect learning and memory.

A number of recent studies have also found that retention is influenced by posttraining systemic administration of enkephalin and endorphin (Martinez & Rigter 1980, Kovács & de Wied 1981, Izquierdo et al 1981, 1982). Conflicting findings have been reported in studies of the effect of posttraining endorphin on retention of an inhibitory avoidance response. Kovács et al (1981a) and Kovács & de Wied (1981) reported that β-endorphin enhances retention. Retention in their studies was also enhanced by α-endorphin and impaired by γ-endorphin. In contrast, Martinez & Rigter (1980) found that β-endorphin impaired retention while α-endorphin was ineffective. While the two experiments used different procedures (i.e. s.c. vs i.p.

injections), it is not clear why opposite results were obtained. It is perhaps worth noting that in these experiments as well as experiments with other hormones, inverted-U dose-response curves are typically found and optimal doses are usually in a narrow dose range. Thus, further studies are needed to resolve these conflicting findings.

In an extensive series of studies, Izquierdo and his colleagues (1981) investigated the effect of posttraining systemic administration of endorphin and enkephalin on retention of an active avoidance response (shuttle responding) and habituation (rearing to a tone) in rats. As was noted above, posttraining naloxone enhanced retention in these tasks, and the effects of naloxone are blocked by morphine (Izquierdo 1979). The additional finding that the effect of naloxone is blocked by pretreatment with α-methyl-p-tyrosine and potentiated by amphetamine strongly suggests that naloxone effects involve adrenergic systems. Specifically, Izquierdo (1980a,b) suggests that naloxone releases adrenergic systems from opioid inhibition. Posttraining enkephalin and endorphin impaired retention in both tasks when administered systemically in low to moderate doses.

Izquierdo et al (1981) also found that training results in decreased β-endorphin immunoreactivity in the brain following training, suggesting that training causes the release and metabolism of β-endorphin. Further, β-endorphin immunoreactivity is also decreased by electroconvulsive shock (ECS) (Dias et al 1981), suggesting that release of β-endorphin in the brain might contribute to the amnestic effect of ECS. This interpretation is supported by the finding that the amnestic effect of ECS is attenuated by naloxone administered after training but prior to the ECS treatment (Carrasco et al 1982). Tortella et al (1981) have also reported that naloxone blocks the posttrial electrophysiological and behavioral effects of ECS. These results are also of interest in view of evidence that the amnestic effect of electrical stimulation of the amygdala is blocked by naloxone injected into the bed nucleus of the stria terminalis (K. C. Liang et al, unpublished data). As is indicated above, Izquierdo has suggested that endogenous opioids impair retention by inhibiting adrenergic systems. Recent findings suggest that the effects of enkephalin are influenced by peripheral epinephrine. Adrenal demedullation blocks the effect of enkephalin on retention. However, amnesia can be obtained in demedullated rats given epinephrine prior to administration of enkephalin (Izquierdo 1982).

CENTRAL EFFECTS OF HORMONES

The studies reviewed here provide extensive evidence that learning and memory are modulated by peripheral as well as central administration of a variety of hormones. If these studies are to contribute to an understanding of the physiology of memory, it will be essential to understand the basis or bases of the modulating influences. A key finding of these studies is that several of the hormones (e.g. epinephrine and ACTH) produce either enhancement or impairment of retention depending upon the training conditions used. Thus, there is clear evidence that posttraining hormones modulate retention. It is not yet clear where and how the hormones act to influence retention. Ultimately, the hormones must influence brain processes underlying memory storage. But do the hormones act directly on the brain or are the effects of the hormones initiated in the periphery?

The problem is complicated by the fact that hormones found to influence memory are synthesized in the brain as well as in the periphery (e.g. Goldstein 1976, Krieger & Liotta 1979). Further, hormones influence retention when administered i.c.v. or into specific brain regions (Huston & Stäubli 1981, Kovács & de Wied 1981, Sagen & Routtenberg 1981, Bohus et al 1982). These findings suggest that hormones of brain origin directly modulate memory by influencing activity in specific brain structures. Further, these findings argue for the view that peripherally administered hormones affect retention because small quantities enter the brain and, like hormones of central origin, influence specific brain regions. According to this view (Bohus & de Wied 1981), the brain is the site of action of peripherally released or peripherally administered hormones. Peripherally administered hormones might influence brain processes through a variety of mechanisms (Kastin et al 1979). It is possible that small amounts of peripheral hormones enter the brain by passing the blood-brain barrier (BBB) or that a metabolic product or fragment of the hormone passes the BBB. However, most evidence indicates that peptide hormones do not readily pass the BBB (Dunn & Gispen 1977, Cornford et al 1978). Hormones might influence the brain by acting on brain regions (e.g. area postrema) poorly protected by the BBB (Lechtensteiger et al 1977). There is some evidence that hormones act by altering the permeability of the BBB. For example, Ermisch et al (1982) reported that vasopressin alters BBB permeability to orotic acid and leucine, and Goldman & Murphy (1981) found that the ACTH analog $ACTH_{4-9}$ (Organon 2766) reduces BBB permeability. Epinephrine administered peripherally (s.c.) produces a pronounced (400%) increase in cerebral blood flow resulting from a pressure-mediated passage of epinephrine across the BBB (Abdul-Rahman et al 1979). It seems likely that peripheral hormones may also act through influences on peripheral receptors on autonomic afferents. Thus, the influence on brain activity may be due to neuronal influences from the periphery rather than, or possibly in addition to, direct entry of the hormones into the brain. Whatever the detailed mechanism of action, it is clear that peripherally administered hormones influence brain activity. As noted above, for example, levels of brain norepinephrine are substantially lowered shortly after peripheral administration of epinephrine or ACTH (Gold & Delanoy 1981).

The modulating influences of many treatments affecting learning and memory appear to be influenced by epinephrine. The effects of peripherally administered peptides are attenuated by adrenal demedullation and restored by epinephrine (Borrell et al 1981, Izquierdo et al 1982). These findings are comparable to those obtained in studies of the effects of posttraining amygdala stimulation (McGaugh et al 1982). It is not clear from the available evidence whether the peptide effects are based on cooperative influences of epinephrine on brain activity, as seems to be the case for amygdala stimulation effects on memory. The possibility that the effects are due to central interactions is suggested by the findings that vasopressin as well as $ACTH_{4-10}$ effects on learning are blocked by amygdala lesions (van Wimersma Greidanus et al 1979) and that epinephrine effects on retention are blocked by lesions of the stria terminalis (Liang & McGaugh 1982). Since it has also been shown that vasopressin effects on retention are blocked by 6-OHDA lesions of the dorsal adrenergic bundle (Bohus et al 1982), it would be interesting to know whether such lesions also block the effects of peripherally administered epinephrine on retention. Recent findings suggest that understanding the bases of peptide-catecholamine interactions in the periphery as well as in the brain is essential for understanding the modulatory influences of hormones on memory.

HORMONES AS ENDOGENOUS MODULATORS OF MEMORY

The findings summarized in this review provide strong evidence that retention is modulated by posttraining administration of hormones. Since several of the hormones that have been used in these experiments are known to be released by stimulation comparable to that used in training, these findings are consistent with the view that memory storage processes are modulated by endogenous hormones released by training experiences (Gold & McGaugh 1975, 1978). But, of course, the fact that exogenous hormones can influence memory does not necessarily mean that endogenous hormones ordinarily play a role in memory storage. According to this hypothesis, 1. training should be expected to release the modulating hormones, 2. retention should be affected by interference with the release of the hormones or the activation of receptors, 3. the effects resulting from interference with release should be attenuated by administration of the hormones, 4. the effects of exogenous hormones should vary with the degree to which endogenous hormones are released by the training, and 5. administration of hormones should be most effective if administered shortly after training, that is, at the time at which endogenous hormones are presumed to be released by the training experience. The findings of studies of epinephrine generally fit well with these expectations. The results of studies of the effects of ACTH and opioid peptides are also generally consistent with these assumptions. While the effects of vasopressin and oxytocin provide strong evidence that these hormones alter memory storage processes, there is less evidence that they normally serve as endogenous memory modulators. More evidence is needed. While studies of the effects of peptide hormone analogs are of considerable interest in that they can reveal the peptide sequences that are critical for the behavioral effects, such studies do not contribute directly to an understanding of the role of endogenous hormones in memory storage.

As I have emphasized, the hormones investigated in these studies are released by electric shock and other forms of intense stimulation. Most of the studies of the effects of hormones on memory have used footshock as motivation during the training. The fact that the experiments have generally used aversive stimulation raises the question of whether the effects of "stress-related" hormones on memory are restricted to retention of aversively motivated learning. The available evidence suggests that these hormones, as well as treatments that affect hormones, do affect retention in appetitive as well as aversive tasks, but this issue deserves more extensive investigation. We need to know not only whether hormones modulate memory for appetitive learning but whether training experiences in nonaversive tasks also release hormones, as would be expected if nonaversively motivated learning is modulated by endogenous hormones.

Several hormones that have been studied, including epinephrine, ACTH, and vasopressin, produce either enhancement or impairment of retention depending upon the training conditions and dose used. There is evidence to suggest that several peptide hormones, oxytocin and the opioid peptides enkephalin and endorphin, may be endogenous amnestic hormones. These hormones appear to impair retention under several testing conditions and with a wide range of doses (van Wimersma Greidanus et al 1981, Izquierdo et al 1982). Since the dose-response curve for memory modulation is typically in the form of an inverted U, it might be that the findings are due to the particular hormone doses investigated. However, if these hormones are found to impair memory consistently, then we will have to consider why amnestic hormones are released by training experiences. Izquierdo et al (1982) have suggested that this provides a mechanism to prevent the storage of an overwhelming amount of information. But why then is there also release of hormones that enhance retention? Is memory modulation a result of a hormonal algebraic process? If so, on what basis is it determined that too much information is being processed? On the basis of available evidence it seems appropriate to conclude only that these hormones influence retention. Further studies are needed to determine whether certain hormones are uniquely amnestic in their effects.

CONCLUSION

There is extensive evidence that hormones can modulate memory, and there is moderately convincing evidence that endogenous hormones modulate memory storage. Further, the findings reviewed here strongly suggest that peripheral hormonal processes may be involved in the physiology of memory. As yet, however, the studies have not revealed the details of the mechanisms by which hormones modulate memory. Such understanding, when obtained, should contribute significantly to a more general understanding of the physiology and cellular neurobiology of memory.

ACKNOWLEDGMENTS

My work is supported in part by Research Grants MH 12526 and AG 00538. I thank my colleagues and students for their contributions to the ideas discussed here and Lynn Brown, Nan Collett, and Lisa Weinberger for preparing the manuscript.

Literature Cited

Abdul-Rahman, A., Dahlgren, N., Johansson, B. B., Siejö, B. K. 1979. Increase in local cerebral blood flow induced by circulating adrenaline: Involvement of blood-brain barrier dysfunction. *Acta Physiol. Scand.* 107:227–32

Alliot, J., Alexinsky, T. 1982. Effects of post-trial vasopressin injection on appetitively motivated learning in rats. *Physiol. Behav.* 28:525–30

Amir, S., Brown, Z. W., Amit, Z. 1980. The role of endorphin in stress: Evidence and speculations. *Neurosci. Biobehav. Rev.* 4:77–86

Archer, T., Ogren, S. O., Fuxe, K., Agnati, L. F., Enroth, P. 1981. On the interactive role of central noradrenaline neurons and corticosterone in two-way active avoidance acquisition in the rat. *Neurosci. Lett.* 27:341–46

Belluzzi, J. D., Stein, L. 1977. Enkephalin and morphine-induced facilitation of long-term memory. *Neurosci. Abstr.* 3:23

Belluzzi, J. D., Stein, L. 1981. Facilitation of long-term memory by brain endorphins. See Martinez et al 1981c, pp. 291–303

Bennett, C., Liang, K. C., McGaugh, J. L. 1982. Epinephrine alters the effect of amygdala stimulation on retention of avoidance tasks. *Neurosci. Abstr.* 8: 459

Berman, R. F., Kesner, R. P. 1981. Electrical stimulation as a tool in memory research. In *Electrical Stimulation Research Techniques*, ed. M. M. Patterson, R. P. Kesner, pp. 173–203. New York: Academic

Bertler, A., Falck, B., Owman, C., Rosengren, E. 1966. The localization of monoaminergic blood-brain barrier mechanisms. *Pharmacol. Rev.* 18: 369–85

Bloch, V., Hennevin, E., Leconte, P. 1977. Interaction between post-trial reticular stimulation and subsequent paradoxical sleep in memory consolidation processes. In *Neurobiology of Sleep and Memory*, ed. R. R. Drucker-Colín, J. L. McGaugh, pp. 255–72. New York: Academic

Bloom, F. E., McGinty, J. F. 1981. Cellular distribution and function of endorphins. See Martinez et al 1981c, pp. 199–230

Bodnar, R. J., Kelly, D. D., Brutus, M., Glusman, M. 1980. Stress-induced analgesia: Neural and hormonal determinants. *Neurosci. Biobehav. Rev.* 4:87–100

Bohus, B. 1977. Effect of desglycinamide-lysnic vasopressin (DG-LVP) on sexually motivated T-maze behavior of the male rat. *Horm. Behav.* 8:52–61

Bohus, B., Conti, L., Kovács, G. L., Versteeg, D. H. G. 1982. Modulation of memory processes by neuropeptides: Interaction with neurotransmitter systems. In *Neuronal Plasticity and Memory Formation*, ed. C. Ajmone Marsan,

H. Matthies, pp. 75–87. New York: Raven. 659 pp.

Bohus, B., de Wied, D. 1981. Actions of ACTH- and MSH-like peptides on learning, performance and retention. See Martinez et al 1981c, pp. 59–77

Bohus, B., Kovács, G. L., de Wied, D. 1978. Oxytocin, vasopressin and memory: Opposite effects on consolidation and retrieval processes. *Brain Res.* 157: 414–17

Borrell, J., Bohus, E. R., de Kloet, E. R., Versteeg, D. H. G., de Wied, D. 1981. Passive avoidance retention deficit following short term adrenalectomy: The effects of post-learning arginine[8]-vasopressin and adrenaline. *Neurosci. Lett.* Suppl. 7, S265

Brewton, C. B., Liang, K. C., McGaugh, J. L. 1981. Adrenal demedullation alters the effect of amygdala stimulation on retention of avoidance tasks. *Neurosci. Abstr.* 11:870

Brown, O. M., Palfai, T., Wichlinski, L. 1981. Effect of an amnesia dose of reserpine, syrosingopine or guanethidine on the levels of whole brain dopamine and norepinephrine in the mouse. *Pharmacol. Biochem. Behav.* 15:911–14

Carrasco, M. A., Dias, R. D., Izquierdo, I. 1982. Naloxone reverses retrograde amnesia induced by electroconvulsive shock. *Behav. Neural Biol.* 34: 352–57

Castellano, C. 1975. Effects of morphine and heroin on discrimination learning and consolidation in mice. *Psychopharmacology* 42:235–42

Cornford, E. M., Brown, L. D., Crane, P. D., Oldendorf, W. H. 1978. Blood-brain barrier restrictions of peptides and low uptake of enkephalins. *Endocrinology* 103:1297–1303

de Wied, D. 1964. Influence of anterior pituitary on avoidance learning and escape behavior. *Am. J. Physiol.* 207:255–59

de Wied, D. 1980. Pituitary neuropeptides and behavior. In *Central Regulation of the Endocrine System*, ed. K. Fuxe, T. Hokfelt, R. Luft, pp. 297–314. New York: Plenum

de Wied, D., Bohus, B. 1966. Long term and short term effects on retention of a conditioned avoidance response in rats by treatment with long acting pitressin and α-MSH. *Nature* 212:1484–86

de Wied, D., Bohus, B., van Ree, J. M., Urban, I. 1978. Behavioral and electrophysiological effects of peptides related to lipotropin (β-LPH). *J. Pharmacol. Exp. Ther.* 204:570–80

Dias, R. D., Perry, M. L. S., Carrasco, M. A., Izquierdo, I. 1981. Effect of electrocon-vulsive shock on β-endorphin immunoreactivity of rat brain, pituitary gland, and plasma. *Behav. Neural Biol.* 32:265–68

Dunn, A. J. 1980. Neurochemistry of learning and memory: An evaluation of recent data. *Ann. Rev. Psychol.* 31:343–90

Dunn, A. J., Gispen, W. H. 1977. How ACTH acts on the brain. *Biobehav. Rev.* 1:15–23

Ermisch, A., Landgraf, R., Heinold, G., Sterba, G. 1982. Vasopressin, blood-brain barrier, and memory. See Bohus et al 1982, pp. 147–53

Everett, J., Roberge, A. G. 1981. Selective changes in the metabolism of biogenic amines after successive discrimination training in cats. *Neuroscience* 6: 1753–57

Fekete, M., de Wied, D. 1982. Potency and duration of action of ACTH$_{4-9}$ analog (ORG-2766) as compared to ACTH$_{4-10}$ and (D-Phe[7]) ACTH$_{4-10}$ on active and passive avoidance behavior of rats. *Pharmacol. Biochem. Behav.* 16:387–92

Fibiger, H. C., Roberts, D. C. S., Price, T. C. 1975. On the role of telencephalic noradrenaline in learning and memory. In *Chemical Tools in Catecholamine Research*, ed. G. Jonsson, T. Malmfers, C. Sachs. Amsterdam: Elsevier/North Holland

Flood, J. F., Jarvik, M. E., Bennett, E. L., Orme, A. E. 1976. Effects of ACTH peptide fragments on memory formation. *Pharmacol. Biochem. Behav.* Suppl. 1, 5:41–51

Flood, J. F., Smith, G. E., Jarvik, M. E. 1980. A comparison of effects of localized brain administration of a catecholamine and protein synthesis inhibitors on memory processing. *Brain Res.* 197: 153–65

Gallagher, M., Kapp, B. S. 1978. Manipulation of opiate activity in the amygdala alters memory processes. *Life Sci.* 23:1973–78

Gallagher, M., Kapp, B. S. 1981a. Influence of amygdala opiate-sensitive mechanisms, fear-motivated responses, and memory processes for aversive experiences. See Martinez et al 1981c, pp. 445–61

Gallagher, M., Kapp, B. S. 1981b. Effect of phentolamine administration into the amygdala complex of rats on time-dependent memory processes. *Behav. Neural Biol.* 31:90–95

Gallagher, M., Kapp, B. S., Musty, R. E., Driscoll, P. A. 1977. Memory formation, evidence for a specific neurochemical system in the amygdala. *Science* 198:423–25

Gallagher, M., Kapp, B. S., Pascoe, J. P., Rapp, P. R. 1981. A neuropharmacology of amygdaloid systems which contribute to learning and memory. In *The Amygdaloid Complex*, ed. Y. Ben-Ari, pp. 343–54. Amsterdam: Elsevier/North Holland

Gold, P. E., Delanoy, R. L. 1981. ACTH modulation of memory storage processes. See Martinez et al 1981c, pp. 79–98

Gold, P. E., McCarty, R. 1981. Plasma catecholamines: Changes after footshock and seizure-producing frontal cortex stimulation. *Behav. Neural Biol.* 31:247–60

Gold, P. E., McCarty, R., Sternberg, D. B. 1982. Peripheral catecholamines and memory modulation. See Bohus et al 1982, pp. 327–38

Gold, P. E., McGaugh, J. L. 1975. A single-trace, two-process view of memory storage processes. In *Short-Term Memory*, ed. D. Deutsch, J. A. Deutsch, pp. 355–78. New York: Academic

Gold, P. E., McGaugh, J. L. 1978. Endogenous modulators of memory storage processes. In *Clinical Psychoneuroendocrinology in Reproduction*, ed. L. Carenza, P. Pancheri, L. Zichella, pp. 25–46. London: Academic

Gold, P. E., Murphy, J. 1980. Brain noradrenergic responses to training and to amnestic frontal cortex stimulation. *Pharmacol. Biochem. Behav.* 13:257–63

Gold, P. E., Reigel, J. A. 1980. Extended retrograde amnesia gradients produced by epinephrine injections administered at the time of cortical stimulation. *Physiol. Behav.* 24:1101–6

Gold, P. E., Sternberg, D. B. 1978. Retrograde amnesia produced by several treatments. Evidence for a common neurobiological mechanism. *Science* 201:367–69

Gold, P. E., Sternberg, D. B. 1980. Neurobiology of amnesia. *Science* 209:836–37

Gold, P. E., van Buskirk, R. 1975. Facilitation of time-dependent memory processes with posttrial amygdala stimulation: Effect on memory varies with footshock level. *Brain Res.* 86:509–13

Gold, P. E., van Buskirk, R. 1976a. Effects of posttrial hormone injections on memory processes. *Horm. Behav.* 7:509–17

Gold, P. E., van Buskirk, R. 1976b. Enhancement and impairment of memory processes with posttrial injections of adrenocorticotrophic hormone. *Behav. Biol.* 16:387–400

Gold, P. E., van Buskirk, R. 1978a. Posttraining brain norepinephrine concentrations: Correlation with retention performance of avoidance training and with peripheral epinephrine modulation of memory processing. *Behav. Biol.* 23:509–20

Gold, P. E., van Buskirk, R. 1978b. Effects of α- and β-adrenergic receptor antagonists on post-trial epinephrine modulation of memory: Relationship to posttraining brain norepinephrine concentrations. *Behav. Biol.* 24:168–84

Goldman, H., Murphy, S. 1981. An analog of ACTH/MSH$_{4-9}$, ORG-2766, reduces permeability of the blood-brain barrier in rats. *Pharmacol. Biochem. Behav.* 14:845–48

Goldstein, A. 1976. Opioid peptides (endorphins) in pituitary and brain. *Science* 193:1081–86

Gorelick, D. A., Bozewiez, T. R., Bridger, W. H. 1975. The role of catecholamines in animal learning and memory. In *Catecholamines and Behavior*, ed. A. J. Friedhoff, 2:1–30. New York: Plenum

Gunne, L., Reis, D. J. 1963. Changes in brain catecholamines associated with electrical stimulation of amygdaloid nucleus. *Life Sci.* 11:804–9

Haycock, J. W., van Buskirk, R., Ryan, J. R., McGaugh, J. L. 1977. Enhancement of retention with centrally-administered catecholamines. *Exp. Neurol.* 54:199–208

Hunter, B., Zornetzer, S. F., Jarvik, M. E., McGaugh, J. L. 1977. Modulation of learning and memory: Effects of drugs influencing neurotransmitters. In *Handbook of Psychopharmacology*, ed. L. Iversen, S. Iversen, S. Snyder, 8:531–77. New York:Plenum

Huston, J. P., Stäubli, U. 1981. Substance P and its effects on learning and memory. See Martinez et al 1981c, pp. 521–40

Iimori, K., Tanaka, M., Kohno, Y., Ida, Y., Nakagawa, R., et al. 1982. Psychological stress enhances noradrenaline turnover in specific brain regions in rats. *Pharmacol. Biochem. Behav.* 16:637–40

Ishikawa, K., Martinez, J. L. Jr., McGaugh, J. L. 1981. Simultaneous determination of 4-hydroxyamphetamine and catecholamines in the same samples of mouse brain. *8th Int. Congr. Pharmacol. Abstr.* In press

Izquierdo, I. 1979. Effect of naloxone and morphine on various forms of memory in the rat: Possible role of endogenous opiate mechanisms in memory consolidation. *Psychopharmacology* 66:199–203

Izquierdo, I. 1980a. Effect of β-endorphin and naloxone on acquisition, memory and retrieval of shuttle avoidance and habituation learning in rats. *Psychopharmacology* 69:111–15

Izquierdo, I. 1980b. Effect of a low and a high dose of β-endorphin on acquisition and retention in the rat. *Behav. Neural Biol.* 30:460–64

Izquierdo, I. 1982. Effect of opioid peptides on learning and memory: Single or dual effect? In *Pharmacology of Learning and Memory,* ed. S. Saito, J. L. McGaugh. In press

Izquierdo, I., Dias, R. D., Perry, M. L., Souza, D. O., Elisabetsky, E., Carrasco, M. A. 1982. A physiological amnestic mechanism mediated by endogenous opioid peptides, and its possible role in learning. See Bohus et al 1982, pp. 89–113

Izquierdo, I., Grandenz, M. 1980. Memory facilitation by naloxone is due to release of dopaminergic and beta-adrenergic systems from tonic inhibition. *Psychopharmacology* 67:265–68

Izquierdo, I., Perry, M. L., Dias, R. D., Souza, D. O., Elisabetsky, E., 1981. Endogenous opioids, memory modulation, and state dependency. See Martinez et al 1981c, pp. 269–90

Jensen, R. A., Martinez, J. L. Jr., Messing, R. B., Spiehler, V., Vasquez, B. J., et al. 1978. Morphine and naloxone alter memory in the rat. *Neurosci. Abstr.* 4:260

Jensen, R. A., Martinez, J. L. Jr., Vasquez, B. J., McGaugh, J. L., McGuinness, T., et al. 1977. Amnesia produced by intraventricular administration of diethyldithiocarbamate. *Neurosci. Abstr.* 3:235

Judge, M. E., Quartermain, D. 1982. Alleviation of anisomycin-induced amnesia by pre-test treatment with lysine vasopressin. *Pharmacol. Biochem. Behav.* 16:463–66

Kasamatsu, T., Pettigrew, J. D. 1976. Depletion of brain catecholamines: Failure of ocular dominance shift after monocular occlusion in kittens. *Science* 194:206–9

Kastin, A. J., Olson, R. D., Schally, A. V., Coy, D. H. 1979. CNS effects of peripherally administered brain peptides. *Life Sci.* 25:401–14

Kastin, A. J., Scollan, E. L., King, M. G., Schally, A. V., Coy, D. H. 1976. Enkephalin and a potent analog facilitates maze performance after intraperitoneal administration in rats. *Pharmacol. Biochem. Behav.* 5:691–95

Kesner, R. P. 1981. The role of amygdala within an attribute analysis of memory. See Gallagher et al 1981, pp. 331–42

Kesner, R. P., Wilburn, M. W. 1974. A review of electrical stimulation of the brain in the context of learning and retention. *Behav. Biol.* 10:259–93

Kety, S. 1972. Brain catecholamine, affective states and memory. In *The Chemistry of Mood, Motivation and Memory,* ed. J. L. McGaugh, pp. 65–80. New York: Plenum

Koob, G. L., Le Moal, M., Bloom, F. E. 1981. Enkephalin and endorphin influences on appetitive and aversive conditioning. See Martinez et al 1981c, pp. 249–67

Kovács, G. L., Bohus, B., de Wied, D. 1981a. Retention of passive avoidance behavior in rats following α- and γ-endorphin administration: Effects of post-learning treatments. *Neurosci. Lett.* 22:79–82

Kovács, G. L., de Wied, D. 1981. Endorphin influences on learning and memory. See Martinez et al 1981c, pp. 231–47

Kovács, G. L., Versteeg, D. H. G., de Kloet, E. R., Bohus, B. 1981b. Passive avoidance performance correlates with catecholamine turnover in discrete limbic regions. *Life Sci.* 28:1109–16

Krieger, D. T., Liotta, A. S. 1979. Pituitary hormones in brain. Where, how and why? *Science* 205:366–72

Lechtensteiger, W., Lienhart, R., Kopp, H. G. 1977. Peptide hormones and central dopamine neuron systems. *Psychoneuroendocrinology* 2:237–48

Leconte, P., Hennevin, E. 1981. Post-learning paradoxical sleep, reticular activation, and noradrenergic activity. *Physiol. Behav.* 26:587–94

Leshner, A. I., Merkle, D. A., Mixon, J. F. 1981. Pituitary-adrenocortical effects on learning and memory in social situations. See Martinez et al 1981c, pp. 159–79

Leshner, A. I., Politch, J. A. 1979. Hormonal control of submissiveness in mice: Irrelevance of the androgens and relevance of the pituitary-adrenal hormones. *Physiol. Behav.* 22:531–34

Lewy, A. J., Seiden, L. S. 1972. Operant behavior changes norepinephrine metabolism in rat brain. *Science* 175:454–55

Liang, K. C., McGaugh, J. L. 1981. Lesions of the stria terminalis attenuate the amnestic effect of amygaloid stimulation on avoidance responses. *Neurosci. Abstr.* 7:652

Liang, K. C., McGaugh, J. L. 1982. Lesions of the stria terminalis attenuate the facilitatory effect of epinephrine on retention in an inhibitory avoidance task. *Neurosci. Abstr.* 8: 321

Luttinger, D., Nemeroff, C. B., Prange, A. J. Jr. 1982. The effects of neuropeptides on discrete-trial conditioned avoidance responding. *Brain Res.* 237:183–92

Mactutus, C. F., Smith, R. L., Riccio, D. C. 1980. Extending the ACTH-induced memory reactivation in an amnestic paradigm. *Physiol. Behav.* 24:541–46

Martinez, J. L. Jr. 1982a. Conditioning: Modulation by peripheral mechanisms. In *Conditioning: Representation of Involved Neural Function,* ed. C. D. Woody. New York: Plenum. In press

Martinez, J. L. Jr. 1982b. Endogenous modulators of memory. In *Theory in Psychopharmacology,* ed. S. J. Cooper, Vol. 2. New York: Academic. In press

Martinez, J. L. Jr., Ishikawa, K., Hannan, T. J., Liang, K. C., Vasquez, B. J., et al. 1981a. Actions of 4 OH-amphetamine on active avoidance conditioning and regional brain concentrations of norepinephrine and dopamine. *Neurosci. Abstr.* 7:523

Martinez, J. L. Jr., Jensen, R. A., McGaugh, J. L. 1981b. Attenuation of experimentally-induced amnesia. *Prog. Neurobiol.* 16:155–86

Martinez, J. L. Jr., Jensen, R. A., Messing, R. B., Rigter, H., McGaugh, J. L., eds. 1981c. *Endogenous Peptides and Learning and Memory Processes.* New York: Academic. 587 pp.

Martinez, J. L. Jr., Jensen, R. A., Messing, R. B., Vasquez, B. J., Soumireu-Mourat, B., et al. 1980a. Central and peripheral actions of amphetamine on memory storage. *Brain Res.* 182:157–66

Martinez, J. L. Jr., Rigter, H. 1980. Endorphins alter acquisition and consolidation of an inhibitory avoidance response in rats. *Neurosci. Lett.* 18:197–201

Martinez, J. L. Jr., Rigter, H., Jensen, R. A., Messing R. B., Vasquez, B. J., McGaugh, J. L. 1981d. Endorphin and enkephalin effects on avoidance conditioning: The other side of the pituitary-adrenal axis. See Martinez et al 1981c, pp. 305–24

Martinez, J. L. Jr., Vasquez, B. J., Jensen, R. A., Soumireu-Mourat, B., McGaugh, J. L. 1979. ACTH$_{4-9}$ analog (ORG 2766) facilitates acquisition of an inhibitory avoidance response in rats. *Pharmacol. Biochem. Behav.* 10:145–47

Martinez, J. L. Jr., Vasquez, B. J., Rigter, H., Messing, R. B., Jensen, R. A., et al. 1980b. Attenuation of amphetamine-induced enhancement of learning by

adrenal demedullation. *Brain Res.* 195:433–43

McCarty, R., Gold, P. E. 1981. Plasma catecholamines: Effects of footshock level and hormonal modulators of memory storage. *Horm. Behav.* 15:168–82

McGaugh, J. L. 1966. Time-dependent processes in memory storage. *Science* 153:1351-58

McGaugh, J. L. 1973. Drug facilitation of learning and memory. *Ann. Rev. Pharmacol.* 13:229–41

McGaugh, J. L. 1976. Neurobiological aspects of memory. In *Biological Foundations of Psychiatry,* ed. R. G. Grenell, S. Gabay, pp. 499–525. New York: Raven

McGaugh, J. L., Gold, P. E. 1976. Modulation of memory by electrical stimulation of the brain. See Rosenzweig & Bennett 1976, pp. 549–60

McGaugh, J. L., Gold, P. E., Handwerker, M. J., Jensen, R. A., Martinez, J. L. Jr., et al. 1979. Altering memory by electrical and chemical stimulation of the brain. In *Brain Mechanisms in Memory and Learning: From the Single Neuron to Man,* ed. M. A. B. Brazier, 4:151–64. New York: Raven

McGaugh, J. L., Gold, P. E., van Buskirk, R., Haycock, J. 1975. Modulating influences of hormones and catecholamines on memory storage processes. In *Hormones, Homeostasis and the Brain,* ed. W. H. Gispen, Tj. B. van Wimersma Greidanus, B. Bohus, D. de Wied, pp. 151–62. Amsterdam: Elsevier/North Holland

McGaugh, J. L., Herz, M. J. 1972. *Memory Consolidation,* pp. 151–62. San Francisco: Albion

McGaugh, J. L., Martinez, J. L. Jr., Jensen, R. A., Hannan, T. J., Vasquez, B. J., et al. 1982. Modulation of memory storage by treatments affecting peripheral catecholamines. See Bohus et al 1982, pp. 311–25

McGaugh, J. L., Martinez, J. L. Jr., Jensen, R. A., Messing, R. B., Vasquez, B. J. 1980. Central and peripheral catecholamine function in learning and memory processes. In *Neural Mechanisms of Goal-Directed Behavior and Learning,* ed. R. F. Thompson, L. H. Hicks, V. B. Shvyrkov, pp. 75–91. New York: Academic

Meligeni, J. A., Ledergerber, S. A., McGaugh, J. L. 1978. Norepinephrine attenuation of amnesia produced by diethyldithiocarbamate. *Brain Res.* 149: 155–64

Messing, R. B., Jensen, R. A., Martinez, J. L. Jr., Spiehler, V. R., Vasquez, B. J., et al.

1979. Naloxone enhancement of memory. *Behav. Neural Biol.* 27:266–75

Messing, R. B., Jensen, R. A., Vasquez, B. J., Martinez, J. L. Jr., Spiehler, V. R., McGaugh, J. L. 1981. Opiate modulation of memory. See Martinez et al 1981c, pp. 431–43

Mondadori, C., Waser, P. G. 1979. Facilitation of memory processing by posttrial morphine: Possible involvement of reinforcement mechanisms? *Psychopharmacology* 63:297–300

Nakagawa, R., Tanaka, M., Kohno, Y., Noda, Y., Nagasaki, N. 1981. Regional response of rat brain noradrenergic neurons to acute intense stress. *Pharmacol. Biochem. Behav.* 14:729–32

Natelson, B. H., Tapp, W. N., Adamus, J. E., Mittler, J. C., Levin, B. E. 1981. Humoral indices of stress in rats. *Physiol. Behav.* 26:1049–54

Oei, T. P. S., King, M. G. 1980. Catecholamines and aversive learning: A review. *Neurosci. Biobehav. Rev.* 4:161–73

Ogren, S. O., Archer, T., Ross, S. B. 1980. Evidence for a role of the locus coeruleus noradrenaline system in learning. *Neurosci. Lett.* 20:351–56

Ogren, S. O., Fuxe, N. 1974. Learning, brain noradrenaline and the pituitary-adrenal axis. *Med. Biol.* 52:399–405

Pfeiffer, W. D., Bookin, H. B. 1978. Vasopressin antagonizes retrograde amnesia in rats following electroconvulsive shock. *Pharmacol. Biochem. Behav.* 9:261–63

Reis, D. J., Gunne, L. M. 1965. Brain catecholamines: Relation to the defense reaction evoked by amygdaloid stimulation in the cat. *Science* 149:450–51

Riccio, D. C., Concannon, J. T. 1981. ACTH and the reminder phenomena. See Martinez et al 1981c, pp. 117–42

Ridley, R. M., Haystead, A. J., Baker, H. F., Crow, T. J. 1981. A new approach to the role of noradrenaline in learning: Problem solving in the marmoset after α-noradrenergic receptor blockade. *Pharmacol. Biochem. Behav.* 14:849–55

Rigter, H., Hannan, T. J., Messing, R. B., Martinez, J. L. Jr., Vasquez, B. J., et al. 1980a. Enkephalins interfere with acquisition of an active avoidance response. *Life Sci.* 26:337–45

Rigter, H., Jensen, R. A., Martinez, J. L. Jr., Messing, R. B., Vasquez, B. J., et al. 1980b. Enkephalin and fear-motivated behavior. *Proc. Natl. Acad. Sci. USA* 77:3729–32

Rigter, H., van Riezen, H. 1975. Anti-amnestic effect of ACTH$_{4-10}$: Its independence of the nature of the amnesic agent and

the behavioral test. *Physiol. Behav.* 14:563–66

Rigter, H., van Riezen, H. 1978. Hormones and memory. In *Psychopharmacology: A Generation of Progress,* ed. M. A. Lipton, A. Di Mascio, K. F. Killam, pp. 677–89. New York: Raven

Riley, A. L., Zellner, D. A., Duncan, H. J. 1980. The role of endorphins in animal learning and behavior. *Neurosci. Biobehav. Rev.* 4:69–76

Roberts, D. C. S., Fibiger, H. C. 1977. Evidence for interactions between central noradrenaline neurons and adrenal hormones in learning and memory. *Pharmacol. Biochem. Behav.* 2:191–94

Rosenzweig, M. R., Bennett, E. L., eds. 1976. *Neural Mechanisms of Learning and Memory,* pp. 549–60. Cambridge, Mass: MIT Press

Sagen, J., Routtenberg, A. 1981. Specific anatomical and synaptic sites of neuropeptide action in memory formation. See Martinez et al 1981c, pp. 541–61

Sahgal, A., Keith, A. B., Wright, C., Edwardson, J. A. 1982. Failure of vasopressin to enhance memory in a passive avoidance task in rats. *Neurosci. Lett.* 28:87–92

Serota, R. G., Roberts, R. B., Flexner, L. B. 1972. Acetoxycycloheximide-induced transient amnesia: Protective effects of adrenergic stimulants. *Proc. Natl. Acad. Sci. USA* 69:340–42

Shashoua, V. E. 1982. Molecular and cell biological aspects of learning: Toward a theory of memory. *Adv. Cell. Neurobiol.* 3:97–141

Soumireu-Mourat, B., Micheau, J., Franc, C. 1981. ACTH$_{4-9}$ analog (ORG 2766) and memory processes in mice. See Martinez et al 1981c, pp. 143–58

Squire, L. R., Davis, H. P. 1981. The pharmacology of memory: A neurobiological perspective. *Ann. Rev. Pharmacol. Toxicol.* 21:323–56

Squire, L. R., Davis, H. P., Spanis, C. W. 1980. Neurobiology of amnesia. *Science* 209:836–37

Stein, L., Belluzzi, J. D., Wise, C. D. 1975. Memory enhancement by central administration of norepinephrine. *Brain Res.* 84:329–35

Sternberg, D. B., Gold, P. E. 1980. Effects of α- and β-adrenergic receptor antagonists on retrograde amnesia produced by frontal cortex stimulation. *Behav. Neural Biol.* 29:289–302

Sternberg, D. B., Gold, P. E. 1981a. Intraventricular adrenergic antagonists: Failure to attenuate retrograde amnesia. *Physiol. Behav.* 27:551–55

Sternberg, D. B., Gold, P. E. 1981b. Retrograde amnesia produced by electrical stimulation of the amygdala: Attenuation with adrenergic antagonists. *Brain Res.* 211:59–65

Sternberg, D. B., Gold, P. E., McGaugh, J. L. 1982. Noradrenergic sympathetic blockade: Lack of effect on memory or retrograde amnesia. *Eur. J. Pharmacol.* 81:133–36

Sternberg, D. B., McGaugh, J. L., Gold, P. E. 1981. Propranolol-induced attenuation of both memory facilitation and amnesia produced by frontal cortex stimulation. *Neurosci. Abstr.* 7:360

Tanaka, M., Kohno, Y., Nakagawa, R., Ida, Y., Takeda, S., Nagasaki, N. 1982. Time-related differences in noradrenaline turnover in rat brain regions by stress. *Pharmacol. Biochem. Behav.* 16:315–19

Tortella, F. C., Cowan, A., Belenky, G. L., Holaday, J. W. 1981. Opiate-like electroencephalographic and behavioral effects of electroconvulsive shock in rats. *Eur. J. Pharmacol.* 76:121–28

U'Prichard, D. C., Reisine, T. D., Mason, S. T., Fibiger, H. C., Yamamura, H. I. 1980. Modulation of rat α- and β-adrenergic receptor populations by lesion of the dorsal adrenergic bundle. *Brain Res.* 187:143–54

Vachon, L., Roberge, A. G. 1981. Involvement of serotonin and catecholamine metabolism in cats trained to perform a delayed response task. *Neuroscience* 6:189–94

van Wimersma Greidanus, Tj. B., Bohus, B., de Wied, D. 1975. The role of vasopressin in memory processes. See McGaugh et al 1975, pp. 135–41

van Wimersma Greidanus, Tj. B., Bohus, B., de Wied, D. 1981. Vasopressin and oxytocin in learning and memory. See Martinez et al 1981c, pp. 413–27

van Wimersma Greidanus, Tj. B., Croiset, G., Bakker, E., Bowman, H. 1979. Amygdaloid lesions block the effect of neuropeptides (vasopressin and ACTH 4-10) on avoidance behavior. *Physiol. Behav.* 22:291–95

van Wimersma Greidanus, Tj. B., de Wied, D. 1976. Modulation of passive avoidance behavior of rats by intracerebroventricular administration of antivasopressin serum. *Behav. Biol.* 18:325–33

Viveros, O. H., Diliberto, E. J. Jr., Hazum, E., Chang, K. J. 1980. Enkephalins as possible adrenomedullary hormones: storage, secretions, and regulation of synthesis. In *Neural Peptides and Neuronal Communications,* ed. E. Costa, M. Trabucchi. New York: Raven

Walsh, T. J., Palfai, T. 1979. Peripheral catecholamines and memory characteristics of syrosingopine-induced amnesia. *Pharmacol. Biochem. Behav.* 11:449–52

Weingartner, H., Gold, P., Ballenger, J. C., Smallberg, S. A., Summers, R., et al. 1981. Effects of vasopressin on human memory functions. *Science* 211:601–3

Wendlant, S., File, S. E. 1979. Behavioral effects of lesions of the locus coeruleus noradrenaline system combined with adrenalectomy. *Behav. Neural Biol.* 26:189–201

Ann. Rev. Psychol. 1983. 34:325–49

COMPREHENSION, PRODUCTION, AND LANGUAGE ACQUISITION

Eve V. Clark and Barbara Frant Hecht

Department of Linguistics, Stanford University, Stanford, California 94305

CONTENTS

INTRODUCTION

Some of the skills we acquire during childhood require that we be able to coordinate what we understand or perceive with what we produce or encode. Others do not. Consider our ability to reach out and pick up an object a few inches away. To do this successfully, we must link what we can see with the fine motor adjustments possible for our hands. This hand-eye coordination is often taken for granted until one observes an infant who has yet to attain it. Or consider the ability to imitate someone else's actions. One has to be able to represent and then reproduce the motor activities observed.

325

0066-4308/83/0201-0325$02.00

In contrast, consider two other activities: bicycling and swimming, both of them skills typically mastered before adulthood. When we say someone can bicycle or can swim, we usually mean he is able to produce the pertinent actions so as to meet some basic criterion, say, staying upright on a bicycle and staying afloat in a swimming pool. These abilities, though, do not require coordination with the ability to recognize that someone else is riding a bicycle or swimming. One can perceive and recognize activities on different occasions as instances of bicycling or swimming without ever learning to bicycle or swim oneself. And one could learn to ride a bicycle or swim without necessarily having seen anyone else doing so. Our point is that producing some behavior and recognizing it in others are two distinct processes, and there is little need in many cases to coordinate them in any way.

Language, however, does require coordination. Since it is a conventional system, its very use demands that two distinct processes—production and comprehension—be coordinated. Without such coordination, speakers would be unable to use language to communicate and to infer intentions. And this in turn suggests that one part of acquisition consists of coordinating what one can produce with what one can understand.

As adults, we tend to take such coordination for granted. Closer inspection, though, reveals many areas of language use in which comprehension and production remain distinct. For example, most speakers of English (and of other languages) understand a range of dialects and accents but can only produce one or two themselves. Many speakers may also understand a second or third language quite well but be unable to produce it. Conversely, in some settings speakers may produce language they cannot understand, for instance Hebrew prayers learned for recitation at a bar mitzvah or (prior to the introduction of vernaculars) the Latin mass. Such examples of production without comprehension are typically tied to specific, often ritual, settings. Nonetheless, such examples show that production can in some sense occur without comprehension, just as comprehension can without production.

The absence of coordination between comprehension and production in such instances suggests that we may represent things linguistic in one way for the process of understanding—essentially recognizing what the speaker intends—and in another for talking—essentially retrieving from memory the necessary elements for constructing an utterance. At the same time, as mature speakers of a language, we have learned to coordinate most of what we can produce with what we can understand. For example, Californians recognize that the word *right* pronounced by an Australian, a South African, a Texan, and a Bostonian are all to be represented as variants of the same linguistic element, and that all these variants are to be coordinated with a Californian production of *right*. And the latter in its turn will be recognized as the word *right* by Australians, South Africans, Texans, and Bostonians even though it doesn't precisely match their productions.

Coordination, then, is part of what children must work on as they acquire language. And the fact that comprehension and production have to be coordinated in itself raises a critical question about how comprehension and production should be defined. In the case of adults, we normally assume full comprehension, regardless of context, and fully appropriate production. Such assumptions simply do not hold for children still acquiring their first language. Children may show some comprehension of an utterance simply by looking toward the object named, or demonstrate greater comprehension by carrying out a series of contrasting instructions. And they may produce a word appropriately in only one context or do so across a range equivalent to the adult's. Since children acquiring a first language start with only partial knowledge of the sound system, the meanings, and the structural forms they are using, one has to establish their degree of comprehension or production in assessing what they have acquired.

Yet investigators typically have not provided explicit criteria for the degree of comprehension or production, from near zero to fully adult-like performance, that children control. Different investigators have relied on different criteria for attributing presumably adult-like performance to children. These criteria often depend on a single observational or experimental setting, and children are usually said to have acquired a particular structure on the basis of comprehension alone, or production alone. A few investigators have tried to compare performance in comprehension with performance in production, but most of these studies have been flawed. Methodologically, the tasks tapping the two processes have made quite different kinds of demands on the children doing them. Theoretically, there has been little attempt to consider why the processes of comprehension and production might differ, or what the developmental consequences of any differences might be.

These methodological and theoretical shortcomings, we suggest, arise in large part from the tendency of most investigators in the field to focus on the *product*—the language itself—rather than on the *processes* language-users rely on. In the present chapter, we will begin by reviewing some of the studies that have looked at both comprehension and production, and claims made about the relations between the two processes. In doing this, we will focus on some of the methodological problems these studies have raised. We will then turn to an approach that starts from processes rather than product, and give a brief account of how production becomes coordinated with comprehension during the course of acquiring a language. This framework can accommodate both discrepancies and similarities in performance tested in comprehension and production. Finally, we will discuss some of the implications of looking at language acquisition in terms of processes instead of in terms of the more traditional product, the language itself.

COMPREHENSION AND PRODUCTION

Anecdotal reports have long favored the view that young children understand more than they produce. This is a common observation in many of the classic diary studies as well as in much of the more recent observational and experimental research (e.g. Huttenlocher 1974, Rescorla 1980). Very young children just beginning to produce recognizable words themselves seem to attend to and respond appropriately to many more words around them. Nonetheless, the question of whether one system is more advanced is complicated by the problem that measures of both comprehension and production may be somewhat overestimated. Adults often forget how many clues to what the child is expected to do may be offered by the actual setting. A small child, told *Now would you put your blocks away* as the adult holds out the box in which the blocks are normally kept, is very likely to put the blocks in the box, but the reasons for his actions may not require any comprehension of the linguistic forms in the request just made (e.g. Shatz 1978). Observers also overestimate what children understand by treating what they say as if their words were equivalent to the adult's in meaning. Children often echo the ends of utterances addressed to them and use stock phrases fluently without understanding the individual words or morphemes. Thus they may appear to have adult-like comprehension both when they respond to adult utterances while actually relying on contextual cues and when they themselves make use of complex constructions that are no more, for them, than unanalyzed routines.

Observers commonly overestimate children's abilities in production too. Children make use of many words and routines that at casual glance may suggest much greater sophistication than they actually possess. For example, a child might use a Wh question like *Where is it?* with the appropriate inversion of subject and auxiliary verb, and be credited with knowledge of the structural properties of Wh forms. Yet the same child, on other occasions, may use forms like *Where is it goes?* or *Where is it the dog?*, both forms that show up the earlier, apparently correct production as an unanalyzed routine.

Comprehension Does Not Match Production

Even a fairly casual glance through the recent acquisition literature reveals a number of studies that report discrepancies between what children seem to understand and what they produce, both in their spontaneous speech and in situations designed to check on comprehension or elicit production.

Recent vocabulary studies offer a case in point. Goldin-Meadow and her colleagues (1976) found that 1- to 2-year-old children often seemed to have different repertoires for the two modes. In a comprehension test of vocabulary, they noted that a child would appear to understand the word *dog,* for example, just as an adult would, and respond appropriately upon hearing it (by pointing to the right picture on a page full of animals, picking up an appropriate toy, and so on). But when the same child was asked to name a picture of a dog, he would only say *wuf-wuf.* [1] At this stage, such children seemed to understand the adult meaning of *dog* but produced only a "child word," or no word at all (see also Rescorla 1980). They also produce some words or phrases they seem not to fully understand. A child may say *bye bye* only when other people leave a particular room, but fail to say it in other appropriate contexts, or say *hi,* initially picked up from an adult making finger puppets speak, only when the child has something covering her hand (Bowerman 1976).

Comprehension does not match production in early overextensions of words either. Like Moore (1896), Thomson and Chapman (1977) found that children aged 1:9 to 2:3 (1 year 9 months to 2 years 3 months) who overextended words like *doggie* to pick out all kinds of four-legged animals or *ball* to pick out all kinds of spherical objects in production, consistently chose only appropriate referents for the same words in comprehension. Thomson and Chapman concluded that the children's production was probably limited because they had difficulty in retrieving the right words, words that may in fact have been known to them. [2] The reliance on overextensions in production, then, marked a lag in production compared to comprehension.

Differences between performance in comprehension and production have also shown up in studies of the acquisition of inflections. Anisfeld and Tucker (1968) looked at 6-year-olds' ability to produce and to understand the various plural morphemes for nouns in English—/-s/, /-z/, and /-iz/ —used on words like *cat, dog,* and *house* respectively. Although the different tasks they used showed no overall advantage for comprehension over

---

[1] It is possible in such cases that the child's production reflected a routine that had emerged as part of reading—the routine of making the appropriate animal noise upon being shown a picture—but the child presumably understands *wuf-wuf* as well as *dog.* However, reliance on routines does not explain the discrepancies noted, for instance, between comprehension and production of simple verbs.

[2] Unfortunately, Thomson and Chapman did not test the children's comprehension of the words that would have been appropriate for the various categories included in the domain of each overextension, nor try to elicit them in other settings.

production, they found different patterns of performance in the two modes. In production, plural /-s/ and /-z/ were the easiest [replicating previous studies such as Berko (1958)], and the syllabic /-iz/ was more difficult. But in comprehension, /-z/ was the easiest and /-s/ and /-iz/ were both more difficult. Anisfeld and Tucker accounted for the different patterns by pointing to the different requirements for production and comprehension. In production, the children had to depend on whatever information they had stored about the forms of noun plurals for English, but in comprehension they could also draw on other generalizations about the forms of English words, for instance, that few singular nouns end in /-z/ so such words must be plural, or that most plurals are longer than singulars.

Finally, comprehension does not match production in studies of children's acquisition of terms like *same*. Karmiloff-Smith (1977) found that young French-speaking children usually interpreted *same* (*même*) in phrases like *the same duck* to mean "same kind" rather than "same one." Only later did they arrive at the "same one" interpretation. Another group of slightly older children, asked to describe the same situations used in the comprehension task, consistently reserved such expressions as *the same duck* (*le même canard*) for "same one," and created separate forms to express the notion "same kind" (e.g. the ungrammatical *le même de canard* "the same of duck" or *un de même de canard* "one of same of duck"). Thus, the earlier preferred interpretation of phrases like *the same duck*, (*le même canard,* taken as meaning "same kind") did not match the forms produced to express that meaning.[3]

These studies, however, do not show whether comprehension is systematically ahead of production or the reverse. Rather, they suggest that the two processes are different. But are there cases of comprehension without production? The answer to this appears to be "yes."

Is Comprehension Systematically Ahead of Production?

Studies of early language in children tend to suggest that children perceive and understand more about the sound structure and meanings of words than they themselves can initially produce. A number of studies have described children who have some comprehension of a term or a construction but still lack productive control over the pertinent forms. Clark and Hecht (1982) found that most of the 3-year-olds they studied understood the suffix *-er*, used to form agent and instrument nouns in English. In production, though, few of these children produced *-er* consistently when forming such

---

[3]It is possible, though unlikely, that the age difference between the children might account for the discrepancy. A more stringent demonstration would call for testing the same children on both comprehension and production.

nouns. They often relied on other linguistic options too. Such data suggest that children attain some comprehension of a form before they start to gain productive control over it (see also Winitz et al 1981). Comprehension, however, need not be complete prior to production. Given data like these, one would simply expect that where there were differences between the two processes, comprehension would be ahead.

Although this pattern of findings has been widely reported, its interpretation has often been difficult. Fraser, Bellugi, and Brown (1963) explicitly compared 3-year-olds' ability to imitate, comprehend, and produce a variety of morphological and syntactic forms in English. In the comprehension task, children were shown pairs of contrasting pictures to test their understanding of the singular-plural distinction and told, say, "One of these pictures is called 'The boy draws' and the other is called 'The boys draw.' " The experimenter then offered one of the two sentences and asked children to identify the appropriate picture, and then did the same with the other sentence. In production, the experimenter elicited descriptions for the same picture pairs. Fraser and his colleagues found that children consistently performed better on the comprehension task than they did on production. (They did better still on an imitation task with the same sentences, thus showing that articulatory demands could not explain the lag in production.) These findings were replicated (e.g. by Lovell & Dixon 1967) and seemed to offer strong support for a general advance of comprehension over production.

This conclusion has been challenged on methodological grounds. Baird (1972) argued that it was inappropriate for Fraser, Bellugi, and Brown to compare raw scores on the different tests directly because the probability of a child's giving a correct response by chance was not equal across tasks (see also Fernald 1972). This problem clearly is a very general one in any comparison of different processes.

More cogent perhaps is the argument that logically comprehension must precede production. To produce an utterance, one must choose the words and structures best suited to conveying one's intention as speaker. But to make the appropriate choices, one must understand the linguistic elements in order to know how they will be interpreted by someone else (see Ingram 1974). Notice that these logical requirements should make some tasks easier than others. In many comprehension tasks, the addressee, the child, listens to and then carries out instructions, an everyday occurrence. But production tasks, especially those that rely on imitation, omit a critical ingredient, namely the speaker's intention. And several investigators have noticed that young children spontaneously produce utterances that they are subsequently unable to imitate (e.g. Slobin & Welsh 1973, Bloom et al 1974). Production relies on the child's own intentions in ways comprehension does not, and such differences between the processes have to be taken into account in studying them.

Direct comparisons of comprehension and production in experimental studies have often been flawed because the tasks are not easily equated. This, of course, may simply reflect the different demands made by the processes of understanding versus producing an utterance. Nonetheless, the logical priority of comprehension over production appears supported by recent studies that have looked at both processes and found that children consistently seem to understand something of a construction before they start to produce it appropriately themselves (e.g. Winitz et al 1981, Clark & Hecht 1982). Where there is a difference, then, comprehension seems to be ahead of production.[4]

Is Production Ever Ahead of Comprehension?

Some investigators have argued for there being production without comprehension. However, what they actually seem to be arguing for is production without full comprehension. Their data are not incompatible with the view that some comprehension must always precede production. What appears critical in these studies are the definitions of production and of comprehension and the criteria used for acquisition.

Keeney and Wolfe (1972) argued from data on English number agreement that children could produce forms in spontaneous speech that they did not yet understand. Keeney and Wolfe looked at 3- and 4-year-olds' imitation, comprehension, and production of subject-verb agreement. In their spontaneous speech, these children usually observed number agreement by producing a singular verb with a singular subject and a plural verb with a plural subject. In comprehension, the children had to select one of a pair of pictures depicting singular or plural referents for nouns. In one task, they heard full sentences to match to a picture (e.g. *The bird flies*), and they all performed nearly perfectly, but as Keeney and Wolfe pointed out, they could have based their responses on their knowledge of plural marking on nouns alone (e.g. *bird* vs *birds*). In the other comprehension task, they heard only the verb (e.g. *flies* or *fly*) and performed very poorly. On the basis of this task alone, Keeney and Wolfe concluded that the children did not yet understand the relation between verb form and singular-plural

[4]Further evidence for comprehension taking precedence over production can be drawn from case studies of abnormal language development. Both Lenneberg (1962) and Fourcin (1975) documented instances of language development through comprehension in the complete absence of production. Fourcin's study is particularly compelling since the true degree of language mastery subsequently became accessible for study when, at age 30, the patient was introduced to a special typewriter and after only a few days began to write in fluent, syntactically perfect English. Prior to this, he had had no medium for producing language.

meaning, and that production of number agreement was therefore ahead of comprehension.

But as Keeney and Wolfe themselves suggested, the verb-only task was a difficult one (see also Bloom & Lahey 1978). What seems critical is its judgmental nature. Inferring that the subject of a verb must be singular or plural from hearing the verb alone could simply be beyond the capacity of 3- or 4-year-olds. A better test would presumably be one more like that in Fraser et al (1963), with irregular nouns, e.g. *the sheep jump* vs *the sheep jumps*. This study, then, gives only the most tenuous support to the view that production precedes comprehension.

Superficially, production may seem to be ahead of comprehension in several domains in early acquisition. Children will produce whole phrases or quite complex utterances at a time when they appear to respond appropriately to—to understand—only single words. However, closer examination reveals that many of these utterances are unanalyzed, well-practiced routines picked up as single chunks from adults. R. Clark (1974) observed one child who would copy whole phrases from adult utterances and maintain them intact, with no substitutions of other lexical items in any slot for several weeks. The same child, aged 2:9 to 3:0, also appeared to rely on well-practiced but unanalyzed chunks such as *Baby Ivan have a bath* and *Let's go see,* to form longer utterances, as in:

Baby Ivan have a bath, let's go see + baby Ivan have a bath

I want + I eat a apple

I don't know + where's Emma gone.

The initial routine character of such chunks gradually became apparent as the child later broke them down and analyzed the constituent parts. Johnson (1981) found a similar reliance on routines in children's early questions. A phrase like *what's that,* for example, would be combined with *the dog* to produce a question, *what's that the dog?,* in contexts where the child seemed to be asking "where's the dog?" or "what's the dog doing?." The child's analysis of the internal structure of such forms—the relation of the auxiliary or copula verb to the subject noun phrase, for example—was very slow to emerge.

Much the same goes for children acquiring their second language. Fillmore (1979) reported extensive initial reliance on unanalyzed routines such as *I wanna play, lemme see, let's go, I dunno, it's my turn,* and so on. Early question routines from these children, e.g. *How do you do dese?,* were gradually analyzed and modified over time, first by the addition of noun phrases or prepositional phrases, as in *How do you do dese + little tortillas?* Next, the routine was reduced to *How do you* with different verbs substituted for *do,* as in *How do you make the flower?,* or *How do you gonna make these?* With the addition of further question routines or "frames," the children's analysis of these previously routine chunks led to errors such as lack of inversion not obvious at earlier stages of production (see also Hakuta 1976).

Children's reliance on such ready-made chunks or routine utterances in both first and second language production shows clearly why children's utterances often should not be taken at face value. Apparently perfect utterance forms can result from reliance on routines; they do not necessarily signal that the child has fully appropriate productive control over the structure in question. Assessing the relation between what children produce and what exactly they understand may be difficult, but the point is that there is no evidence in such productions that *appropriate* production is occurring in the absence of comprehension, much less ahead of comprehension.[5]

Comprehension vs Production: A Qualitative or Quantitative Distinction?

Findings like these have led many researchers over the last decade to argue that comprehension and production are necessarily distinct. But are they distinct qualitatively or quantitatively? Bloom and Lahey (1978) have argued for a quantitative difference. Asymmetries between the two processes, they suggested, are analogous to those between perception and production in other domains: for example, in memory, recognition is more extensive than recall because it is harder to retrieve the details needed for the reproduction required in recall (Maccoby & Bee 1965). These differences in memory appear quantitative rather than qualitative in nature: people can recognize more instances of stimuli they've seen than they can list in a recall task. In the comprehension and production of language, however, the differences appear to be qualitative as well. Anisfeld and Tucker (1968), for instance, did not find any general difference in the level of difficulty children had in comprehending versus producing plural endings on nouns. What they did find were different patterns of errors in the two modes, and from that they argued that comprehension and production tasks tap different aspects of children's linguistic knowledge.

[5]Certain rare language disorders, though, appear to provide evidence for production without or ahead of comprehension. Some brain injuries to adults result in what has been called "pure word deafness" in patients with otherwise normal hearing. They appear to understand nothing but are said to produce normal fluent speech (Rubens 1979, Damasio 1981). It is not clear, however, that their speech is or could be fully appropriate. Another rare type of injury results in alexia where patients can write but not read (Geschwind 1972). Among children, such reports are even rarer but see Yamada (1981). These cases are particularly difficult to evaluate because spontaneous (at times inappropriate) productions are compared to performance on comprehension tasks. As Yamada pointed out, comprehension requires a test-taking ability that production does not.

Qualitative differences were also uncovered by de Villiers and de Villiers (1974) in children's uses of word order to mark subject, verb, and object. They wished to characterize children's tacit knowledge of the rule assigning these relations on the basis of word order in English. In different tasks, however, they arrived at different characterizations of what children (aged 2 to 4) knew. Early production was limited in two-word utterances to potential subject-verb, subject-object, or verb-object sequences. However, it is impossible to tell whether these utterances reflect a syntactic rule or not (Bowerman 1973). In comprehension, children at this stage tended to take the first noun phrase as the subject provided it was human or animate. They therefore still seemed to be relying on semantic rather than syntactic factors in interpreting word order. A little later they began to show good comprehension of subject-verb-object sequences even with reversible active sentences (e.g. *the dog chased the boy* vs *the boy chased the dog*). By now they also produced some subject-verb-object sequences, but these tended to observe the semantic constraints observed earlier in comprehension: subjects were human or animate and objects usually inanimate. The ability to make judgments about whether word order was correct or not emerged even later (see also Gleitman et al 1972), as did the ability to make corrections following such judgments.

As de Villiers and de Villiers pointed out, such data do not provide any simple answer to the question of when children acquire the subject-verb-object word order rule in English. Different kinds of performance—comprehension, production, judgments, and corrections—each yield different points of acquisition for the same rule of grammar. De Villiers and de Villiers concluded that one cannot set up a model for the child's linguistic knowledge in which each rule can simply be "checked off" as it is acquired.

Prior to the acquisition of a linguistic rule, children are usually said to rely on heuristics or strategies for comprehending or producing language. But such strategies may often be isomorphic with the adult's "rules," except in that they apply only in one kind of task, in imitation, say, but not in production, or in comprehension but not in elicited judgments of anomaly or grammaticality, instead of in all domains of language use (see Hecht 1983). This raises two questions: What kinds of heuristic strategies do young children use in comprehension compared to production? And, for those strategies that appear isomorphic with the adult's, how can one tell when children have really acquired the adult-like "rules"?

Strategies for Comprehension and Production

Where children either do not understand what someone says to them or lack the appropriate means to make their own intentions known to someone else, they rely on a variety of heuristics or strategies to get by. Strategies for comprehension, predictably, differ from those for production. The differences between them can be related fairly directly to what has to be represented in memory and where the process in question may break down through incomplete knowledge. For comprehension, children need to be able to locate word shapes in a recognition store that allows considerable latitude in the acoustic forms relatable to particular word shapes. Once word shapes have been located, children can then "look up" what they have stored of the word meanings and how these are linked to each other, to conceptual categories, and to generic knowledge about those categories. For production, children have to be able to retrieve words appropriate to their intentions (words with the relevant meanings) together with the articulatory programs they require (directions for pronunciation) and only then try to produce the words in question.

In comprehension, when children either do not have or cannot find the pertinent information in memory for a particular word or expression, they rely on what they know about whatever seems to be being talked about. They take up the properties of particular objects, their usual roles, and the relations that can hold between them in responding to requests or instructions they do not understand. For example, in studies designed to find out when children could understand various locative prepositions in English, Clark (1973, 1983) found that very young children, aged 1:6–2:0, relied on what they knew about containers and supporting surfaces rather than on any understanding of the words *in* and *on*. They put objects in containers and on surfaces regardless of the preposition in the instructions.

Similar reliance on general knowledge—that instigators of actions are typically animate—also guides children's choices of referents for nonsense words presented as the subjects or objects of particular activity verbs (Dewart 1979; see also Bridges 1980). Reliance on the probable relations between adults and babies, for example, allows very young children to give apparently perfect interpetations of passive sentences like *The baby was fed by the girl.* Only the comparison with *The girl was fed by the baby* or *The baby fed the girl* reveals the degree to which 3-year-olds as well as younger children are relying only on their general knowledge rather than knowledge of English word order (Wetstone & Friedlander 1973, Strohner & Nelson 1974, Chapman & Miller 1975). Young children may also rely on their knowledge of the usual routine in particular circumstances to decide how to act, quite independently of what is actually said (cf Bowerman 1978b, Shatz 1978).

As a result of such strategies, children may seem to understand more than they actually do. A particular problem arises when their strategy-based responses are indistinguishable from the responses adults would give—

where the adults' responses are taken to be based on their interpretations of linguistic forms. For example, children aged 2 and under will consistently pick out the uppermost surface of an unmarked object if asked to touch the top (Clark 1980). Initially such responses suggest they already know the meaning of *top*. However, they will select the same surface when asked to touch the bottom, front, or back, as well. And it is only when their responses to *top* and *bottom,* for instance, contrast with each other, with the upper surface being selected for *top* and the lower one for *bottom,* that one can be sure that the children are responding on the basis of some linguistic knowledge rather than general nonlinguistic organizing principles alone (Clark 1980, 1983). To establish that children understand particular lexical items or constructions, then, is often a difficult matter (see also Chapman 1978).

In production, children rely on rather different strategies. Rather than having to infer another's intention, they themselves begin with a particular intention they wish to convey. They then have to find the right words, and with them the relevant articulatory programs (Kiparsky & Menn 1977, Vihman 1981). If they fail to find the right words, they fall back on one of several alternatives. They may go to general purpose forms and, for picking out objects, produce demonstratives like *this* or *that,* or general purpose nouns like *thing.* And for picking out actions, they may produce general purpose verbs like *do* or *go* (Clark 1983). In both instances, children appear to intend a very precise interpretation for each utterance of such general purpose forms, a meaning only computable in the context of the utterance. Another strategy children have recourse to is the production of largely unanalyzed chunks or routines familiar from previous occasions that bear some resemblance to the present one. This results in more advanced-seeming production in some settings than one would otherwise expect (e.g. R. Clark 1974, Fillmore 1979) or inappropriate production of words or longer expressions on some occasions alongside apparently appropriate uses on others (e.g. Bowerman 1976, 1978a).

Just as in comprehension, children's strategies for producing something to convey their intentions may mislead one about how much they really intend of the words and expressions produced. A 2-year-old may produce completely well-formed questions like *Where is the ball?* or *Can I get down?* But an important clue to whether these are simply formulaic is the form of the other questions asked by the same child. The contrasts among all the interrogatives produced by the child are needed in order to assess the status of those productions that seem appropriate (cf Johnson 1981). However, eliciting and recording contrasting forms in production can be even harder than checking up on contrasting forms in comprehension. What appears critical in both cases, to distinguish nonlinguistic strategy from linguistic knowledge, is that the child be able to contrast a range of forms in compre-hension or in production, and that these contrasts correspond to those made by adults.

COORDINATING COMPREHENSION AND PRODUCTION

Everyday uses of language depend on coordinating what we can produce—to express our intentions as speakers—with what we understand as listeners. Without such coordination, we could not make full use of the conventional nature of language—that, for instance, everyone in the speech community agrees that the word *table* picks out instances of the category "table," that an expression like *would you mind if* introduces a polite request, and so on. For a system to be conventional, such tacit agreements have to be observed by speakers and addressees if they are to use the system to communicate. We have suggested that production and comprehension do not come already coordinated. Children may understand words and expres-sions before they come to produce them appropriately, and they may pro-duce many expressions that they only partially understand. One task during acquisition is to coordinate their comprehension and production.

Matching Representations

One means for matching production to comprehension would be to align certain parts of what is represented for each process. For instance, what children recognize when they hear someone say the word *apple* should contain certain elements in common with what they produce when they want to say *apple*. But this alignment takes time. Initially, young children may produce only forms like *ap* or *apu* rather than the adult *apple*. And upon hearing *ap* or *apu,* they will fail to recognize it as *apple*. On the other hand, they can recognize *apple* even when it is said by unfamiliar adults (Smith 1973, Dodd 1975). Similarly, children at the telegraphic stage of combining words are more likely to respond to more adult-like commands, favoring *Throw me the ball* over the child-like *Throw ball* (Shipley et al 1969). This suggests that children initially rely on more adult-like represen-tations of words and phrases in comprehension that are not reflected in production, and that these representations provide a standard to which they will eventually match their own productions of those same linguistic units.

Evidence for children's representations for comprehension being closer to the adult's than those for production comes from several sources. First, it has long been noted in studies of phonological development that children can discriminate contrasts between sounds that they fail to produce.[6] A classic example is that of a child who correctly distinguishes the words *mouth* and *mouse,* showing comprehension of each, but produces the form [maus] for both (e.g. Smith 1973). Or consider what has been called the *fis* phenomenon. Although young children will often fail to pronounce sounds like the *sh* in *fish* or the *r* in *right* correctly, they become very upset if adults imitate the child pronunciation rather than using the usual form. If the adult says *fis,* following the child's production, the child will reject it, accepting only the adult pronunciation, *fish* (see review in Clark & Clark 1977). Children may also be capable of pronouncing the pertinent sounds, but not yet have coordinated their own production of a word with the adult's. For instance, one child who produced *puggle* for adult *puddle* at the same time produced the form *puddle* for adult *puzzle* (see Smith 1973, Macken 1980). Or consider such metalinguistic comments as *I can't say that* (usually a correct judgment) and the triumphant announcement of mastery once the child achieves the appropriate pronunciation—*I can say X!* (see Clark 1978). These data strongly support the conclusion that what children store in memory about the shapes of words is closer to the adult versions they hear than to their own productions.

A second source of support for the same conclusion is children's corrections or repairs of their own speech. Attempts at correcting one's own production could simply result in random adjustments, some getting closer to the adult forms, some departing still further from them. However, when young children repair their own pronunciation, whether spontaneously or upon request, the majority of their repairs go toward the adult pronunciation. Clark (1982) argued that these data supported the view that children relied on a standard for coordinating their production with comprehension, and that the standard was based on what children have represented in memory so as to recognize words and phrases heard from others. These representations for comprehension provide the measure of whether their own productions of words are adequate.

In setting up a standard of comparison, children presumably go through two main steps. First, they must attend to the adult output and identify recurring sequences of sounds for which they have identified potential referents. They can then set up some representation for these in memory so as to be able to recognize the same sequences on other occasions. Any new words or phrases to which children are exposed can be added to their

---

[6]This finding is not, of course, limited to studies of phonology, but we cite such studies because investigators in this domain have long been aware of the discrepancies between comprehension and production and have noted that children are aware of them too (cf Clark 1978).

memory store. (However, the representations children set up will not necessarily match adult ones, at least not initially, because the child may not yet know which phonetic contrasts, for example, are systematic and which accidental.) These representations then guide the children's comprehension on subsequent occasions and provide the loci to which children can add more information about meanings, reference, sound patterns for recognition, and so on. This store of representations for recognition—for identifying forms heard in the input, from whatever speaker—is continually modified and added to.

Second, these representations in memory can then be used for checking up on the children's own productions when they aim at particular targets, trying to pronounce words as they have heard them from others. But producing a word is a very different matter from hearing and recognizing it. Children may have difficulty retrieving the right words from memory, and even more difficulty, at times, once they have the right words, in producing the appropriate articulatory "programs" for each one (e.g. Kiparsky & Menn 1977). Like making tennis strokes, producing words takes practice. Children have to discover what sequences of articulations will result in the appropriate sequence of sounds. They also have to learn which adjustments have to be made as longer and longer sequences are combined within a single utterance. It is here that children rely on their representations for comprehension: they use them as the targets toward which to aim. Because these targets are represented in memory, children are not dependent on having just heard an adult rendition of the words or phrases being attempted. But to use a representation for comprehension as a target—a standard—toward which to aim in production requires that children be able to monitor what they produce, check it against the standard, and then repair it.

Monitoring Production

Evidence that children monitor what they produce comes from their repairs to their own utterances. To make a repair, children have to detect the word or construction that is mismatched to what they intended to produce. They must therefore detect the problem item and check it against their standard in order to effect some repair. Even 1- and 2-year-olds make frequent repairs, both in response to adult requests (typically *What?* or *Hm?*) and on their own. And when they make repairs, the repaired versions of their utterances are consistently closer in form to adult productions than their initial utterances were (e.g. Käsermann & Foppa 1981). Moreover, the elements that get repaired are ones in need of repair. Children do not simply change something at random when they are queried by adults.

This directionality of repair is just as evident in deliberately elicited

repairs—where adults simply said *What?* at regular intervals—as in naturally occurring exchanges (Gallagher 1977, Stokes 1977, Käsermann &
Foppa 1981). These data also provide evidence against the view that children do not monitor what they say but merely remember their immediately
preceding utterances and, in response to adult queries, go back to forms of
language they feel more sure of. This view predicts that the direction of
repair for younger children should be toward earlier forms developmentally
and thus be regressive. The data show such repairs are in fact progressive.
So if children can repair their own productions and do so in the direction
of more adult-like forms, then they must be able to monitor their own
speech.[7]

The directionality of their spontaneous repairs is also toward the adult
norm (Clark 1982). These spontaneous repairs suggest that children actively monitor their own speech during acquisition, at least until it matches
some standard. The standard, we have suggested, is provided by their
representations for comprehension, in memory. Once children can match
their productions of particular words or phrases to this standard, their
monitoring presumably becomes more automatic, although it will still operate—just as it does for adults—to catch slips of the tongue or wrong word
choices. The fact that children initiate repairs to their own utterances offers
even stronger evidence that monitoring their own speech is not a sporadic
affair. They are systematically trying to match their own productions to
whatever standard they have represented in memory for comprehension,
and these attempts to coordinate their production and comprehension go
on even in the absence of communicative problems. This coordination of the
two processes, then, appears to be an integral part of language acquisition.

Coordination in Acquisition

Coordination appears essential to any account of how children change their
language during production. Their utterances, for instance, progress from
simple one-word forms like *ball* or *juice* to longer more elaborate ones like
I want to play with the ball or *Can you give me some juice?* within as little
as two years. Such changes, which sometimes appear unnecessary from a
communicative point of view, have long puzzled researchers in language
acquisition. What motivates children to acquire the conventional forms of
the language used around them? What we suggest is that the mismatch
detectable between what children understand and what they themselves

---

[7]Although this is generally the case, children sometimes appear to go back from more
advanced forms to simpler ones in production as they analyze previously unanalyzed routines
(e.g. Fillmore 1979) and as they come to rely on new organizing principles discovered in the
semantic relations among words and constructions (e.g. Bowerman 1978a,b).

produce during acquisition provides the impetus for such language change (Clark 1982).

To coordinate production with comprehension takes a long time. Any new information added to the representations stored for comprehension—information about systematic contrasts among sounds, among word meanings, or among word combinations—may temporarily widen the gap between comprehension and production. Children trying to coordinate the two must then narrow that gap again by adding the pertinent information to their representations for production. New routines or formulaic utterances added to the representations for production will also contribute to the gap between production and comprehension. But as children begin to analyze the pertinent forms in comprehension and set up representations of the parts and their meanings, they will both adjust their representations for production and coordinate them with those for comprehension. Each step on the road to coordination advances them toward adult-like uses of language, and not only makes for better coordination of children's comprehension with their own production, but for better coordination with other users of the same language.

To summarize, one essential part of acquiring a language is the coordination of what children produce with what they understand. This coordination is effected by matching certain parts of the memory representations children set up for production to what they already have represented for comprehension. What they understand, then, sets the standard for what they are trying to produce. Explicit evidence for such matching comes from children's recognition of mismatches, along with their skill in identifying adult over child productions, and from the repairs they make to their own utterances.

IMPLICATIONS AND CONCLUSIONS

The prevailing view of language acquisition has focused on the product (the language and its grammar) being acquired. But if we focus instead on the processes of comprehension and production, then we need to reexamine earlier assumptions about, for example, the nature of representations for linguistic knowledge that children store in memory, the effects of linguistic input from mature speakers on children's acquisition of language, and how to tell whether children have acquired particular word meanings or syntactic structures. In this section, we will take up each of these topics—three among many—and consider some of the problems raised or resolved by taking a different perspective.

Memory Representations

What do we represent in memory about the language we use every day? During the last two decades, linguists have usually assumed, either tacitly or explicitly, that speakers maintain a single mental store, a mental lexicon, that can be equated with an idealized grammar of the language. This single set of representations includes information about phonological forms and phonetic realizations of words and idioms, semantic information about the word meanings, and syntactic rules for combining linguistic units. This linguistic knowledge is the speaker's competence, in contrast to his performance—actual uses of language with all its attendant slips and errors, false starts, and mistaken interpretations. But such a view emphasizes the product—the forms of the language—divorced from the processes involved in understanding or producing utterances. This view assumes that whatever the processes invoked, they all draw on the same set of representations.

An alternative to this approach is to start from the perspective of the processes people make use of as they understand and produce language. Speakers need different kinds of information for comprehension and production. In comprehension, they need procedures for identifying dialectal, geographic, stylistic, and historical variants of their first language, access to a much larger recognition store of vocabulary than they use on an everyday basis, the pertinent acoustic information for recognizing linguistic elements, the connections each item (word, idiom, or phrase) has to other linguistic units, and the connections each has to their nonlinguistic knowledge, both generic and specific, about categories of objects, situations, and relations.

In production, speakers need procedures for retrieving words and larger units with meanings appropriate to the speaker's intentions, procedures for combining words and larger units so as to express the desired meanings, and the necessary articulatory programs for pronouncing the resultant utterances (Clark & Clark 1977). These asymmetries in the information needed for comprehension versus production hold for all speakers, but we know very little about how children learn these processing procedures or about how they store linguistic information in memory. Earlier approaches focused on the product—the language as distinct from its users—and ignored most processing considerations, including the differences between comprehension and production.

Focusing on processes in comprehension and production leads to rather different assumptions about how language might be represented in memory. For example, it seems plausible that speakers might draw on at least two sets of memory representations, one for understanding language and one for producing it. Such an assumption would account quite neatly for the discrepancies between comprehension and production in both children and adults. As we have seen, children commonly understand more than they produce during the early stages of acquisition, and they may understand forms of language in the absence of any production. The same holds for adults. They too can understand a larger range of forms and a more extensive vocabulary than they can produce, though this may not be as obvious for their first language as it is for other languages acquired later.

One important argument in earlier discussions for postulating a single set of representations was parsimony. Why have two sets of representations where some of the information will be duplicated and hence redundant? However, what may be parsimonious for descriptions of the product of some process—here, the grammar of a language—may not be parsimonious for an account of processing. Given the enormous amount of information, linguistic and otherwise, we store in memory, there seems to be no a priori reason to assume that we are constrained to make use of only one set of representations for linguistic information. Parsimony, in terms of fewer elements to be represented, does not appear characteristic of human memory (e.g. MacKay 1976, Bolinger 1976, Lukatela et al 1980), so there seems to be little reason to assume it in models of processing.

In principle, of course, one cannot rule out the existence of a more abstract, single set of representations analogous to the kind of linguistic competence postulated by Chomsky (1965, 1976). However, in a processing model with representations in memory for comprehension and for production, an additional, more abstract set of representations combining all such information would appear both redundant and unparsimonious.

In short, greater emphasis on processing may lead us to different theories about how children (and adults) store information about their language, and also about the procedures whereby they make use of that information, both as speakers and as listeners. This approach, we suggest, will also lead to different theories about language acquisition itself. By way of illustration, we will briefly consider one area of research where the contrast between comprehension and production has been ignored, namely in studies of input. Ignoring process in this domain has lead researchers to make certain assumptions that oversimplify what has to be accounted for.

Language Input and Language Acquisition

What relation does language input—the language children hear addressed to them—have to children's acquisition? This question has motivated a large number of studies over the last decade or so (e.g. Snow & Ferguson 1977). In all these studies, researchers have assumed something like the following: adults expose children to particular structures; so to assess the effects of particular inputs, one waits to see when the child in his turn produces those same structures. This "input-becomes-output" class of models, however, appears too simple once one takes into account what children must represent for comprehension compared to what they represent for production.

The initial discrepancies between comprehension and production make the effects of adult input difficult to assess directly. Children may observe and store forms for comprehension for a long time before attempting to produce them, or they may try to produce them almost immediately after hearing them. Up to now, the effects of input have been assessed only by looking at when children begin to *produce* particular forms. But a better measure of the effects of input might be what children understand. Furthermore, any effects of input will probably also depend on which systems or subsystems children are actively monitoring at that moment (Clark 1982). For instance, pronoun forms will be of little immediate use to a child not working on pronouns. And it is not clear that all children work on the same systems in the same sequence during acquisition. These factors make the precise relation between adult input and child mastery more difficult to analyze.

What is needed is some principled account of how children make use of information from input and what determines their attention to some subsystems over others at the same stage of development. This will require much more careful analysis of what might count as pertinent information from input, given the state of the child's system both in production and in comprehension (e.g. see Cross 1977). Input studies to date, however, have focused almost entirely on what children produce, and not on what children understand. Yet input necessarily has its most immediate effects on comprehension rather than production.

Assessing Acquisition

Word meanings and syntactic structures carry with them a whole network of interrelated forms and uses, connections to other segments of the language. Languages are complex systems "òu tout se tient." But many, or even most, of these interconnections take a long time to build up, so that many tests of acquisition are actually only tests of part of the knowledge taken for granted in adult speakers. Researchers tend to look only at comprehension or production of core meanings without regard to the many extensions known to adults.

To assess acquisition, therefore, we need to take into account the degree of coordination between comprehension and production, as well as the gradual nature of the acquisition process itself. First, if comprehension and production are only partially coordinated for a particular domain, one would expect children's performances to differ in tasks tapping one or the other kind of knowledge about language. Indeed, the issue of what has been acquired becomes less of an issue once we accept that mastery is attained at different points for different kinds of processing. With this perspective, differences are assumed rather than regarded as problems to be explained away. Because production and comprehension are only partially coordinated, and because acquisition is gradual, children may find some kinds of tasks easier than others, so that their performance may match the adult's in some places only. As children get older and have their production and comprehension better coordinated, such differences among tasks will become harder to detect.

While children are still acquiring particular constructions and meanings, they usually start by understanding and using forms in very limited domains. They may show some comprehension in one task but not in another, or produce the appropriate descriptions on one occasion but not on another (Hecht 1983). Children have to build up information about the range of uses possible and the different domains in which particular forms contrast. Different tasks may also lend themselves in differing degrees to children's relying on nonlinguistic rather than linguistic knowledge (e.g. Clark 1980), or on routine productions of utterances rather than on forms intended and designed for that occasion.

Language acquisition takes place gradually. Only by taking account of how children build up their representations in memory for comprehension and production can we gauge the differences between the processes of comprehension and production and study their coordination. All too many studies of acquisition assume that comprehension or production of single instances of a construction or a word meaning show that the child has acquired that form and could therefore understand or produce it in other settings. However, there is more and more evidence that learning a language looks rather like accretion of instances to small paradigms rather than global inferences based on single exemplars (e.g. Bybee & Slobin 1982).

In conclusion, we have suggested that theories of acquisition would profit from a perspective that takes account of the differences between the different demands made by comprehension and production. The study of what is acquired in language acquisition, we have argued, requires consideration of more than just the language used, it requires consideration of the novice language *user*. But to take account of language users, one needs to focus on processes as well as products. A focus on process illuminates such phenomena as discrepancies in performance from one task to another, different points of acquisition as assessed in comprehension versus production, and so on. It also complicates theories about such phenomena as the relation of adult input to child acquisition. Most crucial, though, is that such a perspective appears essential if we are to get at the many factors that play a role in the actual process of acquiring a language.

ACKNOWLEDGMENTS

Preparation of this chapter was supported in part by the National Science Foundation (BNS80-07349) and in part by the Spencer Foundation. We are grateful to Kathie Carpenter, Herbert H. Clark, Sophia Cohen, and Susan A. Gelman for many discussions and for helpful comments on earlier drafts.

Literature Cited

Anisfeld, M., Tucker, G. R. 1968. English pluralization rules of six-year-old children. *Child Dev.* 28:1201–17

Baird, R. 1972. On the role of chance in imitation-comprehension-production test results. *J. Verb. Learn. Verb. Behav.* 11:474–77

Berko, J. 1958. The child's learning of English morphology. *Word* 14:150–77

Bloom, L., Hood, L., Lightbown, P. 1974. Imitation in language development: If, when and why. *Cogn. Psychol.* 6:380–420

Bloom, L., Lahey, M. 1978. *Language Development and Language Disorders.* New York: Wiley

Bolinger, D. L. 1976. Meaning and memory. *Forum Linguist.* 1:1–14

Bowerman, M. 1973. Structural relationships in children's utterances: Syntactic or semantic? In *Cognitive Development and the Acquisition of Language,* ed. T. E. Moore, pp. 197–213. New York: Academic

Bowerman, M. 1976. Semantic factors in the acquisition of rules for word use and sentence construction. In *Normal and Deficient Child Language,* ed. D. M. Morehead, A. E. Morehead, pp. 99–179. Baltimore: Univ. Park Press

Bowerman, M. 1978a. Systematizing semantic knowledge: Changes over time in the child's organization of word meaning. *Child Dev.* 49:977–87

Bowerman, M. 1978b. Words and sentences: Uniformity, individual variation, and shifts over time in patterns of acquisition. In *Communicative and Cognitive Abilities—Early Behavioral Assessment,* ed. F. D. Minifie, L. L. Lloyd, pp. 349–96. Baltimore: Univ. Park Press

Bridges, A. 1980. SVO comprehension strategies reconsidered: The evidence of individual patterns of response. *J. Child Lang.* 7:89–104

Bybee, J., Slobin, D. I. 1982. Rules and schemas in the development and use of the English past tense. *Language* 58:265–89

Chapman, R. S. 1978. Comprehension strategies in children: A discussion of Bransford and Nitsch's paper. In *Speech and Language in the Laboratory, School, and Clinic,* ed. J. Kavanaugh, W. Strange, pp. 308–27. Cambridge, Mass: MIT Press

Chapman, R. S., Miller, J. 1975. Word order in early two and three word utterances: Does production precede comprehension? *J. Speech Hear. Res.* 18:355–71

Chomsky, N. 1965. *Aspects of the Theory of Syntax.* Cambridge, Mass: MIT Press

Chomsky, N. 1976. *Reflections on Language.* New York: Random House

Clark, E. V. 1973. Non-linguistic strategies and the acquisition of word meanings. *Cognition* 2:161–82

Clark, E. V. 1978. Awareness of language: Evidence from what children say and do. In *The Child's Conception of Language,* ed. A. Sinclair, R. Jarvella, W. J. M. Levelt, pp. 17–43. New York: Springer

Clark, E. V. 1980. Here's the *top*: Nonlinguistic strategies in the acquisition of orientational terms. *Child Dev.* 51:329–38

Clark, E. V. 1982. Language change during language acquisition. In *Advances in Child Development,* ed. M. E. Lamb, A. L. Brown, 2:173–97. Hillsdale, NJ: Erlbaum

Clark, E. V. 1983. Meanings and concepts. In *Carmichael's Manual of Child Psychology,* Vol. 3: *Cognitive Development,* ed. J. H. Flavell, E. M. Markman; gen. ed., P. H. Mussen. New York: Wiley

Clark, E. V., Hecht, B. F. 1982. Learning to coin agent and instrument nouns. *Cognition* 12:1–24

Clark, H. H., Clark, E. V. 1977. *Psychology and Language.* New York: Harcourt Brace Jovanovich

Clark, R. 1974. Performing without competence. *J. Child Lang.* 1:1–10

Cross, T. G. 1977. Mothers' speech adjustments: The contribution of selected child-listener variables. In *Talking to Children: Language Input and Acquisition,* ed. C. E. Snow, C. A. Ferguson, pp. 151–88. Cambridge: Cambridge Univ. Press

Damasio, A. 1981. The nature of aphasia: Signs and syndromes. In *Acquired Aphasia,* ed. M. Taylor Sarno, pp. 51–65. New York: Academic

de Villiers, J. G., de Villiers, P. A. 1974. Competence and performance in child language: Are children really competent to judge? *J. Child Lang.* 1:11–22

Dewart, M. H. 1979. Children's hypotheses about the animacy of subject and object nouns. *Br. J. Psychol.* 70:525–30

Dodd, B. 1975. Children's understanding of their own phonological forms. *Q. J. Exp. Psychol.* 27:165–72

Fernald, C. D. 1972. Control of grammar in imitation, comprehension, and production: Problems of replication. *J. Verb. Learn. Verb. Behav.* 11:606–13

Fillmore, L. W. 1979. Individual differences in second language acquisition. In *Individual Differences in Language Behavior and Language Ability,* ed. C. J. Fillmore, D. Kempler, W. S.-Y. Wang, pp. 203–28. New York: Academic

Fourcin, A. J. 1975. Language development in the absence of expressive speech. In *Foundations of Language Development,* ed. E. H. Lenneberg, E. Lenneberg, pp. 263–68. New York: Academic

Fraser, C., Bellugi, U., Brown, R. 1963. Control of grammar in imitation, comprehension, and production. *J. Verb. Learn. Verb. Behav.* 7:121–35

Gallagher, T. 1977. Revision behaviors in the speech of normal children developing language. *J. Speech Hear. Res.* 20:303–18

Geschwind, N. 1972. Language and the brain. *Sci. Am.* 226:76–83

Gleitman, L. R., Gleitman, H., Shipley, E. F. 1972. The emergence of the child as grammarian. *Cognition* 1:137–64

Goldin-Meadow, S., Seligman, M. E. P., Gelman, R. 1976. Language in the two-year-old. *Cognition* 4:189–202

Hakuta, K. 1976. A case study of a Japanese child learning English as a second language. *Lang. Learn.* 26:321–51

Hecht, B. F. 1983. *Discrepancies in children's use of the English plural: A study of partial knowledge.* PhD thesis. Stanford Univ., Stanford, Calif.

Huttenlocher, J. 1974. The origins of language comprehension. In *Theories in Cognitive Psychology,* ed. R. L. Solso, pp. 331–68. Potomac, Md: Erlbaum

Ingram, D. 1974. The relationship between comprehension and production. In *Language Perspectives—Acquisition, Retardation, and Intervention,* ed. R. L. Schiefelbusch, L. L. Lloyd, pp. 313–34. Baltimore: Univ. Park Press

Johnson, C. E. 1981. *Children's questions and the discovery of interrogative syntax.* PhD thesis. Stanford Univ., Stanford, Calif.

Karmiloff-Smith, A. 1977. More about the same: Children's understanding of postarticles. *J. Child Lang.* 4:377–94

Käsermann, M. L., Foppa, K. 1981. Some determinants of self-correction. In *The Child's Construction of Language,* ed. W. Deutsch, pp. 77–104. London: Academic

Keeney, T. J., Wolfe, J. 1972. The acquisition of agreement in English. *J. Verb. Learn. Verb. Behav.* 11:698–705

Kiparsky, P., Menn, L. 1977. On the acquisition of phonology. In *Language Learning and Thought,* ed. J. Macnamara, pp. 47–78. New York: Academic

Lenneberg, E. H. 1962. Understanding language without the ability to speak: A case report. *J. Abnorm. Soc. Psychol.* 65:419–25

Lovell, K., Dixon, E. M. 1967. The growth of the control of grammar in imitation, production, and comprehension. *J. Child Psychol. Psychiatry* 8:31–39

Lukatela, G., Gligorijević, B., Kostić, A., Turvey, M. T. 1980. Representation of inflected nouns in the internal lexicon. *Mem. Cognit.* 8:415–23

Maccoby, E. E., Bee, H. 1965. Some speculations concerning the lag between perceiving and performing. *Child Dev.* 36:367–77

MacKay, D. G. 1976. On the retrieval and lexical structure of verbs. *J. Verb. Learn. Verb. Behav.* 15:169–82

Macken, M. A. 1980. The child's lexical representation: the 'puzzle-puddle-pickle' evidence. *J. Ling.* 16:1–17

Moore, K. C. 1896. The mental development of a child. *Psychol. Rev. Monogr. Suppl.* 1(3)

Rescorla, L. 1980. Overextension in early language development. *J. Child Lang.* 7:321–35

Rubens, A. B. 1979. Agnosia. In *Clinical Neuropsychology,* ed. K. M. Heilman, E. Valenstein, pp. 233–67. Oxford: Oxford Univ. Press

Shatz, J. 1978. On the development of communicative understandings: An early strategy for interpreting and responding to messages. *Cogn. Psychol.* 10:271–301

Shipley, E. F., Smith, C. S., Gleitman, L. R. 1969. A study in the acquisition of language: Free responses to commands. *Language* 45:322–42

Slobin, D. I., Welsh, C. A. 1973. Elicited imitation as a research tool in developmental psycholinguistics. In *Studies of Child Language Development*, ed. C. A. Ferguson, D. I. Slobin, pp. 485–97. New York: Holt, Rinehart & Winston

Smith, N. V. 1973. *The Acquisition of Phonology: A Case Study.* Cambridge: Cambridge Univ. Press

Snow, C. E., Ferguson, C. A., eds. 1977. *Talking to Children: Language Input and Acquisition.* Cambridge: Cambridge Univ. Press

Stokes, W. T. 1977. *Motivation and language development: The struggle towards communication.* Presented at Bien. Meet. Soc. Res. Child Dev., New Orleans

Strohner, H., Nelson, K. E. 1974. The young child's development of sentence comprehension: Influence of event probability, nonverbal context, syntactic form, and strategies. *Child Dev.* 45:567–76

Thomson, J. R., Chapman, R. S. 1977. Who is 'Daddy' revisited: The status of two-year-olds' over-extended words in use and comprehension. *J. Child Lang.* 4:359–75

Vihman, M. M. 1981. Phonology and the development of the lexicon: Evidence from children's errors. *J. Child Lang.* 8:239–64

Wetstone, H., Friedlander, B. Z. 1973. The effect of word order on young children's responses to simple questions and commands. *Child Dev.* 44:734–40

Winitz, H., Sanders, R., Kort, J. 1981. Comprehension and production of the /-əz/ plural allomorph. *J. Psycholing. Res.* 10:259–71

Yamada, J. 1981. Evidence for the independence of language and cognition: Case study of a "hyperlinguistic" adolescent. *UCLA Work. Pap. Cogn. Ling.* 3:121–60

Ann. Rev. Psychol. 1983. 34:351–62

ANIMAL COGNITION

David Premack

Department of Psychology, University of Pennsylvania, Philadelphia,
Pennsylvania 19104

CONTENTS

This is a highly selective review of the literature centering around three main topics: social cognition, identity, and imaginal vs abstract representation.

SOCIAL COGNITION

What does one individual know about another individual? How is the information obtained, how is it represented, and what kinds of computations can be made on the representation? Despite the patent significance of social cognition—most species with which psychologists work are ones for which these questions are germane for they are species in which there is recognition at the level of the individual—work of this kind has only begun. A quick way to appreciate the importance of this factor is to turn first to humans where social cognition is highly developed, and then determine which of the capacities and practices found in humans are found in other species.

Humans have vast stores of information about one another. In addition, they attribute at least two kinds of states to others; short-term states—the propositional attitudes such as intention, belief, desire, that are attributed on the basis of the individual's immediate behavior; and long-term states—traits such as honesty, greed, generosity, that require samples of the individual's behavior over some period of time. Exactly how humans arrive at these

351

attributions (and whether they are justified) is contentious and forms an active part of social psychology. Nevertheless, there is not the slightest doubt that humans make such attributions and use them throughout daily life.

What kinds of information do nonhuman species store about one another, and do they too attribute states? Kummer, Cheney, and Seyfarth, Premack and his colleagues, among others, have begun to address questions of this general kind. Kummer, Cheney, and Seyfarth combine field and laboratory techniques. For example, Cheney and Seyfarth record calls of wild vervet monkeys and then observe the behavior of individual monkeys when the calls are played back to them in the field. Two examples will give the idea of the technique and of the kind of information that has been obtained so far (Cheney & Seyfarth 1980, Seyfarth & Cheney 1981). When a vervet hears the calls of another individual, it responds with only routine interest provided the call comes from the area in which it recently observed the individual; but it shows visible surprise if the call comes from a different area. Evidently, one of the things a vervet knows about his conspecific is its location in the field. In another study, the distress calls of different vervet infants were played back to a group of monkeys. Many of the listeners immediately directed their attention to the mother of the infant whose call was heard. Evidently, the vervet can identify the mother of an infant merely from its distress call.

Kummer, who has been a long-time student of the social structure of primate groups (Kummer 1971), has recently begun to ask what the baboon itself may know about the social structure of its group and what use it could make of this information (Kummer 1982). Consider the linear dominance orders characteristic of many social groups including that of the hamadryas baboon. When a new baboon is introduced into a group, must it fight with each member in order to find its position in the group, or are there shortcuts it could take that would lessen the risk to itself? If the new individual combined observational learning with transitive inference, it could appreciably reduce the number of contests in which it engaged. For example, an individual who had found by painful trial that B was stronger than itself, and had observed that A was stronger than B, could by using transitive inference stay clear of A. Many species can benefit from observational learning; in addition, nonhuman primates can apparently engage in transitive inference [shown in monkeys by McGonigle & Chalmers (1977) and confirmed more recently for chimpanzees by Gillan (1981)]. Both demonstrations of transitive inference concern magnitude of food, not strength of aggressors. But the animal's success on the one dimension encourages studying its facility on other dimensions.

Premack and his colleagues, concerned with the short-term states humans attribute to one another, have asked: "What is the minimal evidence that would warrant attributing similar attributions to nonhuman animals?" Children and chimpanzees are shown videotapes depicting human actors confronting problems of various kinds, e.g. trying to reach inaccessible food, to escape a locked cage, to cope with malfunctioning equipment. The terminal image showing the actor in the throes of a problem is put on hold and the subject is given still photographs, one of which constitutes a solution to the problem. Children of about 4 years of age and the language-trained adult chimpanzee Sarah consistently chose the correct photograph on the first trial (Premack & Woodruff 1978, Premack & Premack 1982).

Performance of this kind is taken as evidence for attribution because, in essence, the videotapes do not depict problems but merely a sequence of events. For example, in one of the videotapes the actor is seen jumping up and down below a bunch of bananas. This series of events does not become a problem unless one attributes intention to the actor. Not until the actor is seen as trying to reach the bananas does it become sensible to choose a photograph of the actor stepping onto a chair—as did both Sarah and 4-year-old children when shown this videotape. About 50% of 3-year-old children, in contrast, did not choose either this photograph or any others that constituted solutions. They chose instead photographs of objects physically matching some object in the videotape. Many children at this age evidently do not interpret the videotapes and thus do not perceive a problem. They perceive instead a sequence of events.

Although Sarah passed tests of the above kind, she failed when additional demands were made. For example, she failed to choose different solutions for a young child and an older one, a child and an adult, a person and a chimpanzee, distinctions that children about 4½ years of age draw when tested as Sarah was. In addition, Sarah failed to distinguish between guessing and knowing.

After being shown videotapes in which, on some trials, the actor closely watched which of four containers was baited (and on other trials did not watch at all), Sarah was then given photographs showing the actor choose either the container that was baited on that trial or one that was not baited. Her choices were not determined by whether or not the actor had observed the baiting, and hence would know or could only guess. They were determined instead by her attitude toward the actor who appeared on the videotape. If she liked him, she chose primarily photographs showing him select the container baited on that trial; if she disliked him, the container that was not baited on that trial. This is an interesting outcome, but not one that tells us anything about her ability to distinguish guessing from knowing. Finally, although the chimpanzee may attribute intention to the other one, whether it proceeds beyond and attributes not only intention but attribution itself remains in doubt. In short, we have no evidence that Sarah thinks we think she has intention, the second-order attribution that is highly characteristic of humans.

SAME/DIFFERENT

The study of identity—the conditions under which different species react differentially to items that humans consider to be same or different—has been heating up in recent years. As a new field, it is somewhat casual with its distinctions and runs the risk of bogging down in confusion.

Consider a basic difference between two possible meanings of same. This is exemplified by the difference between presenting the same item on two different occasions and presenting two tokens of one type on the same occasion: for example, $apple_1$ presented at t_1 and t_2; $apple_1$ and $apple_2$ presented at t_1 (the two apples being as much alike physically as possible). The animal literature largely conflates the two cases, calling them both same/different. This would be less unacceptable, even given the clear procedural difference, if the two tasks were of equal difficulty. But they are not —the successive task is far easier than the simultaneous one. It is, I suspect, because (at least as it is carried out by most nonhuman species) the successive task has relatively little to do with same/different. The animal simply reacts to whether or not it has experienced the item before. Old/new or familiar/unfamiliar would be better tags for this case than same/different.

The simultaneous task is one very few individuals can do: in my laboratory only children and three of ten chimpanzees have done it. The three successful apes have in common exposure to language training. Although this training does not instill human language, it appears to enhance the animal's ability to solve certain problems, specifically those that depend on abstract representation (e.g. Premack 1980, 1982, Woodruff & Premack 1981).

In the match-to-sample procedure—the most common approach to the study of identity in nonhuman animals—the subject is presented with one sample and two or more alternatives and is required to select the alternative(s) most like the sample. In the simultaneous same/different procedure, the subject is presented with two items that either are or are not alike, and is required to apply the plastic words "same" to the one case and "different" to the others. One would suppose that when an animal can do the former (not only for training items but for all possible ones), it could easily graduate to the latter, and that in fact both procedures measure essentially the same competence. But this is not the case. Monkeys and apes that readily do generalized match to sample (and pass the successive test) fail the simultaneous task unless given either the language training or a heroic number of training trials.

A true same/different judgment is more complex than may meet the eye. When an individual calls two apples same, two elephants same, two toads same, etc, he is judging that the relation between the apples (same$_1$) is the same as that between the elephants (same$_2$) and that both of these relations are the same as that between the toads (same$_3$). Judging relations between relations is more complex than discriminating between items that have and have not been experienced before or reacting to items on the basis of their physical similarity.

Reacting to items on the basis of their physical similarity is what pigeons appear to do when trained on match-to-sample. A long-standing controversy in the pigeon's learning of match-to-sample and oddity concerned whether the bird solved these problems simply by forming standard associations, e.g. after observing red, peck red (matching), after observing red, peck green (oddity), as Skinner (1950) had proposed and Carter & Werner (1978) revived, or by reacting to the similarity relations between the sample and alternatives. A nice study by Zentall and associates (1981) showed that the pigeon makes use of the similarity relations. This is not a surprise, for Honig (1965)—in what may still be the only application of the simultaneous procedure to nonprimates—successfully trained pigeons to respond differentially to pairs of like and unlike colors. As is usual in the traditional dichotomous controversy—associations vs similarity—the nonexclusive alternative is overlooked, namely, that pigeons use similarity and also learn to approach (and avoid) absolute stimulus values with which reward is (or is not) associated. Responding to the similarity between pairs of items and learning to approach the absolute values of the items that make up the pairs are not logically incompatible; in fact, there are suggestions that pigeons do both (Premack 1978), as there is evidence (Lawrence & DeRivera 1954) that rats respond both to a brightness relation and to the absolute values of the stimuli that instantiate the relation.

The pigeon's poor record on generalized match-to-sample may be due more to experimental artifacts than to limitations in intelligence. If, as seems clear, pigeons like other species learn not only to respond to the similarity between pairs of items but also to approach the absolute values of the items that make up the pairs, then transfer tests must not put familiar alternatives into competition with novel ones. This combination of alternatives will seriously underestimate the animal's ability to do generalized matching, as can be shown even in apes. After juvenile chimpanzees had done generalized match-to-sample with toys (and were therefore responding to similarity), Woodruff interpolated trials on which the samples consisted of highly familiar plants. On all such trials, the animals erroneously chose toys (Premack 1978). To explain these results, we must assume that while learning to choose the alternative that matched the sample, the animal also learned to choose toys, i.e. a class of items with certain properties. Learning does not take place only on the relational (or absolute) level but on both levels. If apes and pigeons differ in this regard, it may be in the relative weights the two species assign the factors; the relational factor being weighted more heavily in the ape. If humans and apes differ in this regard, it may be in the human's ability to decide voluntarily to concentrate on one factor or the other, e.g. to remember categories while ignoring members or vice versa. Although apes learn on both levels, I have not been able to gain conditional control of the two levels and thus, in effect, instruct the ape: "Pay attention to the relations" or "Pay attention to the details." Humans cannot only be instructed by others in this manner but can also instruct themselves.

On the basis of a composite response-selection decision-process model of pigeon matching behavior, Wright & Sands (1982) are also led to conclude that pigeons may be able to do more generalized matching than they have. These writers put the emphasis on the matching criterion the bird uses. Having found the difficulty of the discrimination to affect the number of VTEs the pigeon makes before choosing an alternative, they argue that the strictness of the bird's matching criterion can be affected by payoff and switching effort. I hope this interesting prediction will not go untested.

In view of the wide use that match-to-sample has come to have in the study of identity, it may be well to consider a potential weakness of the procedure. In studying identity, the experimenter wishes the subject to answer questions such as these: 1. Do these items look (sound, smell, etc) alike? 2. Do these items belong to the same class? 3. Do these items instantiate the same relation? In particular, the experimenter does not want to be in the position of assuming that his subject's response constitutes answers to the above questions when in fact they constitute an answer to a much simpler and in any case different question, that is: Is this an item you have seen before? The match-to-sample procedure, however, is readily subject to being used essentially as what I earlier called the "successive procedure." After looking at the sample and choosing the matching alternative, the subject may not choose the item that is the same as the sample—in any of the three senses of same described above—but simply the item that it has seen before or seen most recently. The point is not that this is not a worthwhile question, but that one needs to be clear on what question is being answered.

One way around this problem is to construct the match-to-sample test of pairs of items rather than of single items. Let AA be the sample with BB and CD the alternatives; as well as CD the sample, with EE and GH the alternatives. In matching BB to AA, and GH to CD, the animal must be matching the items that are the same in one of the several senses of same, and not simply selecting the item it has seen most recently. The language-trained chimpanzee Sarah passed problems of this kind, though the nonlanguage-trained chimpanzees did not (Premack 1982).

Judgment of the relation between relations, which is an implicit requirement of the same/different judgment, is made explicit by the analogy. In an analogy, the individual is given two pairs of items arranged in a specific pattern, e.g. A/A' and B/B', and is required to judge whether the relation between them is same or different. Or the animal can be given an incomplete analogy, e.g. A/A' same B/?, and required to complete the analogy by choosing among alternatives. Gillan, Premack & Woodruff (1981) showed that the language-trained chimpanzee Sarah was capable of doing analogies in both formats. In a sense, this is no surprise; animals that can make same/different judgments should be able to do analogies. Rewriting the same/different judgment shows that it is itself an analogy, e.g. $apple_1/apple_2$ same $elephant_1/elephant_2$; one that differs from the standard analogy only in being restricted to the relations of sameness and difference. The standard analogy, in contrast, is not so restricted and can concern any relation. For instance, some of the more interesting relations in the analogies Sarah passed were the functional ones of opening and marking: can opener/can same key/lock; paintbrush/painted surface same pencil/marked paper.

ABSTRACT VS IMAGINAL REPRESENTATION

Although it is nearly 20 years since pigeons were found to form so-called natural concepts (Herrnstein & Loveland 1964), how they do so is still shrouded in mystery. Progress has been slight because the formation of concepts in the pigeon is part of the general field of concept formation, and how any species forms concepts or, indeed, what is a concept, is largely unknown. Some informal consensus exists on some broad issues, but one finds little more than that. 1. Although the perception and representation of every species is constructed from a set of primitives, there are no theories suggesting what these primitives may be, nor, as a result, any sensible (nonheroic) research strategies for finding them. 2. Primitives are combined in some fashion to form larger units; but what the combinatorial rules are (and what exactly a larger unit is) remains unclear. For instance, is object a "larger unit" or itself a kind of primitive; and, on either view, which species perceive and represent objects? 3. Perceptual transformations assure recognition of the same item under changes in size, perspective, and the like; but the conditions under which the transformations operate, the relations among them, which species have which of them, are largely unknown. It is against this background of ignorance that the lack of progress in pigeon concept formation must be understood.

Recent work has increased the number of positive cases (e.g. Herrnstein 1979), though it is not clear what is shown by the new cases that was not shown by the original ones. A serious contrast between concepts the pigeon can and cannot form—which we still lack—could be helpful, though only if it led to systematic differences, such as showing that the primitives the bird used with natural items were inapplicable to artifacts. If simply more positive cases, or even a contrast between positive and negative ones, is not what is needed, what would be helpful?

It may be profitable to deal systematically with the recurrent claim that the pigeon cannot form the concepts from simple features but must use classification rules, perhaps like those that underlie family resemblance. This requires that someone describe classification rules, generate stimuli according to such rules, and then test the bird's ability to form concepts over the generated items. Admitting that there is no end of possible rules, and no criteria for choosing among them, could provide the following benefits: chasten promissory talk about classification rules, actually lead to the discovery of some workable rules, or guide inquiry into other quarters.

An additional frustration with this area is the inability of the reader—who is shown only a few of the test photographs—to judge for himself the author's claim that the concepts could not be formed on the basis of "simple features." I have never found this claim entirely convincing. Consider two objections to the claim. First, pigeons have never been shown to have functional classes—furniture, toys, candy, sports equipment—where class members do not look alike; they only recognize physical classes—trees, humans, birds—where class members do look alike. It is somewhat irrelevant that there are countless humans (or trees, birds, etc)—they all look alike. Second, as to whether simple features could comprise the invariances that underly classification of humans, trees, etc depends, of course, on what counts as "simple." Strictly as an example, consider defining tree on the basis of two "simple features": a trunklike vertical and a leafy horizontal combined in a specified way. Then a trunk with a horizontal composed of newspapers would fail, as would a metal girder with a leafy horizontal. (If the bird accepts leafless trees, we might add the alternative of a trunk plus one or more horizontal "trunks".) In the event "trunk" and "leaves" happened to work, it would be important to know whether these features were primitive or, as seems more likely, could be further decomposed. The problem is not necessarily that simple features will not work, but that too many "simple features" could work, and until some of the possibilities are tested, we could not hope to find them. In addition to the intrinsic defining features, there are extrinsic factors such as background or context. The fact that

Charlie Brown, the cartoon character, posed a more difficult discrimination for the pigeon than an actual person (Cerella 1977) *could* mean that background is important. The bird's discrimination of Charlie Brown might improve if he were presented on a natural background, and/or its discrimination of tree suffer if the photograph around the tree were blotted out. Also, if the tree were inverted or positioned unnaturally in the photograph, e.g. growing from the sky, this could tell us something about both the effect of context and the bird's perceptual transformations. Incidentally, it is not entirely proper to credit the bird with concepts such as human, tree, etc when the only comparisons the bird is given are human vs the absence of human, tree vs the absence of trees, etc. The bird should also be compared on human vs say, ape or scarecrow, as well as "deviant" human (infant, paraplegic, obese person) vs absence of human. Before crediting the bird with human, we need to know something about its false positives and negatives.

Epstein, Lanza & Skinner (1980) have, meantime, been trying to slay mind. The fact that the outcome is somewhat predictable does not deny the project all saving grace. The basic approach has been to find performances in apes or monkeys that are recommended as proofs of mind and then demonstrate the same performance in the pigeon. Although this could backfire (and be taken as showing mind in the pigeon), there is, in fact, a mitigating simplicity in all the performances, and the opposite conclusion is drawn: what need is there for mind when there are contingencies and reinforcement? The project would be silly, as much of the discussion is, were it not for some beneficial side effects.

We are reminded that the original would-be demonstrations of complex cognitive processes leave a good deal to be desired. For example, Savage-Rumbaugh, Rumbaugh & Boysen (1978) claimed to have shown "intentional symbolic communication" in apes. Basically, however, they did nothing more than is represented in the following fictitious example. An ape in North Dakota is trained to press key Y when shown item h, and a second ape in Guam is trained to press key L when shown Y. Both apes are then flown to the south of France, their cages are pressed together, and the Dakota ape is shown h. It promptly presses Y, leading the Guam ape to press key L. Voila: intentional symbolic communication. It did not take long for Epstein et al (1980) to duplicate the outcome with pigeons. We are led to conclude that "intentional symbolic processes" are no more than a combination of contingencies and reinforcement, or that the original demonstration was a far from perfect exemplification of what is meant by "intentional symbolic processes."

Epstein et al (1981) have managed to slay the concept of self along with the communicating apes. Pigeons they find respond appropriately to their mirror images as do chimpanzees (Gallup 1970). Curiously, however, the monkey does not. Does this demonstrate then that pigeons and chimpanzees show evidence for the concept of self, whereas the monkey's failure is based on cognitive frailty? No. More likely it is based on gaze aversion. While apes and humans like to be looked at (humans of some cultures consider it an honor), monkeys resent it and thus respond aggressively to the image they see in the mirror. This demonstration underscores the risk of defining concepts—especially ones as complex as "self"—on the basis of a single measure rather than a convergence of several measures. The present case is more interesting, since it demonstrated the ability of the pigeon to respond to mirror images but provided no comment on the unexpected capacity and why the pigeon might possess it.

The elegant work by Church, Gibbon, and Roberts (Church 1978, Gibbon & Church 1981, Roberts 1982), showing discrimination of time in rats, could, if viewed properly, contribute to an understanding not only of animal cognition but of cognition generally. It could help to differentiate cognitive from associative processes.

Is there any relation between the rat's discrimination of temporal durations and the human system of tense—past, present, future (which, incidentally, has yet to be demonstrated in apes let alone nonprimates)? The experimental contrast of these two cases would seem to provide an excellent opportunity to compare associative and cognitive processes. For example, are the mechanisms humans use when discriminating short intervals comparable to those used by rats? Do humans then use different mechanisms when distinguishing one tense from another and making judgments about time? Do the latter bear any relation to the former—either phylogenetically or ontogenetically—or are they unrelated?

Cognition (as a kind of computation) presupposes abstract representation, and I know of no evidence for representation of this kind in the nonprimate. In the tasks solved by rats and pigeons—for which representation is a defensible inference—e.g. spatial location (Olton & Samuelson 1976) and temporal order (Straub, et al 1979, Weisman et al 1980), the representation could be of the imaginal kind. Furthermore, in tasks these species do *not* solve, the use of abstract representation is an essential requirement.

Clear evidence for the abstract code is provided by the ability to judge the correspondence between a string of "words" and the conditions that the string describes. The language-trained ape, in answering yes/no questions, provides evidence of this kind. The animal can be shown simple conditions, e.g. a red card or a green one, and when interrogated with its plastic words "red or green?" answer "yes" or "no" appropriately. Comparable evidence is provided when an animal makes same/different judgments about analogies; in this case too the animal makes judgments about a relation between relations that do not look alike. The lack of such evidence in nonprimates,

ANIMAL COGNITION   361

along with the improbability of obtaining it, is compatible with the view that these species have only imaginal representation. The boundaries of cognition need close attention. As cognition washes belatedly over the shores of animal learning, there is a tendency to "liberalize" association and to reinterpret it as cognition. This could bring serious confusion because associative and cognitive processes are not equivalent. Nor is one true and the other false. They are distinct processes. Found in various degrees in different species, the greatest challenge to understanding them comes from the primate, where both processes are found. We must ultimately explain how the associative and cognitive processes interact.

Literature Cited

Carter, D. E., Werner, T. J. 1978. Complex learning and information processing by pigeons: A critical analysis. *J. Exp. Psychol: Anal. Behav.* 29:565–601

Cerella, J. 1977. Absence of perspective processing in the pigeon. *Pattern Recognition* 9:65–68

Cheney, D. L., Seyfarth, R. M. 1980. Vocal recognition in free-ranging vervet monkeys. *Anim. Behav.* 28:362–67

Church, R. M. 1978. The internal clock. In *Cognitive Processes in Animal Behavior,* ed. S. H. Hulse, H. Fowler, W. K. Honig, pp. 277–310. Hillsdale, NJ: Erlbaum

Epstein, R., Lanza, R. P., Skinner, B. F. 1980. Symbolic communication between two pigeons (*Columba livia domestica*). *Science* 207:543–45

Epstein, R., Lanza, R. P., Skinner, B. F. 1981. "Self-awareness" in the pigeon. *Science* 212:695–96

Gallup, G. 1970. Chimpanzees: self-recognition. *Science* 167:86–87

Gibbon, J., Church, R. M. 1981. Time left: Linear versus logarithmic subjective time. *J. Exp. Psychol: Anim. Behav. Processes* 7:87–108

Gillan, D. J. 1981. Reasoning in the chimpanzee: II. Transitive inference. *J. Exp. Psychol: Anim. Behav. Processes* 7: 150–64

Gillan, D. J., Premack, D., Woodruff, G. 1981. Reasoning in the chimpanzee: I. Analogical reasoning. *J. Exp. Psychol: Anim. Behav. Processes* 7:1–17

Herrnstein, R. J. 1979. Acquisition, generalization, and discrimination reversal of a natural concept. *J. Exp. Psychol: Anim. Behav. Processes* 5:116–29

Herrnstein, R. J., Loveland, D. H. 1964. Complex visual concept in the pigeon. *Science* 146:549–51

Honig, W. K. 1965. Discrimination, generalization, and transfer on the basis of stimulus differences. In *Stimulus Generalization,* ed. D. J. Mostofsky. Stanford, Calif: Stanford Univ. Press

Kummer, H. 1971. *Primate Societies. Group Techniques of Ecological Adaptation.* Chicago: Aldine

Kummer, H. 1982. Social knowledge in free-ranging primates. In *Animal Mind–Human Mind,* ed. D. R. Griffin. Dahlem Knof. Berlin/Heidelberg/New York: Springer

Lawrence, D. H., DeRivera, J. 1954. Evidence for relational transposition. *J. Comp. Physiol. Psychol.* 47:465–71

McGonigle, B., Chalmers, M. 1977. Are monkeys logical? *Nature* 267:694–96

Olton, D. S., Samuelson, R. J. 1976. Remembrance of places passed: Spatial memory in rats. *J. Exp. Psychol: Anim. Behav. Processes* 2:97–116

Premack, D. 1978. Why it would be difficult to talk to a pigeon. See Church 1978, pp. 423–51

Premack, D. 1980. Characteristics of an upgraded mind. In *Bericht über den 32. Kongress der Deutschen Gesellschaft für Psychologie in Zurich,* ed. W. Michaelis, Band 1, 49–70

Premack, D. 1982. The codes of man and beasts. *The Behavioral and Brain Sciences.* In press

Premack, D., Premack, A. J. 1982. *The Mind of an Ape.* New York: Norton. In press

Premack, D., Woodruff, G. 1978. Does the chimpanzee have a theory of mind? *Behav. Brain Sci.* 4:515–26

Roberts, S. 1982. Cross-modal use of an internal clock. *J. Exp. Psychol: Anim. Behav. Processes* 8:2–22

Savage-Rumbaugh, E. S., Rumbaugh, D. M., Boysen, S. 1978. Intentional symbolic communication in chimpanzee. *Science* 201:640–41

Seyfarth, R. M., Cheney, D. L. 1981. How monkeys see the world: A review of recent research on East African vervet monkeys. In *Primate Communication,* ed. C. Snowdon, C. H. Brown, M. Petersen. Cambridge: Cambridge Univ. Press

Skinner, B. F. 1950. Are theories of learning necessary? *Psychol. Rev.* 57:193–216

Straub, R. O., Seidenberg, M. S., Bever, T. G., Terrace, H. S. 1979. Serial learning in the pigeon. *J. Exp. Anal. Behav.* 32:137–48

Weisman, R. G., Wasserman, E. A., Dodd, P. W., Larew, M. B. 1980. The representation and retention of two-event sequences in pigeons. *J. Exp. Psychol: Anim. Behav. Processes* 6:312–25

Woodruff, G., Premack, D. 1981. Primitive mathematical concepts in the chimpanzee: proportionality and numerosity. *Nature* 293:568–70

Wright, A. A., Sands, S. F. 1982. A model of detection and decision processes during matching to sample by pigeons: Performance with 88 different wavelengths in delayed and simultaneous matching tasks. *J. Exp. Psychol: Anim. Behav. Processes* 7:191–216

Zentall, T. R., Edwards, C. A., Moore, B. S., Hogan, D. E. 1981. Identity: The basis for matching and oddity learning in pigeons. *J. Exp. Psychol: Anim. Behav. Processes* 7:70–86

Ann. Rev. Psychol. 1983. 34:363–400

CROSS-CULTURAL RESEARCH IN PSYCHOLOGY

Richard W. Brislin

Culture Learning Institute, East-West Center, Honolulu, Hawaii 96848

CONTENTS

Introduction

By any conventional standard, the amount of cross-cultural research published since the last treatment in the *Annual Review of Psychology* (Laboratory of Comparative Human Cognition 1979) has been massive. There have been two Handbooks (Triandis et al 1980, Munroe et al 1981); edited collections (Altman et al 1980, Warren 1980, Hamnett & Brislin 1980); proceedings volumes of conferences exclusively devoted to cross-cultural studies (Eckensberger et al 1979, Marsella et al 1979); a textbook (Segall 1979); as well as the usual set of book-length contributions (e.g. Hofstede 1980, Levinson & Malone 1980) and articles in the several journals wherein cross-cultural research reports predictably are to be found. Psychologists are likely to dream about field work in some remote spot not only to gather original data but also for a chance to catch up with the printed word.

363

0066-4308/83/0201-0363$02.00

In the last four to five years cross-cultural studies have been recognized as central to theory development by large numbers of psychologists. They may not have worked in other cultures themselves, but they have accepted the fact that any definition of psychology (e.g. scientific study of human behavior) must take into account the variety of human behavior found in various parts of the world. Exhortations concerning the importance of gathering cross-cultural data have been made by industrial psychologists (Landy & Trumbo 1980), social psychologists (Hollander 1981, Wrightsman & Deaux 1981), and cognitive psychologists (Estes 1975, Piaget 1977, and Medin 1981, who chided a colleague for *not* integrating relevant cross-cultural data). Selected cross-cultural research has also been reviewed in conceptual analyses of a wide range of topics, again by scholars not primarily identified as cross-cultural psychologists. These include music (Davies 1978), obesity (Rodin 1981), everyday conceptions of intelligence (Sternberg et al 1981), and power (Ng 1980). Cultural issues were treated in a special issue of the *American Psychologist* devoted to testing (Olmedo 1981). The integration of cross-cultural studies into various types of psychological research has also been documented in archival studies. In one of the studies of citation impact [perhaps better called sweepstakes (Buffardi & Nichols 1981)], the *Journal of Cross-Cultural Psychology* makes a good showing among the 99 journals studied as being the source of articles frequently cited by authors. On a lighter note, cross-cultural research is apparently well enough established to assist in the creation of parodies and satire. To follow Garcia's (1981) humor, readers have to be familiar with some rather sophisticated concepts in the always-difficult methodological problem area of obtaining equivalent measures of constructs in different cultures.

Fortunately, the relevant literature does not stop with the work of psychologists. Again in the last four or five years, there have been serious treatments of the contributions of psychologists by colleagues in anthropology, and vice versa (Price-Williams 1979, Berry 1980a, Harkness & Super 1980, Munroe & Munroe 1980b). No longer do psychologists merely give lip service to the necessity of studying anthropologists' ethnographies in order to design relevant experiments, and no longer do anthropologists merely make passing references to individual differences, reliability, and validity. The breakdown in mutual name calling and the number of sophisticated analyses combining the efforts of psychologists and anthropologists have been among the most notable developments during the period under review in this chapter.

The range of concepts investigated in cross-cultural studies by people closely associated with the field is also vast. The entire life span of individuals has received attention (Heron & Kroeger 1981, Munroe et al 1981), as has their acquisition of their culture's norms (Erchak 1980), language development (Bowerman 1981), use of leisure time (Crandall & Thompson 1978), psychological disorders (Draguns 1980b), and a host of other critical aspects of human behavior (see Table 1). Cross-cultural research is not confined to one methodological approach, one or even a limited number of topic areas, or one or a few traditional specialties within psychology (e.g. personality, experimental, developmental, social, clinical). Another way of conveying this point is by noting the lack of much effort to establish a separate division of the American Psychological Association. Since cross-cultural data are of relevance to research in any of the present divisions, it makes little sense to have a separate unit. Rather than an identifiable specialty, cross-cultural research is a loosely organized field whose practitioners believe that data gathered from people in all parts of the world will improve theory development in psychology. If there is any agreement, it centers around a set of methodological guidelines for *not* imposing one's own cultural standards when gathering data in another. These guidelines will be reviewed later in this chapter when recent methodological developments are covered.

Another factor contributing to the rich and large literature is the resurrection and development of old concepts. In the period under review, a number of topic areas which long were neglected began to receive invigorating doses of new thinking. After a surprising absence of research on adolescent behavior following Margaret Mead's (1928) observations in Samoa that teenage years are not necessarily stressful and turbulent, Dinges, Trimble & Hollenbeck (1979) gave attention to adolescence among American Indians. Keeping in mind the same problem of possible imposition already mentioned, the authors urged a move away from a behavior-as-social-problem approach to behavior-as-competencies in adjusting to a difficult world. Once a good topic area for choice should one want to lose his or her professional reputation, the relation between culture and personality has been recently reexamined (Draguns 1979b, Morsbach 1980, Shweder 1979a,b, 1980). In attempting to move away from the classic criticism that culture and personality studies yield little but collections of stereotypes, these authors have integrated ideas about individual variability, multimodal distributions, internal dynamics of a society, and the recognition that most aspects of a society can be found somewhere else and that comparisons are a matter of a culture's emphasis rather than the presence or absence of a feature. The controversial problem of cultural evolution, always difficult because of a history of superior-inferior judgments and the ease of making negative attributions based on what "stage" has been reached, has likewise received sensitive treatments (Levinson & Malone 1980, Thompson 1980). A central idea here is the distinction between specific and general evolution, the former being adaptation to identifiable environmental pressures, and the latter involving a "passage from less to greater energy transformation, lower to higher levels of integration, and less to greater all-round adaptability" (Sahlins 1960, p. 38).

Greater research activities in various parts of the world have also increased the range of published studies. Traditionally, the largest amount of research activity was carried out in Africa. This is probably due to a number of factors: British colonial rule allowing (at the time) fairly easy entry; off-shoots from projects centered around worker selection from a pool of African applicants as well as their training for skilled jobs; and the leadership of influential figures such as Frederick Bartlett, Simon Biesheuvel, Gustav Jahoda, and S. H. Irvine. Recently, however, cross-cultural psychology has been the recipient of many good studies and critical analyses from other parts of the world. This is especially notable for Australia (Davidson 1980, Knapp & Seagrim 1981); New Zealand (Mackie 1980, St. George 1980); New Guinea (Feather 1979, St. George & Preston 1980); Hawaii (Werner 1979, Jordan & Tharp 1979); and other parts of the Pacific (Colletta 1980, on Ponape; Lewis 1980, on traditional navigation in the central Caroline Islands).

As a final comment on the range of research, another reason is undoubtedly the confidence and experience of researchers. Large numbers of today's practitioners began by studying a limited set of problems with relatively straightforward tasks to which indigenous people responded in a manner allowing relatively easy interpretation. For instance, two-dimensional visual illusions (Segall et al 1966) were studied by many researchers in the 1960s. These people learned from experience about such central issues as problem conceptualization in cross-cultural terms, equivalence, researcher-participation communication, and sensitivity to the community in which one is working. They then took these lessons and employed them in studying much more complex subject areas (e.g. Berry 1980a on ecological models; Jahoda 1981 on schooling and intellectual skills; and Wagner 1981 on memory development). Even those researchers who stayed in the general area of perception began to study more complex issues (e.g. Deregowski, 1979, 1980b on engineering drawings and the building of three-dimensional models). Many of these early lessons have been communicated in detail so that others can benefit from them (Triandis & colleagues 1980). With the lessons developed from the narrow set of early studies, different researchers have pursued their wide variety of interests to yield the diversity present today. There is no one recognized leader or even set of leaders whose apprentices might work on only those topics deemed worthy by the master(s). Rather, thousands of seeds have been sowed and a hundred flowers have bloomed. There is richness in its diversity together with user frustration in reaping the benefits. Research reports are very widely scattered, as a glance at the bibliography will reveal.

Definitions of Culture

Like a number of concepts long studied by psychologists, such as personality, intelligence, and abnormal behavior, there is no one definition of "culture" which is widely accepted. The most frequently cited definition is probably that of Kroeber & Kluckhohn (1952, p. 181), which includes such elements as "patterns, explicit and implicit, of and for behavior acquired and transmitted by symbols, constituting the distinctive achievements of human groups . . . [and] ideas and their attached values." The definition by Herskovits (1948, p. 17) of culture as "the man-made part of the human environment" has also been influential, especially given Triandis's (1980b) addition based on a distinction between physical and subjective culture. The former would include man-made objects (Altman & Chemers 1980, Altman et al 1980) such as houses and tools, and the latter would include responses to those objects in the form of values, roles, and attitudes (e.g. Davidson & Thomson 1980, Zavalloni 1980). Given the long tradition of psychological research on people's responses to their world, Triandis's use of "culture" is very helpful. Since much cross-cultural research has the goal of understanding concepts as seen by people in the culture under study (Price-Williams 1980a), the influence of work in cognitive psychology has been strong. Much research has been focused on people's knowledge about their world (Posner & Baroody 1979), their communication with one another given their shared knowledge (DeVos 1980), and the transmittal of this knowledge to the next generation (Edwards 1981, McClelland 1981).

Given what many psychologists and anthropologists actually do, then, in terms of focusing on researchable questions, the slightly longer definition of Geertz (1973, p. 89) captures the flavor of much cross-cultural psychological inquiry: "[Culture] denotes an historically transmitted pattern of meanings embodied in symbols, a system of inherited conceptions expressed in symbolic forms by means of which men communicate, perpetuate, and develop their knowledge about and attitudes toward life." To this definition, the Kroeber-Kluckhohn element that these symbolic forms have "attached value" should be added. The fact that symbols are valued leads to ethnocentric thinking, especially concerning subjective elements such as ideology, religion, morality, or law. People feel that what they do is good or right and that members of other cultures are somewhat backward and/or illogical concerning their treatment of those same subjective aspects (e.g. Amir and associates 1978, 1979, 1980, Haque & Lawson 1980). The ethnocentrism then leads to outgrouping and prejudice, both of which may become so intense that the smooth functioning of society becomes threatened (Stening 1979, Brislin 1981). At times, the opposite of ethnocentric elitism is felt concerning material aspects of culture. Here one culture may envy the apparent superiority of another concerning its labor-saving devices, electronic gadgets, and concrete buildings (Altman & Chemers 1980, Yang & Bond 1980). Of course, the inextricable link between physical and subjective culture to which Triandis points means that value-laden elements will be affected by acquisition of the envied physical elements (e.g. Colletta 1980, Madsen & Lancy 1981).

Any definition is useful only insofar as it helps researchers gather more reliable and valid data. While it is gratifying to see the recent widespread use of "culture" as an explanatory variable, the concept is beginning to run the danger of being so broad in its focus as to preclude much usefulness. Reviewing research in developmental psychology, Harkness (1980, p. 11) pointed to the "invisibility of the culture in psychological theory," arguing that the historical neglect of the concept led to an overemphasis on nativist theories of child development. Since so many aspects of culture are not assessed in the typical study *within* any one country, the study's results are too often attributed to genetic factors or to some supposed universal process. Similarly, Touhey (1981, p. 594) pointed to the importance of culture in analyzing failures to replicate studies in social psychology. "A rapidly expanding body of research in cross-cultural psychology has alerted investigators to the possibility that many basic findings on personality and microsocial processes will not generalize across cultures." Expanding on this point, Touhey argues that it is necessary to gather data on the sorts of variables Geertz specifies when researchers make attempts to generalize across subpopulations within a country. The lack of information on such critical aspects of culture as preferences, knowledge about a topic, and salient symbols makes failures to replicate almost impossible to explicate.

The Uses and Benefits of Cross-Cultural Research

Again looking at what psychologists actually do, many formulate their research according to this definition: cross-cultural research is the empirical study of members of various cultural (as defined above) groups who have had significant and identifiable experiences leading to predictable, and theoretically important, similarities and differences in behavior. Ideally, the antecedents and consequences of the behavior can be specified (Triandis 1980b,c). Interestingly, psychologists have spent far more effort analyzing the uses and benefits of cross-cultural research than they have in formulating their own definitions of culture, being happy to borrow the latter from anthropologists. The classic references for "uses and benefits" are Whiting (1954, 1968) and Strodtbeck (1964), and recently others have expanded upon the earlier analyses (Lonner 1979, Berry 1980b, Brown & Sechrest 1980, Kornadt et al 1980, Segalowitz 1981).

INCREASING RANGE OF VARIABLES   The most frequently cited use of cross-cultural research is that the range within independent variables, and a wider range of conceivable responses to dependent variables, can be found in other cultures or by comparisons across cultures (e.g. Sue et al 1979, Ginsburg et al 1981). In a study of social identity, Giles and associates (1979) found that Puerto Rico was an excellent research site. There are many possible identities within the multicultural society which people may choose, and most people can lay claim to more than one because of their family histories. At times the reason for the increased range of variables will be due to poverty, and researchers will feel concerned that they are exploiting people's severe misfortunes. Aram & Piraino (1978) found more support for the Maslow hierarchy of needs theory than is typical in research carried out within highly industrialized countries (Landy & Trumbo 1980). This may be due to the fact that their study was carried out in Chile where there is far less satisfaction of the basic physiological and safety/security needs than in (for instance) the United States. The inclusion of a sample whose members have basic needs unsatisfied increases the range of the independent variables central to Maslow's hierarchy.

OBTAINING QUITE DIFFERENT VARIABLES   At times, variables can be obtained, central to theory development, which are not found within those few countries where the bulk of empirical research has taken place (Pedersen 1979, Kavanagh & Venezky 1980). Studying methods of traditional navigation in the Pacific, Lewis (1980) argued that the navigator's task puts great demands upon memory skills and that a trip (among many other details) was viewed as a moving reference island (etak) progressing from one star position to another. Importantly, the system was shown to be transferable to another part of the Pacific previously unknown to the navigator. Mau Piailug, who developed his skills in the central Caroline Islands (Micronesia), was asked to navigate without instruments from Hawaii south to Tahiti (Polynesia). He did so in a trip carefully documented by Lewis (1980). Studying the relationship between an indigenous naming system based on birth order and Piagetian stages of development, Saxe (1981) skillfully incorporated a variable not found elsewhere. Among Ponam islanders in New Guinea, boys and girls are given sets of names based on their birth order relation to same-sex siblings. To understand the determinate and indeterminate aspects of age relationship, Saxe hypothesized and found that children must have reached a level of operational reasoning (independently assessed) where two relations of differences can be coordinated. Excellent applied research has taken advantage of indigenous practices and knowledge of this sort in the development of school curricula and pedagogical approaches [e.g. Jordan & Tharp (1979) on the teaching of reading in Hawaii].

UNCONFOUNDING VARIABLES   One of the most intriguing possibilities is that variables which occur together in one culture, and hence which are confounded in any statistical analysis, can be studied separately in other cultures (Brown & Sechrest 1980, Bowerman 1981). For instance, there are parts of the world where formal schooling is not required or expected of all children, and where the criteria for distributing the available classroom seats are not based solely on natural aptitude (Rogoff 1981). Thus, there can be studies of the effects of schooling and aptitude, and their interaction, an impossible project in many countries. Feldman, McDonald & Sam (1980) argued that research carried out among young adults in New Zealand allowed a test of stereotype attribution separating the effects of ethnicity (European, Maori, Samoan), origin (urban-rural), and occupation/educational status (manager, skilled tradesman, laborer). In other countries, the variables could be badly confounded; for instance, respondents might not be able to realistically imagine two non-white ethnic groups with both rural and urban members. But without the two non-white groups, researchers might be measuring xenophobia rather than differentiation among non-white groups for specifiable reasons. And without the rural-urban distinction, researchers might be measuring a prejudice toward people "from the sticks."

By studying Asian Americans who had reached different levels of acculturation in the United States and comparing their behavior with that of Caucasians, Sue et al (1979) were able to investigate the differential effects of genetic-racial differences in alcohol sensitivity and cultural differences in attitudes and values toward alcohol use. Results supported interpretations based on the latter set of variables. The inclusion of an acculturated sample of Asian Americans, who showed more alcohol use than less acculturated peers, was the strongest piece of evidence to support the cultural factors hypothesis.

STUDY OF THE CONTEXT IN WHICH BEHAVIOR OCCURS   Few psychologists would disagree that behavior is a function of the person and the environment, but the environment has been notoriously difficult to conceptualize and to operationalize. Cross-cultural researchers have been active in studying the social context in which behavior occurs (McKessar & Thomas 1978, Bilmes & Boggs 1979, Tseng & Hsu 1979, Holtzman 1979, Kilbride 1980; see also quote from Harkness 1980, above.) The study of context can be more productive in other cultures since researchers can more easily "remove" themselves from the cultures they are studying (because of their unfamiliarity) so as to better understand the multiple causes of others' behavior. When working in their own culture, they are so close to the same contexts as research participants that the separation of person from environment is more difficult. In fact, the hypothesis that cross-cultural experiences lead to greater insights into social contexts has itself been suggested (Hall 1977, Brislin 1981). Attempting to draw general conclusions from the large body of research on psychological disorders, Draguns (1980b, p. 155) gave explicit attention to the distinction between invariant aspects of abnormal manifestations across cultures and the various shapings of behaviors demanded by people's needs to fit themselves into their social contexts. For instance, he concluded that manifestations of psychosis are less influenced by culture than are manifestations of nonpsychotic disorders and that (more speculatively) among psychoses, "affective disorders appear to be more susceptible to cultural shaping than are the schizophrenias." One of the major messages of the approach known as "ethnographic cognition" (Laboratory of Comparative Human Cognition 1979, Ciborowski 1980) is that the social context has been underemphasized in much psychological research. Only with an understanding of the context in which people live can researchers design studies in which individuals' competencies can be demonstrated. Without such understanding, researchers may obtain data demonstrating some gross reaction to an imposed, unfamiliar context—hardly a worthwhile study.

MAXIMIZATION OF DIFFERENCES IN RESPONDENTS' ATTRIBUTES
If research hypotheses are supported in studies with very different populations, the findings can be taken more seriously than those hypotheses supported only by studies of homogeneous populations within one country. In cross-cultural studies, variances of respondents' attributes which are *not* directly related to the hypotheses are maximized, and these variances are often extremely difficult to obtain within one research site. But if research findings are supported despite the variance added from the work in other cultures, then the hypotheses must be robust (Foschi 1980). For instance, in studies of the determinants of cooperative and competitive behavior, Madsen & Lancy (1981) have demonstrated that an important factor leading to cooperativeness is primary group identification. Other factors varied across the investigators' ten research sites in New Guinea: homogeneous vs heterogeneous language communities, sex of respondents, rural-urban differences, presence or absence of modern appliances, and length of contact with people from highly industrialized nations. The presence or absence of primary support groups was the major predictor of cooperativeness in

games despite variance within any research site (see also Korte & Ayvalio-glu 1981). The technique of maximizing variance can also be used in attempts to integrate diverse literatures. In their review of the nature, antecedents, and consequences of alienation, Guthrie & Tanco (1980) incorporated research findings from studies of long-term city dwellers, villagers moving from rural to urban settings in many parts of the world, villagers who decided to stay in the places where they were born, Peace Corps volunteers from the United States assigned to rural communities in other countries, the children of Americans stationed overseas, and powerless groups within a highly industrialized country, such as Appalachia within the United States. Interesting parallels were drawn between certain patterns of behavior typical of alienation and the learned helplessness observable in laboratory studies (Seligman 1975). This parallel between certain aspects of alienation and learned helplessness is an example of the mutual enrichment possible between cross-cultural studies and concepts from general psychology. This is a point which will be addressed at greater length later in this chapter.

A similar use of cross-cultural studies might be called "maximizing the types of methodology used." For instance, the participants in the Madsen & Lancy (1981) research knew they were playing a game, and results from games do not necessarily generalize to other aspects of everyday behavior (Sutton-Smith & Roberts 1981). In research by Nadler & associates (1979), on the other hand, children in Israel had a chance to donate a valued commodity to poor children. The children did not know they were participants in a research study at the time of the request. As predicted, kibbutz children gave more than city children. The occasional field study (e.g. Bolton 1979b, Korte & Ayvalioglu 1981) using unobtrusive measures (Bochner 1980) is valuable since it "keeps a hypothesis honest." If a hypothesis is supported by findings only in tightly controlled laboratory studies, it is going to be of limited use in the development of better theories about human behavior. But if the hypothesis is robust enough to be supported in field studies, where there are more sources of extraneous variance, then it is likely to receive the continued attention of psychologists. Several psychologists have commented that hypotheses derived from the prisoners' dilemma paradigm have not received continued attention in recent years since laboratory findings were neither interesting nor replicable (Helmreich et al 1973, Mann 1980). The decision in favor of such unobtrusive cross-cultural studies, of course, assumes that the ethical issues have been analyzed responsibly. Here the issue is the ethics of studying people's behavior (or their children's behavior) when they have not consented to the unobtrusive observations (Warwick 1980).

TRAINING STUDIES TO TRIGGER LATENT COMPETENCIES For many years, hundreds of now mercifully forgotten studies of comparisons across cultures concluded that one group was better than another on such-and-such a competency. Rarely did researchers ask basic questions about the reasons for the poor performance of the low-scoring group. The basic theoretical distinction in linguistics between competence and overt performance (which may or may not demonstrate mastery of the competence to observers) was not taken seriously. The competence-performance distinction, oddly underemphasized until recently in psychology, has achieved the status of a point on which virtually all linguists agree (Hudson 1981, p. 336).

A child's poor performance in formal, threatening, or unfamiliar situations cannot be taken as evidence of impoverished linguistic competence, but may be due to other factors such as low motivation for speaking in that situation, or unfamiliarity with the conventions for use of language in such situations.

Lack of attention to these basic factors in cross-cultural research studies is now sufficient reason to reject articles submitted for publication (Lonner 1980a).

Taking advantage of the rich theoretical possibilities present in this distinction, psychologists influenced by Piaget have pointed to the importance of training studies to trigger latent competencies (Dasen et al 1979, Heron & Kroeger 1981, Dasen & Heron 1981). There are various reasons why competencies may not be manifested in performance, as Hudson points out. Another reason is that people may have never or rarely been in situations in which a certain latent competency was necessary for the accomplishment of some task. The approach of the researcher in examining children and assessing competencies (e.g. that a certain level of reasoning has been reached) is to develop training tasks which encourage the manifestation of latent competencies in overt performance. Dasen & Ngini (1979) reasoned that the rate of learning is also important. Very rapid learning, where the competence is demonstrated quickly, means that training has "actualized" the existing competence. "If the training is successful, but improvement in performance occurs more slowly, it is more likely that the operational structure was not present but was built up during training (Dasen & Ngini 1979, p. 96)." This conclusion, of course, assumes ruling out plausible alternative explanations such as respondents' gradual warming up to the researcher and to the task. The content of training is also theoretically important. In work among Baoule children in West Africa on the assessment of quantity and class conservation, Dasen, Lavallee & Retschitzki (1979) designed procedures to create a conflict among the children's existing schemes so as to encourage the development of new structures. The training task, then, mirrors the everyday life events thought necessary for development along Piagetian stages. It is no accident that studies with data on training show much higher percentages of respondents achieving the highest substage within concrete operations, often equaling the norms from highly industrialized nations (see Dasen 1972 for a review of earlier studies where training was not a component).

WORK WITH LARGE DATA SETS IN LIBRARIES AND COMPUTER STORAGE FACILITIES   For researchers skilled at secondary analyses of data, there are a number of large data sets in libraries and/or on computer tapes. These include: (a) the Human Relations Area Files (HRAF), a compilation of ethnographic data on over 300 culture groups throughout the world (Barry 1980, Naroll et al 1980); (b) the Atlas of Affective Meaning, a set of judgments about the connotation of concepts from over 30 cultural groups (Osgood et al 1975); (c) the study of ethnocentric and intergroup attitudes (Brewer & Campbell 1976), based on interviews with members of 30 ethnic groups in East Africa; (d) in industrial and organizational psychology, data sets on worker values in 40 countries (Hofstede 1980) and the assessment of managers in 12 countries (Bass & associates 1979).

The advantages of working with such data sets are the possibilities of multinational comparisons, opportunities for the investigation of hypotheses with half a sample and cross-validation on the other half, and the opportunity to benefit from the maximizing-of-differences feature of cross-cultural studies, already discussed. The disadvantages are especially clear, thus allowing reasoned decisions by potential investigators, since various critics have discussed the drawbacks of secondary analysis (e.g. Levinson & Malone 1980 for the specific case of HRAF-based studies). The weaknesses are probably no greater than data sets in any one investigator's long-term programmatic research, but somehow flaws are clearer in someone else's data. With HRAF, there is no check on the reliability of the ethnographer's judgment. There are techniques (worthy of study) for determining the general reliability of an observer (Naroll et al 1980), but not the reliability of any specific set of observations. Further, topics on which there is the greatest amount of information are the ones long studied by anthropologists (e.g. kinship, social structure, land tenure), and there may be insufficient information on topics traditionally studied by psychologists. In the Atlas of Affective Meaning, connotative ratings of concepts were made by teenagers attending schools, a dangerous sample from which to generalize to a culture as a whole (Mead 1977). In the Hofstede data, surveys of worker values were done in only one company (branches of a multinational firm) within each of 40 countries. Similar comments could be made about the other data sets. However, various uses could be made of the data files during the planning of field work where original research is to be done. Ethnographic background information on cultures (much of it in publications no longer in print and available only through HRAF) can and should be consulted. The meaning of key terms a researcher is employing certainly affects the data collected, and some of these meanings may be found in the Atlas. Since researchers usually work with host nationals during field work, information about the value of work identified by Hofstede should be useful. These data sets can also be used in teaching. Students can learn to formulate and to test precise hypotheses using the data files so as to be better prepared for the opportunity to gather original data.

The Mutual Enrichment of Cross-Cultural and General Psychology

Another striking aspect of the last few years of cross-cultural research is the large number of concepts developed in general psychology (many of which were themselves formulated in the last 10 years) which have been investigated cross-culturally. The mutual enrichment is that cross-cultural research benefits from the presence of well-thought-out concepts, and general psychology benefits from the sharpening which cross-cultural data can provide. Table 1 lists a variety of concepts actively studied by psychologists, the researchers who have investigated the concepts in other cultures, and the countries in which original data were gathered.

NEED FOR ACHIEVEMENT   A few examples should be presented to demonstrate how the mutual enrichment can work in practice. McClelland's (1961) classic work on achievement motivation places more emphasis on personality and less on "situational and contextual factors, . . . social expectations, norms, task definitions and social cues" than Maehr & Nicholls (1980, p. 223) feel is warranted by data gathered in Iran, Japan, India, Nigeria, and New Zealand. As has been discussed previously, it is exactly the aspects of achievement noted by Maehr & Nicholls (contextual factors, expectations, norms, etc) that are influenced by culture. Whereas the American ideal might be individualistic achievement as a goal, the Japanese concept of achievement is integrally associated with a person's group role and status, especially with respect to one's family. Whereas the American ideal includes good intentions to produce as well as actual output, the Iranian emphasis is on good intentions but does not necessarily demand actual output. The sufficiency of good intentions may be due to the fact that in Iran, strong sensitivities exist regarding moral norms. The demonstration that one is morally proper by having good intentions may be more important than a successful outcome in and of itself. Through additions and

Table 1 A sampling of concepts from general psychology investigated in cross-cultural studies

Concept	Researchers	Culture or cultural groups
A-Act (attitude toward the act)	Callan 1980	Greek and Italian immigrants in Australia
Aggression	Bolton 1976, 1979a	Qolla from Peru-Bolivia
	Jaffe et al 1981	Israel
Attribution theory	Detweiler 1978	Truk
	Fry & Ghosh 1980a,b	Asian immigrants to Canada
	Chandler & associates 1981	India, Japan, South Africa, Yugoslavia
Behavior prediction	Lieberman 1978	West India
	Guthrie 1979	Philippines
Categorization	Detweiler 1980	Truk
Cognitive mediation	Foorman et al 1981	Mexican Americans
	Fry 1982	Japan
Conservative authoritarianism	Miller et al 1981	Poland
Cooperation-competition	Thomas 1978	New Zealand
	Kagan & Knight 1979	Mexican Americans
	Madsen & Lancy 1981	New Guinea
Counseling	Sue et al 1978	Mexican Americans and native Americans
	Fry et al 1980	Black Americans
Delinquency	Yang 1981	Taiwan
Dialectics	Diaz-Guerrero 1979	Mexico
Dream analysis	K. Johnson 1978	Uganda
Emotion	Boucher & Carlson 1980	Malaysia: Malay and Tamuan
Ethnic identity	Morland & Hwang 1981	Taiwan and Hong Kong
	Rich et al 1981	Israel
Helping behavior	Graf et al 1979	Netherlands
	Korte & Ayvalioglu 1981	Turkey
Instrumental-terminal value distinction	Feather 1979, 1980	New Guinea
Intelligence	Gill & Keats 1980	Malaysia
Internal-external locus control	Munro 1979	Zambia, Zimbabwe
	Evans 1981	Japan
	Faustman & Mathews 1980	Sri Lanka
	Khanna & Khanna 1979	India
	Lao 1978	Taiwan
	Saraswathi et al 1970	India
	Niles 1981	Sri Lanka
Language acquisition	Bowerman 1981	Examples drawn from over 25 languages
Learned helplessness	Guthrie 1979	Philippines

Table 1 *(Continued)*

Concept	Researchers	Culture or cultural groups
Learning theory	Childs & Greenfield 1980	Zinacanteco in Mexico
Life satisfaction and the elderly	Fry & Ghosh 1980a	India
Machiavellianism	Dien & Fujisawa 1979	Japan
Memory	Wagner 1981	Morocco
Moral development	Turiel et al 1978 Ziv et al 1978	Turkey Israel
Need for achievement	Duda 1980 Maehr & Nicholls 1980	Navajo native Americans Iran
Need hierarchy (Maslow)	Aram & Piraino 1978	Chile
Nutrition	Palmer & Barba 1981	Philippines
Participative decision making	Drenth & associates 1979	Multinational survey, primarily Europe
Piagetian concepts	Brown et al 1980 Shea & Yerua 1980 Fahrmeier 1978a,b Dasen et al 1979	Malaysia New Guinea Hausa in Africa Baoule in West Africa
Pictorial depth perception	Leach 1978	Shona in Africa
Power	Saraswathi et al 1979	India
Psychological disturbances	Marsella 1979, 1980	Japan, Philippines
Psychometric theory	Irvine 1979, Irvine & Carroll 1980	Various sites in Africa
Social desirability	Fioravanti et al 1981	France, Italy
Worker motivation and values	Hofstede 1980	Multinational survey of 40 countries

refinements to concepts originally developed in one part of the world (in this case of need for achievement, the United States), the work of McClelland is developed and improved.

CAUSAL ATTRIBUTION   In studies of how people interpret their own successes and failures (Miller & Ross 1975), research carried out in the United States and Canada indicates that people attribute success experiences to their own efforts but attribute failures to luck, task difficulty, or idiosyncrasies of the judges. Fry & Ghosh (1980b) felt that these findings, a cornerstone of attribution theory in social psychology, may be affected by cultural variables, especially the socialization patterns to which people are exposed as children. Among Asian Indians, people are taught that they should accept responsibility for all their deeds, both positive and negative. In a cross-cultural comparison, this should be seen in greater attribution of personal responsibility for failure among Indians compared to Caucasian-Americans. This was indeed a result of the Fry and Ghosh study which was carried out in Canada among Indian immigrants and Caucasians. Although not predicted, the researchers also found that Asian Indians claimed less personal responsibility for success than did Caucasian Americans. Fry and Ghosh speculated that this may be due to (a) socialization pressures demanding self-effacement and social denial of an individual's success; or (b) the minority group status of the Asian immigrants leading to a lack of encouragement for self-confidence and self-assurance. Cross-cultural data should not be seen in a gadfly-like guise. The original findings are not denied; indeed, they were replicated among the Caucasian participants. The enrichment of (not detraction from) attribution theory comes from the demonstration that personal factors (e.g. values) and situational factors (e.g. minority status) play an important role in the analysis of causal explanations.

INTELLIGENCE   There is hardly a topic area with a longer history or a more extensive literature in psychology than intelligence, and it has also been the focus of cross-cultural research. While some of the earliest studies tried to compare culture on tests standardized in one country, such research has now achieved the dismissal which it deserves. More recently, psychologists have suggested that studies of everyday conceptions of intelligence in different cultures (Goodnow 1979, 1980) may be a good approach to expanding our understanding. Gill & Keats (1980, p. 241) found that respondents in Malaysia placed more emphasis on social skills, in their own explanations of intelligence, than did respondents in Australia. This finding "may reflect the Islamic idea of integration of oneself into one's environment which seemed to be the basis of Wober's (1974) findings in Uganda with Muslim subjects, who associated intelligence with the terms 'friendly,' 'honorable,' 'happy,' and public.' " As might be expected of people long exposed to schooling in a highly industrialized nation, Australian respondents placed more emphasis on knowledge of academic skills such as speaking, reading, and writing. The emphasis on speaking, especially, causes severe problems when people from one cultural background attend the schools of another (Johnson & Marsella 1978, Thomas 1979). Children in many cultures are not reinforced for speaking freely with adults and so are not prepared for the frequent verbal exchanges between teacher and pupil which are typical of other cultures. Innovative teaching practices have taken advantage of the greater emphasis on the intellectual skills of social sensitivity and sharing among many Pacific and Asian cultures. For instance, Jordan & Tharp (1979; see also Speidel 1981) described the development of cooperative reading groups in Hawaii in which children discuss what they have recently read with each other.

LANGUAGE ACQUISITION   In a retrospective analysis of language acquisition research, an extremely fast moving field whose generalizations of yesterday are the disputations of today, Bowerman (1981) concluded that there are two areas where cross-cultural data have been especially powerful in modifying conclusions based on English language studies. These are the principles known as pivot grammar (McNeil 1970) and telegraphic speech (R. Brown 1973). In the former, children's two-word utterances are said to be composed of a relatively small number of pivot words together with a larger number of "open class" words. Among other features, pivot words have fixed position and do not occur as single-word utterances. Neither of these assertions is true of open class words. Based on her own data from Finnish speaking children, Bowerman found the pivot grammar did not give an adequate account of their competencies. This fact caused her to review her own data on English speaking children, and she concluded that the principles of pivot grammar fared no better. "This example illustrates how an important benefit of the cross-cultural approach can be to force a reappraisal of our conceptions of what takes place in our own culture" (Bowerman 1981, p. 119). Further analysis indicated that a major weakness was pivot grammar's emphasis on only the superficial forms and arrangements of words, not meaning in a social context.

Telegraphic speech was another attempt to account for children's early word combinations. Part of this conceptualization is the functor: these words have grammatical rather than referential functions and are members of small, closed syntactic classes. R. Brown (1973) proposed that there are four determinants of the presence of functors in any given child's speech: perceptual salience, frequency of input from adults, whether the form is constant or affected by verbal context, and the type of semantic role (basic or modulatory, examples of the latter being pluralization or past tense). It is important to note both that these generalizations were influenced by cross-cultural data (English, French, Samoan, Swedish, and Spanish speakers), and are in turn the sorts of assumptions which can benefit from additional cross-cultural data (see previous discussions of the definition of culture). Bowerman (1981) feels that these are major steps forward but that further editing will be necessary. She concludes that children at the two-word utterance stage are capable of conceptualizing and expressing modulations of meaning, but that the exact conditions under which they express these competencies are not yet known. Examples from children learning Swedish, Garo (a Tibeto-Burman language), Hindi, and Dutch are put forward to show possible directions for the necessary modifications.

MACHIAVELLIANISM   In another set of generalizations which was influenced by cross-cultural data and which has consciously incorporated social context variables, Geis (1979) concluded that people high in Machiavellianism can affect the behavioral outcomes of themselves and others in a number of specifiable situations. These include situations in which there is latitude for improvisation, irrelevant affect, and face-to-face interaction. Research by Dien & Fujisawa (1979) in Japan sheds additional light on the first situational factor. Since Japanese women hold lower status in their society than men, they must be able both to create and to take advantage of a latitude of improvisation in order to achieve their goals. To learn such behavior, they would be likely to use their mothers as role models, and this would be especially true for firstborn and only girls given the probable closeness between mother and daughter. Given the opportunities in society already open to men, there would not be the need for males to learn manipulative behaviors from their parents. Dien & Fujisawa found that the Machiavellianism scores of 11-year-old boys was unassociated with that of their parents, but that the scores of 11-year-old girls were positively correlated. Further, the highest correlation was obtained between mothers' scores and the scores of firstborn and only girls. In a concluding comment which also sheds light on the issue of value consistency (Zavalloni 1980), the authors point out one reason why traditional values such as deference and self-effacement may not be related to overt behavior. If people can better achieve their goals through some kind of manipulation rather than through expression of traditional values, they will often opt for the former. More speculatively, Dien and Fujisawa point out that the Japanese girls may have learned to verbalize the traditional values at the same time they have learned to incorporate manipulative techniques into their behavior (see also Morsbach 1980).

Using Concepts from General Psychology: Facilitators or Blinders?

The use of concepts which have been developed and operationalized has both advantages and disadvantages. Given the relatively rare opportunity of doing field research in other cultures, observations can be sharpened and time used most productively if the researcher starts with well-developed concepts. Of course, the concepts can also act as blinders. Especially for concepts with well-established operational definitions (e.g. a scale or experimental procedure), borrowing from general psychology can lead to the imposition of a framework and to an oversight of what is important in and for a given culture (Berry 1980b,c). This seeming contradiction between concepts as contributors to profitable research and concepts as blinders is one of the most important issues in cross-cultural research. The ability to steer a course between the possibilities of concepts-as-facilitators and concepts-as-impositions is a necessary skill demanded of psychologists who regularly engage in cross-cultural studies.

Various general approaches have been formulated to deal with the problem. One is the use of multiple methods (Barry 1980, Naroll et al 1980). The classic paper on this topic is by Donald Campbell (1968), who points out that the inherent weaknesses in any one method can be alleviated if hypotheses are investigated through different methods with different inherent weaknesses. Hypotheses which are robust enough to pass muster through investigation with a variety of methods are then retained. Recent examples include the work of Evans (1981), who employed both the Rotter I-E scale and a word association task to measure locus of control in Japan. The word association data allowed a replication of general findings indicated by the I-E scale scores as well as further probes into the meaning of the external locus indicated by the scale responses. Keeping in mind that different studies of aggression have yielded different results based on choice of methodology, Bolton (1976, 1979a) employed measures of both overt and fantasy aggression in his study of hypoglycemia and its effects on behavior among the Qolla Indians from the Peru-Bolivia border region. Rohner, Rohner & Roll (1980) have studied the relation between parental acceptance-rejection and children's personality by performing secondary data analyses of anthropological data files and by gathering original data in various field sites (see also R. Rohner 1980).

One of the best ways to insure nonimposition of concepts is to work with collaborators who are themselves members of other cultures. Especially when specifically invited to comment and made to feel at ease in their role as critic, they can sharpen and improve research plans (see Brislin 1979, Finley 1979, Drenth & Wilpert 1980, all of whom also discuss difficulties in collaboration). A possible drawback to this approach, which can probably be overcome in many cases, is that indigenous scholars themselves may have been trained in those highly industrialized countries where most research has been done. Colleagues in the countries where advanced degrees were earned, rather than colleagues in their own countries, may become the reference group (Kashoki 1978, Kumar 1979). Concepts learned in other countries may have achieved an overly high status wherein they become near-sacred and hence unmodifiable. This deference is diminishing. Many authors from developing countries have recently put forward very helpful and insightful critiques (Durojaiye 1979a,b, Sinha 1979a,b), as well as excellent data (Zaidi 1979a,b,c, Okonji 1980), and so have provided a counterbalance to the still uncomfortable fact that most cross-cultural research emanates from just a few countries.

Another general approach is to begin research in other cultures with no specific definitions of concepts, and instead to do ethnographic research until possibilities of more controlled observations become clear. The latter might be experiments using materials with which people are familiar and which can be studied in natural contexts similar to those of people's everyday behavior. Most strongly put forward by Cole and his colleagues (Cole 1975, Cole & Means 1981), this approach has had more success as a methodological reminder than as a source of important findings. The ethnographic cognition approach provided a needed corrective to experiments which clearly imposed foreign ideas and procedures and to experiments where there was not adequate communication between researchers and participants. However, the approach's yield of substantive, replicable findings is not impressive (Ciborowski 1979, Berry 1980a). Further, in the development of basic and applied behavioral science research in developing countries (Durojaiye 1979b), there is simply not the time and funding to allow a fresh start from a "zero point." There is no choice but to import and to adapt concepts which have been well researched elsewhere. My own feeling is that the best of the ethnographic cognition approach can be combined with the use of existing concepts, as well as with more recent innovations [e.g. everyday conceptualizations (Goodnow 1980)], to create a smorgasbord of possibilities from which researchers can draw given the demands of a specific research project.

Emics and Etics: Culture-Specific and Culture-General Concepts

The framework which can incorporate a range of methodological possibilities and which has proved very helpful to researchers investigating a variety of topics is known as emics-etics (Lonner 1979, Berry 1980c, Triandis 1980c, Lonner & Triandis 1980, Brislin 1981). It is a metaphor drawn from earlier work in linguistics and anthropology, and another but longer set of terms for the same idea would be "culture-specific and culture-general." The terms are borrowed (and, it should be pointed out, freely adapted) from phonemic and phonetic analysis in linguistics. The goal of phonemic analysis is to document the meaningful sounds in any language, that is, sounds which make a difference in meaning when part of morphemes or words (e.g. pin vs bin). The goal of phonetic analysis is to develop a systematization of sounds meaningful in at least one of the world's languages based on such factors as the exact part of the vocal apparatus used in making the sounds. Consider the example of the distinction between the initial "l" and the initial "r" sound in English: lock vs rock. There is not this distinction in the Japanese language, and consequently there are difficulties when Japanese learn English. They must also invest a good deal of time and energy in order to make the distinction in their speech. Various aspects of the metaphor can be seen when it is applied in actual cross-cultural research projects. There is the search for culture-general or universal concepts (etics), culture-specific concepts (emics), as well as attempts to systematize etics in formal theories (Lonner 1980b). Emics identified by people outside a culture are difficult to understand and to describe because, by definition, they are not part of the outsider's frame of reference. Emics should receive special attention in discussion sections of research reports.

CONSERVATIVE-AUTHORITARIANISM   Research has recently shown that aspects of some general concepts are etic and that others are emic. The example of need for achievement (Maehr & Nicholls 1980) has already been discussed. Achievement includes the etic of goal setting, but the Japanese emic is that the goals can be group oriented and in the United States they are more frequently individual oriented. It should be noted that a combination of etics and emics is necessary for an understanding of a concept as it is found in any given culture. In investigating the meaning of the concept "conservative-authoritarianism" in Poland and the United States, Miller, Slomczynski & Schoenberg (1981) specifically used an emic-etic framework. They found that there was a core set of five scale items (the etic) which were successful, as shown by the application of various construct validity criteria, in measuring the concept in both countries. These items dealt with deference to traditional authority figures such as parents, forefathers, and experts, and acceptance of conventional morality regarding premarital sex. Further, there were two emic scales (one for each country) which were successful in measuring additional aspects of the concept. For Poland, three items measured an aspect called "deference to hierarchial authority which is bureaucratically or legally legitimized." In the United States, four emic items measured two aspects called "use of stereotypes and the endorsement of public intervention in matters ordinarily addressed elsewhere, e.g. in the family or courts" (Miller et al 1981, pp. 186–87). Emic items were shown as measuring aspects of the same concept (within each country) through the use of multivariate statistics relating the core items to the emics. It is no accident that the labels for the emic items are long. Since Miller and her colleagues wanted to communicate their results to readers in both the United States and Poland, they had to introduce unfamiliar aspects of a general concept, a task which often demands lengthy titles and explanatory prose.

DEPRESSION   The concept of depression has been analyzed in culture-general and culture-specific terms by Marsella (1980), and there seems to be less core meaning than might be expected. In comparing the subjective experience of depression among Japanese Americans and Caucasian Americans, the former used external referent words such as dark, cloudy, or rain, while the latter used internal referent words such as sadness, despair, and loneliness. The different connotations of depression are undoubtedly mediated by self images in the two countries [e.g. internal-external locus of control (Evans 1981, reviewed previously)] which influence subjective experience. In reviewing other studies of depression among members of seven cultures, Marsella (1980 p. 243) concluded that there is little in common except that the emotional state is one of concern to people. "This does not mean that depression, as it is defined in the West, is absent in cultures that do not have conceptually equivalent terms but, rather, that it is conceptualized differently and may be experienced differently." Related work has been done, using a culture-general and culture-specific approach within the same analysis, by Boucher (1979) on emotion, Higginbotham (1978) on anxiety, Draguns (1980a) on psychological disorders requiring intervention, and Shizuru & Marsella (1981) on the processing of sensory information among Japanese Americans.

LOCUS OF CONTROL   Other work can be interpreted through an emicetic approach even though the researchers themselves did not use the terms. In another study of locus of control, Lao (1978) argued that the concept is multidimensional rather than unidimensional. She developed three subscales which measured aspects of the original, broader concept: the belief in general internality (one item: "When I make plans, I am almost certain to make them work"); the belief in the influence of powerful others; and beliefs about the role of chance in one's life. She found that these subscales measured common conceptions in the United States, Taiwan, and Japan, and that there were also some emic concerns which must be considered for a fuller understanding. One was that the general internality factor accounted for the most variance with the Taiwan respondents, while the belief in the influence of powerful others accounted for the most variance among respondents in the United States. "This would suggest that general intensity is a more dominant factor for the Chinese (Lao 1978, p. 118)." Another intriguing finding was that the test, originally developed out of a research tradition within the United States, was far more effective in measuring locus of control among the Taiwanese than among the American respondents. The three factors accounted for 76% of the variance among the Chinese but only 33% among the Americans. Other researchers have also found either higher reliabilities, greater predictability, or clearer results with American-developed personality tests used in other cultures compared to similar data from the United States (Aram & Piraino 1978, Ray & Singh 1980, Shizuru & Marsella 1981). Given the controversy and criticism over the last 10 years concerning the propriety of tests standardized in one country but used in another, this is a very surprising set of findings. A speculative possibility is that people in some cultures have a more stable image of their own personalities. Compared to the American ideal of change and development over time, including one's adulthood, people in some cultures may formulate a clear self-image at some point in their lives. Further, they may not consciously entertain the possibility of change to the same extent as Americans.

WORKING WITH EMIC CONCEPTS   In the work with locus of control, researchers started with a possible etic and investigated emic manifestations in different cultures. At times, the research moves in the opposite direction: a possible emic is investigated for more general or etic aspects. Knapp & Seagrim (1981) investigated a striking finding reported by Kearins (1976) on the far greater superiority of Aboriginal Australian children over Caucasian Australian (called "European") children in an experiment measuring visual memory for spatial displays. Far more Aboriginal children made perfect scores on one or more subtasks within the experiment, causing speculation about the possibility of widespread eidetic imagery. After failing to replicate the finding, Knapp and Seagrim, following a lead suggested by Drinkwater (1978), analyzed the possibility that the Aboriginal children in the Kearins study lived in areas where visual memory games were common in their everyday lives. Consequently, the specific skills learned there transferred to the experimental task. The Aboriginal children tested in the replication study were not so familiar with visual games. Interestingly, five European children from the replication study were familiar with a party game involving the memorization of objects from a picture or an array. The results for these children was superior to the performance of the Kearins' group of European children. Knapp & Seagrim (1981, p. 228) concluded:

> . . . it may be unwise to think, as has been the fashion, in terms of exclusive strategies —visual or verbal—being used by different racial groups . . . [we] prefer to consider that a range of coding strategies involving both visual and verbal components is available to all subjects, groups of whom may select from them differently.

Another general point is the danger of generalizing from very specific skills found in an experiment (emic) to a more general strategy of widespread utility. Whereas Kearins suggested tasks such as visual association to teach Aboriginal children to read, Knapp and Seagrim suggest that the skill (which itself is a fragile phenomenon to demonstrate) may be task-specific and unrelated to the verbal skills demanded by reading. The movement between considerations of very specific skills demonstrated by people in different cultures and the analysis of how these skills relate to a broader framework resembles the sort of dialectic analyzed by Altman (1977). Other work on the specific skills-general factors problem has been carried out recently by Biesheuvel (1979), Nachshon (1979), Cummins (1980), Deregowski (1980a,) Jahoda (1980a), and Wagner (1981).

Another use of emics is to integrate them into studies meant to investigate an etic concept. Put another way, the goal of the researcher is to discover emic content (by definition, with which people are familiar) so as to use it in investigating a theoretical construct. It is in the discovery of such emic content where the contributions of ethnographic cognition and everyday behavior analysis (previously reviewed) can be helpful. Without the addition of emic content, researchers may obtain only reactions to unfamiliar material. Bickersteth & Das (1981) investigated the concept of syllogistic reasoning among children in Canada and Sierra Leone. They developed four types of syllogisms in a noteworthy attempt at what might be called "balanced fairness" for all participants. Syllogisms were designed with content relevant to Sierra Leone, such as sugar cane; relevant to Canada, such as Pierre Trudeau and a hockey player; with realistic content of probable equal concern in the two countries, such as field sports; and with unrealistic content, such as flying elephants. Participants worked with all four types of syllogisms in their own language. Sierra Leone children performed as well as Canadian children on all types of items, and they gave equal numbers of explanations for their answers based on their cultural background and the logical relationships of the premises. The concerns for communication with participants and for culture-relevant materials shown by Bickersteth & Das is becoming the norm for research. I have been a reviewer recently of articles submitted to two journals not known as primary outlets for cross-cultural research (*Social Psychology Quarterly* and *American Psychologist*), and the editors circulated copies of the comments by all three reviewers for each submission. For both articles, other reviewers pointed to the issues of communication with participants and interpretative problems when people are faced with materials familiar in one culture but not in another.

Other analysts have written on the issue of developing emic materials within etic frameworks (Jones & Zoppel 1979, Davidson & Thomson 1980) and have given specific examples based on their own research. One variant of this procedure which should receive more attention is the addition of new items to so-called standardized tests. Researchers can start with an existing instrument, but if they feel (based on pretest work or informal observations) that there is an emic coloring to some etic, they can design new items to test their hypotheses. They can relate people's responses to the new and old items using the sort of multivariate statistical procedures described by Miller et al (1981; see also Irvine & Carroll 1980 for application of multivariate statistics).

Universals

Another feature of much cross-cultural research over the last 5 years is that claims have been made and evidence put forth for the existence of culture universals (Lambert & Tan 1979, Triandis 1979, Super 1980, Munroe &

Munroe 1980b). Such studies emphasize the etic aspects of cross-cultural research, although provisions can also be made for emic coloring of concepts within any one culture. Research on universals will undoubtedly be one of cross-cultural psychology's most visible contributions to theory development in the behavioral/social sciences. Solid evidence that a concept is universal or has a universal core meaning is the foundation for any incorporation into a theoretical system. Further, analysis of the reasons for the universality leads to testable hypotheses and later integration of findings into theories. The following discussion of universals is organized according to the typology developed by Lonner (1980b). Slight modifications have been made to maximize the differences across the types of universals, but even with these modifications a given piece of research can be placed in more than one category. The categories are meant to help organize a diverse literature rather than to form the basis of some metatheory.

SIMPLE UNIVERSALS   This category includes facts about culture which are observable in people's behavior. They include the fact that people educate their children (Rogoff 1981), shelter themselves from the elements (Altman & Chemers 1980), and engage in rituals (Peters & Price-Williams 1980). What removes these from the status of boring generalities is the emic manifestations of etics within a given culture (what Lonner 1980b calls "variform universals"). People certainly express emotions (Izard 1980), but this generality becomes much more interesting and important given the results of empirical research. The number of basic, discrete emotions appears to be finite and low [approximately six (Boucher 1979)], and happiness appears to be the clearest in its expression and most easily communicable across cultures (Boucher & Carlson 1980, Keating & Associates 1981). Convergent evidence concerning the central role of happiness comes from the work of Osgood (1979), who points to the universal aspect of evaluation (good-bad for me) as the strongest component of the connotation of concepts.

FUNCTIONAL UNIVERSALS   Different behaviors can have the same consequences, and functional universals refer to behaviors which have the same consequences when cultures are compared. The frequently heard term "functionally equivalent," then, means that different behaviors can be considered comparable if they have the same effects. A good example is current thinking about psychopathology (Draguns 1977, 1980b; see also Sanua 1980, Tseng & Hsu 1980). Four dimensions of abnormal behavior have been suggested as existing in all cultures, with the emphasis for comparative purposes being on the observable effects and the shared beliefs about the behavior within a society. The dimensions (to use Draguns' terms) are convenient labels which will include many different behaviors whenever cultures are compared. The category called "bipolar extremes" of a dimension—which would be based on societal standards (Higginbotham 1979a,b) —and the "pathological extremes" of a dimension (again, as labeled in a society) are the categories which allow analysis of the dimensions according to their functional equivalence across cultures. The dimensions, then, will include many culture-specific items, some of which would be considered pathological in one culture (e.g. beliefs in spirits which have a direct influence on one's behavior) but normal and even desirable in another. For instance, one of Draguns' dimensions is social behavior, with bipolar extremes of reliable and appropriate to untrustworthy and unpredictable, and a pathological extreme of labeled personality disturbances. Wide variations in what is considered appropriate have been identified across cultures [e.g. Rohner (1980) on parental acceptance-rejection, Peters & Price-Williams (1980) on social control mechanisms], with considerable overlap between what one society considers normal and what another considers a matter for outside intervention.

ETHOLOGICALLY ORIENTED UNIVERSALS   Some behaviors may be common to all humans because of a phylogenetic link involving survival value through a long evolutionary process (Thompson 1980). Some behaviors will be universal since all humans have the genetic capabilities and can find sufficient stimulation within any society to activate the behaviors. An example is speech: since all societies have members whose body organs needed to produce speech are sound, the utterances of infants can be compared across cultures (Bowerman 1981). Other behaviors will be universal because of common threats from nature or from other, hostile societies. Examples are the need to organize societies into action for the common good (Boldt 1979, Price-Williams 1979, 1980b) and the consequent effects on words within languages which describe interpersonal relationships (Bond 1979, White 1980).

SYSTEMATIC BEHAVIOR UNIVERSALS: DYNAMIC   When a number of presumed universals have been integrated into a system, with theoretical links between the multiple universals, Lonner (1980b) applies the label "systematic." Historically, the work of Freud attracted a great deal of attention in cross-cultural studies (see Levinson & Malone 1980 for a review), but its influence has waned over the last 20 years. Probable reasons include troubling issues of reliability and validity of measures and concerns that a system foreign to other cultures is being imposed. Maslow's need hierarchy (e.g. Aram & Piraino 1978) is more testable across cultures since the basic needs stem from human demands for food, security, and affiliation.

Given the assumptions about people's basic quest for knowledge and under-standing about aspects of culture beyond their very basic needs, the possible universality of value systems can be tested (McClelland 1981). Attempts have been made to devise explanatory frameworks within which nomothetic and ideographic approaches to value assessment can be combined (Zaval-loni 1980).

SYSTEMATIC BEHAVIOR UNIVERSALS: SEQUENTIAL Some system-atic universals have the component of a hypothesized sequence of stages which are reached over a period of time. The work that has attracted the most attention by cross-cultural psychologists are Kohlberg's stages of moral development (Turiel et al 1978, Ziv et al 1978) and Piaget's stages of cognitive development (Dasen et al 1979, Dasen & Heron 1981). Specific experiences during socialization have been hypothesized as affecting the rate of movement among stages and (much more speculatively) the achieve-ment of the higher stages. For instance, Ziv et al (1978) found that children of the same age in Israel were differentially exposed to models and influ-ences which might affect the development of moral judgments. City chil-dren, exposed to a greater variety of models, were more relativistic in their judgments than were Kibbutz children living in more homogenous environ-ments. Arab children living in Israel demonstrated judgments similar to those of the Kibbutz children. Despite the differences between the Kibbutz and the Arab communities, a common core set of socialization experiences such as homogeneity (within a culture) of norms and strong expectations of children yielded similar outcomes. A probable outcome from further research on the achievement of higher stages within either the Kohlberg or Piagetian systems (assuming that the highest stages are not impositions from Western technology or ideology) will be that people can universally demonstrate the competencies which define the stages (see Jahoda 1980b). Absence of demonstrations that the higher stages are achieved by adults may reflect more upon the researchers' design and measures than people's competencies (please see previous discussion on communication and famil-iar materials). However, there may be fewer demands in the everyday lives of people in different cultures to demonstrate the competencies thought to be part of the higher stages.

SPECULATIVE UNIVERSALS Some presumed universals have been the topics for more cocktail party conversation than empirical research. Lonner (1980b) points out that many such presumed universals are actually labels for very complex concepts (e.g. the proper role of elected or hereditary authority; determinants of and limits on personal freedom; the effects of modernization upon traditional values) which allow some sort of minimal communication among people. Even with the weight of "information" coming from armchair analyses rather than cross-cultural data, some of these extremely difficult topics have been the subject of empirical studies. Munroe & Munroe (1980b) have analyzed altered states of consciousness by demystification through use of more basic concepts such as socialization emphases and coping mechanisms to deal with the contradictions of everyday life. The concept of an enemy, and the potential for war, is a probable universal, and this complex problem has also been interpreted in terms of more basic concepts (Rofe & Lewin 1980). Similar analyses have been done on the phenomena of modernization and acculturation as people incorporate elements of highly industrialized societies into their cultures or actually move across cultures (Paige 1979, Higginbotham 1979a, Szapocznik et al 1980). The concept of subjective culture, central to Triandis's (1980a,b,c) attempts to develop a broad, integrative framework to explain human behavior in cross-cultural perspective, has been clearly operationalized in research on personal symbols (Valadez 1978).

What Problems Will Cross-Cultural Research Always Have?

Given the obvious complexities of working in other cultures, there will always be difficulties with which researchers must deal. None will ever automatically go away, yet there have been excellent discussions of approaches to dealing with the difficulties. There will always be a larger number of plausible rival hypotheses to account for data compared to studies within the researcher's own country, but there are also lists of common plausible rival explanations which researchers can consult (Brown & Sechrest 1980). There will always be temptations to use one's own standards in interpreting data and thus temptations to write with a judgmental tone (discussed by Jordan & Tharp 1979, Zaidi 1979a, St. George 1980, Triandis 1980b). Researchers can acquaint themselves with the literature on culture relativity (Lonner 1980b, Shweder & Bourne 1982), so that at least they know when they are being judgmental. Closely related, there will always be ethical concerns centering around the choice of topic for study, funding sources, the people with whom one works, the uses to which publications will be put, reciprocity in the research endeavor, and a host of other issues (Doob 1980, Goodenough 1980, Warwick 1980). There will always be difficulties in making comparisons across cultures (Bochner 1980, Pareek & Rao 1980), determining equivalence of measures (Brislin 1980, S. H. Irvine & Carroll 1980), and interpreting the meaning of what people in various cultures are saying to the researcher (e.g. the exchange between J. Irvine 1978 and Greenfield 1979). As Malpass (1977) has pointed out, these issues are not merely methodological sore spots. Any solution to methodological problems is also likely to be a substantive contribution to theoretical issues such as communication, semantics, and values.

Future Needs

Major advances have been made in both substantive contributions and methodological breakthroughs, yet there are many issues which are in need of further study. More longitudinal research is needed such as the 20-year follow-up of children raised in the Kibbutz (Beit-Hallahmi et al 1979). More collaborative efforts in which data are gathered in many countries and shared among a number of collaborators are needed (Campbell 1968, Drenth & Wilpert 1980, Keating et al 1981). Data from many cultures are easier to interpret than data from one or two since there are fewer plausible rival hypotheses, above and beyond the investigators' preferred explanation, to account for the findings. At the same time, if multiple data sets are analyzed so as to be reported at the level of cultures or countries (as has been done by Berry 1980a, Hofstede 1980, Welch et al 1981), then the classic problem of inferring individual differences from ecological correlations comes to the forefront (Robinson 1950). This problem is in need of further analysis as it applies to cross-cultural psychology. There must also be more thinking about obtaining input from members of different cultures concerning the concepts to be investigated and the methods to be used, as well as their reactions (prior to publication) about a study's findings (some comments on this issue by Draguns 1979a, Triandis 1979). Such additional input should provide a balance to the inevitable biases which any outsider brings to the study of another culture.

There are also some mistakes which cross-cultural research does not need to perpetuate. One is premature conclusions about questionable data. Kagan & associates (1979) were unable to replicate earlier (Kagan & Klein 1973) and widely cited (e.g. Whiting 1981) research in Guatemala which was initially interpreted as indicating that children can "catch up" in cognitive functioning despite unfavorable early experiences. Kagan et al (1979, p. 59) concluded that if the performance differences across two research sites in Guatemala are ". . . the product of differences in nutrition, health, and the variety of experiences during infancy, then our earlier suggestion that the effects of infant experience can be overcome by later events is challenged in a major way." The problem with the earlier data set was that the tests had a rather obvious ceiling problem. Commenting on the later study and the overinterpretation of the earlier Guatemalan data, Greenbaum (1979, p. 69) pointed out that ". . . such a situation demands care in drawing conclusions. This was lacking in the authors' previous statements."

In addition to ceiling effects, other methodological problems have continued despite very detailed treatments in the literature. Whenever researchers work with intact samples, there is the temptation to equate through matching. This procedure was treated as if it was a methodological plus in some places (e.g. Bronfenbrenner 1979), despite detailed warnings that it creates regression artifacts (Campbell & Stanley 1966). A balanced treatment concerning the issue of matched samples in cross-cultural studies is provided by Draguns (1980b, pp. 114–15). Post hoc analyses of data continue to prove that psychologists can provide an explanation for just about any piece of data (Pitariu 1981). Following in the tradition of Serpell (1976), some writers have emphasized the difficulties of cross-cultural comparisons without putting forward any positive suggestions for what they would consider a better alternative (e.g. Cole & Means 1981). There is a difference between concluding that (*a*) cross-cultural studies have not shed much light on a writer's very specific research interest and (*b*) cross-cultural studies have not made contributions. Conclusion *a* has been confused with conclusion *b*. My own impression is that there is a positive relationship between people's favorable vs unfavorable conclusions and the scope of their reading.

Conclusions

Cross-cultural studies have been able to make contributions to the development of many topic areas in psychology (see Table 1). Lessons learned and suggested future guidelines have been conveniently collected (Triandis et al 1980). There is a great deal of mutual enrichment between anthropology and psychology (Munroe & Munroe 1980b, Shweder & Bourne 1982). More and more notable cross-cultural studies are emanating from countries which previously were only the sites for research (e.g. Saraswathi et al 1979). Applications have been made in a variety of areas such as bilingual education (Cummins 1980), management career development (Wakabayashi & associates 1980), alcohol abuse (Sue et al 1979), and education (Price-Williams & Gallimore 1980). The future will undoubtedly see even more widespread acceptance of sophisticated methodological standards for any study which calls itself cross-cultural. More true collaborations will occur as social scientists in other countries become less deferent to imported concepts and instead put forward their own alternatives. Given the presence of methodological guidelines and model studies, the future will see even more give and take between cross-cultural and general psychology focused on various theoretical ideas.

ACKNOWLEDGMENTS

I would like to thank Graham Davidson, Susan Goldstein, Walter J. Lonner, Anthony Marsella, Lanette Shizuru, and Geoffrey White for their helpful comments on early drafts of this chapter.

Literature Cited

Altman, I. 1977. Privacy regulation: culturally universal or culturally specific? *J. Soc. Issues* 33(3):66–84

Altman, I., Chemers, M. 1980. Cultural aspects of environment-behavior relationships. See Triandis et al 1980, 5:335–93

Altman, I., Rapoport, A., Wohlwill, J., eds. 1980. *Human Behavior and Environment: Environment and Culture.* New York: Plenum. 351 pp.

Amir, Y., Bizman, A., Ben-Ari, R., Rivner, M. 1980. Contact between Israelis and Arabs: a theoretical evaluation of effects. *J. Cross-Cult. Psychol.* 11:426–43

Amir, Y., Sharan, S., Bizman, A., Rivner, M., Ben-Ari, R. 1978. Attitude change in desegregated Israeli high schools. *J. Educ. Psychol.* 70:129–36

Amir, Y., Sharan, S., Rivner, M., Ben-Ari, R., Bizman, A. 1979. Group status and attitude change in desegregated classrooms. *Int. J. Intercult. Relat.* 3:137–52

Aram, J., Piraino, T. 1978. The hierarchy of needs theory: an evaluation in Chile. *Interam. J. Psychol.* 12:179–88

Barry, H. 1980. Description and uses of the Human Relations Area Files. See Triandis et al 1980, 2:445–78

Bass, B., Burger, R., Doktor, R., Barrett, G. 1979. *Assessment of Managers: An International Comparison.* New York: Free Press. 206 pp.

Beit-Hallahmi, B., Nevo, B., Rabin, A. 1979. Family and communally raised (Kibbutz) children 20 years later: biographical data. *Int. J. Psychol.* 14:215–23

Berry, J. 1980a. Ecological analyses for cross-cultural psychology. See Warren 1980, 2:157–89

Berry, J. 1980b. Introduction to methodology. See Triandis et al 1980, 2:1–28

Berry, J. 1980c. Social and cultural change. See Triandis et al 1980, 5:211–79

Bickersteth, P., Das, J. 1981. Syllogistic reasoning among school children from Canada and Sierra Leone. *Int. J. Psychol.* 16:1–11

Biesheuvel, S. 1979. The development of psychomotor skills: cross-cultural and occupational implications. *J. Cross-Cult. Psychol.* 10:271–93

Bilmes, J., Boggs, S. 1979. Language and communication: the foundations of culture. See Marsella et al 1979, pp. 47–76

Bochner, S. 1980. Unobtrusive methods in cross-cultural experimentation. See Triandis et al 1980, 2:319–87

Boldt, E. 1979. On aligning actions in simple societies. *Can. Rev. Soc. Anthropol.* 16:249–259

Bolton, R. 1976. Hostility in fantasy: a further test of the hypoglycemia-aggression hypothesis. *Aggressive Behav.* 2:257–74

Bolton, R. 1979a. Differential aggressiveness and litigiousness: social support and social status hypotheses. *Aggressive Behav.* 5:233–55

Bolton, R. 1979b. Machismo in motion: the ethos of Peruvian truckers. *Ethos* 7:312–42

Bond, M. 1979. Dimensions used in perceiving peers: cross-cultural comparisons of Hong Kong, Japanese, American and Filipino University students. *Int. J. Psychol.* 14:47–56

Boucher, J. 1979. Culture and emotion. See Marsella et al 1979, pp. 159–78

Boucher, J., Carlson, G. 1980. Recognition of facial expression in three cultures. *J. Cross-Cult. Psychol.* 11:263–80

Bowerman, M. 1981. Language development. See Triandis et al 1981, 4:93–185

Brewer, M., Campbell, D. 1976. *Ethnocentrism and Intergroup Attitudes: East African Evidence.* Beverly Hills, Calif: Sage. 218 pp.

Brislin, R. 1979. The problems and prospects of cross-cultural research as seen by experienced practitioners. See Eckensberger et al 1979, pp. 219–35

Brislin, R. 1980. Translation and content analysis of oral and written materials. See Triandis et al 1980, 2:389–444

Brislin, R. 1981. *Cross-Cultural Encounters: Face-to-Face Interaction.* New York: Pergamon. 373 pp.

Bronfenbrenner, U. 1979. *The Ecology of Human Development.* Cambridge: Harvard Univ. Press. 330 pp.

Brown, C., Keats, J., Keats, D., Seggie, I. 1980. Reasoning about implication: a comparison of Malaysian and Australian subjects. *J. Cross-Cult. Psychol.* 11:395–410

Brown, E., Sechrest, L. 1980. Experiments in cross-cultural research. See Triandis et al 1980, 2:297–318

Brown, R. 1973. *A First Language: The Early Stages.* New York: Free Press. 437 pp.

Buffardi, L., Nichols, J. 1981. Citation impact, acceptance rate, and APA journals. *Am. Psychol.* 36:1453–56

Callan, V. 1980. The value and cost of children: Australian, Greek, and Italian couples in Sydney, Australia. *J. Cross-Cult. Psychol.* 11:482–97

Campbell, D. 1968. A cooperative multinational opinion sample. *J. Soc. Issues* 24(2):245–56

Campbell, D., Stanley, J. 1966. *Experimental & Quasi-Experimental Designs for Research.* Chicago: Rand-McNally. 84 pp.

Chandler, T., Shama, D., Wolf, F., Planchard, S. 1981. Multiattributional causality: a five cross-national samples study. *J. Cross-Cult. Psychol.* 12:207–21

Childs, C., Greenfield, P. 1980. Informal modes of learning and teaching: the case of Zinacanteco weaving. See Warren 1980, 2:269–316

Ciborowski, T. 1979. Cross-cultural aspects of cognitive functioning: culture and knowledge. See Marsella et al 1979, pp. 101–16

Ciborowski, T. 1980. The role of context, skill, and transfer in cross-cultural experimentation. See Triandis et al 1980, 2:279–95

Cole, M. 1975. An ethnographic psychology of cognition. In *Cross-cultural Perspectives on Learning,* ed. R. Brislin, S. Bochner, W. Lonner, pp. 157–75. Beverly Hills, Calif: Sage. 336 pp.

Cole, M., Means, B. 1981. *Comparative Studies of How People Think: An Introduction.* Cambridge: Harvard Univ. Press. 208 pp.

Colletta, N. 1980. Ponape: cross-cultural contact, formal schooling, and foreign dominance. See Hamnett & Brislin 1980, pp 61–69

Crandall, R., Thompson, R. 1978. The social meaning of leisure in Uganda and America. *J. Cross-Cult. Psychol.* 9:469–81

Cummins, J. 1980. Psychological assessment of immigrant children: logic or intuition? *J. Multiling. Multicult. Educ.* 1:97–111

Dasen, P. 1972. Cross-cultural Piagetian research: a summary. *J. Cross-Cult. Psychol.* 3:23–39

Dasen, P., Heron, A. 1981. Cross-cultural tests of Piaget's theory. See Triandis et al 1981, 4:295–341

Dasen, P., Lavallee, M., Retschitzki, J. 1979. Training conservation of quantity (liquids) in West African (Baoule) children. *Int. J. Psychol.* 14:57–68

Dasen, P., Ngini, L. 1979. Cross-cultural training studies of concrete operations. See Eckensberger et al 1979, pp. 94–104

Davidson, A., Thomson, E. 1980. Cross-cultural studies of attitudes and beliefs. See Triandis et al 1980, 5:25–71

Davidson, G. 1980. Psychology and Aborigines: the place of research. *Aust. Psychol.* 15:111–21

Davies, J. 1978. *The Psychology of Music.* Stanford, Calif: Stanford Univ. Press. 240 pp.

Deregowski, J. 1979. Lack of applied perceptual theory: the case of engineering drawings. See Eckensberger et al 1979, pp. 15–26

Deregowski, J. 1980a. Experienced and inexperienced model makers: model-making and drawing in Rhodesia. *J. Cross-Cult. Psychol.* 11:189–202

Deregowski, J. 1980b. Perception. See Triandis et al 1980, 3:21–115

Detweiler, R. 1978. Culture, category width, and attributions: a model-building approach to the reasons for cultural effects. *J. Cross-Cult. Psychol.* 9:259–84

Detweiler, R. 1980. Intercultural interaction and the categorization process: a conceptual analysis and behavioral outcome. *Int. J. Intercult. Relat.* 4:275–93

DeVos, G. 1980. Ethnic adaptation and minority status. *J. Cross-Cult Psychol.* 11:101–24

Diaz-Guerrero, R. 1979. The development of coping style. *Hum. Dev.* 22:320–31

Dien, D., Fujisawa, H. 1979. Machiavellianism in Japan: a longitudinal study. *J. Cross-Cult. Psychol.* 10:508–16

Dinges, N., Trimble, J., Hollenbeck, A. 1979. American Indian adolescent socialization: a review of the literature. *J. Adolesc.* 2:259–96

Doob, L. 1980. The inconclusive struggles of cross-cultural psychology. *J. Cross-Cult. Psychol.* 11:59–73

Draguns, J. 1977. Mental health and culture. In *Overview of Intercultural Education, Training, and Research,* ed. D. Hoopes, P. Pedersen, G. Renwick, pp. 57–73. Washington DC: Georgetown Univ. (SIETAR). 152 pp.

Draguns, J. 1979a. Culture and personality. See Marsella et al 1979, pp. 179–207

Draguns, J. 1979b. Culture and personality: old fields, new directions. See Eckensberger et al 1979, pp. 131–42

Draguns, J. 1980a. Introduction to psychopathology. See Triandis et al 1980, 6:1–8

Draguns, J. 1980b. Psychological disorders of clinical severity. See Triandis et al 1980, 6:99–174

Drenth, P., Koopman, P., Rus, V., Odar, M., Heller, F., Brown, A. 1979. Participative decision making: a comparative study. *Ind. Relat.* 18:295–309

Drenth, P., Wilpert, B. 1980. The role of 'social contracts' in cross-cultural research. *Int. Rev. Appl. Psychol.* 29:293–305

Drinkwater, B. 1978. A reply to Kearins. *Aust. J. Psychol.* 30:115–18

Duda, J. 1980. Achievement motivation among Navajo students: a conceptual analysis with preliminary data. *Ethos* 8:316–31

Durojaiye, M. 1979a. Ethics of cross-cultural research viewed from third world perspective. *Int. J. Psychol.* 14:137–41

Durojaiye, M. 1979b. The need for international cooperation in cross-cultural psychology with special reference to action research in Africa. See Eckensberger et al 1979, pp. 3–11

Eckensberger, L., Lonner, W., Poortinga, Y., eds. 1979. *Cross-Cultural Contributions to Psychology*. Amsterdam: Swets & Zeitlinger. 441 pp.

Edwards, C. 1981. The comparative study of the development of moral judgment and reasoning. See Munroe et al 1981, pp. 501–28

Erchak, G. 1980. The acquisition of cultural rules by Kpelle children. *Ethos* 8:40–48

Estes, W., ed. 1975. *Handbook of Learning and Cognitive Processes,* Vol. 1. Hillsdale, NJ: Erlbaum. 303 pp.

Evans, H. 1981. Internal-external locus of control and word association: research with Japanese and American students. *J. Cross-Cult. Psychol.* 12:372–82

Fahrmeier, E. 1978a. The development of concrete operations among the Hausa. *J. Cross-Cult. Psychol.* 9:23–44

Fahrmeier, E. 1978b. The decline of egocentrism in Hausa children. *J. Cross-Cult. Psychol.* 9:191–200

Faustman, W., Mathews, W. 1980. Perception of personal control and academic achievement in Sri Lanka: cross-cultural generality of American research. *J. Cross-Cult. Psychol.* 11:245–52

Feather, N. 1979. Accuracy of judgment of value systems: a field study of own and attributed value priorities in Papua New Guinea. *Int. J. Psychol.* 14:151–62

Feather, N. 1980. Value systems and social interaction: a field study in a newly independent nation. *J. Appl. Soc. Psychol.* 10:1–19

Feldman, J., MacDonald, F., Sam, I. 1980. Stereotype attribution in two ethnic groups. *Int. J. Intercult. Relat.* 4:185–202

Finley, G. 1979. Collaborative issues in cross-cultural research. *Int. J. Intercult. Relat.* 3(1):5–13

Fioravanti, M., Gough, H., Frere, L. 1981. English, French, and Italian adjective check lists: a social desirability analysis. *J. Cross-Cult. Psychol.* 12:461–72

Foorman, B., Arias-Godinez, B., Gonzales, J. 1981. Language and cognition: English and Spanish-speaking children's performance on perceptual and communication tasks. *J. Cross-Cult. Psychol.* 12:304–26

Foschi, M. 1980. Theory, experimentation, and cross-cultural comparisons in social psychology. *Can. J. Sociol.* 5:91–102

Fry, P. 1982. Cognitive mediators between life stress and depression in the elderly: a cross-cultural comparison of Asian and Caucasians. *Int. J. Psychol.* 17: In press

Fry, P., Ghosh, R. 1980a. Attributional differences in the life satisfactions of the elderly: a cross-cultural comparison of Asian and United States subjects. *Int. J. Psychol.* 15:201–12

Fry, P., Ghosh, R. 1980b. Attributions of success and failure: comparison of cultural differences between Asian and Caucasian children. *J. Cross-Cult. Psychol.* 11:343–63

Fry, P., Knopf, G., Coe, K. 1980. Effects of counselor and client racial similarity on the counselor's response patterns and skills. *J. Couns. Psychol.* 27:130–37

Garcia, J. 1981. The logic and limits of mental aptitude testing. *Am. Psychol.* 36:1172–80

Geertz, C. 1973. Thick description: toward an interpretive theory of culture. In *The Interpretation of Cultures.* New York: Basic Books. 470 pp.

Geis, F. 1979. Machiavellianism: a cross-cultural perspective of manipulative social behavior. See Eckensberger et al, pp. 151–62

Giles, H., Llado, N., McKirnan, D., Taylor, D. 1979. Social identity in Puerto Rico. *Int. J. Psychol.* 14:185–201

Gill, R., Keats, D. 1980. Elements of intellectual competence: judgments by Australian and Malay university students. *J. Cross-Cult. Psychol.* 11:233–43

Ginsburg, H., Posner, J., Russell, R. 1981. The development of knowledge concerning written arithmetic: a cross-cultural study. *Int. J. Psychol.* 16:13–34

Goodenough, W. 1980. Ethnographic field techniques. See Triandis et al 1980, 2:29–55

Goodnow, J. 1979. "Conventional wisdom": everyday models of cognitive development. See Eckensberger et al 1979, pp. 55–68

Goodnow, J. 1980. Everyday concepts of intelligence and its development. See Warren 1980, 2:191–219

Graf, R., Freer, S., Plaizier, P. 1979. Interpersonal perception as a function of help-seeking: a United States-Netherlands contrast. *J. Cross-Cult. Psychol.* 10:101–10

Greenbaum, C. 1979. Commentary and discussion (of the Kagan et al 1979 monograph). *Monogr. Soc. Res. Child Dev.* 44(5) No. 180:67–73

Greenfield, P. 1979. Response to "Wolof 'magical' thinking: culture and conservation revisited" by Judith I. Irvine. *J. Cross-Cult. Psychol.* 10:251–56

Guthrie, G. 1979. A cross-cultural odyssey: some personal reflections. See Marsella et al 1979, pp. 349–68

Guthrie, G., Tanco, P. 1980. Alienation. See Triandis et al 1980, 6:9–59

Hall, E. 1977. *Beyond Culture.* Garden City, NY: Anchor. 298 pp.

Hamnett, M., Brislin, R., eds. 1980. *Research in Culture Learning: Language and Conceptual Studies.* Honolulu: Univ. Press Hawaii. 183 pp.

Haque, A., Lawson, E. 1980. The mirror image phenomenon in the context of the Arab-Israeli conflict. *Int. J. Intercult. Relat.* 4:107–15

Harkness, S. 1980. The cultural context of child development. *New Dir. Child Dev.* 8:7–13

Harkness, S., Super, C. 1980. Child development theory in anthropological perspective. *New Dir. Child Dev.* 8:1–5

Helmreich, R., Bakeman, R., Scherwitz, L. 1973. The study of small groups. *Ann. Rev. Psychol.* 24:337–54

Heron, A., Kroeger, E. 1981. Introduction to developmental psychology. See Triandis et al 1981, 4:1–15

Herskovits, M. 1948. *Man and His Works.* New York: Knopf. 678 pp.

Higginbotham, H. 1978. Review of *Cross-Cultural Anxiety,* ed. C. Spielberger, R. Diaz-Guerrero (1976). *J. Cross-Cult. Psychol.* 9:499–502

Higginbotham, H. 1979a. Culture and mental health services. See Marsella et al 1979, pp. 307–32

Higginbotham, H. 1979b. Cultural issues in providing psychological services for foreign students in the United States. *Int. J. Intercult. Relat.*

Hofstede, G. 1980. *Culture's Consequences: International Differences in Work-Related Values.* Beverly Hills, Calif: Sage. 480 pp.

Hollander, E. 1981. *Principles and Methods of Social Psychology.* New York: Oxford Univ. Press. 558 pp.

Holtzman, W. 1979. Culture, personality development, and mental health in the Americas. *Interam. J. Psychol.* 13: 27–49

Hudson, R. 1981. Some issues on which linguists can agree. *J. Ling.* 17:333–43

Irvine, J. 1978. Wolof "magical thinking": culture and conservation revisited. *J. Cross-Cult. Psychol.* 9:300–10

Irvine, S. H. 1979. The place of factor analysis in cross-cultural methodology and its contribution to cognitive theory. See Eckensberger et al 1979, pp. 300–41

Irvine, S. H., Carroll, W. 1980. Testing and assessment across cultures: issues in methodology and theory. See Triandis et al 1980, 2:181–244

Izard, C. 1980. Cross-cultural perspectives on emotion and emotional communication. See Triandis et al 1980, 3:185–221

Jaffe, Y., Shapir, N., Yinon, Y. 1981. Aggression and its escalation. *J. Cross-Cult. Psychol.* 12:21–36

Jahoda, G. 1980a. Sex and ethnic differences on a spatial-perceptual task: some hypotheses tested. *Br. J. Psychol.* 71: 425–31

Jahoda, G. 1980b. Theoretical and systematic approaches in cross-cultural psychology. See Triandis et al 1980, 1:69–141

Jahoda, G. 1981. The influence of schooling on adult recall of familiar stimuli: a study in Ghana. *Int. J. Psychol.* 16: 59–71

Johnson, F., Marsella, A. 1978. Differential attitudes toward verbal behavior in students of Japanese and European ancestry. *Genet. Psychol. Monogr.* 97:43–76

Johnson, K. 1978. Modernity and dream content: a Ugandan example. *Ethos* 6: 212–20

Jones, E., Zoppel, C. 1979. Personality differences among Blacks in Jamaica and the United States. *J. Cross-Cult. Psychol.* 10:435–56

Jordan, C., Tharp, R. 1979. Culture and education. See Marsella et al 1979, pp. 265–85

Kagan, J., Klein, R. 1973. Cross-cultural perspectives on early development. *Am. Psychol.* 28:947–61

Kagan, J., Klein, R., Finley, G., Rogoff, B., Nolan, E. 1979. A cross-cultural study of cognitive development. *Monogr. Soc. Res. Child Dev.* 44(5) No. 180. 66 pp.

Kagan, S., Knight, G. 1979. Cooperation-competition and self-esteem: a case of cultural relativism. *J. Cross-Cult. Psychol.* 10:457–67

Kashoki, M. 1978. *Indigenous scholarship in African universities: the human factor* (research paper). New York: Wenner-Gren Found. 32 pp.

Kavanagh, J., Venezky, R., eds. 1980. *Orthography, Reading, and Dyslexia.* Baltimore: Univ. Park Press. 342 pp.

Kearins, J. 1976. Skills of desert aboriginal children. In *Aboriginal Cognition: Retrospect and Prospect,* ed. G. Kearney, D. McElwain, pp. 199–221. Canberra: Aust. Inst. Aboriginal Stud. 418 pp.

Keating, C., Mazur, A., Segall, M., Cysneiros, P., Divale, W., et al. 1981. Culture and the perception of social dominance from facial expression. *J. Pers. Soc. Psychol.* 40:615–26

Khanna, P., Khanna, J. 1979. Locus of control in India: a cross-cultural perspective. *Int. J. Psychol.* 14:207–14

Kilbride, P. 1980. Sensorimotor behavior of Baganda and Samia infants: a controlled comparison. *J. Cross-Cult. Psychol.* 11:131–52

Knapp, P., Seagrim, G. 1981. Visual memory in Australian aboriginal children and children of European descent. *Int. J. Psychol* 16:213–31

Kornadt, H., Eckensberger, L., Emminghaus, W. 1980. Cross-cultural research on motivation and its contribution to a general theory of motivation. See Triandis et al 1980, 3:223–321

Korte, C., Ayvalioglu, N. 1981. Helpfulness in Turkey: cities, towns, and urban villages. *J. Cross-Cult. Psychol.* 12:123–41

Kroeber, A., Kluckhohn, C. 1952. Culture: a critical review of concepts and definitions 47(1). Cambridge, Mass: Peabody Mus. 223 pp.

Kumar, K., ed. 1979. *Bonds Without Bondage: Explorations in Transcultural Interactions.* Honolulu: Univ. Press Hawaii. 302 pp.

Laboratory of Comparative Human Cognition. 1979. What's cultural about cross-cultural cognitive psychology? *Ann. Rev. Psychol.* 30:145–72

Lambert, W., Tan, A. 1979. Expressive styles and strategies in the aggressive actions of children of six cultures. *Ethos* 7: 19–36

Landy, F., Trumbo, D. 1980. *Psychology of Work Behavior.* Homewood, Ill: Dorsey. 626 pp.

Lao, R. 1978. Levenson's IPC (Internal-External Control) scale: a comparison of Chinese and American students. *J. Cross-Cult. Psychol.* 9:113–24

Leach, M. 1978. Pictorial depth and space: procedural, instrumental, cultural, and experiential factors contributing to their perception by Shana children. *J. Cross-Cult. Psychol.* 9:417–38

Levinson, D., Malone, M. 1980. *Toward Explaining Human Culture.* Buffalo, NY: HRAF. 397 pp.

Lewis, D. 1980. Mau Piailug's navigation of *Hokule'a* from Hawaii to Tahiti. See Hamnett & Brislin 1980, pp. 3–25

Lieberman, D. 1978. Language use in a bilingual West Indian community: analysis of behavior and attitudes. *Ethos* 6: 221–41

Lonner, W. 1979. Issues in cross-cultural psychology. See Marsella et al 1979, pp. 17–45

Lonner, W. 1980a. A decade of cross-cultural psychology: JCCP, 1970-1979. *J. Cross-Cult. Psychol.* 11:7–34

Lonner, W. 1980b. The search for psychological universals. See Triandis et al 1980, 1:143–204

Lonner, W., Triandis, H. 1980. Introduction to basic processes. See Triandis et al 1980, 3:1–20

Mackie, D. 1980. A cross-cultural study of intra-individual and interindividual conflicts of centration. *Eur. J. Soc. Psychol.* 10:313–18

Madsen, M., Lancy, D. 1981. Cooperative and competitive behavior: experiments related to ethnic identity and urbanization in Papua New Guinea. *J. Cross-Cult. Psychol.* 12:389–408

Maehr, M., Nicholls, J. 1980. Culture and achievement motivation: a second look. See Warren 1980, 2:221–67

Malpass, R. 1977. Theory and method in cross-cultural psychology. *Am. Psychol.* 32:1069–79

Mann, L. 1980. Cross-cultural studies of small groups. See Triandis et al 1980, 5:155–209

Marsella, A. 1979. Cross-cultural studies of mental disorders. See Marsella et al 1979, pp. 233–62

Marsella, A. 1980. Depressive experience and disorder across cultures. See Triandis et al 1980, 6:237–89

Marsella, A., Tharp, R., Ciborowski, T., eds. 1979. *Perspectives on Cross-Cultural Psychology.* New York: Academic. 413 pp.

McClelland, D. 1961. *The Achieving Society.* Princeton, NJ: Van Nostrand. 512 pp.

McClelland, D. 1981. Childrearing versus ideology and social structure as factors in personality development. See Munroe et al 1981, pp. 73–90

McKessar, C., Thomas, D. 1978. Verbal and non-verbal help-seeking among urban Maori and Pakeha children. *NZ J. Educ. Stud.* 13:29–39

McNeil, D. 1970. *Acquisition of Language: the Study of Developmental Psycholinguistics.* New York: Harper & Row. 183 pp.

Mead, M. 1928. *Coming of Age in Samoa.* New York: 297 pp.

Mead, M. 1977. Comments from an anthropologist. *Ann. NY Acad. Sci.* 285:501-4

Medin, D. 1981. Review of Vol. 14, *The Psychology of Learning and Motivation. Contemp. Psychol.* 26:762-63

Miller, D., Ross, M. 1975. Self-serving biases in the attribution of causality: fact or fiction. *Psychol. Bull.* 82:213-25

Miller, J., Slomczynski, K., Schoenberg, R. 1981. Assessing comparability of measurement in cross-national research: authoritarianism-conservatism in different sociocultural settings. *Soc. Psychol. Q.* 44:178-91

Morland, J., Hwang, C. H. 1981. Racial/ethnic identity of preschool children: comparing Taiwan, Hong Kong, and the United States. *J. Cross-Cult. Psychol.* 12:409-24

Morsbach, H. 1980. Major psychological factors influencing Japanese interpersonal relations. See Warren 1980, 2:317-44

Munro, D. 1979. Locus-of-control attribution: factors among Blacks and Whites in Africa. *J. Cross-Cult. Psychol.* 10:157-72

Munroe, R. H., Munroe, R. L. 1980a. Infant experience and childhood affect among the Logoli: a longitudinal study. *Ethos* 8:295-315

Munroe, R. L., Munroe, R. H. 1980b. Perspectives suggested by anthropological data. See Triandis et al 1980, 1:253-317

Munroe, R. H., Munroe, R. L., Whiting, B., eds. 1981. *Handbook of Cross-Cultural Human Development.* New York: Garland STPM. 888 pp.

Nachshon, I. 1979. Directional scanning of visual stimuli: sex effects and sex differences among subjects with opposite reading habits. *J. Cross-Cult. Psychol.* 10:231-42

Nadler, A., Romek, E., Shapira-Friedman, A. 1979. Giving in the Kibbutz: prosocial behavior of city and Kibbutz children as affected by social responsibility and social pressure. *J. Cross-Cult. Psychol.* 10:57-72

Naroll, R., Michik, G., Naroll, R. 1980. Holocultural research methods. See Triandis et al 1980, 2:479-521

Ng, S. H. 1980. *The Social Psychology of Power.* London: Academic. 280 pp.

Niles, F. 1981. Dimensionality of Rotter's I-E scale in Sri Lanka. *J. Cross-Cult. Psychol.* 12:473-79

Okonji, M. 1980. Cognitive styles across cultures. See Warren 1980, 2:1-50

Olmedo, E. 1981. Testing linguistic minorities. *Am. Psychol.* 36:1078-85

Osgood, C. 1979. From Yang and Yin to *and* or *but* in cross-cultural perspective. *Int. J. Psychol.* 14:1-35

Osgood, C., May, W., Miron, M. 1975. *Cross-Cultural Universals of Affective Meaning.* Urbana: Univ. Ill. Press. 580 pp.

Paige, R. 1979. The learning of modern culture: formal education and psychosocial modernity in East Java, Indonesia. *Int. J. Intercult. Relat.* 3:333-64

Palmer, C., Barba, C. 1981. Mental development after dietary intervention: a study of Philippine children. *J. Cross-Cult. Psychol.* 12:480-88

Pareek, Y., Rao, T. 1980. Cross-cultural surveys and interviewing. See Triandis et al 1980, 2:127-79

Pedersen, P. 1979. Non-Western psychology: the search for alternatives. See Marsella et al 1979, pp. 77-98

Peters, L., Price-Williams, D. 1980. Towards an experiential analysis of Shamanism. *Am. Ethnol.* 7:397-418

Piaget, J. 1977. Preface. In *Piagetian Psychology: Cross-Cultural Contributions,* ed. P. Dasen, pp. ix-xi. New York: Gardner. 379 pp.

Pitariu, H. 1981. Validation of the CPI Feminity scale in Romania. *J. Cross-Cult. Psychol.* 12:111-17

Posner, J., Baroody, A. 1979. Number conservation in two West African societies. *J. Cross-Cult. Psychol.* 10:479-96

Price-Williams, D. 1979. Modes of thought in cross-cultural psychology: an historical overview. See Marsella et al 1979, pp. 3-16

Price-Williams, D. 1980a. Anthropological approaches to cognition and their relevance to psychology. See Triandis et al 1980, 3:155-84

Price-Williams, D. 1980b. Toward the idea of a cultural psychology: a superordinate theme for study. *J. Cross-Cult. Psychol.* 11:75-88

Price-Williams, D., Gallimore, R. 1980. The cultural perspective. *Adv. Spec. Educ.* 2:165-92

Ray, J., Singh, S. 1980. Effects of individual differences on productivity among farmers in India. *J. Soc. Psychol.* 112:11-17

Rich, Y., Amir, Y., Ben-Ari, R. 1981. Social and emotional problems associated with integration in the Israeli junior high school. *Int. J. Intercult. Relat.* 5:259-75

Robinson, W. 1950. Ecological correlations and the behavior of individuals. *Am. Soc. Rev.* 15:351-57

Rodin, J. 1981. Current status of the internal-external hypothesis for obesity. *Am. Psychol.* 36:361-72

Rofe, Y., Lewin, I. 1980. Attitudes toward an enemy and personality in a war environment. *Int. J. Intercult. Relat.* 4:97–106

Rogoff, B. 1981. Schooling and the development of cognitive skills. See Triandis et al 1981, 4:233–94

Rohner, E., Rohner, R., Roll, S. 1980. Perceived parental acceptance-rejection and children's reported behavioral dispositions: a comparative and intracultural study of American and Mexican children. *J. Cross-Cult. Psychol.* 11: 213–31

Rohner, R. 1980. Worldwide tests of parental acceptance-rejection theory: an overview. *Behav. Sci. Res.* 15:1–21

Sahlins, M. 1960. Evolution: specific and general. In *Evolution and Culture,* ed. M. Sahlins, E. Service, pp. 12–44. Ann Arbor: Univ. Mich. Press. 131 pp.

St. George, R. 1980. The language skills of New Zealand Polynesian children: from deficiency to diversity. *Ethnic Racial Stud.* 3:89–98

St. George, R., Preston, R. 1980. Psychological testing in Papua New Guinea: a critical appraisal of the work of the Psychological Services Branch. *Aust. Psychol.* 15:57–69

Sanua, V. 1980. Familial and sociocultural antecedents of psychopathology. See Triandis et al 1980, 6:175–236

Saraswathi, T., Takker, D., Kaur, I. 1979. Perceived maternal disciplinary practices and their relation to moral judgment in 10–13-year-old Indian children. See Eckensberger et al 1979, pp. 345–52

Saxe, G. 1981. When fourth can precede second: a developmental analysis of an indigenous numeration system among Ponam islanders in Papua New Guinea. *J. Cross-Cult. Psychol.* 12:37–50

Segall, M. 1979. *Cross-Cultural Psychology: Human Behavior in Global Perspective.* Monterey, Calif: Brooks-Cole. 269 pp.

Segall, M., Campbell, D., Herskovits, M. 1966. *The Influence of Culture on Visual Perception.* Indianapolis: Bobbs-Merrill. 268 pp.

Segalowitz, N. 1981. Issues in the cross-cultural study of bilingual development. See Triandis et al 1981, 4:55–92

Seligman, M. 1975. *Helplessness.* San Francisco: Freeman. 250 pp.

Serpell, R. 1976. *Culture's Influence on Behavior.* London: Methuen. 144 pp.

Shea, J., Yerua, G. 1980. Conservation in community school children in Papua New Guinea. *Int. J. Psychol.* 15:11–25

Shizuru, L., Marsella, A. 1981. The sensory processes of Japanese-American and Caucasian-American students. *J. Soc. Psychol.* 114:147–58

Shweder, R. 1979a. Rethinking culture and personality theory. Part I: a critical examination of two classical postulates. *Ethos* 7:255–78

Shweder, R. 1979b. Rethinking culture and personality theory. Part II: a critical examination of two more classical postulates. *Ethos* 7:279–311

Shweder, R. 1980. Rethinking culture and personality. Part III: From genesis and typology to hermeneutics and dynamics. *Ethos* 8:60–94

Shweder, R., Bourne, E. 1982. Does the concept of the person vary cross-culturally? In *Cultural Conceptions of Mental Health and Therapy,* ed. A. Marsella, G. White, pp. 97–137. Dordrecht, The Netherlands: Reidel. 389 pp.

Sinha, D. 1979a. Cognitive and psychomotor skills in India: a review of research. *J. Cross-Cult. Psychol.* 10:324–55

Sinha, D. 1979b. Perceptual style among nomadic and transitional agriculturalist Birhors. See Eckensberger et al 1979, pp. 83–93

Speidel, G., ed. 1981. KEEP: Kamehameha Early Education Program. *Educ. Perspect.* 20(1), entire issue. 48 pp.

Stening, B. 1979. Problems in cross-cultural contact: a literature review. *Int. J. Intercult. Relat.* 3:269–313

Sternberg, R., Conway, B., Ketron, J., Bernstein, M. 1981. People's conceptions of intelligence. *J. Pers. Soc. Psychol.* 41: 37–55

Strodtbeck, F. 1964. Considerations of metamethod in cross-cultural studies. *Am. Anthropol.* 66:223–29

Sue, S., Allen, D., Conaway, L. 1978. The responsiveness equality of mental health care to Chicanos and Native Americans. *Am. J. Community Psychol.* 6:137–46

Sue, S., Zane, N., Ito, J. 1979. Alcohol drinking patterns among Asian and Caucasian Americans. *J. Cross-Cult. Psychol.* 10:41–56

Super, C. 1980. Cognitive development: looking across at growing up. *New Dir. Child Dev.* 8:59–69

Sutton-Smith, B., Roberts, J. 1981. Play, games, and sports. See Triandis et al 1981, 4:425–71

Szapocznik, J., Kurtines, W., Fernandez, T. 1980. Bicultural involvement and adjustment in Hispanic-American youths. *Int. J. Intercult. Relat.* 4:353–65

Thomas, D. 1978. Cooperation and competition among children in the Pacific Islands and New Zealand: the school as an agent of social change. *J. Res. Dev. Educ.* 12:88–96

Thomas, D. 1979. Social organization in the classroom: the competitive ethic and the Pacific way. *Directions* 2:1–7

Thompson, W. 1980. Cross-cultural uses of biological data and perspectives. See Triandis et al 1980, 1:205–52

Touhey, J. 1981. Replication failures in personality and social psychology: negative findings or mistaken assumptions? *Pers. Soc. Psychol. Bull.* 7:593–95

Triandis, H. 1979. The future of cross-cultural psychology. See Marsella et al 1979, pp. 389–410

Triandis, H. 1980a. A theoretical framework for the study of bilingual-bicultural adaptation. *Int. Rev. Appl. Psychol.* 29:7–16

Triandis, H. 1980b. Introduction. See Triandis et al 1980, 1:1–14

Triandis, H. 1980c. Reflections on trends in cross-cultural research. *J. Cross-Cult. Psychol.* 11:35–58

Triandis, H., Lambert, W., Berry, J., Lonner, W., Heron, A., Brislin, R., Draguns, J., eds. 1980–1981. *Handbook of Cross-Cultural Psychology,* six vol. Boston: Allyn & Bacon. 2507 pp.

Tseng, W. S., Hsu, J. 1979. Culture and psychotherapy. See Marsella et al, 1979, pp. 333–45

Tseng, W. S., Hsu, J. 1980. Minor psychological disturbances of everyday life. See Triandis et al 1980, 6:61–97

Turiel, E., Edwards, C., Kohlberg, L. 1978. Moral development in Turkish children, adolescents, and young adults. *J. Cross-Cult. Psychol.* 9:75–86

Valadez, J. 1978. Personal symbols: their heuristic importance for the analysis of militant political groups and artists in six Western cultures. *J. Cross-Cult. Psychol.* 9:439–54

Wagner, D. 1981. Culture and memory development. See Triandis et al 1981, 4:187–232

Wakabayashi, M., Minami, T., Hashimoto, M., Sano, K., Graen, M., Novak, M. 1980. Managerial career development: Japanese style. *Int. J. Intercult. Relat.* 4:391–420

Warren, N., ed. 1980. *Studies in Cross-Cultural Psychology,* Vol. 2. London: Academic. 357 pp.

Warwick, D. 1980. The politics and ethics of cross-cultural research. See Triandis et al 1980, 1:319–71

Welch, M., Page, B., Martin, L. 1981. Sex differences in the ease of socialization: an analysis of the efficiency of child training processes in preindustrial societies. *J. Soc. Psychol.* 113:3–12

Werner, E. 1979. Subcultural differences in ability, achievement, and personality factors among Oriental and Polynesian children on the island of Kauai, Hawaii. See Eckensberger et al 1979, pp. 163–79

White, G. 1980. Conceptual universals in interpersonal language. *Am. Anthropol.* 82:759–81

Whiting, J. 1954. The cross-cultural method. In *Handbook of Social Psychology* ed. G. Lindzey, 1:523–31. Reading, Mass: Addison-Wesley. 588 pp.

Whiting, J. 1968. Methods and problems in cross-cultural research. In *Handbook of Social Psychology,* ed. G. Lindzey, E. Aronson, 2:693–728. Reading, Mass: Addison-Wesley. 819 pp. 2nd ed.

Whiting, J. 1981. Environmental constraints on infant care practices. See Munroe et al 1981, pp. 155–79

Wober, M. 1974. Towards an understanding of the Uganda concept of intelligence. In *Culture and Cognition: Readings in Cross-Cultural Psychology,* ed. J. Berry, P. Dasen, pp. 260–80. London: Methuen. 465 pp.

Wrightsman, L., Deaux, K. 1981. *Social Psychology in the 80s.* Monterey, Calif: Brooks-Cole. 650 pp.

Yang, K. 1981. Problem behavior in Chinese adolescents in Taiwan: a classificatory-factorial study. *J. Cross-Cult. Psychol.* 12:179–93

Yang, K., Bond, M. 1980. Ethnic affirmation by Chinese bilinguals. *J. Cross-Cult. Psychol.* 11:411–25

Zaidi, S. 1979a. Autostereotypes of Pakistani adults. *Psychologia* 22:84–87

Zaidi, S. 1979b. Perception of parental sex preference by Nigerian children. *J. Soc. Psychol.* 108:267–68

Zaidi, S. 1979c. Values expressed in Nigerian children's drawings. *Int. J. Psychol.* 14:163–69

Zavalloni, M. 1980. Values. See Triandis et al 1980, 5:73–120

Ziv, A., Green, D., Guttman, J. 1978. Moral judgment: differences between city, Kibbutz and Israeli Arab preadolescents on the realistic-relativistic dimension. *J. Cross-Cult. Psychol.* 9:215–26

Ann. Rev. Psychol. 1983. 34:401–30

PSYCHOPATHOLOGY: BIOLOGICAL APPROACHES[1]

Monte S. Buchsbaum

Section on Clinical Psychophysiology, National Institute of Mental Health, Bethesda, Maryland 20205

Richard J. Haier

Section of Psychiatry and Human Behavior, Brown University, and Butler Hospital, Providence, Rhode Island 02906

CONTENTS

401

0066-4308/83/0201-0401$02.00

INTRODUCTION

The Implications of Genetics and Drug Treatment

Genetic transmission and drug response research continue to inspire biological approaches to the puzzles of psychopathology. Fifteen years ago, for example, the Denmark adoption studies of schizophrenia delivered a dramatic triad of findings: there was more schizophrenia in the biological relatives of adoptees, who themselves were schizophrenic, than in the adoptive families (Kety et al 1968); the adopted-away offspring of schizophrenic parents were at greater risk for schizophrenic illness than were controls adopted away from normal parents (Rosenthal et al 1968); and children of normal parents adopted away into homes where an adoptive parent became schizophrenic were not at greater risk for psychiatric problems (Wender et al 1974). In recent years, adoption strategies have examined affective disorders, alcoholism, and criminality. Each of these studies reports evidence supporting some genetic component, but much clarification and refinement are necessary. Nonetheless, any degree of genetic transmission between generations requires biological mechanisms. For this reason the genetic studies of psychopathology have encouraged the search for biological factors.

Most such research has focused on the action of drugs which ameliorate behavioral symptoms. Early findings established links between drug action and neurotransmitter systems. In schizophrenia, clinical alleviation of symptoms appears related to the action of dopamine as a chemical messenger from one nerve cell synapse to the next. Similarly, tricyclics used to alleviate depression affect various stages of the serotonin and norepinephrine synaptic transmission systems. Again, none of these stories are completely understood, but the repeated empirical associations between synaptic events difficult to measure (even indirectly) and the complex clinical conditions of psychopathology help explain the intense pursuit of biological approaches. This enthusiasm notwithstanding, researchers are critically examining the contrast between the rapid advances in understanding synaptic neuropharmacology and the great difficulty in discovering a chemical basis for schizophrenia and other disorders.

In this review, we examine the theoretical models implied in a biological test for a psychiatric illness, review the current state of some of the most widely researched candidates for such a test, and examine recent progress to ascertain whether alternative strategies may be better suited to new conceptualizations of psychopathology and their relation to normal variation. Recent reviews and research reports in 1981 and 1982 are given emphasis because of the rapidly evolving technology and diagnostic developments.

Medical Methods and Psychiatry

The traditional medical model assumes discrete categories for well and ill individuals and that a single biological factor overwhelms psychosocial factors. The clinical interview in all branches of medicine typically begins with the chief complaint: "Doctor, I feel so x all the time." From this point, the onset, course, and severity of symptom x are probed, other aspects of the patient's health queried, and tentative diagnoses listed. Next, laboratory tests are ordered to confirm diagnoses and follow the course of the illness and its response to treatment. Laboratory tests play an increasingly central role in the patient care process, slowly superseding the physician's dependence on the patient's reported symptoms. This is not only because of frustratingly vague reports (e.g. x = tired), but because impressive advances in chemical, electrophysiologic, and imaging techniques give us increasingly specific information concerning each organ, metabolic pathway, or possible pathogen.

Tests typically provide three types of sometimes overlapping information: anatomic, functional, and diagnostic. Thus, an X-ray CT scan of the brain may give an anatomic locale of a space-occupying lesion (right temporal lobe) but not the etiology (benign tumor, cyst, or malignancy?). An elevated level of creatinine in the urine may indicate reduced kidney function but not pinpoint the right or left kidney or its etiology. An elevated uric acid level confirms the diagnosis of gout without locating the joint affected or assessing the owner's ability to run a 6 minute mile. Of the three types of information, it is the diagnostic that generally is the most powerful. Medical diagnosis often provides an etiological understanding of the pathophysiology, suggests future course or prognosis, and implies a specific therapy. Thus, in a clinical visit in this paradigm, the patient starts by saying "Doctor, I feel so sore in my toe all the time." The doctor orders a uric acid level and the laboratory reports an elevated value. A diagnosis is made of gout—an inherited metabolic disease which leads to elevations of uric acid in the blood and its subsequent and painful deposition in joints. Knowledge of the abnormality in uric acid metabolism allows dietary control and precise pharmacotherapy. In the psychologist's or psychiatrist's office, the analogous complaint is, "Doctor, a voice tells me my toe is evil." In gout, the clinician had an observable physical finding, the red and enlarged joint, sometimes containing deposits of uric acid as a validation for the blood test. In schizophrenia, the physical sign is absent, no laboratory test is available, and validation of the symptom or diagnosis uncertain.

Many biological tests for psychiatric illness have already been discovered, although their discovery has redefined the illness as syphilis or pernicious anemia, and transferred the patient to another medical subspeciality. Will continued progress in identifying ever more intricate or subtle brain disturbances eliminate the need for psychology and psychiatry as clinical disciplines? The mere lumping of patients without a brain disease detectable with current technology into the major category of "mental illness" is an inauspicious starting point for the biological researcher, the patient, and this review. Subdivision of the category by symptoms reported by the diseased organ itself similarly seems an uncertain second step. Nonetheless, some progress has been made by biological researchers using this approach. We will begin with concepts and criteria fundamental for understanding and evaluating how this progress came about.

Biological Markers

A biological marker is a measurable indicator of a disease which may or may not be causal. A marker may be stable over time irrespective of the overt presence of the illness—a trait marker. Or it may be dependent on the disease episode, appearing just before, during, or after an illness—a state marker. Biological markers can be divided into four general types, not necessarily mutually exclusive.

ETIOLOGICAL INDICATORS   Most of the variables studied by biological researchers are chosen with the hope that they are intimately related to the pathophysiology of a disease. Thus their identification as a diagnostic test would provide an etiological explanation for the illness and have implications for treatment. Unfortunately, the inaccessibility of the brain tissue, and its direct measurement, leads to the study of peripheral blood and urine components, often many steps removed from the primary phenomena hypothesized as etiological.

DISEASE PRODUCTS   The substance measured as the marker may not be the cause of the pathology but only the product of an abnormal metabolic process. Thus, an excess of the neurotransmitter norepinephrine could cause elevations of abnormal synaptic transmission; its metabolic product 3-methoxy-4-hydroxyphenylglycol (MHPG), an index of increased norepinephrine production, is harmless in itself. It is particularly difficult to know if a marker is a disease product or an etiological factor. Increased size of the brain's ventricular space measured by X-ray computed tomographic scans, for example, may result from having schizophrenia, or schizophrenic symptoms may result from brain atrophy reflected by increased ventricles.

CHALLENGE MARKERS   Abnormalities in biological systems may be detectable only when challenged to respond at a physiological limit. In diabetes, blood sugar level may not be diagnostic unless preceded by a provocative sugar meal as in the glucose tolerance test. In psychiatric research, psychotropic drugs or hormones are given and the response of neurotransmitter or endocrine systems can be measured. Examples include the administration of neuroleptics and the measurement of the hormone prolactin (Meltzer et al 1981), the administration of the steroid dexamethasone with measurement of cortisol (Carroll et al 1980), administration of apomorphine (Rotrosen et al 1979) or clonidine, and measurement of growth hormone (Matussek et al 1980). Siever et al (1981) present a useful review.

LINKAGE MARKERS   A biological marker may not have any physiological relationship to the metabolic abnormality, but may merely appear as a characteristic on the same chromosome. Such a linkage marker would not only run in the families of patients with the illness but would occur more often in those relatives who actually are ill. A linkage marker is the result of crossing over during chromosomal recombination; the closer the marker is on the chromosome to the actual gene for the illness, the more frequently it is associated with the illness in a family pedigree. The genes for color blindness (Gershon & Bunney 1976) and glucose-6-phosphate dehydrogenase (Mendlewicz et al 1980) are examples of such linkage markers for affective illness, but their association has not been clearly demonstrated. The group of human leukocyte antigen (HLA) genes, located on the short arm of chromosome six, are other examples of possible linkage markers (Weitkamp et al 1981). Note that in a single pedigree, a particular HLA antigen could be present in individuals with the illness, but in another pedigree, it could be absent in individuals with the illness. Linkage markers are not necessarily completely nonetiological. Genes related or complementary in function may reside close together on chromosomes, and HLA linkage could suggest some aberrant immunologic phenomena in depression. Similarly, color blindness is a central nervous system (CNS) deficit, and the same region of the X-chromosome could control another CNS deficit related to depression. Lastly, a linked gene could be a contributory etiological factor associated with the disease. Association with specific HLA antigens has been reported both for schizophrenia and for affective disorders (Gattaz et al 1981, McGuffin et al 1981).

The Development of a Laboratory Test

The psychometric development of psychological tests is extremely advanced, but has been applied to biological markers only in rudimentary form. In addition to the standard psychometric requirements, biological markers are frequently tested with respect to etiological significance, heritability, and robustness from the pervasive artifacts of drug administration, institutionalization, and other factors associated with being mentally ill.

INTERNAL CONSISTENCY   A laboratory test clearly must measure the substance or phenomenon reproducibly; for example, the same sample of blood divided in two aliquots, or alternate trials of an electrophysiological procedure. Assessment of reproducibility is necessary to decide the minimum number of replicate assays, trials, or aliquots necessary. Reproducibility is frequently reported as the coefficient of variation between duplicates.

RELIABILITY OVER TIME   Unless individual differences in a measure are stable over time, it cannot be a useful trait indicator. Product moment correlations between two values obtained two or more weeks apart assess this tendency for an individual to maintain his level relative to others. Typical measures such as urinary 3-methoxy-4-hydroxyphenylglycol (MHPG) have test-retest correlations in the 0.6-0.7 range indicating about 50% of the variation is due to individual traits (Hollister et al 1978, Buchsbaum et al 1981). Normal populations typically show somewhat smaller ranges than patients, which may lead to spurious underestimation of reliability. Transient environmental factors, especially diet and exercise, are systematically different in hospitalized patients, and their effect on the marker must be assessed. An episode marker might only appear while the patient is ill and would need to be assessed during two separate episodes, or twice in rapid succession during a single episode.

HERITABILITY   Genetic transmission is not necessary for a marker. For example, a traumatic birth may damage a specific brain area and leave some deficit. However, because of the observed genetic factors in the major psychoses, it has been assumed that a valid etiological marker would have some heritability. This can be assessed by comparison of monozygotic and dizygotic twins, family pedigrees, adoption studies, sib-sib correlations, or other designs. Typically, measurement of neurotransmitters, metabolites, or enzymes shows continuous distributions; parent-offspring correlations are significant, but a clear dominant or recessive inheritance is often not revealed (see Gershon et al 1980, Nurnberger & Gershon 1982.) The fact that putative markers do not follow simple Mendelian patterns is completely consistent with analyses of the pattern of occurrence of psychiatric illness in family pedigrees (Gottesman & Shields 1982).

RELATIONSHIP TO CNS FUNCTION   To be applicable to living patients and normal controls, most markers must be assessed indirectly in blood, urine, or cerebrospinal fluid. A marker's validity is strengthened by a knowledge of its direct relevance to CNS function, especially to brain systems also affected by drugs which ameliorate the condition.

ARTIFACTS OF DRUG EFFECTS   Most severely ill patients have been treated with drugs and controls have not. This is the most pervasive and critical source of artifact facing marker research. Restricting testing to patients who have never had drugs may result in an extremely biased and perhaps diagnostically questionable sample. Short time periods off drugs in the range of 1–7 days may be insufficient, since the brain chronically adapts to drugs and sudden drug discontinuation may change synaptic sensitivity, creating an opposite neurochemical effect (see Bunney 1981). A period of 14 days or more off psychoactive medication is usually necessary to avoid medication effects. An alternative strategy is to examine marker presence in nonpatient populations. Since the majority of psychiatric disorders are untreated in the mental health system (Weissman & Myers 1980), biologically based case finding is a possibility. Screening populations for low platelet monoamine oxidase has been one example of this approach (Buchsbaum et al 1976, Baron et al 1980b, Demisch et al 1982).

SENSITIVITY AND SPECIFICITY   Sensitivity of a test refers to the proportion of individuals with a disorder who show a positive test result. The specificity of a test refers to the proportion of people without a disorder who show a negative test result. Diagnostic confidence is the proportion of people with a positive test who have the disorder. These numbers provide criteria for comparing markers and all three are necessary for a complete report. Thus, a marker with a sensitivity of 90% is not useful for the administration of a treatment if the specificity is 20% (80% of noncases would then receive treatment in addition to the 90% of the cases). The balance between sensitivity and specificity desired depends on the costs of missing a case or the risk of applying treatment to a noncase. Thus, in screening a population for a dangerous disease to locate cases for full diagnostic workup, one would desire a test with high sensitivity; testing inpatients for an intrusive but effective therapy requires high specificity.

DIAGNOSTIC SUBTYPES   The repeated failure to find that every individual within a major diagnostic category shows a biological marker has led many investigators to divide their sample into more narrow categories. This division is typically made on symptomatic features or family history in the hope of discovering a one-to-one correspondence between the marker and some diagnostic category. Traditional subtypes are acute/chronic and paranoid/nonparanoid in schizophrenia and unipolar/bipolar and endogenous/nonendogenous in affective illness. Biological data have tended to validate these subtypes in that group differences between subtypes have been demonstrated, but individual diagnostic power remains low.

EXAMPLES OF MARKER RESEARCH

Platelet Monoamine Oxidase: A Trait Marker?

Three factors make platelet monoamine oxidase (MAO) an especially suitable example for illustration of biological approaches to psychopathology: the strong theoretical basis for its relevance, the worldwide replication of the finding of low MAO in psychopathology, and the continuing controversy after 10 years of research. The groups of drugs (neuroleptics, tricyclic antidepressants, MAO inhibitors) which are used clinically in the major psychoses, schizophrenia and affective illness, affect the synaptic dynamics of the biogenic amines. Thus, an enzyme which catalyzes the metabolism (oxidative deamination) of biogenic amines would seem a critical marker to investigate. Low MAO levels in schizophrenia would be consistent with the dopamine theory of schizophrenia (i.e. less oxidation = excess dopamine) and trace amine (i.e. abnormal amines not oxidized) hypotheses.

In 1972, Murphy and Weiss reported low levels of platelet MAO in patients with bipolar affective disorder. Shortly after this, Murphy & Wyatt (1972) also found low MAO in patients with schizophrenia. Wyatt et al (1973) found low MAO in both members of pairs of identical twins discordant for schizophrenia. A series of replications followed—14 by 1977 (Buchsbaum & Rieder 1979) and 44 by 1982 (De Lisi et al 1982)—the great majority showing low MAO in the patient groups. The development of the MAO marker, because of its widespread initial success, was broad enough to cover each of the steps in the development of a marker we have outlined.

INTERNAL CONSISTENCY   Determination of platelet MAO activity in two samples of blood from the same sample yielded high reliability [$r = 0.98$, $n = 52$ (Murphy et al 1976)]. While the absolute levels of the MAO activity depend on many details of the assay, such major modifications as altering the centrifugal separation of the platelets or shifting to an alternate amine substrate leave the ranking of individuals preserved $r = 0.95$, between differential and Corash centrifugation (Arora et al 1982); $r = 0.89$ between benzylamine and tryptamine (Murphy et al 1976). Thus, having controls and patients done in the same laboratory is an important methodological feature.

TEST-RETEST RELIABILITY   Normal individuals vary over a 20-fold range (Murphy et al 1976). Test retest variation across 1–2 weeks was 0.94 ($n = 26$) and two months was 0.86 ($n = 42$) in normal volunteers (Murphy et al 1976). Small changes occur during the menstrual cycle (Belmaker et al 1974, Baron et al 1980a), but studies of the effects of diet and physical exercise are not known to us. Comparisons of patients with depression, mania, or acute schizophrenia studied at the time of hospital admission and again at discharge did not yield greater differences than normals studied twice (Carpenter et al 1975, Murphy et al 1976, 1977).

HERITABILITY   MAO shows higher concordance in identical than fraternal twins (Nies et al 1973, Murphy et al 1974, Winter et al 1978). Parents of probands selected for low or high MAO showed corresponding MAO values (Puchall et al 1980), and within-family variance was significantly lower than among families of patients with affective illness (Gershon et al 1980) or normal adults (Pandey et al 1979). Despite these findings, the inheritance of MAO activity levels does not fit an autosomal dominant or recessive model (Gershon et al 1980). While Breakefield & Edelstein (1980) and Breakefield et al (1981) suggested an X-chromosome locus, no suggestion of X-linkage is seen in mother-son correlations (Puchall et al 1980).

RELATIONSHIP TO CNS FUNCTION   Since the platelet is a cell of the peripheral blood, the question of relationship to synaptic sites in the brain must be raised. The very aspect which makes platelet MAO (type B) activity so intriguing is its presence in human but not most mammalian species. This makes experimental approaches involving direct sampling of brain and blood in the same individuals difficult. Nevertheless, as reviewed elsewhere (Murphy & Kalin 1980), drugs which inhibit brain MAO inhibit platelet MAO as well. Platelet MAO is correlated with individual differences in neuroendocrine indices of central biogenic amine metabolism such as prolactin (Kleinman et al 1979).

ARTIFACTS OF DRUG EFFECTS   Initial reports (Murphy et al 1974) did not indicate any effect of neuroleptics on MAO levels, and reports on patient groups both on and off neuroleptic medication appeared quite similar in finding low MAO. Subsequent studies have found either no effect (Wyatt & Murphy 1976, Wyatt et al 1978, Mann & Thomas 1979), increased activity (Brockington et al 1976), or decreased activity (Takahashi et al 1975, Becker & Shaskan 1977, Friedhoff et al 1978, Mann & Chiu 1978, Jackman & Meltzer 1980, De Lisi et al 1981). In the studies where patients are studied both on and off drugs (De Lisi et al 1981), a typical MAO reduction with drug is 23%, roughly comparable to the 27% reduction that is seen across 14 studies (Buchsbaum & Rieder 1979). The problem of assessing the drug artifacts in these studies is confounded by illness severity, diagnostic features, and chronicity. In a typical sequence, a patient becomes ill, is diagnosed, is placed on medication, and improves to some variable degree over months. A design which compares patients who happen to be treated and those who are not may be contrasting severity, presence of socially disruptive symptoms, or propensity for drug side effects (leading to drug cessation and inclusion in a drug-free sample). A design contrasting patients before and during drug treatment may confound symptom presence and absence, or physiological features changing during a disease episode. If patients were on medication at first contact, then withdrawal from drug for the before condition, as in De Lisi et al (1981), could spuriously affect the baseline. No study to date has used a drug/placebo random assignment trial with repeated measures in the same individual (a crossover design). Even with such a sophisticated design, however, the interpretation of a lowered MAO with neuroleptics for the biological marker issue is unclear. If platelet MAO is indeed an important indicator of central catecholamine economy, then a powerful catecholamine drug might well be expected to affect the marker. The work of De Lisi et al (1981), showing a relationship between clinical drug response and the extent of neuroleptic effect on platelet MAO, suggests a fine physiological link between marker and the etiological process.

SENSITIVITY AND SPECIFICITY   These criteria have not been reported directly for MAO but can be calculated from studies which publish the raw distribution. Using only the unmedicated patients and normal controls from Murphy & Wyatt's (1972) early report, and a cutoff equal to the mean of the schizophrenic population, we calculate a 59% sensitivity, a 96% specificity, and a 77% diagnostic confidence. Subsequent studies of drug-free patients yielded figures which ranged from 100% on all three measures [no overlap (Domino & Khanna 1976)] to 50% [same mean value (Takahashi et al 1975)]. Low MAO has been found in bipolar affective illness. Murphy et al (1982) review nine studies of bipolar affective illness, five of which show significant reduction. In 48 male and 23 female off-medication patients with bipolar affective disorders, significant reduction of MAO was shown in both groups (Murphy et al 1982). This would lower the specificity of the MAO marker for schizophrenia.

DIAGNOSTIC SUBTYPES   Noting that the drug amphetamine, similar in structure to naturally occurring amine substrates of MAO, could cause paranoid symptoms in normal individuals, Wyatt et al (1981) focused on the paranoid/nonparanoid subtypes. In their initial study (Wyatt et al 1978), 7 of 25 low MAO schizophrenics (MAO less than 9.16) received DSM-II diagnoses of paranoid schizophrenia whereas 0 of 11 high MAO schizophrenics received this diagnosis. A prospective study of 42 additional chronic schizophrenics similarly confirmed that patients with paranoid schizophrenia and with paranoid features both had lower platelet MAO activity (Potkin et al 1978) although another study failed to do so (Berger et al 1978). Patients with nonaffective schizophrenic disorders (most of whom were paranoid), characterized by auditory hallucinations and delusions, had lower MAO activity than controls (Orsulak et al 1978, Schildkraut et al 1980). Even when consecutive admissions were studied, including patients regardless of race, ethnic background, or initial psychiatric diagnosis, low MAO activity was associated with auditory hallucinations (Adler et al 1980). Becker & Shaskan (1977) found hallucinations more frequent in low MAO subjects. Meltzer et al (1980) also found lower MAO in hallucinating patients although the paranoid/nonparanoid distinction just missed statistical significance. As auditory hallucinations and paranoid features may enhance the probability of neuroleptic treatment, the subsequent possibility that the low MAO/paranoid association is a drug artifact must be entertained. The Meltzer study used patients off medication at least 7 days, a feature not present in the original Wyatt et al (1978) and Potkin et al (1978) studies. Thus, further studies in patients off medication longer are necessary to clarify this finding. In an entirely unmedicated volunteer sample, Haier et al (1979) actually found the reverse correlation between the MMPI Pa scale and MAO, suggesting a complex linkage. The distinction between a drug artifact and an etiological marker becomes especially blurred in this example. Paranoid features and hallucinations are especially sensitive clinically to neuroleptic treatment; paranoid features and hallucinations are elicited by amine substrates of MAO. MAO is low specifically in patients with paranoid features and hallucinations, and MAO is specifically affected by drugs which affect amine neurotransmitters. Could the drug effect on MAO actually be additional evidence of the marker's validity? If drugs did not change MAO, would this be evidence that catecholamines are not involved in schizophrenia?

Dexamethasone Suppression Test: A State Marker

In affective disorders, the neuroendocrine approach to identifying markers of illness episodes and, perhaps, even of diagnostic subtypes currently shows considerable progress. One challenge marker, plasma cortisol response to dexamethasone, is of current interest. Most research on the dexamethasone suppression test (DST) in psychiatry is focused on diagnostic specificity and sensitivity and the ability of the test to follow the course of the illness. The mechanics of the DST are simple. A 1 or 2 mg oral dose of dexamethasone (a synthetic steroid) is given at midnight. Plasma cortisol is measured at 4 and 11 pm the following day. The cortisol assay is available routinely and inexpensively from commercial laboratories. In normal individuals control of cortisol production by the adrenal gland is maintained by the secretion of adrenocorticotropic hormone (ACTH) by the pituitary gland. ACTH stimulates cortisol production and cortisol in turn decreases ACTH release, an example of negative feedback as in a household thermostat. Dexamethasone acts on the pituitary to suppress ACTH production, which in turn suppresses cortisol. In pituitary or adrenal diseases like Cushing's and Addison's, however, negative feedback is missing and cortisol is not suppressed following dexamethasone. The DST is useful in diagnosing such neuroendocrine diseases. It is of interest in psychiatry because many patients with affective disorder fail to suppress cortisol after dexamethasone.

INTERNAL CONSISTENCY AND TEST-RETEST RELIABILITY   The between- and within-assay variation in cortisol determination is generally in the range of 5 to 10% (e.g. Brown & Qualls 1981). The test-retest correlation is a more complex issue. No reports on reliability on two DSTs done in the same week are available, and depressed patients can change their clinical state rapidly. Brown & Qualls (1982) tested patients on two consecutive hospital admissions for depression separated by several months, and noted that of 11 patients (6 suppressors and 5 nonsuppressors) 10 had the same DST result on retest.

HERITABILITY   Schlesser et al (1979, 1980) compared DST results in 86 unipolar depressed patients divided into three groups on the basis of family history. The patients with a first-degree relative with depression (but no first-degree relatives with mania, alcoholism, or antisocial personality) are called familial pure depressive disease. Of these 28 patients, 23 or 82% showed DST nonsuppression. Of the 35 patients with sporadic depressive disease (i.e. no psychiatric illness in first-degree relatives), 13 or 37% were DST nonsuppressors. The third group was labeled depression spectrum disease (i.e. alcoholism and/or antisocial personality in a first-degree relative) and only one of these 23 or 4% was a DST nonsuppressor. This study also reported that none of 80 manic and schizophrenic controls were nonsuppressors. It would seem that a genetic subtype of depression may be identified with the DST although replication attempts are inconsistent (Carroll et al 1980, Coryell et al 1982, Rudorfer et al 1982).

No studies of twin or family correlations have yet been reported. These might need to be done while individuals are in a depressive episode, although the possibility that a slightly increased incidence of nonsuppression would appear in well relatives has not been ruled out.

RELATIONSHIP TO CNS   It is unclear whether DST abnormalities indicate a primary hypothalamic dysfunction or are connected with noradrenergic control of ACTH (Sachar & Baron 1979, Matussek et al 1980, Sachar et al 1980, Checkley 1980; see also review by Siever et al 1981). In the context of neuroendocrine studies, a possible role for the endogenous opiates in depression should also be mentioned. The DST works by challenging the hypothalamic-pituitary-adrenal (HPA) axis, suppressing the production of ACTH which regulates cortisol. ACTH and β-lipotropin are thought to derive from the same parent molecules and β-lipotropin yields β-endorphin. Neuroendocrine dysfunctions assessed by the DST may thus reflect problems with endogenous opiate system regulation of some neuroendocrine functions. Depressed patients as a group show decreased sensitivity to pain, which is thought to be mediated by the endogenous opiate system, especially β-endorphins (Davis et al 1979). Haier (1982) reported that depressed inpatients showing DST nonsuppression were less pain sensitive than depressed patients with DST suppression. If so, sensitivity to painful stimuli may be as useful as the DST as a laboratory test to identify meaningful subgroups.

ARTIFACTS OF MEDICATION   As with platelet MAO, most studies of the DST have been done on patients medicated with psychoactive drugs, in this case given to treat depression. Since patients with depression receive drugs with a wider range of pharmacological effects (tricylic antidepressants, lithium, MAO inhibitors, antianxiety drugs, as well as neuroleptics) the problem is even more complex than with schizophrenia. In a typical examination of the drug effect, Schlesser et al (1980) report increased incidence of DST nonsuppression in individuals off medication, but they have only 8 (of a total 60) patients available.

SENSITIVITY AND SPECIFICITY   A number of studies have shown that a sizable portion of psychiatric patients fail to suppress cortisol on the DST. Carroll et al (1981) have reported that more DST nonsuppression occurs in patients with endogenous depression. They also report that a 1 mg DST has a sensitivity of 67%, and that most psychiatric patients with other kinds of depression or other diagnoses like schizophrenia show normal suppression of cortisol following the DST. The specificity of a 1 mg DST is reported as 96% (Carroll et al 1981), although not all studies find either this high rate or a specificity advantage of the 1 mg (62%) over the 2 mg (79%) DST (Haier & Keitner 1982). It is interesting to compare the 67% sensitivity and 96% specificity to the 59% and 96% figures calculated for platelet MAO. Relatively high rates of DST nonsuppression have also been noted in conditions such as obsessive-compulsive disorder (Insel et al 1982).

To enhance diagnostic specificity, Carroll et al (1981) recommended, for example, exclusion of patients with severe weight loss to avoid false positive, nonsuppression results known from medical studies. The symptom of decreased appetite had the highest item weight in a discriminant function separating endogenous and nonendogenous depression (Feinberg & Carroll

1982). Since weight loss is a cardinal symptom of endogenous depression, could DST nonsuppression be merely an artifact of the physiological effects of depressed patients skipping meals? It might equally be argued that the symptom of weight loss in depression suggests an HPA axis dysfunction, confirmed by the DST findings. Also, DST nonsuppression findings in anorexia nervosa or bulimia (Roy-Byrne 1982) rather than being artifacts to be diagnostically excluded could be taken as evidence of some common HPA pathophysiology shared with depression.

The concept of artifact in marker studies is borrowed loosely from the nineteenth century pathology where reagents for slide staining may introduce structures not present in life. In the complex network of physiological and behavioral mechanisms, cause and effect may not be so easily separable. The neuroleptic artifact in MAO research and the weight loss artifact in DST research are both examples of how premature closure on artifacts may possibly prevent an understanding of the psychobiology of a promising marker.

DIAGNOSTIC SUBTYPES   As with MAO and the paranoid subgroup of schizophrenia, the relatively high rate of DST nonsuppression in cases of endogenous depression can help validate that clinical subgroup. However, since as many as 50% or 60% of some samples of endogenous depression do not show nonsuppression, additional possibilities can be considered. For example, in studies of endogenous depression, suppressors can be regarded as DST failures (i.e. false negatives) or as clinically misdiagnosed cases (i.e. they really did not have endogenous depression), or as a separate subgroup (perhaps with a different etiology). This last possibility is suggested by some reports of treatment response differences between clinically matched (i.e. all with endogenous depression) samples of suppressors and nonsuppressors, but no replication studies have been reported (Brown & Shuey 1980, Brown et al 1980, Brown & Qualls 1981). The possibility that schizophrenics or other nondepressed patients who are DST nonsuppressors respond clinically to treatments for affective disorder (e.g. ECT, lithium, or tricyclics) is a significant use of the biological marker strategy (Carman et al 1980). It may be that a homogeneous group of psychiatric patients can be identified on the basis of HPA axis dysfunction irrespective of clinical symptoms. Studies exploring this possibility would not a priori exclude cases without evidence of endogenous depression. In fact, one use of the DST may be in identifying clinically undetectable affective disorder. In the future, we may label such cases as having an HPA axis disease. For the present time, however, the clinical use of DST results has not yet been fully established either with respect to subtyping or to treatment.

DIFFICULTIES OF SINGLE MARKER STUDIES

As seen in our overview of the two most researched markers, there is great difficulty in going beyond statistical group differences to understanding individuals. Many patients with a diagnosis fail to show the marker, and some normals and patients with other diagnoses do show the marker. These problems are at the heart of the question of validity, unnecessarily limiting scientific progress because of four possibly unwarranted assumptions.

Diagnosis as Marker Validation

A patient with auditory hallucinations, bizarre behavior, and flat affect for 183 days has a positive DST on admission. The researcher is forced to count this case as a failure of DST specificity since the clinician does not adjust his diagnosis to affective illness in the presence of clear DSM III-criteria for schizophrenia. This may not be the best way of establishing a relationship between specific and accurate measures of cortisol and subtle and intricate aspects of human behavior cataloged in a diagnostic category. These symptoms are influenced by a myriad of psychosocial and experiential considerations and may differ from the atomic behaviors counted in animal pharmacology.

The validity of a psychiatric diagnostic category evolves from the apparent clustering of symptoms assumed to be pathonomonic for the category. Even for the major categories of schizophrenia and affective disorder, however, the respective symptom clusters are neither mutually exclusive (Pope & Lipinski 1978) nor does a sharp boundary with respect to outcome occur (Kendell & Brockington 1980). Statistical methods of clustering have been applied to problems of schizophrenia (Strauss et al 1973) and endogenous depression (Matussek et al 1981), but these clusters may differ somewhat from traditional classifications. Since there is more than one cluster solution using differing statistical methods, even if they did confirm traditional classifications, their validity also needs to be determined independently. Carpenter et al (1976) applied cluster analysis to subtypes of schizophrenia without confirmatory results, and all traditional subtypes were apparently lumped together. Symptom clusters developed by Farmer et al (1983) similarly did not fully resemble traditional subtypes, but they were validated against family concordance. It should be noted that the clinician has normally been trained on the traditional symptom clusters and that most cluster attempts do not gather symptom assessments from interviews blind to the historical concept of the disease. Thus, clusters may validate the efficacy of education rather than the natural history of psychosis.

A genetic strategy has been used to validate diagnosis with mixed results. Spectrum, mild, or atypical cases predominate among the ill relatives of schizophrenics (Rosenthal et al 1968) and alcoholics among relatives of patients with affective disorders (Winokur et al 1978). After classifying 288 unipolar depressives by family history, although finding greater premorbid personality disturbances associated with a positive history, Behar et al (1981) conclude that one "cannot classify familial subtypes to a clinically useful extent."

We, and others, have proposed the identification of groups on a biological anomaly or feature and then validation of such classification on the basis of prediction of drug treatment response, pedigree analysis, prediction of clinical course, or even symptom clustering (e.g. Buchsbaum & Haier 1978). This strategy of using biological independent variables has a number of advantages. First, it is more efficient for detecting biological etiologies since statistical effects are not diluted by irrelevant cases misclassified because of similar symptoms. Second, many individuals with atypical or less severe symptom manifestations, currently excluded from research studies which rely on strict symptom-based diagnoses, could be studied if they met a biological criterion. Third, the biological strategy allows the study of non-hospitalized, unmedicated individuals, avoiding the possible artifacts of hospitalization and prior drug treatment which plague reports of biological differences. Family members and children at risk can be assessed prospectively.

Biological Heterogeneity

The assumption that there is only one salient marker for each DSM-III category is probably incorrect. Bound by the paradigmatic straightjacket of symptom-based diagnostic homogeneity, researchers search for the elusive one-to-one correspondence between specific biological factors and specific symptoms. But if the heterogeneity in the major categories reflects diverse multiple etiologies with similar symptoms, as in mental retardation, then this course will not elucidate the biological factors of the illness. We already suspect from the wide individual differences in response to psychoactive drugs that a single neurochemical disturbance may produce quite different symptoms from one person to another. Davidson & Bagley (1969) maintain that "distinguishing clinical features between these psychoses and 'true schizophrenia' are largely illusory." Even if one eliminates the numerous known organic conditions (not always specifically excluded in clinical studies), there is no compelling reason to consider the residual patient group homogeneous; certainly variability in drug response, clinical course, genetic transmission, and other factors suggests quite the opposite. Indeed, symptoms could be the worst features for biological researchers to anchor on, since they may be primarily determined by interpersonal psychosocial factors, as many nonbiologically oriented researchers have suggested. What Kraepelin put together on the basis of clinical symptoms and course of illness is ready to be torn apart on the basis of biological markers.

Diagnostic Distinctiveness

The strategy of using biological marker variables to identify membership in diagnostic categories requires the categories to be distinct entities. The research evidence for the distinctiveness of schizophrenia and affective illness is relatively weak. Kendell & Brockington (1980), for example, could find no discontinuity in outcome or course variables between these groups; Braden et al (1982) found no powerful distinction in lithium response; Pope & Lipinski (1978) found limited symptom differences. In genetic studies, some overlap exists, with schizophrenics appearing in the offspring of marriages where both parents were hospitalized, but neither for schizophrenia (Fischer & Gottesman 1980), although Gershon & Rieder's (1980) review supports the distinction. Many biological markers, in addition to MAO and the DST, are positive in both schizophrenia and affective illness [e.g. smooth pursuit eye movements (Holzman & Levy 1977)], leading some critics to disparage the validity of the marker. There are two other equally viable possibilities: (a) misdiagnosis because of the difficulties in symptomatic criteria discussed above, and (b) the existence of an underlying general vulnerability to psychosis, the clinical form of which could depend on experiential or additional biological factors.

Statistical Power and Single Marker Studies

Most marker studies that have been reported follow a set design: A new and sophisticated marker is measured in a small group of patients and normal controls, and the results are then compared by t-test. Investigators' results usually differ from one university center to another, and failure to replicate is common. Reviews of the field tally up the positive and negative studies, and researchers move on to the next exciting neurochemical.

Even if one assumes that only a single marker is involved in a diagnostic grouping, the consequences of low statistical power have rarely been considered. Rothpearl et al (1981) evaluated statistical power and found that the majority of studies on cerebrospinal fluid (CSF) metabolites in depressives and controls had less than a 50% chance of detecting a medium size difference (0.5 SD). They provide power curves for the major CSF metabolites, e.g. homovanillic acid (HVA), 5-hydroxyindoleacetic acid (5HIAA), based on normative data and an extensive review of current studies. But what if a psychiatric disease is not biologically unitary but heterogeneous?

We have investigated the statistical power for t-tests assuming only two independent biological factors using a computer simulation (Buchsbaum & Rieder 1979). The model assumed a deficit, low levels of "enzyme M," to be found in only a fraction of schizophrenics. We constructed a normally distributed control population with a mean value of 10 units and a SD of 2 units. We then obtained synthetic enzyme level measurements for each "normal control subject" from a generator of normally distributed random numbers. The schizophrenic population was constructed to consist of some fraction of individuals with "normal levels of enzyme M" (drawn from the same distribution as the controls) and the remainder having "enzyme M deficiency disease," drawn from a population with a mean level of six units and an SD of two units. The mean enzyme activity for this abnormal pool was thus 2 SD below the mean of controls. (The choice of 10 and 6 as mean enzyme values for the two populations is for illustration; the following results would apply to all comparisons of homogeneous and heterogeneous populations with the subgroups separated by 2 SD.) We next determined the sample sizes of schizophrenic patients and controls that investigators would need to be able to expect a statistically significant (P < .05, two-tailed t-test) difference in 50% and 95% of their studies, given different fractions of schizophrenics coming from the low-enzyme-M-level pool. For simplicity, the number of cases in the control and schizophrenic samples was held equal. Our procedure was to simulate the results of 1000 experiments and count how many yielded a significant t value (P < .05, two-tailed t test) with the degrees of freedom equal to the number of controls plus schizophrenics minus two. The sample size was progressively raised until exactly 500 t-values were significant and then exactly 950 were significant. This was done for different percentages of enzyme M deficiency, ranging from 80% to 10% in steps of 10%. For example, if 38% of schizophrenics have enzyme M deficiency, and 1000 research teams across the world do studies on the enzyme with 20 normal subjects and 20 controls, then approximately 500 research reports would conclude that enzyme M levels were significantly low (P < .05, two-tailed t-test) in schizophrenia and approximately 500 research reports would conclude that they "failed to replicate" the low enzyme M level finding. With a lower percentage having the enzyme deficiency, or with sample sizes below 20, the majority of investigators would fail to replicate these results. The curve rises rapidly, and very large sample sizes become necessary to demonstrate significant group differences consistently when a small percentage of patients have the deficiency.

Our simulations point out the difficulty of demonstrating associations between psychiatric disorders and biological deviations, even though they "really" exist in our population because we have structured the simulation to include them. The reader should note that our assumption of the mean difference between subgroup pools (2 SD) underlies our simulation. While this assumption appears to be reasonable, the real situation for any given biological variable may vary.

Multifactor Etiology

While the concept of an interacting biological deficiency and environmental stress [e.g. stress-diathesis model (Rosenthal 1970)] has been considered frequently, multiple interacting biological factors also need to be considered. For example, two neurotransmitter enzyme deficiencies might interact to enhance a problem. Monoamine oxidase and dopamine-beta-hydroxylase (DBH) are an example of such a pair (see Wyatt 1978). Both are under genetic control and both metabolize phenylethylamine, a naturally occurring amphetamine-like substance which may be higher in some psychotic patients (e.g. Karoum et al 1982). If an individual had low levels of both enzymes, higher PEA might occur or other monoamine dysfunctions with possibly concomitant psychosis. We examined individuals with low MAO and below average DBH and found attentional deficits, a hallmark of schizophrenic vulnerability (Buchsbaum et al 1978). Simultaneous evaluation of related markers is a serious need for the field.

Serotonin Depression: Reversing the Independent Variable

Researchers studying serotonin and its metabolite (5HIAA) in depression have taken a strongly biological view and provide an example of reversing the traditional approach in marker research and focusing on serotonin, not diagnosis, as the independent variable.

Van Praag & Korf (1971) proposed a biochemical classification of patients with depression based on 5HIAA levels in CSF. Åsberg et al (1975) also noted a bimodal distribution in cerebrospinal fluid concentration of 5HIAA and boldly named the low group "serotonin depression." While patients with high or low 5HIAA did not differ clinically in the extent of their depression, the lower group's level of depression did correlate with 5HIAA levels. Post et al (1980) review CSF serotonin studies comprehensively.

Traskman et al (1981) note 5HIAA as a predictor of suicide attempts in both depressed and nondepressed patients, and Sedvall et al (1980) found a higher incidence of patients with depressive disorders in the relatives of healthy volunteers with low CSF 5HIAA. Ignoring diagnostic criteria, but sorting patients into high and low 5HIAA groups, Rydin et al (1982) found more anxiety and hostility in Rorschach ratings of low 5HIAA patients.

If serotonin depression is a low serotonin dysfunction, then substances from which serotonin is made might be expected to increase serotonin and ameliorate depression. This has been attempted with the amino acid tryptophan, yielding a targeted clinical response restricted to low CSF 5HIAA patients (Van Praag & de Haan 1980).

VULNERABILITY AND PERSONALITY

Genetic Models

If some psychiatric disorders result, at least in part, from neuroendocrine, neurotransmitter, or other biologically based problems, and if nearly all such markers show normal and overlapping distributions in general populations and patients, a continuum of biological risk can be conceptualized. This empirical finding seems consistent with the threshold models of genetic transmission of psychiatric illness (see Reich et al 1972, Baron et al 1981) which assume a liability continuously distributed. "Presence or absence" of a marker really depends on an empirically determined cutoff score. Individuals in the normal population can be identified on the basis of having marker values close to or even over the cutoff associated with patients. Are such individuals bona fide psychiatric cases that have escaped previous identification or treatment? Or are they at risk to become cases, or show milder forms of psychopathology, or abnormal personality traits? Given that as many as half of monozygotic twins can be discordant for psychiatric illnesses (Gottesman & Shields 1982) and that epidemiological studies show high rates of previously untreated and unreported affective disorders in community samples (Weissman et al 1980), it is quite possible that psychiatric inpatients represent only the tip of the iceberg of all people at risk for psychopathology.

MAO in Normal Populations

Only a few studies have investigated biological variables identified as putative markers of psychiatric problems in nonpatient samples. Buchsbaum and co-workers (1976) screened 375 college volunteers on platelet MAO activity. Since low MAO had been associated with chronic schizophrenia and bipolar affective disorder, the investigators hypothesized that if low MAO was related to psychopathology, then so-called normals selected for equally low MAO should be vulnerable to similar psychopathology, abnormal personality, or even exhibit milder forms of schizophrenia or affective disorder. A comparison of the lowest and highest MAO students indicated that the low group had more signs of psychiatric problems. These included more previous contacts with mental health professionals, more trouble with the law, higher MMPI scales, and more suicide attempts among their first-degree relatives. Two-year followup confirmed these trends although frank DSM-III schizophrenia did not emerge (Coursey et al 1982). Possible artifacts of neuroleptic administration were clearly not a factor in these findings (Coursey et al 1982).

Further analysis of this sample used cortical evoked potential (EP) techniques to measure sensory inhibition (Coursey et al 1979, Haier et al 1980). Subjects whose EP amplitudes increase markedly with increases in stimulus intensity are said to show augmenting, a pattern associated with sensitivity to pain and a hypothesized lack of sensory inhibition. The other pattern, reducing, is a relative lack of EP amplitude change with stimulus intensity; it is associated with pain tolerance and the presence of sensory inhibition (Buchsbaum 1971, 1978, Von Knorring 1978a,b, Zuckerman et al 1974). Groups of patients with unipolar depression and acute schizophrenia tend to show the reducing EP pattern; bipolar patients, paranoid schizophrenics, and alcoholics show augmenting (Buchsbaum et al 1973, Buchsbaum 1975, Schooler et al 1976, Coger et al 1976, Von Knorring 1978a,b). More psychiatric patient-like MMPI profiles (interpreted without knowledge of MAO/AR group membership) occurred in students having the combinations of either low MAO with augmenting (LA) or high MAO with reducing (HR) than in students characterized by either low MAO with reducing (LR) or high MAO with augmenting (HA) [79% vs. 49%; males and females combined; $p < .05$ (Haier et al 1980)].

A second independent study of male college volunteers screened for normal and extreme MMPI scores (Haier et al 1980) replicated this finding and showed that affective disorders (assessed using the SADS-L and the RDC) were more frequent in the same specific LA and HR combinations than in the combinations of LR and HA (52% vs 6%, $p < .005$). The "vulnerable" combinations had a sensitivity of 92% and a specificity of 60%. A follow-up of these students (conducted without knowledge of subgroup membership) showed that the LA and HR combinations were predictive of new episodes of major depression and/or hypomania during the 18 months after the initial interviews and biological determinations (Haier et al 1980). In the combined LA and HR groups, 67% had subsequent episodes of these affective disorders compared to 18% of LR and HA students ($p < .012$). The follow-up sensitivity was 88% and the specificity was 56%. This follow-up also suggested that individuals in the LA and the HR groups (but particularly the LA group) who did not meet RDC for any affective disorder at the initial interview were more likely to have an episode of major depression and/or hypomania during the subsequent 18 months than such individuals in the LR or HR groups.

The stimulus-seeking and extraversion correlates of MAO (i.e. low MAO is related to high stimulus-seeking) demonstrated both in students (Schooler et al 1978, Fowler et al 1980, Gattaz & Beckmann 1981) and in monkeys

(Redmond et al 1979) and the characterization of AR as a dimension of sensory inhibition (Buchsbaum 1971, Zuckerman et al 1974, Lukas & Siegel 1977) suggest a vulnerability/protection model for consideration (Haier et al 1980). In this model, the four biological combinations (LA, LR, HA, HR) are described as types on the basis of the presence or absence of stimulus-seeking and sensory inhibition. Low MAO/augmenting individuals are hypothesized as high sensation seekers who lack sensory protection (with the possible correlate of overarousal). High MAO/reducers are low sensation seekers with strong sensory inhibition (underarousal may be associated with this combination). Both the LA and the HR groups or "quadrants" are associated with vulnerability to psychopathology, especially depression. In the remaining two groups, a congruence or balance is hypothesized between high sensation seeking with sensory inhibition (LR) and low sensation seeking with the lack of sensory inhibition (HA). In fact, the LR and the HA combinations may be "protective" in the sense that few individuals in these groups meet the RDC for psychopathology.

If individuals with the vulnerable combinations of LA or HR are biologically predisposed to psychopathology, the actual development of symptomatology is likely an interaction of these biological variables with psychosocial factors, particularly levels of stress. For example, an individual with low MAO and augmenting (i.e. sensation seeking with lack of sensory inhibition) may not develop symptomatology if, as a result of psychosocial factors, his/her behavior is restricted and stress levels are kept minimal. But increased levels of stress in interaction with the vulnerable biochemistry are more likely to produce difficulties. Thus, for maximal prediction of risk, both biological and psychosocial factors need to be assessed (see Zubin & Spring 1977).

As we have noted, major problems in the study of possible biological risk factors of psychiatric illness include the lack of specificity between the factor and a single diagnostic category and the failure of all individuals within a category to show the same factor. The approach illustrated in these MAO studies of vulnerability addresses these problems by defining "diagnostic" subgroups on the basis of biological homogeneity (see Buchsbaum & Haier 1978), thus using the biological measures as independent variables and clinical symptoms as dependent variables. We believe that this strategy will help elucidate relationships between biological and clinical variables.

The study of biological markers of psychopathology in nonpatient samples raises many interesting questions concerning possible relationships between biological systems and normal personality variations. There are not many studies of neuroendocrine function or neurotransmitters and personality variables in normals, but a few studies are intriguing. The trait of sensation seeking is reported to be negatively correlated with MAO (Murphy et al 1977, Schooler et al 1978), and Zuckerman has proposed that monoamine systems "constitute the biological determinants of the basic dimensions of personality" (Zuckerman 1982). Some preliminary results of an NIMH study of normal volunteers show a number of relationships between biological measures (e.g. CSF norepinephrine, MHPG, DBH, MAO, cortisol) and personality tests (e.g. sensation seeking, Eysenck's E, N, and P). These relationships are difficult to summarize, but they tentatively support the idea that individual differences in normal personality are related to variations in neurotransmitter systems. The application of findings from research on the biological basis of psychopathology to research on the biological basis of personality has much potential and may be an expanding area for the 1980s.

FUTURE MARKERS

There are hundreds of potential markers currently under study. This review selected the most widely studied to illustrate the strategies and problems in getting any one accepted as valid and useful. Markers from psychophysiology, noncatecholamine neurotransmission, and anatomic features also need to meet the tests suggested and may equally profit from using the marker, not diagnosis, as a starting point in biopsychosocial investigation. New markers will capitalize on dramatically advancing technology but may similarly be swept away without a sophistication of experimental design and behavioral assessment to match.

Local Cerebral Function

Blood, urine, and cerebrospinal fluid, although valuable reflectors of the neurochemical and neuropharmacological activity of the brain, are removed in time and place from the disordered thought and diluted by the products of both functional and dysfunctional brain systems. Biopsy studies, which have aided internist study of functional disorders of organs such as the liver, are destructive to the brain and less useful because of the brain's complex and varied structure.

Positron emission tomography (PET) is a versatile approach utilizing the mathematics of X-ray transmission scanning (CT scans) to produce slice images of radioisotope distribution (Brownell et al 1982). Positron emitters such as carbon-11 or fluorine-18 can be used to tag glucose, amino acids, drugs, neurotransmitter precursors, and many other molecules the brain uses. The first substance studied in patients with schizophrenia is a synthetic sugar; sugar is the food the brain uses for energy to work.

Initial studies suggest a pattern of relatively reduced glucose use in the frontal lobes and left caudate nucleus of schizophrenics (Buchsbaum et al

1982). Despite the complexity and cost, the tests of a good marker will need to be met before this new and exciting technology can be judged. Another new technique, nuclear magnetic resonance (NMR), images variation in water distribution (Brownell et al 1982). With this technique, central areas important in the study of schizophrenia and affective illness are brought into clarity unattainable by conventional CT. NMR, which imposes a brief magnetic field on the head and reconstructs the picture from radio signals emitted from perturbed atoms, adds no radiation and thus is especially suitable for combination with PET studies.

Electroencephalographic measures can also be an imaging technqiue when data from enough electrodes are used. Maps of the cortical surface can be constructed using mathematical interpolation methods. The possibilities for exploring the entire cortex and better defining neurophysiological and pharmacological effects are great. This entirely hazard-free technology will be enhanced significantly by combination with PET and NMR imaging to provide a strengthened functional basis for interpretation.

Genetic Technology

The research strategies described here depend on conventional observation of the phenotype. Molecular genetics opens a more direct approach to describe genes and their products. Recombinant DNA methods can be used for genetic mapping and cells from human biopsy can be cultured and studied (see Gershon 1981). These new techniques may unravel the now clear but only weakly statistical familial associations seen in psychiatric illnesses.

Psychological Technology

If a strategy of choosing the marker as the independent variable and the clinical status as the dependent variable is adopted, the success will depend equally on the biological methods and the assessments of the clinical manifestation. Neuropsychological tests, for example, can lead to better characterizations of thought disorder. Electromyographic recording of facial muscles may quantitate flat affect. Computerized activity monitors can define psychomotor retardation. Laboratory psychophysical tasks can specify perceptual abnormalities. The methods of experimental psychology and ethology may form a new core for a clinical psychology sensitized to these strategy innovations.

SUMMARY

The current state of the biological approaches to psychopathology is chaotic; no markers have been accepted despite the fact that dozens have resulted in promising, if not dramatic, results. Under the current requirement for diagnostic specificity, we suspect that no marker will ever be accepted. As we have suggested, research using alternative views of diagnosis, vulnerability, and heterogeneity may hold greater promise for the 1980s. Psychiatric diagnosis will be metamorphosized by research shifting the biological marker from dependent variable to independent criterion. New diagnostic categories may be created around marker rather than symptom variables. This could lead to new labels for old familiar and perhaps pejorative categories. Similarly, treatment would be aimed at understanding specific brain dysfunction of each distressed individual. This would be done with laboratory tests of neurotransmitter, neuroendocrine, and metabolic function. Psychophysiological and psychological testing would complete such an evaluation. The response would be an individualized combination of somatic and nonsomatic treatment. At the present time, several markers are just at the edge between research tools and clinical usefulness (see review by Uytdenhoef et al 1982); new strategies may bring one or more into clinical practice. Finally, the use of markers in relatives or even the general population will open new opportunities for prevention in vulnerable individuals.

Literature Cited

Adler, S. A., Gottesman, I. I., Orsulak, P. J., Kizuka, P. P., Schildkraut, J. J. 1980. Platelet MAO activity: Relationships to clinical and psychometric variables. *Schizophr. Bull.* 6:226–31

Arora, R. C., Sahai, S., Meltzer, H. Y. 1982. Correlation between platelet monoamine oxidase activity obtained by single centrifugation and the Corash method. *Psychiatry Res.* In press

Åsberg, M., Thorén, P., Träskman, L. 1975. "Serotonin depression"—A biochemical subgroup within the affective disorders? *Science* 191:478–80

Baron, M., Klotz, J., Mendlewicz, J., Rainer, J. 1981. Multiple-threshold transmission of affective disorders. *Arch. Gen. Psychiatry* 38:79–84

Baron, M., Levitt, M., Perlman, R. 1980a. Human platelet monoamine oxidase and the menstrual cycle. *Psychiatry Res.* 3:323–27

Baron, M., Levitt, M., Perlman, R. 1980b. Low platelet monoamine oxidase activity: A possible biochemical correlate of borderline schizophrenia. *Psychiatry Res.* 3:329–35

Becker, R. E., Shaskan, E. G. 1977. Platelet monoamine oxidase activity in schizophrenic patients. *Am. J. Psychiatry* 134:512–17

Behar, D., Winokur, G., Van Valkenburg, C., Lowry, M., Lachenbruch, P. A. 1981. Clinical overlap among familial subtypes of unipolar depression. *Neuropsychobiology* 7:179–84

Belmaker, R. H., Murphy, D. L., Wyatt, R. J., Loriaux, L. 1974. Human platelet monoamine oxidase changes during the menstrual cycle. *Arch. Gen. Psychiatry* 31:553

Berger, P. A., Ginsburg, R. A., Barchas, J. D., Murphy, D. L., Wyatt, R. J. 1978. Platelet monoamine oxidase in chronic schizophrenic patients. *Am. J. Psychiatry* 135:95–98

Braden, W., Fink, E. B., Qualls, C. B., Ho, C. K., Samuels, W. O. 1982. Lithium and chlorpromazine in psychotic inpatients. *Psychiatry Res.* 7:69–81

Breakefield, X. O., Edelstein, S. B. 1980. Inherited levels of A and B types of monoamine oxidase activity. *Schizophr. Bull.* 6:282–88

Breakefield, X. O., Edelstein, S. B., Grossman, M. H. 1981. Variations in MAO and NGF in cultured human skin fibroblasts. In *Genetic Research Strategies in Psychobiology and Psychiatry*, ed. E. S. Gershon, S. Matthysse, X. O. Breakefield, R. D. Ciaranello, pp. 129–42. Pacific Grove, Calif: Boxwood

Brockington, I., Crow, T. J., Johnstone, E. C., Owen, F. 1976. An investigation of platelet monoamine oxidase activity in schizophrenia and schizo-affective psychosis. *Monoamine Oxidase and Its Inhibition.* CIBA Found. Symp. 39: 353–62

Brown, W. A., Qualls, C. B. 1981. Pituitary-adrenal disinhibition in depression: *Psychiatry Res.* 4:115–28

Brown, W. A., Haier, R. J., Qualls, C. B. 1980. Dexamethasone suppression test identifies subtypes of depression which respond to different antidepressants. *Lancet* 1:928–29

Brown, W. A., Qualls, C. B. 1982. Pituitary-adrenal regulation over multiple depressed episodes. *Psychiatry Res.* 7:265–69

Brown, W. A., Shuey, I. 1980. Response to dexamethasone and subtype of depression. *Arch. Gen. Psychiatry* 37:747–51

Brownell, G. L., Budinger, T. F., Lauterbur, P. C., McGeer, P. L. 1982. Positron tomography and nuclear magnetic resonance imaging. *Science* 215:619–26

Buchsbaum, M. S. 1971. Neural events and psychophysical law. *Science* 172:502

Buchsbaum, M. S. 1975. Average evoked response augmenting/reducing in schizophrenia and affective disorders. In *Biology of the Major Psychoses: A Comparative Analysis,* ed. D. X. Freedman, pp. 129–42. New York: Raven

Buchsbaum, M. S. 1978. Neurophysiological studies of reduction and augmentation. In *Individuality in Pain and Suffering,* ed. A. Petrie, pp. 141–57. Chicago: Univ. Chicago Press. 2nd ed.

Buchsbaum, M. S., Coursey, R. D., Murphy, D. L. 1976. The biochemical high risk paradigm: Behavioral and familial correlates of low platelet monoamine oxidase activity. *Science* 194:339–41

Buchsbaum, M. S., Haier, R. J. 1978. Biological homogeneity, symptom heterogeneity, and the diagnosis of schizophrenia. *Schizophr. Bull.* 4:473–75

Buchsbaum, M. S., Ingvar, D. H., Kessler, R., Waters, R. N., Cappelletti, J., et al. 1982. *Arch. Gen. Psychiatry* 39:251–59

Buchsbaum, M. S., Landau, S., Murphy, D., Goodwin, F. 1973. Average evoked response in bipolar and unipolar affective disorders: Relationship to sex, age of onset and monoamine oxidase. *Biol. Psychiatry* 7:199–212

Buchsbaum, M. S., Murphy, D. L., Coursey, R. D., Lake, C. R., Ziegler, M. G. 1978. Platelet monoamine oxidase, plasma dopamine-beta-hydroxylase and atten-tion in a "biochemical high risk" sample. *J. Psychiatr. Res.* 14:215–24

Buchsbaum, M. S., Muscettola, G., Goodwin, F. K. 1981. Urinary MHPG, stress response, personality factors and somatosensory evoked potentials in normal subjects and patients with major affective disorders. *Neuropsychobiology* 7:212–24

Buchsbaum, M. S., Rieder, R. O. 1979. Biologic heterogeneity and psychiatric research: Platelet MAO as a case study. *Arch. Gen. Psychiatry* 36:1163–69

Bunney, W. E. Jr. 1981. Neuronal receptor function in psychiatry: Strategy and theory. In *Neuroreceptors—Basic and Clinical Aspects,* ed. E. Usdin, W. E. Bunney Jr., J. M. Davis, pp. 241–55. New York: Wiley

Carman, J. S., Crews, E. L., Wyatt, E. S., Dohn, H. H., Hall, K. R. 1980. Prediction of response to psychotropic medications. *Ala. J. Med. Sci.* 17:161–65

Carpenter, W. T. Jr., Bartko, J. J., Carpenter, C. L., Strauss, J. S. 1976. Another view of schizophrenia subtypes. *Arch. Gen. Psychiatry* 33:508–16

Carpenter, W. T. Jr., Murphy, D. L., Wyatt, R. J. 1975. Platelet monoamine oxidase activity in acute schizophrenia. *Am. J. Psychiatry* 132:438–41

Carroll, B. J., Curtis, G. C., Mendels, J. 1976. Neuroendocrine regulation in depression. *Arch. Gen. Psychiatry* 33:1051–58

Carroll, B. J., Feinberg, M., Greden, J. F., Tarika, J., Albala, A. A., et al. 1981. A specific laboratory test for the diagnosis of melancholia. *Arch. Gen. Psychiatry* 38:15–22

Carroll, B. J., Greden, J. F., Feinberg, M., James, N. McI., Haskett, R. F., et al. 1980. Neuroendocrine dysfunction in genetic subtypes of primary unipolar depression. *Psychiatry Res.* 2:253–64

Checkley, S. A. 1980. Neuroendocrine tests of monoamine function in man: A review of basic theory and its application to the study of depressive illness. *Psychol. Med.* 10:35–53

Coger, R. W., Dymond, A. M., Serafetinides, E. A., Lowenstam, I., Pearson, D. 1976. Alcoholism: Averaged visual evoked response amplitude-intensity slope and symmetry in withdrawal. *Biol. Psychiatry* 11:435–43

Coryell, W., Gaffney, G., Burkhardt, P. E. 1982. The dexamethasone suppression test and familial subtypes of depression —a naturalistic replication. *Biol. Psychiatry* 17:33–40

Coursey, R. D., Buchsbaum, M. S., Murphy, D. L. 1979. Platelet MAO activity and evoked potentials in the identification of subjects biologically at risk for psychiatric disorders. *Br. J. Psychiatry* 134: 372–81

Coursey, R. D., Buchsbaum, M. S., Murphy, D. L. 1982. Two-year follow-up of subjects and their families defined as at risk for psychopathology on the basis of platelet MAO activities. *Neuropsychobiology* 8:51–56

Davidson, K., Bagley, C. R. 1969. Schizophrenia-like psychoses associated with organic disorders of the central nervous system: A review of the literature. In *Current Problems in Neuropsychiatry*, ed. R. N. Hemington. Ashford, Kent: Headley

Davis, G. C., Buchsbaum, M. S., Bunney, W. E. Jr. 1979. Analgesia to painful stimuli in affective illness. *Am. J. Psychiatry* 136:1148–51

De Lisi, L. E., Wise, C. D., Bridge, T. P., Phelps, B. H., Potkin, S. G., Wyatt, R. J. 1982. Monoamine oxidase and schizophrenia. In *Biological Markers in Psychiatry and Neurology*, ed. E. Usdin, I. Hanin, pp. 79–96. New York: Pergamon

De Lisi, L. E., Wise, C. D., Bridge, T. P., Rosenblatt, J. E., Wagner, R. L., et al. 1981. A probable neuroleptic effect on platelet monoamine oxidase in chronic schizophrenia patients. *Psychiatry Res.* 4:95–107

Demisch, L., Georgi, K., Patzke, B., Demisch, K., Bochnick, H. J. 1982. Correlation of platelet MAO activity with introversion: A study on a German rural population. *Psychiatry Res.* 6:303–12

Domino, E. F., Khanna, S. S. 1976. Decreased blood platelet MAO activity in unmedicated chronic schizophrenic patients. *Am. J. Psychiatry* 133:323–26

Farmer, A. E., McGuffin, P., Spitznagel, E. L. 1983. Heterogeneity in schizophrenia: A cluster analytic approach. *Psychiatry Res.* In press

Feinberg, M., Carroll, B. J. 1982. Separation of subtypes of depression using discriminant analysis. *Br. J. Psychiatry* 140:384–91

Fischer, M., Gottesman, I. I. 1980. A study of offspring of parents both hospitalized for psychiatric disorders. In *The Social Consequences of Psychiatric Illness*, ed. E. Robins, P. Clayton, J. Wing, pp. 75–90. New York: Brunner/Mazel

Fowler, C. J., Von Knorring, L., Oreland, L. 1980. Platelet monoamine oxidase activity in sensation-seekers. *Psychiatry Res.* 3:273–79

Friedhoff, A. J., Miller, J. C., Weisenfreund, J. 1978. Human platelet MAO in drug-free and medicated schizophrenic patients. *Am. J. Psychiatry* 135:952–55

Gattaz, W. F., Beckmann, H. 1981. Platelet MAO activity and personality characteristics: A study in schizophrenia patients and normal individuals. *Acta Psychiatr. Scand.* 63:479–85

Gattaz, W. F., Beckmann, H., Mendlewicz, J. 1981. HLA antigens and schizophrenia: A pool of two studies. *Psychiatry Res.* 5:123–28

Gershon, E. S. 1981. The uses of genetic variation in psychobiology. See Breakefield et al. 1981, pp. 1–14

Gershon, E. S., Bunney, W. E. 1976. The question of X-linkage in bipolar manic-depressive illness. *J. Psychiatr. Res.* 13:99–117

Gershon, E. S., Goldin, L. R., Lake, C. R., Murphy, D. L., Guroff, J. J. 1980. Genetics of plasma dopamine-β-hydroxylase (DBH) erythrocyte catechol-O-methyl transferase (COMT), and platelet monoamine oxidase (MAO) in pedigrees of patients with affective disorders. In *Enzymes and Neurotransmitters in Mental Disease*, ed. E. Usdin, T. L. Sourkes, M. B. H. Youdim, pp. 281–99. New York: Wiley

Gershon, E. S., Rieder, R. O. 1980. Are mania and schizophrenia genetically distinct? In *Mania: An Evolving Concept*, ed. R. H. Belmaker, H. M. Van Praag, pp. 97–109. Jamaica, NY: Spectrum

Gottesman, I. I., Shields, J. 1972. *Schizophrenia and Genetics: A Twin Study Vantage Point*. New York: Academic. 307 pp.

Gottesman, I. I., Shields, J. 1982. *Schizophrenia: The Epigenetic Puzzle*. Cambridge: Cambridge Univ. Press

Haier, R. J., Buchsbaum, M. S., Murphy, D. L. 1980. An 18-month followup of students biologically at risk for psychiatric problems. *Schizophr. Bull.* 6:334–37

Haier, R. J., Buchsbaum, M. S., Murphy, D. L., Gottesman, I. I., Coursey, R. D. 1980. Psychiatric vulnerability, monoamine oxidase and the averaged evoked potential. *Arch. Gen. Psychiatry* 37: 340–45

Haier, R. J., Keitner, G. 1982. Sensitivity and specificity of 1 and 2 mg dexamethasone suppression tests. *Psychiatry Res.* 7:271–76

Haier, R. J., Murphy, D. L., Buchsbaum, M. S. 1979. Paranoia and platelet monoamine oxidase in normals and non-schizophrenic psychiatric groups. *Am. J. Psychiatry* 136:308–10

Hollister, L. E., Davis, K. L., Overall, J. E., Anderston, T. 1978. Excretion of MHPG in normal subjects. *Arch. Gen. Psychiatry* 35:1410–15

Holzman, P. S., Levy, D. L. 1977. Smooth pursuit eye-movements and functional psychoses: A review. *Schizophr. Bull.* 3:15–27

Insel, T. R., Kalin, N. H., Guttmacher, L. B., Cohen, R. M., Murphy, D. L. 1982. The dexamethasone suppression test in patients with primary obsessive-compulsive disorder. *Psychiatry Res.* 6:153–60

Jackman, H. L., Meltzer, H. Y. 1980. Factors affecting determination of platelet monoamine oxidase activity. *Schizophr. Bull.* 6:259–66

Karoum, F., Linnoila, M., Potter, W. Z., Chuang, L. W., Goodwin, F. K., Wyatt, R. J. 1982. Fluctuating high urinary phenylethylamine excretion rates in some bipolar affective disorder patients. *Psychiatry Res.* 6:215–22

Kendell, R. E., Brockington, I. F. 1980. The identification of disease entities and the relationship between schizophrenic and affective psychoses. *Br. J. Psychiatry* 137:324–31

Kety, S. S., Rosenthal, D., Wender, P. H., Schulsinger, F. 1968. The types and prevalence of mental illness in the biological and adoptive families of adopted schizophrenics. *J. Psychiatr. Res.* 6:345–62

Kleinman, J. E., Potkin, S., Rogol, A., Buchsbaum, M. S., Murphy, D. L., et al. 1979. A correlation between platelet monoamine oxidase activity and plasma prolactin concentration in man. *Science* 206:479–81

Lukas, J. H., Siegel, J. 1977. Cortical mechanisms that augment or reduce evoked potentials in cats. *Science* 198:73–75

Matussek, N., Ackenheil, M., Hippius, H., Muller, F., Schroder, H., et al. 1980. Effect of clonidine on growth hormone release in psychiatric patients and controls. *Psychiatry Res.* 2:25–36

Matussek, P., Soldner, M., Nagel, D. 1981. Identification of the endogenous depressive syndrome based on the symptoms and the characteristics of the course. *Br. J. Psychiatry* 138:361–72

Mann, J., Chiu, E. 1978. Platelet monoamine oxidase activity in Huntington's chorea. *J. Neurol. Neurosurg. Psychiatry* 41:809–12

Mann, J., Thomas, J. M. 1979. Platelet monoamine oxidase activity in schizophrenia. *Br. J. Psychiatry* 134:366–71

McGuffin, P., Farmer, A. E., Yonance, A. H. 1981. HLA antigens and subtypes of schizophrenia. *Psychiatry Res.* 5:115–22

Meltzer, H. Y., Arora, R. C., Jackman, J., Pscheidt, G., Smith, M. D. 1980. Platelet monoamine oxidase and plasma amine oxidase in psychiatric patients. *Schizophr. Bull.* 6:213–19

Meltzer, H. Y., Busch, D. A., Creese, I. R., Snyder, S. H., Fang, V. S. 1981. Effect of intramuscular chlorpromazine on serum prolactin levels in schizophrenic patients and normal controls. *Psychiatry Res.* 5:95–105

Mendlewicz, J., Linkowski, P., Wilmotte, J. 1980. Linkage between glucose-6-phosphate dehydrogenase deficiency and manic-depressive psychosis. *Br. J. Psychiatry* 137:337–42

Murphy, D. L., Belmaker, R., Carpenter, W. T., Wyatt, R. J. 1977. Monoamine oxidase in chronic schizophrenia: Studies of hormonal and other factors affecting enzyme activity. *Br. J. Psychiatry.* 130:151–58

Murphy, D. L., Belmaker, R., Wyatt, R. J. 1974. Monoamine oxidase in schizophrenia and other behavioral disorders. *J. Psychiatr. Res.* 11:221–47

Murphy, D. L., Coursey, R. D., Haenel, T., Aloi, J., Buchsbaum, M. S. 1982. Platelet monoamine oxidase as a biological marker in the affective disorders and alcoholism. See De Lisi et al. 1982

Murphy, D. L., Kalin, N. H. 1980. Biological and behavioral consequences of alterations in monoamine oxidase activity. *Schizophr. Bull.* 6:357–67

Murphy, D. L., Weiss, R. 1972. Reduced monoamine oxidase activity in blood platelets from bipolar depressed patients. *Am. J. Psychiatry* 128:1351–57

Murphy, D. L., Wright, C., Buchsbaum, M. S., Nichols, A., Costa, J. L., Wyatt, R. J. 1976. Platelet and plasma amine oxidase activity in 680 normals: Sex and age differences and stability over time. *Biochem. Med.* 16:254–65

Murphy, D. L., Wyatt, R. J. 1972. Reduced monoamine oxidase activity in blood platelets from schizophrenic patients. *Nature* 238:225–26

Murphy, D. L., Wyatt, R. J. 1975. Enzyme studies in the major psychiatric disorders: I. Catechol-O-methyl-transferase, monoamine oxidase in the affective disorders, and factors affecting some behavior-related enzyme activities. See Buchsbaum 1975, pp. 277–88

Nies, A., Robinson, P. S., Lamborn, K. R., Lampert, R. P. 1973. Genetic control of platelet and plasma monoamine oxidase activity. *Arch. Gen. Psychiatry* 28: 834–38

Nurnberger, J. I., Gershon, E. S. 1982. Genetics. In *Handbook of Affective Disorders*, ed. E. Paykel, pp. 126–45. Livingston, England: Churchill

Orsulak, P. J., Schildkraut, J. J., Schatzberg, A. F., Herzog, J. M. 1978. Differences in platelet monoamine oxidase activity in subgroups of schizophrenic and depressive disorders. *Biol. Psychiatry* 13: 637–47

Pandey, G. N., Dorus, E., Shaughnessy, R., Davis, J. M. 1979. Genetic control of platelet monoamine oxidase activity: Studies on normal families. *Life Sci.* 25:1173–78

Papakostas, Y., Fink, M., Lee, J., Irwin, P., Johnson, L. 1981. Neuroendocrine measures in psychiatric patients: Course and outcome with ECT. *Psychiatry Res.* 4:55–64

Pope, H. J., Lipinski, J. F. 1978. Diagnosis in schizophrenia of manic-depressive illness. *Arch. Gen. Psychiatry* 35:811–28

Post, R. M., Ballenger, J. C., Goodwin, F. K. 1980. Cerebrospinal fluid studies of neurotransmitter function in manic and depressive illness. In *Neurobiology of Cerebrospinal Fluid*, ed. J. H. Wood, pp. 685–717. New York: Plenum

Potkin, S. G., Cannon, H. E., Murphy, D. L., Wyatt, R. J. 1978. Are paranoid schizophrenics biologically different from other schizophrenics? *N. Engl. J. Med.* 298:61–66

Puchall, L. B., Coursey, R. D., Buchsbaum, M. S., Murphy, D. L. 1980. Parents of high risk subjects defined by levels of monoamine oxidase activity. *Schizophr. Bull.* 6:338–46

Redmond, D. E. Jr., Murphy, D. L., Baulu, J. 1979. Platelet monoamine oxidase activity correlates with social affiliative and agonistic behaviors in normal Rhesus monkeys. *Psychosom. Med.* 41:87–100

Reich, T., James, J. W., Morris, C. A. 1972. The use of multiple thresholds in determining the mode of transmission of semi-continuous traits. *Ann. Hum. Genet.* 36:163–84

Rosenthal, D. 1970. *Genetic Theory and Abnormal Behavior.* New York: McGraw-Hill

Rosenthal, D., Wender, P. H., Kety, S. S., Schulsinger, F., Welner, J., Ostergaard, L. 1968. Schizophrenic's offspring reared in adoptive homes. In *The Transmission of Schizophrenia*, ed. D. Rosenthal, S. S. Kety, pp. 377–91. Oxford: Pergamon

Rothpearl, A. B., Mohs, R. C., Davis, K. L. 1981. Statistical power in biological psychiatry. *Psychiatry Res.* 5:257–66

Rotrosen, J., Angrist, B., Gershon, S., Paquin, J., Branchey, L., et al. 1979. Neuroendocrine effects of apomorphine: Characterization of response patterns and application to schizophrenia research. *Br. J. Psychiatry* 135:444–56

Roy-Byrne, P. 1982. *Neuroendocrine tests in bulimia.* Presented at Am. Psychiatr. Assoc. Ann. Meet., Toronto, Canada

Rudorfer, M. V., Hwu, H. G., Clayton, P. J. 1982. Dexamethasone suppression test in primary depression: Significance of family history and psychosis. *Biol. Psychiatry* 17:41–48

Rydin, E., Schalling, D., Åsberg, M. 1982. Rorschach ratings in depressed and suicidal patients with low CSF 5HIAA. *Psychiatry Res.* 7:229–43

Sachar, E. J., Asnis, G., Nathan, R. S., Halbreich, U., Tabrizi, M., Halpern, F. S. 1980. *Arch. Gen. Psychiatry* 37:755–57

Sachar, E. J., Baron, M. 1979. The biology of affective disorders. *Ann. Rev. Neurosci.* 2:505–18

Schildkraut, J. J., Orsulak, P. J., Schatzberg, A. F., Herzog, J. M. 1980. Platelet monoamine oxidase activity in subgroups of schizophrenic disorders. *Schizophr. Bull.* 6:220–25

Schlesser, M. A., Sherman, B. M., Winokur, G. 1979. Genetic subtypes of unipolar primary depressive illness distinguished by hypothalamic-pituitary-adrenal axis activity. *Lancet* 1:739–41

Schlesser, M. A., Winokur, G., Sherman, B. M. 1980. Hypothalamic-pituitary-adrenal axis activity in depressive illness. *Arch. Gen. Psychiatry* 37:737–43

Schooler, C., Buchsbaum, M. S., Carpenter, W. T. 1976. Evoked response and kinesthetic measures of augmenting/reducing in schizophrenics: Replications and extensions. *J. Nerv. Ment. Dis.* 163: 221–32

Schooler, C., Zahn, T. P., Murphy, D. L., Buchsbaum, M. S. 1978. Psychological correlates of monoamine oxidase activity in normals. *J. Nerv. Ment. Dis.* 166:177–86

Sedvall, G., Fyro, B., Gullberg, B., Nyback, H., Wiesel, F. A., Wode-Helgodt, B. 1980. Relationships in healthy volunteers between concentration of monoamine metabolites in cerebrospinal fluid and family history of psychiatric morbidity. *Br. J. Psychiatry* 136:366–74

Siever, L., Insel, T., Uhde, T. 1981. Noradrenergic challenges in the affective disorders. *J. Clin. Psychopharmacol.* 1: 193–206

Strauss, J. S., Bartko, J. J., Carpenter, W. T. 1973. The use of clustering techniques for the classification of psychiatric patients. *Br. J. Psychiatry* 122:531–40

Takahashi, S., Tani, N., Yamane, H. 1975. Monoamine oxidase activity in blood platelets in alcoholism. *Folia Psychiatr. Neurol. Jpn.* 30:455–62

Träskman, L., Åsberg, M., Bertilsoon, L., Sjöstrand, L. 1981. Monoamine metabolites in CSF and suicidal behavior. *Arch. Gen. Psychiatry* 38:631–36

Uytdenhoef, P., Linkowski, P., Mendlewicz, J. 1982. Biological quantitative methods in the evaluation of psychiatric treatment: Some biochemical criteria. *Neuropsychobiology* 8:60–72

Van Praag, H., de Haan, S. 1980. Depression vulnerability and 5-hydroxytryptophan prophylaxis. *Psychiatry Res.* 3:75–83

Van Praag, H., Korf, J. 1971. Endogenous depressions with and without disturbances in the 5-hydroxytryptamine metabolism: A biochemical classification. *Psychopharmacologia* 19:148–52

Von Knorring, L. 1978a. An experimental study of visual averaged evoked responses (V. AER) and pain measures (PM) in patients with depressive disorders. *Biol. Psychol.* 6:27–38

Von Knorring, L. 1978b. Visual averaged evoked responses in patients with bipolar affective disorders. *Neuropsychobiology* 4:314–20

Weissman, M. M., Myers, J. K. 1980. Psychiatric disorders in a U.S. community: The application of research diagnostic criteria to a resurveyed community sample. *Acta Psychiatr. Scand.* 62:99–111

Weitkamp, L. R., Stancer, H. C., Persad, E., Flood, C., Guttormsen, S. 1981. Depressive disorders and HLA: A gene on chromosome 6 that can affect behavior. *N. Engl. J. Med.* 305:1301–6

Wender, P. H., Rosenthal, D., Kety, S. S., Schulsinger, F., Welner, J. 1974. Cross-fostering: A research strategy for clarifying the role of genetic and experiential factors in the etiology of schizophrenia. *Arch. Gen. Psychiatry* 30:121–28

Winokur, G., Behar, D., Van Valkenburg, C., Lowry, M. 1978. Is a familial definition of depression both feasible and valid? *J. Nerv. Ment. Dis.* 166:764–68

Winter, H., Herschel, M., Propping, P., Friedl, W., Vogel, F. 1978. A twin study on three enzymes (DBH, COMT, MAO) of catecholamine metabolism. *Psychopharmacology* 57:63–69

Wyatt, R. J. 1978. Is there an endogenous amphetamine? A testable hypothesis of schizophrenia. In *The Nature of Schizophrenia: New Approaches to Research and Treatment,* pp. 116–25. New York: Wiley

Wyatt, R. J., Murphy, D. L. 1976. Low platelet monoamine oxidase activity and schizophrenia. *Schizophr. Bull.* 2:77–89

Wyatt, R. J., Murphy, D. L., Belmaker, R., Cohen, S., Donnelly, C. H., Pollin, W. 1973. Reduced monoamine oxidase activity in platelets: A possible genetic marker for vulnerability to schizophrenia. *Science* 179:916–18

Wyatt, R. J., Potkin, S. G., Kleinman, J. E., Weinberger, D. R., Luchins, D. J., Jeste, D. V. 1981. The schizophrenia syndrome: Examples of biological tools for subclassification. *J. Nerv. Ment. Dis.* 169:100–12

Wyatt, R. J., Potkin, S. G., Walls, P. D., Nichols, A., Carpenter, W., Murphy, D. 1978. Clinical correlates of low platelet monoamine oxidase in schizophrenic patients. In *Psychiatric Diagnosis: Exploration of Biological Predictors,* ed. H. S. Akiskal, W. L. Webb, pp. 279–97. New York/London: Spectrum

Zubin, J., Spring, B. 1977. Vulnerability—A new view of schizophrenia. *J. Abnorm. Psychol.* 86:103–26

Zuckerman, M. 1982. The neurobiology of some dimensions of personality. *Int. Rev. Neurobiol.* 24: In press

Zuckerman, M., Murtaugh, T., Siegel, J. 1974. Sensation-seeking and cortical augmenting-reducing. *Psychophysiology* 11:535–42

Ann. Rev. Psychol. 1983. 34:431–63

PERSONALITY STRUCTURE AND ASSESSMENT

Leonard G. Rorer

Department of Psychology, Miami University, Oxford, Ohio 45056

Thomas A. Widiger

Department of Psychology, University of Kentucky, Lexington, Kentucky 40506

CONTENTS

Until the editors told them not to do it anymore, authors of chapters for the *Annual Review of Psychology* used to start by apologizing for the fact that they could not possibly cover all the literature in the time period that had been assigned to them. Goldberg (1974) pointed out that just publishing his bibliography of MMPI studies would have exceeded his page limit. We have had no such problem, because we have studiously avoided most of the literature that is typically included under this topic, on the grounds that it

431

0066-4308/83/0201-0431$02.00

deserves to be avoided. If one were to outline the field in terms of our order of priority and importance, it would go from the most basic, abstract, and theoretical to the most specific and applied. Most of the work in the area tends to be in the latter areas having to do with implementation and application, and those are the areas that have been covered in previous reviews.

To be more specific, the bulk of the current literature is in the traditional areas that we do not cover: development of new tests, empirical correlates of scores and patterns on established tests, measurement of constructs, and the psychological, attitudinal, and personality correlates of almost anything you can imagine.

We could have summarized the research on such tests as the Rorschach, TAT, MMPI, SCT, Hand Test, Szondi, etc (e.g. Wolman 1978, Butcher 1979, McReynolds 1981). We also could have summarized the recent positive and negative findings on the constructs of achievement motivation, assertiveness, authoritarianism, cognitive styles, extraversion, field dependence, moral development, locus of control, loneliness, mindlessness, etc. It would be impossible, however, to integrate this research into a theory of personality structure. As London & Exner (1978) acknowledge in the introduction to their anthology:

> There obviously has been no overreaching plan or theory, implicit or explicit, guiding the selection of topics for trait researchers. Indeed the editors were forced to organize the book by means of the unsophisticated tactic of simply placing chapters in alphabetical order (p. xiv).

Wiggins (1980) sums it up well: "The last 25 years of personality study may be characterized as a period of construct elaboration in which a variety of single dimensions of personality . . . have been studied in depth in experimental, correlational, and field designs" (p. 285).

> The choice of which two constructs are to be related is not informed by theoretical considerations. Rather, it appears to be determined by an author's reading of the zeitgeist in terms of the *frequency* with which the names of the two constructs have appeared in the titles of journal articles. . . . Thus, if it is a vintage year for "fear of success" and "field dependence," a study of "The relationship between fear of success and field dependence in student nurses" is surefire (p. 286).

As a result, literature reviews appear to be disparate conglomerations rather than cumulative or conclusive integrations. Our assessment is that this literature constitutes a negligible increment to our understanding of personality structure.

It is the aim of this review to acquaint you with a set of minority opinions in a literature that you might otherwise have overlooked. The literature is inconclusive, but it does contain new ideas. Our goal is not to convince you of anything, but to persuade you to try thinking about things in a different way. We believe that if you read and think about some of this literature, it will be difficult for you to return to your old beliefs. Even if you continue doing some of the same things, you will most likely think about them in different ways.

It is no secret that personality assessment has been in big trouble as it has come under attack from both expert and lay critics. Assessment takes up a decreasing proportion of the professional practitioner's time, occupies a place of decreasing importance in the university graduate curriculum, and has been legally outlawed in many selection situations. Many have reacted by jumping what they believe to be a sinking ship. Others have come to the defense of the establishment, and have argued that with a few refinements we can continue with business as usual (Korchin & Schuldberg 1981).

Clearly (to these reviewers), it is not a time for business as usual. Nor is it a time to abandon ship. Rather, it is a time to question our basic assumptions. While it has been commonplace for years to give lip service to the statement that the field of personality assessment is enormously complicated, this complexity has seldom been sufficiently appreciated. Having intoned that the enterprise is enormously complicated, practitioners have gone right back to their simple-minded methods. For many applied assessment situations, simple-minded methods are quite sufficient and are the methods of choice. In general, if you want information from someone, the best way to get it is to ask them (e.g. Shrauger & Osberg 1981). Assuming that they understand the question, that they have the information, and that they are not motivated to deceive you, that is not only the simplest and least expensive, but also the most accurate procedure. That fact is often threatening to those who are at pains to make the enterprise seem complicated and mysterious so as to support the idea that one needs highly trained professionals to administer and interpret obtuse and highly convoluted protocols.

Trying to understand personality and to measure personality structure is another matter. We have tried to use assessment (individual differences) models that are inappropriate to the task, which is more complicated than has been realized. The complications are conceptual, and understanding them requires a significant change in orientation.

PHILOSOPHICAL ISSUES

Our thesis is that psychology is burdened with an outmoded philosophy, and a distorted view of science, to both of which it adheres with messianic fervor. Presumably the model that psychology seeks to emulate is that of physics, as opposed to that of religion or mysticism. Consider, therefore, what is probably the most famous experiment of the century: the test of the first or special theory of relativity. Scientists assembled and noted the apparent position of several stars during an eclipse of the sun. They observed an apparent deflection of the stars' positions. A prediction had been confirmed. Could this be science? There was no control group. No subjects were assigned randomly to conditions. Though the observations were variable, no test was performed to determine if the result was statistically significant. There was no check on the demand characteristics to see if the investigators' observations had been biased by their theoretical expectations. Science, indeed! In psychology the whole affair would be pejoratively described as merely observational, and poorly controlled at that. Can you imagine a respectable journal publishing such findings? Certainly not until the investigator succeeded in bringing the project into the laboratory and confirming it there.

And what of the physics of today? Certainly they have cleaned up their act? In the hope of dispelling an illusion, "No!" Physicists have no qualms about considering quarks and black holes, things that are not operationally definable, or even, in principle, observable. Can a scientist really deal with something that is neither observable nor operationally definable? In a word, "Yes!" Psychology in general, and personality theory and assessment in particular, have paid a high price for refusing to follow physics' model.

Psychology is emulating an illusion in adhering to a philosophy of science that may never have existed. We have described it only indirectly, but we are all so familiar with the litany about operational definitions and the experimental method that describing it in detail seems like reciting the mass to the Pope. The logical empiricists abandoned operationism when Carnap's (1936, 1937) classic paper, *Testability and Meaning,* was published. It is one of those ironies of scientific history that the position was presented to psychology in its classic form just a few years later when Koch's master's thesis was published in the *Psychological Review.* During the 1940s, psychology adopted logical empiricism while philosophy abandoned it. Logical empiricism in its weakened forms may be said to have endured into the 1950s, by which time the logical empiricists themselves were demonstrating the untenability of their previous position, and Koch (1977, 1981) had joined those calling for a change. We are not going to try to explain why psychology has fallen somewhere between 25 and 45 years behind what is known in philosophy (a fascinating problem that can only be addressed under a revised philosophy of science), and we do not have space to provide an explication of more modern theories, but we can try to provide a road map for those who are inclined to follow it.

A good place to start is Mahoney (1976, chap. 7). Even though there are deep divisions among philosophers with respect to ontology (theories about the essence or structure of reality), cosmology (theories of causal influence), and epistemology (theories of knowledge), on a number of issues there is a consensus that may constitute a shock or revelation to most psychologists, who tend to believe that science progresses via the accumulation of facts, which constitute the foundation of knowledge and on the basis of which theories are constructed. As facts accumulate, we inductively generalize to theories, from which hypotheses are logically derived, and the theories are retained or rejected on the basis of experimental tests of these hypotheses. Philosophers agree that all of the above can be shown to be false. Mahoney explains why, and provides clear and compelling examples.

Psychologists seem to suffer from a pathological fear of being nonscientific. Philosophers refer to the distinction between science and nonscience as the demarcation problem. Most agree that no attempt at demarcation has been successful—with the possible exception of their own. Clearly, anyone who fears something that cannot be identified is going to develop strong defenses to ward off the chronic anxiety. Those who would like a brief introduction to the problem would do well to try Grünbaum (1978a). His short piece contrasts the conventional inductivist view of theory confirmation with Popper's falsificationist position. The inductivist view is that a theory is scientific to the extent that it is consistent with the facts, whereas its rivals are not. Popper suggested as an alternative criterion that theories are scientific to the extent that they are falsifiable. His motivation was to show that astrology and psychoanalysis were unscientific, something he believed that his theory could do and that the inductivists' theory was unable to do. Grünbaum disagrees on both counts, and further points out that black holes and other postulated entities may be inductively confirmable but pseudoscientific under Popper's criterion. The fact that we have not found something yet does not mean that we may not find it somewhere else at another time. Thus, any theory postulating the existence of something is never disconfirmable, and is, therefore, pseudoscientific under Popper's criterion—a severe problem for the criterion! Universal generalizations (e.g. all persons are mortal) pose the same problem for Popper's criterion.

Although Grünbaum is a philosopher, he writes in a way that should be understandable to most psychologists, and many of his articles are on psychologically relevant topics. If the above whets your appetite, Grünbaum has more detailed treatments of the problem (Grünbaum 1976b, 1978b). Other articles of interest to psychologists include those dealing with determining the falsity of a scientific hypothesis, the role of auxiliary hypotheses in falsificationism (a topic we shall consider shortly), psychoanalysis, and the role of psychological explanations in the rejection or acceptance of scientific theories (Grünbaum 1971, 1976a, 1979, 1980).

Most psychologists are only dimly aware that the two procedures that they believe to be *the* methods of science, theory confirmation and induction, are illogical and unjustifiable. Theory confirmation involves the logical fallacy of affirming the consequent (e.g. Mahoney 1976), and, as Hume pointed out, the use of induction can be justified only by using induction. Popper attempted to deal with the first problem by requiring that tests of theories involve predictions of low a priori probability, as in the test of the special theory of relativity (see Meehl 1978). However, it is hard to see how the procedure can survive in the face of the dilemmas presented by Salmon (1973, 1975), who proves that two experiments, each individually confirming an hypothesis (theory), may nevertheless conjunctively refute it! Even negative outcomes are not conclusive, Popper's famous modus tollens notwithstanding. As Duhem (1962/1906) pointed out, and most philosophers now agree, every experiment tests not only the hypothesis of interest, but many auxiliary hypotheses as well. Thus, it is possible for a negative result to be due to an erroneous auxiliary hypothesis. "By skillful manipulation of auxiliary theories and assumptions about unobservable initial conditions, ... the most mundane scientific theory not only can be 'saved' no matter what the evidence, but can also be made to account for any possible (relevant) evidence" (Maxwell 1975, p. 158). That, by itself, is bad enough. It is, however, possible for a negative outcome to confirm each of the hypotheses independently while refuting their conjunction! We are not going to show you how, because we want you to read Salmon for yourself. His examples are straightforward and involve nothing more complicated than conditional probabilities. His results clearly make a shambles of contemporary accounts of scientific method as involving the corroboration or disconfirmation of theories by the accumulation of positive or negative results by different investigators. Salmon opts for a Bayesian alternative, as does one of the authors of this chapter. Meehl (1978), Glymour (1980), and others disagree. Maxwell (1975) provides a good account of a Bayesian frequentist position in the same volume in which Salmon's article appears.

There are two ways to go in understanding the demise of logical positivism. One is to become familiar with the position and then to follow the attacks on the various parts of the position. An excellent short summary was provided in Schlagel's address to the APA in 1979, but copies may not be readily available. Suppe (1977), in an introduction to a volume of papers that were presented at a symposium in 1969, offers a moderately technical summary of the received view (as logical empiricism came to be called), of the attacks on it, and of the alternatives that have been offered. He considers such issues as formalization, the analytic-synthetic distinction, the distinction between observational and theoretical terms, the attempts to develop correspondence rules, and the adequacy of the received view for analyzing scientific theories. A number of the papers also make interesting reading, but may offer more than the average psychologist wants to know about the subject. While the introduction seems to us even-handed and fair, the afterword (written for the second edition in 1976), suggesting a current consensus of opinion, is a disappointment. Skip it.

A second approach is offered by Weimer (1979), whose work was strongly influenced by Bartley (1962). Weimer offers a summary of both rationalism and empiricism, and then goes straight for the jugular without slugging through all the battles summarized by Suppe. Weimer points out that empiricism falls by its own criterion that all knowledge is justifiable knowledge, because there is no way to justify empiricism! Empiricism and rationalism alike ultimately depend on an unjustifiable commitment, a leap of faith. Science does not differ from religion—an ironical result, given that the motivation for empiricism was precisely to distinguish science from mysticism.

Weimer's solution is to embrace comprehensively critical rationalism, the only position that has the virtue of being consistent. Comprehensively critical rationalism holds that no statement can be justified; all claims are subject to criticism and challenge, including comprehensively critical rationalism. Weimer's book has a kind of Catch-22 characteristic, in that you may not find it either understandable or convincing if you are not at least somewhat familiar with the work on which it is based, whereas if you are already familiar with the work on which it is based, you may not learn much from the book. Nevertheless, we believe that most psychologists would get their money's worth from the bibliography alone, and that reading the book will make almost any open-minded reader want to consult the works in the bibliography, if for no other reason than to understand what Weimer said.

The following references are somewhat less general. Leahey (1980) gives a moderately technical history of operationism, in which he argues that operational definitions are neither operational nor definitional, but really low-level laws. He concludes that "continued advocacy and pretended use of operational definitions is merely liturgical, and obscures important aspects of actual scientific practice" (p. 127). Kantorovich (1978) describes an idealization of a Lakatosian research program that has both Bayesian and Popperian features. For an historical summary specifically dealing with psychology, we recommend Mischel (1976), who does a good job of relating psychological theories to their philosophical underpinnings at a nontechnical level.

Physics' status as the premier science hinges at least in part on the doctrine of reductionism, that is, the notion that all other sciences, including psychology, are ultimately reduceable to physics, so that psychological events will someday be describable in terms of electrical and chemical events. Davidson (1980) and Peele (1981) are among those arguing that such reduction is, in principle, impossible.

If you want to get beyond logical empiricism to some more current viewpoints, consider Block's (1980) two-volume collection of *Readings in Philosophy of Psychology*. Among other things, it will acquaint you with functionalism, a currently important ism, and with the growing conviction among philosophers that the solution of many long-standing philosophical puzzles depends on advances in psychology. It is clear that physics and philosophy profoundly influenced each other in the first half of this century. Current findings in quantum mechanics are inconsistent with traditional logic (Hughes 1981) and with our conceptions of an independent reality (d'Espagnat 1979), and may require further changes in philosophical truths that have been considered self-evident for years. Likewise, solutions to problems such as that of the mind may come as much from psychological and physiological discoveries as from philosophical analysis (e.g. Churchland 1980).

Looking to the future, Royce (1982) sounds the same theme. His view is that other disciplines, such as physics, have broken away from philosophy because they have been able to solve their problems scientifically rather than by rational analysis (philosophically), and he forecasts that psychology will do the same. He is in accord with Weimer (1979) in believing that epistemology may turn out to be a psychological, rather than a philosophical, problem. He forecasts that "psychology's indigenous philosophy will take some form of what I have called *constructive dialectics,* where *dialectic* has to do with maintaining the tension between viable conceptual alternatives" (p. 259). He believes that if psychology is to advance, the *"need for theoretical-philosophical expertise is critical"* (p. 264), and suggests that APA Division 24 actively promote this expertise by sponsoring workshops, seminars, and awards.

Causality

The cornerstone of the argument for the experimental method as the sine qua non of science is that it is the only way to establish causal relationships. But just what is a cause? And what is a causal relationship? Unknown to most psychologists, the original empiricist position was that there is no such thing as a cause; Hume viewed it as a theoretical term to which one could attach no meaning beyond that of a high correlation between two events. Although this revelation may come as a shock to psychologists who are used to distinguishing "merely correlational" relationships from experimental ones, the distinction is nonexistent.

Since Hume there have been numerous other attempts to solve the riddle of causality. Just as there is a basic split between realists and instrumentalists, so there is no basic agreement as to whether causes are real or linguistic (theoretical) entities, though it is generally conceded even by realists that we can never know or observe causes directly, but must infer them. There is general agreement that any adequate treatment of causes must allow for both probabilistic relationships and multiple determination, that effects either follow or are instantaneous with causes (a nontrivial and thorny problem), and that many cause-effect relationships are reversible. There is at least a strong minority opinion that causes are theoretical, linguistic, or functional relationships, and hence do not exist independent of the theory in which they are imbedded. There is probably majority agreement that causes cannot be established by experiments any more than by any other method. In any case, one makes inferences as to which things are constant and which are varied (causal), and experiments are not qualitatively different from other observations.

For the psychologist who thinks that causality is a simple, obvious, or noncontroversial concept, some reading is in order. A good place to start is Cook & Campbell (1979, Chap. 2). They present a readable summary of some of the major positions, with good examples of some of the difficulties. Meehl (1977) provides clear examples of probabilistic and multiple determination, shows that the notion of etiology (causality) is used in many different ways, and provides quantitative definitions in terms of necessary and sufficient conditions for the different meanings that he identifies.

Meehl (1977) also discusses the use of cause to refer to a nonspecific etiology, a use that is widespread in medicine and social science and especially in psychotherapy and personology. Suppose a factory burns, and the investigator now has the job of determining a cause of the fire. Was it arson, or was it a short in the fuse box? Suppose the investigator concludes that the fire was caused by a short in the fuse box. Most of us would regard that as a meaningful statement, even though it cannot be experimentally verified. What is at issue is not whether a short in the fuse box could cause a fire —we acknowledge that it could—but whether, on this occasion, it did. Clearly, shorts in fuse boxes do not always cause fires, and fires may be caused in many ways. Thus, a short is neither a necessary nor a sufficient condition for causing the fire. Briefly, what is sufficient is the entire set of conditions, of which a short in the fuse box is one. Under these conditions, the short is necessary, because without it the fire would not have occurred, and we say that the short caused the fire, even though the other conditions were also necessary. The applicability of this model to answering questions about the reasons for a person's actions should be obvious. Meehl's article should be required reading.

A slightly more technical survey of theoretical analyses of causality is available in the introductory section of Brand (1976), preceding the collection of papers on which the summary is based. Be prepared to conclude that you do not understand causality. Psychologists should also be especially interested in the papers by Mackie (1976), on whose work Meehl (1977) is based, and Davidson (1976), who discusses the logical form of singular causal statements. Anyone who still thinks that experiments establish causal relationships should recall the Duhemian dilemmas and Salmon's paradoxes.

As an illustration of the pitfalls of combining muddy thinking about causality with slavish devotion to pseudo-rigorous experimentalism, consider the personality-judgment and clinical studies that are being reported in the social psychology literature under the rubrics of attribution theory and attitude change, respectively. Typically, these studies involve two groups, one of which is subjected to some manipulation and the other of which is not. The mean scores of the groups are compared, and if they differ, it is concluded that the manipulation caused the individuals to shift their opinions, attitudes, attributions, or whatever; for example, that listening to someone read an essay influenced the way in which that person was subsequently described. At least two things should be noted about this dreadful literature. First, between-persons data are being used to make an inference of a within-individual effect. Second, a group effect (summed over persons) is being used to infer a causal effect whose nexus is located within the individual. Neither inference is warranted. A moment's reflection will reveal that the data themselves indicate that the causal inference is unwarranted at the individual level, because some scores are higher, some are lower, and some are the same when the two groups are compared. Even in those (more appropriate) studies in which the same individual is tested twice, some subjects shift their responses in each direction and some remain the same. If one wishes to make a causal inference, the inference must be that the manipulation caused the group, but not any individual, to change. One could say that the manipulation caused some subjects to increase, some to decrease, and some to remain the same; and that it caused some to increase, and some to decrease, more than others; but there is no constant effect for which the manipulation can be said to be the cause. All that can be said is that the manipulation caused whatever the particular subject did, but that is a tautological statement that could be made without any observation whatsoever, much less without performing an experiment!

Psychologists' Discontents

In the psychological literature there have been recent and increasing signs of discontent with the stultifying influences of the epistemological zeitgeist. The cumulative impact of these articles has been lessened because (a) they have been scattered; (b) broad calls for change tend to be made within the context of the current framework, rather than challenging the basic epistemological assumptions; and (c) the calls for basic epistemological change tend to be focused on one or another specific issue, rather than the entire framework. We have assembled some of them for you.

Hilgard (1980) chronicled the resurgence of interest in consciousness and cognition, topics that were taboo 10 years ago. Natsoulas (1978, 1981) and Lieberman (1979) were among those joining in the call for the study of consciousness. Tyler (1981) also noted the new areas of research, and called, in addition, for research designs that are appropriate for the study of individuals and individuality at a sufficient level of complexity as to be generalizable outside the laboratory. She noted the need for a liberalization of theory, and discussed probabilistic functionalism (Petrinovich 1979), general systems theory, and contextualism as alternatives to mechanistic models. Levine (1980) offered investigative reporting as a research model.

In several papers, Gergen (1978, 1980, 1981, Gergen & Morawski 1980) has clearly described a number of shortcomings in the empiricist position, especially the notion that there are facts that one can observe, and on the basis of which one can build theories that are uninfluenced by values. He has called for the abandonment of empiricism on the grounds that it does not lead to the generation of new ideas or theories. His 1980 paper offers a particularly clear illustration and discussion of the extent to which facts are constructions, and shows that we are interested not in the basic behavioral act, but in the meaning of the act.

Greenwald (1975) and Greenwald & Ronis (1981) proposed a distinction between operational and conceptual disconfirmability, apparently without realizing that they correspond to attributing disconfirmation to the auxiliary and main hypotheses, respectively. The exchange in the literature (Leary 1979, Rakover 1981) amounted to a discussion of the Duhemian thesis, though no one mentioned it by name.

Zuriff's (1980) description of "Radical behaviorist epistemology" deserves careful reading, because it carefully distinguishes the various epistemological positions that behaviorists have taken, and because the final position that the author describes is a nonjustificationist one in which the criterion of truth is interpreted in the same way that radical behaviorists interpret values, that is, not as something that ought to be, but rather as something that emerges as a result of the activity. The criterion of truth cannot be justified any more than values can. It simply exists. While the author describes this position as empirical, it is also nonjustificationist and seems to be compatible with comprehensive critical rationalism. For those who want a short, careful treatment of epistemology from a behaviorist viewpoint, this is the best piece of which we know.

Messick (1981) explained once again that in personality assessment we are dealing with constructs, and then presented three different models of the possible relationships between traits, constructs, and test and nontest behaviors. He explains clearly and carefully how these different formulations lead to different assessment strategies, thus showing that our epistemological position does make a difference in what we do. In discussing psychiatric classifications, Skinner (1981) stresses the need for a continual interplay between theory development and empirical analysis. His framework for an integrated paradigm is based on the principles of construct validation rather than blind empiricism.

Wachtel (1980) repeats his earlier (1973) observation that the experimental method gives misleading answers to many questions, because it describes the effects of situations on behavior without allowing for the fact that people choose their situations. He also argues persuasively that the premium placed on (vacuous) productivity leads to the study of trivial rather than important issues, and that the pressure to obtain research grants leads to data gathering instead of theorizing, even though new conceptualizations may be needed before we can know what data to gather. His suggestion that salary and promotional decisions be made on the basis of the person's three best articles within the last 5 (7, 10, pick your number) years, so as to reward quality rather than quantity, merits serious consideration.

The single most important theoretical and methodological article in the psychological literature in recent years is Meehl's (1978). Unfortunately, the article will probably be difficult for most psychologists to understand. Though Meehl's writing is clear and concise, he is forced to assume background knowledge that most of us do not possess. Fortunately, the problem is easily solved by reading Meehl (1967) and Golden & Meehl (1979). Meehl's (1978) is not a philosophical paper; it is a methodological paper about the conduct of psychological science on a day-to-day basis. Meehl classifies himself as a neo-Popperian, which means that he sees the basic method of science as being the attempt to subject theories to refutation. In a nutshell, Meehl argues that the slow progress of soft psychology is due to our failure to subject our theories to such tests. Conventional methodology in psychology involves setting up a null hypothesis that one wishes to refute in order to confirm the theory. Because the null hypothesis is (quasi) always false, improved precision leads to a greater chance of rejecting the null hypothesis and hence of confirming the theory. Contrariwise, sloppy research may lead to failure to reject the null, and hence rejection of perfectly good theories. Clearly, something is wrong. Meehl's prescription is to emulate the hard sciences, in which point estimates are made. In this case the methodology works the way that it should, because increased precision leads to an increased chance of rejecting the theory, that is, to a more, instead of a less, stringent test (Meehl 1967). Meehl (1978) does not mince words in stating his conclusion: "I believe that the almost universal reliance on merely refuting the null hypothesis as the standard method for corroborating substantive theories in the soft areas is a terrible mistake, is basically unsound, poor scientific strategy, and one of the worst things that ever happened in the history of psychology" (p. 817). This is not a soft-headed antiscientific humanist talking; this is a dustbowl empiricist who endorses actuarial methods and rigorous research. Take heed! Get the article and read it once a week for six weeks.

Meehl is not alone in noting problems with current hypothesis testing procedures. Novick & Jackson (1974) have described them as "giving a misleading answer to a question which nobody is asking" (p. 245), a point the Bayesians have been making for years (e.g. Edwards et al 1963). Pitz (1978, 1980) notes that an hypothesis cannot be tested in isolation, but only in comparison to some other hypothesis. When a precise hypothesis is compared with an imprecise alternative, conventional procedures often lead to erroneous conclusions, such as rejecting the null hypothesis when its likelihood is actually greater than that of the alternative.

Why Change?

Based on our personal experience, psychologists seem to insist on consistency, hard-headedness, justifiability, logic, meaningfulness, rationality, rigor, and all those other good scientific things, but not to be the least bit perturbed that their implicit, if not explicit, methodological and philosophical position is inconsistent, unjustifiable, and just plain muddle-headed *by their own standards.* Is their indifference justified? We think not.

The major result of clinging to an outmoded philosophy and methodology has been the trivialization of the discipline by restricting both the methods of investigation and the range of topics that are considered appropriate. Broadly, topics have been considered inappropriate if they cannot be studied experimentally and objectively. Nowhere have the results been more disastrous than in personality and social psychology. The obsession with pseudo-rigor has resulted in well-controlled studies that are virtually irrelevant to the questions they are supposed to answer. Indeed, most of the studies seem to have little to do with substantive questions of interest at all, but to focus instead on the minutiae of the experimental manipulations in previous studies. Pencil (1976) offers a devastating parody that will make you laugh and cry at the same time.

One of the important implications of recent philosophical analysis is that there is no single method of science and no rule to specify the nature of the data or the means of data acquisition that is correct. Laboratory experiments are not the only, or even the preferred, road to knowledge. Little of the interesting or exciting work on personality theory and assessment is being done in laboratories. It is being done in clinics by clinicians. It was widely recognized that psychoanalysis constituted not only a method of treatment, but also a theory of personality. So it is with its competitors. Behaviorism, social-learning theory (e.g. Bandura 1977), and rational-emotive therapy (Ellis 1979), to cite three examples, also constitute implicit theories of personality that are being made progressively more explicit, and the attempts to apply those therapies constitute tests of those theories. The significant debates concerning the epistemological foundations of personality theory are taking place in the clinical literature between proponents of the behavioral and cognitive points of view (e.g. Ledwidge 1978, 1979, Kazdin 1979, Mahoney & Kazdin 1979, Messer & Winokur 1980, Liotti & Reda 1981, Ross 1981).

THEORETICAL ISSUES

Personality Theory and Traits

If one is going to assess something, it might seem reasonable to expect that one would know what it is that one is assessing. Not so with personality. Or with traits. Given the deep divisions among philosophers with respect to realist as opposed to instrumentalist views, and the numerous variations on those positions, it is hardly surprising that there is little agreement as to what personality is or whether it exists. For this review, personality is simply considered to be a collection of traits.

Hirschberg (1978) has provided an understandable and philosophically sound summary of competing views of traits. She rejects the simple summary and dispositional views of traits in favor of a causal-dispositional formulation. It is meaningful to speak of a trait causing a behavior, and to say that the behavior is thereby explained, because the behavior might have occurred for other reasons. If there was a perfect relationship between traits and behaviors, then it would be tautological to explain a behavior by saying that it was caused by the trait. From Hirschberg's discussion, it follows that a particular behavior can be the result of many different traits, and that a trait can be expressed by many behaviors (see also Runyan 1981). As shown in the above discussion of causality, most relationships are probabilistic and multiply determined. Further discussion of the status of traits would take us into a discussion of personality theory, which is properly Loevinger's topic.

Trait vs Situations in the Determination of Behavior

Mischel (1968) is usually credited with having started the trait vs situation debate with statements such as "With the possible exception of intelligence, highly generalized behavioral consistencies have not been demonstrated, and the concept of personality traits as broad dispositions is thus untenable"

(1968, p. 146). The conclusion was consistent with the tenor of the times, especially the behavioral modification movement, and was widely accepted. The observation that correlations between traits, as measured by leading objective tests, and behaviors rarely exceeded .30 was taken as convincing evidence.

In one sense this widespread acceptance seems strange, because we have never met anyone who, from a behavioral viewpoint, was not a trait theorist. If one really believes that situations determine behavior, then there is no reason to test or interview prospective employees for jobs such as police officer; it is only necessary to structure the job situation properly. Picking a mate would simply be a matter of finding someone whose physical characteristics appeal to you. In a properly managed class all students would work up to their abilities. Do you know anyone who believes these things? Obviously not. Why, then, have so many intelligent people come to espouse a theoretical point of view that none of them practices? We will argue that it is because the problem has not been properly formulated, and that once the problem is properly formulated, the seeming difficulties vanish.

Another possible response is that we are all acting on the basis of an illusion. Indeed, this position has been taken by those who argue that trait ratings are made on the basis of implicit personality theories without basis in fact. Passini & Norman (1966) showed that trait ratings of strangers did not differ in structure from those of close acquaintances. Norman & Goldberg (1966) subsequently showed that while the structure was the same, the factor loadings and rating reliabilities were quite different. Nevertheless, D'Andrade and Shweder have continued to push what they term the systematic distortion hypothesis, and those who wish to defend the validity of personality inventories have continued to argue with them. The data indicate that the structure of trait ratings of persons and the structure of semantic ratings of trait descriptors are the same, a result that is consistent with either the view that semantic structures exist because they reflect veridical relationships or the view that the structure of trait ratings is due to the semantic structure of the trait descriptors. Given the confounds, it is not clear that there is any evidence that could not be explained by either side and that would, therefore, be considered conclusive proof of the other position. For those who wish to pursue the technical intricacies of this puzzle, the following chronological list of references should more than suffice: Shweder (1977a), Block (1977b), Shweder (1977b), Jackson et al (1979), Paunonen & Jackson (1979), Block, Weiss & Thorne (1979), Shweder & D'Andrade (1979), Kim & Rosenberg (1980), Shweder & D'Andrade (1980), Lamiell et al (1980), Shweder (1980), Lamiell (1980), Gara & Rosenberg (1981), and Shweder (1982).

A great deal of nonsense has been written on the trait-situation topic, and as far as we can tell all the data that have been collected are irrelevant to solving the problem, which is conceptual. Let's start with the basics. It is clear that one does not go to a restaurant to get one's hair cut. One does not have sexual intercourse in the church during church services. It is unusual to find anyone reading a book during a movie. People at football games do not usually sleep. If these are examples of what behaviorists mean when they say that behavior is primarily determined by situations, then they are correct, and we have never heard of a trait theorist who disagreed. (Note that this is an observational, not an experimental fact.) On the other hand, one's traits may determine whether one goes to a movie or to a football game, or if one stays home and sleeps or reads a book. And that fact cannot be discovered by experiments in which people are put into the situations in which their behavior is observed (e.g. Wachtel 1973).

PROBLEMS OF ANALYSIS   The first result of Mischel's book was a rash of ANOVA studies. Psychologists suddenly discovered ω^2 and set about calculating ω^2 for traits, situations, and interactions in an attempt to determine which accounted for the most variance in behavior. It was eventually pointed out that the results were inconclusive, because the variance ratios could be made arbitrarily large or small by making the variance for traits or situations arbitrarily large or small (e.g. Bowers 1973). There was a lot of talk about how to sample traits and situations so as to get a proper estimate, but about the same time that it was realized that there was no way to do that it was also becoming clear that even if one could sample traits and situations, the answer would not be very interesting.

In a paper that has been widely ignored, Golding (1975) demonstrated that the relative importance of traits and situations for predicting behavior could be estimated better by generalizability theory than by ω^2. For any population it can be true simultaneously that traits and environments each have a perfectly predictable effect on behavior, that is, there is perfect generalizability across both persons and situations. For example, behavior tends to become more loud and boisterous as one goes from a church to a school to a meeting to a bar to a football game. Though an individual's behavior may change from situation to situation, that individual's rank order on any number of traits may remain constant in the group. Given that the variability among people may be perfectly specifiable for any situation, and that the effect of situations may be perfectly specifiable for any person, the proportions of variance attributable to traits and situations can still be made arbitrarily large or small. In other words, generalizability coefficients answer the question of interest, and ω^2s do not.

Bem & Allen (1974) initiated a different line of investigation that is still continuing. They suggested that the nomothetic approach should be modified to allow for the possibility that the trait descriptors appropriate for describing an individual's behavior may vary from individual to individual; that is, not all traits are equally relevant for describing any particular person's behavior. Subjects were asked to indicate how consistent they were on a number of traits (friendliness and conscientiousness were the traits of interest). Self and peer ratings on these traits were then compared with a number of behavioral ratings, and the correlations for those who indicated that the trait was relevant for them (that they were consistent on it) were significantly higher than for those who said that the trait was not relevant.

Kenrick & Stringfield (1980) presented data to support their conclusion that correlations between trait ratings and behaviors increase as a function of both self-ratings of consistency on the trait and the observability of the trait. The conclusions of both Bem & Allen and Kenrick & Stringfield have been challenged on the grounds that the correlations are due to the use of self-rating measures rather than more objective behavioral measures (Lutsky et al 1979) and that consistency is confounded with trait extremity (Rushton et al 1981). Several responses, including the last one cited, seem motivated by a fear that pursuit of Bem & Allen's approach will lead to an idiographic rather than a nomothetic approach, and that this, in turn, spells the end of personology and personality assessment as a science. Others (e.g. Harris 1980) would welcome an idiographic approach. Meanwhile, Kenrick & Braver (1982) have replied to the issues raised by Rushton et al (1981).

Tellegen et al (1982) point out that Bem & Allen's proposal to use individual differences in consistency to improve predictions is equivalent to saying that consistency constitutes a moderator variable. Using simulated data in a sequential regression analysis, they demonstrate once again how difficult it is to improve on an additive linear model, and suggest that such attempts will likely be successful only when they are guided by cogent theoretical considerations. Cogent thinking, here.

An important statistical-methodological response of another kind has come most notably from Epstein (1979, 1980), but also from others (e.g. Whitely 1978), who have pointed out that behavioral measures have the status, and hence the reliability, of one-item tests. Given the constraints imposed by such low reliabilities, correlations between traits and behaviors could not be expected to be higher. The solution is to pool or aggregate behaviors so as to raise reliability. When this is done, correlations rise dramatically. However, there is continuing controversy as to whether the pooling has been cross-situational or just cross-time (Mischel 1979). In view of increasing evidence of consistency of traits over time (Block 1977a, Costa et al 1980, McCrae et al 1980, Shaie & Parham 1976), that issue seems to have become relatively noncontroversial, but the cross-situational question remains unresolved, for good reason, as will be discussed below.

By far the single most important paper in this area is the one by Lamiell (1981).

The argument, in a nutshell, is that the assessment of differences between individuals on various common attributes, and the study of the stabilities (and instabilities) of those differences over time and across situations, fails to confront what is clearly the most basic problem of all within the discipline: the development of a framework for empirically *describing* the personality of any given individual (p. 276). In the individual differences model, an individual's score on a variable has meaning only in relation to the scores of others. "Having generated data that reflect differences between individuals along some common attribute *a*, an investigator normally seeks to determine the stability of those differences over time and across situations" (Lamiell 1981, p. 277).

Lamiell is certainly correct that this is the model that is generally accepted today as being appropriate for assessing the extent to which individuals are consistent in their manifestations of behaviors, that is, the degree of relationship between traits and behaviors. It is the model that has been used in all the research studies dealing with the issue, including the research on which Mischel based his critique and the research that has been carried out in response to his critique.

Lamiell points out that all the statistics calculated on the basis of the standard persons X variables (X situations X times) matrix "are *aggregate* indices, computed on the basis of data summed *across* individuals, [and] that virtually precludes their appropriateness as grounds on which to infer anything about the consistency or inconsistency of any *one* individual . . ." (p. 279). Lamiell also notes that Epstein (and others) do report (in addition to conventional intersubjective coefficients) correlations between attributes within individuals over time. These coefficients do indicate the covariation between traits over time, but do not indicate the consistency with which an individual exhibits an attribute, as can be seen by noting that if an individual is perfectly consistent on either of the traits, the coefficient will be zero. In order to get substantial correlations, there must be substantial behavioral variability. In other words, in this case increasing correlations are not indications of increasing behavioral consistency, as has been claimed.

Lamiell argues that an individual's personality is best described, not in contrast with what others do, but in contrast with what the person does not do but could do. He proposes as an index of a person's status on an attribute the ratio of the person's attitude-consistent behaviors to the domain of all possible attribute-relevant behaviors in that situation. These ratios could be compared across persons, resulting in what Lamiell terms an idiothetic psychology of personality.

The observation that traditional analyses of persons X variables matrices are irrelevant to answering questions of personality structure was made previously by Norman (1967) and Gollob (1968a,b,c). The particular problem that Norman chose as an example was the relationship between a person's rating of his or her status on an attribute and his or her rating of the social desirability of the same attribute. He showed that the persons X attributes covariance matrix can be decomposed in the same way that the variance matrix is usually decomposed in an ANOVA. Given a persons X attributes matrix, the expected mean products for the correlations over either persons or attributes contain components of variance that are a measure of heterogeneity in the sample. The principle is the same as that involved in calculating ω^2 for traits and situations. By making the sample variances large or small, the relational indices can be made correspondingly large or small. Counterintuitively (because of our erroneous training), it is the correlation based on the interaction terms (the residuals after the main effects have been removed) that indexes the relationship of interest.

Gollob developed the same point with respect to factor analysis. In his FANOVA model, ANOVA and FA are combined. ANOVA is used to remove the main effects, and the factor analysis is then performed on the residuals to give an estimate of the relationship between variables within the person. The concept of the structure of personality certainly applies to a structure within the individual, not to a populational structure; yet it is the latter and not the former that is being estimated in all current studies. The papers by Lamiell, Norman, and Gollob should be required reading in every graduate psychology program.

CONCEPTUAL PROBLEMS   All of the above critiques have to do with methods of analysis. They do not get to the heart of the matter: a false implicit premise in the formulation of the question. That premise came from an operationist philosophy of science that holds that concepts (in this case traits) should be reducible to observables (in this case behavior). The power and utility of constructs lies precisely in the fact that they are not operationalizable; they have neither an explicit definition nor an infallible indicator. If traits were reducible to behaviors, then they would have little utility. Traits are valuable precisely because they are not reducible to behaviors. Traits are explanatory because the relationship between traits and behaviors is probabilistic. Any behavior might occur for some reason other than that the person possesses the trait. One may confidently predict that a passive-aggressive person will do something that will screw up a project, even though one may have no idea how that result will be brought about.

The last example also illustrates that we do not classify behaviors, but rather the results or the inferred intentions of behaviors. Even the radical behaviorists did not deal with behaviors; they dealt with behavioral results, namely bar presses. They were not interested in how the bar was pressed. It did not matter if the rat used its left forepaw, its right forepaw, or its arse to get the bar down. Useful studies of human behavior, such as those of Patterson, have similarly used judges to categorize behaviors (e.g. Jones et al 1975). If one's hand comes in contact with someone's arm, it may be a greeting, a hit, a tease, a seduction, an accident, a signal for attention, a twitch, or an attempt to chase a mosquito. We are not interested in the behavior, but in the inference concerning the behavioral intent (Gergen & Morawski 1980, Rychlak 1981, Rorer & Widiger 1982). It is the latter that is almost always intended in discussions of the relationship between traits and behavior, but the word behavior is used ambiguously to suggest a greater degree of objectivity than there is. Behaviorists are interested in an intended effect, and that is not an objectively observable entity.

We need to note another problem. Descriptors are relative—even physical descriptors. A person who is tall in the classroom may be short on the basketball team. We have heard contestants in the Miss America and similar beauty contests described as ugly. We automatically understand the meaning of the descriptor because we automatically relate it to the appropriate reference group. Yet it is precisely this problem that causes trait theorists trouble when they call someone cheerful or depressed without specifying the reference group. Clearly the attributes and behaviors that are implied vary as a function of the group relative to which the description is made.

There is a further problem with the relationship between traits and behaviors and it has to do with what Rorer & Widiger (1982) call ascription rules: the implicit rules that we use for ascribing traits or other descriptors to individuals. Consider the traits honest and murderous. Gacey, who murdered some 30 persons over a period of two or three years, is the most murderous person known to us. This person was noted for being active in church, boy scouts, and other community related activities, was seen as an upstanding citizen, and was generally well liked. If someone had followed him around taking behavior samples, it would have been found that in the overwhelming proportion of instances he was not engaged in murdering anyone. Yet this low relationship would in no way lead us to withdraw the descriptor murderous. Indeed one, or maybe two, instances of murderous behavior is all that is needed for most of us to be willing to ascribe the trait murderous to an individual. But now consider honesty. Most people would require that the person's assertions be consistently honest, and only one or two instances in which one finds that one is unable to depend on a person's report suffice for us to be unwilling to continue to ascribe the trait honest to that person. We tend to think of sociopaths as completely untrustworthy;

yet most of the statements that they make are true. In other words, it takes only a few positive instances of murderous behavior to warrant the ascription of the trait murderous, whereas it takes only a few negative instances of dishonest behavior to preclude the ascription of the trait honest. Ascription rules vary with the trait.

Once one starts thinking along these lines, there are clearly further complications. The examples that have been given seem to be ones for which the *number* of instances of the behavior is the relevant consideration, but other descriptors such as friendly seem to relate to the *frequency* with which the behavior is exhibited rather than to the absolute number of instances. It is not sufficient that one has been friendly some number of times; one must continue to be friendly with some frequency. Still other traits, such as cheerful or sad, may relate to the *proportion* of time that one exhibits cheerful as opposed to sad behavior. It also seems likely that sequence effects are important. If an individual whom we have known and trusted over an extended period of time deceives us, we are likely to discount the behavior and to say that the person wasn't really him or herself and to continue to describe the person as honest or trustworthy. If, on the other hand, an individual deceives us during our initial acquaintance, it may be impossible for that person ever to overcome our doubts concerning his or her trustworthiness.

When we begin to consider implicit rules for ascribing traits with probabilistic references we encounter the issues raised by the situationist or behaviorist. We have little trouble believing that a man might be described as bold and adventuresome by the men he led on a mountain-climbing expedition, and yet be described as shy and timid by the women he met at social gatherings—or in the bedroom. It is our hunch that in making ascriptions people typically look for confirming instances (e.g. Tversky & Kahneman 1974). If ascription is primarily dependent on the occurrence of confirmatory instances, it is perfectly reasonable to ascribe seemingly contradictory traits to the same person.

The attribution of a trait may be dependent upon the situation in which the behavior occurs, but the relevance of the situation to a trait attribution is dependent upon the ascription rule for that trait. Situational variables are relevant precisely through an ascription rule, and these rules vary with the trait being ascribed. Many of the problems in personality assessment seem to stem from the failure to specify the population, environment, and situation relative to which the trait description is being made. Does the situational variability mean that traits do not exist, or that they are not useful? Certainly not. But it does mean that the simplistic model underlying most assessment instruments needs to be modified.

Similar problems emerged in Pepper's (1981) analysis of the meaning of frequency expressions. People vary in their definitions in relation to the base rate of the event that is being described. For example, the meaning of "very often" drops from 86% when no context is specified to 39% when it relates to the frequency of earthquakes. When applied to earthquakes, "almost never" means a little over 1%; but in relation to shooting in westerns, it means 10%. "Sometimes," when it relates to shooting in westerns, has a higher frequency definition than "very often" in relation to earthquakes. This is the relativity effect we mentioned above with a vengeance.

Pepper's review of the literature on frequency terms indicates widely different results between studies and between subjects within studies. Rorer & Widiger's (1982) results showed such wide individual differences in subjects' reports of their ascription rules that they concluded that other means were needed to study the phenomenon.

In sum, the data, on the basis of which the question of the relationship between traits and behaviors was raised, are irrelevant to the question, and the question assumes a relationship between traits and behaviors that does not exist in the meaning of the words. Any meaningful investigation is going to have to take ascription rules into account, and is going to have to use data and analyses that relate to intraindividual relationships.

METHODOLOGICAL INNOVATIONS

We have said that traditional formulations and methods are inadequate, and that the experimental method does not warrant the haloed position it has been given. Have there been any advances in methods to deal with hypothetical constructs (open sets) in nonexperimental settings? Fortunately, the answer is yes. This is not a statistical review, so in what follows we concentrate on conceptualization and methodology that are relevant to assessment.

Causal Modeling

Bentler's (1980) description of causal modeling procedures is excellent, but the exposition in subsequent studies may be equally helpful in understanding the concepts and procedures (e.g. Bagozzi 1981, Bentler & Speckart 1979, 1981).

Conceptually, causal modeling may be thought of as involving a combination of path analysis and confirmatory factor analysis. Path models specify contingencies (pathways) between measured variables under the assumptions of a causal model; that is, given certain assumptions concerning the causal relationships among a set of variables, what would the relationships between those variables be? These relationships can be estimated by simultaneous regression equations, and the estimates compared with the predictions of the competing models. Two useful references on the assumptions and uses of path analysis at a nontechnical level are Billings & Wroten (1978) and James (1980).

The problem with path analysis is that it does not deal with the fact that postulated relationships are usually between constructs, not variables. Hence, we need a procedure that will allow for multiple measures of hypothetical constructs (latent entities) among which the relationships are postulated to hold. Intuitively, it should seem reasonable that factor analytic procedures could be used to extract the common variance from each set of variables hypothesized to index a construct, and that these factors could then be taken to represent the construct. Relationships among these factors (constructs, latent entities) could then be calculated. Again, different causal assumptions lead to different hypothesized relationships among the constructs. When these are specified, confirmatory factor analysis can be used to determine which of the models fits the data best. Essentially, one is determining whether the addition (deletion) of a causal entity or pathway results in a significant improvement (decrement) in explaining the results, that is, a significantly better (worse) fit of the model to the data. Though significance tests for goodness of fit are available, the emphasis is on comparing models rather than on testing for significance (Bentler & Bonett 1980).

A companion procedure that is distinct from path analysis, but often confused with it, is cross-lagged correlation (CLC; Billings & Wroten 1978). Rogosa (1980) provides examples to show that "when reciprocal causal effects are absent, the difference between the cross-lagged correlations may be either small or large, and when reciprocal causal effects are present, the difference between the cross-lagged correlations may be either small or large" (p. 257). His conclusion is straightforward: "No justification was found for the use of CLC. In CLC both determinations of spuriousness and attributions of causal predominance are unsound" (p. 257).

Taxometric Methods

Most psychometric models assume that one is measuring traits that are continuously (and normally) distributed in the population, e.g. cheerfulness, extraversion, sociability, and intelligence. Test theory tends to be based on such models. But what do we do for cases such as the flu, where you either have it or you don't, but if you have it, you may have anything from a mild to a severe case? Schizophrenia is an example for which there is a sizable body of opinion that holds that the group is qualitatively distinct. Genetic theories postulate that one either has or does not have the predisposition to schizophrenia. A group such as those with the predisposition to schizophrenia may be called a taxon. How does one go about identifying members of such a group? There is no way to know for certain who is or is not a member of the group, and there is no agreement on any sure signs that guarantee either membership in or exclusion from the group. Clearly, we cannot use standard criterion group experimental methods. What do we do?

One method that has been overlooked is mixed group validation (Dawes & Meehl 1966), of which traditional criterion group validation is a special case. Mixed group validation involves comparing sign rates with base rates in groups for which the base rates are known and unequal. The basic logic of mixed group validation can be understood by considering the limiting case. Suppose we have two groups for which the base rate is known, but it is not the same in the two groups. Now suppose we have a perfect sign. Clearly, the probability of the sign in each group will match the base rate for that group. What is not immediately obvious is that if this condition occurs, that is, if the sign rate matches the base rate in each of the groups, then the sign must be *perfectly* valid. Dawes (1967) suggested one potential application that has not been exploited. Clinical judgment could be used to form two groups, such as those who are more or less likely to commit suicide, to have successful marriages, or to do well with a particular kind of therapy. Clearly, we cannot know for which cases the classification is correct and for which it is not, but if we know the proportion in each group for which it is correct, then mixed group validation can be used to look for signs that, because of the bootstraps effect, may have higher validities than the original judgments.

Golden & Meehl (1978, 1979) have presented a series of methods for identifying taxa. If it is assumed that there exists a set of indicators that discriminate members of a taxon from nonmembers, but are independent within the taxon and nontaxon groups, then Meehl has shown that a number of consequences can be deduced. Iterative selection methods can then be used to identify indicators (items) whose characteristics match those of the ideal model. Each item so selected can be used to predict (for example) the base rate (prevalence) of the taxon in the population under study, and the adequacy of the items can be determined by noting the consistency of the predicted values. Golden & Meehl (1979) used the method with MMPI items to differentiate the sexes (a trial with a known criterion) and to estimate the prevalence of schizotypia among a nonschizophrenic male psychiatric inpatient sample. In the first case, the estimates were shown to be reasonably accurate, and in the second to be consistent with each other and with prior theoretical predictions. Miller et al (1982) found that a linear combination of the MMPI items identified by Golden & Meehl did not significantly discriminate schizophrenics from nonschizophrenics. The relevance of this result to the original study is indeterminate, especially in light of the fact that Golden & Meehl speculated that some of the items might reverse themselves for purposes of detecting schizophrenics rather than compensated schizotypes.

MAXCOV-HITMAX (Meehl 1973) involves calculating the covariance of two potential indicators at each of a number of levels of a third indicator. Meehl proves that the interval for which the covariance is a maximum is the optimum cutting point on the third variable. The underlying logic is that the maximum covariance occurs with a 50% base rate. The point at which there is an even mixture of the taxonomic and nontaxonomic classes is the intersection of the frequency functions for the two variables. Having determined the cutting point on one variable, the roles of the variables can be switched, until cutting points have been established for each variable.

The normal method involves assuming parameter values for two (or more) underlying distributions on a single variable and then checking the empirical distributions to determine which set of assumed values has the best fit. In other words, this is a maximum likelihood procedure and requires distributional assumptions (normality).

A summary of the experimental studies and of the logic of Meehl's research program is now available in Meehl & Golden (1982). This integrated presentation is a considerable help in understanding the methods. Many of Meehl's theoretical mathematical papers on taxometric methods are unpublished, and are available only as research reports. They will presumably be available one day in a book that was referenced as "in press" five years ago, but has more recently been downgraded to "in preparation." When it appears, buy it.

Base Rates and Bootstraps

In a fundamental sense, there is no way to separate decision theory from assessment. Each can be conceptualized as a subcategory of the other. Given the outcome of some assessment procedure (a score), one makes a decision to apply some descriptor such as accepted, schizophrenic, or cheerful. As Meehl & Rosen pointed out long ago, the decision (inference) associated with a score is a function of the population relative to which the decision is made (Meehl & Rosen 1955, Dawes 1962, Rorer et al 1966). It follows that if one uses a test in a situation for which the base rates are significantly different from those used to determine the cutting scores in the test manual (typically 50%), then one needs to revise the cutting score.

Rorer & Dawes (1982) have now shown that by observing the proportion of positive cases identified by the cutting score in the test manual, it is possible to estimate the base rate in the current situation even though criterion cases cannot be identified. This value can be used, in turn, to obtain a revised cutting score appropriate for that situation.

Prototypes

Cantor et al (1980) distinguish between what they call the classical and the prototypic views of categorization. In the former a category is defined by a number of necessary and sufficient rules, whereas in the latter the defining "features need only be correlated with category membership" (p. 184), with the result that classification in the first case is determinate, whereas in the second it is probabilistic. The authors credit Wittgenstein (1953) with having been the first to emphasize the problems of the classical definition in philosophy, and offer prototypes as the more appropriate model for traits (e.g. Cantor & Mischel 1979) and psychiatric diagnoses (Cantor et al 1980, Horowitz et al 1981a,b). In other words, traits and diagnoses are hypothetical constructs and are not operationally definable. Do you suppose that Cronbach and Meehl smiled just a little bit when they read these articles? Now that hypothetical constructs have been renamed, maybe research on them will become not only acceptable but respectable. What Cantor et al (1980) have to say may not be new, but it is both clear and correct.

POTPOURRI

An *Annual Review of Psychology* chapter provides a substantive summary of selected topics; it also serves as a guide to the literature. With the latter intent, we offer the following in no particular order. If you have no better alternative than reading during your evening hours, any of the following should do nicely.

Norman began, and Goldberg is continuing, an attempt to develop a comprehensive taxonomy of trait descriptive terms. Obviously, Webster's Dictionary does a good job of that, so the problem is first to reduce the taxonomy to manageable proportions without losing significant terms, and then to find a structure for those terms so that the taxonomy is useful. Our above analysis would suggest that Goldberg faces monumental problems in developing a useful instrument, but he is making heroic efforts (for an introduction, see Goldberg 1981a,b,c).

With the growing interest in cognitive theories generally, George Kelly's personal construct theory, with its idiographic emphasis and its rejection of much of the logical empiricist position, has come to be accepted by many as a classic that was ahead of its time. The first two chapters in Landfield & Leitner (1980) provide an excellent introduction to both the theory and the metatheory, and the remaining chapters give a good sampling of the theory in use today.

Most of us learned at some time that two variables can be negatively related within levels of some third variable, while having a positive relationship over levels of the third variable, but it is easy to forget that simple truism when drawing conclusions from studies. For example, if we are told that men benefit from a treatment, and that women also benefit from that treatment, we are inclined to conclude that it must be the case that men and women combined benefit from the treatment. Not so! If you don't believe it, see Novick (1980), whose paper is worth reading for other reasons as well. Messick & van de Geer (1981) describe a number of forms of this reversal paradox, as they call it, and show that it has some important theoretical implications.

We were going to talk about circumplex models, particularly the interpersonal adaptations of Benjamin (e.g. McLemore & Benjamin 1979), but Wiggins (1980, 1982) has summarized that area so well that we decided to defer to him. We would hate to do something second best.

Fiske (1981) has edited a useful little book called *Problems with Language Imprecision.* The title indicates what the chapters have in common, but fails to convey what they are about. In addition to the contributions by Goldberg (1981a) and Pepper (1981) that we have already cited, there are discussions of the meanings of statistical terms, ways to reduce the variability of subjects' interpretations of questionnaire items, and the use of subject-generated descriptors.

Classical test theory has been in trouble for some time. Practitioners and researchers should both be aware of these problems and of some recent attempts at alternative models. Lumsden (1976) and Weiss & Davison (1981) provide useful guides to both. Cliff's (1979) "Test Theory Without True Scores?" is a good example of an alternative approach.

Several articles in the last 10 years have purported to show that low reliability is not necessarily related to low power or validity. The trick is to get the right reliability. Sutcliffe (1980) does much to clear up the confusion. Regression toward the mean is another of those topics about which it is easy to become confused. Humphreys (1978) offers clarification for the simple case, but Nesselroade et al (1980) show that for longitudinal sequences of observations the results depend on the model that is assumed. The variation in results is complex and far from intuitively obvious. Gaito (1980) tries to lay to rest the notion that statistical procedures require measurement scales with particular properties. Will Stevens's (1946) fallacy never die?

Researchers often want to obtain sensitive or possibly embarrassing information from respondents. Randomized response techniques involve giving respondents two questions—the question of interest and another question —and a randomizing device that determines which question they should answer. The idea is that the respondent will answer honestly, because the researcher has no way of knowing which question any particular subject answered. Statistical techniques allow one to estimate the proportions of the population responding to each question. Himmelfarb & Edgell (1980) summarize previous techniques and offer some new ones of their own.

WHAT OF THE FUTURE?

If the field were to accept the point of view that has been presented here (and we think it will—slowly, kicking and screaming all the way), what would the science of personology look like? The changes would start at the level of graduate training, where logical empiricism would be replaced by more contemporary philosophical positions on methodology; analysis of variance, null hypothesis significance testing, and classical test theory would be replaced by taxometric methods, Bayesian statistics, analysis of covariance structures (including causal modeling), generalizability theory, decision theory, and other methods appropriate for construct validation; sole reliance on the experimental method would be replaced by an emphasis on using methods appropriate for the study of personality structure, in particular those of clinical psychology; and theoretical and integrative papers would be encouraged in place of the fragmented laboratory studies of unrelated personality traits that have added so little to our knowledge.

Beyond the graduate program the distinction between professional and research psychologists would become blurred, and practitioner-researchers would collaborate on integrated research based upon multiple kinds of data. Publication priority would be given to theoretical and integrative articles; publication decisions would be made on the basis of the article's contribution to our knowledge, rather than on whether some statistical test reached a significant level; and promotion and tenure decisions would be made on the basis of the quality rather than the quantity of a scholar's published research.

Finally, and most difficult of all, we would become comfortable with the idea that there is no test that can separate science from nonscience, and consequently that science is distinguished from religion precisely by the fact that it does not require acceptance of certain beliefs as an act of faith.

ACKNOWLEDGMENTS

Craig Beaver and Bobbie Hopes made substantial contributions to the preparation of this manuscript. All errors of either omission or commission should be brought to the attention of Lewis R. Goldberg, who is ultimately responsible for this chapter having been written.

Literature Cited

Bagozzi, R. P. 1981. Attitudes, intentions, and behavior: A test of some key hypotheses. *J. Pers. Soc. Psychol.* 41:607–27

Bandura, A. 1977. Self-efficacy: Toward a unifying theory of behavioral change. *Psychol. Rev.* 84:191–215

Bartley, W. W. III. 1962. *The Retreat to Commitment.* New York: Knopf. 223 pp.

Bem, D. J., Allen, A. 1974. On predicting some of the people some of the time: The search for cross-situational consistencies in behavior. *Psychol. Rev.* 81:506–20

Bentler, P. M. 1980. Multivariate analysis with latent variables: Causal modeling. *Ann. Rev. Psychol.* 31:419–56

Bentler, P. M., Bonett, D. G. 1980. Significance tests and goodness of fit in the analysis of covariance structures. *Psychol. Bull.* 88:588–606

Bentler, P. M., Speckart, G. 1979. Models of attitude-behavior relations. *Psychol. Rev.* 86:452–64

Bentler, P. M., Speckart, G. 1981. Attitudes "cause" behaviors: A structural equation analysis. *J. Pers. Soc. Psychol.* 41:226–38

Billings, R. S., Wroten, S. P. 1978. Use of path analysis in industrial/organizational psychology: Criticisms and suggestions. *J. Appl. Psychol.* 63:677–88

Block, J. 1977a. Advancing the psychology of personality: Paradigmatic shift or improving the quality of research? In *Personality at the Crossroads*, ed. D. Magnusson, N. S. Endler, pp. 37–64. New York: Wiley. 454 pp.

Block, J. 1977b. An illusory interpretation of the first factor of the MMPI: A reply to Shweder. *J. Consult. Clin. Psychol.* 45:930–35

Block, J., Weiss, D. S., Thorne, A. 1979. How relevant is a semantic similarity interpretation of personality ratings? *J. Pers. Soc. Psychol.* 37:1055–74

Block, N., ed. 1980. *Readings in Philosophy of Psychology*, Vols. 1, 2. Cambridge, Mass: Harvard Univ. Press. 318 pp., 372 pp.

Bowers, K. S. 1973. Situationism in psychology: An analysis and a critique. *Psychol. Rev.* 80:307–36

Brand, M. 1976. *The Nature of Causation.* Urbana: Univ. Illinois Press. 387 pp.

Butcher, J. N., ed. 1979. *New Developments in the Use of the MMPI.* Minneapolis: Univ. Minnesota Press. 416 pp.

Cantor, N., Mischel, W. 1979. Prototypes in person perception. *Adv. Exp. Soc. Psychol.* 12:4–52

Cantor, N., Smith, E. E., French, R. D., Mezzich, J. 1980. Psychiatric diagnosis as prototype categorization. *J. Abnorm. Psychol.* 89:181–93

Carnap, R. 1936, 1937. Testability and meaning. *Philos. Sci.* 3:419–71, 4:1–40

Churchland, P. S. 1980. A perspective on mind-brain research. *J. Philos.* 77:185–207

Cliff, N. 1979. Test theory without true scores? *Psychometrika* 44:373–93

Cook, T. D., Campbell, D. T. 1979. *Quasi-Experimentation: Design and Analysis Issues for Field Settings.* Chicago: Rand McNally. 405 pp.

Costa, P. T. Jr., McCrae, R. R., Arenberg, D. 1980. Enduring dispositions in adult males. *J. Pers. Soc. Psychol.* 38:793–800

Davidson, D. 1976. Causal relations. See Brand 1976, pp. 353–68

Davidson, D. 1980. Mental events. See Block 1980, pp. 107–19

Dawes, R. M. 1962. A note on base rates and psychometric efficiency. *J. Consult. Psychol.* 26:422–24

Dawes, R. M. 1967. How clinical judgment may be used to validate diagnostic signs. *J. Clin. Psychol.* 23:403–10

Dawes, R. M., Meehl, P. E. 1966. Mixed group validation: A method for determining the validity of diagnostic signs without using criterion groups. *Psychol. Bull.* 66:63–67

d'Espagnat, B. 1979. The quantum theory and reality. *Sci. Am.* 241(5):158–81

Duhem, P. 1962. [*The Aim and Structure of Physical Theory*]. Original in French as *La Theorie Physique: Son Objet, Sa Structure*, 1906. Transl. 2nd ed., Princeton Univ. Press, 1954. Reprinted, New York: Atheneum. 344 pp.

Edwards, W., Lindman, H., Savage, L. J. 1963. Bayesian statistical inference for psychological research. *Psychol. Rev.* 70:193–242

Ellis, A. 1979. Toward a new theory of personality. In *Theoretical and Empirical Foundations of Rational-Emotive Therapy*, ed. A. Ellis, J. M. Whiteley, pp. 7–32. Monterey, Calif: Brooks/Cole. 274 pp.

Epstein, S. 1979. The stability of behavior: I. On predicting most of the people much of the time. *J. Pers. Soc. Psychol.* 37:1097–1126

Epstein, S. 1980. The stability of behavior: II. Implications for psychological research. *Am. Psychol.* 35:790–806

Fiske, D. W., ed. 1981. *Problems with Language Imprecision.* San Francisco: Jossey-Bass. 107 pp.

Gaito, J. 1980. Measurement scales and statistics: Resurgence of an old misconception. *Psychol. Bull.* 87:564–67

Gara, M. A., Rosenberg, S. 1981. Linguistic factors in implicit personality theory. *J. Pers. Soc. Psychol.* 41:450–57

Gergen, K. J. 1978. Toward generative theory. *J. Pers. Soc. Psychol.* 36:1344–60

Gergen, K. J. 1980. Towards intellectual audacity in social psychology. In *The Development of Social Psychology,* ed. R. Gilmour, S. Duck, pp. 239–70. New York: Academic. 355 pp.

Gergen, K. J. 1981. The meager voice of empiricist affirmation. *Pers. Soc. Psychol. Bull.* 7:333–37

Gergen, K. J., Morawski, J. 1980. An alternative metatheory for social psychology. *Rev. Pers. Soc. Psychol.* 1:326–52

Glymour, C. 1980. *Theory and Evidence.* Princeton: Princeton Univ. Press. 383 pp.

Goldberg, L. R. 1974. Objective diagnostic tests and measures. *Ann. Rev. Psychol.* 25:343–66

Goldberg, L. R. 1981a. Developing a taxonomy of trait-descriptive terms. See Fiske 1981, pp. 43–66

Goldberg, L. R. 1981b. Language and individual differences: The search for universals in personality lexicons. In *Review of Personality and Social Psychology,* ed. L. Wheeler, 2:141–65. Beverly Hills, Calif: Sage. 295 pp.

Goldberg, L. R. 1981c. Unconfounding situational attributions from uncertain, neutral, and ambiguous ones: A psychometric analysis of descriptions of oneself and various types of others. *J. Pers. Soc. Psychol.* 41:517–52

Golden, R. R., Meehl, P. E. 1978. Testing a single dominant gene theory without an accepted criterion variable. *Ann. Hum. Genet.* 41:507–14

Golden, R. R., Meehl, P. E. 1979. Detection of the schizoid taxon with MMPI indicators. *J. Abnorm. Psychol.* 88:217–33

Golding, S. L. 1975. Flies in the ointment: Methodological problems in the analysis of the percentage of variance due to persons and situations. *Psychol. Bull.* 82:278–88

Gollob, H. F. 1968a. Confounding of sources of variation in factor-analytic techniques. *Psychol. Bull.* 70:330–44

Gollob, H. F. 1968b. Rejoinder to Tucker's "Comments on 'Confounding of sources of variation in factor-analytic techniques.' " *Psychol. Bull.* 70:355–60

Gollob, H. F. 1968c. A statistical model which combines features of factor analytic and analysis of variance techniques. *Psychometrika* 33:73–115

Greenwald, A. G. 1975. On the inconclusiveness of "crucial" cognitive tests of dissonance versus self-perception theories. *J. Exp. Soc. Psychol.* 11:490–99

Greenwald, A. G., Ronis, D. L. 1981. On the conceptual disconfirmation of theories. *Pers. Soc. Psychol. Bull.* 7:131–37

Grünbaum, A. 1971. Can we ascertain the falsity of a scientific hypothesis? In *Observation and Theory in Science,* ed. E. Nagel, S. Bromberger, A. Grünbaum, pp. 69–129. Baltimore: Johns Hopkins Press. 134 pp.

Grünbaum, A. 1976a. *Ad hoc* auxiliary hypotheses and falsification. *Br. J. Philos. Sci.* 27:329–62

Grünbaum, A. 1976b. Is the method of bold conjectures and attempted refutations *justifiably* the method of science? *Br. J. Philos. Sci.* 27:105–36

Grünbaum, A. 1978a. How is science distinguished from pseudo-science?: Two views. *Proc. Pa. Acad. Sci.* 52:96–98

Grünbaum, A. 1978b. Popper vs. inductivism. In *Progress and Rationality in Science,* ed. G. Radnitzky, G. Andersson, pp. 117–42. Boston: Reidel. 416 pp.

Grünbaum, A. 1979. Is Freudian psychoanalytic theory pseudo-scientific by Karl Popper's criterion of demarcation? *Am. Philos. Q.* 16:131–41

Grünbaum, A. 1980. The role of psychological explanations of the rejection or acceptance of scientific theories. *Trans. NY Acad. Sci.* Ser. II, 39:75–90

Harris, J. G. 1980. Nomovalidation and idiovalidation: A quest for the true personality profile. *Am. Psychol.* 35:729–44

Hilgard, E. R. 1980. Consciousness in contemporary psychology. *Ann. Rev. Psychol.* 31:1–26

Himmelfarb, S., Edgell, S. E. 1980. Additive constants model: A randomized response technique for estimating evasiveness to quantitative response questions. *Psychol. Bull.* 87:525–30

Hirschberg, N. 1978. A correct treatment of traits. In *Personality: A New Look at Metatheories,* ed. H. London, pp. 45–68. New York: Wiley-Halsted. 174 pp.

Horowitz, L. M., Post, D. L., French, R. S., Wallis, K. D., Siegelman, E. Y. 1981a. The prototype as a construct in abnormal psychology: 2. Clarifying disagreement in psychiatric judgments. *J. Abnorm. Psychol.* 90:575–85

Horowitz, L. M., Wright, J. C., Lowenstein, E., Parad, H. W. 1981b. The prototype as a construct in abnormal psychology: 1. A method for deriving prototypes. *J. Abnorm. Psychol.* 90:568–74

Hughes, R. I. G. 1981. Quantum logic. *Sci. Am.* 245(4):202–13

Humphreys, L. G. 1978. To understand regression from parent to offspring, think statistically. *Psychol. Bull.* 6:1317–22

Jackson, D. N., Chan, D. W., Stricker, L. J. 1979. Implicit personality theory: Is it illusory? *J. Pers.* 47:1–10

James, L. R. 1980. The unmeasured variables problem in path analysis. *J. Appl. Psychol.* 65:415–21

Jones, R. R., Reid, J. B., Patterson, G. R. 1975. Naturalistic observation in clinical assessment. In *Advances in Psychological Assessment,* ed. P. McReynolds, 3:42–95. San Francisco: Jossey-Bass. 555 pp.

Kantorovich, A. 1978. An ideal model for the growth of knowledge in research programs. *Philos. Sci.* 45:250–72

Kazdin, A. E. 1979. Fictions, factions, and functions of behavior therapy. *Behav. Ther.* 10:629–54

Kenrick, D. T., Braver, S. L. 1982. Personality: Idiographic *and* nomothetic! A rejoinder. *Psychol. Rev.* 89:182–86

Kenrick, D. T., Stringfield, D. O. 1980. Personality traits and the eye of the beholder: Crossing some traditional philosophical boundaries in the search for consistency in all of the people. *Psychol. Rev.* 87:88–104

Kim, M. P., Rosenberg, S. 1980. Comparison of two structural models of implicit personality theory. *J. Pers. Soc. Psychol.* 38:375–89

Koch, S. 1977. *Vagrant confessions of an asystematic psychologist: An intellectual autobiography.* Presented at Ann. Conv. Am. Psychol. Assoc., 85th, San Francisco

Koch, S. 1981. The nature and limits of psychological knowledge: Lessons of a century qua "science." *Am. Psychol.* 36:257–69

Korchin, S. J., Schuldberg, D. 1981. The future of clinical assessment. *Am. Psychol.* 36:1147–58

Lamiell, J. T. 1980. On the utility of looking in the "wrong" direction. *J. Pers.* 48:82–88

Lamiell, J. T. 1981. Toward an idiothetic psychology of personality. *Am. Psychol.* 36:276–89

Lamiell, J. T., Foss, M. A., Cavenee, P. 1980. On the relationship between conceptual schemes and behavior reports: A closer look. *J. Pers.* 48:54–73

Landfield, A. W., Leitner, L. M., eds. 1980. *Personal Construct Psychology: Psychotherapy and Personality.* New York: Wiley. 330 pp.

Leahey, T. H. 1980. The myth of operationism. *J. Mind Behav.* 1:127–43

Leary, M. R. 1979. Levels of disconfirmability and social psychological theory: A response to Greenwald. *Pers. Soc. Psychol. Bull.* 5:149–53

Ledwidge, B. 1978. Cognitive behavior modification: A step in the wrong direction? *Psychol. Bull.* 85:353–75

Ledwidge, B. 1979. Cognitive behavior modification or new ways to change minds: Reply to Mahoney and Kazdin. *Psychol. Bull.* 86:1050–53

Levine, M. 1980. Investigative reporting as a research method. *Am. Psychol.* 35:626–38

Lieberman, D. A. 1979. Behaviorism and the mind: A (limited) call for a return to introspection. *Am. Psychol.* 34:319–33

Liotti, G., Reda, M. 1981. Some epistemological remarks on behavior therapy, cognitive therapy and psychoanalysis. *Cogn. Ther. Res.* 5:231–36

London, H., Exner, J. E. 1978. *Dimensions of Personality.* New York: Wiley. 620 pp.

Lumsden, J. 1976. Test theory. *Ann. Rev. Psychol.* 27:251–80

Lutsky, N., Peake, P., Wray, L., Frable, D. 1979. *Subjective assessments of individual personality: Panning for consistency in human behavior.* Presented at Ann. Conv. Am. Psychol. Assoc., 87th, New York

Mackie, J. L. 1976. Causes and conditions. See Brand 1976, pp. 307–44

Mahoney, M. J. 1976. *Scientist as Subject: The Psychological Imperative.* Cambridge, Mass: Ballinger. 249 pp.

Mahoney, M. J., Kazdin, A. E. 1979. Cognitive behavior modification: Misconceptions and premature evacuation. *Psychol. Bull.* 86:1044–49

Maxwell, G. 1975. Induction and empiricism: A Bayesian-frequentist alternative. In *Induction, Probability, and Confirmation,* ed. G. Maxwell, R. H. Anderson, pp. 106–65. Minneapolis: Univ. Minnesota Press. 551 pp.

McCrae, R. R., Costa, P. T. Jr., Arenberg, D. 1980. Constancy of adult personality structure in males: Longitudinal, cross-sectional, and times-of-measurement analyses. *J. Gerontol.* 35:877–83

McLemore, C. W., Benjamin, L. S. 1979. Whatever happened to interpersonal diagnosis? A psychosocial alternative to DSM-III. *Am. Psychol.* 34:17–34

McReynolds, P., ed. 1981. *Advances in Psychological Assessment,* Vol. 5. San Francisco: Jossey-Bass. 564 pp.

Meehl, P. E. 1967. Theory-testing in psychology and physics: A methodological paradox. *Philos. Sci.* 34:103–15

Meehl, P. E. 1973. MAXCOV-HITMAX: A taxonomic search method for loose genetic syndromes. In *Psychodiagnosis: Selected Papers,* ed. P. E. Meehl. Minneapolis: Univ. Minnesota Press. 359 pp.

Meehl, P. E. 1977. Specific etiology and other forms of strong influence: Some quantitative meanings. *J. Med. Philos.* 2: 33–53

Meehl, P. E. 1978. Theoretical risks and tabular asterisks: Sir Karl, Sir Ronald, and the slow progress of soft psychology. *J. Consult. Clin. Psychol.* 46:806–34

Meehl, P. E., Golden, R. R. 1982. Taxometric methods. In *Handbook of Research Methods in Clinical Psychology,* ed. P. C. Kendall, J. N. Butcher, pp. 127–82. New York: Wiley. 728 pp.

Meehl, P. E., Rosen, A. 1955. Antecedent probability and the efficiency of psychometric signs, patterns, or cutting scores. *Psychol. Bull.* 52:194–216

Messer, S. B., Winokur, M. 1980. Some limits to the integration of psychoanalytic and behavior therapy. *Am. Psychol.* 35: 818–27

Messick, S. 1981. Constructs and their vicissitudes in educational and psychological measurement. *Psychol. Bull.* 89: 575–88

Messick, D. M., van de Geer, J. P. 1981. A reversal paradox. *Psychol. Bull.* 90: 582–93

Miller, H. R., Streiner, D. L., Kahgee, S. L. 1982. Use of the Golden-Meehl indicators in the detection of schizoid-taxon membership. *J. Abnorm. Psychol.* 91: 55–60

Mischel, T. 1976. Psychological explanations and their vicissitudes. In *1975 Nebraska Symposium on Motivation,* ed. W. J. Arnold, 23:133–204. Lincoln: Univ. Nebraska Press. 586 pp.

Mischel, W. 1968. *Personality and Assessment.* New York: Wiley. 365 pp.

Mischel, W. 1979. On the interface of cognition and personality: Beyond the person-situation debate. *Am. Psychol.* 34: 740–54

Natsoulas, T. 1978. Consciousness. *Am. Psychol.* 33:906–14

Natsoulas, T. 1981. Basic problems of consciousness. *J. Pers. Soc. Psychol.* 41: 132–78

Nesselroade, J. R., Stigler, S. M., Baltes, P. B. 1980. Regression toward the mean and the study of change. *Psychol. Bull.* 88:622–37

Norman, W. T. 1967. On estimating psychological relationships: Social desirability and self-report. *Psychol. Bull.* 67: 273–93

Norman, W. T., Goldberg, L. R. 1966. Raters, ratees, and randomness in personality structure. *J. Pers. Soc. Psychol.* 4:681–91

Novick, M. R. 1980. Statistics as psychometrics. *Psychometrika* 45:411–24

Novick, M. R., Jackson, P. H. 1974. *Statistical Methods for Educational and Psychological Research.* New York: McGraw-Hill. 456 pp.

Passini, F. T., Norman, W. T. 1966. A universal conception of personality structure? *J. Pers. Soc. Psychol.* 4:44–49

Paunonen, S. V., Jackson, D. N. 1979. Nonverbal trait inference. *J. Pers. Soc. Psychol.* 37:1645–59

Peele, S. 1981. Reductionism in the psychology of the eighties: Can biochemistry eliminate addiction, mental illness, and pain? *Am. Psychol.* 36:807–18

Pencil, M. 1976. Salt passage research: The state of the art. *J. Commun.* 26:31–36

Pepper, S. 1981. Problems in the quantification of frequency expressions. See Fiske 1981, pp. 25–42

Petrinovich, L. 1979. Probabilistic functionalism: A conception of research method. *Am. Psychol.* 34:373–90

Pitz, G. F. 1978. Hypothesis testing and the comparison of imprecise hypotheses. *Psychol. Bull.* 85:794–809

Pitz, G. F. 1980. Using likelihood ratios to test imprecise hypotheses. *Psychol. Bull.* 87:575–77

Rakover, S. S. 1981. Social psychological theory and falsification. *Pers. Soc. Psychol. Bull.* 7:123–30

Rogosa, D. 1980. A critique of cross-lagged correlation. *Psychol. Bull.* 88:245–58

Rorer, L. R., Dawes, R. M. 1982. A base-rate bootstrap. *J. Consult. Clin. Psychol.* 50:419–25

Rorer, L. G., Hoffman, P. J., LaForge, G. E., Hsieh, K. C. 1966. Optimum cutting scores to discriminate groups of unequal size and variance. *J. Appl. Psychol.* 50:153–64

Rorer, L. G., Widiger, T. A. 1982. *Ascription rules for trait descriptive adjectives.* Presented at Ann. Conf. Midwest. Psychol. Assoc., 54th, Minneapolis

Ross, A. O. 1981. Of rigor and relevance. *Prof. Psychol.* 12:318–27

Royce, J. R. 1982. Philosophical issues, Division 24, and the future. *Am. Psychol.* 37:258–66

Runyan, W. M. 1981. Why did Van Gogh cut off his ear? The problem of alternative explanations in psychobiography. *J. Pers. Soc. Psychol.* 40:1070–77

Rushton, J. P., Jackson, D. N., Paunonen, S. V. 1981. Personality: Nomothetic or idiographic? A response to Kenrick and Stringfield. *Psychol. Rev.* 88:582–89

Rychlak, J. F. 1981. Logical learning theory: Propositions, corollaries, and research evidence. *J. Pers. Soc. Psychol.* 40: 731–49

Salmon, W. C. 1973. Confirmation. *Sci. Am.* 228(5):75–83

Salmon, W. C. 1975. Confirmation and relevance. See Maxwell 1975, pp. 3–36

Schaie, K. W., Parham, I. A. 1976. Stability of adult personality traits: Fact or fable? *J. Pers. Soc. Psychol.* 34:146–58

Schlagel, R. H. 1979. *Revolution in the philosophy of science: Implications for method and theory in psychology.* Presented at Ann. Meet. Am. Psychol. Assoc., 87th, New York

Shrauger, J. S., Osberg, T. M. 1981. The relative accuracy of self-predictions and judgments by others in psychological assessment. *Psychol. Bull.* 90:322–51

Shweder, R. A. 1977a. Illusory correlation and the MMPI controversy. *J. Consult. Clin. Psychol.* 45:917–24

Shweder, R. A. 1977b. Illusory correlation and the MMPI controversy: Reply to some of the allusions and elusions in Block's and Edward's commentaries. *J. Consult. Clin. Psychol.* 45:936–40

Shweder, R. A. 1980. Factors and fictions in person perception: A reply to Lamiell, Foss, and Cavenee. *J. Pers.* 48:74–81

Shweder, R. A. 1982. Fact and artifact in trait perception: The systematic distortion hypothesis. *Prog. Exp. Pers. Res.* 11: In press

Shweder, R. A., D'Andrade, R. G. 1979. Accurate reflection or systematic distortion? A reply to Block, Weiss, and Thorne. *J. Pers. Soc. Psychol.* 37: 1075–84

Shweder, R. A., D'Andrade, R. G. 1980. The systematic distortion hypothesis. In *Fallible Judgment in Behavioral Research,* ed. R. A. Shweder. In series, *New Directions for Methodology of So-*
cial and Behavioral Science, 4:37–58. San Francisco: Jossey-Bass. 97 pp.

Skinner, H. A. 1981. Toward the integration of classification theory and methods. *J. Abnorm. Psychol.* 90:68–87

Stevens, S. S. 1946. On the theory of scales of measurement. *Science* 103:677–80

Suppe, F. 1977. *The Structure of Scientific Theories.* Urbana: Univ. Illinois Press. 818 pp. 2nd ed.

Sutcliffe, J. P. 1980. On the relationship of reliability to statistical power. *Psychol. Bull.* 88:509–15

Tellegen, A., Kamp, J., Watson, D. 1982. Recognizing individual differences in predictive structure. *Psychol. Rev.* 89: 95–105

Tversky, A., Kahneman, D. 1974. Judgment under uncertainty: Heuristics and bias. *Science* 185:1124–30

Tyler, L. E. 1981. More stately mansions— Psychology extends its boundaries. *Ann. Rev. Psychol.* 32:1–20

Wachtel, P. L. 1973. Psychodynamics, behavior therapy, and the implacable experimenter: An inquiry into the consistency of personality. *J. Abnorm. Psychol.* 82:324–34

Wachtel, P. L. 1980. Investigation and its discontents: Some constraints on progress in psychological research. *Am. Psychol.* 35:399–408

Weimer, W. B. 1979. *Notes on the Methodology of Scientific Research.* Hillsdale, NJ: Erlbaum. 257 pp.

Weiss, D. J., Davison, M. L. 1981. Test theory and methods. *Ann. Rev. Psychol.* 32:629–58

Whitely, S. E. 1978. Individual inconsistency: Implications for test reliability and behavioral predictability. *Appl. Psychol. Meas.* 2:571–79

Wiggins, J. S. 1980. Circumplex models of interpersonal behavior. See Gergen & Morawski 1980, 1:265–94

Wiggins, J. S. 1982. Circumplex models of interpersonal behavior in clinical psychology. See Meehl & Golden 1982, pp. 183–222

Wittgenstein, L. 1953. *Philosophical Investigations.* (G. E. M. Anscombe, transl.) Oxford, England: Blackwell. 232 pp.

Wolman, B. B., ed. 1978. *Clinical Diagnosis of Mental Disorders. A Handbook.* New York: Plenum. 921 pp.

Zuriff, G. E. 1980. Radical behaviorist epistemology. *Psychol. Bull.* 87:337–50

Ann. Rev. Psychol. 1983. 34:465–509

SOCIAL AND PERSONALITY DEVELOPMENT

Ross D. Parke and Steven R. Asher

Department of Psychology (R.D.P.) and Department of Educational Psychology
(S.R.A.), University of Illinois, Champaign, Illinois 61820

CONTENTS

INTRODUCTION

In examining the recent literature in social-personality development over the past 5 years, a number of themes or issues have emerged, including increased attention to biological determinants, the role of affect in social development, cognitive models, and social interactional analyses. These themes often cut across traditional topical categories of social development such as aggression, sex-typing, and achievement, and we have organized our review around these themes to underscore their emergence. We also will highlight methodological changes during recent years. Advances have been made in research designs and measures. Also, a multivariate focus has

465

become increasingly common in which researchers assess a wide range of behavioral domains in a single study or series of studies. This trend has permitted a sensitivity to the multidimensionality of the social-personality domain and a recognition that advances are most likely to be forthcoming from the mapping of relationships among different but connected behavioral systems. A healthy attention to differing determinants, antecedents, developmental courses, and behavioral functions of behavior is evident. Finally, we highlight the recent emphasis on ecological concerns—an emerging hallmark of the social-personality development area. This emphasis has several manifestations, including research on major life events and social policy issues.

That research on personality and social development is flourishing is evident from the growing number of research articles and the number of edited scholarly volumes that have been published within the past several years on specific personality and social development topics. The growth of literature makes the task of surveying the literature more formidable for the beginning graduate student (and for the annual reviewer) than it would have been previously. Fifteen years ago it would have been possible to design a study based on a particular theoretical view, or just plain common sense, and to proceed with minimal worries that the study would duplicate earlier efforts. Such studies often made a contribution. Today the situation is quite different. For any topic there are likely to be several research traditions that address the problem, making it essential that researchers inform themselves through a careful reading of the literature (see note on p. 509).

Furthermore, on many topics, considerable relevant literature lies outside the traditional boundaries of psychology. This is particularly true of the area of social development, where sociologists, anthropologists, and medical researchers substantially overlap in terms of their research and applied interests. Collaborative, interdisciplinary studies are increasingly seen to be necessary for adequate exploration of many problems. Nonetheless, given the nature of this volume, we have confined our review to the more recent psychological literature. The last review of this topic in the *Annual Review of Psychology* appeared in 1978, although a partial review appeared in Volume 32 in Masters' (1981) treatment of the more general area of developmental psychology. Our emphasis here will be on literature from 1979 to the present. Furthermore, since other *Annual Review* chapters emphasize adolescence and adulthood, our focus will be on infancy to preadolescent years.

An extremely valuable way to gain an appreciation for the scope of the field is to read the fourth edition of *Carmichael's Manual of Child Psychology*, edited by Mussen (1983). This work, published in two volumes in 1970, now consists of four volumes, with one volume, edited by Hetherington, exclusively devoted to social and personality development. Some traditional topics in the field such as aggression, sex-typing, and peer interaction remain, but many new topics, including self-concept, achievement motivation, play, and prosocial behavior, are sufficiently mature to warrant separate chapters. While basic developmental issues continue to predominate, topics of clinical and applied relevance also are evident in this recent edition. These include atypical development and intervention and treatment. In light of the strong influence of cognitive psychology on personality and social development research, it is not surprising that the cognitive development volume of the *Manual,* edited by Flavell and Markman, also contains topics such as moral development and social cognition which could easily have been included in the social development volume. The volume devoted to infancy, edited by Campos and Haith, contains a number of chapters of interest to the social developmentalist as well. We have described this important reference work in some detail because its topics serve to illustrate the breadth of the field of personality and social development and because the currency of the fourth edition will make it an invaluable source for those wishing to gain access to recent literature.

In keeping with this spirit, we reference throughout this chapter many of the major edited volumes that have appeared recently on particular aspects of children's social and personality development. These volumes should be useful for the student seeking reference points to the burgeoning primary literature.

CURRENT RESEARCH THEMES

Biological Determinants

A review of the current dialogue between geneticists and environmentalists finds environmentalists increasingly retreating to allow models of social development to include genetic-constitutional factors. This is exemplified by two areas of research: temperament research and twin studies.

TEMPERAMENT   The search for better measures of individual differences in temperament and for clues concerning how temperamental differences affect social development continues. A number of thoughtful, integrative reviews have recently appeared (Bates 1980, Rothbart & Derryberry 1981) as well as two major measurement schemes for assessing temperament in infants. Bates and his colleagues (Bates et al 1979) have developed a caregiver rating instrument, the Infant Characteristics Questionnaire, which has yielded four internally consistent and cross-validated factors for describing infant "difficultness"—a dimension originally identified in the New York Longitudinal Study (Thomas et al 1968, Thomas & Chess 1977). These factors include: 1. fussy/difficult, 2. unadaptable, 3. dull, and 4. unpredictable. A second infant temperament measure, the Infant Behavior Questionnaire, comes from Rothbart (1982) for use with 3-, 6-, 9-, and 12-month-old infants. Both Bates's and Rothbart's temperament measures have historical roots in the Thomas and Chess work, although Rothbart also draws on earlier work in animal heritability and human twin studies (Fuller & Thompson 1960, Gray 1971). Moreover, in contrast to the Bates focus on "difficultness," Rothbart's scale covers a wider range of temperamental dimensions: activity level, soothability, fear (distress and latency to approach intense or novel stimuli), distress in response to limitations (anger/-frustration), smiling and laughter, and duration of orienting. The careful attention to psychometric and conceptual properties by Rothbart and Bates promises that these new measures will be useful to infancy researchers.

One of the problems that has limited the value of earlier scales is the lack of external validation of parent-reported infant temperament. Both Bates and Rothbart provide data on this issue. Bates et al report significant correlations between mothers' and fathers' reports of infant temperament, while Rothbart (1980), using a second adult in the household (father or baby-sitter), reported similar satisfactory evidence of external validity for her scale.

Most interesting is the evidence concerning the predictive utility of the new scales. Specifically, Bates et al found evidence that parents' perceptions of "difficult" behaviors in the infant reflects characteristics of the parent (e.g. parity, extraversion, and achievement orientation) as well as observable behavior of the infant, such as fussy/difficult (Bates et al 1979, Bates et al 1982). Similarly, Rothbart (1980) showed some modest links between parental temperament ratings and home observations. The low to moderate and scattered pattern of these relationships underscores the fact that further refinements in measurement of temperament may be necessary and/or more careful selection and measurement of infant behaviors may be required before sizable relationships between temperament and behavior are uncovered. Alternatively, temperament's role in socially relevant behavior may, in fact, be significant but modest.

A third new measure of temperament which may be of particular value to researchers using a life-span developmental framework has been developed by Lerner and associates (1982). The five-factor scale, the Dimensions of Temperament Survey (DOTS), includes the following scales: activity level, attention span/distractibility, adaptability/approach withdrawal, rhythmicity and reactivity. These scales were shown to be applicable from early childhood to young adulthood.

Other recent issues concerning temperament measurement include cross-cultural differences in temperament. For example, in a cross-cultural extension of the Carey and McDevitt (1978) questionnaire completed with

Chinese infants (Hsu et al 1981), the Chinese babies were rated in a similar pattern to American samples, but clear racial differences were evident. Chinese babies were less difficult, easier, and slower to warm up than their American counterparts.

Problems remain with cross-cultural temperament research, including the possibility of response biases in cross-cultural ratings of temperament, which could, of course, be ruled out by independent observations. However, this approach assumes that observed (real) differences in temperament are the most important determinants of treatment by social agents. As many have argued before (e.g. Parke 1978, Sameroff 1980), "mothers' perception of temperamental characteristics may prove to be more significant than the actual characteristics themselves" (Hsu et al 1981, p. 1340). In combination with the recent finding (Sameroff et al 1982) that maternal characteristics such as social status, anxiety level, and mental health status were more powerful predictors of ratings of infant temperament than child behavior, more attention needs to be given to the role of maternal perceptions in studies of temperament. Finally, the interesting issue of the different ways the same temperamental characteristics may be responded to within different cultural contexts remains unanswered.

TWIN STUDIES   The use of twins continues to be a frequent means of isolating genetic influences on social development. An analysis of longitudinal temperament data from 350 pairs of twins from the Collaborative Perinatal Project represents the largest data base that has been analyzed to address this issue (Goldsmith & Gottesman 1981). Behavorial ratings of identical and fraternal twins at 8 months and 4 and 7 years of age were examined. Although the results demonstrated that, in general, nonfamilial factors accounted for at least 50% of the observed variance across ages, there was interesting variation in the relative contribution of genetic and environmental factors at each age point. At 8 months, individual differences in a broadly based "activity" factor showed evidence of moderate genetic influence. At 4 years, IQ showed appreciably greater familial influence than any of the composites of temperament ratings, but significant genetic effects were apparent for "task persistence" and "irritability." Finally, at 7 years some evidence for genetic effects on "active adjustment" and "fearfulness" factors was present. This study underscores the value of carefully monitoring the interplay of environmental and genetic influences over development and over different behavioral domains. A second recent example is the report of Matheny and co-workers (1981) of the Louisville Twin Study. Using semistructured interviews with mothers over the first 6 years of the twins' lives, these investigators isolated a set of behaviors related to negative aspects of temperament and a set of behaviors related to sociability at 6 months, which were replicated at later ages. Concordance rates for the identical twin pairs were uniformly higher than for fraternal pairs, suggesting that genotype similarity was associated with intrapair similarity for aspects of emotionality and sociability.

In summary, there is still considerable interest in specifying the relative contributions of biological and environmental factors in social development, especially for the purpose of understanding how their interaction is reflected in behavior.

The Role of Affect

Throughout psychology, the role of affect is becoming an issue of increasing concern (e.g. Zajonc 1980, Bower 1981). The investigation of the developmental origins of both the production and recognition of emotions as well as the role of emotional expressions in the regulation of social interaction continue to be central concerns of developmental psychology, especially infancy researchers.

PRODUCTION AND RECOGNITION OF EMOTIONS   Under the continuing guidance of the writings of Ekman, (Ekman & Friesen 1978, Ekman & Oster 1979), and Izard (e.g. Izard 1977, 1978, 1982; Buechler & Izard 1980), the older assumption that there are no facial response patterns specific to discrete emotional states is being discounted. Evidence suggests that facial expressions may be, at least in part, governed by genetically encoded programs—an implication of the finding of universality of facial expression recognition (Izard 1971, Ekman 1973).

Recent investigators have extended prior work to assess how early facial expressions and discrete emotional expressions are related, and how general are prior findings derived from actor-posed facial displays (see Oster 1981 for a review). Hiatt, Campos & Emde (1979) found that 10- to 12-month-old infants yielded some specific facial patterns of emotion, especially happiness and surprise but less so for fear. Almost all situations, however, elicited blends rather than discrete emotions.

Evidence of specificity for other emotions, such as anger, is available as well. Angry facial expressions can be detected reliably in 7-month-olds (Stenberg et al 1982). These studies represent a general trend toward the use of ecologically valid contexts for the study of emotion (e.g. Izard's 1978 use of the innoculation situation as a way of studying the development of infants' emotional reactions to painful stimulation).

Developmental tuning of both production and discrimination of emotional states continues beyond infancy (Field & Walden 1981, 1982). Skills vary across specific emotions as indicated by judges' greater accuracy in reading happy than angry and fearful expressions. For three- to five-year-olds, adults were more accurate raters of children's elicited emotional productions than were other children, which suggests that developmental progress in children's productions of expressions may be superior to their discrimination of expressions. Children's production skills were also related to sociometric ratings by their peers and expressivity ratings by their teachers, suggesting that the regulation of affective expression may be one ingredient in the emergence of social competence.

AFFECT AND SOCIAL BEHAVIOR   The shift toward recognition of the role of emotional expression in the regulation of social behavior is one of the most important shifts in the past few years (e.g. Camaras 1977, Emde & Brown 1978). The extensive studies on face-to-face interaction of parents and infants (e.g. Brazelton et al 1974, Stern 1977) illustrate how parents and possibly infants modify their patterns of stimulation in response to each others' emotional signals. Both Stern and the Brazelton group have shown how shifts in the interaction intensity of stimulation are modified by infant arousal levels; however, the precise emotional cues which are used in regulating interaction patterns are not yet specified. These patterns are evident in both mother-infant (Tronick 1982) and father-infant (Power & Parke 1982, Yogman 1982) interaction. Through experimental modifications of typical affective displays (e.g., frown or still-face presentations), Tronick (1982) has demonstrated that infants are sensitive to shifts in affect; infants become agitated, may turn away, or possibly cry in response to violations of usual affective displays. A number of volumes have appeared recently that address these issues (Schaffer 1977, Bullowa 1979, Field & Fogel 1982, Tronick 1982).

Children's social behavior is modified by affective displays not only in direct face-to-face encounters, but through observing the emotional expressions of third parties. Using naturally occurring as well as simulated anger and affection displays of others in the home, Cummings, Zahn-Waxler & Radke-Yarrow (1981) found that 1- to 2½-year-old bystanders reacted with distress to anger and with affection and overt signs of pleasure to affection. Interparent anger occasionally led to intervention efforts by the children. As early as one year of age, children are not only aware of others' angry and affectionate interactions but are also likely to react emotionally to them.

One of the most interesting ways in which the social regulatory effects of emotions has been demonstrated is through the notion of "social referencing" (Campos & Stenberg 1981, Feinman & Lewis 1981a, Klinnert et al 1982). "Social referencing" concerns the tendency of a person to seek out emotional information from a significant other in the environment and to use that information to make sense of an event that is otherwise ambiguous or beyond the person's own intrinsic appraisal capabilities (Klinnert et al 1982, p. 12). In support of the construct, investigators have shown that infants' reactions to novel toys (Klinnert 1981), the visual cliff (Sorce et al 1981), and adult strangers (Feinman & Lewis 1981b) can be modified by the nature of the mother's facial expressions with positive expressions, such as happiness eliciting approach behavior and negative emotional displays such as fear leading to avoidance. A detailed analysis of the developmental course of social referencing and the possible requisite skills has recently appeared (Klinnert et al 1982). Investigations of infants and children with various types and severity of developmental delays, such as Down's Syndrome infants (Sorce et al 1982) and physically handicapped infants (Lewis & Michalson 1983), may be a promising approach to the general relationship between cognition and emotion (Zajonc 1980).

EMPATHY AS AFFECT   The development of empathy is a research area which continues to generate considerable interest. Although developmental studies of empathy are important in their own right, the study of children's empathic development also offers a rich opportunity to explore the relationships between affect and behavior and between affect and cognition.

Following much debate during the early 1970s (Aderman & Berkowitz 1970, Borke 1971, 1973, Chandler & Greenspan 1972), it is now generally agreed that empathy is best understood as a construct involving complex interactions between cognitive and affective components which vary according to such factors as age, the nature of the emotion, and situational factors.

Both Feshbach (1978, 1982) and Hoffman (1978, 1982) have introduced models to further our understanding of the nature of empathy. Feshbach's model has three components involving both cognitive and affective elements. The first component is the ability to discriminate and label affective states in others. The second component is the ability to assume the perspective and role of another person. The third component concerns emotional capacity and responsiveness. Feshbach argues that all three elements are necessary in order for empathic reponses to occur. With development, these elements and the way in which they interact are likely to change, thus modifying the nature of empathic responses. Hoffman has formulated a developmental model that also integrates affective and cognitive elements. He has defined empathy "in terms of the arousal of affect in the observer that is not a reaction to his own situation but a vicarious response to another person's situation" (Hoffman 1978, p. 229). Such a response may be the result of a number of different processes. He suggests that different modes of empathic arousal require different perceptual and cognitive abilities. Cognitive development enables qualitative changes and a progression to "higher forms of empathic arousal." Thus empathic responses cannot be understood in isolation from cognitive factors.

Two hypotheses with respect to the relationship between empathy and social behavior have been explored by researchers in this area. The first, that children who are emotionally empathic should be less aggressive, has not been supported consistently by recent data (Sawin 1979) in spite of earlier positive results (Feshbach & Feshbach 1969). Neither has a second hypothesis, which suggests that empathic children should demonstrate a greater degree of altruistic behavior (Buckley et al 1979, Marcus et al 1979, Eisenberg-Berg & Lennon 1980). No compelling model has emerged to reconcile discrepant findings. Attention should now be focused on the multidimensionality of the empathy construct and the particular social behaviors that are likely to be influenced by variations in specific dimensions of empathy.

Recent efforts in the study of children's empathy also have been addressed to measurement issues. Bryant (1982a) has refined an empathy measure designed by Mehrabian and Epstein (1972) to allow its use by children and adolescents. This index was found to be significantly related to aggressiveness among first and fourth grade boys, to have significant test-retest reliability at first, fourth, and seventh grades, and to relate significantly to children's acceptance of individual differences in other children. In contrast, Sawin (1979) has suggested that multiple measures of empathy are necessary. He notes that "when physiological and facial reactions to affect are combined with children's labeling of their feelings, the multiple measure may prove to be a more powerful predictor of their social behavior toward peers than any single index of emotional empathy" (p. 8). Physiological measures (e.g. shifts in heart rate, galvanic skin response) are free of social desirability bias although they lack precision and provide little information concerning the particular affect children are experiencing. Subjective ratings of affect in children's faces and voices when responding to affect displays of others show promise as an index of empathic arousal. In addition to being free of social desirability bias, this measure can be used in naturalistic settings and allows for some discrimination between emotions.

Cognitive Perspectives

A major feature of recent social and personality development literature is the influence of cognitive perspectives on theory and research. This influence has multiple manifestations, including stage models, information processing approaches, studies of social knowledge, and research on attribution processes.

STAGE MODELS   There is continuing interest in stage models of cognitive development and the relationship of cognitive stages to modes of social functioning. Traditionally most of this work had been focused on moral development. Recently, however, extensions have been made into other domains, especially children's knowledge of social roles (Fischer 1980, Watson & Fischer 1980) and children's expectations about friendship (Berndt 1979, Selman 1980, Youniss 1980). In Selman's (1980) research, for example, the emphasis is on levels of children's perspective-taking ability and the relationship of these levels to the child's understanding of the basis of friendship.

Another area in which stage models have played a role is in research on achievement attributions. Nicholls (1978) has outlined a four-level model of how children come to understand that effort and ability covary to produce achievement outcomes. His study showed that children aged 5 and 6 did not distinguish effort and ability; they assumed that smarter people also try harder. Children gradually come to distinguish the two causes, seeming to understand effort as a separate cause. Nicholls' results showed that it was not until children reached age 11 or 12 that they fully understood that being smart means one has to try less hard to do well. As Nicholls points out, children did not fully understand these causes until they attained formal operations.

A variant of stage models can be found in other recent research on children's moral reasoning (Eisenberg-Berg & Neal 1979, Eisenberg-Berg & Roth 1980) and person perception processes (Barenboim 1981). Here, too, the emphasis is on changes over age in children's conceptions; however, the "stage" construct is used more metaphorically and there is less interest in linking cognitions to structural changes in cognitive development. For example, Barenboim (1981) examined changes over age in children's perceptions of others. Younger children tend to use behavioral constructs, whereas in later stages children use psychological constructs and then psychological comparisons.

INFORMATION PROCESSING APPROACHES   Another manifestation of the cognitive influence is the upsurge of interest in information processing perspectives. An information processing view emphasizes not stages of development but phases of processing that an individual moves through in responding to a cognitive or social task. For example, Rest (1983) has recently adopted an information processing perspective in considering the production of moral behavior. Rest suggests a four-step process: (1) "interpreting the situation in terms of how people's welfare is affected by possible action of the subject; (2) figuring out what the ideal moral course of action would be; (3) deciding what one actually intends to do; and (4) executing and implementing what one intends to do." This model not only serves in Rest's review to organize previous literature on moral judgment and moral behavior, it also calls attention to relatively neglected issues, especially issues relevant to the first component. Rest's model is in the same intellectual tradition as Flavell's (1974) paper on components underlying perspective taking and should have enormous impact on future research.

Another promising extension of an information processing perspective is Dodge's work on children's processing of social information and the relationship of processing style to aggressive behavior (Dodge 1980, 1981, Dodge & Frame 1982). Dodge has proposed a five-step process (decoding of social cues, interpretation, response search, selecting an optimal response, enactment) and has done research showing how distortions during the early phases can lead to aggressive behavior. In particular, Dodge (1980) has demonstrated that aggressive boys are more likely to perceive another's actions as hostile when there is ambiguity concerning intention. Furthermore, when aggressive boys are given an opportunity to search for cues to determine intent, they respond more quickly and perform a less diligent search (see also Dodge & Newman 1981).

Somewhat related to information processing accounts, is research on social and personality development conducted from a task-analytic perspective. This perspective has been adopted in much of the research on referential communication. Task-analytic research considers the competencies that children need to deal with the particular social tasks at hand. Certain competencies are quite task specific (for example, comparison processing on referential communication tasks; see Asher & Wigfield 1981). Other competencies are more general "metacognitive" types of processes such as the ability to reflect on or monitor one's own communication processes and make necessary adjustments, as required (see Flavell 1981).

The applications of a task-analytic perspective have been limited primarily to referential communication tasks which are perhaps more cognitive than they are social. However, the perspective could well have utility in contexts that are clearly social. For example, Asher, Renshaw & Hymel (1982) have suggested that peer relations can be thought of as involving skills concerning the tasks of initiation of relationships, maintenance, and conflict resolution. Fine-grained observations are needed of the types of interpersonal tasks children face and the types of skills they develop to cope with these tasks.

SOCIAL KNOWLEDGE RESEARCH   The influence of cognitive perspectives on the field is also seen in the upsurge of research on children's social knowledge. Some of this work has incorporated elements of script theory (Nelson 1981). This perspective is potentially quite valuable because it highlights not only the content of children's knowledge but the way that knowledge is organized temporally. Further, it focuses attention on the purposeful nature of social behavior. Children's scripts involve plans for particular goals; thus, it is critical that social knowledge research attend to the way children formulate goals as well as plans for specific goals (Higgins et al 1981, Stein & Goldman 1981, Renshaw & Asher 1982). Social development research has frequently ignored the goal selection process by providing children with a goal and studying the strategies children use to pursue the goal. Yet an inherent part of life in social situations, which are often ill defined (Greene 1976), is deciding what goals to pursue. For example, Higgins et al (1981) have noted that referential communication is only one goal in communication situations. Other goals include social relationship goals (initiating or maintaining a social bond), social reality goals (achieving consensus about reality), presentation-of-self goals, entertainment goals (conversation for the sake of recreation), task goals, and persuasion goals. Studying the way children select and pursue these goals would help to broaden the study of children's communication processes beyond those studied thus far in the referential communication work.

Research on social knowledge is proceeding in several directions. One of these is literature on children's social problem solving (see Urbain & Kendall 1980, Krasnor & Rubin 1981). The earlier research in this area emphasized the simple numerosity of children's strategies, but more recent work is beginning to attend to the actual content of children's strategies for specific social situations. Another area that emphasizes the content of children's knowledge involves studies of children's knowledge of specific aspects of the social world—for example, children's knowledge about kinship networks (Jordan 1980) and perceptions of economic earnings and needs associated with different occupational roles (Siegal 1981).

ATTRIBUTION PROCESSES   The impact of cognitive perspectives also is evident in research on attributional processes and children's achievement motivation. The attribution approach to achievement motivation (see Weiner 1979, Frieze 1980, 1981) is concerned with how beliefs about the causes of success and failure determine subsequent achievement behavior. Throughout the 1970s, the attribution model developed by Weiner and associates (1971) has been highly influential. Recently the model has been revised; for instance, Weiner (1979) has added a new attribution dimension (called "intentionality") to his original two-dimensional taxonomy. There also has been increasing interest in the development of attributional processes. Nicholls (1979, 1980) has shown that young children seem to overestimate their attainment in school and often cannot judge which of a set of tasks is more difficult. Parsons et al (1982) found that young children maintain higher expectancies after failing than do older children. Similarly, in a study of the development of "learned helpless" responses to failure, Rholes and co-workers (1980) found that the learned helpless pattern was not evident in kindergarten, first and third grade children, but did appear in fifth grade. Taken as a whole, these results show that young children do not make attributions in the way adults do, and they do not respond as negatively to failure feedback.

Other studies in the attribution tradition have shown that children's attributions tend to become more internal across age (Ruble et al 1979). Attributions also tend to be situation specific; Frieze & Snyder (1980) found that children's attributions for other children's performance varied greatly depending upon the kind of activity the other child was engaged in (e.g. a school test versus catching frogs). Finally, Diener & Dweck (1978) showed that children differ greatly in their tendency to engage in attributions; in response to failure, children classified as "mastery oriented" actually were less likely to make attributions than children classified as "learned helpless."

While much progress has been made in understanding how children make attributions, results of other recent research pose some interesting problems with the attribution model. A basic assumption of that model is that attributions determine subsequent behavior in achievement situations. In a study with adults, Covington & Omelich (1979) found that attributions accounted for little of the variance in college students' subsequent performance on an exam. Similar results were found by Parsons and her colleagues (1982) with late elementary through high school age students. Thus caution is needed concerning the causal role played by attributions.

Much of the research in this tradition consists of analog tasks in laboratory settings. An important issue is whether results from laboratory type studies have external validity. For instance, many laboratory studies (e.g. Dweck & Reppucci 1973) have found sex differences in attributions with boys attributing success more to ability and girls attributing failure more to lack of ability. Results of recent field studies show no such sex differences (see Parsons et al 1982). The discrepancy in results between field and lab studies clearly warrants further investigation.

Social Interactional Perspectives

There have been substantial conceptual and methodological advances in three major realms of children's social interactions: parent-child, sibling, and peer interaction.

PARENT-CHILD INTERACTION   Conceptually, new views of the context of parent-child relations are emerging. Although studies of parent-child dyads, especially the mother-child dyad, continue to dominate the literature, a variety of conceptual schemes have been offered which call for an expansion of our models to include triads (Parke et al 1979, Belsky 1981). Of particular importance is the greater recognition given to the husband-wife relationship as a neglected but important dyad that may, in turn, affect how parents execute their roles as mothers and fathers. Belsky (1981) has proposed a model which provides a useful integrative scheme to guide investigation in this area and, in contrast to merely adding the marital relationship to the list of factors to consider in family studies, careful attention is being given to exploring ways in which this dyadic relationship affects the infant's social/emotional development. The finding of Pedersen, Anderson & Cain (1980) of a positive relationship between negative affect between spouses and the amount of negative affect directed to the infant underscores the importance of examining the husband-wife dyad. Similarly, numerous studies (Goldberg 1982; see Lamb 1979 for a review) have demonstrated second-order effects in triads, such as a decrease in parent behavior as a result of the presence of a spouse on either mother-infant or father-infant behavior. More research is required on the impact of these triadic interactions and of marital relationships for infant and child development. Accompanying these conceptual shifts in the study of parent-child interaction is the recognition that the paths of influence are often indirect as well as direct, and efforts to conceptualize and quantify these alternative influence paths are under way (Parke et al 1979, Belsky 1981, Lewis & Feiring 1981).

The embeddedness of families in larger networks of social systems also is increasingly gaining recognition. Two themes emerge. First, efforts continue to characterize the type and amount of social contacts outside the family with both informal and formal agents and agencies (Cochran & Brassard 1979, Parke & Tinsley 1982). Second, and more important for social development researchers, the impact of differing degrees of connectedness to, utilization of, and satisfaction with social support on individual family members and, in turn, on the infant and child's social-emotional development is being studied (Lewis & Feiring 1979, Lewis 1982). Illustrative of this trend is Crockenberg's (1981) finding that maternal social support was the best predictor of secure mother-infant attachment. Moreover, researchers are finding that satisfaction with the quantity and quality of social support is more significant in determining beneficial effects of support than objective assessments of availability and usage of support resources. Wahler (1980), for example, found that both the identity of the support agents and the conditions which governed contact were important determinants of the impact of social support. Families with contact with mainly relatives, who in turn often initiated the contact, fared less well in maintaining gains from a child-rearing modification treatment program than mothers who used a wider network of agents and who perceived themselves as able to control the timing and amount of contact.

Advances are also taking place methodologically. Studies which attempt to characterize in quantifiable terms, using microanalytic techniques, the nature of dyadic interchange between adults and infants and/or children continue. However, this research has moved beyond the early descriptive stage which showed the mutual regulatory character of early social relationships (Stern 1977, Tronick et al 1980). In fact, some investigators (e.g. Gottman & Ringland 1981) have questioned how balanced the interchanges really are between infants and parents. Alternative explanations suggest that much of the early work on dyadic communicative behavior may be more a testimony of maternal sensitivity and less a marker of infant social precocity. Although neither the measurement issues nor the interpretative controversies are settled, researchers are examining the predictive value of these early interchanges for understanding later social development. A particularly impressive entry in this domain is a monograph report by Martin (1981) of a longitudinal study of the consequences of early mother-infant interaction at 10 months for child behavior at 22 and 42 months. Using structural equations methodology—an approach to the analysis of parent-infant interaction advocated earlier by Thomas & Martin (1976)—Martin found that mother, child, and dyadic characteristics, as measured at 10 months, were shown to be predictors for the child's compliance, coerciveness, willingness to explore behind a barrier, and willingness to let the mother leave the room.

Other indications of both the methodological and conceptual sophistication of research in parent-child relations come from the continuing work of Patterson (1981, 1982), who has provided further empirical support for his model of coercive family interaction for the development of aggressive, antisocial behavior of boys. Reliance on careful in situ observational measures combined with the sophisticated application of sequential analytic techniques continues to make this an exemplary research project. A longitudinal perspective, however, is still lacking, and major progress may be limited without knowledge of the predictive value of coercive interchanges among family members.

Another methodological innovation appears in Olweus's (1980) research on the development of aggression in young adolescents. While limited by his reliance on retrospective interview techniques to assess child-rearing tactics, his use of a path-analytic approach to examine the impact of child rearing on current aggression is noteworthy. Olweus's research confirms the importance of maternal negativism, power assertion disciplinary tactics, and permissiveness, and also demonstrates the role of temperamental characteristics in determining aggressive behavior. The attraction of specifying relative weights to different child-rearing factors as well as articulating a possible causal chain is clear. This research is probably best viewed as hypothesis generating; both experimental and longitudinal analysis are necessary to support firm conclusions concerning the temporal sequence in the development of aggression.

The development of attachment Research on parent-child attachment
continues to flourish with a particular emphasis on the predictive value of
various types of attachment patterns as identified by the Ainsworth Strange
Situation (Ainsworth et al 1978). Sroufe, Waters, and their colleagues have
provided impressive support for the predictive power of the attachment
construct. In a series of four studies (Matas et al 1978, Arend et al 1979,
Waters et al 1979, Sroufe 1982), a link between attachment and developmental outcome has been established. Securely attached infants, in contrast
to their anxiously attached age mates, differed on (*a*) ego resiliency and
curiosity during the preschool years (Arend et al 1979); (*b*) problem-solving
behavior and quality of play at 2 years of age (Matas et al 1978); and (*c*)
measures of peer competence at 3½ years of age (Waters et al 1979). Others
(Easterbrooks & Lamb 1979, Pastor 1981) have provided support for the
link between quality of infant-to-mother attachment and later peer interactive competence.

While quality of attachment has been found to show considerable stability in nonstressed middle-class families (Waters 1978), less stability is evident in families encountering stressful life circumstances (Vaughn et al
1979, Thompson et al 1982). In their sample of disadvantaged families,
Vaughn et al found that a change from secure to anxious attachment was
associated with higher stressful-event scores. However, as Thompson et al
(1982) show, changes in family circumstances, such as maternal employment or regular nonmaternal care, are associated with shifts in attachment
classification, but not necessarily toward attachment insecurity. Instead,
shifts occurred toward greater security of attachment in some cases, while
evidence of greater insecurity was present in other families. Reconciliation
of these two sets of data requires closer attention to the degree of stress
encountered in the families as well as further information concerning the
coping strategies and social supports available to the families. These two
studies provide important evidence concerning the modifiability of attachment relationships, a finding which is consistent with the developmental
emphasis of ethological attachment theory. As Vaughn et al note, "like any
other affectional relationship, infant-mother attachments arise from interaction; they continue to develop even after an affective bond has formed
and they are responsive to changes in the behavior of either partner"
(Vaughn et al 1979, p. 975).

Some conditions that fail to affect quality of attachment adversely have
also been identified. In contrast to earlier predictions concerning the potentially negative impact of minimal maternal-infant contact and prolonged
separation following birth or later infant attachment relationships (Klaus
& Kennell 1976), Rode and associates (1981) found no differences in the
attachment classifications of prematurely born infants and infants who were
not separated from their mothers at birth. The data suggest that attachment

patterns are influenced by maternal-infant interaction over a period of time and provide evidence for the resiliency of infants in their formation of attachment patterns. Other investigators are also questioning the contention that close physical contact between mother and infant in the first few hours of life is necessary for parent-to-infant attachment or bonding (Svejda et al 1980, Campbell & Taylor 1980, Grossmann et al 1981).

Although attachment theorists (Ainsworth et al 1978) have asserted that the development of attachment is a process of mutual influence, most of the evidence to date has illuminated the mother's role and little information has been forthcoming concerning the infant's contribution. To correct the imbalance, Waters, Vaughn & Egeland (1980) assessed the relationship between newborn behavior as indexed by the Brazelton Neonatal Behavioral Assessment Scale (Brazelton 1973, Als et al 1978) and the infant's attachment classification at one year of age. In comparison with the secure attachment group, anxious/resistant infants scored lower on orientation, motor maturity, and physiological regulation at day 7. These data suggest that early neonatal difficulties may reflect problems in integrative and adaptive mechanisms which continue to influence behavior, interaction, and later attachment relationships. The fact that these infants may be more difficult from an early age may help explain the earlier characterization (Ainsworth et al 1978) of mothers with anxious/resistant infants as unskilled in holding, face-to-face interaction, and feeding. Certain types of infants, it appears, may be more difficult to teach interactive behaviors and perhaps more difficult to learn from as well. More research concerning the role of individual and perhaps constitutionally based differences among infants would represent an important contribution to our understanding of the bidirectionality of the attachment process. Progress in the classification of infants and children in their physical attractiveness also may yield further insights into the infant's role in early social relations (Langlois & Stephan 1981).

Early maltreatment has been isolated as an important determinant of later quality of attachment (Egeland & Sroufe 1981). Infants with a history of either extreme neglect or abuse, in contrast to infants with a history of excellent care, were characterized by a low proportion of secure attachment at 12, but not at 18, months. Stability from 12 to 18 months was greater in the excellent care group while over half of the mistreated infants changed classifications. Some of the conditions which are associated with secure attachment within the maltreatment group include the presence of a supportive family member, less chaotic life style, and in some instances, a robust infant.

Evidence continues to accumulate against a monotropic view of early attachment relationships. Not only are fathers increasingly recognized as important attachment figures (see Parke, 1978, 1981, Lamb 1981, for reviews), but it is becoming increasingly clear that it is necessary to consider the relationships that the infant develops with *both* mother and father in order to fully appreciate early social development. In an important study, Main & Weston (1981) measured the quality of attachment of infants to both parents and showed that one-year-olds develop distinctly different relationships with mothers and fathers. Infants were securely or insecurely attached to either parent or both parents. Infants who were securely attached to both parents were more responsive to a friendly clown than those who were securely attached to only one parent and insecurely attached to the other; babies who were insecurely attached to both parents were the least sociable with the clown. This study suggests that a less than optimal relationship with one parent can be compensated for by a better relationship with the other parent—and to study either fathers or mothers alone provides an insufficient window upon early social development. Using the family as the unit of analysis and recognition of the family as a social system seems a more promising research strategy (Parke et al 1979, Belsky 1981, Pedersen, 1981).

Further support for the relationship between the availability of external social support systems and the quality of infant-parent attachment is available. As discussed earlier, Crockenberg (1981) found that social support was the best predictor of secure attachment and that it was most important for mothers with irritable babies. Other evidence suggests that social support may mitigate against the effects of unresponsive mothering by providing the infant with a responsive substitute. This study is an interesting demonstration of the interplay between temperamentally based factors and social contextual variables and offers further support for a transactional view of early social development (Sameroff & Chandler 1975). The Crockenberg research is consistent with other work using the HOME Scale (Elardo et al 1975) which has demonstrated links between social support and the adequacy of the home environment, including the quality of the parenting with infants (Unger & Powell 1980) and with 3-year-olds (Pascoe et al 1981). These two studies gain particular significance in view of the previously established positive relationship between the HOME Scale and mental test performance (Bradley & Caldwell 1976). However, none of these studies has yet explored the relative contribution of different members of the social network to these outcomes. Some conceptual progress of this type is being made (Lewis 1982, Parke & Tinsley 1982, Tinsley & Parke 1983).

Special populations   Another theme in parent-child interaction is the upsurge of interest in special child populations, especially infants at risk for later development, such as premature infants, infants with various physical handicaps, and Down's Syndrome babies (see Kopp 1983 for a review). A number of volumes have appeared recently (Field et al 1979, 1980, Sawin et al 1980, Taylor 1980, Friedman & Sigman 1981) and testify to the increasingly interdisciplinary character of this research, especially between developmental psychology and medical specialities such as pediatrics and obstetrics. In addition, these reports on special populations provide further demonstrations of the bidirectionality of parent-child relations, and at a more specific level, they provide an interesting test of the impact of parent-infant interaction patterns for later social functioning. Numerous studies (Bakeman & Brown 1980, Field 1980, Goldberg et al 1980, Kopp 1983) document the ways in which parental treatment of preterm and fullterm infants differs. Although there is evidence that these differences in interaction have short-term effects on infant cognitive and socio-emotional development, evidence of long-term effects is less impressive.

In a recent report of an important longitudinal analysis of preterm infant development, Bakeman & Brown (1980) found that preterm and full-term infants do not differ in sociability and social relationships by three years of age. Moreover, although early parent-infant interaction patterns differed for preterms and full-term infants, in general these differences did not predict social or cognitive ability at age 3. Birth status (preterm/full-term) did predict cognitive but not social ability, with preterms scoring lower in cognitive performance—a finding which suggests that the antecedents of social and cognitive development need to be considered separately. Moreover, these data suggest that the preterm may be more at risk for cognitive than social development. Although prediction from infancy was not very successful, relationships between parent-toddler interaction and social and cognitive development at 3 years were more robust; specifically, children of mothers who were more emotionally and verbally responsive at 20 months exhibited more social and cognitive competence at 36 months. The non-predictability of parental treatment in the first year of life for later development led the investigators to suggest that young infants may be "buffered" from reproductive and caretaking insults during the early months of life. Other evidence in support of this general view is available (Dunn 1975), at least for early infancy.

Cross-cultural variations Another characteristic of parent-child research is the interest in cross-cultural variation in parent-infant interaction patterns (Leiderman et al 1977, Field et al 1981). This research highlights the role of contextual constraints on social development, including parent-child interaction patterns (Yarrow & Waxler 1979, Hess 1981). It also under-scores the necessity of recognizing the multiple paths leading to "normal" or optimal development and the important role of belief systems in other cultures as well as our own culture in organizing child-care environments and as mediators of parental behavior. (Parke 1978, Goodnow 1979, McGillicuddy-DeLisi et al 1979, Sameroff 1980, Hess 1981). In addition, these reports raise serious questions about the universality of some of the modal paradigms of the last decade. For example, in some cultures, face-to-face interactions with the mother rarely occur since the infant is typically placed outward to relate to other members of the social group, or because the sibling is considered the primary social interaction partner (e.g. Martini & Kirkpatrick 1981).

SIBLING INTERACTION   The role of sibling interaction in children's social development has often been ignored. Two recently reported major research programs are significantly reducing this deficit: the Abramovitch program in Canada and the Dunn project in England. Both utilize observational longitudinal strategies, and their findings are somewhat similar. Older sibs serve as models for their younger brothers and sisters, which suggests that siblings may play an underestimated role in the socialization process. Older children initiate both prosocial and agonistic behaviors more often than younger children. Modest variations in spacing do not appear to have major effects on sib interaction, and the sibling interaction patterns are relatively stable over time (Abramovitch et al 1979, 1980, Pepler et al 1981). Both Dunn (e.g. Dunn & Kendrick 1981a) and Abramovitch (e.g. Pepler et al 1981) found that sex composition of the dyads matters, with more frequent positive behavior evident in same-sex pairs, while more frequent negative behavior is evident in different-sex pairs.

Just as peer interaction is not independent of the quality of the mother-child relationship (e.g. Sroufe 1979, Pastor 1981), sib relationships are clearly linked to both the quality and quantity of mother-infant interaction. Both the relationship that the mother has developed with the older child and the nature of the relationship that the mother evolves with a second infant will significantly modify sibling relationships.

Interestingly, in families where there is a particularly intense and playful exchange between mother and firstborn girl, not only is the behavior of the older sibling relatively hostile and aggressive to the younger sib, but by 14 months the behavior of the second child is more negative to the firstborn (Dunn & Kendrick 1981b). Similarly, the extent to which the mother interacts and plays with her secondborn infant is negatively related to positive interactions between older and younger siblings—especially for girls. Close relationships between mother and child, it appears, do not necessarily ensure harmonious sibling relations—an interesting update on the longstanding problem of sibling rivalry.

PEER INTERACTION   Research on children's peer relationships has accelerated rapidly within the past several years, and a dominant theme within the area has been the development of social competence and the relationship of social competence to status in the peer group.

Early manifestations of competence   Precocity of infants has been a continuing theme for the last decade as new techniques and conceptualizations permit a finer grained and more acute examination of infant skills. The peer relations area is no exception as studies continue to uncover the developing social skills of young infants and toddlers with their peers.

A variety of studies over the last few years have documented that young infants express interest in one another, react differentially to other infants in contrast to adults, and vary their interactions across social contexts (presence or absence of mother), physical settings (familiar vs unfamiliar setting), and presence or absence of toys (see Mueller & Vandell 1979, Rubin & Ross 1982, Hartup 1983).

Even in the first year of life, evidence of rudimentary social skills is apparent, although the frequency and complexity of infant-infant interchanges are limited. Vandell, Wilson, and Buchanan (1980) studied the interaction of pairs of 6-, 9-, and 12-month-old infants and found that single social acts (e.g. a smile, a vocalization) were just as common as sequences of social actions (i.e. actions followed within a brief period by social actions from the other infant) or semisocial acts (actions centered around a shared toy without involving the other infant). Although social behavior is still limited in the second half year of life, the nature of the interactive elements changes over this period. Looking appears earliest, followed by touching and reaching, and only later does coordinated activity appear. As Hartup (1983) notes "To a considerable extent, the appearance of these social elements parallels changes occurring in the baby's reactions to the mother as well as to inanimate objects. Early child-child interaction is thus embedded in more general developmental change." Ross and her colleagues (Goldman & Ross 1978, Hay & Ross 1979, Ross 1982) have made considerable progress by analyzing social games between 18-month-olds with a 12- or 24-month old partner. A variety of features of games were isolated using naturally occurring ball games, including (*a*) mutual involvement, (*b*) turn-taking, (*c*) repetition of a two-partner sequence, and (*d*) nonliterality (i.e. the activities incorporated in a game were not meant literally). These authors also note a high degree of similarity between the games that toddlers played with adults vs peers, which suggests that an adult partner is not necessary to support these types of social exchanges. Others (e.g. Eckerman & Stein 1982) have offered further theoretical and empirical analyses of the toddler's emerging interactive skills.

Relationship of competence to peer status   The relationship of children's social interaction style to their status in the peer group is a topic of long-standing interest to developmental psychologists. The typical research strategy has been to collect sociometric data on children's status in the peer group and then to relate status data to observations of the child's social interaction patterns in the group. This methodology has traditionally yielded modest but statistically significant relationships between prosocial behavior and sociometric acceptance, and between negative or antisocial behavior and sociometric rejection (see Asher & Hymel 1981 for a recent review). An oft-cited limitation of these studies has been the difficulty in drawing causal inferences: Is ineffective social behavior the cause of low status or the consequence?

Several studies have begun to address the issue by especially creating new groups in order to study the emergence of status and the behaviors that lead to acceptance versus rejection (Coie & Kupersmidt 1981, Dodge 1982, Putallaz 1982). Findings indicate that when children are placed in a new group their status soon correlates with their status in their regular class-room situation. Furthermore, there are clear patterns of positive versus negative behavior that bring about status. As in earlier literature, a neces-sary distinction must be made between children who are neglected by their peers and those who are rejected. These two groups of children show different interaction styles, and it appears that rejected status is more stable from one year or group to the next (Coie & Dodge 1982).

An important methodological innovation has been the increasing use of analog procedures to study situations and events that occur infrequently in the classroom yet are important contexts for the development of peer rela-tionships. The analog laboratory situation also lends itself more readily to videotaping and the more fine-grained observation of behavior that results. In an exemplary study, Putallaz & Gottman (1981) used an analog situation to study the way in which children go about entering a group. They found that unpopular children were less likely to adopt the ongoing frame of reference of the participants and also engaged in behaviors that drew atten-tion to self but were less likely to be successful in gaining entry.

That low-status children are deficient in social skills is further suggested by two other lines of research. Interview studies in which children are asked about their ideas about social interaction also find that unpopular children's ideas are more unique, are more aggressive in conflict situations, and exhibit less independent resourcefulness in initiation and maintenance situations (Ladd & Oden 1979, Asher & Renshaw 1981). Intervention studies also provide support for the "social skill deficit hypothesis" (Asher & Renshaw 1981) in that unpopular children who are taught social skills make signifi-cant gains in social status in the peer group (Gresham & Nagle 1980, Ladd 1981).

Thus, considerable progress has been made in studying the relationship of social competence to social acceptance. An area for future work will be in conceptualizing more carefully the dimensions of social competence and in studying the relationship of specific dimensions of competence to peer acceptance. Some theoretical and empirical work is beginning to emerge along these lines. Goetz & Dweck (1980) have studied the relationships of children's attributional processes to their social coping styles. Children who attribute social rejection to their own personal inadequacies are less likely to cope effectively by changing their strategies. In a related study, Wheeler & Ladd (1982) report that popular children feel more efficacious in social situations than do unpopular children.

Another dimension receiving attention is children's goals for social interaction. Asher & Renshaw (1981) have speculated that unpopular children's problems in social interaction may result not necessarily only from lack of knowledge about what to do in various social situations but from the way they construe goals in certain social situations. For example, in a game situation unpopular children might center on the goal of defeating their play partner and ignore the goal of ensuring that they and their play partner have a good time and develop a positive relationship. In a test of this hypothesis, Renshaw & Asher (1982) interviewed children about their goals and found some evidence that popular children suggested more friendly assertive goals than unpopular children.

Research on the competence correlates of sociometric status have adopted a trait-like view of competence; children are assigned scores based on their average observed interaction style, and these scores are correlated with children's overall level of status in the peer group. Masters & Furman's (1981) data provide an implicit challenge to this perspective. These investigators found that the sociometric ratings a child (P) gave to another child (O) could be predicted based on the particular interactive history child P had with O, but could not be predicted based on the type of interactions O had with other children in the same group. This suggests that social interaction processes and social competence need to be studied at the level of the dyadic relationship. It is conceivable that children will display competence in some relationships and not others, and these displays both produce attraction and result from it.

It also continues to be clear that sociometric status may be affected by factors other than social competence. Work on physical attractiveness continues to show positive relationships between children's attractiveness and their social status and social behavior (Langlois & Downs 1979, Vaughn & Langlois 1982). Children's status in the peer group is also mediated by their academic performance. Green and co-workers (1980) have recently reported moderate correlations between standardized achievement test performance and sociometric status. This replicates earlier research on this topic and strongly suggests that psychologists comparing extreme groups of popular and unpopular children on social competence may in part be comparing high- and low-achieving children. A related study by McMichael (1980) also points to the need to take academic performance into account. McMichael found that low-achieving, low-sociometric-status boys tended to nominate one another as friends. These children may perhaps turn out to be the children identified by Coie, Dodge & Coppotelli (1982) as "controversials"—that is, children who receive several positive and several negative nominations from children in the group.

Finally, as in the case of parent-child interaction, there is growing interest in the peer relations of children with handicapping conditions (Greenspan 1981, Strain 1981, Taylor 1982). Retarded children in particular repeatedly have been found to be rejected by the peer group, and this problem has become of particular concern in light of the current mandate for the main-streaming of handicapped children in regular classrooms. In her review of the social competence of retarded children, Taylor (1982) draws heavily on both social-cognitive and motivational literature to outline several dimensions of competence that may be problematic for handicapped youngsters. The dimensions include: (a) children's goals in interpersonal situations, (b) the personal-motivational orientations which activate goal-directed behavior, (c) the social inference and role-taking abilities which contribute to goal formulation and management of social encounters, and (d) the interpersonal strategies or tactics employed to achieve interpersonal goals. This type of analysis hopefully will lead to both descriptive and intervention research focused on specific processes rather than simply more global behavioral or sociometric outcome research.

METHODOLOGICAL INNOVATIONS

Productive diversity characterizes the methodology found in recent social and personality development research: there is variety in designs, settings, measures, and data analysis techniques employed. We will briefly highlight certain trends.

Designs and Settings

The arguments between advocates of experimentation in the laboratory and advocates of description in the field have subsided. There is a growing recognition of the contributions of experimental and descriptive research in both field and laboratory settings (Parke 1979). Indeed, in several areas of recent personality and social development literature, there are excellent examples of descriptive research followed by experimental tests of hypothesized processes. For example, Dweck and associates (1978) found that teachers gave different types of feedback to boys and girls in the classroom. These patterns were hypothesized to be related to particular attributional styles, and in a second study Dweck et al (1978) found that experimentally manipulating type of feedback indeed led to the hypothesized attributional style. Similarly, Carpenter & Huston-Stein (1980) observed differences in the level of activity structure experienced by boys and girls in the preschool.

Subsequent manipulations of activity structure (Carpenter et al 1982) produced anticipated effects on children's involvement with adults. The work by Dweck et al illustrates the sequence of field-descriptive work followed by experimental laboratory research, whereas the research by Carpenter and Huston follows field-descriptive inquiry with experimental manipulation in the field as well as laboratory setting. Both lines of research illustrate the sequence of using descriptive research to generate hypotheses and experimental research to test them.

Longitudinal research designs are being used more extensively in personality and social development research. Eaton (1979) has demonstrated how longitudinal data can be used to differentiate children in terms of the trend of their response over time. In a study of children's test anxiety, Eaton found that within-subject change in children's anxiety over 3 years was a better predictor of arithmetic test performance than was children's current level of anxiety or average level over the 3 years.

Also noteworthy is the increasing exploration of children's personality and social development in new settings (Medrich et al 1982). The home and nursery school continue to dominate as preschool settings, and the elementary school remains popular as a site for research in middle childhood. Still, other settings are receiving deserved attention, including neighborhoods (Bryant 1982b), camps (Furman & Childs 1982), hospitals (Parke et al 1980), playgrounds (Smith & Connolly 1980), and organized sports (Fine 1981). Relatively little research exists on socialization contexts such as church groups and clubs. Still less exists on behavior across contexts, although research on parent attachment and peer relations, reviewed above, is an exception.

Measurement and Analysis

REPORTS BY SIGNIFICANT OTHERS   Parents continue to be utilized as informants about their children's behavior, but unlike an earlier era when retrospective accounts predominated, the current emphasis is on collecting contemporaneous information. For example, Cummings, Zahn-Waxler & Radke-Yarrow (1981) trained parents to observe and report how their toddlers responded to expressions of anger and affection by others. Achenbach & Edelbrock (1981) made extensive use of more formal parent ratings in order to chart social and personality adjustment across the years of 4 to 16.

Teacher reports on children's social behavior are also being utilized somewhat more widely (e.g. Green et al 1980, Connolly & Doyle 1981). There is generally good interjudge agreement in behavior ratings, and teachers are probably valid reporters, particularly when they have been asked to observe children closely for a period of time before making the ratings (Wheeler & Ladd 1982). A virtue of teacher reports, like parent reports, is that infrequently occurring but psychologically significant events can be captured due to the teacher's long period of contact with the child being rated. The utility of teacher ratings is illustrated in a study by Rubin (1982), who found that children who engage in a high degree of solitary play that is constructive are not rated by teachers as maladjusted; however, children whose solitary activities were characterized by dramatic play were more likely to be viewed as maladjusted. This is an important finding in light of continuing interest in infrequently interacting children, referred to in the literature as socially withdrawn (e.g. Furman et al 1979). Apparently, some children whose interaction rates are well below average may be quite competent while others are not (see Asher et al 1981).

Finally, peer ratings continue to play an important role in the literature. Peer ratings are used to learn about a child's behavior (peer assessment) and to study interpersonal attraction (sociometric assessment). A rating-scale sociometric recently adapted for preschoolers appears to be highly reliable (test-retest) with 4-year olds and far more reliable than the traditional best-friends nomination measure (Asher et al 1979). A paired-comparison sociometric technique has been used recently with preschoolers by Vaughn & Waters (1981) and is also showing very high reliability. These new instruments will likely stimulate increased research on interpersonal attraction in the preschool years.

That peers can be useful information sources for behavioral assessment is also evident. Knight (1981) had fourth- through sixth grade children predict how their classmates would respond to a laboratory measure of social orientation. Children were successful at predicting whether their peers would exhibit a cooperative, competitive, or individualistic orientation. Coie, Dodge & Coppotelli (1982) recently have exploited the advantages of peer assessment to study developmental changes in the qualities children like and dislike in a peer.

SELF-REPORT   Children continue to be used as reporters concerning their own psychological functioning. Two scales assessing children's perceptions of their own competence have appeared recently; both have sound psychometric properties. Harter (1982) has developed a scale which examines self-concept in four distinct domains: social, academic, physical, and general. She has found that children as young as 8 make meaningful differentiations among the four domains.

Wheeler & Ladd (1982) have developed a social self-concept measure that focuses on children's feelings of efficacy in conflict and nonconflict situations with peers. Children's reports of self-efficacy were found to be correlated with sociometric status, teacher ratings of social competence, and a child's self-report measure of anxiety. Furthermore, Wheeler and Ladd found that children feel less efficacious in conflict than in nonconflict situations.

INTERVIEWS Until recently, interviews with children have been underutilized in the personality and social development literature. However, the current focus on social cognition has fostered considerable interest in various interview methods. For example, interviews are being used to study children's knowledge about social relations such as friendship or authority relations (Selman 1980, Youniss 1980) and to explore children's ability to discriminate between conventional versus moral transgressions (Nucci & Turiel 1978). Concerning the latter, it appears that very young children make a distinction between events that are wrong because they violate a social norm (e.g. failing to pick up one's toys) versus behaviors that are wrong because of their moral implications [e.g. hitting another person (Weston & Turiel 1980, Smetana 1981)].

One significant development in interview methodology is the development of on-the-spot interviewing methods in contrast to what Selman (1980) terms the reflective reasoning interview. Whereas the latter typically involves showing children hypothetical social situations and probing their reasoning about such situations, on-the-spot interviewing involves studying reasoning in action. For example, Eisenberg-Berg & Neal (1979) approached children when they helped another child and inquired about their reasons. Children reported a variety of motives for their prosocial behavior including taking into account the needs of others, that both children would benefit, and that a friendly relationship would develop. In the literature on conventional versus moral reasoning, children were also interviewed "on the spot" about their perceptions of a transgression that has just occurred in the classroom (Nucci & Turiel 1978).

ANALYSIS OF INTERACTIONAL DATA Observational studies of social interaction continue to be an increasingly common strategy for assessing children's social and personality development. In addition to formal observational strategies using precoded categories, precise time lines, and videotaped records, ethnographic observational traditions are still evident as strategies from other fields such as linguistics, sociology, and anthropology continue to be incorporated into the methodological repertoire of developmental psychology.

A number of major volumes and reviews describing, debating, and illustrating the value and limitations of observational methodological strategies have appeared (Sackett 1978, 1979, Cairns 1979, Lamb et al 1979, Hess 1981). Recent advances, however, are less on data collection than on data analysis. Two sets of major analytic strategies, sequential analysis and time series analysis, have received attention. Debate continues on the optimal strategy for analyzing social interactional data. Although a variety of alternative strategies for handling sequential data have been offered by a number of contributors (see Bakeman et al 1979, Castellan 1979, Gottman & Bakeman 1979), comparative analysis of different sequential strategies has been a rarer event. An exception is the recent work of Martin et al (1981), who compared several microanalytic methods for analysis of mother-child interaction at 18 months. Standard sequential probability analysis, which has the limitation of confounding perseverative effects with partner effects, was compared with a multiple regression procedure which corrects this problem but has other limitations. A third approach which focuses on the independent analyses of onsets and offsets was developed and overcomes limitations of the other procedures. In general, Martin et al confirmed earlier findings (Altmann 1965), namely that a large proportion of the information yielded by a sequential analysis is available in the first intervals of a new behavior sequence, and little information is gained by carrying sequential analysis over several time periods.

One of the persistent problems with all of the methods of sequential analysis involves the presence of serial dependency or autocorrelation among the sequentially occurring behaviors. Recent advances in the application of time series analysis to social interaction data may help in better estimating the contribution of this serial dependency. See Gottman & Ringland (1981) and Lester, Hoffman & Brazelton (1982) for recent illustrations and Gottman (1982) for an excellent introduction to these techniques for the mathematically shy researcher.

Finally, some other trends in observational research are discernible. Multi-method strategies including the use of ratings are increasingly common, and in some cases serve as a protective net against failure to detect interesting patterns which may not appear at the microanalytic level. The value of global ratings is being appreciated more fully, and the utility of macro and micro levels of analysis for different questions is being recognized (Cairns & Green 1979). Evidence, not just speculation, may be driving the field to this new openness to a wide range of methods. A number of recent researchers have found that ratings of parental behavior yield better prediction of either later social behavior (Bakeman & Brown 1980) or later cognitive assessments (Jay & Farran 1981) than more microanalytic and more expensive measures of parent-child interaction. Further delineation of the types of questions for which various levels of observational analysis are most useful would constitute a major methodological contribution.

META-ANALYSIS   The use of a recently developed aid to the reviewer-integrator of prior research, namely meta-analysis (Glass 1978), is finding its way into the social development literature. Smith & Glass (1980) illustrate the utility of meta-analysis in their review of the class size literature. In spite of much skepticism to the contrary, these researchers demonstrated that small classes yield beneficial effects on teacher and pupil attitudes as well as instruction and achievement. Children have higher self-concepts, greater interest in school, and participate more in class activities in small classes. Maccoby & Jacklin (1980) offer a further illustration of the effective use of meta-analysis in their review of observational studies of aggression between young children by showing clear sex differences in aggression—a finding which successfully challenged Tieger's (1980) contrary claim. The use of meta-analysis in this case was not merely to summarize prior findings, but was used as a powerful tool for settling a theoretical dispute. Although the utility of this approach has been demonstrated, the implications of combining studies of varying levels of quality into a single set for analysis purposes still warrants systematic examination.

ECOLOGICAL CONCERNS

Although there has been a long tradition of concern about the ecological validity of research in children's social development, stemming at least in part from the early work and theory of Kurt Lewin and Roger Barker, new impetus to this viewpoint has been provided by the recent writings of Bronfenbrenner (1977, 1979). His 1979 monograph, *The Ecology of Human Development,* was an important call for more ecologically sensitive research and conceptualization. This general strategy is reflected in a number of different ways. Life events research, which takes advantage of naturally occurring planned and unplanned transitions such as divorce, birth, and unemployment is one example. A further illustration derives from an increasing interest in social policy issues such as racial attitudes, day care, and child abuse.

Life Events Research

Research in this area not only has roots in the ecological tradition but reflects the influence of a life-span developmental viewpoint as well (Baltes et al 1980). Transitions in life and their effects on child development are often the focus of this type of research. Examples of recent research on life events are studies of the transition to parenthood and divorce.

TRANSITION TO PARENTHOOD   The transition to parenthood issue—a long-time favorite of sociologists (e.g. Le Masters 1957, Russell 1974)—recently has come under scrutiny by psychologists (Cowan et al 1978, Vincent et al 1980, Osofsky & Osofsky 1983, Power & Parke 1983). Two major research projects have been completed which represent an increasingly sophisticated conceptualization of the transition issue. Entwisle &

Doering (1981) and Grossman, Eichler & Winicoff (1980) report longitudinal analyses of how couples change as a result of the birth of an infant. Although limited by a reliance on verbal report measures, their multivariate conceptualization of the transition process, including increased focus on the father, moves this research area significantly beyond the retrospective reports of the past two decades. The Grossman et al study is of particular interest since these investigators show ways in which the couples' management of the transition affects the infant's development. Both projects underscore the significance of preparation for and management of the birth process as important determinants of how a couple copes with this transition. Both teams of investigators find, for example, clear evidence that preparation for childbirth and presence of the father are important as well as the type of childbirth. Caesarean section deliveries have increased rapidly over the past decade. In contrast to mothers who delivered vaginally, mothers of C-section-delivered infants experienced longer postpartum depressions and were less positive about caring for their infant. Possibly in response to the mother's delayed capacity for assuming caretaking responsibility, C-section delivery is associated with increased father involvement in caregiving (Entwisle & Doering 1981, Grossman et al 1980, Pedersen et 1981) at least through the first half year; differences tend to be absent by 12 months (Grossman et al 1980).

One twist in the transition to parenthood research is the investigation of the impact of the second infant on the family, especially the mother-firstborn relationship. In a series of papers from studies discussed earlier in the sibling interaction section. Dunn & Kendrick (1980, 1982; Kendrick & Dunn 1980) have reported decreases in maternal attention and play with the firstborn and an increase in negative, prohibitory, and confrontational behaviors after the arrival of a second infant. In contrast to earlier studies of transition to parenthood which relied on parental retrospective reports, the use of home-based observational analyses in these studies places them in the forefront of current research in early social relations.

DIVORCE   Interest in the impact of divorce on children has culminated in reports of two large-scale studies by Hetherington, Cox & Cox (1979, 1982) and Wallerstein & Kelley (1981). The Hetherington project suggests that divorce has clear disruptive impact on children's social relations in the family and in extrafamilial contexts. In this study of mother custody, boys were affected more than girls, although other evidence indicates that the impact of divorce on boys may be less if the father has custody (Santrock & Warshak 1979). Peer relations of children of divorced parents were affected as well. These children, especially boys, demonstrated less imaginative, cooperative, and constructive play patterns (Hetherington et al 1979). Moreover, these boys chose younger play partners and exhibited patterns of low physical and high verbal aggression, a pattern more commonly seen in girls. Even after 2 years, negative effects were still present for boys, although the impact on girls was no longer evident. One of the important determinants of children's postdivorce adjustment appears to be the nature of the father's continued support and contact with the family (Hess & Camara 1979, Hetherington 1979, 1981). The Wallerstein & Kelley (1981) project, although more clinically oriented, provides useful clues concerning the differential impact of divorce on children at differing developmental levels. However, more systematic research on the developmental aspects of divorce is necessary.

Another closely related issue, namely the impact of step-parents on children's development, is beginning to receive attention. This is an important but little understood issue. The fact that over six million children in the United States now live in step-parent homes suggests that this is a topic worthy of study. Santrock and associates (1982) found that the step-parenting arrangement affects boys and girls differently, with boys appearing to benefit more than girls. Moreover, these investigators found that the social behavior of children is not necessarily less competent in step-parent families than in intact families and argue that the quality of postdivorce family functioning as indexed by such factors as the adequacy of parenting behavior and marital conflict is more important than family structure per se. Other family issues such as the impact of joint custody are beginning to receive attention as well (Clingenpeel & Reppucci 1982).

Social Policy

As Sears (1975) has pointed out, child psychology was born in large part as an applied discipline, and from its beginnings researchers investigated diverse substantive problems of considerable practical significance. Research on personality and social development, like developmental psychology more generally, has recently returned to its more problem-oriented origins, following an era characterized almost exclusively by process-oriented inquiry. The field is infused with a variety of important developmental problems and policy issues, and in many areas the empirical and methodological advances have been considerable. Traditional policy concerns such as racial attitudes and day care endure while problems such as child abuse are attracting more attention from psychologists.

RACIAL ATTITUDES   There has been a discernible shift in the research methods by which racial attitudes are explored. The earlier methods of using children's doll or picture preferences to infer racial attitudes are increasingly giving way to the study of interracial attitudes in the context of real-life relationships. This has involved more use of direct observations of behavior, sociometric surveys, and interview and ethnographic methods.

Although no direct comparisons have been made, it appears that assessments in the context of children's everyday peer groups are yielding more positive pictures of children's cross-race relations. For example, observational and sociometric research by Singleton & Asher (1979) and Schofield & Francis (1982) finds that elementary school black and white children generally accept one another in work and play situations, even though they don't necessarily choose one another as best friends. Indeed, the degree of racial bias children evidence is small compared to the degree of sex bias children show in the same studies.

Still, race bias exists and longitudinal data indicate significant increases over age (Singleton & Asher 1979). Schofield (1982) has studied the elements of children's perceived identities that may lead to cross-race cleavage. White children are more likely to perceive blacks as threatening and aggressive, whereas blacks are more likely to see whites as conceited and "standoffish." These identity elements can lead to attributional biases in ambiguous situations. For example, Sagar & Schofield (1980) found that given an ambiguous action that could be interpreted as aggressive, children were more likely to make this attribution when the actor was black.

DAY CARE   The tremendous current and projected rise in the need for day care for young children has not been matched by the amount of empirical evidence documenting the effects of day care on children's development (Children's Defense Fund 1982). Demographic increases in the number of women with young children entering the job force and the increase of households headed by single mothers (as a result of divorce or by choice) emphasize the importance of focusing research on this topic. Two recent efforts warrant discussion, both included in an important interdisciplinary edited volume on empirical and social policy issues of day care (Zigler & Gordon 1982).

One is a comprehensive review by Rutter (1982) of the social and emotional consequences of day care for young children. Rutter suggests that there is no good evidence that high quality day care is disruptive to the parent-child relationship, but that there is some consistency in the available data base to suggest that day care modifies children's interactive behavior. However, the behaviors modified and the direction in which they are modified (i.e. positively or negatively) varies between studies. Moreover, Rutter suggests, as have others, that the ways in which day care affects children's development are probably mediated by characteristics of day care (e.g. small groups of children with one caregiver vs larger groups of children with several caregivers) and characteristics of the children (e.g. age, sex, prior experience, ordinal position). The review calls for more detailed analysis concerning the match between components of day care and specific child variables. It also includes a discussion of the social policy implications of such research findings.

A report by McCartney and associates (1982) on an exemplary large-scale day care study conducted in Bermuda is also included in the Zigler & Gordon volume (1982). The study compared the effects of differences in the quality of day care on developmental outcomes. One important finding from this study is that a high degree of verbal interaction between caregivers and children is a significant component in day-care children's verbal skills and overall emotional development. As findings from such studies as McCartney et al accumulate, developmental psychologists may be able to make reliable recommendations concerning the optimal environment for young children in group settings such as day care. For a thoughtful contribution in this direction, see Clarke-Stewart (1982).

CHILD ABUSE   Child abuse and neglect continue to be of interest, with reviews emphasizing both the developmental aspects of abuse and the need for a multilevel analysis of abuse (Starr 1979, Belsky 1980, Parke & Lewis 1981). At the empirical level, most progress has been made in delineating the different family interaction styles of abusive and neglectful parents (Burgess & Conger 1978, Starr 1979, Reid et al 1982). Reid, Patterson & Loeber (1982), for example, found that abusive parents, especially mothers, displayed more verbal and physical aggression toward their children, used more negative commands, and were less discriminating in their use of positive feedback. These analyses have led to systematic research efforts to modify these patterns (Reid et al 1981).

Increasingly, the child's role in abuse is being recognized (Friedrich & Boriskin 1976, Belsky 1980, Parke & Lewis 1981). Evidence of the child's influence comes from a series of laboratory analog studies which illustrate how aversive behavior of the children can lead to the escalation of the intensity of punitive adult behavior (Passman & Mullhern 1977, Mullhern & Passman 1979, Vasta & Copitch 1981). While these studies provide clear results in an area not noted for tidy findings, their value is limited by the artificiality of the paradigms employed. In conjunction with field-based observational analyses, however, this type of analog study is of value.

Moreover, abusive parents seem to react differently even to infants' ordinary social signals. In a novel approach to this issue, Frodi, Lamb & Anderson (1980) compared the reactions of abusing and nonabusing parents to videotapes of crying and smiling infants and reported that the abusive parents rated themselves more annoyed by and less sympathetic toward the crying infant than did the nonabusers. Interestingly, the abusers also reported being less attentive, happy, and willing to interact with the smiling baby than the nonabusers. Moreover, the psychophysiological patterns of the two groups differed, with the abusive parents showing little autonomic discrimination to the two types of events, although the abusive parents experienced greater increases in heart rate than nonabusive parents in response to the crying infants. In sum, abusers appear to react to any social stimulus—positive or negative—as aversive. In light of earlier findings (e.g. Berkowitz 1974) which suggest that "stimuli perceived as aversive are more likely to elicit aggression" (Frodi et al 1980), this negative attributional bias of abusive parents may, in part, contribute to their pattern of abusive treatment.

As a complement to the continuing interest in the interaction patterns of abusive and nonabusive families, a number of researchers have moved beyond earlier clinical and anecdotal data (Galdston 1971, Green 1978) to a systematic examination of the impact of being abused on later socioemotional development. In a well-executed observational study, George & Main (1979) showed that abused children tend to be more aggressive with their peers as well as their teachers and show ambivalent and wary reactions to adult caregivers. Others (e.g. Lewis & Schaeffer 1981) have failed to find differences in the amount of aggressive behavior exhibited by abused and nonabused children; the difference between studies may be due to the highly differentiated measures of aggressive behavior used by George and Main.

The interplay between ecological variables and child abuse is well illustrated in the work of Garbarino, who has shown that rates of abuse vary with the amount of poverty and the availability of social support (Garbarino & Crouter 1978, Garbarino & Gilliam 1980). While demonstrations that there are correlations between abuse and general socioeconomic indicators are important, recent work has moved beyond this descriptive phase by demonstrating that disruptive economic change in particular is likely to be causally linked to abuse. Steinberg, Catalano & Dooley (1981) found over a 30-month period that increases in child abuse are preceded by periods of high job loss. This exemplary study replicated the finding in two distinct metropolitan communities under very conservative criteria which ruled out most "third variable" explanations. Although archival economic and social data are only beginning to be used by developmental psychologists (e.g. Bronfenbrenner 1977), increased utilization is likely as our models of social development increasingly expand in scope and complexity to include multiple determinants beyond the immediate family unit.

CONCLUSION

Recent research on personality and social development is being shaped by diverse theoretical perspectives and methodological traditions, and the area is experiencing considerable vitality and growth. The reasons for this growth include factors inherent in the recent history of psychology more generally and factors in the larger society in which the discipline functions. For both intellectual and sociopolitical reasons, research on children's social and personality development has moved center stage in recent years. Whether it continues to flourish will depend not only on its intellectual dynamism but on the continuation of national support for social science research. Sears (1975) has described the way in which World War II adversely affected the enormous research effort in developmental psychology that was launched in the late 1920s. Hopefully, the current constrictions in federal support and university hiring will be temporary and the field will continue to build on the exciting developments of recent years.

ACKNOWLEDGMENTS

The authors wish to thank Barbara Tinsley for her excellent editorial suggestions on early drafts, and Tim Hill, Barbara Tinsley, and Allan Wigfield for their substantial contributions to the empathy (Hill), day care (Tinsley), and attribution processes (Wigfield) sections of this chapter. Thanks also to Carma Diel, Joan Neef, and Jo Powell for typing the manscript.

Work on this review was greatly facilitated by support from National Institute of Child Health and Human Development training grant HD 07205-01 and research grant HEW PH5 059591, and from a research grant from the National Foundation March of Dimes.

Literature Cited

Abramovitch, R., Corter, C., Lando, B. 1979. Sibling interaction in the home. *Child Dev.* 50:997–1003

Abramovitch, R., Corter, C., Pepler, R. D. 1980. Observations of mixed-sex sibling dyads. *Child Dev.* 51:1268–71

Achenbach, T. M., Edelbrock, C. S. 1981. Behavioral problems and competencies reported by parents of normal and disturbed children aged four through sixteen. *Monogr. Soc. Res. Child Dev.* 47(1) Ser. 194

Aderman, D., Berkowitz, L. 1970. Observational set, empathy and helping. *J. Pers. Soc. Psychol.* 14:141–48

Ainsworth, M., Blehar, M., Waters, E., Wall, S. 1978. *Patterns of Attachment.* Hillsdale, NJ: Erlbaum. 391 pp.

Als, H., Tronick, E., Lester, B. M., Brazelton, T. B. 1979. Specific neonatal measures: The Brazelton Neonatal Behavioral Assessment Scale. In *Handbook of Infant Development,* ed. J. D. Osofsky, pp. 185–215. New York: Wiley. 954 pp.

Altmann, S. A. 1965. Sociobiology of rhesus monkeys. II: Stochastics of social communication. *J. Theor. Biol.* 8:490–522

Arend, F., Gove, F. L., Sroufe, L. A. 1979. Continuity of individual adaptation from infancy to kindergarten: A predictive study of ego-resiliency and curiosity in preschoolers. *Child Dev.* 50:950–59

Asher, S. R., Hymel, S. 1981. Children's social competence in peer relations: Sociometric and behavioral assessment. In *Social Competence,* ed. J. D. Wine, M. D. Smye, pp. 125–57. New York: Guilford. 399 pp.

Asher, S. R., Markell, R. A., Hymel, S. 1981. Identifying children at risk in peer relations: A critique of the rate-of-interaction approach to assessment. *Child Dev.* 52:1239–45

Asher, S. R., Renshaw, P. D. 1981. Children without friends: Social knowledge and social skill training. In *The Development of Children's Friendships,* ed. S. R. Asher, J. M. Gottman, pp. 273–96. New York: Cambridge Univ. Press. 347 pp.

Asher, S. R., Renshaw, P. D., Hymel, S. 1982. Peer relations and the development of social skills. In *The Young Child: Reviews of Research,* ed. S. G.

Moore, C. R. Cooper, 3:137–58. Washington DC: Natl. Assoc. Educ. Young Child. 304 pp.

Asher, S. R., Singleton, L. C., Tinsley, B. R., Hymel, S. 1979. A reliable sociometric measure for preschool children. *Dev. Psychol.* 15:443–44

Asher, S. R., Wigfield, A. 1981. Training referential communication skills. In *Children's Oral Communication Skills,* ed. W. P. Dickson, pp. 105–26. New York: Academic. 394 pp.

Bakeman, R., Brown, J. V. 1980. Early interaction: Consequences for social and mental development at three years. *Child Dev.* 51:437–44

Bakeman, R., Cairns, R. B., Appelbaum, M. 1979. Note on describing and analyzing interactional data: Some first steps and common pitfalls. See Cairns 1979, pp. 227–34

Baltes, P. B., Reese, H. W., Lipsitt, L. P. 1980. Lifespan developmental psychology. *Ann. Rev. Psychol.* 31:65–110

Barenboim, C. 1981. The development of person perception in childhood and adolescence: From behavioral comparisons to psychological constructs to psychological comparisons. *Child Dev.* 52:129–44

Bates, J. E. 1980. The concept of difficult temperament. *Merrill-Palmer Q.* 26:299–319

Bates, J. E., Bennett-Freeland, C. A., Lounsbury, M. L. 1979. Measurement of infant interactions. *Child Dev.* 50:794–803

Bates, J. E., Olson, S. L., Pettit, G. S., Bayles, K. 1982. Dimensions of individuality in the mother-infant relationship at six months of age. *Child Dev.* 53:446–61

Belsky, J. 1980. A family analysis of parental influence on infant exploratory competence. See Pedersen et al 1980, pp. 87–110

Belsky, J. 1981. Early human experience: A family perspective. *Dev. Psychol.* 14:3–23

Berkowitz, L. 1974. Some determinants of impulsive aggression: Role of mediated associations with reinforcements for aggression. *Psychol. Rev.* 81:165–76

Berndt, T. J. 1979. *Children's conceptions of friendship and the behavior expected of friends.* Unpublished manuscript. Yale Univ.

Borke, H. 1971. Interpersonal perception of young children: Egocentrism or empathy? *Dev. Psychol.* 5:263–69

Borke, H. 1973. The development of empathy in Chinese and American children between three and six years of age: A cross-cultural study. *Dev. Psychol.* 9:102–8

Bower, G. H. 1981. Mood and memory. *Am. Psychol.* 36:129–48

Bradley, R. H., Caldwell, B. M. 1976. Early home environment and changes in mental test performance in children from 6 to 36 months. *Dev. Psychol.* 12:93–97

Brazelton, T. B. 1973. *Neonatal Behavioral Assessment Scale.* London: Heinemann Med. Books. 66 pp.

Brazelton, T. B., Koslowski, B., Main, M. 1974. The origins of reciprocity: The early mother-infant interaction. In *The Effect of the Infant on its Caregiver,* ed. M. Lewis, L. Rosenblum, pp. 49–76. New York: Wiley. 264 pp.

Bronfenbrenner, U. 1977. The changing American family. In *Contemporary Readings in Child Psychology,* ed. E. M. Hetherington, R. D. Parke, pp. 315–31. New York: McGraw-Hill. 441 pp.

Bronfenbrenner, U. 1979. *The Ecology of Human Development.* Cambridge: Harvard Univ. Press. 330 pp.

Bryant, B. K. 1982a. An index of empathy for children and adolescents. *Child Dev.* 53:413–25

Bryant, B. K. 1982b. *The neighborhood walk: A developmental perspective on sources of support and aspects of psychological well-being in middle childhood.* Unpublished manuscript. Univ. Calif. Davis

Buckley, N., Siegel, L. S., Ness, S. 1979. Egocentrism, empathy, and altruistic behavior in young children. *Dev. Psychol.* 15:329–30

Buechler, S., Izard, C. E. 1980. Anxiety patterns in childhood and adolescence. In *Handbook on Stress and Anxiety,* ed. I. L. Kutash, L. B. Schlessinger. San Francisco: Jossey-Bass. 580 pp.

Bullowa, M., ed. 1979. *Before Speech.* Cambridge: Cambridge Univ. Press. 400 pp.

Burgess, R. L., Conger, R. D. 1978. Family interaction in abusive, neglectful and normal families. *Child Dev.* 49:1163–73

Cairns, R. B., ed. 1979. *The Analysis of Social Interactions: Methods, Issues, and Illustrations.* Hillsdale, NJ: Erlbaum. 243 pp.

Cairns, R. B., Green, J. A. 1979. How to assess personality and social patterns: Observations or ratings? See Cairns 1979, pp. 81–116

Camaras, L. A. 1977. Facial expressions used by children in a conflict situation. *Child Dev.* 48:1431–35

Campbell, S. B., Taylor, P. M. 1980. Bonding and attachment: theoretical issues. See Taylor 1980, pp. 3–24

Campos, J. J., Stenberg, C. 1981. Perception, appraisal, and emotion: The onset of social referencing. In *Infant Social Cognition: Empirical and Theoretical Considerations*, ed. M. E. Lamb, L. R. Sherrod, pp. 273–314. Hillsdale, NJ: Erlbaum. 433 pp.

Carey, W. B., McDevitt, S. C. 1978. Revision of the infant temperament questionnaire. *Pediatrics* 61:735–39

Carpenter, C. J., Huston-Stein, A. C. 1980. Activity structure and sex-typed behavior in preschool children. *Child Dev.* 51:862–72

Carpenter, C. J., Huston, A. C., Petrowsky, K. 1982. *An experimental analysis of the effects of activity structure on sex-typed behavior in preschool children.* Presented at Ann. Meet. Am. Psychol. Assoc., Washington DC

Castellan, N. J. 1979. The analysis of behavior sequences. See Cairns 1979, pp. 80–116

Chandler, M., Greenspan, S. 1972. Ersatz egocentrism: A reply to H. Borke. *Dev. Psychol.* 7:104–6

Children's Defense Fund. 1982. *Employed Parents and Their Children: A Data Book.* Washington DC: Children's Defense Fund. 92 pp.

Clarke-Stewart, K. A. 1982. *Daycare.* Cambridge: Harvard Univ. Press. 173 pp.

Clingenpeel, W. G., Reppucci, N. D. 1982. Joint custody after divorce: Major issues and goals for research. *Psychol. Bull.* 91:102–27

Cochran, M. M., Brassard, J. A. 1979. Child development and personal social networks. *Child Dev.* 3:601–16

Coie, J. D., Dodge, K. A. 1982. *Continuities of children's social status: A five year longitudinal study.* Unpublished manuscript. Duke Univ.

Coie, J. D., Dodge, K. A., Coppotelli, H. 1982. Dimensions and types of social status: A cross-age perspective. *Dev. Psychol.* 18:557–70

Coie, J. D., Kupersmidt, J. 1981. *A behavioral analysis of emerging social status in boys' groups.* Presented at Bien. Meet. Soc. Res. Child Dev., Boston

Connolly, J., Doyle, A. 1981. Assessment of social competence in preschoolers: Teachers versus peers. *Dev. Psychol.* 4:454–62

Covington, M. V., Omelich, C. L. 1979. Are causal attributions causal? A path analysis of the cognitive model of achievement motivation. *J. Pers. Soc. Psychol.* 37:1487–1504

Cowan, C. P., Cowan, P. A., Coie, L., Coie, J. D. 1978. Becoming a family: The impact of a first child's birth on the couple's relationship. In *The First Child and Family Formation*, ed. W. B. Miller, L. F. Newman, pp. 296–324. Chapel Hill, NC: Carolina Population Center. 466 pp.

Crockenberg, S. B. 1981. Infant irritability, mother responsiveness, and social support influences on the security of infant-mother attachment. *Child Dev.* 52:857–65

Cummings, E. M., Zahn-Waxler, C., Radke-Yarrow, M. 1981. Young children's responses to expressions of anger and affection by others in the family. *Child Dev.* 52:1274–82

Diener, C. I., Dweck, C. S. 1978. An analysis of learned helplessness: Continuous changes in performance strategy, and achievement cognitions following failure. *J. Pers. Soc. Psychol.* 36:451–62

Dodge, K. A. 1980. Social cognition and children's aggressive behavior. *Child Dev.* 51:162–70

Dodge, K. A. 1981. *Social competence and aggressive behavior in children.* Presented at Midwest. Psychol. Assoc., Detroit

Dodge, K. A. 1982. Behavioral antecedents of peer social status. *Child Dev.* In press

Dodge, K. A., Frame, C. L. 1982. Social cognitive biases and deficits in aggressive boys. *Child Dev.* 53:620–35

Dodge, K. A., Newman, J. P. 1981. Biased decision-making processes in aggressive boys. *J. Abnorm. Psychol.* 90:375–79

Dunn, J. 1975. Consistency and change in styles of mothering. In *Parent-Infant Interaction.* Ciba Found. Symp. 33, pp. 155–70. New York: Assoc. Sci. Publ. 324 pp.

Dunn, J., Kendrick, C. 1980. The arrival of a sibling: Changes in patterns of interactions between mother and first-born child. *J. Child Psychol. Psychiatry* 21: 119–32

Dunn, J., Kendrick, C. 1981a. Social behavior of young siblings in the family context: Differences between same-sex and different-sex dyads. *Child Dev.* 52: 1265–73

Dunn, J., Kendrick, C. 1981b. Interaction between young siblings: Association with the interaction between mother and firstborn child. *Dev. Psychol.* 3: 336–43

Dunn, J., Kendrick, C. 1982. *Siblings: Love, Envy and Understanding.* Cambridge: Harvard Univ. Press. 304 pp.

Dweck, C. S., Davidson, W., Nelson, S., Enna, B. 1978. Sex differences in learned helplessness: II. The contingencies of evaluative feedback in the classroom and III. An experimental analysis. *Dev. Psychol.* 14:268–76

Dweck, C. S., Reppucci, N. D. 1973. Learned helplessness in reinforcement responsibility in children. *J. Pers. Soc. Psychol.* 25:109–16

Easterbrooks, M. A., Lamb, M. 1979. The relationship between quality of infant-mother attachment and infant competence in initial encounters with peers. *Child Dev.* 50:380–87

Eaton, W. O. 1979. Profile approach to longitudinal data: Test anxiety and success-failure experience. *Dev. Psychol.* 15:344–45

Eckerman, C. O., Stein, M. R. 1982. The toddler's emerging interactive skills. See Rubin & Ross 1982

Egeland, B., Sroufe, L. A. 1981. Attachment and early maltreatment. *Child Dev.* 52:44–52

Eisenberg-Berg, N., Lennon, R. 1980. Altruism and the assessment of empathy in the preschool years. *Child Dev.* 51:552–57

Eisenberg-Berg, N., Neal, C. 1979. Children's moral reasoning about their own spontaneous prosocial behavior. *Dev. Psychol.* 15:228–29

Eisenberg-Berg, N., Roth, K. 1980. Development of young children's prosocial moral judgment: A longitudinal followup. *Dev. Psychol.* 16:375–76

Ekman, P., ed. 1973. *Darwin and Facial Expression.* New York: Academic. 273 pp.

Ekman, P., Friesen, W. 1978. *Facial Action Coding System.* Palo Alto, Calif: Consult. Psychol. Press

Ekman, P., Oster, H. 1979. Facial expressions of emotion. *Ann. Rev. Psychol.* 30:527–54

Elardo, R., Bradley, R., Caldwell, B. 1975. The relation of infants' home environments to mental test performance from six to thirty-six months: A longitudinal analysis. *Child Dev.* 46:71–76

Emde, R. N., Brown, C. 1978. Adaptation to the birth of a Down's syndrome infant: Grieving and maternal attachment. *J. Am. Acad. Child Psychiatry* 17:299–323

Entwisle, D. R., Doering, S. G. 1981. *The First Birth: A Family Turning Point.* Baltimore: Johns Hopkins Univ. Press. 331 pp.

Feinman, S., Lewis, M. 1981a. *Social referencing and second-order effects in 10-month-old infants.* Presented at Meet. Soc. Res. Child Dev., Boston

Feinman, S., Lewis, M. 1981b. Maternal effects on infants' response to strangers.

Unpublished manuscript. Educ. Test. Serv., Princeton, NJ

Feshbach, N. D. 1978. Studies of empathic behavior in children. In *Progress in Experimental Personality Research,* ed. B. A. Maher, 8:1–47. New York: Academic. 344 pp.

Feshbach, N. D. 1982. Sex differences in empathy and social behavior in children. In *The Development of Prosocial Behavior,* ed. N. Eisenberg-Berg, pp. 315–59. New York: Academic. 403 pp.

Feshbach, N. D., Feshbach, S. 1969. The relationship between empathy and aggression in two age groups. *Dev. Psychol.* 1:102–7

Field, T. M. 1980. Interactions of preterm and term infants with their lower and middle-class teenage and adult mothers. See Field et al 1980

Field, T. M., Fogel, A., eds. 1982. *Emotion and Early Interactions.* Hillsdale, NJ: Erlbaum. In press

Field, T. M., Goldberg, S., Stern, D., Sostek, A. M. 1980. *High Risk Infants and Children: Adult and Peer Interactions.* New York: Academic. 387 pp.

Field, T. M., Sostek, A. M., Goldberg, S., Shuman, H. H., eds. 1979. *Infants Born at Risk.* New York: Spectrum. 498 pp.

Field, T. M., Sostek, A. M., Vietze, P., Leiderman, P. H., eds. 1981. *Culture and Social Interactions.* Hillsdale, NJ: Erlbaum. 615 pp.

Field, T. M., Walden, T. A. 1981. Production and perception of facial expressions in infancy and early childhood. In *Advances in Child Development,* ed. H. Reese, L. Lipsitt, 16:169–211. New York: Academic. 330 pp.

Field, T. M., Walden, T. A. 1982. Production and discrimination of facial expressions by preschool children. *Child Dev.* 53:1299–1311

Fine, G. A. 1981. Friends, impression management, and pre-adolescent behavior. See Asher & Renshaw 1981, pp. 29–52

Fischer, K. W. 1980. A theory of cognitive development: The control and construction of hierarchies of skill. *Psychol. Rev.* 87:477–531

Flavell, J. H. 1974. The development of inferences about others. In *Understanding Other Persons,* ed. T. Mischel, pp. 66–115. Totowa, NJ: Rowan & Littlefield. 266 pp.

Flavell, J. H. 1981. Monitoring social cognitive enterprises: Something else that may develop in the area of social cognition. In *Social Cognitive Development: Frontiers and Possible Futures,* ed. J. H. Flavell, L. Ross, pp. 272–87. New

York: Cambridge Univ. Press. 322 pp.

Friedman, S. L., Sigman, M., eds. 1981. *Preterm Birth and Psychological Development.* New York: Academic. 438 pp.

Friedrich, W. N., Boriskin, J. A. 1976. The role of the child in abuse: A review of the literature. *Am. J. Orthopsychiatry* 46:580–90

Frieze, I. H. 1980. Beliefs about success and failure in the classroom. In *The Social Psychology of School Learning,* ed. J. H. McMillan, pp. 39–78. New York: Academic. 266 pp.

Frieze, I. H. 1981. Children's attributions for success and failure. In *Developmental Social Psychology,* ed. S. M. Kassin, F. X. Gibbons, pp. 51–71. Oxford: Oxford Univ. Press. 376 pp.

Frieze, I. H., Snyder, H. N. 1980. Children's beliefs about the causes of success and failure in school settings. *J. Educ. Psychol.* 72:186–96

Frodi, A. M., Lamb, M. E., Anderson, C. W. 1980. Child abuser's responses to infant smiles and cries. *Child Dev.* 51:238–41

Fuller, J. L., Thompson, W. R. 1960. *Behavior Genetics.* New York: Wiley. 396 pp.

Furman, W., Childs, M. K. 1981. *A temporal perspective on children's friendship.* Presented at Soc. Res. Child Dev., Boston

Furman, W., Rabe, D. F., Hartup, W. W. 1979. Rehabilitation of socially withdrawn preschool children through mixed-age and same-age socialization. *Child Dev.* 4:915–22

Galdston, R. 1971. Violence begins at home: The parents' center project for the study and prevention of abuse. *Am. Acad. Child Psychiatry* 10:336–50

Garbarino, J., Crouter, A. 1978. Defining the community context of parent-child relations: The correlates of child maltreatment. *Child Dev.* 49:604–16

Garbarino, J., Gilliam, G. 1980. *Understanding Abusive Families.* Lexington, Mass: Lexington Press. 263 pp.

George, C., Main, M. 1979. Social interactions of young abused children: Approach, avoidance and aggression. *Child Dev.* 50:306–18

Glass, G. V. 1978. Integrating findings: The meta-analysis of research. In *Review of Research in Education,* ed. L. Shulman, pp. 351–79. Itasca, Ill: Peacock. 399 pp.

Goetz, T. E., Dweck, C. S. 1980. Learned helplessness in social situations. *J. Pers. Soc. Psychol.* 39:246–55

Goldberg, S., Brachfield, S., DiVitto, B. 1980. Feeding, fussing and play: Parent-infant interaction in the first year as a function of prematurity and perinatal problems. See Field et al 1980

Goldberg, W. A. 1982. *Marital quality and child-mother, child-father attachments.* Presented at Int. Conf. Infant Stud., Austin, Texas

Goldman, D. B., Ross, H. S. 1978. Social skills in action: An analysis of early peer games. In *The Development of Social Understanding,* ed. J. Glick, K. A. Clarke-Stewart, pp. 177–212. New York: Gardner. 288 pp.

Goldsmith, H. H., Gottesman, I. I. 1981. Origins of variation in behavioral style: A longitudinal study of temperament in young twins. *Child Dev.* 52:91–103

Goodnow, J. J. 1979. Conventional wisdom: Everyday models of cognitive development. In *Cross-cultural Contributions to Psychology,* ed. L. H. Eckensberger, W. J. Lonner, Y. H. Poortinga. Amsterdam: Swets & Zeitlinger

Gottman, J. M. 1982. *Time-Series Analysis.* Cambridge: Cambridge Univ. Press. 400 pp.

Gottman, J. M., Bakeman, R. 1979. The sequential analysis of observational data. See Lamb et al 1979, pp. 185–206

Gottman, J. M., Ringland, J. T. 1981. The analysis of dominance and bidirectionality in social development. *Child Dev.* 52:393–412

Gray, J. A. 1971. *The Psychology of Fear and Stress.* New York: McGraw Hill. 256 pp.

Green, A. H. 1978. Psychopathology of abused children. *J. Am. Acad. Child Psychiatry* 17:92–103

Green, K. D., Forehand, R., Beck, S. J., Vosk, B. 1980. An assessment of the relationship among measures of children's social competence and children's academic achievement. *Child Dev.* 51:1149–56

Greene, D. 1976. Social perception as problem solving. In *Cognition and Social Behavior,* ed. J. S. Caroll, J. W. Payne, pp. 155–61. Hillsdale, NJ: Erlbaum. 290 pp.

Greenspan, S. 1981. Defining childhood social competence: A proposed working model. In *Advances in Special Education,* Vol. 3: *Socialization Influences on Exceptionality,* ed. B. K. Keogh, pp. 1–39. Greenwich, Conn: JAI Press. 235 pp.

Gresham, F. M., Nagle, R. J. 1980. Social skills training with children: Responsiveness to modeling and coaching as a function of peer orientation. *J. Consult. Clin. Psychol.* 18:718–29

Grossman, F. K., Eichler, L. S., Winicoff, S. A. 1980. *Pregnancy, Birth and Parent-*

hood. San Francisco: Jossey-Bass. 306 pp.

Grossman, K., Thane, K., Grossman, K. E. 1981. Maternal tactual contact of the newborn after various postpartum conditions of mother-infant contact. *Dev. Psychol.* 17:158–61

Harter, S. 1982. The perceived competence scale for children. *Child Dev.* 53:87–97

Hartup, W. W. 1983. The peer system. In *Carmichael's Manual of Child Psychology,* 4th ed., editor-in-chief P. H. Mussen. Vol. 4: *Social Development,* ed. E. M. Hetherington. New York: Wiley. In press

Hay, D. F., Ross, H. S., Goldman, D. B. 1979. Social games. In *Play and Learning,* ed. B. Sutton-Smith. New York: Gardner

Hess, R. D. 1981. Approaches to the measurement and interpretation of parent-child interaction. In *Parent-Child Interaction,* ed. R. W. Henderson, 207–33. New York: Academic. 335 pp.

Hess, R. D., Camara, K. A. 1979. Post-divorce family relationships as mediating factors in the consequences of divorce for children. *J. Soc. Issues* 35:79–96

Hetherington, E. M. 1979. Divorce: A child's perspective. *Am. Psychol.* 34:851–58

Hetherington, E. M. 1981. Children and divorce. In Hess 1981, pp. 33–58

Hetherington, E. M., Cox, M., Cox, R. 1979. Play and social interaction in children following divorce. *J. Soc. Issues* 35:26–49

Hetherington, E. M., Cox, M., Cox, R. 1982. Effects of divorce on parents and children. In *Nontraditional Families: Parenting and Child Development,* ed. M. E. Lamb, pp. 233–88. Hillsdale, NJ: Erlbaum. 364 pp.

Hiatt, S., Campos, J., Emde, R. 1979. Facial patterning and infant emotional expression: Happiness, surprise, and fear. *Child Dev.* 50:1020–35

Higgins, E. T., Fondacaro, R., McCann, C. D. 1981. Rules and roles: The "communication game" and speaker-listener processes. See Asher & Wigfield 1981, pp. 289–312

Hoffman, M. L. 1978. Toward a theory of empathic arousal and development. In *The Development of Affect,* ed. M. Lewis, L. A. Rosenblum, pp. 227–56. New York: Plenum. 426 pp.

Hoffman, M. L. 1982. The measurement of empathy. See Izard 1982, pp. 279–96

Hsu, C., Soong, W., Stigler, J. W., Hong, C., Liang, C. 1981. The temperamental

characteristics of Chinese babies. *Child Dev.* 52:1337–40

Izard, C. E. 1971. *The Face of Emotion.* New York: Appleton-Century-Crofts. 468 pp.

Izard, C. E. 1977. *Human Emotions.* New York: Plenum. 495 pp.

Izard, C. E. 1978. On the development of emotions and emotion-cognition relationships in infancy. See Hoffman 1978, pp. 389–414

Izard, C. E., ed. 1982. *Measuring Emotions in Infants and Children.* New York: Cambridge Univ. Press. 349 pp.

Jay, S., Farran, D. C. 1981. The relative efficacy of predicting IQ from mother-child interactions using ratings versus behavioral count measures. *J. Appl. Dev. Psychol.* 2:165–77

Jordan, V. B. 1980. Conserving kinship concepts: A developmental study in social cognition. *Child Dev.* 51:146–55

Kendrick, C., Dunn, J. 1980. Caring for a second baby: Effects on interaction between mother and firstborn. *Dev. Psychol.* 16:303–11

Klaus, M. H., Kennell, J. H. 1976. *Maternal-Infant Bonding.* St. Louis: Mosby

Klinnert, M. D. 1981. *Infants' use of mothers' facial expressions for regulating their own behavior.* Presented at Meet. Soc. Res. Child Dev., Boston

Klinnert, M. D., Campos, J. J., Sorce, J. F., Emde, R., Svejda, M. 1982. Emotions as behavior regulators: Social referencing in infancy. In *Emotions in Early Development,* Vol. 2: *The Emotions,* ed R. Plutchik, H. Kellerman. New York: Academic. In press

Knight, G. P. 1981. Behavioral and sociometric methods of identifying cooperators, competitors, and individualists: Support for the validity of the social orientation construct. *Dev. Psychol.* 4:430–33

Kopp, C. 1983. Development of at-risk infants. In *Carmichael's Manual of Child Psychology,* 4th ed., editor-in chief P. H. Mussen. Vol. 2: *Infancy,* ed J. J. Campos, M. Haith. New York: Wiley. In press

Krasner, L. R., Rubin, K. H. 1981. The assessment of social problem-solving skills in young children. In *Cognitive Assessment,* ed. C. Glass, M. Genest, pp. 452–76. New York: Guilford. 532 pp.

Ladd, G. W. 1981. Effectiveness of a social learning method for enhancing children's social interaction and peer acceptance. *Child Dev.* 50:171–78

Ladd, G. W., Oden, S. 1979. The relationship between peer acceptance and children's ideas about helpfulness. *Child Dev.* 2:402-7

Lamb, M. E. 1979. The effects of the social context on dyadic social interaction. See Lamb et al 1979, pp. 253-68

Lamb, M. E., ed. 1981. *The Role of the Father in Child Development.* New York: Wiley. 582 pp.

Lamb, M. E., Suomi, S. J., Stephenson, G. R. 1979. *Social Interaction Analysis: Methodological Issues.* Madison: Univ. Wisconsin Press. 320 pp.

Langlois, J. H., Downs, A. C. 1979. Peer relations as a function of physical attractiveness: The eye of the beholder or behavioral reality? *Child Dev.* 50:409-18

Langlois, J. H., Stephan, C. W. 1981. Beauty and the beast: The role of physical attractiveness in the development of peer relations and social behavior. In *Developmental Social Psychology,* ed. S. S. Brehm, S. M. Kassin, F. X. Gibbons, pp. 152-68. New York: Oxford. 376 pp.

Leiderman, P. H., Tulkin, I. R., Rosenfeld, A., eds. 1977. *Culture and Infancy: Variations in the Human Experience.* New York: Academic. 615 pp.

Le Masters, E. E. 1957. Parenthood as crisis. *Marriage Fam. Living* 19:352-55

Lerner, R. M., Palermo, M., Spiro, A. III, Nesselroade, J. R. 1982. Assessing the dimensions of temperamental individuality across the life span: The dimensions of temperament survey (DOTS). *Child Dev.* 53:149-59

Lester, B. M., Hoffman, J., Brazelton, T. B. 1982. *Spectral analysis of mother-infant interaction in term and preterm infants.* Presented at Int. Conf. Infant Stud., Austin, Texas

Lewis, M. 1982. The social network systems model. In *Review of Human Development,* ed. T. M. Field, A. Huston, H. C. Quay, L. Troll, G. E. Finley, pp. 180-214. New York: Wiley. 664 pp.

Lewis, M., Feiring, C. 1979. The child's social network: Social object, social functions and their relationship. In *The Child and Its Family,* ed. M. Lewis, L. A. Rosenblum, pp. 9-27. New York: Plenum. 304 pp.

Lewis, M., Feiring, C. 1981. Direct and indirect interactions in social relationships. In *Advances in Infancy Research,* Vol. 1, ed. L. Lipsitt, pp. 129-61. New York: Ablex. 267 pp.

Lewis, M., Michalson, L. 1983. *Children's Emotions and Moods: Theory and Measurement.* New York: Plenum. In press

Lewis, M., Schaefer, S. 1981. Peer behavior and mother-infant interaction in maltreated children. In *The Uncommon Child: The Genesis of Behavior,* Vol. 3, ed. S. M. Lewis, L. Rosenblum, pp. 193-223. New York: Plenum. 342 pp.

Maccoby, E. E., Jacklin, C. N. 1980. Sex differences in aggression: A rejoinder and reprise. *Child Dev.* 51:964-80

Main, M., Weston, D. R. 1981. The quality of the toddler's relationship to mother and to father: Related to conflict behavior and the readiness to establish new relationships. *Child Dev.* 52:932-40

Marcus, R. F., Telleen, S., Roke, E. J. 1979. Relation between cooperation and empathy in young children. *Dev. Psychol.* 15:346-47

Martin, J. A. 1981. A longitudinal study of the consequences of early mother-infant interaction: A microanalytic approach. *Monogr. Soc. Res. Child Dev.* 46(3) Ser. 190

Martin, J. A., Maccoby, E. E., Baran, K. W., Jacklin, C. N. 1981. Sequential analysis of mother-child interaction at 18 months: A comparison of microanalytic methods. *Dev. Psychol.* 2:146-157

Martini, M., Kirkpatrick, J. 1981. Early interactions in the Marquesas Islands. See Field et al 1981, pp. 189-214

Masters, J. C. 1981. Developmental psychology. *Ann. Rev. Psychol.* 32:117-51

Masters, J. C., Furman, W. 1981. Popularity, individual friendship selection, and specific peer interaction among children. *Dev. Psychol.* 3:344-50

Matas, L., Arend, R. A., Stroufe, L. A. 1978. Continuity of adaptation in the second year: The relationship between quality of attachment and later competence. *Child Dev.* 49:547-56

Matheny, A. P. Jr., Wilson, R. S., Dolan, A. B., Krans, J. A. 1981. Behavioral contrasts in twinships: Stability and patterns of differences in childhood. *Child Dev.* 52:579-88

McCartney, K., Scarr, S., Phillips, D., Grajek, S., Schwarz, J. D. 1982. Environmental differences among day care centers and their effects on children's development. See Zigler & Gordon 1982, pp. 126-51

McGillicuddy-De Lisi, A. V., Sigel, I. E., Johnson, J. E. 1979. The family as a system of mutual influences: Parental beliefs, distancing behaviors, and children's representational thinking. See Lewis & Feiring 1979, pp. 91-106

McMichael, P. 1980. Reading difficulties, behavior, and social status. *J. Educ. Psychol.* 72:76-86

Medrich, E. A., Roizen, J., Rubin, V., Buckley, S. 1982. *The Serious Business of Growing Up.* Berkeley: Univ. Calif. Press. 402 pp.

Mehrabian, A., Epstein, N. 1972. A measure of emotional empathy. *J. Pers.* 40: 523–43

Mueller, E., Vandell, D. 1979. Infant-infant interaction. See Als et al 1979, pp. 591–622

Mullhern, R. K., Passman, R. H. 1979. The child's behavioral pattern as a determinant of maternal punitiveness. *Child Dev.* 3:815–20

Mussen, P. H., ed. 1983. *Carmichael's Manual of Child Psychology.* New York: Wiley. 4th ed.

Nelson, K. 1981. Social cognition in a script framework. See Flavell 1981, pp. 97–118

Nicholls, J. G. 1978. The development of the concepts of effort and ability, perception of academic attainment, and the understanding that difficult tasks require more ability. *Child Dev.* 49: 800–14

Nicholls, J. G. 1979. Development of perception of own attainment and causal attributions for success and failure in reading. *J. Educ. Psychol.* 1:94–99

Nicholls, J. G. 1980. The development of the concept of difficulty. *Merrill-Palmer Q.* 26:271–81

Nucci, L. P., Turiel, E. 1978. Social interactions and the development of social concepts in preschool children. *Child Dev.* 49:400–7

Olweus, D. 1980. Familial and temperamental determinants of aggressive behavior in adolescent boys: A causal analysis. *Dev. Psychol.* 16:644–60

Osofsky, J. D., Osofsky, H. J. 1983. Psychological and developmental perspectives on expectant and new parenthood. In *Review of Child Development Research,* Vol. 7, ed. R. D. Parke, R. N. Emde, H. McAdoo, G. P. Sackett. Chicago: Univ. Chicago Press. In press

Oster, H. 1981. "Recognition" of emotional expression in infancy? See Campos & Stenberg 1981, pp. 85–125

Parke, R. D. 1978. Parent-infant interaction: Progress, paradigms and problems. In *Observing Behavior,* Vol. 1: *Theory and Applications in Mental Retardation,* ed. G. P. Sackett, pp. 69–95. Baltimore: Univ. Park Press. 416 pp.

Parke, R. D. 1979. Interactional designs. See Cairns 1979, pp. 15–35

Parke, R. D. 1981. *Fathers.* Cambridge, Mass: Harvard Univ. Press. 136 pp.

Parke, R. D., Hymel, S., Power, T. G., Tinsley, B. R. 1980. Fathers and risk: A hospital based model of intervention. See Sawin et al 1980, pp. 174–89

Parke, R. D., Lewis, N. G. 1981. The family in context: A multi-level interactional analysis of child abuse. See Hess 1981, pp. 169–204

Parke, R. D., Power, T. G., Gottman, J. 1979. Conceptualizing and quantifying influence patterns in the family triad. See Lamb et al 1979, pp. 231–55

Parke, R. D., Tinsley, B. R. 1982. The early environment of the at-risk infant: Expanding the social context. In *Intervention With At-Risk and Handicapped Infants: From Research to Application,* ed. D. Bricker, pp. 153–77. Baltimore: Univ. Park Press. 317 pp.

Parsons, J. D., Adler, T. F., Futterman, R., Goff, S. B., Kaczala, C. M., et al. 1982. Expectancies, values and academic behaviors. In *Assessing Achievement,* ed. J. T. Spence. San Francisco: Freeman. In press

Pascoe, J. M., Loda, F. A., Jeffries, V., Earp, J. A. 1981. The association between mothers' social support and provision of stimulation to their children. *Dev. Behav. Pediatr.* 2:15–19

Passman, R. H., Mullhern, R. K. 1977. Maternal punitiveness as affected by situational stress: An experimental analogue of child abuse. *J. Abnorm. Psychol.* 86:565–69

Pastor, D. L. 1981. The quality of mother-infant attachment and its relationship to toddlers' initial sociability with peers. *Dev. Psychol.* 17:326–35

Patterson, G. R. 1981. Mothers: The unacknowledged victims. *Monogr. Soc. Res. Child Dev.* 45(5), Serial No. 186

Patterson, G. R. 1982. *Coercive Family Processes.* Eugene: Castilia Press

Pedersen, F. A. 1981. Father influences viewed in a family context. In *The Role of the Father in Child Development,* ed. M. E. Lamb, pp. 295–317. New York: Wiley. 582 pp.

Pedersen, F. A., Anderson, B. J., Cain, R. L. Jr. 1980. Parent-infant and husband-wife interactions observed at age five months. In *The Father-Infant Relationship,* ed. F. A. Pedersen, pp. 71–86. New York: Praeger. 185 pp.

Pedersen, F. A., Zaslow, M. J., Cain, R. L., Anderson, B. J. 1981. Caesarean childbirth: Psychological implications for mothers *and* fathers. *Infant Ment. Health J.* 2:257–63

Pepler, D. J., Abramovitch, R., Corter, C. 1981. Sibling interaction in the home: A longitudinal study. *Child Dev.* 52: 1344–50

Power, T. G., Parke, R. D. 1982. Play as a context for early learning: Lab and home analyses. In *The Family as a Learning Environment,* ed. I. E. Sigel, L. M. Laosa. New York: Plenum. In press

Power, T. G., Parke, R. D. 1983. Social network factors and the transition to parenthood. *Sex Roles.* In press

Putallaz, M. 1982. Predicting children's sociometric status from their behavior. *Child Dev.* In press

Putallaz, M., Gottman, J. M. 1981. An interactional model of children's entry into peer groups. *Child Dev.* 52:986–94

Reid, J. B., Taplin, P. S., Lorber, R. 1981. A social interactional approach to the treatment of abusive families. In *Violent Behavior: Social Learning Approaches to Prediction, Management and Treatment,* ed. R. B. Stuart. New York: Brunner/Mazel

Reid, J. R., Patterson, G. R., Loeber, R. 1982. The abused child: Victim, instigator, or innocent bystander? In *Response Structure and Organization,* ed. J. Berstein, pp. 47–68. Lincoln: Univ. Nebraska Press. 267 pp.

Renshaw, P. D., Asher, S. R. 1982. Social competence and peer status: The distinction between goals and strategies. See Rubin & Ross 1982, pp. 375–95

Rest, J. R. 1983. Morality. In *Carmichael's Manual of Child Psychology,* 4th ed., editor-in-chief P. H. Mussen, Vol. 3: *Cognitive Development,* ed. J. H. Flavell, E. Markman. New York: Wiley. In press

Rholes, W. S., Blackwell, J., Jordan, C., Walter, C. 1980. A developmental study of learned helplessness. *Dev. Psychol.* 16:616–24

Rode, S. S., Chang, P-N., Fisch, R. O., Sroufe, L. A. 1981. Attachment patterns of infants separated at birth. *Dev. Psychol.* 17:188–91

Ross, H. S. 1982. The establishment of social games among toddlers. *Dev. Psychol.* 18:509–18

Rothbart, M. K. 1980. *Longitudinal home observation of infant temperament.* Presented at Int. Conf. Infant Stud., New Haven

Rothbart, M. K. 1982. Measurement of temperament in infancy. *Child Dev.* In press

Rothbart, M. K., Derryberry, D. 1981. Development of individual differences in temperament. In *Advances in Developmental Psychology,* ed. M. E. Lamb, A.

L. Brown, pp. 37–86. Hillsdale, NJ: Erlbaum. 248 pp.

Rubin, K. H. 1982. Nonsocial play in preschoolers: Necessary evil? *Child Dev.* 53:651–57

Rubin, K. H., Ross, H. S., eds. 1982. *Peer Relationships and Social Skills in Childhood.* New York: Springer. In press

Ruble, D. N., Feldman, N. S., Higgins, E. T., Karlovac, M. 1979. Focus of causality and the use of information in the development of causal attributions. *J. Pers.* 47:596–614

Russell, C. S. 1974. Transition to parenthood: Problems and gratifications. *J. Marriage Fam.* 36:294–301

Rutter, M. 1982. Social-emotional consequences of day care for preschool children. See Zigler & Gordon 1982, pp. 3–32

Sackett, G. P., ed. 1978. *Observing Behavior,* Vol 2: *Data Collection and Analysis Methods.* Baltimore: Univ. Park Press. 110 pp.

Sackett, G. P. 1979. The lag sequential analysis of contingency and cyclicity in behavioral interaction research. See Als et al 1979, pp. 623–49

Sagar, H. A., Schofield, J. W. 1980. Racial and behavioral cues in black and white children's perceptions of ambiguously aggressive acts. *J. Pers. Soc. Psychol.* 39:590–98

Sameroff, A. J. 1980. Issues in reproductive and caretaking risk: Review and current status. See Sawin et al 1980, pp. 343–59

Sameroff, A. J., Chandler, M. J. 1975. Reproductive risk and the continuum of caretaking casualty. In *Review of Child Development Research,* ed. F. D. Horowitz, 4:187–244. Chicago: Univ. Chicago Press. 579 pp.

Sameroff, A. J., Seifer, R., Elias, P. K. 1982. Sociocultural variability in infant temperament ratings. *Child Dev.* 53:164–73

Santrock, J. W., Warshak, R. A. 1979. Father custody and social development in boys and girls. *J. Soc. Issues* 35:112–25

Santrock, J. W., Warshak, R. A., Lindbergh, C., Meadows, L. 1982. Children's and parents' observed social behavior in stepfather families. *Child Dev.* 53: 472–80

Sawin, D. B. 1979. *Assessing empathy in children: A search for an elusive construct.* Presented at bien. meet. Soc. Res. Child Dev., San Francisco

Sawin, D. B., Hawkins, R. C., Walker, L. O., Penticuff, J. H., eds. 1980. *Exceptional Infant: Psychosocial Risks in Infant-Environment Transitions,* Vol. 4. New York: Brunner/Mazel. 461 pp.

Schaffer, H. R. 1977. *Mothering.* Cambridge: Harvard Univ. Press

Schofield, J. W. 1982. *Black and White in Schools: Trust, Tension, or Tolerance?* New York: Praeger. In press

Schofield, J. W., Francis, W. D. 1982. An observational study of peer interaction in racially mixed "accelerated" classrooms. *J. Educ. Psychol.* In press

Sears, R. S. 1975. Your ancients revisited: A history of child development. In *Review of Child Development Research,* ed. E. M. Hetherington, 5:1–73. Chicago: Univ. Chicago Press. 615 pp.

Selman, R. L. 1980. *The Growth of Interpersonal Understanding: Developmental and Clinical Analyses.* New York: Academic. 343 pp.

Siegal, M. 1981. Children's perceptions of adult economic needs. *Child Dev.* 52:379–82

Singleton, L. C., Asher, S. R. 1979. Racial integration and children's peer preferences: An investigation of developmental and cohort differences. *Child Dev.* 50:936–41

Smetana, J. G. 1981. Preschool children's conceptions of moral and social rules. *Child Dev.* 52:1333–36

Smith, M. L., Glass, G. 1980. Meta-analysis of research on class size and its research to attitudes and instruction. *Am. Educ. Res. J.* 17:419–33

Smith, P. K., Connolly, K. J. 1980. *The Ecology of Preschool Behaviour.* Cambridge: Cambridge Univ. Press. 383 pp.

Sorce, J. F., Emde, R. N., Frank, M. 1982. Maternal referencing in normal and Down's syndrome infants: A longitudinal study. In *The Development of Attachment and Affiliative Systems,* ed. R. N. Emde, R. Harmon. New York: Plenum. In press

Sorce, J. F., Emde, R. N., Klinnert, M. D., Campos, J. J. 1981. *Maternal emotional signaling: Its effect on the visual cliff behavior of one-year-olds.* Presented at bien. meet. Soc. Res. Child Dev., Boston

Sroufe, L. A. 1979. The coherence of individual development: Early care, attachment, and subsequent developmental issues. *Am. Psychol.* 34:834–41

Sroufe, L. A. 1982. Infant caregiver attachment and patterns of adaptation in preschool: The roots of maladaptation and competence. *Minn. Symp. Child Psychol.* In press

Starr, R. H. Jr. 1979. Child abuse. *Am. Psychol.* 34:872–78

Stein, N. L., Goldman, S. R. 1981. Children's knowledge about social situations: From causes to consequences. See Asher & Renshaw 1981, pp. 297–321

Steinberg, L. D., Catalano, R., Dooley, P. 1981. Economic antecedents of child abuse and neglect. *Child Dev.* 52: 975–85

Stenberg, C., Campos, J. J., Emde, R. N. 1982. The facial expression of anger in seven-month-olds. *Child Dev.* In press

Stern, D. 1977. *The First Relationship.* Cambridge: Harvard Univ. Press. 149 pp.

Strain, P., ed. 1981. *The Utilization of Classroom Peers as Behavior Change Agents.* New York: Plenum. 366 pp.

Svejda, M. J., Campos, J. J., Emde, R. N. 1980. Mother-infant "bonding": Failure to generalize. *Child Dev.* 51:775–79

Taylor, A. R. 1982. Social competence and interpersonal relations between retarded and nonretarded children. In *International Review of Research in Mental Retardation,* Vol. 11, ed. N. R. Ellis. New York: Academic. In press

Taylor, P. M., ed. 1980. *Parent-Infant Relationships.* New York: Grune & Stratton. 371 pp.

Thomas, A., Chess, S. 1977. *Temperament and Development.* New York: Brunner/Mazel. 270 pp.

Thomas, A., Chess, S., Birch, H. G. 1968. *Temperament and Behavior Disorders in Children.* New York: New York Univ. Press. 309 pp.

Thomas, E. A. C., Martin, J. A. 1976. Analyses of parent-infant interaction. *Psychol. Rev.* 83:141–56

Thompson, R. A., Lamb, M. E., Estes, D. 1982. Stability of infant-mother attachment and its relationship to changing life circumstances in an unselected middle-class sample. *Child Dev.* 53:144–48

Tieger, T. 1980. On the biological basis of sex differences in aggression. *Child Dev.* 51:943–63

Tinsley, B. R., Parke, R. D. 1983. Grandparents as support and socialization agents. In *Beyond the Dyad,* ed. M. Lewis. New York: Plenum. In press

Tronick, E., ed. 1982. *Social Interchange in Infancy: Affect, Cognition, and Communication.* Baltimore: Univ. Park Press. 224 pp.

Tronick, E. Z., Als, H., Brazelton, T. B. 1980. Monadic phases: A structural descriptive analysis of infant-mother face to face interaction. *Merrill-Palmer Q.* 26:3–24

Unger, D. G., Powell, D. R. 1980. Supporting families under stress: The role of social networks. *Family Relat.* 29:566–74

Urbain, E. S., Kendall, P. C. 1980. Review of social-cognitive problem-solving interventions with children. *Psychol. Bull.* 88:109–43

Vandell, D. L., Wilson, K. S., Buchanan, N. R. 1980. Peer interaction in the first year of life: An examination of its structure, content, and sensitivity to toys. *Child Dev.* 51:481–88

Vasta, R., Copitch, P. 1981. Simulating conditions of child abuse in the laboratory. *Child Dev.* 52:164–70

Vaughn, B. E., Egeland, B., Sroufe, L. A., Waters, E. 1979. Individual differences in infant-mother attachment at twelve and eighteen months: Stability and change in families under stress. *Child Dev.* 50:971–75

Vaughn, B. E., Langlois, J. H. 1982. Physical attractiveness as a correlate of peer status and social competence in preschool children. *Dev. Psychol.* In press

Vaughn, B. E., Waters, E. 1981. Attention structure, sociometric status, and dominance: Interrelations, behavioral correlates, and relationships to social competence. *Dev. Psychol.* 17:275–88

Vincent, J. P., Cook, N. I., Messerly, L. 1980. A social learning analysis of couples during the second postnatal month. *Am. J. Fam. Ther.* 8:49–68

Wahler, R. G. 1980. Parent insularity as a determinant of generalization success in family treatment. In *The Ecosystem of the "Sick" Child,* ed. S. Slazinger, J. Antrobus, J. Glick, pp. 187–99. New York: Academic. 308 pp.

Wallerstein, J. S., Kelly, J. B. 1981. *Surviving the Breakup.* New York: Basic Books. 341 pp.

Waters, E. 1978. The reliability and stability of individual differences in infant-mother attachment. *Child Dev.* 49: 483–94

Waters, E., Vaughn, B. E., Egeland, B. R. 1980. Individual differences in infant-mother attachment relationships at age one: Antecedents in neonatal behavior in an urban, economically disadvantaged sample. *Child Dev.* 51:208–16

Waters, E., Wippman, J., Sroufe, L. A. 1979. Attachment, positive affect, and competence in the peer group: Two studies in construct validation. *Child Dev.* 3: 821–29

Watson, M. W., Fischer, K. W. 1980. Development of social roles in elicited and spontaneous behavior during the preschool years. *Dev. Psychol.* 16:483–94

Weiner, B. 1979. A theory of motivation for some classroom experiences. *J. Educ. Psychol.* 1:3–25

Weiner, B., Frieze, I., Kukla, A., Reed, A., Rest, S., Rosenbaum, L. 1971. *Perceiving the Causes of Success and Failure.* Morristown, NJ: Gen. Learn. Corp.

Weston, D. R., Turiel, E. 1980. Act-rule relations: Children's concepts of social rules. *Dev. Psychol.* 16:417–24

Wheeler, V. A., Ladd, G. W. 1982. Assessment of children's self-efficacy for social interactions with peers. *Dev. Psychol.* In press

Yarrow, M. R., Waxler, C. Z. 1979. Observing interaction: A confrontation with methodology. See Cairn 1979, pp. 37–66

Yogman, M. W. 1982. Development of the father-infant relationship. In *Theory and Research in Behavioral Pediatrics,* Vol. 1, ed. H. Fitzgerald, B. Lester, M. W. Yogman. New York: Plenum. 530 pp.

Youniss, J. 1980. *Parents and Peers in Social Development: A Sullivan-Piaget Perspective.* Chicago: Univ. Chicago Press. 301 pp.

Zajonc, R. B. 1980. Feeling and thinking: Preferences need no inferences. *Am. Psychol.* 35:151–75

Zigler, E. F., Gordon, E. W., eds. 1982. *Day Care: Scientific and Social Policy Issues* Boston: Auburn House. 515 pp.

NOTE ADDED IN PROOF   Word has just been received that the publication referred to as *Carmichael's Manual of Child Psychology* (Paul Mussen, Editor-in-Chief) has been retitled *Handbook of Child Psychology.*

Ann. Rev. Psychol. 1983. 34:511–42
Copyright © 1983 by Annual Reviews Inc. All rights reserved

SOCIAL INFERENCE

Reid Hastie

Department of Psychology, Northwestern University, Evanston, Illinois 60201

CONTENTS

INTRODUCTION

This is a review of research published during 1979, 1980, and 1981 on the psychology of social inference. A standard dictionary defines "inference" as: "1. The act or process of inferring. 2. Something inferred; a conclusion based on a premise" (*American Heritage,* 1969). A more technical source provides the definition "Inference. Derivation of a proposition (the conclusion) from a set of other propositions (the premises). When the inference is acceptable the premises afford good reasons to assert, or render certain, the conclusion" (Brody 1967). Thus, an inference has three components: (*a*) a set of premises, usually represented as sentences, verbal propositions, or

0066-4308/83/0201-0511$02.00

formal propositions; (*b*) a conclusion, represented in the same format; (*c*) rules, principles, templates, or procedures which connect the premises to the conclusion in a "reasonable" manner.

One important function served by philosophical analysis in the development of psychological theory is as a source of optimal or normative inference models (e.g. Quine 1970) and hypotheses about everyday reasoning (e.g. Cohen & Nagel 1934). Many psychological theories of inference start with normative models from logic (e.g. Braine 1978) or mathematics (Edwards 1968) and then alter the inference rules and add principles of inference processing (e.g. specifying the order in which rules will be invoked, the form in which premises and conclusions will be represented, and the limits on processing and representation capacities throughout the inference process).

A second important function of philosophical analysis might be to evaluate psychological theories for completeness and consistency (Suppes 1960). However, this type of evaluation has rarely been performed at all in social psychology, and it has usually come from within the field (e.g. Harris 1976).

Taxonomies of Inference Types

Philosophers have traditionally divided inferences into two general forms, induction and deduction, although there are several problematic forms (Peirce's abduction, Quine's eduction, etc). A second general taxonomy that distinguishes among logical, probabilistic, and plausible inference forms has been cited in the cognitive science literature (e.g. Hutchins 1981). Psychologists concerned with text processing have suggested additional inference taxonomies that are useful in understanding sentence and narrative story comprehension. For example, Nicholas & Trabasso (1980) distinguish among lexical, spatiotemporal, extrapolative, and evaluative inferences. We will divide the present review into four topics according to inference content: inferences involving category membership relations, causal relations, moral imperatives, and structural balance relations. Many relevant inference types will not be covered because of length requirements on chapters in the *Annual Review of Psychology*.

Systematic Theoretical Positions

Three approaches to social inference can be identified as major systematic theoretical positions, each providing a unified view of research methodology and a theoretical vocabulary that spans several judgment tasks: the Information Integration Theory approach (N. H. Anderson 1981), the judgment heuristics approach (Nisbett & Ross 1980), and the information processing approach (Wyer & Carlston 1979).

Information Integration Theory includes theoretical analyses of stimulus selection and valuation (psychophysical relations), information integration (cognitive algebra), and response generation (psychomotor laws). The focus of theoretical and empirical work has been on the integration stage, and a system of simple algebraic rules (adding, multiplying, averaging, etc) provides a parsimonious, precise, and general analysis of many social inference phenomena. The basic psychological model, with its emphasis on numerical stimulus representation and processing rules, is paired with a systematic and practical (functional) measurement theory.

Information Integration Theory is the most complete and coherent theoretical position in social psychology, and it is also the most firmly grounded in empirical research. The basic psychological mechanisms are stated concisely as general algebraic equations that can be clearly related to other models expressed in the same "language," as well as to more informal theoretical analyses. The general framework of the theory includes the molar processing stages that must be part of any cognitive model. Thus, the theoretical and methodological solutions presented by Information Integration Theory define questions that must be addressed by any adequate cognitive theory. This is a very sobering implication for social psychologists who do not acknowledge measurement, stimulus valuation, identifiability, and process model sufficiency problems, much less propose solutions to them.

There are limitations on current Information Integration Theory approaches (N. H. Anderson 1981) that derive from the fact that the theoretical structure is concerned with molar processing stages. On one hand, this is an advantage in that considerable theoretical progress can be made at a global level, leaving finer processing questions for solution when more detailed process models are available. However, this top-down approach frustrates many researchers, especially those who are interested in more molecular processing questions. For example: In what order (in real time) are integration operations performed when impression formation, causal attribution, or distributive justice judgments are "calculated"? What mental operations correspond to the adjustment of weights, multiplying, and adding operations in averaging integration? What process and representation principles apply when verbal (e.g. an adjective) or visual (e.g. a photograph) stimuli are translated into quantitative values? A second class of limits on the approach derives from the current lack of theoretical principles that prescribe which alternative processing rules, within the general model, will characterize integration in specific tasks. For example, the Information Integration approach does not "predict" that an averaging rule will describe the integration of trait adjectives to yield a likeability judgment. Rather, the approach allows the researcher to identify the integration rule empirically by comparing alternate rules (adding, multiplying, or averaging rules) once the proper experiments have been conducted. We should note that Anderson and his colleagues have identified these limitations and proposed reasonable solutions to many of them.

The second major theoretical position in research on social inference is exemplified by information processing models drawn from traditional cognitive psychology (Bower 1975, Hastie & Carlston 1980). Wyer & Carlston (1979) provide the clearest and most general exposition of this approach to social cognition. The information processing approach, like Information Integration Theory, begins with a molar stage framework, but it goes into finer detail by specifying a variety of representational formats and structures, memory systems, and elementary information processes. A core of basic concepts (e.g. sensory register, short-term memory, long-term memory) that are common to the many theorists subscribing to this approach has begun to develop, although there is still considerable laboratory-to-laboratory variation and no uniform measurement theory (e.g. Estes 1979).

The Information processing approach to social cognition is also limited. First, the approach outlines a general theory of the mind, but few exact predictions for behavior in specific task environments can be derived from the basic theoretical principles. Rather, specific classes of models must be defined, using the general theoretical concepts, and these task-specific models can be tested competitively (e.g. J. R. Anderson 1976, Newell & Simon 1972). Second, the general theory is not committed to a uniform representational calculus, and many implementations of task-specific models are stated as verbal principles. This means that the derivation of unequivocal, precise empirical hypotheses may be difficult. The solution to the derivation problem advocated by many theorists is the use of computer program simulation models (Abelson 1968, J. R. Anderson 1980).

The third general theoretical approach to social inference is based on the judgment heuristics introduced by Tversky & Kahneman (1974, Kahneman et al 1982). Four Judgment heuristics—availability, representativeness, anchoring and adjustment, and simulation—are hypothesized to account for a great range of judgment phenomena, including many examples of (allegedly) irrational behavior (Nisbett & Ross 1980). Context-dependent inference schemata (knowledge structures) are also cited to account for additional inference phenomena (cf Schank & Abelson 1977, Abelson 1981). Although current versions of the judgment heuristics approach are relatively incomplete and unrigorous as psychological models, they have stimulated a flood of intriguing research.

The major limits on the judgment heuristic approach derive from its newness. Basic research on the properties of the heuristic mechanisms, the conditions that invoke them, and the types of tasks in which they occur has only just begun. Furthermore, although the heuristics have enormous intuitive plausibility and after-the-fact explanatory power, they lack predictive power. Falsifiable empirical predictions from this approach are almost non-existent in the social literature.

CATEGORY MEMBERSHIP INFERENCES

Philosophical analyses concerned with reasoning about the attributes of categories can be divided into models for induction, reasoning from specific instances to generic category characteristics, and deduction, reasoning from general category characteristics to specific instance properties. Recently, philosophical analyses of induction have concentrated on the logic of statistical inference (e.g. Hacking 1965). Some social psychologists (Nisbett & Ross 1980) have attempted to compare the behavior of human subjects to performance prescribed by normative statistical models for the experimental tasks.

A sound argument that humans have deviated from a normative performance standard depends on several subarguments. First, a normative model specifying optimal performance that is appropriate to the subject's task must be identified. Second, the application of the model to the task must be proper, with model inputs and outputs correctly mapped onto information in the task environment and the subject's responses. Third, the subject must define the task in the same manner as the researcher. For example, the subject's goals must match the goals the experimenter uses when applying the normative model to calculate an optimal performance strategy. These three conditions are exceedingly difficult to satisfy in the complex, information-rich environments studied by social psychologists. There is considerable disagreement on the first two issues when probability theory is the source of normative analyses (Stich & Nisbett 1980, Cohen 1981), and there has been little attention to the issue of subject-researcher agreement on task definition (Miller & Cantor 1982). Our opinion is that none of the applications to social judgment provide compelling arguments that human reasoning deviates from normative model prescriptions. Nonetheless, it also seems clear that certain aspects of statistical logic are not appreciated by subjects in social judgment tasks.

Collins (1978) suggested a framework within which to view categorical inference and the validity of inductive and uncertain deductive inference. In his work, three components are specified: (a) a memory representation which encodes structural and statistical properties; (b) inference processes; and (c) conditions which affect the certainty of each type of inferential conclusion, and that relate characteristics of the memory representation to characteristics of an observation. For example, an inductive generalization is more certain when variance among category members is small, when sample size is large, and so forth. As yet, Collins's theory of plausible reasoning is not complete in specifying conditions that affect inference certainty. Therefore, its role as a normative model is also not clear. However, it serves, at a minimum, as an outline of the issues that any adequate theory of inference must address.

Member-to-Category Inferences

Several reports of research studying inferences about a population or about generic category from information about one instance or several instances appeared during the period under review. An experiment by Hamill et al (1980) provided a demonstration that subjects are insensitive to characteristics of sampling when drawing general conclusions about the attributes of a population such as an occupation group. Zuckerman & Mann (1979) report an important demonstration that the extent to which a perceiver will generalize from one actor's behavior (to other people, stimuli, or occasions) depends on the causal explanation for the original behavior. Generalization to other people (consensus or baserate generalization) was relatively insensitive to the causal attribution compared to generalization across stimuli or occasions.

Quattrone & Jones (1980) also studied the process whereby a perceiver reasons from information about a single instance to a conclusion about population characteristics (in their case, undergraduate student bodies). They concluded that generalization from the instance to the group only occurred under certain conditions: when the group was a relatively unfamiliar outgroup and when the subject had no clear preconceptions concerning attributes of the group. Quattrone & Jones made interesting suggestions about the manner in which the perceived homogeneity or heterogeneity of a social group would facilitate or impede generalization from an instance, although they note that no strong empirical evidence for this mediator was obtained. A companion experiment by Jones et al (1981) also found that generalization concerning an outgroup, given information about one of its members, is more facile than generalization concerning an ingroup. Again, no clear evidence for the perceived homogeneity-heterogeneity of the group as a mediator was provided.

Research on induction involving two (or more) categories or populations has also been reported. Crocker (1981) has reviewed the developing literature on perception of covariation between attributes such as typical behavior and group membership. She has also emphasized the difficulty of using statistical models (e.g. the Neuman-Pearson correlation coefficient) to draw conclusions about human failings in judgment. Two recent experiments (Hamilton & Rose 1980, McArthur & Friedman 1980) study subjects' tendencies to induce correlations between group membership (e.g. race or occupation group) and typical behavior (e.g. socially desirable or socially undesirable) when there was no systematic variation in the stimulus materials (zero correlation). In both series of experiments evidence was found that subjects' preconceptions concerning characteristics of the groups influenced judgments of covariation. In both cases, deduction-like processes appeared to lead subjects to see correlations between racial category, occupation group, age category, or gender category and desirable or undesirable behaviors. Peterson (1980) makes a point concerning covariation perception in a nonsocial judgment task (perceiving contingencies between adjacent trials in a sequence of light bulb flashes) that may have implications for the illusory correlation tasks. Peterson concluded that even in an artificial, nonsocial judgment task subjects do not conceive of relationships among classes of events as probabilistic but rather as deterministic. This deterministic model for the sequence generation process prevents subjects from (correctly) perceiving noncontingencies between adjacent light bulb flashes. If we accept the implications of Peterson's result for the illusory correlation task, it would seem that discovery of the "models" (probabilistic, deterministic, etc) that subjects have of the relationship between category membership and behavior should be a prime focus in future research on categorical reasoning.

Category-to-Member Inferences

Several experiments on the reasoning of subjects from population characteristics to member characteristics have shown the influence of statistical properties of the population on inferences. Linville & Jones (1980) studied the influence of information about a member's racial group on inferences about a law school applicant's evaluation. These researchers concluded that an ingroup (to which the judge was also a member) was perceived as more heterogeneous than an outgroup and that evaluations reflected heterogeneity in that more moderate evaluations were generated for the members of more heterogeneous groups. This conclusion needs to be qualified by the fact that all subjects were whites judging white or black law-school applicants; thus, the result may not reflect a general ingroup-outgroup difference, but rather a white-group versus black-group difference (e.g. it is plausible that the white racial group is more heterogeneous given that it is almost ten times larger than the black racial group). Locksley et al (1980b) also studied ingroup-outgroup evaluations for artificial, laboratory groups created by an arbitrary lottery. Even in this minimal ingroup-outgroup situation, subjects made inferences about personal characteristics of the members of their own and other groups on the basis of only group membership information. Locksley et al found that negative evaluations were associated with outgroups and positive evaluations with ingroups, but that this discrimination depended on the actual rewardingness (in terms of monetary payoffs) of the experimental ingroups and outgroups. Pettigrew (1979) has provided a somber comment on ingroup-outgroup perceptions by speculating that an "ultimate attribution error" may occur when an outgroup member performs a negative act such that a negative act is attributed to the disposition of the actor or even to the actor's genetic characteristics.

A virtual industry has developed to identify the conditions under which perceivers are influenced by baserate or consensus information when making category classification judgments (e.g. Is Fred an engineer?) or estimating magnitudes (e.g. How many days will it take to write an *Annual Review* chapter?). Kahneman & Tversky (1972) showed that subjects' category membership judgments were relatively insensitive to baserate information when any case-specific information was also presented. Many investigators have been able to demonstrate that baserate information does influence judgments (as did Kahneman & Tversky) but that the degree of influence is critically dependent on characteristics of the judgment task or problem statement and that baserate information has less impact than the normative Bayesian model requires (Manis et al 1980, 1981).

Locksley et al (1980a) have reported an apparent non-use of baserate information in reasoning about member attributes given information about gender category and individual behavior. Based on an application of Bayes's theorem, Locksley et al concluded that gender category preconceptions had no influence on judgments of individuals when any case-specific information was also presented. Unfortunately, the Bayes's theorem analysis is inconclusive; the authors' analysis was based on mean data for groups of subjects, which is not appropriate to test their hypothesis concerning individual subjects' judgments.

Several researchers have concluded that the use of baserate information depends on its relationship (e.g. causal versus noncausal) to the to-be-judged outcome (Bar-Hillel 1980a, Tversky & Kahneman 1980); the sample size (Kassin 1979a); the source (Kassin 1979b, Kulik & Taylor 1980) of the baserate information; or other contextual factors. Others (Ginosar & Trope 1980) have argued that baserate information will be used only when there is a fundamental reconceptualization of the judgment task. One theoretical question that remains open concerns the manner in which baserate information will be processed under those conditions where it does influence judgments. For example, in research by Bar-Hillel involving judgments of a traffic accident, when baserate information is labeled causally relevant it has a sizeable impact on the judgment; otherwise there is little impact. Bar-Hillel & Fischhoff (1981), following Kahneman & Tversky, suggest that the representativeness heuristic explains the influence of case-specific information, but they do not discuss the manner in which baserate information is used. However, to our knowledge no explicit mechanism has been suggested to describe the judgment process (Bayesian probability revision, averaging, anchoring and adjustment, etc), that utilizes baserate information.

Comment on Probabilistic Inferences

Research on probabilistic reasoning about social categories and their members has been primarily phenomena-driven. Many practically important and theoretically provocative phenomena have been identified. The judgment heuristics approach (Nisbett & Ross 1980) has been a major source of insights concerning the existence of judgment phenomena. However, as yet no general process models have been proposed that account for several types of phenomena or yield precise theoretical predictions.

One weakness of the heuristics approach is the lack of research on the nature and instigating conditions of the basic heuristic mechanisms. The papers by Beyth-Marom & Fischhoff (1977) on availability and by Bar-Hillel (1980a,b) on representativeness virtually exhaust the literature since the original work by Kahneman and Tversky. These papers show that we do not yet have clear conceptions of the fundamental heuristic mechanisms, and without clarity on the basic mechanisms, unequivocal theoretical prediction and testing is impossible. Furthermore, research on the conditions that elicit processing by one heuristic or another is almost nonexistent. We know of only one experiment (Tversky & Kahneman 1974, study 7) that attempts to identify conditions under which the availability or representativeness heuristic will be selected. Without principles to predict heuristic use or to identify heuristic use, tests of theories based on the heuristic mechanisms will be difficult or impossible.

We can indicate some of the problems that must be addressed by an adequate process model. First, clear theoretical principles must be stated for the representation of categories and members. Are they theoretically structured as lists of features (necessary and sufficient or prototypical), coordinates of a space, templates, or what? What types of statistical information (central tendency, heterogeneity, numerosity, baserate) are represented with a category and its members and in what format? Second, what processes operate on these types of information, how are they retrieved from memory? What comparisons, transformations, and restructuring operations are permitted? We have cited Collins's (1978) fragments of a theory of inference as one of the most useful outlines for a process model. Rips (1975) provides an illustration of a theoretical analysis in which structure and process principles are combined to yield predictions for the judged certainty of inductive inferences.

Social Stereotypes

Most of the major developments, in the social psychology of stereotype inferences during the period under review are presented in chapters in a volume edited by Hamilton (1981). Six research programs are summarized that attempt to apply principles from (nonsocial) cognitive psychology to elucidate complex social stereotyping phenomena. Furthermore, many important phenomena that doubtless occur in real world reasoning as well as in the laboratory tasks under study are captured under controlled, repeatable laboratory conditions.

There are two general characteristics of more mature cognitive theories, such as information processing and algebraic models, that are missing from contributions in the Hamilton volume. First, only the chapters by Ashmore (1981) and Ashmore & Del Boca (1981) deal rigorously with the representation of stereotype concepts. They provide a general conceptual definition of stereotype "as a set of beliefs about the personal attributes of a group of people." They operationalize the definition using personality trait adjectives as attributes and Euclidian (multidimensional scaling) and hierarchical geometric models of the relationships among traits attributed to social categories (gender categories in their examples). Ashmore and Del Boca discuss many of the limits on their geometric models, and it is obvious that most of the phenomena discussed and identified in other chapters in the volume would require more elaborate representation models. Until the representation issue is addressed and clear commitments are made to representations and their contents, no unequivocal predictions can be made concerning processing of stereotype information (cf Smith & Medin 1981).

A second weakness of the theoretical analyses included in the volume derives from the problem of integrating the implications of many molecular hypotheses concerning stereotype reasoning to yield unequivocal and consistent predictions for behavior. The theoretical analyses can all be summarized as lists of principles that are relevant to stereotype reasoning. These lists range from a crisp 7 in the Taylor (1981) chapter to at least 20 in the Wilder (1981) chapter. An example of one of the principles is, "when stereotyping categorization of individuals into groups occurs, within group differences will be minimized and between group differences will be exaggerated." Of course, there is nothing objectionable about this principle or about the procedure of starting a general theory of stereotyping inferences from a set of defensible principles. However, theoretical derivation and testing become unwieldy when several verbal principles are combined and their joint implications are assessed. The difficulty of assessing the joint implications of several principles is increased by the lack of explicit commitments to representational structures. This criticism is not a rejection of the research reported in the Hamilton volume; rather, it is an admonition to social psychologists to move beyond relatively loose verbal statements to more precise formulations that will facilitate theoretical reasoning.

Syllogistic Deduction

One of the oldest formal logical systems, Aristotle's syllogism, was designed to handle categorical reasoning and modern logic provides a number of formal sentential and predicate calculuses which accept quantified or unquantified categorical terms as arguments. Intuitively, there are a number of inference types that are typical of categorical or set membership reasoning that appear in social category inferences. Some of these examples include "synonymic deductions": John is the Chief of Police, the Chief of Police is a Baptist, therefore John is a Baptist. Reasoning by mutual exclusivity: John is a man, therefore John is not a woman. Reasoning by set inclusion: John is a policeman, policemen have guns, therefore John has a gun. Recently, cognitive psychologists have developed a number of process models to accout for deductive reasoning; J. R. Anderson (1980), and Revlin & Mayer (1978) provide useful introductions to this literature.

In 1960 McGuire proposed a process model for syllogistic reasoning that combined elements of Aristotle's analysis with elementary probability theory. Wyer & Goldberg (1970) and Wyer et al (1979) have extended McGuire's theoretical and empirical work on this model. O'Malley & Thistlethwaite (1980) varied the order in which the terms of a syllogism were presented (embedded among dozens of other syllogisms) and used reaction times and ratings to test hypotheses about the basis for the Socratic effect, whereby an individual's evaluation of the terms of a syllogism moved toward greater consistency (defined by the McGuire syllogism-probability theory model) after they have been activated in an initial rating session. The authors concluded that the increase in consistency could be explained with reference to inferences from premises to conclusions in the spirit of the McGuire process model. Wyer & Hartwick summarize research in their own laboratory and reach a conclusion consistent with the O'Malley & Thistlethwaite inference model.

CAUSAL INFERENCES

Several recent developments in the philosophy of causation have important implications for the psychology of causal reasoning, but they are still uncited in the social literature. These developments include a clarification of the conditional relations involved in causal reasoning, introduction of the concept of causal field, and development of the role of regularity in causal reasoning and causal schema induction (J. Anderson 1938, Hart & Honore 1959, Suppes 1970, Mackie 1974). Mackie (1974) has made the major contribution, and we will present a short synopsis of some of his conclusions concerning the perception of causation (his volume also includes an analysis of causation "in the objects"). Unlike some analysts, Mackie considers singular causal events, arguing that unique occurrences are perceived causally and that causal reasoning is not restricted to general cases. Mackie also argues that there is a unity to the perception of causal relations that applies both to physical causation (e.g. a stone falls on a chestnut and causes it to flatten) and to interpersonal causal relations (e.g. one person causes another person to take an action). The focus of his analysis is on the differences between temporal sequences of events that are labeled causal and sequences that are not labeled causal. One illustration is the analysis of a constellation of events that causes a house to catch on fire (p. 37). There are three events that combined to cause the fire: the flow of electric current through wire, decayed insulation on the wire, and the presence of flammable material near the decayed spot in the wire. Other associated factors are relevant to the cause-effect relationships, for instance, the presence of oxygen in the air, and the lack of a fire-preventing sprinkler system, but these factors are not perceived as causes.

Mackie claims that four general conditions must be fulfilled for the perception of a causal relation between an event X and an event Y. 1. Event X and event Y are distinct. 2. Event X occurred and event Y occurred. 3. In the circumstances, Y would not have occurred if X had not occurred. 4. X was causally Prior to Y. We can explicate Mackie's theory by examining each of these conditions with reference to his house fire example. First, the events X and Y are taken as states of the world (or changes in states of the world) with the concept of an event as an unanalyzed primitive in the analysis. These events can include quantitatively specified conditions (e.g. the flow of electricity with a certain level of voltage and amperage) as well as the absence of conditions (e.g. the absence of insulation on the wire or the absence of a sprinkler system).

Second, the notion of cause is defined with reference to contrary-to-fact conditionals (if S had not occurred, then . . .) Mackie goes further with his discussion of contrary-to-fact conditionals and suggests that reasoning with conditionals is dependent on a human capacity for imaginative transfer, the ability to picture the actual causal field while denying the occurrence of an antecedent. In Mackie's words, "The key item is a picture of what would have happened if things had been otherwise, and this is borrowed from some experience where things were otherwise. It is a contrast case rather than the repetition of like instances that contributes most to our primitive concept of causation" (Mackie 1974, p. 57).

Third, and perhaps most important, Mackie develops the notion of causal field (introduced by J. Anderson 1938). This notion is referenced by the expression "in the circumstances."

> Causal statements are commonly made in some context, against a background which includes the assumption of some causal field ... Both cause and effect are seen as differences within a field; anything that is a part of the assumed (but commonly unstated) description of the field itself will then be automatically ruled out as a candidate for the role of cause ... What is said to be caused, then, is not just an event, but an event in a certain field, and some "conditions" can be set aside as not causing this event in this field simply because they are part of the chosen field, though if a different field were chosen, in other words if a different causal question were being asked, one of those conditions might well be said to cause this event in that other field (Mackie 1974, pp. 34–35).

In our illustration of the house fire, some conditions such as the presence of oxygen in the air, and the lack of a sprinkler system, could be taken to be part of an assumed causal field. Although they are necessary conditions for the fire they would not be perceived as causes. In the full text, Mackie actually distinguished among three types of factors or events with reference to a perceiver. (a) Candidates for causes that are insufficient but nonredundant (necessary) parts of a constellation of factors that is an unnecessary but sufficient condition to produce the effect. In our house fire example, the electric current passing through the wire, the frayed insulation, and the presence of flammable material are all candidates for these insufficient nonredundant parts of an unnecessary but sufficient condition to produce the fire. (b) Some of these causal candidates and perhaps other highly associated factors will not be treated as causes but will rather be seen as conditions for the effect because they are not perceptually salient, because of conversational conventions (a speaker and listener may assume certain shared knowledge), and so forth. In the house fire example, a perceiver might acknowledge that the flow of electric current through the wire is a candidate for a causal factor but ignore it when discussing causes because "everyone" would assume that the wires were used to conduct electricity or because the flow of electricity is a nonsalient standing condition (i.e. a state that is relatively constant). (c) There will be factors or events that are not perceived as causally relevant because they are part of the causal field. We noted in the house fire example that the presence of oxygen in the air and the lack of a fire sprinkler system might be examples of circumstances of this type.

Mackie also notes that the propositions that characterize our reasoning about causal events tend to be "elliptical" or "gappy." Causal analyses are incomplete in that no perceiver's representation of a causal situation could include all of the causal factors and circumstances that truly characterize the situation. This elliptical property of our reasoning about causation becomes critical when Mackie attempts to account for how we learn causal schemata.

Fourth, Mackie provides an original analysis of the concept of causal priority, his last condition for the identification of causal relations. He is persuasive that something beyond mere temporal priority underlies causation "in the object world"; however, his analysis is not convincing with reference to the perception of causation.

Mackie's analysis of causality implies that psychological models for causal reasoning should be extended to account for the nature and determinants of the causal field. Some branches of attribution theory, those concerned with salience effects on causal attribution, already include considerations of context effects. However, one implication of Mackie's analysis is that the salience effects that have been obtained (e.g. Taylor & Fiske 1975, McArthur & Post 1977) probably involve perceptual processes rather than memory retrieval processes [McArthur (1980) appears to concur while Fiske et al (1982) appear to disagree].

Mackie also provides useful suggestions concerning a psychological process model for the identification of causes of an effect. Major social attribution models (Jones & Davis 1965, Kelley 1967) have been criticized because they lack well-defined procedures, applicable to a range of situations, that tell a perceiver how to process information about plausible causes to identify the perceived causes. [We might contrast this theoretical situation with the relatively clear computational rules provided by N. H. Anderson's (1974, 1981) algebraic models for causal inference.] Mackie presents what he describes as a process of "progressive localization of cause" that is a method of eliminative induction. This method is familiar to psychologists through research on general hypothesis-testing models for learning and perception (e.g. Lashley 1929, Bruner et al 1956, Campbell 1960, Restle 1962, Levine 1971). The model has also influenced a number of attribution theorists (e.g. Kelley 1973, Snyder & Swann 1978, Smith & Miller 1979a, Hansen 1980, Kruglanski 1980); however, we know of no clear statement of the full conceptual model in the social attribution literature.

In its general form the model can be viewed as including five stages: (a) generating hypotheses (e.g. candidates for causal events) called the abduction process by philosophers; (b) the sampling of hypotheses, from the pool of generated hypotheses, for further consideration; (c) testing a sampled hypothesis by evaluating it with relevant evidence; (d) rejection of hypotheses that fall when tested against relevant evidence; (e) retaining a record of previously rejected hypotheses. Many of the current social attribution models can be combined with this hypothesis-testing process model to yield relatively clear information processing models for attribution.

Cognitive Factors

We can classify the major contributions of attribution research with reference to the stage within the hypothesis-testing model to which they pertain. For example, Kelley (1967), Pruitt & Insko (1980), Read & Stephan (1979), Tillman & Carver (1980), Jones & Davis (1965), Enzle et al (1980), Weiner (1972), Elig & Frieze (1979), Meyer (1980), Touhey & Villemez (1980), Kruglanski (1975, 1979), Buss (1978, 1979), Harvey & Tucker (1979), Locke & Pennington (1982), and other theorists have made fundamental contributions by characterizing the types of hypotheses that will be generated and sampled in early stages of the model (e.g. situation or disposition; person, stimulus, or modality; ability, motivation, task difficulty, or luck; intrinsic or extrinsic motivation factors; cause or reason). Research on perceptual salience (Taylor et al 1979, Smith & Miller 1979b, McArthur & Ginsberg 1981, Schwarz & Strack 1981), priming (Ferguson & Wells 1980), and set (Yarkin et al 1981) can be interpreted with reference to hypothesis generation and sampling mechanisms (McArthur 1980).

Miller & Porter (1980) and Moore et al (1979) provide an intriguing riddle in that their research on the effects of temporal distance on attribution to the person or the situation has reached almost opposite conclusions using similar research methods. Both groups favor interpretations of their respective findings that can be expressed in terms of hypothesis generation or sampling processes. Their theoretical analyses illustrate the flexibility of availability heuristic interpretations; virtually opposite behaviors are cited as evidence for the availability mechanism.

Jones & Davis were relatively clear about some of the logics that would be used to test whether or not a hypothesis would be retained, while Kelley referred to Mill's methods (covariation analysis) but was not explicit about test procedures. Snyder (1981) claimed that social hypothesis testing is subject to "confirmatory" biases, and others (Hansen 1980, Kruglanski 1980, Major 1980) have found biases in information acquisition to test causal hypotheses. Snyder has not presented a clear conceptual definition of "confirmatory" evidence and, although systematic patterns of information seeking have been identified, no strong argument for a "confirmatory bias" exists in the social literature. Schustack & Sternberg (1981) present evidence that subjects were sensitive to both confirmatory and disconfirmatory evidence when testing causal hypotheses. Regrettably, these experiments did not include materials involving individual social behavior. Reeder & Brewer (1979, Reeder 1979, Reeder & Fulks 1980) have made a major contribution in their discussion of the logic that underlies tests of dispositional hypotheses given behavioral evidence.

One implication of the general hypothesis-testing model is that the hypothesis that has been sampled will guide the retrieval of information from long-term memory or the perceptual search for information in the environment. Thus, information associated with or relevant to the current hypothesis will dominate the testing stage. However, we see no reason to expect that confirmatory information will invariably be selected, and there are many obvious examples of the use of both confirmatory and disconfirmatory information to test attributional hypotheses.

We can also account for the "fundamental attribution error" (the perceiver's preference for person attributions when explaining another person's behavior) in terms of the hypothesis-testing model. Our account is close to the explanation presented by Jones and his colleagues (Jones 1979, Jones et al 1979, A. G. Miller et al 1979, 1981; also see Harvey et al 1981, Jellison & Green 1981). It is plausible that characteristics of the person (either self or other) are likely candidates for generation and sampling in the causal judgment process. The extensive knowledge available about the self frequently leads to the rejection of self attribution hypotheses; however, person attributions about another person are harder to reject because less relevant information is available. Thus, person attributions for another's behavior are often retained.

There are two processes that lie outside of the traditional hypothesis-testing model but that appear to be related to other induction processes, sometimes referred to as enumerative induction. First, there are processes that are often called "adjustment and anchoring" following the Tversky & Kahneman (1974) heuristic label (e.g. Jones 1979). It seems natural to think of anchoring and adjustment with reference to the hypothesis-testing model; the anchor is a nonrejected hypothesis and, if the hypothesis refers to a magnitude or a quantity, it is reasonable to think of inferences that adjust the magnitude. However, adjustment processes seem to be outside of any conventional version of the eliminative induction model. Because the experimental and intuitive support for the adjustment process is compelling, we believe that the hypothesis-testing model should be elaborated to allow the adjustment of a current hypothesis. To date we know of no analyses within the literature on judgment heuristics that specify the nature, limits, and applicability of adjustment processes.

Second, there is a class of models that are represented by the extensive work of Anderson and his colleagues on cognitive algebra (1974, 1981). Algebraic models for perception of causes have received a massive amount of empirical support and are also intuitively convincing (most recently, Singh et al 1979, Surber 1981a,b). We would argue that this is a second set of processes involved in causal reasoning and, for the moment, distinguish them from the hypothesis-testing processes. Algebraic models may also be treated as models for the adjustment of a hypothesis rather than for hypothesis generation or testing. It is plausible that the enumerative induction models describe a class of processes that operate once a hypothesis has been selected for test and that their significance and pervasiveness is far greater than the label "adjustment" would indicate.

Motivational Factors

Several programs of research have studied the role played by motivational and emotional factors in determining causal judgments. Most theoretical interpretations of these phenomena are expressed with reference to cognitive processing; motivation and emotion change the inputs or rates of cognitive processing, but do not fundamentally alter or replace processes in the hypothesis-testing framework.

Three recent papers studying the conditions that elicit attributional reasoning (Lau & Russell 1980, Pyszczynski & Greenberg 1981, Wong & Weiner 1981) support previous conclusions that unexpected events are likeliest to instigate attribution processes. Wollert (1979) and Bernstein et al's (1979) findings concerning the conditions under which expectations change in natural (academic performance) situations are also consistent with this conclusion.

A number of studies have explored the phenomenon of self-serving attributional tendencies: People perceive themselves as causes of positive outcomes to a greater degree than as causes of negative outcomes. The phenomenon has been obtained in a great variety of situations both in the laboratory and the outside world (Bernstein et al 1979, Cunningham et al 1979, Green & Gross 1979, Carver et al 1980, Lau & Russell 1980, Mirels 1980, Sherman 1980, Smith & Manard 1980, Weary 1980). The search for explanatory analyses has been hampered by the lack of a general process model, but it seems likely that information availability (Ross & Sicoly 1979, Tyler 1980, Weinstein 1980, Ross 1981, Thompson & Kelley 1981), attribution rules (Tyler & Devinitz 1981), and self-presentation strategies (Weary 1979, Arkin et al 1980) are all involved in some manifestations of the tendency. Evidence for the role of availability is strongest, but it is as yet unclear which stage(s) of the hypothesis-testing model (e.g. generation, sampling, testing, adjustment) is (are) susceptible to availability influences.

Weiner's discussion of the relationships between emotional response and causal attribution has stimulated several investigations of these correlations (Weiner et al 1979, Weiner 1980). Weiner and his colleagues have shown that subjects, when judging hypothetical cases, infer particular emotions will follow from situational conditions and that particular situational conditions are present given certain emotional responses. Weiner's hypothesis that emotional response is a determinant of the actions that follow performance feedback in achievement tasks has received support from experimental results obtained by Stephan & Gollwitzer (1981) but not from correlational analyses of performance in academic test settings (Covington & Omelich 1979).

Causal attribution appears to be an important determinant of belief persistence (C. A. Anderson et al 1980) and of the influence of expectancies on action (Sherman et al 1981). The application of results from research on causal attribution to the study of attitude change and persistence (Cook & Flay 1978) and self-control (Bandura 1982, Alloy & Seligman 1979) is an important development.

Methodology

Probably the major methodological issue concerning social psychologists during the years under review was raised by Nisbett & Wilson (1977), who argued that people have no awareness of cognitive processes and that causal self-reports will almost all be inaccurate. Several theoretical (Cotton 1980, White 1980, Sabini & Silver 1981) and empirical (Smith & Miller 1978, Wright & Rip 1981) replies to Nisbett & Wilson have appeared, and Ericsson & Simon (1980) have outlined an information-processing model that would account for the generation of self-report responses as well as judgments and decisions. The general effect of the self-report controversy has been to motivate researchers to be more critical of measures designed to index cognitive processes (see also F. D. Miller et al 1981, Elig & Frieze 1979).

MORAL INFERENCES

The proper subject of ethics or moral philosophy has always been variously conceived by philosophers and psychologists. However, there is wide agreement that moral reasoning is concerned with how a person ought to act and how the actor should consider the needs and values of others when selecting a course of action. Two topics have received attention during the years under review: judgments of fairness of the division of resources in groups and judgments of deservingness of the recipients of help or harm.

Distributive Justice

Research on the topic of distributive justice is social psychology's most sophisticated contribution to research on moral reasoning. The fundamental question addressed by social psychologists in this area has been the nature of an allocation rule, often expressed algebraically, that captures subjects' sense of a fair distribution of the outputs or profits from a joint endeavor. Harris and his colleagues (Harris 1980, Harris & Joyce 1980) have extended their rational analysis of equity formulas to include empirical research on subjects' judgments of hypothetical work situations involving small groups of four or five co-workers. Harris's linear formula was a clear winner in competition against other equity formulas, particularly when judgments about negative-input group members (group members who detracted from the group's production) were included in the analysis. Harris points out that his general linear formula includes several other popular equity formulas as special cases and that it has several parameters giving it an advantage in competitive goodness-of-fit tests. A major problem for the linear formula (as noted by Messick & Sentis 1979, Harris et al 1981) is that theoretical work remains to be done to explain subjects' "use" of the formula with more basic psychological principles and to develop a process model, summarizing the mental processes subjects perform when reasoning according to the formula. Harris, Messick, and their colleagues are sophisticated in this regard and have introduced considerations of self-interest and cognitive economy to explain some features of their results, usually departures from the basic algebraic models. Harris (in Harris et al 1981) has made a suggestion that research on distributive justice in small work groups and research on outcome allocation in differential power coalition games may both be interpreted with the same equity models. Harris provides an example of the generality of his linear formula in a reanalysis of data from Kormorita & Kravitz's (1979) experiments on coalition formation. However, Kormorita & Kravitz do not provide an ideal case to develop this analogy because their definition of power (as comparison level for alternatives) and some of their parameter estimates did not afford easy generalization from coalition games to resource distribution tasks.

A review by Hook & Cook (1979) makes an important contribution to the literature on equity judgments by relating the complexity of cognitive processes necessary to make some equity judgments to the extant literature on the development of cognitive capacities in children. Farkas & Anderson (1979) have made another important contribution by presenting empirical findings from a study in which subjects were asked to allocate rewards in a hypothetical judgment task with two-person work groups. When subjects were given two types of input information, effort information and performance information for the two workers, they appeared to make separate equity judgments and then to integrate those judgments to produce a final reward allocation decision. The alternative integration strategy, integrating judgments of the inputs and then making one equity judgment, appeared to be followed when the two types of input were conceptually commensurate (i.e. two performances rather than separate effort and performance information).

There have been a number of studies of subjects' reactions to perceived inequity, often testing derivations from relative deprivation principles.

Bernstein & Crosby (1980) conducted an experiment in which subjects evaluated hypothetical educational or business situations and the outcomes that a student or employee received. The protagonist in each of the vignettes was described as having information about several relevant conditions including the presence of a comparison other who possessed a desired outcome, the sense of entitlement of the protagonist to a desired outcome, the past of future feasibility of receiving the desired outcome, and the extent to which the protagonist felt personally responsible for failing to obtain the desired outcome. Information about the presence of a comparison other, perceived entitlement to an outcome, and past and future feasibility of obtaining the outcome all affected subjects' ratings of felt deprivation. Subjects were asked to estimate the types of emotional reactions that the protagonists might exhibit in the vignettes. Manipulations of information about the comparison other and about feasibility of obtaining the outcome had effects on estimates of negative emotional reactions and on expectations for resentment in the protagonist. However, the role of these emotional states as a mediator of felt deprivation was not clearly established.

DeCarufel (deCarufel 1979, deCarufel & Schopler 1979) has conducted research studying situations in which subjects participate in simulations of industrial tasks where over a series of trials outcome is manipulated to provide variation of equitable treatment. In all of this work, an equality standard is the most plausible fairness principle, and subjects are induced to feel a sense of inequity by being paid less than a peer who also participates in the simulated task. DeCarufel studied the effects of providing subjects with a "voice" to express dissatisfaction, to request reimbursement, or to threaten for reimbursement. Subjects were more satisfied when they were able to express their dissatisfaction with their inequitable treatment, and they were most satisfied when their requests for compensation yielded a normatively appropriate compensation in line with their request (i.e. an equality standard was applied on later trials in the experimental task). Folger et al (1979) also studied the effects of "voice" on perceptions of inequity in a simulated industrial work situation. They argued that allowing subjects to express their dissatisfaction had two effects, an effect on perceived fairness of the procedure and an effect of satisfying the subject that others had been informed of their plight. They found that allowing subjects to express themselves increased satisfaction only if the subject was uncertain that others knew of their inequitable treatment.

Furby (1981) summarized data collected by Morawetz (1977) from residents in two small Israeli communities. In one community the distribution of family incomes was flat (equal-income) and in the other the distribution was positively skewed. The average "rated happiness" in the equal-income community was higher than the average happiness in the skewed-distribution community. Morawetz found a negative relationship between income level and happiness, such that the higher the income in the positive skew community, the lower the satisfaction. This result contradicts a prediction made by Brickman (1975), based on an adaptation-level principle, that a positive correlation should prevail. Furby interpreted this result as support for the hypothesis that happiness ratings were determined by perceived fairness.

Clark & Mills (1979) have introduced a distinction between two types of relationships, exchange relationships and communal relationships, that may be important when considering the domains of applicability of the various fairness rules. The empirical work reported by Clark and Mills is concerned with requests for help, rather than the distribution of rewards, but their conceptual conclusion may be generalizable to the resource distribution experiments. They found that reciprocation of a benefit was essential for satisfaction in exchange relationships but that reciprocation often produced negative reactions in communal relationships. The implication is that equity principles may apply in marketplace or exchange relationships, but not in communal relationships, for example, among members of a family.

Three experiments are relevant to the effects of self-attention or self-awareness on adherence to equity norms in distributing rewards. Carles & Carver (1979) conducted an experiment in which partners performed an ESP judgment task with a subject either performing at a higher or lower level than his or her partner. The subject was then asked to allocate a reward. The partner was made salient as a person in one condition by the presentation of a short personality description, and in other conditions the subject-partner role relationship was emphasized or the experimental task was emphasized. Male subjects tended to give themselves a greater portion of the reward for performance when the other person was made salient as compared to the other two salience conditions. Female subjects did just the reverse, allocating more of the reward to their partner under person salient conditions than under the role or task salient conditions. In an experiment by Greenberg (1980), attentional focus was manipulated while a reward was being allocated by placing the subject in a booth surrounded by mirrors or by opaque surfaces. When the subject felt responsible for his outcomes while competing with another subject, reward distribution tended to follow an equity-like rule reflecting performance (in nonresponsible conditions the typical allocation tended to follow an equality rule). This tendency for reward distribution to reflect performance differences was amplified when attention was focused on the self during reward allocation. In contrast to Carles & Carver, Greenberg obtained no gender differences in his research. Diener & Srull (1979) also used the subject's own image to manipulate self-awareness, but without the presence of a partner. When subjects were asked to award monetary wages to themselves at the end of the experimental session, self-aware subjects were more sensitive to information about social or public standards for performance than non-self-aware subjects.

On the surface this pattern of findings is somewhat puzzling, particularly the lack of gender effects in the Diener & Srull study and the Greenberg study as compared to the Carles & Carver study. Callahan-Levy & Messé (1979) found that under a variety of conditions females paid themselves less than did males and even paid themselves less than they paid other females. However, task conditions varied across the different experiments, as did the experimental operations manipulating self-awareness. There is a hint from all three experiments that when subjects are made self-aware they will be likelier to reflect public standards of fairness rather than self-serving standards. Further research on the gender differences in allocation behavior should be conducted for both theoretical and practical reasons.

Deservingness Judgments

A large segment of the moral reasoning literature deals with the consequences of interactions between (usually two) people with a concentration on helping and harming responses. Forsyth (1980) has extended the theoretical analysis initiated in his research on college students' moral judgments of the ethics of psychological research on obedience (Schlenker & Forsyth 1977). He has proposed a two-dimensional (idealism by absolutism) taxonomy of ethical ideologies and constructed a test to identify an individual's ideology. Forsyth's method appears to have some validity as a predictor of individual differences in judgments of a hypothetical actor's responsibility for negative or positive events (Forsyth 1981). However, Forsyth has not yet connected his work to other analyses of individual differences in moral reasoning (e.g. Kohlberg 1969, Rawls 1971, Turiel 1977, Rest 1979) or demonstrated the relative superiority of his predictive method.

Kulik & Brown (1979) conducted a study of the relationships among frustration, blame attribution, and aggression, finding that responses to frustration were influenced by the perceived legitimacy of the frustrator's actions and by other attributional factors. The experiment is important because it includes an ingenious new method to elicit and measure aggressive responses that avoids the artificiality of the shock machine and hypothetical situation questionnaires that have pervaded research on frustration and aggression. The remainder of the small social literature on moral reasoning has focused on situational determinants of deservingness judgments such as retaliation severity (Harvey 1981), participant-observer status (Janoff-Bulman et al 1979, Eisenberg-Berg & Neal 1981), or on age differences (Suls et al 1981).

Empirical research on deservingness judgments is impeded by the lack of model inference rules for moral reasoning. Many researchers have recognized this problem, and we have cited several individual difference taxonomies that are based on broad distinctions between types of moral reasoning. However, as yet no generally popular logic for moral reasoning has been presented. Moral reasoning is dependent on individual perceptions of the goodness or value of actions or outcomes of actions. It is possible that there are not special inference rules that are invoked in rendering moral judgments. Rather, it may be that other forms of inference (e.g. categorical, causal, balance, etc) underlie moral judgments which involve distinctive contents concerned with the needs and desires of the self and others. This view would be consistent with some applications of economic models to ethical reasoning (e.g. Braithwaite 1955), the views of developmental psychologists who have emphasized the continuity between cognitive and moral development, and it is analogous to the theoretical position of the proponents of algebraic models for distributive justice (reviewed above).

STRUCTURAL BALANCE INFERENCES

Heider's (1946) principle of structural balance is one of social psychology's original contributions to the social science literature of inference models. The balance principle is of special importance because of its incorporation of logical and evaluative factors. In a sense, it is one of the few clear examples of a logic for reasoning about emotional responses. Although balance principle derivations are usually represented in terms of graph theory formalizations, several theorists have concerned themselves with a symbolic sentential representation (Abelson & Rosenberg 1958). Thus, Heider's model can be conceived of as a set of inference rules that prescribe conclusions that will be reached when certain binary relationships are presented as premises.

Tashakkori & Insko (1979, 1981) have conducted a series of experiments that explore a quantitative generalization of the original balance model. They compare three alternative models that predict quantitative degrees of positive sentiment relationships between P and O from information about P-X and O-X relationships also expressed quantitatively. Insko & Adewole (1979), staying with the simpler signed relationship model, have explored some of the conditions affecting balance inferences. For example, they found that balance relationships tended to influence cognitive and expectation ratings more than affect ratings for inferred (not presented) relationships. They also found that information concerning P-O contact (interpersonal interaction among hypothetical entitles described in experimenter-provided premises) influenced affective ratings in some attraction (pairwise) relationships.

An important insight into subjects' reasoning when presented with balance triad information was provided by Aderman (1969) when he noted that subjects may "import" premises into an inferential system by assuming relationships among the entities in the hypothetical triad. Insko & Adewole investigated the effects of providing information about P-O contact and found that when such information is not provided subjects occasionally infer it. Two other papers explored assumptions subjects might "import" in balance reasoning tasks: C. E. Miller (1979) used a talk-aloud method to show that subjects frequently "misconstrued" situations described in the balance task materials by adding assumptions concerning agreement or disagreement among the hypothetical P and O characters. Gerbing & Hunter (1979) also found subjects went beyond the information given by the experimenter to infer common interests (or lack of common interests) between the hypothetical P and O characters.

One deserved criticism of much of the research on the balance principle is that it has overemphasized definitional questions and technical questions concerned with the application of formal models. Recent papers by Sentis & Burnstein (1979) and Cacioppo & Petty (1981) make major contributions to the development of a model of the mental processes underlying balance principle effects. Sentis & Burnstein used subjects' reaction times to verify conclusions concerning imbalanced or balanced relationship triads to draw conclusions about the mnemonic representation of information about the to-be-judged triad. They outlined an explicit model for the information processes necessary to yield inferences in the balance task and found that qualitative features of the results were consistent with the model. One of the remarkable predictions of the model was that for imbalanced sets reaction times to questions increased as the number of to-be-retrieved relations increased; however, with balanced information reaction times actually decreased as the number of to-be-retrieved relations increased. This finding is reminiscent of several results in the fact retrieval literature concerned with reaction times to retrieve facts from unintegrated or logically integrated sets of propositions (e.g. Smith et al 1978). Cacioppo & Petty (1981) varied study time or motivation to draw inferences and found parallel effects on attraction (one binary relationship), agreement (two binary relationships), and balance (three binary relationships) inferences. Their conclusion was that the three types of inferences were generated independently and ordered in time from simplest (attraction) to most complex (balance). They note that this temporal sequence puts strong constraints on plausible inference process models for the balance reasoning task and that theoretical analyses by Heider and Insko do not predict these temporal order effects.

Gollob's extension of the balance model to inferences concerning subject-verb-object sentences is the most important methodological and theoretical development of Heider's principle since its original statement (Gollob 1974). Regrettably, only a handful of papers on the subject-verb-object approach to social cognition were published during the period under review. Thompson et al (1980) showed that three-way balance affects plausibility inferences and time to acquire a concept (balance concept) in a discrimination learning task (particularly when the balance relationship is defined on a common evaluative dimension). Kravitz & Wyer (1979) applied the subject-verb-object method to subjects' inferences about the admirableness of an actor or the recipient of an action described in short sentences. The sentences included information about each character, the intentions of the actor, and the consequences of the actor's action. The method allowed the researchers to infer which items of information or configurations of information, influenced the admirableness judgment. In a second experiment social desirability (virtuousness) and competence were shown to underlie the admirableness judgment. Gollob (1979) and N. H. Anderson (1979) authored two parts of a heated and instructive exchange concerning the merits of the subject-verb-object approach. The level of discourse in this exchange is remarkably sophisticated, but accessible, and it exemplifies the discussion of methodological and theoretical issues in the context of a well-specified theoretical approach. The major focus of the exchange, the need for clear theoretical principles to motivate algebraic models, is relevant to virtually all models of social inference.

CONCLUSION

There has been progress in research on social inference processes. Three major theoretical positions are taking form and phenomenon-specific hypotheses are being integrated into general explanatory principles. At present no important alternatives to cognitive models are popular in social psychology.

The problem of extending current cognitive models to account for the influence of emotional and motivational factors on inference processes will probably be the major source of theoretical questions during the next few years (Zajonc 1980, Bower 1981). The role of emotional responses as "mediators" in inference processes has been cited but not thoroughly analyzed in research on attribution, relative deprivation, and evaluative balance. Even more formidable questions lie ahead when the relationships between mood states and inference processes and the influence of needs and desires on the selection of goals for behavior are explored.

ACKNOWLEDGMENTS

The author is grateful to Thomas Ostrom, Nancy Pennington, Robert Schwartz, Susan Sugarman, and Roger Tourangeau for suggestions on the contents of this review and to Charlotte Pieters for careful preparation of the manuscript.

Literature Cited

Abelson, R. P. 1968. Simulation of social behavior. In *The Handbook of Social Psychology*, ed. G. Lindzey, E. Aronson, 2:274–356. Reading, Mass: Addison-Wesley. 819 pp.

Abelson, R. P. 1981. Psychological status of the script concept. *Am. Psychol.* 36:715–29

Abelson, R. P., Rosenberg, M. J. 1958. Symbolic psycho-logic: A model of attitudinal cognition. *Behav. Sci.* 3:1–13

Aderman, D. 1969. Effects of anticipating future interaction on the preference for balanced states. *J. Pers. Soc. Psychol.* 11:214–19

Alloy, L. B., Seligman, M. E. P. 1979. On the cognitive component of learned helplessness and depression. *Psychol. Learn. Motiv.* 13:219–76

Anderson, C. A., Lepper, M. R., Ross, L. 1980. Perseverance of social theories: The role of explanation in the persistence of discredited information. *J. Pers. Soc. Psychol.* 39:1037–49

Anderson, J. 1938. The problem of causality. *Australas. J. Philos.* 2:127–42

Anderson, J. R. 1976. *Language, Memory, and Thought.* Hillsdale, NJ: Erlbaum. 546 pp.

Anderson, J. R. 1980. *Cognitive Psychology and its Implications.* San Francisco: Freeman. 386 pp.

Anderson, N. H. 1974. Cognitive algebra. *Adv. Exp. Soc. Psychol.* 7:1–101

Anderson, N. H. 1979. Indeterminate theory: Reply to Gollob. *J. Pers. Soc. Psychol.* 37:950–52

Anderson, N. H. 1981. *Foundations of Information Integration Theory.* New York: Academic. 423 pp.

Arkin, R. M., Appelman, A. J., Burger, J. M. 1980. Social anxiety: Self-presentation and the self-serving bias in causal attribution. *J. Pers. Soc. Psychol.* 38:23–35

Ashmore, R. D. 1981. Sex stereotypes and implicit personality theory. See Hamilton 1981, pp. 1–36

Ashmore, R. D., Del Boca, F. K. 1981. Conceptual approaches to stereotypes and stereotyping. See Hamilton 1981, pp. 37–82

Bandura, A. 1982. Self-efficacy mechanism in human agency. *Am. Psychol.* 37:122–47

Bar-Hillel, M. 1980a. The baserate fallacy in probability judgments. *Acta Psychol.* 44:211–33

Bar-Hillel, M. 1980b. What features make samples seem representative? *J. Exp. Psychol: Human Percept. Perform.* 6:578–89

Bar-Hillel, M., Fischhoff, B. 1981. When do base rates affect predictions? *J. Pers. Soc. Psychol.* 41:671–80

Bernstein, M., Crosby, F. 1980. An empirical examination of relative deprivation theory. *J. Exp. Soc. Psychol.* 16:442–56

Bernstein, W. M., Stephan, W. G., Davis, M. H. 1979. Explaining attributions for achievement: A path analytic approach. *J. Pers. Soc. Psychol.* 37:1810–21

Beyth-Marom, R., Fischhoff, B. 1977. Direct measures of availability and frequency judgments. *Bull. Psychon. Soc.* 9:236–38

Bower, G. H. 1975. Cognitive psychology: An introduction. See Estes 1979, pp. 25–80

Bower, G. H. 1981. Mood and memory. *Am. Psychol.* 36:129–48

Braine, M. D. S. 1978. The relation between the natural logic of reasoning and standard logic. *Psychol. Rev.* 85:1–12

Braithwaite, R. B. 1955. *Theory of Games as a Tool for the Moral Philosopher.* London: Cambridge Univ. Press. 75 pp.

Brickman, P. 1975. Adaptation level determinants of satisfaction with equal and unequal distributions in skill and chance situations. *J. Pers. Soc. Psychol.* 32:191–98

Brody, B. A. 1967. Glossary of logical terms. In *Encyclopedia of Philosophy*, ed. P. Edwards, 5:57–77. New York: Wiley. 553 pp.

Bruner, J. S., Goodnow, J. J., Austin, G. A. 1956. *A Study of Thinking.* New York: Wiley. 330 pp.

Buss, A. R. 1978. Causes and reasons in attribution theory: A conceptual critique. *J. Pers. Soc. Psychol.* 36:1311–21

Buss, A. R. 1979. On the relationship between causes and reasons. *J. Pers. Soc. Psychol.* 37:1458–64

Cacioppo, J. T., Petty, R. E. 1981. Effects of extent on thought on the pleasantness ratings of P-O-X triads: Evidence for three judgmental tendencies in evaluating social situations. *J. Pers. Soc. Psychol.* 40:1000–9

Callahan-Levy, C. M., Messé, L. A. 1979. Sex differences in the allocation of pay. *J. Pers. Soc. Psychol.* 37:433–46

Campbell, D. T. 1960. Blind variation and selective retention in creative thought as in other knowledge processes. *Psychol. Rev.* 67:380–400

Carles, E. M., Carver, C. S. 1979. Effects of person salience versus role salience on reward allocation in a dyad. *J. Pers. Soc. Psychol.* 37:2071–80

Carver, C. S., DeGregorio, E., Gillis, R. 1980. Field-study evidence of an ego-defensive bias in attribution among two categories of observers. *Pers. Soc. Psychol. Bull.* 6:44–50

Clark, M. S., Mills, J. 1979. Interpersonal attraction in exchange and communal relationships. *J. Pers. Soc. Psychol.* 37:12–24

Cohen, L. J. 1981. Can human irrationality be experimentally demonstrated? *Behav. Brain Sci.* 4:317–70

Cohen, M. R., Nagel, E. 1934. *An Introduction to Logic and the Scientific Method.* New York: Harcourt, Brace. 467 pp.

Collins, A. 1978. Fragments of a theory of human plausible reasoning. In *Proceedings of Conference on Theoretical Issues in Natural Language Processing II,* ed. D. Waltz. Urbana: Univ. Illinois Press

Cook, T. D., Flay, B. R. 1978. The persistence of experimentally induced attitude change. *Adv. Exp. Soc. Psychol.* 11:1–57

Cotton, J. L. 1980. Verbal reports on mental processes: Ignoring data for the sake of the theory? *Pers. Soc. Psychol. Bull.* 6:278–81

Covington, M. V., Omelich, C. L. 1979. Are causal attributions causal? A path analysis of the cognitive model of achievement motivation. *J. Pers. Soc. Psychol.* 37:1487–1504

Crocker, J. 1981. Judgment of covariation by human perceivers. *Psychol. Rev.* 90:272–92

Cunningham, J. D., Starr, P. A., Kanouse, D. E. 1979. Self as actor, active observer , and passive observer: Implications for causal attributions. *J. Pers. Soc. Psychol.* 37:1146–52

deCarufel, A. 1979. Factors affecting the evaluation of improvement: The role of normative standards and allocator resources. *J. Pers. Soc. Psychol.* 37:847–57

deCarufel, A., Schopler, J. 1979. Evaluation of outcome improvement resulting from threats and appeals. *J. Pers. Soc. Psychol.* 67:662–73

Diener, E., Srull, T. K. 1979. Self-awareness, psychological perspective, and self-reinforcement in relation to personal and social standards. *J. Pers. Soc. Psychol.* 37:413–23

Edwards, W. 1968. Conservativism in human information processing. In *Formal Representations of Human Judgment,* ed. B. Kleinmuntz, pp. 17–98. New York: Wiley. 267 pp

Eisenberg-Berg, N., Neal, C. 1981. Children's moral reasoning about self and others: Effects of identity of the story character and cost of helping. *Pers. Soc. Psychol. Bull.* 7:17–23

Elig, T. W., Frieze, I. H. 1979. Measuring causal attributions for success and failure. *J. Pers. Soc. Psychol.* 37:621–34

Enzle, M. E., Harvey, D. M., Wright, E. F. 1980. Personalism and distinctiveness. *J. Pers. Soc. Psychol.* 39:542–52

Ericsson, K. A., Simon, H. A. 1980. Verbal reports as data. *Psychol. Rev.* 87:215–51

Estes, W. K. 1979. The information processing approach to cognition. In *Handbook of Learning and Cognitive Processes,* ed. W. K. Estes, 5:1–18. Hillsdale, NJ: Erlbaum. 337 pp.

Farkas, A. J., Anderson, N. H. 1979. Multidimensional input in equity theory. *J. Pers. Soc. Psychol.* 37:879–96

Ferguson, T. J., Wells, G. L. 1980. Priming of mediators in causal attribution. *J. Pers. Soc. Psychol.* 38:461–70

Fiske, S. T., Kenny, D. A., Taylor, S. E. 1982. Structural models for the mediation of salience effects on attribution. *J. Exp. Soc. Psychol.* 18:105–27

Folger, R., Rosenfield, D., Grove, J., Corkran, L. 1979. Effects of "voice" and peer opinions on responses to inequity. *J. Pers. Soc. Psychol.* 37:2253–61

Forsyth, D. R. 1980. A taxonomy of ethical ideologies. *J. Pers. Soc. Psychol.* 39:175–84

Forsyth, D. R. 1981. Moral judgment: The influence of ethical ideology. *Pers. Soc. Psychol. Bull.* 7:218–23

Furby, L. 1981. Satisfaction with outcome distributions: Studies from two small communities. *Pers. Soc. Psychol. Bull.* 7:206–11

Gerbing, D. W., Hunter, J. E. 1979. Phenomenological bases for the attribution of balance to social structure. *Pers. Soc. Psychol. Bull.* 5:299–302

Ginosar, Z., Trope, Y. 1980. The effects of base rates and individuating information on judgments about another person. *J. Exp. Soc. Psychol.* 16:228–42

Gollob, H. F. 1974. The Subject-Verb-Object approach to social cognition. *Psychol. Rev.* 81:286–321

Gollob, H. F. 1979. A reply to Norman H. Anderson's critique of the Subject-Verb-Object approach to social cognition. *J. Pers. Soc. Psychol.* 37:931–49

Green, S. K., Gross, A. E. 1979. Self-serving biases in implicit evaluations. *Pers. Soc. Psychol. Bull.* 5:214–17

Greenberg, J. 1980. Attentional focus and locus of performance causality as determinants of equity behavior. *J. Pers. Soc. Psychol.* 38:579–85

Hacking, I. 1965. *The Logic of Statistical Inference.* London: Cambridge Univ. Press. 232 pp.

Hamill, R., Wilson, T. D., Nisbett, R. E. 1980. Insensitivity to sample bias: Generalizing from atypical cases. *J. Pers. Soc. Psychol.* 39:578–89

Hamilton, D. L., ed. 1981. *Cognitive Processes in Stereotyping and Intergroup Behavior.* Hillsdale, NJ: Erlbaum. 369 pp.

Hamilton, D. L., Rose, T. L. 1980. Illusory correlation and the maintenance of stereotypic beliefs. *J. Pers. Soc. Psychol.* 39:832–45

Hansen, R. D. 1980. Commonsense attribution. *J. Pers. Soc. Psychol.* 39:996–1009

Harris, R. J. 1976. The uncertain connection between verbal theories and research hypotheses in social psychology. *J. Exp. Soc. Psychol.* 12:210–19

Harris, R. J. 1980. Equity judgments in hypothetical, four-person partnerships. *J. Exp. Soc. Psychol.* 16:96–115

Harris, R. J., Joyce, M. A. 1980. What's fair? It depends on how you phrase the question. *J. Pers. Soc. Psychol.* 38:165–79

Harris, R. J., Messick, D. M., Sentis, K. P. 1981. Proportionality, linearity, and parameter constancy: Messick and Sentis reconsidered. *J. Exp. Soc. Psychol.* 17:210–25

Hart, H. L. A., Honoré, A. M. 1959. *Causation and the Law.* London: Oxford Univ. Press. 454 pp.

Harvey, J. H., Town, J. P., Yarkin, K. L. 1981. How fundamental is "The fundamental attribution error"? *J. Pers. Soc. Psychol.* 40:346–49

Harvey, J. H., Tucker, J. A. 1979. On problems with the cause-reason distinction in attribution theory. *J. Pers. Soc. Psychol.* 37:1441–46

Harvey, M. D. 1981. Outcome severity and knowledge of "Ought": Effects on moral evaluations. *Pers. Soc. Psychol. Bull.* 7:459–66

Hastie, R., Carlston, D. E. 1980. Theoretical issues in person memory. In *Person Memory: The Cognitive Basis of Social Perception,* ed. R. Hastie et al, pp. 1–53. Hillsdale, NJ: Erlbaum. 308 pp.

Heider, F. 1946. Attitudes and cognitive organization. *J. Psychol.* 21:107–12

Hook, J. G., Cook, T. D. 1979. Equity theory and the cognitive ability of children. *Psychol. Bull.* 86:429–45

Hutchins, E. 1981. *Culture and Inference.* Cambridge, Mass: Harvard Univ. Press. 143 pp.

Insko, C. A., Adewole, A. 1979. The role of assumed reciprocation of sentiment and assumed similarity in the production of attraction and agreement effects in p-o-x triads. *J. Pers. Soc. Psychol.* 37:790–808

Janoff-Bulman, R., Lang, L., Johnston, D. 1979. Participant-observer differences in attributions for an ambiguous victimization. *Pers. Soc. Psychol. Bull.* 5:335–39

Jellison, J. M., Green, J. 1981. A self presentation approach to the fundamental attribution error: The norm of internality. *J. Pers. Soc. Psychol.* 40:643–49

Jones, E. E. 1979. The rocky road from acts to dispositions. *Am. Sci.* 34:107–17

Jones, E. E., Davis, K. E. 1965. From acts to dispositions: The attribution process in social perception. *Adv. Exp. Soc. Psychol.* 2:219–266

Jones, E. E., Riggs, J. M., Quattrone, G. 1979. Observer bias in the attitude attribution paradigm: Effect of time and information order. *J. Pers. Soc. Psychol.* 37:1230–38

Jones, E. E., Wood, G. C., Quattrone, G. A. 1981. Perceived variability of personal characteristics in in-groups and out-groups: The role of knowledge and evaluation. *Pers. Soc. Psychol. Bull.* 7:523–28

Kahneman, D., Slovic, P., Tversky, A. 1982. *Judgment under Uncertainty: Heuristics and Biases.* New York: Cambridge Univ. Press. 576 pp.

Kahneman, D., Tversky, A. 1972. Subjective probability: A judgment of representativeness. *Cogn. Psychol.* 3:430–54

Kassin, S. M. 1979a. Base rates and prediction: The role of sample size. *Pers. Soc. Psychol. Bull.* 5:210–13

Kassin, S. M. 1979b. Consensus information, prediction, and causal attribution: A review of the literature and issues. *J. Pers. Soc. Psychol.* 37:1966–81

Kelley, H. H. 1967. Attribution theory in social psychology. *Neb. Symp. Motiv.* 15:192–238

Kelley, H. H. 1973. The process of causal attribution. *Am. Psychol.* 28:107–28

Kohlberg, L. 1969. Stage and sequence: The cognitive-developmental approach to socialization. In *Handbook of Socialization Theory and Research,* ed. D. Goslin, pp. 347–480. Chicago: Rand McNally. 1182 pp.

Kormorita, S. S., Kravitz, D. A. 1979. The effects of alternatives in bargaining. *J. Exp. Soc. Psychol.* 15:418–34

Kravitz, D. A., Wyer, R. S. Jr. 1979. The effects of behavioral intentions and consequences on judgments of the actor and other: An S-V-O analysis. *J. Pers. Soc. Psychol.* 37:1561–75

Kruglanski, A. W. 1975. The endogenous-exogenous partition in attribution theory. *Psychol. Rev.* 82:387–406

Kruglanski, A. W. 1979. Causal explanation, teleological explanation: On radical particularism in attribution theory. *J. Pers. Soc. Psychol.* 37:1447–57

Kruglanski, A. W. 1980. Lay epistemo-logic —process and contents: Another look at attribution theory. *Psychol. Rev.* 87:70–87

Kulik, J. A., Brown, R. 1979. Frustration, attribution of blame, and aggression. *J. Exp. Soc. Psychol.* 15:183–94

Kulik, J. A., Taylor, S. E. 1980. Premature consensus on consensus? Effects of sample-based versus self-based consensus information. *J. Pers. Soc. Psychol.* 38:871–78

Lashley, K. S. 1929. *Brain Mechanisms and Intelligence.* Chicago: Univ. Illinois Press. 186 pp.

Lau, R. R., Russell, D. 1980. Attributions in the sports pages. *J. Pers. Soc. Psychol.* 39:29–38

Levine, M. 1971. Hypothesis theory and non-learning despite ideal S-R reinforcement contingencies. *Psychol. Rev.* 78:130–40

Linville, P. W., Jones, E. E. 1980. Polarized appraisals of out-group members. *J. Pers. Soc. Psychol.* 38:689–703

Locke, D., Pennington, D. 1982. Reasons and causes: Their role in attribution processes. *J. Pers. Soc. Psychol.* 42:212–23

Locksley, A., Borgida, E., Brekke, N., Hepburn, C. 1980a. Sex stereoptyes and social judgment. *J. Pers. Soc. Psychol.* 39:821–31

Locksley, A., Ortiz, V., Hepburn, C. 1980b. Social categorization and discriminatory behavior: Extinguishing the minimal intergroup discrimination effect. *J. Pers. Soc. Psychol.* 39:773–83

Mackie, J. L. 1974. *The Cement of the Universe.* London: Oxford Univ. Press. 329 pp.

Major, B. 1980. Information acquisition and attribution processes. *J. Pers. Soc. Psychol.* 39:1010–23

Manis, M., Avis, N. E., Cardoze, S. 1981. Reply to Bar-Hillel and Fischhoff. *J. Pers. Soc. Psychol.* 41:681–83

Manis, M., Dovalina, I., Avis, N. E., Cardoze, S. 1980. Base rates can effect individual predictions. *J. Pers. Soc. Psychol.* 38:231–48

McArthur, L. Z. 1980. Illusory causation and illusory correlation: Two epistemological accounts. *Pers. Soc. Psychol. Bull.* 6:507–19

McArthur, L. Z., Friedman, S. A. 1980. Illusory correlation in impression formation: Variations in the shared distinctiveness effect as a function of the distinctive person's age, race, and sex. *J. Pers. Soc. Psychol.* 39:615–24

McArthur, L. Z., Ginsberg, E. 1981. Causal attribution to salient stimuli: An investigation of visual fixation mediators. *Pers. Soc. Psychol. Bull.* 7:547–53

McArthur, L. Z., Post, D. L. 1977. Figural emphasis and person perception. *J. Exp. Soc. Psychol.* 13:520–35

McGuire, W. J. 1960. A syllogistic analysis of cognitive relationships. In *Attitude Organization and Change,* ed. M. J. Rosenberg et al, pp. 65–111. New Haven: Yale Univ. Press. 239 pp.

Messick, D. M., Sentis, K. P. 1979. Fairness and preference. *J. Exp. Soc. Psychol.* 15:418–34

Meyer, J. P. 1980. Causal attribution for success and failure: A multivariate investigation of dimensionality, formation, and consequences. *J. Pers. Soc. Psychol.* 38:704–18

Miller, A. G., Baer, R., Schonberg, P. 1979. The bias phenomenon in attitude attribution: Actor and observer perspectives. *J. Pers. Soc. Psychol.* 37:1421–31

Miller, A. G., Jones, E. E., Hinkle, S. 1981. A robust attribution error in the personality domain. *J. Exp. Soc. Psychol.* 17:587–600

Miller, C. E. 1979. Using hypothetical P-O-X situations in studies of balance: The problem of "misconstrual". *Pers. Soc. Psychol. Bull.* 5:303–6

Miller, D. T., Porter, C. A. 1980. Effects of temporal perspective on the attribution process. *J. Pers. Soc. Psychol.* 39:532–41

Miller, F. D., Smith, E. R., Uleman, J. 1981. Measurement and interpretation of situational and dispositional attributions. *J. Exp. Soc. Psychol.* 17:80–95

Miller, G. A., Cantor, N. 1982. Review: Human Inference by Nisbett & Ross. *Soc. Cognit.* 1:78–93

Mirels, H. L. 1980. The avowal of responsibility for good and bad outcomes: The effects of generalized self-serving biases. *Pers. Soc. Psychol. Bull.* 6:299–306

Moore, B. S., Liu, T. J., Underwood, B. 1979. The dispositional shift in attribution over time. *J. Exp. Soc. Psychol.* 15: 553–69

Morawetz, D. 1977. Income distribution and self-rated happiness: Some empirical evidence. *Econ. J.* 87:511–22

Newell, A., Simon, H. A. 1972. *Human Problem Solving.* Englewood Cliffs, NJ: Prentice-Hall. 920 pp.

Nicholas, D. W., Trabasso, T. 1980. Toward a taxonomy of inferences for story comprehension. In *Information Integration by Children,* ed. F. Wilkening, J. Becker, T. Trabasso, pp. 243–65. Hillsdale, NJ: Erlbaum. 299 pp.

Nisbett, R., Ross, L. 1980. *Human Inference: Strategies and Shortcomings of Social Judgment.* Englewood Cliffs, NJ: Prentice-Hall. 334 pp.

Nisbett, R., Wilson, T. 1977. Telling more than we can know: Verbal reports on mental processes. *Psychol. Rev.* 84: 231–59

O'Malley, M., Thistlethwaite, D. L. 1980. Inference in inconsistency reduction: New evidence on the "Socratic effect." *J. Pers. Soc. Psychol.* 39:1064–71

Peterson, C. 1980. Recognition of noncontingency. *J. Pers. Soc. Psychol.* 38:727–34

Pettigrew, T. F. 1979. The ultimate attribution error: Extending Allport's cognitive analysis of prejudice. *Pers. Soc. Psychol. Bull.* 5:461–76

Pruitt, D. J., Insko, C. A. 1980. Extension of the Kelley attribution model: The role of comparison-object consensus, target-object consensus, distinctiveness, and consistency. *J. Pers. Soc. Psychol.* 39:39–58

Pyszczynski, T. A., Greenberg, J. 1981. Role of disconfirmed expectancies in the instigation of attributional processing. *J. Pers. Soc. Psychol.* 40:31–38

Quattrone, G. A., Jones, E. E. 1980. The perception of variability within in-groups and out-groups: Implications for the law of small numbers. *J. Pers. Soc. Psychol.* 38:141–52

Quine, W. V. 1970. *The Philosophy of Logic.* Englewood Cliffs, NJ: Prentice-Hall. 109 pp.

Rawls, J. 1971. *A Theory of Justice.* Cambridge, Mass: Harvard Univ. Press. 607 pp.

Read, S. J., Stephan, W. G. 1979. An integration of Kelley's attribution cube and Weiner's achievement attribution model. *Pers. Soc. Psychol. Bull* 5:196–200

Reeder, G. D. 1979. Context effects for attributions of ability. *Pers. Soc. Psychol. Bull.* 5:65–68

Reeder, G. D., Brewer, M. B. 1979. A schematic model of dispositional attribution in interpersonal perception. *Psychol. Rev.* 86:61–79

Reeder, G. D., Fulks, J. L. 1980. When actions speak louder than words: Implicational schemata and the attribution of ability. *J. Exp. Soc. Psychol.* 16:33–46

Rest, J. R. 1979. *Development in Judging Moral Issues.* Minneapolis: Univ. Minnesota Press. 305 pp.

Restle, F. 1962. The selection of strategies in cue learning. *Psychol. Rev.* 69:329–43

Revlin, R., Mayer, R. E. 1978. *Human Reasoning.* Washington DC: Winston. 252 pp.

Rips, L. J. 1975. Inductive judgments about natural categories. *J. Verb. Learn. Verb. Behav.* 14:665–81

Ross, M. 1981. Self-centered biases in attributions of responsibility: Antecedents and consequences. In *Social Cognition, the Ontario Symposium,* ed. E. T. Higgins, C. P. Herman, M. P. Zanna, 1:305–22. Hillsdale, NJ: Erlbaum. 437 pp.

Ross, M., Sicoly, F. 1979. Egocentric biases in availability and attribution. *J. Pers. Soc. Psychol.* 37:322–36

Sabini, J., Silver, M. 1981. Introspection and causal accounts. *J. Pers. Soc. Psychol.* 40:171–79

Schank, R., Abelson, R. P. 1977. *Scripts, Plans, Goals, and Understanding.* Hillsdale, NJ: Erlbaum. 248 pp.

Schlenker, B. R., Forsyth, D. R. 1977. On the ethics of psychological research. *J. Exp. Soc. Psychol.* 13:369–96

Schustack, M. W., Sternberg, R. J. 1981. Evaluation of evidence in causal inference. *J. Exp. Psychol. Gen.* 110:101–20

Schwarz, N., Strack, F. 1981. Manipulating salience: Causal assessment in natural setting. *Pers. Soc. Psychol. Bull.* 6:554–58

Sentis, K. P., Burnstein, E. 1979. Remembering schema-consistent information: Effects of a balance schema on recognition memory. *J. Pers. Soc. Psychol.* 37:2200–11

Sherman, S. J. 1980. On the self-erasing nature of errors of prediction. *J. Pers. Soc. Psychol.* 39:211–21

Sherman, S. J., Skov, R. B., Hervitz, E. F., Stock, C. B. 1981. The effects of explaining hypothetical future events: From possibility to probability to actuality and beyond. *J. Exp. Soc. Psychol.* 17:142–58

Singh, R., Gupta, M., Dalal, A. K. 1979. Cultural difference in attribution of performance: An integration-theoretical analysis. *J. Pers. Soc. Psychol.* 37: 1342–51

Smith, E. E., Adams, N., Schorr, D. 1978. Fact retrieval and the paradox of interference. *Cogn. Psychol.* 10:438–64

Smith, E. E., Medin, D. L. 1981. *Categories and Concepts.* Cambridge, Mass: Harvard Univ. Press. 203 pp.

Smith, E. R., Manard, B. B. 1980. Causal attributions and medical school admissions. *Pers. Soc. Psychol. Bull.* 6:644–50

Smith, E. R., Miller, F. D. 1978. Limits on perception of cognitive processes: A reply to Nisbett & Wilson. *Psychol. Rev.* 85:355–62

Smith, E. R., Miller, F. D. 1979a. Attributional information processing: A response time model of causal subtraction. *J. Pers. Soc. Psychol.* 37:1723–31

Smith, E. R., Miller, F. D. 1979b. Salience and the cognitive mediation of attribution. *J. Pers. Soc. Psychol.* 37:2242–52

Snyder, M. 1981. Seek, and ye shall find: Testing hypotheses about other people. See Ross 1981, 1:277–303

Snyder, M., Swann, W. B. 1978. Hypothesis-testing processes in social interaction. *J. Pers. Soc. Psychol.* 36:1202–12

Stephan, W. G., Gollwitzer, P. M. 1981. Affect as a mediator of attributional egotism. *J. Exp. Soc. Psychol.* 17: 443–58

Stich, S. P., Nisbett, R. 1980. Justification and the psychology of human reasoning. *Philos. Sci.* 47:188–202

Suls, J., Witenberg, S., Gutkin, D. 1981. Evaluating reciprocal and nonreciprocal prosocial behavior: Developmental changes. *Pers. Soc. Psychol. Bull.* 7:25–31

Suppes, P. 1960. A comparison of the meaning and uses of models in mathematics and the empirical sciences. *Synthese* 12:287–301

Suppes, P. 1970. *A Probabilistic Theory of Causality.* Amsterdam: North-Holland. 130 pp.

Surber, C. F. 1981a. Necessary versus sufficient causal schemata: Attributions for achievement in difficult and easy tasks. *J. Exp. Soc. Psychol.* 17:569–86

Surber, C. F. 1981b. Effects of information reliability in predicting task performance using ability and effort. *J. Pers. Soc. Psychol.* 40:977–89

Tashakkori, A., Insko, C. A. 1979. Interpersonal attraction and the polarity of similar attitudes: A test of three balance models. *J. Pers. Soc. Psychol.* 37:2262–77

Tashakkori, A., Insko, C. A. 1981. Interpersonal attraction and person perception: Two tests of three balance models. *J. Exp. Soc. Psychol.* 17:266–85

Taylor, S. E. 1981. A categorization approach to stereotyping. See Hamilton 1981, pp. 83–114

Taylor, S. E., Crocker, J., Fiske, S. T., Sprinzen, M., Winkler, J. D. 1979. The generalizability of salience effects. *J. Pers. Soc. Psychol.* 37:357–68

Taylor, S. E., Fiske, S. T. 1975. Point-of-view and perceptions of causality. *J. Pers. Soc. Psychol.* 32:439–45

Thompson, E. G., Gard, J. W., Phillips, J. L. 1980. Trait dimensionality and "balance" in Subject-Verb-Object judgments. *J. Pers. Soc. Psychol.* 38:57–66

Thompson, S. C., Kelley, H. H. 1981. Judgments of responsibility for activities in close relationships. *J. Pers. Soc. Psychol.* 41:469–77

Tillman, W. S., Carver, C. S. 1980. Actors' and observers' attributions for success and failure: A comparative test of predictions from Kelley's cube, self-serving bias, and positivity bias formulations. *J. Exp. Soc. Psychol.* 16:18–32

Touhey, J. C., Villemez, W. J., 1980. Ability attribution as a result of variable effort and achievement motivation. *J. Pers. Soc. Psychol.* 38:211–16

Turiel, E. 1977. Distinct conceptual and moral domains: Social-convention and morality. *Nebr. Symp. Motiv.* 25: 133–71

Tversky, A., Kahneman, D. 1974. Judgments under uncertainty: Heuristics and biases. *Science* 185:1124–31

Tversky, A., Kahneman, D. 1980. Causal schemas for judgments under uncertainty. In *Progress in Social Psychology,* ed. M. Fishbein, 1:49–72. Hillsdale, NJ: Erlbaum. 240 pp.

Tyler, T. R. 1980. Impact of directly and indirectly experienced events: The origin of crime-related judgments and behaviors. *J. Pers. Soc. Psychol.* 39:13–28

Tyler, T. R., Devinitz, V. 1981. Self-serving bias in the attribution of responsibility: Cognitive versus motivational explanations. *J. Exp. Soc. Psychol.* 17:408–16

Weary, G. 1979. Self-serving attributional biases: Perceptual or response distortions? *J. Pers. Soc. Psychol.* 37:1418–20

Weary, G. 1980. Examination of affect and egotism as mediators of bias in causal attributions. *J. Pers. Soc. Psychol.* 38:348–57

Weiner, B. 1972. *Theories of Motivation: From Mechanism to Cognition.* Chicago: Rand-McNally. 474 pp.

Weiner, B. 1980. A cognitive attribution-emotion-action model of motivated behavior: An analysis of judgments of help-giving. *J. Pers. Soc. Psychol.* 39:186–200

Weiner, B., Russell, D., Lerman, D. 1979. The cognition-emotion process in achievement-related contexts. *J. Pers. Soc. Psychol.* 37:1211–20

Weinstein, N. D. 1980. Unrealistic optimism about future life events. *J. Pers. Soc. Psychol.* 39:806–20

White, P. 1980. Limitations on verbal reports of internal events: A refutation of Nisbett & Wilson and of Bem. *Psychol. Rev.* 87:105–12

Wilder, D. A. 1981. Perceiving persons as a group: Categorization and intergroup relations. See Hamilton 1981, pp. 213–58

Wollert, R. W. 1979. Expectancy shifts and the expectancy confidence hypothesis. *J. Pers. Soc. Psychol.* 37:1888–1901

Wong, P. T. P., Weiner, B. 1981. When people ask "why" questions, and the heuristics of attributional search. *J. Pers. Soc. Psychol.* 40:650–63

Wright, P., Rip, P. D. 1981. Retrospective reports on the causes of decisions. *J. Pers. Soc. Psychol.* 40:601–14

Wyer, R. S. Jr., Carlston, D. 1979. *Social Cognition, Inference, and Attribution.* Hillsdale, NJ: Erlbaum. 388 pp.

Wyer, R. S. Jr., Carlston, D., Hartwick, J. 1979. The role of syllogistic reasoning in inferences based upon new and old information. See Wyer & Carlston 1979, pp. 221–76

Wyer, R. S. Jr., Goldberg, L. 1970. A probabilistic analysis of the relationships between beliefs and attitudes. *Psychol. Rev.* 77:100–20

Yarkin, K. L., Harvey, J. H., Bloxom, B. M. 1981. Cognitive sets, attribution and social interaction. *J. Pers. Soc. Psychol.* 41:243–52

Zajonc, R. B. 1980. Feeling and thinking: Preferences need no inferences. *Am. Psychol.* 35:151–75

Zuckerman, M., Mann, R. W. 1979. The other way around: Effects of causal attributions on estimates of consensus, distinctiveness, and consistency. *J. Exp. Soc. Psychol.* 15:582–97

Ann. Rev. Psychology. 1983. 34:543–75

PSYCHOLOGY OF ADULT DEVELOPMENT AND AGING

James E. Birren

Ethel Percy Andrus Gerontology Center, University of Southern California, Los Angeles, California 90007

Walter R. Cunningham

Department of Psychology, University of Florida, Gainesville, Florida 32611

Koichi Yamamoto

Laboratory of Psychology, Osaka Gakuin University, Osaka 564, Japan

CONTENTS

543

0066-4308/83/0201-0543$02.00

BACKGROUND

We have attempted to examine the organization and content of the psychology of adult development and aging, which implies an overview of the content, journals, trends, issues, and theoretical biases and preoccupations of the field. Two approaches were taken. One was a detailed analysis of all of the previous reviews of the topic in the *Annual Review of Psychology*, and the second was an analysis of the literature written since the last relevant review. There is now a span of activities of about 30 years from which the beginnings of a historical perspective can be developed (Shock 1951, Lorge 1956, Birren 1960, Chown & Heron 1965, Botwinick 1970, Schaie & Gribbin 1975, and Baltes et al 1980).

In the seven reviews spanning 30 years, 247 different journals were cited. Apparently the literature on adult development and aging comes from a wide range of journal sources. About half of the journals now commonly cited were not in existence at the time of the first review (Shock 1951). By far the most widely cited journal has been the *Journal of Gerontology*, founded in 1946, with 409 articles cited over the 30 year period. There were 52 journals cited five or more times over the 30 year span for a total number of 1229 citations, compared with total citations from all journals of 1571. In the reviews, journal citations represent 80% of the materials and citations from books 20%.

In 1980, Baltes, Reese & Lipsitt cited the *Journal of Gerontology* only 7 times, whereas in 1975 Schaie cited it 86 times. This gives rise to the question of how aging fits into a life-span perspective since Baltes, Reese & Lipsitt (1980) took a life-span point of view.

The 1975 review by Schaie & Gribbin cited frequently the five most commonly cited journals, with the median citation being 24 times. In contrast, Baltes, Reese & Lipsitt (1980) had median journal citations of only six. It is obvious that at this stage of sophistication of the subject matter contemporary authors vary in the extent to which they feel obliged to reflect content of the current literature on a topic.

The analysis of the seven reviews indicates that, with one exception, a coherence of the field developed about 1960. Of interest is the fact that the American Psychological Association (APA) journals lagged in publication of material on adult development and aging. *Developmental Psychology* was founded in 1969 and was first cited in 1975. Even in the two most recent reviews, the frequency of citation of *Developmental Psychology* (an APA publication) is far below that of the *Journal of Gerontology* for the same period. This would suggest that the activity of psychologists doing research on adult development and aging arose outside the major professional and scientific organization, the APA. If the amount of material published and cited in APA journals defines the orthodoxy of psychology, then adult development and aging is unorthodox and child development is orthodox.

One measure of the degree of orthodoxy of an area, or the degree of coherence, is the number of different journals cited to achieve the median number of citations. Over the 30 year period there was a citation of 1571 articles of which the first 13 journals produced 50% of the citations—an operational definition of a coherence of the field would be the narrowness of the journal citation distribution. Undeveloped or emerging research fields would tend to have many journals with few citations. At present, the psychology of adult development and aging is a field with a great range of inputs in types of journals and in the national origin of the journals frequently cited. For example, of the ten most frequently cited journals, one was published in Great Britain and another in Switzerland.

The present reviewers searched available data bases for relevant articles and books published between 1975 and 1981. There were 30 topics isolated from the previous chapters in the *Annual Review of Psychology*. A search of the available data bases for relevant material published between 1975 and 1981 resulted in an identification of over 4057 articles and books. Given the limitations of space and time, the average current review in this series can deal with less than 10% of the published volume in this area. Obviously, with so much selectivity there is much that is not being subjected to evaluation and integration with a core of growing knowledge.

A detailed analysis was made of the seven reviews of the 30 year period in terms of the subject matter covered, the number of lines used, the number of citations, and the number of articles cited. Generally there is close agreement between these three indicators of emphasis in a review. Ranked in order of the amount of space devoted to "theoretical content," the authors are, from most to least: Botwinick (1970), Birren (1960), Schaie & Gribbin (1975), Chown & Heron (1965), Baltes, Reese & Lipsitt (1980), Shock (1951), and Lorge (1956).

The one topic which all seven reviews developed in considerable detail was that of intellectual abilities or intelligence. Three of the seven authors gave more line space to this topic than to any other and two of the seven gave it the second most line space. Running close behind in emphasis are the combined topics of memory and learning. Clearly the psychology of adult development aging has for 30 years been dominated by a focus of attention on cognitive processes. A cluster of recurring topics of lesser line space than intellectual abilities are those defined by personality, social adjustment, and attitude. Furthermore, an emphasis on either psychobiology or social psychological processes tends to exclude treatment of the other topic. Also, an emphasis on sensation and perception tends to be associated with a discussion of age-related changes in health and survival, but with only a small treatment of the social aspects of aging. An example of the analysis of the reviews by emphasis is illustrated by the Baltes, Reese & Lipsitt (1980) review. In choosing a life-span orientation, they gave over four times the total line space to infant, child, and adolescent development compared with adult development and aging.

The 1970 review of Botwinick and the 1975 review of Schaie and Gribbin seem to be most representative of contemporary research on adult development and aging, with stress on methods and attention to a psychobiology of adult development and aging, which includes the correlates of survival and psychological functioning. With exceptions, we are currently faced with the choice of either a social orientation or a biological one. Unfortunately, for the training of investigators in understanding how behavior is organized, mankind is both a social and a biological organism, and how development and aging progress must be an interaction of both (Birren & Schaie 1977, Birren 1980).

STATUS OF THEORY

Learning and Memory

Two major theoretical orientations employed in recent memory research are the *associationist* and *cognitive processing* approaches. Walsh (1975) has noted a decline in the amount of research in the earlier associative approach and an increase within the cognitive processing framework. This trend is clearly continuing. Within the latter approach, there are several alternative views of memory processes. The older version is the serial stage model (Craik 1977), which continues to be influential. Three of the more important alternatives are levels of processing, multiple codes, and single-trace fragility theory. The merits of the levels of processing approach are emphasized in Craik's (1977) scholarly review. Hines & Fozard (1980), however, cite results that seem to pose problems for this formulation, calling attention to the advantages of the multiple codes approach and single-trace fragility theory. Many researchers are becoming interested in the possibility that attention may be an important source of memory deficits (Hasher & Zacks 1979, Poon et al 1980) although some reviewers are skeptical (e.g. Fredericksen 1980).

There is continuing interest by information processing researchers in Birren's views on changes in speed of processing in the aging nervous system (Birren et al 1980). Salthouse (1980) and Waugh & Barr (1980) suggest that changes in timing may account to a substantial extent for age differences in performance, although it seems unlikely that any single principle will account for all deficits. The use of Birren's concept is increasingly less global, and work is now beginning to be focused on more analytical issues including testing of the concept that speed of processing is a limiting factor for cognition rather than just a performance factor. In this sense cognition and age are intrinsically linked to speed of behavior.

Intellectual Abilities

There has been insufficient emphasis on previous theoretical development in this area. Birren's views continue to be regarded as important (Botwinick 1977, Cunningham 1980a,b). Horn (1976, 1978) continues to conceptually refine and empirically enhance the theory of fluid and crystallized intelligence. His emphasis is on what are called the "vital years"—ages 20 to 50, and most of the studies carried out under this theoretical motivation have been concerned with young or middle adult subjects. Greater application of these concepts to intellectual functioning in the elderly is desirable. It is of interest that unusually high correlations are (e.g. Heron & Chown 1967) observed between indicators of fluid intelligence and perceptual speed. Such relations argue against a nonintellective interpretation of speed changes in the elderly. Horn (1978), for example, has found that decline in perceptual speed appears to be related to fluid intelligence decline, based on partial correlational analyses. It is conceivable that decrements in fluid intelligence and perceptual speed may have a similar neurophysiological basis.

Several studies (reviewed in the empirical advances section) have found high interrelationships between different test measures of intellectual functioning. The dedifferentiation model (see Reinert 1970 for a review) involves a reduction in the number of ability factors in old age, as a counterpart for the differentiation model in early childhood (see Guilford 1967 for a critical review). The term "neointegration" has recently been employed (e.g. Baltes et al 1980) to evade the idea of ontogenetic regression. Finally, the term "greater interdependence" has been introduced (Cunningham 1980a,b, 1981) to reflect the fact that there is no convincing statistical evidence for an actual reduction in the number of ability factors in the elderly, even though the factors do appear to become more interdependent with age.

It is apparent, even on brief reflection, that the modest status of theory in the psychology of aging involves an excessive reliance on models conceptualized and operationalized within the context of young adulthood. Arlin (1975) and Schaie (1977–78) have attempted to develop some ideas which provide a basis for legitimate theories germane to the circumstances of the older adult. Similarly Baltes's ideas (e.g. Baltes et al 1980, Baltes & Willis 1982) about plasticity may provide the stimulus for further theoretical development. In this area generally, there is a need for greater theoretical articulation and related operational development of the concept of plasticity, to distinguish it from learning, habituation, and other forms of adaptation.

There also seems to be a need for a more searching, conceptual analysis of the age variable. There is a widespread recognition of the limitations of chronological age as the exclusive indicator of aging, both at a conceptual level and in terms of a technically rigorous interpretation of descriptive research. Recent technical advances in linear structural equation modeling allow for consideration of various latent variables which are aspects of aging, e. g. primary aging, health status, and longevity, or of a broad latent age construct, in which chronological age would be only one indicator, accompanied by indices of health status, physiological vigor, and other possible variables.

Finally, there has been and will continue to be much discussion regarding "cohort differences" (Rosow 1978). It is emphasized that we lack a theory of cohort differences and coordinated methods of empirical realizations. Such developments, though undoubtedly extremely difficult, are badly needed. Currently, every ambiguity of data, method, or occasion is eligible to be nominated as a potential cohort difference or cultural change. Unfortunately, such assertions cannot be evaluated empirically in our current state of relative ignorance regarding the nature of such cohort differences. The development of coherent concepts of cohort differences and related operationalizations are critical to allow for separation of the wheat from the chaff in particular, and to advance our level of understanding in general.

Psychobiology

In explaining the changes in behavior with age, psychologists have to recognize that heredity contributes to the age-related variance in behavior as well as to length of life and age-related disease. Since characteristics of an organism appearing after the age of reproduction cannot be subjected directly to selective pressure; genetic control over late life traits must arise as counterparts of characteristics which were selected at the time of reproduction. With these issues in mind, Birren (1964) proposed the "counterpart theory" to account for the genetic control over late life patterns of change. In a psychological sense as well as a biological, late life is a counterpart of early development. The difficult research task is to detect the ordered transmutation of that which went before.

One psychobiological phenomenon much studied in animals and in human infants is bonding or attachment (e.g. Bowlby 1969, Gewirtz 1972, Alloway et al 1977). Since adults have strong attachments to other persons they meet after maturity, it is surprising that human adult relationships are mostly described in terms of interpersonal relationships as though their only qualities arise from reinforcement and do not involve affective attachments, though there is some sign of the beginnings of research on adult attachments by Munnichs & van den Heuve (1976). Given the fact that research on the social networks of older adults is now popular, it makes more important the incorporation of bonding or attachment theory in our views of the social behavior of mature and older adults.

EMPIRICAL ADVANCES

Intellectual Abilities

Relationships between aging and abilities continues to be a strong area of interest and controversy. Two distinct kinds of emphasis have emerged. The first, and more traditional viewpoint, takes decline with age in intellectual functioning seriously and seeks to understand the nature of the phenomenon (Horn & Donaldson 1976, Botwinick 1977). A second, newer viewpoint emphasizes evidence for stability of functioning among the elderly (e.g. Baltes & Schaie 1976, Baltes & Willis 1982). Advocates of this position tend to be skeptical of evidence for decline, and emphasize alternative explanations while interpreting results of intervention studies optimistically. Although there are considerable data and soundly reasoned arguments on both sides of this issue, neither the absolute rigor of the extant designs nor the depth of our substantive understanding justifies absolute conclusions. An emerging viewpoint recognizes the reality of both cohort differences and age declines (Eisdorfer 1977, Hultsch & Deutsch 1981).

STRUCTURAL STUDIES   A fundamental assumption of most age-comparative research is that the test instruments or other procedures employed measure the same underlying construct in the same way (Cunningham 1982). Labouvie (1980) has considered conceptual equivalence, metric equivalence, equality of error variances, and also systematic errors of observation. These characteristics are usually studied by applications of factor analysis.

Cunningham & Birren (1980) reanalyzed Owens's (1953, 1966) longitudinal data for college students at approximately ages 20, 50, and 60. The number of factors and the basic pattern of simple structure was approximately the same with a tendency toward greater factor interrelationships with age. A further important result from this study was that when additional data on young adults in the 1970s were compared with data obtained by Owens on young people in 1919, unusually similar factor structures were identified. This raised the possibility that covariance structures may be highly similar across generation and time of measurement, although this problem has not been studied in the elderly. Further cross-sectional work (Cunningham, 1980a,b, 1981) confirmed the previous patterns of results: (a) no change in the number of factors or the basic patterns of the simple structure, (b) the same or only small changes in the magnitude of the factor loadings, but (c) a distinct tendency toward greater factor covariances. These increased factor covariances became most pronounced in the decade of the seventies. The role of speed was further clarified by the employment of three batteries, which varied speed demands: a highly speeded battery, an intermediate battery, and a much less speeded battery. As predicted, increased factor covariances were largest in the less speeded battery. These results appear to be reliable for batteries of short, timed tests with multiple indicators for each primary factor. How well such results generalize to other types of tests and measurement variables remains to be seen.

Baltes et al (1980) reported high intercorrelations within an elderly sample. Various models were considered and a preference was expressed for a general ("g") factor model. However, bearing in mind that "g" factor models can almost always be imposed on ability data (e.g. Guilford 1967, p. 56) even in young adults, it is difficult to accept the conclusion of a more integrated structure in the absence of cross-age comparisons. Hayslip & Sterns (1979) have also reported increasing correlations across age groups for composites of fluid and crystallized intelligence. An apparent discrepant finding was reported by Cunningham et al (1975). Cross-section comparisons showed a decreased correlation with age between a vocabulary measure and Raven's Progressive Matrices (RPM). Such correlational comparisons may be artifactually dependent on the large variability observed for RPM within the elderly sample, reflecting greater variation in neurological integrity, variations in sampling, extraneous performance deficits, or some combination thereof. However, when the covariances within age groups are scaled by equivalent estimates of variance pooled across age groups, the scaled covariances *increase* with age. These results are then in accord with the other findings reviewed in this section. Finally, Cohen et al (1977) considered sex differences in factor structure in an elderly sample. When uniformly scaled covariance matrices were analyzed, highly similar structures resulted.

DESCRIPTIVE STUDIES OF MEAN LEVELS   The review by Schaie & Gribbin (1975) emphasized the sequential findings of Schaie et al (1973) and Schaie & Labouvie-Vief (1974), concluding that the results challenge the view that there is generalized intellectual deficit in the elderly and that cohort differences are in general of greater magnitude than age changes. This conclusion, together with a nontechnical article appearing in a magazine (Baltes & Schaie 1974) sparked considerable controversy.

Horn & Donaldson (1976) critized these conclusions on various grounds, particularly sampling bias. Also, Botwinick (1977) reanalyzed data from Schaie's study and concluded that selective dropout was an important source of bias in longitudinal studies. While it was conceded that relative stability characterized those actually retested in longitudinal studies, it was questioned whether such results generalized to the population at large. This viewpoint was further reinforced by Botwinick & Siegler (1980), Siegler & Botwinick (1979) and also Rudinger (1976). These discussions have emphasized the need for: (a) greater rigor in sampling procedures, (b) intensive study of initial volunteering behavior and age, and (c) further study of selective attrition within longitudinal studies. The findings of Hertzog et al (1978) are interesting in this regard. It was found that individuals who developed cardiovascular disease were more likely to drop out of the study than healthy individuals. There is great need for more research along these lines as well as innovatively designed research primarily oriented toward the issues raised by Botwinick (1977). Until these problems are resolved, doubts will remain regarding the extent of the bias in both repeated measures longitudinal studies and independent sampling longitudinal studies, which may even be biased by differential initial volunteering across age groups. Interesting in this regard is the study of special groups which are clearly not of elite status (e.g. Troll et al 1976).

Botwinick & Arenberg (1976) also argued that wide cross-sectional age ranges and limited longitudinal comparisons could bias sequential designs in terms of increasing the likelihood of detecting greater cross-sectional differences, which could be inappropriately construed as cohort differences. However, Schaie & Parham (1977) concluded that even when the sequential comparisons were balanced, similar results were obtained. Further support for cohort differences was obtained by Cunningham & Birren (1976), who reported strong cohort effects for females on a Number Factor in a 28 year followup, which was supplemented by a time-lag comparison. Although parallel one standard deviation decrements were found for the highly speeded Relations Factor, this was a different pattern than was found for a very similar earlier cohort (Owens 1953; see also Cunningham & Owens 1982). Schaie (1979) has provided analyses of the performance of elderly individuals in comparison with performance levels of a young cohort and concludes that the cohort obsolescence is larger than the age decrements. Looking broadly at the literature, including the long-term time lag comparisons by Owens (1966) and Cunningham & Birren (1976), it seems difficult to avoid the conclusion that cohort membership is a potentially important variable. However, whether or not such cohort effects are greater than age changes in truly or even relatively more representative samples rather than extant volunteer samples remains to be seen. Also, the issue of cohort differences across the life span needs to be evaluated more analytically. Are cohort differences relatively less important in the old as compared with the middle-aged? The Botwinick & Siegler (1980) results raise the possibility that this may be the case, though further study is clearly needed.

Our conclusion is that Schaie's work represents an important beginning, but that the absolute quality of the existing studies does not justify simple, unqualified conclusions. Further work, with a variety of designs and a plurality of emphases, including decrement models, is needed to clarify the course of intellectual abilities in adulthood. It also seems necessary to say that these issues will be better illuminated by development of innovative and forward going new designs and approaches, rather than elaborate posturing which has characterized some of the previous exchanges on these issues.

With regard to specific abilities, there seems to be rather good consensus that intellectual tasks involving a high-speed component usually tend to show age decrements in most individuals fairly early, usually in the thirties. Ability tasks that are commonly utilized in everyday life tend to be insensitive to age. This includes not only vocabularly tests as usually scored (see Botwinick & Storandt 1974b and Botwinick et al 1975 for potentially important caveats), but also tasks such as arithmetic facility, which is both nonverbal and highly speeded, but extensively practiced. The tasks which remain at the center of controversy are those such as Figural Induction or Letter Series tasks, which mark Fluid Intelligence. These show rather different patterns cross-sectionally and longitudinally. Horn & Donaldson (1976), while significantly conceding that some individuals may avoid declines to a substantial extent, argue that others may begin showing losses in the period of 20 to 50 years. However, various longitudinal studies show that most individuals who continue in such studies show little or no decline until the early sixties. Clearly, the possibility of differential patterns of development should be carefully scrutinized, and if such patterns are found to be common, identification of possible mechanisms (health, life style, longevity, and cohort) should be pursued.

PIAGETIAN STUDIES   As with abilities, there are wide individual differences in the elderly (Papalia & Bielby 1975). Cross-sectional results usually show age differences (Clayton & Overton 1976, Sinnott 1975, Cicirelli 1976) but not always (Sinnott & Guttmann 1978). Longitudinal and sequential studies would clearly be useful. Community residents tend to perform better than noncommunity residents (Chap & Sinnott 1977–78). Also, more highly educated persons tend to perform better, even in minority groups (Finley & Delgado 1979). For some tasks, it appears to be quite feasible to improve performance in the elderly (Denney 1974, Hornblum & Overton 1976, Schultz & Hoyer 1976). Delgado (1980) even showed that simple elicitation procedures produced higher level categorizing behavior in the elderly.

PRETEST ACTIVITY   Furry & Baltes (1973) used a simulation technique to investigate fatigue effects on intellectual test performance. This article was widely cited as an example of an extraneous variable which might negatively bias the estimation of abilities in the elderly. However, subsequent work with actual tests (Cunningham et al 1978) showed no reliable fatigue effects even for quite lengthy test batteries. Hayslip & Sterns (1979) also failed to find significant effects when varying test order. Further work lead Furry & Schaie (1979) to conclude that pretest activity was a less potent variable than had earlier been suspected.

TRAINING STUDIES   There has been a considerable increase in interest in training studies. (For a general background, see Labouvie-Vief 1976, 1977, Lavouvie-Vief & Chandler 1978, Blieszner et al 1981, Willis & Baltes 1981). Krauss et al (1980) found that performance on a spatial rotation task could be improved by easing memory requirements and providing for practice. Berg et al (1982) allowed practice in a mental rotation task over several days. Although speed improved with practice, age differences were not eliminated. Other examples of interventions include Birkhill & Schaie (1975), and Labouvie-Vief & Gonda (1976). Plemons et al (1978) employed a hierarchical transfer design in an attempt to modify fluid intelligence. Their conclusions were sharply attacked by Donaldson (1981) on several issues. His basic contention was that the design of the Plemons et al (1978) study was not adequate to support the contention that fluid intelligence (as a higher order construct) has been modified. Although Willis & Baltes (1981) replied point by point, further work (Willis et al 1981) could only demonstrate minimal transfer within the figural relations primary ability factor. In further discussion, the earlier claims that: (a) fluid intelligence as a higher order construct had been modified, and (b) that this could represent some kind of "challenge" to fluid intelligence theory, appear to have been abandoned (Baltes & Willis 1982). The inclusion of young adult comparison groups seems useful in such studies and could result in an enhanced interpretation of the results.

PROBLEM SOLVING   This area has been reviewed recently by Rabbitt (1977) and Giambra & Arenberg (1980). In a particularly significant study, Arenberg (1974) reported a 6 year longitudinal study of logical problem solving. Age changes were found in the proportion of correct solutions for all three problems considered. These changes became larger after age 60. Survival relationships were also found. Lee & Pollack (1978) found large age differences in the Embedded Figures Test for females in their fifties. Kesler et al (1976) reported relationships between education and nonverbal intelligence.

CREATIVITY, COGNITIVE STYLES, AND WISDOM   Alpaugh (1976) and Alpaugh & Birren (1975, 1977) found age differences for both divergent thinking and preference for complexity measures (see also Ruth 1980). They suggested that both creative ability and motivation decline with age. Kogan (1974) has found relatively complex relationships between cognitive style and aging. Kogan (1979) also provides an interesting review on creativity and cognitive style, emphasizing the complexities of research in this area.

Clayton & Birren (1980) developed the concept of wisdom in relation to age and culture. They concluded that characteristics attributed to wise persons are useful to both old and young. Wisdom clearly is an important topic to which insufficient attention has been paid.

Learning and Memory

In view of the plethora of recent reviews (e.g. Poon et al 1980, Kubanis & Zornetzer 1981), we intend to present a highly selected treatment, emphasizing what appear to be particularly significant papers. Although animal studies are important (e.g. Elias 1980), the focus here is on studies of human memory.

A particularly useful review from an associationist viewpoint was provided by Arenberg & Robertson-Tchabo (1977). Treat & Reese (1976) examined imagery and pacing using a paired associate learning task. They found that imagery instructions benefited both young and old, but the latter required greater retrieval time. In an unusually thorough study, Botwinick & Storandt (1974a) examined the relationship between verbal learning and interference. Age differences were smallest with word list materials of high associative strength, but substantial differences occurred on higher difficulty level lists. The results of a study by Okun et al (1978) raised the possibility that cautiousness plays a role (albeit a complex one) in part of the age differences in verbal learning. A review by Elias & Elias (1977) considered, among other topics, the roles of motivation, anxiety, and arousal.

The information processing approach to memory and aging appears to be a rapidly growing enterprise. Craik's (1977) scholarly review highlights levels of processing view, while Waugh & Barr (1980), Fozard (1980), and Salthouse (1980) underscore the role of speed of processing. The relatively few studies of sensory memory suggest that what age decrements have been identified (Schonfield & Wenger 1975, Walsh & Thompson 1978, Cerella et al 1982) are not as large as found in other memory processes (Craik 1977), although more work is clearly needed (Walsh & Prasse 1980, Crowder 1980). Age differences in primary memory appear relatively small except when reorganization or divided attention are required (Craik 1977, Hartley et al 1980, Hultsch & Deutsch 1981). Much recent effort has been focused on secondary memory, which appears to be an area of more substantial age differences (Hultsch & Craig 1976, Earhard 1977, Smith 1977, 1980, Perlmutter 1978, 1979, Mason 1979, Sanders et al 1980, Hultsch & Pentz 1980, Burke & Light 1981). Although there is considerable debate with regard to mechanisms, and there are intrinsic problems in sorting out the impact of memory problems at various processing stages, most results do not categorically refute either encoding differences or retrieval deficits, but storage deficits do not seem plausible (Smith 1980, Smith & Fullerton 1981). Speed of retrieval also appears to decline with age for unfamiliar materials, but such differences are reduced or eliminated for highly familiar stimuli (Poon & Fozard 1978, Thomas et al 1978). Many memory researchers are becoming increasingly interested in the role of attention in memory deficits (Hasher & Zacks 1979, Craik & Simon 1980, Hoyer & Plude 1980, Madden & Nebes 1980, Burke & Light 1981, Wright 1981).

Arenberg's (1978, 1982) longitudinal study of visual retention for designs identified age changes which were small for younger adults, moderate for persons in their fifties and sixties, but substantial in persons beyond the age of 70. Cohort differences were judged to be small. More longitudinal work is desirable, particularly for topics such as rehearsal strategies, which may plausibly reflect cohort differences (e.g. Sanders et al 1980).

Another rapidly emerging approach emphasizes learning and memory in the context of everyday life. The contextual approach is largely concerned with ecologically valid tasks that are significant in the day-to-day lives of older adults: knowledge actualization, comprehension of sentences and retention of prose material, etc (Cohen 1979, Lachman et al 1979, Robinson & House 1979, Taub 1979, Botwinick & Storandt 1980, Hultsch & Pentz 1980, Lachman & Lachman 1980, Ribovich & Erickson 1980, Meyer & Rice 1981). A common finding from this literature is that when individuals are assessed on familiar tasks that have a meaningful context, age differences are smaller than with traditional laboratory tasks, and sometimes are negligible (e.g. Walsh & Baldwin 1977, Waddell & Rogoff 1981).

Psychophysiology

An expanding area of research in the psychology of aging is that of event-related electrical protentials (ERP), and there is a new thrust in attempting to link sensory-evoked potentials, as well as contingent negative variation to age differences in information processing, attention, and arousal. The analyses usually divide potentials into three groups: those occuring in the first 100 milliseconds after the stimulus, those occuring between 100 and 300 milliseconds, and those occurring after 300 milliseconds. The positive potentials recorded after 300 milliseconds appear to be associated with attention (Bowman 1980). Early components are increased in amplitude whereas the components after 100 milliseconds are decreased in amplitude with age (Marsh & Thompson 1977). For example, the amplitude differences in late components are found in auditory evoked potentials, but not in visual evoked potentials. In addition to amplitude, the latency of the wave components has also been found to change with age (Schenkenberg 1970, Drechsler 1978), with late components showing larger age differences. When the experimental conditions require subjects to control their attention the latency of response may show no differences (Brent et al 1977, Goodin et al 1978, Ford et al 1979). A reduction in central inhibition has been credited for the increase in amplitude of response in the early components of the ERP (Dustman & Beck 1969, Shagass 1972, Drechsler 1977). One of the more striking findings is that age differences in ERP components are most significant when subjects are required to engage in the performance of a psychological task.

The contingent negative variation (CNV) is a slow negative shift in electrical potential that occurs in time intervals between two stimuli that are contingently related, as in a reaction time experiment which consists of a warning signal followed by a fixed period before a signal to which the subject should respond. CNV is interpreted as reflecting the development of expectation or the preparation of a response to an expected stimulus. Distraction reduces the amplitude of the CNV. Tecce (1980a,b) linked the evidence of a reduced CNV phenomenon to a lessened capacity to switch attention.

Under some experimental conditions investigators have reported no age differences in the amplitude of the CNV (Thompson & Nowlin 1973), while other investigators have reported age differences (Loveless & Sanford 1974). Other attempts to analyze CNV components in relation to age have been reported by Schaie & Syndulko (1978), and Nakamura et al (1979). The inconsistencies in these findings have been discussed by Smith, Thompson & Michalewski (1980). Under conditions of passive processing or stimulation age differences are shown, whereas under active stimulation the elderly and the young appear to show the same levels of cortical excitability. An important inference is that there may be a decreased capacity in the elderly to sustain arousal levels.

Under conditions of appropriate stimulation older subjects can sustain high arousal level, and minimum age differences are shown in electrical potentials. Therefore, the age differences in performance may not result from a change in the primary information transmitting system of the brain, but in a modulating system.

Motivation

HUNGER AND THIRST   Elias & Elias (1977) regarded the review by Botwinick (1959) as being the most "comprehensive" in summarizing the early investigations on the effects of hunger and thirst-induced drive. Investigations of food deprivation on weight loss were consistent with growth rates and metabolic rates (Jerome 1959, Kleiber et al 1956, Jakubczak 1969), but there are strain differences, for example, among C57 BL/6J, Fisher and ACI/Mai's results.

As Jakubczak's 1970 study showed, loss of weight from water deprivation through death is approximately 100 percent for all ages. There was a close relation between the percents of weight loss and survival time. It appears that weight loss is the best index of both hunger and thirst drive level in studies of age differences in drive level (Elias & Elias 1977).

EATING AND DRINKING HABITS   Recently Peng, Jiang & Hsu (1980) reported their experiments on eating, drinking, and running wheel activity using male Long-Evans rats. They recorded total activity and food and water intake per day. They found a reduction with age in running activity and food intake that "water intake decreased from four months to 17 months of age and later increased with advancing age" (p. 339). "Water and food intake had a significant correlation among rats below 20 months old, but not over this age" (Peng et al 1980, p. 346). "In a few old animals circadian rhythms of these three kinds of behavior (light-dark rhythm, odd intake, and water intake) are not entrained to the light cycle with coincidental phase relationship" (p. 346; see also Zucker 1971, Paxinos 1976).

In Schiffman & Pasternak's (1979) experiment on food discrimination, young students aged 19–25 and healthy elderly subjects aged 72–78 "related the order similarity for all 91 combinations of pairs of 14 commercial food flavors" (p. 73). They confirmed Schiffman's (1979) hypothesis, and found that older subjects preferred fruits and also were better in discriminating fruits and the stimuli.

Wigdor (1980) emphasized that drinking and eating are lifelong habits and are based on interpersonal relationships and societal patterns, and that they relate "not only to the need to satisfy hunger and thirst, but to the needs for affiliation, recognition, self-esteem and affection" (p. 250).

Activity and Exploration

RUNNING ACTIVITY   Wax (1975) used 5-month-old young and 27-month-old senescent C57BL/6J strain mice in an experimental study on running wheel activity under constant light or constant dark conditions. He was testing the hypothesis that "transferring the mice to constant light or constant dark should disrupt the rhythmic behavior of senescent mice more than that of young mice due to differential stress of adaptation to the changed environmental and internal conditions" (p. 22). The independent variables were age, treatment (12 : 12 LL, LD, DD.), and time blocks (first 4 days, next 5 days, final 5 days). The three measures of running activity were periodicity, activity-rest ratios, and amplitude. The results were interpreted as indicating that Aschoff's Rules (Aschoff et al 1971) applied to "nocturnal animals such as the mouse should show shorter periodicity, increased amplitude, and increased activity-rest ratios under constant dark" (Wax 1975, p. 26). The reverse effect under constant light conditions was predicted and observed "not only in mature young mice, but also in senescent mice." Peng et al (1980) concluded from their results that the "ability to keep the day/night rhythm of running activity, food intake and water intake or the ability to recover the day/night rhythm when the light-dark schedule is reversed are still well preserved in most of the rats ranging from 18 months of age to 33 months of age" (p. 347).

Wax's (1975) results of the first experimental series pointed to "rigidity" of old mice (Goodrick 1966), but in the second series of light-dark conditions, old mice were "more reactive" than young mice. That was interpreted as a confirmation of the greater "emotionality" of old animals.

LOCOMOTOR ACTIVITY   In free food and water access schedules, activity decreased with increasing age, females being "generally more active than males" (C57BL/6J and DBA/2J) (Elias & Elias 1977, p. 363). There appeared to be species differences in activity and length of life, for example, between C57BL/6J and DBA/2J (Sprott & Eleftheriou 1974, Elias et al 1975, Eleftheriou 1974, Elias & Elias 1977).

EXPLORATION   Goodrick (1966) observed exploratory behavior of albino rats and found that deprivation increased "exploratory behavior across all age groups and reduced the magnitude of differences among age groups," while control animals decreased exploratory behavior with increasing age.

Elias et al (1975) used 2-, 5-, 6-, 12-, and 24-month-old C57B1/6J and DBA/2J mice in observations of the "number of crossings to and from an illuminated area and a dark area." The results were interpreted as indicating that C57BL/6J mice decreased their exploratory behavior between 2.5 and 6.5 months of age, while in DBA/2J mice no differences in exploratory scores were observed with increasing age (Elias & Elias 1977, p. 366).

Sexuality

SEX HORMONES   In considering the earlier results of Jakubczak (1967) and Timiras & Meisami (1972), Elias & Elias (1977) pointed out that "there were age decrements in the mechanisms that mediate the temporal summation of excitatory neuronal impulses from the CNS which lead to ejaculation, and that age changes in mediating mechanisms in the CNS occurred earlier in the life of the animal than did changes in androgen levels" (Elias & Elias 1977, p. 372).

While human sexual behavior is more complex (Timiras & Meisami 1972), Elias & Elias (1977) emphasized that it should not be concluded that "complex social factors do not affect the mating behaviors of lower animals" (p. 372).

Corby & Solnick (1980) have reviewed research on sexual behavior of older adults from psychosocial and physiological points of view. Both the production of estrogen and progesterone by the postmenopausal ovary and the amount of androgens have been discussed as the main aspects of female hormonal changes (Timiras & Meisami 1972, Vermeulen 1976, Monroe & Menon 1977). However, Weg (1978) pointed out that the role of the estrogen level in menopausal symptoms "had been exaggerated," because "75% of a sample reported no symptoms" (Corby & Solnick 1980, p. 893).

"Recently the decline in secretion of androgens in the male with advancing age has been questioned about the accurate measure of serum and urine testosterone and the complexity of androgen metabolism" (Eisdorfer & Raskind 1975; Corby & Solnick 1980, p. 893). The role of testosterone level has been discussed (Cooper et al 1970, Raboch et al 1975), and Corby & Solnick (1980) concluded that many results about testosterone have been presented, but there is no "clear evidence that androgen therapy was effective in the long term alternation of either libido or sexual responsiveness" (p. 895).

SEXUAL ACTIVITY   Pfeiffer (1978) stated the importance of sexual activity for old persons because sexual interest and activity play major roles in contributing to life satisfaction and problems of sexual expression in later life have not been resolved.

Hite's (1976) conclusions were important because according to her data, the "vasocongestive increase in clitoral shaft diameter and retraction of the clitoral shaft and glands as the female reached high levels of excitement did not change with age," though many other changes were found in individuals over 50 years old (Corby & Solnick 1980, p. 895).

Solnick & Birren (1977) improved the problems of sampling and controlling stimuli in relation to the research of Masters & Johnson (1966). They presented the same erotic film to young and old subjects. Of the potential subjects approached, 85 percent of the young group and 70.6 percent of the older group agreed to be the subjects. Results indicated that the younger men responded rapidly to a particular scene in the movie, then partially lost the erection, while the older men gradually increased the erectile response though it never reached the maximum levels attained by younger men.

Solnick (1978) tested the effect of both fantasy and biofeedback on the male erectile response changes. His results stated that fantasy played an important role in sexual practice, and that the procedure of biofeedback was helpful "to make him aware of what fantasies are most effective to arouse him" (Solnick 1978, p. 40). Although the studies of sexual interest and the frequency of masturbation stated that women's capacity for sex might remain intact throughout life, fewer women than men remained sexually active (Hite 1976, Corby & Solnick 1980).

PSYCHOSOCIAL FACTORS   Pfeiffer (1978) pointed out that the feeling which "all of us harbor regarding sexual expression in our parent generation, and more specifically in our own parents" influences the sexual expression of old persons in our society (p. 27).

The sexual interests of youth may continue into old age (Masters & Johnson 1966). Marital status does not affect men's sexual activity, but men's sexual activities were different from women's because older women's opportunities for sexual expression are greatly restricted, because of the death of their spouses (Kinsey et al 1953, Masters & Johnson 1966, Pfeiffer 1969, 1974, 1978, Botwinick 1978, Corby & Solnick 1980).

Studies of sexual interest (Verwoerdt et al 1969, Pfeiffer & Davis 1972, Cameron & Biber 1973, Hegeler 1976) and sexual dreams (Christenson & Gagnon 1965, Martin 1975) presented evidence about the increasing gap with age between sexual activity and interest.

Comfort (1974) emphasized that old people were "still capable of experiencing sexual pleasure" and "sexuality in the aged should not be rigidly suppressed ... as it is at present in most nursing homes and other institutions" (p. 440; see also Keller et al 1978, and White & Catania 1981).

Personality

CAUTIOUSNESS AND ANXIETY   Botwinick (1978) developed the concept of cautiousness in relation to the elderly and pointed out that in relation to the work of Welford (1951) "accuracy of the elderly was often greater than that of the young only in a relative sense, and often the youngest subjects were both speedy and accurate" (p. 115).

Okun (1976) reviewed the literature on age differences in cautiousness, particularly that which used the choice dilemma instrument. This instrument requires subjects to make decisions on a hypothetical situation. He regards the need for achievement as a relevant factor. Okun, Siegler & George (1978) found that young adults made more correct responses and fewer omission errors and took greater risks than older subjects.

It has also been pointed out that anxiety can raise the arousal of an individual beyond an optimal level and result in more erroneous responses (Eisdorfer 1977). Anxiety can also "result in cautiousness which delays decision processes" and slows responses (Thomae 1980, p. 292).

Costa et al (1976) presented data on the relation between three cognitive ability factors—Information Processing Ability (IPA), Manual Dexterity (MD), and Pattern Analysis Capability (PAC)—and three personality dimensions—Anxiety, Extroversion, and Openness to Experience. "High anxiety scores related to low levels of all three cognitive factors," high scores on openness to experience to high IPA and PAC, and introversion to high PAC. Older subjects performed less well than younger ones on MD and PAC, but not on IPA (p. 663) which they called crystallized intelligence and which was unaffected by the aging process (see also Costa & McCrae 1976, Zarit 1980)

Anxiety of the elderly was reported to be related to a high crime rate in urban areas (Lebowitz 1975, Jarvik & Russell 1979, Thomae 1980). McCrae, Bartone & Costa (1976) reported that anxiety influenced self-reported health; the greater the anxiety the poorer the self-reported health.

HAPPINESS   Graney (1975) reported a close relationship between social activity and happiness of elderly women, and Cameron (1975) reported that happiness was influenced by age, sex, social class, and situational differences (see also Reedy et al 1981). It is also of interest that the subject of humor is beginning to be discussed in relation to age (Schaier & Circirelli 1976, Davies 1977, Weber & Cameron 1978). Humor may be one of the strategies that individuals use in adapting to the stresses of life.

EXTERNAL AND INTERNAL ORIENTATION   The hypothesis that there should be a continuous change with age from extroversion to introversion was proposed by Thomae (1980) in relation to internal control. In this regard, Schaie & Parham (1976) pointed out that their oldest cohort was the least outgoing.

According to Gutmann's (1977) cross-cultural data, men move from active to passive mastery modes, but women move in the opposite direction, from passive to active. It may be that Gutmann's (1975, 1977) findings can be replicated in other cultures (Neugarten 1977).

Lao (1974) tested Rotter's (1966) Internal versus External locus of control and found that internal locus of control increased from young to middle age with no change from middle to old age. Ryckman & Malikosi (1975) confirmed their results although Kuypers (1972) did not find age differences between internals and externals.

Other reports (Levinson 1975, Kivett et al 1977, Reid et al 1977) have examined age differences in other variables such as self-rated health, ego strength, and some specific socialization factors (Thomae 1980, p. 292). Other factors may also influence adaptation and the locus of control such as changes in job status (Back & Morris 1974), retirement (Friedmann & Orbach 1974), widowhood (Lopata 1973), and menopause (Neugarten et al 1965).

HEALTH AND SURVIVAL   One of the distinguishing features of the literature on adult development and aging, in contrast to that on child development, is an emphasis on the health of the subjects. A consistent relationship has been shown between the health status of subjects and intellectual abilities as well as other behavioral variables (Botwinick & Birren 1963, Correll et al 1966). More recently, problem solving and health research were studied in subjects 40 to 79 years of age (LaRue et al 1979, LaRue & Waldbaum 1980, 1981). Health status was determined by medical examinations. A negative correlation (0.28) was reported between a measure of composite formal thinking and systolic blood pressure. Earlier reports linked hypertension to impairment on a variety of functions (Goldman et al 1974, Wilkie et al 1976, Light 1978). The research of Light rather conclusively links slowing of reaction time with cerebral vascular disease and hypertension.

Since individuals with cardiovascular and cerebral vascular disease are likely to have lower intellectual test scores and slower reaction time, it is plausible that psychological measures should be related to the likelihood of survival. A variety of studies have, in fact, indicated that low test scores are related to a lower probability of survival (e.g. Granick 1971). Hertzog, Schaie & Gribbin (1978) showed that low test scores, and particularly a loss in cognitive performance in longitudinal studies, are related to a lower likelihood of survival. Of considerable importance are the findings on identical twins beyond the age of 80 that loss in performance on psychological tests is no longer related to the likelihood of survival (LaRue et al 1979, Steuer et al 1981). Conceivably the pacing effect with age of vascular disease on cognitive function washes out in the very aged. This, in turn, raises the question of what are the dominant pacemakers of mortality in the very aged. We have identified here an increasingly important research area in which psychophysiological mechanisms must be sought to link cognition, mood, age, and health status (Tredway 1978, Birren & Renner 1981, Woods 1981). A relevant study of the effects of the environment on patterns of cognitive performance and on other adult characteristics was reported by Boutourline, Young, and Ferguson in *Puberty to Manhood in Italy and America* (Young & Ferguson 1981). They studied 339 male adolescents growing up in Boston, Rome, and Palermo, Palermo being the community of origin. The study began with boys aged 10 to 14 and followed them for 11 years into manhood. Of particular significance is a conclusion that "the broad course of adolescent development is very much the same living in Italy and in America. The phenomena of human physical and mental growth showed a limited plasticity to environmental change—at least the kind of change provided by the "natural" experiment of migration from southern Italy on which we capitalized" (p. 225). It is to be hoped that these men can be followed into their middle years when cardiovascular and other diseases may become expressed and can be related to environmental influences. The study would then overlap the work by George Vaillant (1977) on Harvard undergraduates who were followed into their middle years.

METHODOLOGICAL ADVANCES

Design and Data Analysis

Earlier discussions of developmental designs (Schaie 1965, Baltes 1968, Schaie 1970, Buss 1973, Botwinick 1978) have continued and expanded without a satisfactory resolution. Adam (1978) provided a severe critique of Schaie's (1965) decision rules in an analysis of variance context. Schaie & Hertzog (1982) in a forthright, articulate, and important chapter have acknowledged that this approach is dated, emphasizing that an atheoretical exploratory attempt to estimate relationships for age, cohort, and period is not realistic. In a general way, this corresponds to Botwinick's (1978) review on this particular issue.

During this period of continuing controversy, there has been an unusually rapid development of technologies for the evaluation of correlational data, and longitudinal data in particular. The structural equation approach (Jöreskog 1979, Jöreskog & Sörbom 1979, Bentler 1980) has wide potential applicability and shows considerable promise for developmental and gerontological research. The various computer programs which have been developed (LISREL IV, Jöreskog & Sörbom, 1978, and the related programs:

COFAMM, Sörbom & Jöreskog 1976, EFAP, Jöreskog & Sörbom 1976) are likely to have an important impact on the aging field. A new version —LISREL V—is now in the process of being introduced, and is said to be easier to use and to contain new options for obtaining statistics useful in the evaluation of model fit, which has been a thorny problem in the application of these techniques (Bentler & Bonett 1980). There have been important advances in appreciating the technical complexities of longitudinal data analysis methods (Nesselroade & Baltes 1979, Kessler & Greenberg 1981, Schaie & Hertzog 1982). Two texts on causal modeling have also resulted in a wider appreciation of applications in empirical research (Heise 1975, Kenny 1979).

The furious onrush of new models and statistical methods for studying longitudinal and sequential data (e.g. Sörbom 1975, Nesselroade & Baltes 1979) has created a situation of considerable uncertainty regarding what approaches are truly optimal. It is apparent that some of the LISREL approaches have important advantages over more traditional applications of analysis of variance, but they clearly come at potential costs (Horn & McArdle 1980, Cliff 1980). Clarifications and refinements in the understanding of previous methods are also progressing rapidly (e.g. Rogosa 1979). Some methodologists seem to feel that there is a "correct understanding" (e.g. Schaie & Hertzog 1982) of how developmental studies should be designed and analyzed. We perceive no truly general consensus. Further, in view of the large number of new model approaches (e.g. Nesselroade & Baltes 1979, among others), many of which lack sufficient empirical, substantive application to evaluate in practice their pragmatic strengths and weaknesses, such a consensus, even if present, would doubtless be premature. New and innovative approaches should continue to be encouraged.

A problem that has been increasingly emphasized by those skeptical of longitudinal methods (e.g. Botwinick 1978) is selective attrition, which is widely believed to weaken the external validity of simple longitudinal studies and repeated measures aspects of sequential studies (Botwinick 1977, Siegler & Botwinick 1979, Botwinick & Siegler 1980, Schaie & Hertzog 1982). Some discussions (e.g. Horn & Donaldson 1976) have even drawn attention to the potentially biased nature of initial volunteer samples in simple cross-sectional studies. Such behavior may interact in complex ways with age. Although volunteering behavior has been studied in more general contexts (Rosenthal & Rosow 1975), there is a clear need for such scrutiny of the volunteering behavior of older adults, particularly with regard to the type of study (memory or other complex cognitive tasks vs attitudes, for example). Encouraging is the very promising development of models which explicitly consider study drop-out in longitudinal contexts (Woodbury & Clive 1974, Woodbury et al 1978, as well as further unpublished work by Woodbury and his colleagues).

New Observations and Measurement Techniques

There continue to be suggestions for intelligence tests oriented toward the unique capabilities and experiences of elderly adults (Schaie & Schaie 1977, Schaie 1977–78), but little actual test development has occurred. It is likely that such work awaits development or refinement of actual theories of intellectual functioning that are rooted in and are truly germane to the life-space of elderly persons.

A number of papers (e.g. Hertzog et al 1978) imply a need for greater sophistication in the measurement of health. Wider awareness (Harbin & Cunningham 1978, Siegler et al 1980) of the complexity of health measurement issues appears to be occurring, although many researchers prefer to carry out research with the "healthy elderly," with some cost (perhaps substantial, but usually unassessed) in terms of generalizability. In terms of neurological assessment, the advance which has resulted in the most change in practice (Drachman 1980) is computerized axial tomography (New & Scott 1975, deLeon et al 1980).

Biography is currently being given much scholarly attention (Paul 1982) and autobiographies are pointed to as a valuable source of research data as well as being of therapeutic value (Birren & Hateley 1982). It seems prudent for investigators to take into account individuals' purposes or intentions. If one accepts the fact that individuals are in part self-constructing, then it is important to know their concept of what it is that they are striving for as a basis for behavior choices. Autobiography supplements external observational methods and offers a way of studying intentionality as well as a method of inducing change in individuals.

A new approach to isolating development issues is the study of males in midlife by Merriam (1980). She did a content analysis of novels and dramas written by distinguished authors in the conviction that literary materials could lead to an inductive theory about development in middle age. This comparative literary approach appears to have the capacity to identify some of the focal points of midlife change that would be missed by more conventional methods.

APPLICATIONS

The growth of research literature on the psychology of aging provides a knowledge basis for a large number of derivative applications to such areas as education (Peterson & Birren 1981), mental health (Birren & Sloane 1980), death and dying (Kalish 1981), and to the emerging field of personal management of health behaviors (Hussian 1981).

The growth in research literature on adult life and aging has been accompanied by an increase in textbooks for college level instruction. Several trends can be seen. One is an increase in textbooks on adulthood and old age (Huyck & Hoyer 1982, Hultsch & Deutsch 1981), and the other trend is toward books which take a life-span approach (Birren et al 1981).

SUMMARY

The psychology of adult development and aging continues to show an explosive growth in research and published literature. In searching the literature for this review, existing information systems yielded over 4000 articles of potential relevance. Obviously, it is inceasingly difficult to form a perspective in a field that is expanding rapidly and which tends to be organized into pockets of subinterests with little cross-citation or theoretical integration. Relative isolation of the subdisciplinary activities is not unlike the developmental psychology of childhood. There seems little momentum in the conceptual or theoretical basis for an integrative developmental psychology at this time. Research is moving forward either by the indepth study of particular behavioral processes or by intensive study of a particular problem of an epoch in the life span, e.g. the newborn, the adolescent, midlife, or the aged.

The most active area of interest remains that of intellectual abilities. This area is also marked by disputes as to the reality and extent of declines in intellectual abilities with age. Resolution of the differences in the interpretation of research findings seems within grasp if the protagonists adopt a less polemical style.

A significant emergent area of research is the study of the relations of cognition to recorded electrical brain potentials, i.e. the event-related potentials and the contingent negative variation. Both types of measurement seem to give promise of linking the level of individual performance to age changes in brain structures. Another area of research that is growing rapidly is that on health status and intellectual functioning. Furthermore, newer experimental research is also examining the effects of exercise and physical fitness on mood and intellectual performance of adults of different ages.

Questions about lifelong patterns of behavior and motivation remain of great significance, but at the moment such research is not showing much progress in methodology. Of some promise is the use of autobiographical and biographical studies in attempting to uncover new issues and relationships that later can be examined with other methods.

Literature Cited

Adam, J. 1977. Statistical bias in cross-sequential studies of aging. *Exp. Aging Res.* 3:325–33

Adam, J. 1978. Sequential strategies and the separation of age, cohort, and time-of-measurement contributions to developmental data. *Psychol. Bull.* 85:1309–16

Alloway, T., Pliner, P., Krames, L., eds. 1977. *Attachment Behavior.* New York: Plenum

Alpaugh, P. K. 19 .. *The creative process in adulthood and old age: An exploratory study.* PhD thesis. Univ. South. Calif., Los Angeles

Alpaugh, P. K., Birren, J. E. 1975. Are there sex differences in creativity across the adult life span? *Hum. Dev.* 18:461–65

Alpaugh, P. K., Birren, J. E. 1977. Variables affecting creative contributions across the adult life span. *Hum. Dev.* 20: 240–48

Arenberg, D. 1974. A longitudinal study of problem solving in adults. *J. Gerontol.* 29:650–58

Arenberg, D. 1978. Differences and changes with age in the Benton Visual Retention Test. *J. Gerontol.* 33:534–40

Arenberg, D. 1982. Estimates of age changes on the Benton Visual Retention Test. *J. Gerontol.* 37:87–90

Arenberg, D., Robertson-Tchabo, E. A. 1977. Learning and aging. See Birren & Schaie 1977, pp. 421–49

Arlin, P. K. 1975. Cognitive development in adulthood: A fifth stage? *Dev. Psychol.* 11:602–6

Aschoff, J., Gerecke, U., Kureck, A., Pohl, H., Rieger, F., et al. 1971. Interdependent parameters of circadian activity rhythms in birds and man. In *Biochronometry,* ed. M. Menaker. Washington DC: Natl. Acad. Sci.

Back, K. W., Morris, J. D. 1974. Perception of self and the study of whole lives. In *Normal Aging II: Reports from the Duke Longitudinal Studies, 1970–1973,* ed. E. Palmore, pp. 216–21. Durham, NC: Duke Univ. Press

Baltes, P. B. 1968. Longitudinal and cross-sectional sequences in the study of age and generation effects. *Hum. Dev.* 11:145–71

Baltes, P. B., Cornelius, S. W., Spiro, A. III, Nesselroade, J. R., Willis, S. L. 1980. Integration vs. differentiation of fluid-crystallized intelligence in old age. *Dev. Psychol.* 16:625–35

Baltes, P. B., Reese, H. W., Lipsitt, L. P. 1980. Life-span developmental psychology. *Ann. Rev. Psychol.* 31:65–110

Baltes, P. B., Schaie, K. W. 1974. Aging and IQ: The myth of the twilight years. *Psychol. Today* 40:35–38

Baltes, P. B., Schaie, K. W. 1976. On the plasticity of intelligence in adulthood and old age: Where Horn and Donaldson fail. *Am. Psychol.* 31:720–25

Baltes, P. B., Willis, S. L. 1982. Plasticity and enhancement of intellectual functioning in old age: Penn State's Adult Development and Enrichment Project (ADEPT). In *Aging and Cognitive Processes,* ed. F.I.M. Craik, S. E. Traub. New York: Plenum. In press

Bentler, P. M. 1980. Multivariate analysis with latent variables: Causal modeling. *Ann. Rev. Psychol.* 31:419–56

Bentler, P. M., Bonett, D. G. 1980. Significance tests and goodness of fit in the analysis of covariance structures. *Psychol. Bull.* 87:588–606

Berg, C., Hertzog, C., Hunt, E. 1982. Age differences in the speed of mental rotation. *Dev. Psychol.* 18:95–107

Birkhill, W. R., Schaie, K. W. 1975. The effect of differential reinforcement of cautiousness in intellectual performance among the elderly. *J. Gerontol.* 30:578–82

Birren, J. E. 1960. Psychological aspects of aging. *Ann. Rev. Psychol.* 11:161–98

Birren, J. E. 1964. *The Psychology of Aging.* Englewood Cliffs, NJ: Prentice-Hall

Birren, J. E., ed. 1980. *Relations of Development and Aging.* New York: Arno. Reprint ed.

Birren, J. E., Hateley, B. J. 1982. Guided autobiography: A special method of life review. In *The Art of Life and Family Writing: A Practical Guide to Autobiography, Biography and Family History,* ed. R. H. Blum. Portola Valley, Calif: Am. Lives Endowment. In press

Birren, J. E., Kinney, D. K., Schaie, K. W., Woodruff, D. S. 1981. *Developmental Psychology: A Life-Span Approach.* Boston: Houghton Mifflin

Birren, J. E., Renner, V. J. 1981. Concepts and criteria of mental health. *Am. J. Orthopsychiatry* 51:242–54

Birren, J. E., Schaie, K. W., eds. 1977. *Handbook of the Psychology of Aging.* New York: Van Nostrand Reinhold

Birren, J. E., Sloane, R. B., eds. 1980. *Handbook of Mental Health and Aging.* Englewood Cliffs, NJ: Prentice-Hall

Birren, J. E., Woods, A. M., Williams, M. V. 1980. Behavioral slowing with age. In *Aging in the 1980s,* ed. L. W. Poon. Washington DC: Am. Psychol. Assoc.

Blieszner, R., Willis, S. L., Baltes, P. B. 1981. Training research in aging on the fluid ability of inductive reasoning. *J. Appl. Psychol.* 2:247–65

Botwinick, J. 1959. Drives, expectancies and emotions. In *Handbook of Aging and the Individual*, ed. J. E. Birren, pp. 739–68. Chicago: Univ. Chicago Press

Botwinick, J. 1970. Geropsychology. *Ann. Rev. Psychol.* 21:239–72

Botwinick, J. 1977. Intellectual abilities. See Birren & Schaie 1977, pp. 580–605

Botwinick, J. 1978. *Aging and Behavior.* New York: Springer

Botwinick, J., Arenberg, D. 1976. Disparate time space in sequential studies of aging. *Exp. Aging Res.* 2:55–66

Botwinick, J., Birren, J. E. 1963. Cognitive processes: Mental abilities and psychomotor responses in healthy aged men. In *Human Aging*, ed. J. E. Birren, R. N. Butler, S. W. Greenhouse, L. Sokoloff, M. Yarrow. Washington DC: GPO

Botwinick, J., Siegler, I. C. 1980. Intellectual ability among the elderly: Simultaneous cross-sectional and longitudinal comparisons. *Dev. Psychol.* 16:49–53

Botwinick, J., Storandt, M. 1974a. *Memory, Related Functions and Age.* Springfield: Thomas

Botwinick, J., Storandt, M. 1974b. Vocabulary ability in later life. *J. Genet. Psychol.* 125:303–8

Botwinick, J., Storandt, M. 1980. Recall and recognition of old information in relation to age and sex. *J. Gerontol.* 35:70–76

Botwinick, J., West, R., Storandt, M. 1975. Qualitative vocabulary test responses and age. *J. Gerontol.* 30:574–76

Bowlby, J. 1969. *Attachment.* New York: Basic Books

Bowman, T. E. 1980. *Electrocortical and Behavioral Aspects of Visuo-Spatial Processing and Cognitive Orientation in Young, Middle Aged and Elderly Females.* PhD thesis. Univ. South. Calif., Los Angeles

Brent, G. A., Smith, D. B. D., Michalewski, H. J. 1977. Differences in the evoked potential in young and old subjects during habituation and dishabituation procedures. *Psychophysiology* 14:96–97

Burke, P. M., Light, L. L. 1981. Memory and aging: The role of retrieval processes. *Psychol. Bull.* 90:513–46

Buss, A. R. 1973. An extension of developmental models that separate ontogenetic change and cohort differences. *Psychol. Bull.* 80:446–79

Cameron, P. 1975. Mood as an indicant of happiness: Age, sex, social class, and situational differences. *J. Gerontol.* 30:216–24

Carp, F. H., Carp, A. 1981. Mental health characteristics and acceptance-rejection of old age. *Am. J. Orthopsychiatry* 51:230–41

Cerella, J., Poon, L. W., Fozard, J. C. 1982. Age and the iconic read-out. *J. Gerontol.* 37:197–202

Chap, J. P., Sinnott, J. D. 1977–78. Performance of institutionalized and community-active old persons on concrete and formal Piagetian tasks. *Int. J. Aging Hum. Dev.* 8:269–78

Chown, S. M., Heron, A. 1965. Psychological aspects of ageing in man. *Ann. Rev. Psychol.* 16:417–50

Christenson, C. V., Gagnon, J. H. 1965. Sexual behavior in a group of older women. *J. Gerontol.* 20:351–56

Cicirelli, V. G. 1976. Categorization behavior in aging subjects. *J. Gerontol.* 31:676–80

Clayton, V. P., Birren, J. E. 1980. The development of wisdom across the life-span: A reexamination of an ancient topic. In *Life-Span Development and Behavior*, ed. P. B. Baltes, O. G. Prim Jr., 3:104–35. New York: Academic

Clayton, V. P., Overton, W. F. 1976. Concrete and formal operational thought processes in young adulthood and old age. *Int. J. Aging Hum. Dev.* I:237–45

Cliff, N. 1980. *Some cautions concerning the application of causal modeling methods.* Presented at special national workshop, Res. Methodol. Crim. Just. Prog. Eval. Natl. Inst. Just., Baltimore

Cohen, D., Schaie, K. W., Gribbin, K. 1977. The organization of spatial abilities in older men and women. *J. Gerontol.* 32:578–85

Cohen, G. 1979. Language comparisons in old age. *Cognit. Psychol.* 11:412–29

Comfort, A. 1974. Sexuality in old age. *J. Am. Geriatr. Soc.* 22:440–42

Cooper, A. J., Ismail, A. A. A., Smith, C. G., Loraine, J. A. 1970. Androgen functions in "psychogenic" and "constitutional" types of impotence. *Br. Med. J.* 3:17–20

Corby, N., Solnick, R. L. 1980. Psychosocial and physiological influences on sexuality in the older adult. See Birren & Sloane 1980, pp. 893–921

Correll, R. E., Rokosz, S., Blanchard, B. M. 1966. Some correlates of WAIS performance in the elderly. *J. Gerontol.* 21:544–49

Costa, P. T., Fozard, J. L., McCrae, R. R., Bosse, R. 1976. Relations of age and personality dimensions to cognitive ability factors. *J. Gerontol.* 31:663–69

Costa, P. T., McCrae, R. R. 1976. Age differences in personality structure: A cluster analysis approach. *J. Gerontol.* 31: 564–70

Craik, F. I. M. 1977. Age differences in human memory. See Birren & Schaie 1977, pp. 384–420

Craik, F. I. M., Simon, E. 1980. Age differences in memory: The roles of attention and depth of processing. See Poon et al 1980, pp. 95–112

Crowder, R. G. 1980. Echoic memory and the study of aging memory systems. See Poon et al 1980, pp. 181–204

Cunningham, W. R. 1978. Principles for identifying structural differences: Some methodological issues related to comparative factor analysis. *J. Gerontol.* 33:82–86

Cunningham, W. R. 1980a. Age comparative factor analysis of ability variables in adulthood and old age. *Intelligence* 4:133–49

Cunningham, W. R. 1980b. Speed, age, and qualitative differences in cognitive functioning. See Poon 1980, pp. 327–31

Cunningham, W. R. 1981. Ability factor structure differences in adulthood and old age. *Multivar. Behav. Res.* 16:3–22

Cunningham, W. R. 1982. Factorial invariance. *Exp. Aging Res.* 8:61–65

Cunningham, W. R., Birren, J. E. 1976. Age changes in human abilities: A 28 year longitudinal study. *Dev. Psychol.* 12: 81–82

Cunningham, W. R., Birren, J. E. 1980. Age changes in the factor structure of intellectual abilities in adulthood and old age. *Educ. Psychol. Meas.* 40:271–90

Cunningham, W. R., Clayton, V. P., Overton, W. F. 1975. Fluid and crystallized intelligence in young and old. *J. Gerontol.* 30:53–55

Cunningham, W. R., Owens, W. A. 1982. The Iowa State Study of the Adult Development of Intellectual Abilities. In *Longitudinal Studies of Psychological Development*, ed. K. W. Schaie. New York: Guilford. In press

Cunningham, W. R., Sepkoski, C. M., Opel, M. R. 1978. Fatigue effects on intelligence test performance in the elderly. *J. Gerontol.* 33:541–45

Davies, J. 1977. Attitudes toward old age and aging as shown by humor. *Gerontologist* 17:220–26

deLeon, M. J., Ferris, S. H., George, A. F., Reisberg, B., Krichoff, I. I., Gershon, S.

1980. Computed tomography evaluations of brain-behavior relationships in senile dementia of the Alzheimer's type. *Neurobiol. Aging* 1:69–79

Delgado, M. A. 1980. *Categorization behavior among children and old adults.* MA thesis. Univ. Florida, Gainesville

Denney, N. W. 1974. Classification abilities in elderly. *J. Gerontol.* 29:309–14

Donaldson, G. 1981. Letter to the editor. *J. Gerontol.* 36:634–38

Drachman, D. A. 1980. An approach to the neurology of aging. See Birren & Sloane 1980, pp. 501–19

Drechsler, F. 1977. Determination of neurophysiological parameters of the aging CNS. I. Evoked potentials. *Akt Gerontol.* 7:273–83

Drechsler, F. 1978. Quantitative analysis of neurophysiological processes of the aging CNS. *J. Neurol.* 218:197–213

Dustman, R. E., Beck, E. C. 1969. The effects of maturation and aging on the waveform of visually evoked potentials. *EEC Clin. Neurophysiol.* 26:2–11

Earhard, M. 1977. Retrieval failure in the presence of retrieval cues: A comparison of three age groups. *Can. J. Psychol.* 31:139–50

Edwards, A. E., Husted, J. R. 1976. Penile sensitivity, age, and sexual behavior. *J. Clin. Psychol.* 32:697–700

Eisdorfer, C. 1977. Intelligence and cognition in the aged. In *Behavior and Adaptation in Late Life*, ed. E. W. Busse, E. Pfeiffer, pp. 212–27. Boston: Little Brown

Eisdorfer, C., Raskind, M. 1975. Aging, hormones, and human behavior. In *Hormonal Correlates of Behavior*, ed. B. E. Eleftheriou, R. L. Sprott, pp. 369–94. New York: Plenum

Ektrom, R. B., French, J., Harman, H., Derman, D. 1976. *Manual for List of Factor-Referenced Tests.* Princeton, NJ: Educ. Test. Serv.

Eleftheriou, B. E. 1974. Changes with age in pituitary adrenal responsiveness and reactivity to mild stress in mice. *Gerontologia* 20:224–30

Elias, M. F. 1980. Animal models for the study of hypertension and behavior. In *Hypertension and Cognitive Processes*, ed. M. F. Elias, D. H. P. Streeten, pp. 137–58. Mt. Desert, Maine: Beech Hill

Elias, M. F., Elias, P. K. 1977. Motivation and activity. See Birrer & Schaie 1977, pp. 357–83

Elias, P. K., Elias, M. F., Eleftheriou, B. E. 1975. Emotionality, exploratory behavior, and locomotion in aging inbred strains of mice. *Gerontologia* 21:46–55

Finley, G. E., Delgado, M. 1979. Formal education and intellectual functioning in the immigrant Cuban elderly. *Exp. Aging Res.* 5:149–54

Ford, J. M., Hink, R. F., Hopkins, W. F. III, Roth, W. T., Pfefferbaum, A., Kopell, B. S. 1979. Age effects on event-related potentials in a selective attention task. *J. Gerontol.* 34:388–95

Fozard, J. L. 1980. The time for remembering. See Poon 1980, pp. 273–87

Frederiksen, J. D. 1980. Some cautions we might exercise in attributing age deficits in memory to attentional dysfunctions. See Poon et al 1980, pp. 131–34

Friedmann, E. A., Orbach, H. L. 1974. Adjustment to retirement. In *American Handbook of Psychiatry*, ed. S. Arieti. New York: Basic Books

Furry, C. A., Baltes, P. B. 1973. The effect of age differences in ability-extraneous performance variables on the assessment of intelligence in children, adults and the elderly. *J. Gerontol.* 28:73–80

Furry, C. A., Schaie, K. W. 1979. Pretest activity and intellectual performance in middle-aged and older persons. *Exp. Aging Res.* 5:413–21

Gewirtz, J., ed. 1972. *Attachment and Dependency.* Washington DC: Winston

Giambra, L. M., Arenberg, D. 1980. Problem solving, concept learning and aging. See Poon 1980, pp. 253–59

Goldman, H., Kleinman, K. M., Snow, M. Y., Bidus, D. R., Korol, B. 1974. Correlation of diastolic blood pressure and signs of cognitive dysfunction in essential hypertension. *Dis. Nerv. Syst.* 35: 571–72

Goodin, D. S., Squires, K. C., Henderson, B. H., Starr, A. 1978. Age-related variations in evoked potentials to auditory stimuli in normal human subjects. *EEG Clin. Neurophysiol.* 44:447–58

Goodrick, C. L. 1960. Learning, retention, and extinction of a complex maze habit for mature-young and senescent Wistar albino rats. *J. Gerontol.* 23:298–304

Goodrick, C. L. 1966. Activity and exploration as a function of age and deprivation. *J. Genet. Psychol.* 108:239–52

Goodrick, C. L. 1971. Variables affecting free exploration responses of male and female Wistar rats as a function of age. *Dev. Psychol.* 4:440–46

Graney, M. J. 1975. Happiness and social participation in aging. *J. Gerontol.* 30:701–6

Granick, S. 1971. Psychological test functioning. In *Human Aging II: An Eleven-Year Follow-up Biomedical and Behavioral Study*, ed. S. Granick, R. D. Patterson, pp. 49–62. Washington DC: GPO

Guilford, J. P. 1967. *The Nature of Human Intelligence.* New York: McGraw-Hill

Gutmann, D. 1977. The cross-cultural perspective: Notes toward a comparative psychology of aging. See Birren & Schaie 1977, pp. 302–26

Gutmann, D. 1974. Alternatives to disengagement: aging among the highland Druze. In *Culture and Personality: Contemporary Readings*, ed. R. LeVine, pp. 232–45. Chicago: Aldine

Gutmann, D. L. 1975. Parenthood: Key to the comparative psychology of the life cycle? In *Life-Span Developmental Psychology: Normative Life Crises*, ed. N. Datan, L. Ginsberg. New York: Academic

Harbin, T. J., Cunningham, W. R. 1978. Influence of contextual variables on blood pressure in the elderly. *Exp. Aging Res.* 6:521–24

Hartley, J. T., Harker, J. O., Walsh, D. A. 1980. Contemporary issues and new directions in adult development of learning and memory. See Poon 1980, pp. 239–52

Harwood, E., Naylor, G. F. K. 1977. A longitudinal study in retrospect. *Proc. 13th Ann. Conf. Aust. Assoc. Gerontol.* 24:297–303

Hasher, L., Zacks, R. T. 1979. *J. Exp. Psychol.* 108:356–88

Hayslip, B. Jr., Sterns, H. L. 1979. Age differences in relationships between crystallized and fluid intelligence and problem solving. *J. Gerontol.* 34:404–14

Hegeler, S. 1976. *Sexual behavior in elderly Danish males.* Presented at Int. Symp. Sex Educ. Ther., Stockholm, Sweden

Heise, D. R. 1975. *Causal Analysis.* New York: Wiley

Heron, A., Chown, S. 1967. *Age and Function.* Boston: Little, Brown

Hertzog, C., Schaie, K. W., Gribbin, K. 1978. Cardiovascular disease and changes in intellectual functioning from middle to old age. *J. Gerontol.* 33:872–83

Hines, T. M., Fozard, J. L. 1980. Memory and aging: Relevance of recent developments for research and application. In *Ann. Rev. Gerontol. Geriatr.* 1:97–120

Hite, S. 1976. *The Hite Report.* New York: MacMillan

Horn, J. L. 1976. Human abilities: A review of research and theory in the early 1970s. *Ann. Rev. Psychol.* 27:437–85

Horn, J. L. 1978. Human ability systems. In *Life-Span Development and Behavior*, Vol. 1, ed. P. B. Baltes. New York: Academic

Horn, J. L., Donaldson, G. 1976. On the myth of intellectual decline. *Am. Psychol.* 31:701–19

Horn, J. L., McArdle, J. J. 1980. Perspectives on mathematical/statistical model building (MASMOB) in research on aging. See Poon 1980, pp. 503–41

Hornblum, J. N., Overton, W. F. 1976. Area and volume conservation among the elderly: Assessment and training. *Dev. Psychol.* 12:68–74

Hoyer, W. J., Plude, D. J. 1980. Attentional and perceptual processes in the study of cognitive aging. See Poon 1980, pp. 227–38

Hultsch, D. F., Craig, E. R. 1976. Adult age differences in the inhibition of recall as a function of retrieval cues. *Dev. Psychol.* 12:83–84

Hultsch, D. F., Deutsch, F. 1981. *Adult Development and Aging.* New York: McGraw-Hill

Hultsch, D. F., Pentz, C. A. 1980. Encoding, storage, and retrieval in adult memory: The role of model assumptions. See Poon et al 1980, pp. 73–94

Hussian, R. A. 1981. *Geriatric Psychology.* New York: Van Nostrand Reinhold

Huyck, M. H., Hoyer, W. J. 1982. *Adult Development and Aging.* Belmont, Calif: Wadsworth

Jakubczak, L. F. 1967. Age, endocrines and behavior. In *Endocrines and Aging,* ed. L. Gitman, pp. 1–15. Springfield, Ill: Thomas

Jakubczak, L. F. 1969. Effects of age and activity restriction on body weight loss of rats. *Am. J. Physiol.* 216:1081–83

Jakubczak, L. F. 1970. Age differences in the effects of water deprivation on activity, water loss, and survival of rats. *Life Sci.* 9:771–80

Jarvik, F. J., Russell, D. 1979. Anxiety, aging and the third emergency reaction. *J. Gerontol.* 34:197–200

Jerome, E. A. 1959. Age and learning—experimental studies. See Botwinick 1959, pp. 655–99

Jöreskog, K. G. 1979. Statistical estimation of structural models in longitudinal-developmental investigations. See Nesselroade & Baltes 1979, pp. 303–51

Jöreskog, K. G., Sörbom, D. 1976. *Exploratory Factor Analysis Program.* Chicago: Natl. Educ. Resour.

Jöreskog, K. C., Sörbom, D. 1978. *Analysis of Linear Structural Relationships by the Method of Maximum Likelihood.* Chicago: Natl. Educ. Resour.

Jöreskog, K. G., Sörbom, D. 1979. *Advances in Factor Analysis and Structural Equation Models.* Cambridge, Mass: ABT Books

Kalish, R. A. 1981. *Death, Grief, and Caring Relationships.* Monterey, Calif: Brooks-Cole

Keller, J. F., Fakes, F., Hinkle, D., Hughston, G. A. 1978. Sexual behavior and guilt among women: A cross-generational comparison. *J. Sex. Marital Ther.* 4:259–65

Kenney, D. A. 1979. *Correlation and Causality.* New York: Wiley

Kesler, M. S., Denney, N. W., Whitely, S. E. 1976. Factors influencing problem-solving in middle-aged and elderly adults. *Hum. Dev.* 19:310–20

Kessler, R. C., Greenberg, D. F. 1981. *Linear Panel Analysis.* New York: Academic

Kinsey, A. C., Pomeroy, W. B., Martin, C. E., Gebhard, P. H. 1953. *Sexual Behavior in the Human Female.* Philadelphia: Saunders

Kivett, V. R., Watson, J. A., Busch, J. G. 1977. The relative importance of physical, psychological and social variables to locus of control orientation in middle age. *J. Gerontol.* 32:203–10

Kleiber, M., Smith, A. H., Chernikoff, H. N. 1956. Metabolic rate of female rats as a function of age and body size. *Am. J. Physiol.* 186:9–12

Kogan, N. 1974. Categorizing and conceptualizing styles in younger and older adults. *Hum. Dev.* 17:218–30

Kogan, N. 1979. Creativity and cognitive style. In *Life-Span Developmental Psychology: Personality and Socialization,* ed. P. B. Baltes, K. W. Schaie. New York: Academic

Krauss, I. K., Quayhagen, M., Schaie, K. W. 1980. Spatial rotation in the elderly: Performance factors. *J. Gerontol.* 35:199–206

Kubanis, P., Zornetzer, S. F. 1981. Age related behavioral and neurobiological changes: A review with an emphasis on memory. *Behav. Neurol. Biol.* 31:115–72

Kuypers, J. A. 1972. Internal-external locus of control and ego functioning, and personality characteristics in old age. *Gerontologist* 12(2), part 1:168–73

Labouvie, E. W. 1980. Identity versus equivalence of psychological measures and constructs. See Poon 1980, pp. 493–502

Labouvie-Vief, G. 1976. Toward optimizing cognitive competence in later life. *Educ. Gerontol.* 1:75–92

Labouvie-Vief, G. 1977. Adult cognitive development: In search of alternative interpretations. *Merrill-Palmer Q.* 23:227–63

Labouvie-Vief, G., Chandler, M. 1978. Cognitive development and life-span developmental theories: Idealistic vs. contextual perspectives. See Horn 1978, pp. 181–210

Labouvie-Vief, G., Gonda, J. N. 1976. Cognitive strategy training and intellectual performance in the elderly. *J. Gerontol.* 31:327–32

Lachman, J. L., Lachman, R. 1980. Age and the actualization of world knowledge. See Poon et al 1980, pp. 285–312

Lachman, J. L., Lachman, R., Thronesbery, C. 1979. Metamemory through the adult life-span. *Dev. Psychol.* 15:543–51

Lao, I. 1974. The developmental trend of the locus of control. *Pers. Soc. Psychol. Bull.* 1:348–50

LaRue, A. 1979. *Older women and younger men: Differing cognitive approaches.* Presented at Ann. Meet. Am. Psychol. Assoc., New York

LaRue, A., Bank, L., Jarvik, Hetland, M. 1979. Health in old age: How do physicians' ratings and self-ratings compare? *J. Gerontol.* 34:687–91

LaRue, A., Jarvik, L. F. 1982. Old age and biobehavioral changes. In *Handbook of Developmental Psychology,* ed. B. B. Wolman, pp. 791–806. Englewood Cliffs, NJ: Prentice-Hall

LaRue, A., Waldbaum, A. 1980. *Aging vs. illness as predictors of Piagetian problem solving in older adults.* Presented at Ann. Int. Conf. Piagetian Theory Helping Prof., 10th, Los Angeles

Lebowitz, B. D. 1975. Age and fearfulness: Personal and situational factors. *J. Gerontol.* 30:696–700

Lee, J. A., Pollack, R. H. 1978. The effects of age on perceptual problem strategies. *Exp. Aging Res.* 4:37–54

Levinson, E. J. 1975. *Correlates of the internal-external locus of control scale in an aging population.* Presented at Ann. Meet. Gerontol. Soc., San Diego

Light, K. C. 1978. Effects of mild cardiovascular and cerebrovascular disorders on serial reaction time performance. *Exp. Aging Res.* 4:3–22

Lopata, H. 1973. *Widowhood in an American City.* Cambridge: Schenkman

Lorge, I. 1956. Gerontology (later maturity). *Ann. Rev. Psychol.* 7:349–64

Loveless, N. E., Sanford, A. J. 1974. Effects of age on the contingent negative variation and preparatory set in a reaction time task. *J. Gerontol.* 29:52–63

Madden, D. J., Nebes, R. D. 1980. Aging and the development of automaticity in visual search. *Dev. Psychol.* 16:377–84

Marsh, G. R., Thompson, L. W. 1977. Psychophysiology of aging. See Birren & Schaie 1977, pp. 219–48

Martin, C. E. 1975. Marital and sexual factors in relation to age, disease, and longevity. In *Life History Research in Psychopathology,* ed. R. D. Wirt, G. Winokur, M. Roff, 4:326–47. Minneapolis: Univ. Minn. Press

Mason, S. E. 1979. Effects of orienting tasks on the recall and recognition performance of subjects differing in age. *Dev. Psychol.* 15:467–69

Masters, W. H., Johnson, V. E. 1966. *Human Sexual Response.* Boston: Little, Brown

McCrae, R. R., Bartone, P. T., Costa, P. T. 1976. Age, anxiety, and self-reported health. *Int. J. Aging Hum. Dev.* 7:49–58

Mellstrom, D. 1981. *Life Style, Ageing and Health Among the Elderly.* Goteborg, Sweden: Univ. Goteborg Press

Merriam, S. B. 1980. *Coping with Male Mid-Life.* Washington DC: Univ. Press Am.

Meyer, B. J. F., Rice, G. E. 1981. Information recalled from prose by young, middle, and old adult readers. *Exp. Aging Res.* 7:253–68

Monroe, S. F., Menon, K. M. J. 1977. Changes in reproductive hormone secretion during the climacteric and postmenopausal periods. *Clin. Obstet. Gynecol.* 20:113–22

Munnichs, J. M. A., van den Heuve, W. J. A., eds. 1976. *Dependency or Interdependency in Old Age.* The Hague: Nijhoff

Nakamura, M., Fukui, Y., Kadobayashi, I., Katoh, N. 1979. A comparison of CNV in young and old subjects: Its relation to memory and personality. *EEG Clin. Neurophysiol.* 46:337–44

Nesselroade, J. R., Baltes, P. B., eds. 1979. *Longitudinal Research in the Study of Behavior and Development.* New York: Academic

Neugarten, B. L. 1977. Personality and aging. See Birren & Schaie 1977, pp. 626–49

Neugarten, B. L., Moore, J. W., Lowe, J. C. 1965. Age norms, age constraints, and adult socialization. *Am. J. Sociol.* 70:710–17

New, P. F. J., Scott, W. R. 1975. *Computed Tomography of the Brain and Orbit.* Baltimore: Williams & Williams

Okun, M. A. 1976. Adult age and cautiousness in decision: A review of the literature. *Hum. Dev.* 19:220–33

Okun, M. A., Siegler, I. C., George, L. K. 1978. Cautiousness and verbal learning in adulthood. *J. Gerontol.* 33:94–97

Owens, W. A. 1953. Age and mental abilities:

A longitudinal study. *Genet. Psychol. Monogr.* 48:3–54

Owens, W. A. 1966. Age and mental ability: A second adult follow-up. *J. Educ. Psychol.* 57:311–25

Papalia, D. F., Bielby, D. D. V. 1975. Cognitive functioning in middle and old age adults: A review of research based on Piaget's theory. *Hum. Dev.* 17:424–43

Paul, A. 1982. 'Biography' is one sign of what may be new life in the art of recounting lives. *Chron. Higher Educ.* 24:19–21

Paxinos, G. 1976. Interruption of septal connections: Effects on drinking, irritability and copulation. *Physiol. Behav.* 17: 81–88

Peng, M. T., Jiang, M. J., Hsu, H. K. 1980. Changes in running-wheel activity, eating and drinking and their day/night distributions throughout the life-span of the rat. *J. Gerontol.* 35:339–47

Perlmutter, M. 1978. What is memory aging the aging of? *Dev. Psychol.* 14:330–45

Perlmutter, M. 1979. Age differences in adults' free recall, cued recall, and recognition. *J. Gerontol.* 34:533–39

Peterson, D. A., Birren, J. E. 1981. The impact of aging on institutions of higher learning. In *Issues in Higher Education and the Professions in the 1980s,* ed. M. Boaz, pp. 129–49. Littleton, Colo: Libraries Unlimited

Pfeiffer, E. 1969. Sexual behavior in old age. See Busse & Pfeiffer 1969, pp. 130–41

Pfeiffer, E. 1974. Sexuality in the aging individual. *J. Am. Geriatr. Soc.* 22:481–84

Pfeiffer, E. 1978. Sexuality in the aging individual. In *Sexuality and Aging,* ed. R. L. Solnick. Los Angeles: Univ. South. Calif. Press

Pfeiffer, E., Davis, G. C. 1972. Determinants of sexual behavior in middle and old age. *J. Am. Geriatr. Soc.* 20:4

Plemons, J. K., Willis, S. L., Baltes, P. B. 1978. Modifiability of fluid intelligence in aging: A short-term longitudinal training approach. *J. Gerontol.* 33: 224–31

Poon, L. W., ed. 1980. *Aging in the 1980s.* Washington DC: Am. Psychol. Assoc.

Poon, L. W., Fozard, J. L. 1978. Speed of retrieval from long term memory in relation to age, familiarity and datedness of information. *J. Gerontol.* 33:711–17

Poon, L. W., Fozard, J. L., Cermak, L. S., Arenberg, D. Thompson, L. W., eds. 1980. *New Directions in Memory and Aging.* Hillsdale, NJ: Erlbaum

Rabbitt, P. 1977. Changes in problem solving in old age. See Birren & Schaie 1977, pp. 605–25

Raboch, J., Mellem, J., Starka, L. 1975. Plasma testosterone in male patients with sexual dysfunctions. *Arch. Sex. Behav.* 4:541–45

Reedy, N. R., Birren, J. E., Schaie, K. W. 1981. Age and sex difference in satisfying love relationships across the adult life span. *Hum. Dev.* 24:52–66

Reid, D. W., Haas, G., Douglas, H. 1977. Locus of desired control and positive concept of the elderly. *J. Gerontol.* 32:441–51

Reinert, G. 1970. Comparative factor analytic studies of intelligence throughout the human life-span. In *Life-Span Developmental Psychology: Research and Theory,* ed. L. R. Goulet, P. B. Baltes. New York: Academic

Ribovich, J. K., Erikson, L. 1980. A study of lifelong reading with implications for instructional programs. *J. Read.* 24:20–26

Robinson, R. D., House, A. M. B. 1979. The reading process and the elderly. *Educ. Gerontol.* 4:223–28

Rogosa, D. 1979. Causal models in longitudinal research: Rationale, formulation, and interpretation. See Nesselroade & Baltes 1979, pp. 263–302

Rosenthal, R., Rosow, R. L. 1975. *The Volunteer Subject.* New York: Wiley

Rosow, I. 1978. What is a cohort and why? *Hum. Dev.* 21:65–78

Rotter, J. B. 1966. Generalized expectancies for internal versus external control of reinforcement. *Psychol. Monogr.* 80: 1–28

Rudinger, G. 1976. Correlates of changes in cognitive functioning. In *Patterns of Aging: Findings from the Bonn Longitudinal Study,* ed. H. Thomae. New York: Karger

Ruth, J. E. 1980. *Creativity as a cognitive construct: The effects of age, sex, and testing practice.* PhD thesis. Univ. South. Calif., Los Angeles

Ryckman, R. M., Malikosi, M. X. 1975. Relationship between locus of control and chronological age. *Psychol. Rep.* 36: 655–58

Salthouse, T. A. 1980. Age and memory: Strategies for localizing the loss. See Poon et al 1980, pp. 47–65

Sanders, R. F., Murphy, M. D., Schmitt, F. A., Walsh, K. K. 1980. Age differences in free recall rehearsal strategies. *J. Gerontol.* 35:550–58

Schaie, J. P., Syndulko, K. 1978. Age differences in cortical activity associated with preparation to respond. *Int. J. Behav. Dev.* 1:255–61

Schaie, K. W. 1965. A general model for the study of developmental problems. *Psychol. Bull.* 64:92–107

Schaie, K. W. 1970. A reinterpretation of age-related changes in cognitive structure and functioning. See Reinert 1970, pp. 485–507

Schaie, K. W. 1977–78. Toward a stage theory of adult cognitive development. *J. Aging Hum. Dev.* 8:129–38

Schaie, K. W. 1979. The primary mental abilities in adulthood: An exploration in the development of psychometric intelligence. In *Life-Span Development and Behavior*, ed. P. B. Baltes, O. G. Brim Jr., 2:67–115. New York: Academic

Schaie, K. W., Gribbin, K. 1975. Adult development and aging. *Ann. Rev. Psychol.* 26:65–96

Schaie, K. W., Hertzog, C. 1982. Longitudinal methods. See La Rue & Jarvik 1982, pp. 91–115

Schaie, K. W., Labouvie-Vief, G. 1974. Generational versus ontogenetic components of change in adult cognitive functioning: A fourteen-year cross-sequential study. *Dev. Psychol.* 10:305–20

Schaie, K. W., Labouvie-Vief, G., Buech, B. U. 1973. Generation and cohort-specific differences in adult cognitive functioning: A fourteen year study of independent samples. *Dev. Psychol.* 9:151–66

Schaie, K. W., Parham, I. A. 1976. Stability of adult personality traits: Fact or fable? *J. Pers. Soc. Psychol.* 13:649–53

Schaie, K. W., Parham, I. A. 1977. Cohort-sequential analyses of adult intellectual development. *Dev. Psychol.* 13:649–53

Schaie, K. W., Schaie, J. P. 1977. Clinical assessment and aging. See Birren & Schaie 1977, pp. 692–723

Schaier, A. H., Circirelli, V. G. 1976. Age differences in humor comprehension and appreciation in old age. *J. Gerontol.* 31:577–82

Schenkenberg, T. 1970. *Visual, Auditory and Somatosensory Evoked Responses of Normal Subjects from Childhood to Senescence.* PhD thesis. Univ. Utah, Salt Lake City

Schiffman, S. 1979. Food recognition by the elderly. *J. Gerontol.* 32:586–92

Schiffman, S., Pasternak, N. 1979. Decreased discrimination of food odors in the elderly. *J. Gerontol.* 34:73–79

Schonfield, D., Wenger, L. 1975. Age limitation of perceptual span. *Nature* 253:377–78

Schultz, N. R., Hoyer, W. J. 1976. Feedback effects on spatial egocentrism in old age. *J. Gerontol.* 31:73–75

Shagass, C. 1972. *Evoked Brain Potentials in Psychiatry.* New York: Plenum

Shock, N. W. 1951. Gerontology (later maturity). *Ann. Rev. Psychol.* 2:353–70

Siegler, I. C., Botwinick, J. 1979. A long-term longitudinal study of intellectual ability of older adults: The matter of selective attrition. *J. Gerontol.* 34:242–45

Siegler, I. C., Nowlin, J. B., Blumenthal, J. A. 1980. Health and behavior: Methodological considerations for adult development and aging. See Poon 1980, pp. 599–612

Sinnott, J. D. 1975. Everyday thinking and Piagetian operativity in adults. *Hum. Dev.* 18:430–43

Sinnott, J. D., Guttmann, D. 1978. Piagetian logical abilities and older adults' abilities to solve everyday problems. *Hum. Dev.* 21:327–33

Smith, A. D. 1977. Adult age differences in cued recall. *Dev. Psychol.* 13:326–31

Smith, A. D. 1980. Introduction to cognitive issues: Advances in the cognitive psychology of aging. See Poon 1980, pp. 223–25

Smith, A. D., Fullerton, A. M. 1981. Age differences in episodic and semantic memory: Implications for language and cognition. In *Communication Processes and Disorders*, ed. D. S. Beasley, G. A. Davis. New York: Grune & Stratton

Smith, D. B. D., Thompson, L. W., Michalewski, H. J. 1980. Averaged evoked potential research in adult aging—status and prospects. See Poon 1980, pp. 135–51

Solnick, R. L. 1978. Alteration of human male erectile response and sexual behavior. *Diss. Abstr. Int. Sect. B* 38:5045–46

Solnick, R. L., Birren, J. E. 1977. Age and male erectile responsiveness. *Arch. Sex. Behav.* 6:1–10

Sörbom, D. 1975. Detection of correlated errors in longitudinal data. *Br. J. Math. Stat. Psychol.* 28:138–51

Sörbom, D., Jöreskog, K. G. 1976. *Confirmatory Factor Analysis with Model Modification.* Chicago: Natl. Educ. Resour.

Sprott, R. L., Eleftheriou, B. E. 1974. Open-field behavior in aging inbred mice. *Gerontologia* 20:155–60

Steuer, J., LaRue, A., Blum, J. E., Jarvik, L. F. 1981. "Critical loss" in the eighth and ninth decades. *J. Gerontol.* 36:211–13

Taub, H. A. 1979. Comprehension and memory of prose by young and old adults. *Exp. Aging Res.* 5:3–13

Tecce, J. J., Yrehik, D. A., Meinbresse, C. L., Cole, J. O. 1980a. CNV rebound and aging. I. Attention functions. In *Motivation, Motor and Sensory Processes of the Brain: Electrical Potentials, Behavior and Clinical Use*, ed. H. H. Kornhuber, L. Deecke, pp. 562–73. New York: Elsevier Biomed. Press

Tecce, J. J., Yrehik, D. A., Meinbresse, C. L., Cole, J. O. 1980b. CNV rebound and aging. II. Type A and B CNV shapes. See Tecce et al 1980a, pp. 552–61

Thomae, H. 1980. Personality and adjustment to aging. See Birren & Sloane 1980, pp. 285–309

Thomas, J. C., Waugh, N. C., Fozard, J. L. 1978. Age and familiarity in memory scanning. *J. Gerontol.* 33:528–33

Thompson, L. W., Nowlin, J. B. 1973. Relation of increased attention to control and autonomic nervous system states. In *Intellectual Functioning in Adults: Psychological and Biological Influences*, ed. L. F. Jarvik, C. Bisdorfer, J. E. Blum, pp. 107–24. New York: Academic

Timiras, P. S., Meisami, E. 1972. Changes in gonadal function. In *Developmental Physiology and Aging*, ed. P. S. Timiras, pp. 527–41. New York: Macmillan

Treat, N. J., Reese, H. W. 1976. Age, pacing and imagery in paired-associate learning. *Dev. Psychol.* 12:119–24

Tredway, V. A. 1978. *Mood and exercise in older adults.* PhD thesis. Univ. South. Calif., Los Angeles

Troll, L. E., Saltz, R., Dunin-Markiewicz, A. 1976. A seven year follow-up of intelligence test scores of foster grandparents. *J. Gerontol.* 31:583–85

Vaillant, G. E. 1977. *Adaptation to Life.* Boston: Little, Brown

Vermeulen, A. 1976. The hormonal activities of the postmenopausal ovary. *J. Clin. Endocrinol. Metab.* 42:247–53

Verwoerdt, A., Pfeiffer, E., Wang, H. S. 1969. Sexual activity in senescence: Changes in sexual activity and interest of aging men and women. *J. Geriatr. Psychiatry* 1:163–80

Waddell, K. J., Rogoff, B. 1981. Effect of contextual organization on spatial memory of middle-aged and older women. *Dev. Psychol.* 17:878–85

Walsh, D. A. 1975. Age differences in learning and memory. In *Aging: Scientific Perspectives and Social Issues*, ed. D. S. Woodruff, J. E. Birren. New York: Van Nostrand Reinhold

Walsh, D. A., Baldwin, M. 1977. Age differences in integrated semantic memory. *Dev. Psychol.* 13:509–14

Walsh, D. A., Prasse, M. J. 1980. Iconic memory and attentional processes in the aged. See Poon et al 1980, pp. 153–80

Walsh, D. A., Thompson, L. W. 1978. Age differences in visual sensory memory. *J. Gerontol.* 33:383–87

Waugh, N. C., Barr, R. A. 1980. Memory and mental tempo. See Poon et al 1980, pp. 251–60

Wax, T. M. 1975. Runwheel activity patterns of mature-young and senescent mice: The effect of constant lighting conditions. *J. Gerontol.* 30:22–27

Weber, T., Cameron, P. 1978. Humor and aging—a response. *Gerontologist* 18: 73–75

Weg, R. B. 1978. The physiology of sexuality in aging. In *Sexuality and Aging*, ed. R. L. Solnick, pp. 48–65. Los Angeles: Univ. South. Calif. Press

Welford, A. T. 1951. *Skill and Age: An Experimental Approach.* London: Oxford Univ. Press

White, C. B., Catania, J. A. 1981. *Psychoeducational intervention for sexuality with the aged, family members of the aged, and people who work with the aged.* Presented at Ann. Meet. Am. Psychol. Assoc., Los Angeles

Wigdor, P. T. 1980. Drives and motivations with aging. See Birren & Sloane 1980, pp. 245–61

Wilkie, F., Eisdorfer, C., Howlin, J. B. 1976. Memory and blood pressure in the aged. *Exp. Aging Res.* 2:3–16

Willis, S. L., Baltes, P. B. 1981. Letter to the editor. *J. Gerontol.* 36:636–38

Willis, S. L., Blieszner, R., Baltes, P. B. 1981. Intellectual training research in aging: Modification of performance on the fluid ability of figural relations. *J. Educ. Psychol.* 73:41–50

Woodbury, M. A., Clive, J. 1974. Clinical pure types as a fuzzy partition. *J. Cybernetics* 4:111–21

Woodbury, M. A., Clive, J., Garson, A. 1978. Mathematical typology: A grade of membership technique for obtaining disease definition. *Comp. Biomed. Res.* 11:277–98

Woods, A. M. 1981. *Age Differences in the Effect of Physical Activity and Postural Changes on Information Processing Speed.* PhD thesis. Univ. South. Calif., Los Angeles

Wright, R. 1981. Aging, divided attention, and processing capacity. *J. Gerontol.* 36:605–14

Young, H. B., Ferguson, L. R. 1981. *Puberty to Manhood in Italy and America.* New York: Academic

Zarit, S. H. 1980. *Aging and Mental Disorders.* New York: Free Press

Zucker, I. R. 1971. Light-dark rhythms in rat eating and drinking behavior. *Physiol. Behav.* 6(2):115–26

AUTHOR INDEX

(Names appearing in capital letters indicate authors of chapters in this volume.)

SUBJECT INDEX

598

CUMULATIVE INDEXES

CONTRIBUTING AUTHORS, VOLUMES 30-34

CHAPTER TITLES, VOLUMES 30–34